The Campaigns and History

of the

Royal Irish Regiment

THE NORTH TRANSEPT OF ST PATRICK'S CATHEDRAL, DUBLIN.
CONTAINING THE COLOURS AND MEMORIALS OF THE ROYAL IRISH REGIMENT.

The Campaigns and History

of the

Royal Irish Regiment

From 1684 to 1902

BY

Lieutenant-Colonel G. le M. GRETTON

LATE 3RD BATTALION, LEICESTERSHIRE REGIMENT

NAMUR, 1695	BLENHEIM	RAMILLIES
OUDENARDE	MALPLAQUET	EGYPT
CHINA	PEGU	SEVASTOPOL
NEW ZEALAND	AFGHANISTAN, 1879-80	EGYPT, 1882
TEL-EL-KEBIR	NILE, 1884-5	SOUTH AFRICA, 1900-02

SECOND THOUSAND

William Blackwood and Sons
Edinburgh and London
1911

PREFACE.

THIS history of the war services of the Royal Irish regiment has been written at the request of the officers of that very distinguished corps. When I accepted the task, I knew that I had undertaken a delightful but difficult piece of work, for it is no easy matter to do justice to the achievements of a regiment which has fought in Europe, in Asia, in Africa, in America, and in Australasia. After serving with credit in William III.'s war in Ireland, the Royal Irish won undying laurels in the Siege of Namur in 1695. They formed part of the British contingent in the army commanded by Marlborough in the Low Countries and in Germany, and fought, not only at the great battles of Blenheim, Ramillies, Oudenarde, and Malplaquet, but in the long series of desperate but now forgotten sieges by which fortress after fortress was wrested from the French. A detachment took part in the defence of Gibraltar in 1727: the whole regiment was involved in the disasters of the campaign of 1745: the flank companies encountered foemen worthy of their steel at Lexington and Bunker's Hill. In the first phase of the great war with France the Royal Irish were in the Mediterranean: they served in the defence of Toulon; they helped Nelson and Moore to expel the French from Corsica, and they were sent to the mainland of Italy where for some months they established themselves firmly at Piombino, a port on the Tuscan coast. A few years later they fought under Abercromby in Egypt, but then their good luck changed, for they were ordered to the West Indies, where they remained till the end of the Napoleonic war.

In 1840, the outbreak of the first war with China re-opened the gates of the Temple of Janus to the XVIIIth; and during the last sixty years almost every decade has seen the regiment employed on active service, for after the Chinese war came the second war in Burma; the Crimea; the Indian Mutiny; the New Zealand war; the second Afghan war; the campaign of Tel-el-Kebir; the Nile expedition; campaigns on the north-west frontier of India; and the war with the Dutch republics in South Africa.

secretary of the Historical Committee, Lieutenant-Colonel A. R. Savile, who for many years devoted himself to the collection of information from officers who had served with the regiment in these campaigns. Probably no one but the man who has profited by Colonel Savile's exertions can appreciate adequately the energy and perseverance he displayed in this labour of love for his regiment. He has also prepared two appendices; one giving an epitome of the services of the Colonels of the regiment, the other describing the memorials which have been raised by the officers and men of the Royal Irish to the memory of those of their comrades who died on active service. Nor is this all for which I have to thank him: his collection of historical matter relating to the regiment at all periods of its existence has proved of great help to me:—indeed in all honesty I may say that if this book meets with success a great part of that success will be due to the "spade work," the results of which Colonel Savile has generously placed at my disposal.

Many of the past and present officers of the Royal Irish regiment have given me great assistance in the later campaigns by preparing for me statements recording their personal recollections, and by lending me their diaries and letters, written at the seat of war; and several non-commissioned officers have supplied me with interesting details about episodes in South Africa.

With the officers who form the Historical Committee I have worked in perfect harmony and identity of views, and I have to thank them warmly for the unfailing support they have given to me during the two years which it has taken me to prepare this book.

I have to express my sense of obligation to the Librarians of the War Office, the India Office, the United Service Institution, and the Royal Colonial Institute, and the officials at the Record Office for their friendly help.

To Mr Rudyard Kipling the warm thanks of the regiment are due for his kindness in allowing the reproduction of his ballad on the second battalion of the Royal Irish in the Black Mountain campaign.

In the compilation of this record very many books have been consulted. Among them stands out pre-eminently the 'History of the British Army,' by the Hon. John Fortescue, who, by his masterly descriptions of the campaigns he has dealt with up to the present, has made the path of a regimental historian comparatively smooth.

SHERBORNE, DORSET.

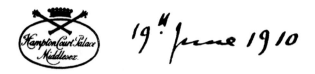

Hampton Court Palace
Middlesex.

19th June 1910

My dear Gregorie

I am indeed very glad
to hear that the History of
the Royal Irish Regiment
is soon to be published. Its
story cannot fail to be a
fine one. Every Soldier
who like myself, had the
honour of fighting, I may
say shoulder to shoulder
with it, will read this
new work with the deepest

interest — were it to be my good fortune to lead a Storming party this afternoon I should indeed wish it were to be largely composed of your celebrated Corps. Believe me to be very sincerely yours

Wolseley

To General C. F. Gregorie
C.B.
Royal Irish Regiment.

CONTENTS.

LIST OF ILLUSTRATIONS.

LIST OF MAPS.

CORRIGENDA.

---

page	line				
40	24	*for*	Lieut. G. Roberts	*read*	S. Roberts.
69	10	,,	Colonel Crosby	,,	Cosby.
70	1 of footnote	,,	,, ,,	,,	,,
121	10	,,	,, Lieut. D. Edwards	,,	Edwardes.
128	4	,,	,, Lieut. C. W. Davis	,,	G. W. Davis.
147 {	3	,,	,, Lieut. H. J. Stephenson	,,	H. F. Stephenson.
	15	,,	,, Lieut. G. W. Stackpoole	,,	G. W. Stacpoole.
	17	,,	,, Ens. T. E. Esmond	,,	T. E. Esmonde.
160	28		,, Lieut. W. F. Cockburn	,,	W. P. Cockburn.
165	4 of footnote	,,	Capt. G. W. Stackpole	,,	G. W. Stacpoole.

The Campaigns and History of
The Royal Irish Regiment.

————•————

CHAPTER I.

1684-1697.

THE RAISING OF THE REGIMENT: AND THE WARS OF WILLIAM III.

THE Royal Irish regiment was raised on April 1, 1684, by Charles II., when he reorganised the military forces of Ireland, which had hitherto consisted of a regiment of foot guards and a number of "independent" troops of cavalry and companies of infantry maintained to garrison various important points in the island. Charles formed these independent troops and companies into regiments of horse and foot; and as many of the officers had seen service on the Continent in foreign armies, and a large number of the rank and file were descendants of Cromwell's veterans, Arthur, Earl of Granard,[1] when granted the commission of colonel in one of the newly raised infantry regiments, took command not of a mob of recruits with everything to learn, but of a body of soldiers of whom any officer might be proud. Of the corps thus raised all but one had an ephemeral existence. During the struggle between James II. and William III. for the possession of Ireland some followed the example of the foot guards, joined the Stuart king in a body, and then took service in France, while others broke up, officers and men ranging themselves as individuals on the side of the monarch with whose religious or political views they were in sympathy. The one bright exception was the regiment formed by Lord Granard, which under the successive names of Forbes', Meath's, Hamilton's, the Royal regiment of Foot of Ireland, the XVIIIth, and the

[1] See Appendix 9.

A

Royal Irish regiment, has earned undying laurels in every part of the world.

Though brought over to England to help in the suppression of Monmouth's rebellion against James II., Granard's took no part in the operations by which the rising was crushed at Sedgemoor, and in the autumn of 1685 returned to Ireland,[1] where evil days awaited it. With James's attempt against the liberties of his English subjects it is not the province of a regimental historian to deal; but it is necessary to explain that the King, desiring ardently to own an army upon which he could count to obey him blindly in the political campaign he was planning, proposed to drive from the Colours all officers and men upon whom he could not rely implicitly to carry out his schemes. He decided to begin operations in Ireland, where he gave the Earl of Tyrconnel unlimited power to remodel the *personnel* of the troops. In 1686, Tyrconnel summarily dismissed from many regiments all the Protestants in the ranks, whom he stripped of their uniforms and turned penniless and starving upon the world. The officers fared little better: two of Granard's captains, John St Leger and Frederick Hamilton, were "disbanded" solely on account of their religious beliefs. As a protest against these proceedings Lord Granard resigned his commission, to which his son Arthur, Lord Forbes, was appointed on March 1, 1686. Next year the regiment "underwent a further purge," thus described by Brigadier-General Stearne,[2] who was then one of Forbes's officers. "Tyrconnel made a strict review of each troop and company, wherein he found a great many descendants of the 'Cromelians,' as he termed them, who must turn out also, and took the name of every man who was to be of the next disbandment, so that every soldier of an English name was marked down. As soon as the camp broke up and the army returned into winter quarters, most of the officers as well as soldiers were disbanded, and only a few kept in for a while to discipline those that supplied their places." Tyrconnel rid himself of about four thousand of all ranks, or considerably more than half the Irish army; the men he replaced with peasants, good in physique but without discipline or training, while the officers he appointed were of a very inferior class, who in the war of 1690-91 failed in many cases to turn to good account the splendid fighting qualities of their soldiers. It is, however, only fair to Tyrconnel's memory to mention that while he thus reduced the efficiency of the Irish army, he increased its power of expansion by devising a short service and reserve system by which many thousand men could be recalled to the Colours in case of need.

Thanks to the political influence and strong personality of Forbes, a "bold

---

[1] In Appendix No. 1 is given a list of the stations where the regiment has been quartered in time of peace.

[2] Brigadier-General Robert Stearne, Brigadier-General Richard Kane, Captain Robert Parker, and Sergeant John Millner, all of the Royal Irish regiment, wrote histories or journals of the wars of William III. and of Anne.

and daring man," who had learned the trade of war first in the army of France under the great Turenne, and later in a campaign against the Turks in Hungary, the regiment in the general ruin suffered less than any other corps. In defiance of Tyrconnel, Forbes succeeded in retaining more of his old officers and soldiers than any other colonel, and in 1688, when the regiment, 770 strong, was ordered to England to meet the invasion threatened by the Prince of Orange, it still contained a number of good officers, sergeants, and old soldiers, whose united efforts had welded into shape the mass of recruits recently poured into its ranks. For the next few months the strain upon these veterans must have been great, as they had to keep the young soldiers in order in a country where Irish troops at that time were looked upon with deep suspicion and hostility by the people, and not as now heartily welcomed by all classes. After being stationed for some time in London the regiment marched to Salisbury, where James had concentrated his troops to meet the Prince of Orange; and when the King, deserted by his generals, statesmen, and courtiers, abandoned his army and fled to France, Forbes kept his men together and returned to the neighbourhood of London, where he was quartered at the village of Colnbrook, near Hounslow. From the Prince of Orange, who by this time was actually, though not yet legally, King of England, Forbes received orders to disband the Roman Catholics of his regiment, and after five hundred officers and men had been disarmed and sent to Portsmouth *en route* for the Isle of Wight, several officers, many sergeants, corporals, and drummers, and about a hundred and thirty private soldiers, remained with the Colours.

Soon after this turning of the tables the regiment had an experience, probably unique in military history—an examination in theology, in which all ranks passed with high honours. The adventure is thus described in Stearne's journal :—

"A report spread through the whole kingdom that the Irish were murdering, burning and destroying the whole country, insomuch that there was not one town in the whole nation that had not an account they were committing all these cruelties in the very next town or village to them. Sir John Edgworth, who was our major, commanded the regiment at this time (Lord Forbes being with the Prince of Orange in London); he was quartered at Lord Oslington's house near Colnbrook, and upon the first of this flying report, sent for all the regiment to repair immediately to his quarters where there was a large walled court before the door, in which he drew them up with the design to keep them there until this rumour was over, but the country people, hearing that an Irish regiment was there, came flocking from all parts to knock us on the head : but Sir John bid them at their peril, not to approach, and told them we were not Irish Papists but true Church of England men; and seeing among the crowd a gentleman, called to him and desired he would send to the minister of the parish to read prayers to us, and if the minister did not convince them we were all of the Church of England, we would submit to their mercy. The minister was soon sent for, and to prayers we went, repeating the responses of the Liturgy so well and so exactly that the minister declared to the mob he never before heard the responses of the Church of England prayers repeated so distinctly and with so much devotion, upon which the mob gave a huzza, and cried 'Long live the Prince of Orange,' and so returned home."

In February 1689, the regiment was re-equipped,[1] and in anticipation of the recruits who in a few months began to refill its depleted ranks, weapons were issued for its full establishment. Five hundred and seventy-nine men were to be armed with flint-lock muskets and bayonets, while two hundred and forty were still to carry long pikes for the protection of the musketeers against cavalry on the battlefield and on the march. The pike, however, was a dying weapon, and was soon superseded completely by the bayonet. No mention is made of hand-grenades, though these missiles were already carried by the grenadier company, composed of men chosen from their comrades in the regiment for height, strength, and courage.

During the winter of 1688-89 Lord Forbes resigned his commission, on the ground that having sworn allegiance to James II. he could bear arms for no other king during his old master's lifetime.[2] For a few weeks Major Sir John Edgworth replaced him, but owing to financial scandals compromising to himself and several of his subordinates he was obliged to retire,[3] and Edward, Earl of Meath, was appointed to the vacancy on May 1, 1689, when William III. completed his arrangements for re-officering the regiment, which was numbered the Eighteenth of the infantry of the line. He issued forty-one new commissions, some to the seniors who had escaped disbandment at Tyrconnel's hands, others to officers who had been expelled from the army during James's reign, others again to young men with no previous military experience. The names of the officers are given in the footnote.[4]

[1] An order to the Master-General of Ordnance, dated 14th February 1689, for the re-equipment of the regiment, gives these figures—

	Firelocks.	Pikes.	Halberts.	Drums.	Bandalers (= i.e. Bandoliers.)	Bayonets.	Flints.	Tents.
The full number of arms for the regiment	579	240	39	26	516	579	1000	156
Whereof the officers have already	60	0	7	5	16	79	0	0
Remain to complete the regiment	519	240	32	21	500	500	1000	156

[2] See Appendix 9. [3] See Appendix 9.
[4] (The names followed by a star are those of officers who had been disbanded by Tyrconnel.)
Colonel—Edward, Earl of Meath.
Lieutenant-Colonel—G. Newcomen (sometimes spelled Newcomb).

One of the results of the revolution by which James II. was deposed and William and Mary placed upon the throne was to plunge England into the vortex of Continental politics. As Prince of Orange, William had been the moving spirit in the coalition of States formed to curb the ambition of the French king, Louis XIV., who throughout his life strove to aggrandise himself at the expense of his neighbours; and when James II. took refuge in France, Louis saw his opportunity to strike a heavy blow at William. By long and careful attention to his navy he had made it superior to the combined fleets of the English and the Dutch—the great naval powers of the time—and, thanks to his command of the sea, was able to land James at Kinsale with five thousand excellent French soldiers to give backbone to the forty thousand men collected by Tyrconnel in anticipation of his Royal master's arrival. So slow was communication in those days that, though James disembarked at Kinsale in March 1689, the news of the invasion did not reach England for several weeks, when William had already despatched most of his best troops to swell the forces of the Allies facing the French in the Low Countries. William hurriedly raised more regiments, but it was not until August that Marshal Schomberg, the veteran selected for the command of the expedition, landed near Belfast, where in a few days he was joined by Meath's[1] regiment, which for some months had been quartered in Wales. The army was sent to Ireland utterly unprepared to take the field. There was no transport, the commissariat was wretched, the artillery was short of horses; guns, muskets, and powder, food, clothing, and shoes alike were bad. No wonder, therefore, that after taking the town of Carrickfergus, Schomberg refused to give battle to James, and fell back upon an entrenched camp at Dundalk to await reinforcements of every kind. Before the autumnal rains set in the General ordered his troops to build themselves huts, and the foreigners in William's pay—old warriors, who had bought their experience in many campaigns—worked with a will; but the English regiments, composed of lazy, careless, and ignorant recruits, whose officers were no better soldiers

Major—Fred[k.] Hamilton.*
Captains—Robert Stearne, F. Preston, Chichester Philips,* J. Worsopp, G. Hamilton, Parsons Hoy*, Cuth[t.] Wilkinson, John Yarner,* R. Needham, F. Rolleston.
Captain-Lieutenant—R. Pointz.*
Lieutenants—W. Flower,* G. Connock, Ant. Brabazon, W. Usher,* J. Porter, Peter Latham,* Ch. Hubblethorne,* H. West, John Culliford,* N. Carteret,* Ch. Brabazon, Robert Blakeney,* W. Underhill.
Ensigns—J. O'Bryen, J. I. Chichester, G. Brabazon, T. Weldon,* T. Allen, John Philips, Ed. Corker, J. Stroud, J. Leigh, H. Brabazon, T. Wilbraham, R. Kane, R. Pigott.
Surgeon—R. Weldon.
    —(Dalton's British Army Lists and Commission Registers.)

[1] Although the regular regiments were now numbered, it continued to be the fashion for many years to ignore their numbers and call them by the names of their colonels. At the risk of committing an anachronism, the author will at once adopt the modern system, and write of the regiment as the XVIIIth or the Royal Irish.

than their men, would not take the trouble to run up shelters or dig trenches to drain their camping-grounds.   Fever soon broke out with appalling results. Out of the 14,000 troops assembled at Dundalk, 1700 died on the spot, 800 perished on the waggons in which the sick were carried to the coast, 3800 died in the hospitals of Belfast.   The losses in the XVIIIth regiment are not known, but from Schomberg's confidential report on the troops under his command it seems to have suffered less than other corps.   Writing on October 23, 1689, the Marshal says: "Meath's (18th Foot), best regiment of all the army, both as regards clothing and good order, and the officers generally good.   The soldiers being all of this province, the campaign is not so hard on them as on others."

Early in November James gave up the attempt to entice Schomberg out of his entrenchments and went into winter quarters.   The Marshal promptly followed his example, holding the country between Lough Erne and Belfast with a chain of fortified posts, and establishing his headquarters at Lisburn, where the XVIIIth was placed in charge of his personal safety.   The staff of the regiment must have been hard-worked in the spring of 1690, for recruits streamed in so fast that in June it was nearly the strongest corps in the British army, standing on parade six hundred and seventy-eight officers and men.   For several months there was constant skirmishing along the line of outposts; but no movements of importance took place until June, when William III. arrived at Carrickfergus with two hundred and eighty-four transports and many vessels laden with stores.   Though this great mass of shipping was escorted by a ludicrously small squadron of only six men-of-war, it was not attacked on the voyage, for the French had neglected to send a fleet to cruise in the Irish seas, thus leaving the line of communication across St George's Channel uninterrupted.   When the reinforcements brought by the King had landed, the army in Ireland reached the respectable total of about 37,000 men, of whom 21,000 were British, and the remainder Huguenots, Dutch, and Danes—continental mercenaries whom William had imported to lend solidity to his recently raised English regiments.

The French officers in James's army had repeatedly urged him to retire into Connaught and defend the line of the Shannon, but on political grounds he declined to accept this excellent advice, and after some manœuvring took up a position on the river Boyne, near Oldbridge and Duleek.   Here he entrenched himself, but on the 1st of July William attacked and routed him with considerable loss.   As the XVIIIth regiment played no important part in the engagement, if, indeed, it came under fire at all, it is only necessary to say that though some of James's troops fought with distinguished gallantry in this battle, others did not show the fine qualities they exhibited later at Limerick and Aughrim.   Covered by a rear-guard of Frenchmen, the defeated army fell back upon the Shannon.   James, for the second time, deserted his soldiers and fled to France, while William occupied Dublin, and matured his plans for the next phase of the campaign. By a great victory over the Anglo-Dutch fleet at Beachy Head the King of France won for the moment the absolute command of the British Channel, and thus could throw reinforcements at will into the south and west of Ireland by the ports of Waterford, Cork, Kinsale, Limerick, and Galway. These towns were, there-fore, essential to William; and hardly less important was Athlone, the entrance to the wild districts of Connaught, to which he hoped to confine the future operations of the war. A strong detachment under General Douglas was therefore sent against Athlone, while William himself led the greater part of his army towards Limerick, where a large number of James's troops had been concentrated. Though these regiments had worked hard to improve the fortifications of the city, its defences were still so imperfect that when the French heard that William was approaching they pronounced the place to be untenable and moved off to Galway, leaving the Irish, about 20,000 strong, to defend it, under the command of General Boisleau, an officer who had learned to appreciate the good qualities of his allies, and Sarsfield, an Irish soldier of great brilliancy and courage. Reinforced by Douglas, whose detachment had failed to make any impression on Athlone, William appeared before Limerick on August 9, and after brushing away the enemy's skirmishers pitched camp within a quarter of a mile of the city wall, expecting little resistance from a place so weak that the French had declared it "could be taken by throwing apples at it." In eight days William opened his batteries, though with very inferior ordnance, for by a daring raid Sarsfield had swooped on the convoy bringing up his siege-train and destroyed nearly all his heavy guns. On the 20th the grenadiers of the XVIIIth and Cutts's regiments greatly distinguished them-selves by the capture of a strong redoubt near John's Gate. A sudden rush from the trenches brought them to the foot of the work, into which they hurled a shower of hand-grenades, and then scrambling over the parapet under heavy fire, dislodged the defenders with the bayonet. As it was known that the redoubt had an open gorge, a quantity of fascines had been collected in the trenches, with which the grenadiers filled up the gap, and then held the redoubt against a determined sally until they were relieved by other troops. The affair cost the victors two hundred and seventy-one killed and wounded; but though it is known that the grenadiers suffered heavily, the only casualty recorded in the XVIIIth is the death of Captain Needham, who was killed by a random shot at the end of the engagement.

This success was followed by the capture of another outlying work; the trenches were pushed close to the walls, and six batteries played upon the defences, which, near John's Gate, began to crumble under the bom-bardment. This breach William determined to assault, though he was warned by some of his officers that Limerick was not yet sufficiently shaken to be stormed. According to many historians, his reasons for hurrying on the attack were that his supply of ammunition was running low, and that with the example of Dundalk before him, he could not venture to expose his troops to the terrible rains which had set in. "At times the downpour was such that the men could not work the guns, and to mount fresh batteries soon became an impossibility: the trenches were knee-deep in mud: the soldiers were never dry from morning till night and from night till morning: sickness, which had been prevalent in the camp before, increased to a plague: the tenting ground became a mere swamp, and those who could afford it kept down the overwhelming damp only by burning bowls of spirits under the canvas." [1] On the 27th the breach appeared to be practicable, and William ordered Douglas to deliver the assault. Half the grenadiers of each regiment, five hundred men in all, were to lead, supported by the XVIIIth and five other infantry corps: on the left of the main attack was another column of infantry: and drawn up in rear stood a strong force of cavalry. At half-past three in the afternoon the grenadiers dashed out of the trenches, hurled themselves against the palisade of the counterscarp, and carried it after fierce fighting; then, gaining the covered way, they dropped into the ditch, scrambled up the breach, and pursued its defenders headlong into the town. So far all had gone well: the impetuous valour of the grenadiers had carried all before it, and victory was within William's grasp, when a mistaken interpretation of orders ruined the day's work. The supporting infantry should have followed the grenadiers up the breach, but, allowing themselves to be drawn into pursuit of some of the enemy along the covered way, they left the grenadiers without reinforcements. When the defenders saw that no more troops were pressing up the breach, they rallied, and, excited by witnessing the destruction of one of William's foreign battalions by an accidental explosion, they drove the remnants of the grenadiers back into the covered way. If the failure to carry the breach was to be redeemed even partially, it was essential that the covered way should remain in the attackers' hands, and round this part of the fortifications raged a fierce fight, in which both sides showed splendid courage; but, after three hours' indecisive combat, Douglas found that his men had used nearly all their ammunition, and drew off to camp with a loss of at least five hundred dead and a thousand wounded. In this unsuccessful assault the XVIIIth suffered severely; [2] more than a hundred sergeants, corporals, and "sentinels" (as private soldiers were then termed) were killed or wounded, and, though the officers of the regiment who left accounts of this war are not agreed as to the exact casualties among the commissioned ranks, it appears certain that

[1] Walton's 'History of the British Standing Army,' p. 135.
[2] See Appendix 2 (A).

six were killed and eight wounded.[1] Though all their names have not been recorded, it is known that Captain Charles Brabazon, Lieutenant P. Latham, and Ensign . . . Smith were killed; Lieutenant-Colonel G. Newcomb (or Newcomen) died of his wounds, and Colonel the Earl of Meath, Lieutenants R. Blakeney and C. Hubblethorne, were wounded.

Dispirited by his reverse, William raised the siege, ordered his army into winter quarters, and after handing over the command to Ginkell, a Dutch general, returned to England after a campaign in which he had scored only one marked success—the victory at the Boyne. He had failed to capture Athlone and Limerick, and, with the exception of Waterford, all the ports in the south and west were still open to the French navy. In September, however, the arrival of Marlborough with an expedition from England improved the situation: Cork and Kinsale surrendered, and thus the harbours of Limerick and Galway alone remained available for the enemy's operations. Ginkell's first step was to establish himself on a line which, starting at Ballyshannon in the north-west, ran through Enniskillen, Longford, Mullingar, Cashel, and Fermoy to Castletown-Berehaven in the south-west. The regiment was ordered to Mullingar, where it passed the winter—very unpleasantly, according to Stearne, who states that, " in the month of December our garrison being reinforced by several regiments of Horse and Foot, marched towards the enemy's frontier, where after having fatigued the troops for upwards of three months in this bad season of the year in ravaging and burning the country we returned to our quarters."

Ginkell opened the campaign of 1691 by an attack on Athlone, a town built on both sides of the Shannon, and enclosed by walls, not in good condition but still by no means to be despised. On the right or Connaught bank a grim old castle frowned down upon a stone bridge, the only permanent means of communication across the river, for though there was a ford it was practicable only in very dry weather. After a short cannonade, Ginkell breached and stormed the defences on the Leinster side of the river, and, driving the enemy before him across the bridge, made himself master of the eastern half of Athlone. But now his real difficulties began. Batteries bristled on the bank above the ford; the guns of the castle commanded the bridge, which was so narrow that a few men could hold it against a regiment; and General St Ruth, a French officer of great experience, from his camp hard by could reinforce the garrison without hindrance from the besiegers. Ginkell rapidly threw up batteries, and opened so vigorous a fire with fifty guns and mortars that one side of the castle crumbled away and the houses on the Connaught bank were knocked to pieces. But until he had crossed the

---

[1] Thanks to the industry of Mr Dalton, the compiler of ' British Army Lists and Commission Registers,' it is possible to trace with some degree of accuracy the casualties among the officers of the regiment in many, though by no means all the battles and sieges between 1690 and 1712.

river he could not close with his enemy; his pontoons were far behind him, and he had no transport to bring them to the front; and the defence of the bridge was so stubborn that he gained ground there only a few inches at a time. St Ruth scoffed at the idea of the place being in serious danger, decrying Ginkell as an old soldier who ought to know better than to waste time and men on a hopeless enterprise. "His master," he said, "ought to hang him for trying to take Athlone, as my master ought to hang me if I lose it." But the Dutch general determined to ascertain if the river was fordable, and, in the words of Stearne, instead of calling for volunteers,

"promised three Danish soldiers who lay under sentence of death, their lives and a reward if they would attempt fording the river, which they gladly accepted, and at noonday put on armour, and entered the river a little below the bridge, and went at some distance from each other; the enemy took them for deserters, and we from our trenches fired seemingly at them, but over their heads at the enemy; when they had passed the depth of the water, and almost on the other side, they turned back, which when the enemy perceived they fired at them as hard as they could, but our cannon which was reserved for that purpose, as also our small shot, fired so briskly upon them that they could not hold up their heads to take aim at the men, by which they were saved, two being only slightly wounded. The General finding the river fordable (which it had not been for many years) resolved to try and pass it, upon which he gave orders for 40 Grenadiers from each company and 80 choice men out of each Battalion of the whole army to march as privately as possible into the trenches, and the whole army to be under arms to sustain the attack should there be occasion.

"On the 20th June[1] the detachments marched into the trenches (I being one of the Captains who commanded ours) with all the privacy we could, but notwithstanding all our caution, St Ruth had notice of our motion and design by the appearance of crowds of people on the hills to see the action, upon which he marched down his whole army to the bank of his part of the town, and filled the Castle and trenches with as many men as it could well hold; our General perceiving this, put off the attack till another time, ordering our detachments back to Camp, but at the same time gave private orders that not a man should stir from his Regiment, or be put on any other duty, but to be all ready at a minute's warning. St Ruth seeing us draw off, was persuaded that our General dare not pass the River at this time, and in this security marched his Army back to Camp, leaving only a slight body of men to guard their works and the Castle. The next day a soldier of our Army (whether sent by the General, or he went of himself, I can't say) went over to the enemy and was carry'd before St Ruth, and told him that the common report in our Camp was that the General finding it was not practicable to pass the River at this time resolved to try what he could do at Banagher which lay ten miles down the River, and that everything was getting

---

[1] In this and many other quotations from the regimental historians the dates are according to the "old style," and do not correspond with those in this book, which are in the "new style."

ready for the march. St Ruth, easily persuaded with this notion, and finding all things very quiet in our Camp, made a splendid entertainment for all the Ladies and Gentlemen, the Officers of the Town, and the Camp. The same day, being 22nd June, our General sent private orders along the Line for all the detachments to march directly into the trenches, and to keep under all the cover they could, at the same time he posted several sentries on the hills to prevent anybody appearing to the enemy. About 3 o'clock, when St Ruth was at the height of his merryment, we began the attack by jumping into the River, and whilst we were wading over, our Cannon and small shot played with great fury over our heads on the enemy, insomuch that they did us but little hurt in passing, and when we got over they made but little or no resistance but fled immediately.

"At the same time we jumped into the River, part of our detachments attacked the Bridge, and laid planks over the arch that had been broken down upon our taking the first town, so that before St Ruth had any account of our design we were in possession of the town ; however he marched his army down to try if he could force us back again, but he committed a grand error which he found out too late, and that was leaving the works at the back of the town stand, which became a fortification against himself, for had it not been for this, we should never have been able to maintain the town against his army, as we were not in possession of the Castle. When St Ruth found there was no forcing us back without a formal siege he returned to his camp, and those in the Castle seeing him march off immediately surrendered at discretion, and next day very early St Ruth decamped and marched off with great precipitation. In this action we had only 27 men killed, and about as many wounded, and not one Officer of note hurt."

Ginkell now proposed to take the town of Galway and then turn southwards against Limerick, but before this plan could be put into execution it was necessary to dislodge St Ruth from the strong defensive position he had taken up near Ballinasloe, where he was determined to fight a pitched battle in the hope of retrieving the reputation he had lost on the banks of the Shannon. His left rested on the castle of Aughrim, a few miles south of Ballinasloe ; his right was marked by the village of Urachree ; his centre ran along the slopes of a green and fertile hill, well suited for counter-attacks by horse and foot. Much of the ground he occupied was surrounded by bogs, crossed by a few tracks, of which only two were fit for cavalry, while all were under the fire of his guns. Between the foot of the hill and the bogs were many little patches of cultivation enclosed by hedges and ditches, some of which St Ruth levelled to allow his cavalry free movement, while he left others intact in order to give cover to his marksmen, to break the enemy's formations, and to conceal the movement of his troops upon the field of battle. The infantry held the centre ; the cavalry were on the flanks with a strong reserve in rear of the left under Sarsfield, who had specific instructions not to move without a distinct order from St Ruth himself. On July 11, the armies, each about

20,000 strong, were within touch, but owing to a heavy fog it was not until the afternoon of the 12th that the battle began with a sharp skirmish, which revealed to Ginkell the strength of St Ruth's position, and convinced him that his only hope of success lay in turning the enemy's left. He accordingly made a feigned attack upon the Frenchman's right, launched the remainder of his infantry against the centre and left, and sent his cavalry to force their way past the Castle of Aughrim. The troops directed against the centre were to halt when they had crossed the bog, and on no account to push on until the column on their right was safely over the quagmire and the cavalry had turned the enemy at Aughrim. But when the soldiers, after floundering thigh-deep in mud and slime, reached firm ground they got out of hand, and forgetting their orders rushed forward, carrying everything before them until a sudden charge of cavalry swept them backwards in confusion, while the column for which they should have waited was still struggling in the bog. When this supporting column, of which the XVIIIth regiment formed part, had scrambled through the quagmire and re-formed its ranks, it moved towards the hill over a part of the field apparently deserted by the enemy, but really filled with sharpshooters, who, hidden in hedges and ditches, with admirable coolness held their fire until the leading companies were within twenty yards of them. Then a storm of bullets smote the head of the column; men dropped in scores, and for a moment the advance was checked, but the troops quickly rallied, and hurling themselves against the first hedge carried it against a resolute defence. Hedge after hedge, ditch after ditch, were charged and won, but by the time the last obstacle was surmounted the infantry had fallen into great confusion: the regiments "were so intermingled together that the officers were at a loss what to do," and at that moment St Ruth's cavalry came thundering down upon them. Under this charge the disorganised infantry gave way, and were being driven backwards into the bog, when St Ruth's horsemen were themselves assailed in rear by some of Ginkell's cavalry, who, after a daring march and still more daring passage of a stream under the walls of Aughrim Castle, reached the battlefield in time to save the foot soldiers from annihilation. During this cavalry combat occurred an interesting instance of the value of steady barrack-square drill. Throughout the winter of 1690-91 the infantry had been practised in regaining its formation rapidly after a charge, and now, when relieved from the pressure of the enemy, the battalions re-formed with comparative ease, and then attacked along the whole line. At this moment victory trembled in the balance, for though the losses on both sides had been heavy, the defenders, on the whole, had had the best of the day, and in Sarsfield's strong body of cavalry they possessed a reserve which had not yet been called into action. Had Sarsfield then struck into the battle his troopers might have turned the scale, but he was fettered by his instructions not to move except on St Ruth's own order, and St Ruth, struck down by a stray cannon-ball, was lying a headless corpse upon the ground. The absence of the French general's directing hand was soon felt, though his death was concealed as long as possible; and when the attacking infantry began to gain ground steadily, and the cavalry turning movement was fully developed, the men who for hours had so valiantly defended their position lost heart and began to fall back in disorder. Then their discipline failed them, and they broke, rushing in panic towards Limerick and Galway, with Ginkell's cavalry and dragoons spurring fiercely after them.

The losses in this battle were very heavy. In William's army 73 officers were killed and 109 wounded; of the other ranks 600 were killed and 908 wounded. The XVIIIth escaped lightly: only one officer, Captain . . . Butler was killed; a major, a captain, and two subalterns were wounded; among the non-commissioned officers and men seven were killed and eight wounded.[1] On the subject of the casualties in the army commanded by St Ruth historians differ widely; but 7000 appears to be the number fixed upon by those least given to exaggeration. Whatever the actual figures were, however, there can be no doubt that James's soldiers were so completely routed that in their retreat they strewed the roads with their discarded weapons. A reward of sixpence was offered for every musket brought into Ginkell's camp; in a short time so many waggon-loads were collected that the price was reduced to twopence, and great numbers of firearms still came in.[2] The dispersal of St Ruth's army was the death-blow to the Stuart cause: Galway made little resistance, and though the garrison of Limerick fought stoutly for a month it was obliged to surrender on October 3, 1691. The French officers were allowed to return to their own country, accompanied by those of James's soldiers who wished to enter the French army, and with their departure ceased all organised opposition in Ireland to the rule of William III., who was thus free to transfer his troops to the Low Countries.

The regiment, however, did not go abroad at once. After wintering at Waterford it was ordered in the spring of 1692 to Portsmouth, to reinforce the garrison of England against an invasion threatened by Louis XIV., and after the French fleet had been beaten at the battle of Cape La Hogue the XVIIIth was one of the regiments selected for a raid against the seaport towns of France; but the coast proved so well guarded that it was impossible to land, and the transports sailed to the Downs and thence to Ostend, where the troops disembarked and marched towards the towns of Furnes and Dixmude, which the French evacuated without waiting to be attacked. While employed in strengthening the walls of Dixmude the

[1] See Appendix 2 (A).   [2] Story's Continuation.

XVIIIth had a curious experience: there was an earthquake, so violent that the soldiers thought the French were blowing up the place with hidden mines, while the Flemish peasants, who were working as navvies, became paralysed with terror and declared that the end of the world was come. In a few weeks the greater part of the troops re-embarked for England, but not all reached land in safety, for a great storm scattered the transports, several of which went to the bottom. The XVIIIth regiment, however, was fortunate enough to escape all loss.

In the course of the winter Lord Meath retired,[1] and was succeeded in the colonelcy by Lieutenant-Colonel Frederick Hamilton; Major Ormsby became Lieutenant-Colonel, and Captain Richard Stearne was promoted to the Majority. In 1693, the regiment, which now was known as Frederick Hamilton's, was turned for a few months into a sea-going corps.

"In May, 1693, we marched to Portsmouth, and embarked on board the Grand Fleet, commanded by three joynt Admirals (viz., Sir Ralph Delaval, Sir Cloudesley Shovel, and Admiral Killigrew) when we served this summer as Marines. Our rendezvous was Spithead; in June we sailed to Torbay, where we waited for the Fleet which was to go under the command of Sir George Rooke who had twenty Men of War to convoy them up the Mediterranean. About the latter end of June Sir George joyned us, and the whole Fleet set sail together, and was looked upon to be the greatest that had been in one sea for many years; there being in all with Men of War and Merchantmen, English and Dutch, near 800 sail: the Men of War with their tenders stretching in one line between the Coast of France and the Merchantmen. The Grand Fleet kept Sir George company till they passed the Bay of Biscay, being the utmost limits of our Admirals' orders, notwithstanding they very well knew that the French Fleet had sailed out of Brest, and was lying before them to intercept Sir George. Yet their orders were such that they dare not sail any farther, but then parted and returned to Torbay.

"The French, who never wanted intelligence from our Courtiers, had an exact account to what degree our Grand Fleet had orders to convoy Sir George, therefore lay by with their Grand Fleet about eighteen hours sail beyond the limit of our Grand Fleet; they upon first sight believed that our Grand Fleet had still kept Sir George company, which put them into such a consternation that for some time they stood away, which gave Sir George an opportunity of making signals to his Merchant ships to shift for themselves and make the best of their way back, whilst he with his Men of War sailed after them in very good order. As soon as the Enemy discovered their mistake they made all sail they could after him, but Sir George, keeping astern of his Merchant ships, made a running fight of it, by which means he saved his whole fleet except a few heavy sailers which were picked up by their Privateers.

"After this the French Fleet made the best of their way to Brest,

---

[1] See Appendix 9.

and the account coming to our Court, orders were sent to the Grand Fleet to sail immediately in quest of them, upon which our Admirals sailed immediately to Brest to try if they could get there before the enemy, but in vain, for they had got in several days before we left Torbay. This affair being over we returned to our port, and in September the Land Forces were put on shore. Our Regiment was landed part at Chatham and part at Southampton, and joyned at Norwich in October. In December we marched to London, and were reviewed in Hide Park by the King; two days after we embarked at Red House, and sailed for Flanders and landed at Ostend in December 1693." [1]

The regiment was now to play a distinguished part in the war with France, which with a breathing space of five short years lasted until 1712. With the exception of the campaign of 1704 in Germany, the fighting in which the XVIIIth was concerned took place chiefly in the country now called Belgium, but then known as Flanders.[2] Its soil was fertile, and cultivated by a large and industrious population. Its numerous cities were celebrated throughout Europe for the wealth of their traders, whose merchandise was carried to the sea over a network of canals and navigable rivers. Every town was walled, and the whole country was studded with fortresses, with many of which the regiment was to become well acquainted in the course of the next twenty years. On the French side of the frontier a chain of forts stretched from Dunkirk to the Meuse, and Louis had further strengthened his border by a great line of field-works, in the hope of making an invasion of France impossible. In a country so highly fortified the war necessarily became one of sieges. Each side tried to breach the other's line of defences by capturing fortresses. There were ceaseless marches and counter-marches, and gigantic attempts to relieve the besieged strongholds, met by equally strenuous efforts to prevent the relieving forces from fulfilling their mission. Flanders, however, was by no means the only part of Europe affected by the war, for sooner or later the French armies invaded nearly every country unfortunate enough to be within their reach. To describe the whole of Louis's struggle for supremacy, and to explain the means by which he induced some of the Allies to abandon the coalition and range themselves on his side, would be far outside the scope of a regimental history. It is enough to say that though the conflict raged from the shores of the North Sea to the south of Spain, where a few thousand British soldiers served for several years, it was in Flanders that Marlborough won most of his splendid victories over the French.

The XVIIIth's first campaign on the Continent—for the few weeks spent at Dixmude in 1692 cannot be dignified by this name—was uneventful. There were no great battles, and the only operation of importance was the

[1] Stearne. [2] See Map No. 2.

siege of Huy, where the regiment was employed with the covering force. In the spring of 1694 the order of precedence among the regiments of the British army was settled in a way very displeasing to Hamilton's officers and men, who ever since the camp at Dundalk had claimed for their corps the numerical position due to its having been raised in April 1684.[1] Kane chronicles the decision in a few words.

"A Dispute arose about the Rank of our Regiment in particular, which were (sic) regimented 1 April 1684 from the old Independent Companies in Ireland, and had hitherto taken Rank of all the Regiments raised by King James the Second, but now those Regiments disputed Rank with us: the King referred the Affair to a Board of General Officers; and most of them being Colonels of those Regiments, would not allow us any other Rank than our first coming into England, which was some time before the King landed, when he came over Prince of Orange on the Revolution, by which we lost Rank of eleven Regiments, taking Rank after those raised by King James, and before all those raised by King William. The King thought the General Officers had acted with great Partiality, but as he had referred the Affair to them, he confirmed it."

The whole question of precedence was re-opened in 1713, and the colonel of the XVIIIth made a strong effort to obtain rank for the regiment from the date of its formation in 1684, but without success.

[1] A letter preserved among the archives of the Brabazon family shows that as early as 1689 the Earl of Meath was trying to obtain for his regiment its proper place in the army.

To WILLIAM BLATHWAYTE Esq.
    Secretary att warr
att his house in Snt James Parke
        London.

LISNEGARNEY *Alias* LISBURNE
Nov. ye 18th (89)
DUKE SCHOMBERG'S HED QUARTERS
IRELAND.

Upon my Request to Duke Schomberg Concerning ye post of my Regiment; he told mee all the oather Regiments was posted as ye King had ordered him; of which he could make no allteration tell he knew farther his Mag^ties pleashure in ye pertickuler of Myne; his Grace appoynted Count Soalmes to enquier farther into this matt^r & since by ye Dukes appoyntment bid me give you ye State of my Case; which ye Enclosed Certyfies by our Commissary Generall, (Yarner,) & y^t when you ofered it before ye King he doubted not but y^t you would procure me an order, to be posted as appeeres by ye Inclosed. I beg ye favour in ye affaire, & y^t you will give me a line in aneswer directed to me in this place; which will be a great kindnesse dun to

Y^e asshured ffaith^ll servant

MEATH.

I doe hereby Certifie that the R^t. hon^ble the Earle of Granard's Regiment of foot was form'd into a Regiment the first of April 1684, which was afterwards given to his son the Lord Forbese, and afterwards, as I am informed, to Sr John Edgworth, and now to the R^t hon^ble the Earle of Meath; Dated this 27 day of September 1689.

ABR: YARNER
mujt^r Gcn^ll of their
Maj^ts Forces in Jreland.

When William III. took the field in 1695, he commanded an army of 124,000 men, composed of contingents from England, Holland, Denmark, and many of the German States. The British numbered about 29,000, and as the King employed them on every occasion when desperate courage and bull-dog tenacity were needed, it is clear that, however much he despised the English politicians who intrigued against him with Louis XIV., he appreciated his British soldiers at their true worth. As his object was the recapture of the fortress of Namur, taken by the French three years before, he began a series of manœuvres designed to decoy Marshal de Villeroi, the French Commander-in-Chief, so far into the western half of the theatre of war that the Allies would be able to dash upon Namur and invest it before their intention was discovered. William was so far successful that he was able to surround the fortress on June 23, but not before the French had thrown in strong reinforcements under Marshal de Boufflers, who took command of the garrison of thirteen or fourteen thousand excellent troops. The citadel stands on a rocky height at the end of the tongue of land formed by the junction of the rivers Sambre and Meuse. The town is built on the left bank of the Sambre; and in the fortification of both citadel and town the highest military art had been displayed—first, by the Dutch engineer Cohorn, who planned and built the works; and later, by his French rival Vauban, who had extended and improved them so greatly that Namur was now considered to be impregnable. A hundred and twenty-eight guns and mortars were mounted on its walls, and its arsenals and storehouses were well supplied in every way. On June 28th, William began his trenches, and five days later opened fire upon the town, which after desperate fighting surrendered on July 24, one of the conditions being that the garrison should be allowed to retire into the citadel with full power to take part in its defence.

During this, the first phase of the siege, the XVIIIth was part of the covering detachment of 20,000 men with which the Prince de Vaudemont, one of William's trusted lieutenants, protected the operations of the besiegers so successfully that during several weeks he engrossed the attention of the French Commander-in-Chief's vastly superior force of 90,000 troops. Before quoting Kane's interesting account of the way de Vaudemont "sparred for time," it must be explained that the French were in no hurry to relieve Namur, where they thought de Boufflers could hold his own indefinitely. De Villeroi accordingly marched against de Vaudemont, who had entrenched himself on the river Lys, nine or ten miles south of Ghent; but

> "finding him stand his Ground, he proceeded with the more Caution, and halted about two Leagues short of him, till he had sent to Lille for some Battering-Cannon. This took up some Time which was what Vaudemont wanted to keep him in Play till the King could fix himself before Namur. At length Villeroy advanced within less than half a League of us, and

finding the Prince still keep his Ground, ordered a great many Fascines to be cut in order to attack us early next Morning. He also sent Lieutenant-General Montal with a strong Body of Horse round by our Right, to fall in our Rear, and cut off our Retreat from Ghent, which was three Leagues in the Rear of us. Now the Prince had three trusty Capuchin Fryars for his Spies, one of whom kept constantly about Villeroy's Quarters, who found Means to inform himself of all his Designs; the other two plied constantly between both Camps without ever being suspected, who gave Vaudemont an Account of everything. Now the Prince having drawn Villeroy so near him, thought it high Time to make his Retreat; he therefore, as soon as Villeroy appeared, sent off all the heavy Baggage and Lumber of the Camp to Ghent, and about Eight in the Evening he ordered part of the Cavalry to dismount and take the Intrenchments, and the Infantry to march privately off with their Pikes and Colours under-hand, lest the Enemy should discover us drawing off; and as soon as it grew duskish the Cavalry mounted and marched after the Foot. Soon after Villeroy's Advance-Guard finding our Works very quiet, ventured up to them; who finding the Birds fled, sent to acquaint the General; on which they marched after us as fast as they could. Montal, who by this time had got into our Rear, finding us marching off, thought to have fallen on our Flank; but Sir David Collier, with two Brigades of Foot, gave them so warm a Reception, that they were obliged to retire with considerable Loss. Next Morning all our Army got safe under the Works of Ghent, at which Time the Enemy's Horse began to appear within a Mile of us; whereupon we past the Canal that runs from thence to Bruges, along which a Breast-Work had been thrown up. . . . Vaudemont had now a very difficult Part to act in Defence of this Canal against so powerful an Army. Villeroy marched immediately down to the Canal, where, for upwards of three Weeks, by Marches and Countermarches he harassed our small Army off their Legs; however, he could not make the least Movement, or form any Design, but the Prince had timely Notice of it; which was very surprising if we consider the Canal that was between us, so that the French said he dealt with the Devil.[1] Villeroy finding he could not pass the Canal on the Prince, at length turned towards Dixmude, where the Prince could give no manner of Assistance; here he succeeded beyond his most sanguine Expectations."

After an easy victory at Dixmude, which the Governor surrendered without firing a shot, de Villeroi turned towards Brussels, where the wealth of the citizens promised much loot to his soldiers; but here he was again foiled by de Vaudemont, who out-marched him and took up a position which saved the city from capture, though not from a savage and unnecessary bombardment. After his artillery had devastated a large part of Brussels, de Villeroi drew off to await orders from Paris, thus giving the covering detachment the opportunity of joining hands with the main army before Namur, where William was assiduously battering the citadel with a

---

[1] Surely the highest compliment ever paid to the Intelligence Department of an Army!

hundred and thirty-six heavy guns and fifty-eight mortars, whose fire towards the end of the siege cost de Boufflers three hundred men a day. On the 10th of August, the XVIIIth and three other British regiments were transferred to the besieging force, to replace corps shattered in the earlier operations, and at once began duty in the trenches. A few days later de Villeroi advanced, hoping to defeat William in a pitched battle, and thus to relieve the garrison which he had so long neglected, but he found the King so well posted and the covering army so heavily reinforced by the besieging troops that he did not venture to attack. While the French Commander-in-Chief was beginning to realise that in leaving de Boufflers so long unrescued he had made an irreparable mistake, William gave orders for a general assault upon the citadel, where the works had been breached in several places. During the night of the 19th, six thousand men from the covering detachment filed into the trenches, where before daybreak they were joined by the greater part of the besiegers. Seven hundred British grenadiers and four regiments—the 17th,[1] the XVIIIth, and Buchan's and Mackay's, two corps which have long since disappeared from the Army List,—under the command of General Lord Cutts, were to assault the work called the Terra Nova; while the Bavarians, Hessians, Brandenburgers,[2] and Dutch were to make simultaneous attacks on the other breaches. As the trenches could not hold all the troops poured into them, the XVIIIth and Buchan's were sent to conceal themselves in the abbey of Salsine, about half a mile from the foot of the Terra Nova breach.

At 10 A.M. on August 20, the explosion of a barrel of gunpowder gave the signal for the attack, and from Cutts's trenches began to emerge the red coats, to whom the most dangerous duty had, as usual, been entrusted; four sergeants, each followed by fifteen picked men, led the column; the grenadiers were close behind them; the 17th and Mackay's followed in support, with the XVIIIth and Buchan's in reserve. It was a desperate enterprise. Between the trenches and the Terra Nova was a stretch of several hundred yards of ground—smooth, coverless, and swept by frontal and cross fire, and before the grenadiers had crossed it they had left behind them a long trail of killed and wounded. Owing to a mistake in the organisation of the attack, the grenadiers and the 17th assailed the breach before the other regiments were at hand to support them, and by the time the XVIIIth came up the assault had been repulsed with heavy loss; many of the officers had been hit, and Cutts, the idol of the troops, was wounded and for the moment incapable of giving orders. Undismayed by the confusion and depression around them, the Irishmen with a yell rushed at the breach. At first they had to scramble over the bodies of those who

[1] The modern names of the old numbered regiments are given in Appendix 11.
[2] *I.e.*, Prussians.

fell in the first attempt, but half-way up they reached the grenadiers' high-water mark, and thence struggled upwards over ground covered by no corpses but those of the XVIIIth. From the neighbouring works they were tormented by cross fire, but yet pushed on, to the admiration of their foes who through the clouds of smoke watched them gradually winning their way up the breach, the Colours high in air, despite the carnage among the officers who carried them. Mad with excitement, determined to win at all cost, the regiment by a splendid effort reached the top of the breach, where the Colours were planted to show the King, who from a hill behind the abbey eagerly watched the progress of his British troops, that the Terra Nova was his. But as the men surged forward they found themselves faced by a retrenchment undamaged by the bombardment. The officers, holding their lives as nothing for the honour of their country and their corps, led rush after rush against this retrenchment, but in vain. They could not reach it; guns posted on the flank of the breach mowed down whole ranks; infantry fired into them at close range. All that men could do the XVIIIth had done, but nothing could withstand such a torrent of lead; the second attack failed, and the remnants of the regiment were driven backwards down the breach, and then charged by a counter-attack of horse and foot which the French let loose upon them.

Shaking themselves clear of the enemy, the survivors fell back towards the spot where Cutts, on resuming the command after his wound was dressed, had ordered his broken regiments to reassemble. While the British were retreating they learned that the Bavarians had not fared much better than themselves; badly led, they had missed their proper objective, the breach in a work called the Coehorne, and had attacked the covered way at a spot where the garrison was in great force; and after two hours' hard fighting they reported that unless help came at once they could not hold their ground. Cutts, who from his love of a "hot fire" had earned for himself the nickname of the Salamander, instantly determined to go to the rescue of the Bavarians, and halting, turned towards the Coehorne and re-formed his column. To the onlookers it seemed impossible that troops fresh from the costly failure at the Terra Nova would face another breach, but Cutts knew what British soldiers could do, and his call for volunteers for a forlorn hope was answered by two hundred men, who headed this fresh attack, followed by Mackay's, with the XVIIIth and the other regiments behind them in support. The assault was successful; the covered way was seized and held by the British, and all along the line victory smiled upon the Allies, who by five o'clock in the afternoon were lodged solidly within the enemy's works.

To reward the XVIIIth for the magnificent courage it showed at the Terra Nova the King formally conferred upon it the title of the Royal

Regiment of Foot of Ireland, with the badge of the Lion of Nassau and the motto "Virtutis Namurcensis Præmium."[1] In the year 1832, the Royal Irish received the somewhat belated official permission to emblazon this motto on their Colours; and it was not until 1910, two hundred and fifteen years after the capture of the fortress, that the regiments who took part in the siege were allowed to add Namur to their battle honours. In these matters our Government does not move with undue haste; it was only in 1882, that the Royal Irish were granted leave to commemorate on their Colours the fact that they had shared in the glories of Blenheim, Ramillies, Oudenarde, and Malplaquet, the last of which was won in 1709!

The distinctions given by William were dearly earned, for though the authorities differ as to the actual numbers of the casualties in the XVIIIth, all agree that they were enormous. According to the army chaplain D'Auvergne, who wrote one of the best accounts of William III.'s wars in Flanders, the regiment lost twenty-five officers and two hundred and seventy-one non-commissioned officers and men. Parker and Kane give the same figures, but as both these officers were severely wounded it is probable that the returns had been sent in long before they came back to duty, and that in their books they adopted D'Auvergne's numbers without investigation. In Stearne's unpublished journal he states that twenty-six officers (whose names he does not mention) and three hundred and eighty of the other ranks were killed or wounded; and as Stearne was one of the few senior officers left with the regiment on the evening of the 20th of August, he must have had every opportunity of knowing the exact numbers. Two theories have been advanced to explain this discrepancy: the first, that Stearne included in his total all who were wounded, while the other historians took count only of the men who were gravely injured and admitted into the base hospital at Liege; the other is that among his four hundred and six casualties were the officers and men hit in the trenches after the XVIIIth joined the besieging army and before the day of the assault, or in other words that his figures show the regiment's losses during the whole of the siege. But even taken on the lower, and therefore safer estimate, the percentage of loss is astonishingly high. At the beginning of a campaign a regiment was seldom more than 600 strong; indeed, many historians consider that 500 was the average strength. Since the XVIIIth had taken the field in June it had done much marching and

[1] When Lord Granard raised the regiment in 1684 a corps of Foot Guards, called the Royal Regiment of Ireland, was on the Irish establishment; in the war between James II. and William III. it sided with the Stuart King, and after the surrender of Limerick it sailed for France to join the army of Louis XIV., where it retained its old name in its new service. The regiments were destined to meet at Malplaquet in 1709.

some work in the trenches, so that Hamilton's ranks cannot have been quite full when he gave the order to storm the breach; but assuming that Hamilton had with him about 600 men, more than 49 per cent, or very nearly half the regiment, were killed or wounded on August 20, 1695. If the strength be taken at 500, the percentage shows that about six men out of every ten were hit; while if Stearne's casualties are adopted the percentage is 81, more than eight men killed or wounded out of every ten who went into action.   As it is impossible to ascertain definitely the strength of the XVIIIth, or to pronounce on the accuracy of the rival chroniclers, it is enough to say that the regiment suffered more heavily than any of the other British corps in Cutts's column, whose losses, including those of the grenadiers, amounted at the least to thirteen hundred and forty-nine officers and men.[1]

In the XVIIIth Lieutenant-Colonel A. Ormsby; Captains B. Purefoy, H. Pinsent, and N. Carteret; Lieutenants C. Fitzmorris and S. Ramme; Ensigns A. Fettyplace, . . . Blunt, H. Baker, and S. Hayter were killed. Captain John Southwell, Ensign B. Lister (or Leycester), and an officer whose name cannot be traced, died of their wounds. Colonel Frederick Hamilton; Captains R. Kane, F. Duroure, H. Seymour, and W. Southwell; Lieutenants L. La Planche, T. Brereton, C. Hybert (or Hibbert), and A. Rolleston; Ensigns T. Gifford, J. Ormsby, and W. Blakeney were wounded.[2]

The result of the assault convinced de Boufflers that he could not resist a renewed attack, and early on the 22nd he made signals of distress to de Villeroi, who finding it impossible to relieve him, retired to Mons, leaving the garrison of Namur to make the best terms it could.   De Boufflers accordingly ordered his drummers to beat the *Chamade*, the recognised signal that a fortress desired to parley with the enemy, and after two or three days' negotiations surrendered: the troops were to be allowed to return to France, the citadel, artillery, and stores remaining in the hands of the victors.   On the 26th, the French, reduced by the two months' siege

[1] Regiment.	Officers killed.	Officers wounded.	Other ranks killed.	Other ranks wounded.	Total.
Grenadiers (drawn from thirteen regiments)	8	10	150	150 about	318
17th	3	8	101	149	261
XVIIIth	12	13	86	185	296
Mackay's	2	15	73	166	256
Buchan's	4	9	65	140	218
	29	55	475	790	1349

[2] See Appendix 2 (A).

to less than five thousand effectives, marched out with all the honours of war—drums beating, Colours flying, and arms in their hands—and after filing through a double line of the allied troops were escorted to Givet, the fortress to which they had safe conduct. With the fall of Namur the campaign of 1695 virtually came to an end, for though there was some marching and counter-marching nothing came of these manœuvres, and the Allies went into winter quarters early in the autumn.

The campaigns of 1696 and 1697 were spent in operations unproductive of any affairs of importance, and the finances of all the combatants were so much exhausted by the strain of this long war that peace was signed at Ryswick in September of the latter year. The British contingent was sent to Ostend to await ships from England to take them home, and on December 10, the XVIIIth sailed on an adventurous voyage, thus described by Stearne.

"The ship I was in, with one more, having got near the Coast of Ireland, there came up with us a Sallee Man of War of about 18 guns, carrying Zealand colours.[1] When the master of our ship saw her bearing down upon us, he called up all the Officers and told us what danger we were in of being made slaves for ever. We thought it a very hard case after getting over so many dangers as we had gone through, upon which we all resolved to die rather than be taken, and having got all our men to arms, we made them lye close under the gunnel, that they might not discover what we were, and called to the other ship, and told them that in case she boarded us, that then they should lay her on board the other side, and that we would do the like in case they boarded them; and our Seamen were to be all ready with ropes to lash us together as soon as they laid us on board. At the same time we were to jump into her, and so take our fate. By the time she came up with us we had got everything ready to put our design in execution, but she fell in the wake of us, we being much the larger ship, and hailed our Master to go on board her, who answered that he would not leave his ship, and so kept on his course. The Sallee Man of War kept us company about an hour, and was once, as we thought, coming up to board us; however, she thought better of it, fell astern, and stood off without firing a shot, being prevented by the wind which blew very fresh, so that they could not put a gun out of their ports.

"This affair had not been long over when we made the Land, but it put our Master in such a fright, that he went quite out of his course, so that the Old Head of Kinsale which was the first land we made, he took to be the Highlands of Dungarvon, which made him

---

[1] This was probably an Algerian pirate, one of the swarm of Moorish vessels which for centuries preyed upon the merchantmen of southern and western Europe. When they captured a European ship, the crew and passengers were carried off to Algiers and sold as slaves; if there were women on board, they were bought for the *harems* of rich Moors. In 1816 England sent a great fleet to Algiers and after a very heavy bombardment, effectually crippled the sea-power of its freebooting population.

stand away to the Southward, instead of directly in to the Shore, untill our Master was quite got out of his knowledge, and night coming on we were obliged to stand out to sea, the wind rising till it blew a storm, insomuch that we were in great danger of foundering at sea in an old rotten ship. Next morning we stood in towards the shore, the wind still continuing very high, and not a soul on board knew where we were, and though we made signals of Distress, yet the wind was so high that no boat dare venture out to our relief, and had it not been for one of our Lieutenants who had been formerly in the West Indies, and who remembered something of the Coast, we should certainly have perished the night following; by his directions we made shift to get into Bantry Bay before night, and very fortunate it was, for that night the wind blew so violent that it was with much difficulty our Ship could ride it out, with all the anchors and cables we had. Next day, being the 24th December, we landed at Bantry, and from there marched to Cork, where the other part of the Regiment landed some days before."

CHAPTER II.

1701-1717.

MARLBOROUGH'S CAMPAIGNS IN THE WAR OF THE SPANISH SUCCESSION.

ALMOST before the troops from Flanders had shaken down into their winter quarters, the anti-military party in England raised the cry of " No standing army " with such vigour that Parliament insisted on the disbandment of many regiments; in each of the remainder three companies were entirely suppressed, and the others cut down to a strength of two sergeants, two corporals, a drummer, and thirty-four private soldiers, while officers at the rate of one for every ten men were allowed to remain with the Colours. In 1701 war again broke out on the Continent. This war, known as that of the Spanish Succession, was but a sequel to the conflict ended at Ryswick, and was again caused by Louis XIV.'s determination to conquer the best part of Europe. Without waiting for a formal declaration of hostilities, Louis struck hard and quick; and occupied the fortresses of Ostend, Nieuport, Oudenarde, Ath, Mons, Charleroi, Namur, and Luxemburg, and nearly all the strongholds on the Meuse from Namur to Venloo, thus threatening at once the southern border of Holland and the keys to its south-eastern frontier, the fortresses of Grave, Nimeguen, and Fort Schenk. The Allies again took up arms; in June the XVIIIth and eleven other regiments were sent off to Holland under Marlborough's command; and Parliament decided that England should furnish a contingent of forty thousand men, of whom eighteen thousand were to be British and the remainder foreigners, taken temporarily into our pay.

Before the English troops settled down into their winter quarters, William III. reviewed the infantry, whose uniform was at that time both comfortable and picturesque. They wore loosely-fitting red coats, cut long enough to protect the thighs from wet and cold; waistcoats, visible when the skirts of the coat were buttoned back to allow the legs free play in marching; breeches with gaiters, buttoning high above the knee, and shoes. Their head-dress was a cocked-hat, like that of a Chelsea pensioner, and their hair was plaited in a pig-tail, which was plastered with powder and tied up with bows.

At the beginning of 1702, the Allies discovered that though Louis had echeloned considerable numbers of troops along the Rhine and the lower Scheldt, his immediate object was to gain possession of the fortresses of Grave, Nimeguen, and Fort Schenk: and a force of 25,000 men, among whom were the XVIIIth and most of the other British regiments, was assembled at Cranenburg, a few miles from Nimeguen, to watch a French army, 60,000 strong, encamped some twenty miles to the southwards. In the absence of Marlborough, who was detained at the Hague by diplomatic business, the army on the Meuse was under the Earl of Athlone, as Ginkell was now called: the French were commanded nominally by the Duke of Burgundy, but really by de Boufflers, who accompanied this royal prince as military adviser. The old Marshal had not forgotten his humiliation at Namur in 1695; and finding out that Athlone's intelligence department and system of patrolling were equally bad, by a sudden swoop so nearly surprised his camp that his troops had to abandon their camp and baggage and hasten for shelter to Nimeguen, where their reception was the reverse of cordial. The Governor was indignant with the Dutch Government for having promoted Athlone over his head; he was suspected of having sold himself to the enemy, and either from treachery or from the wish to see his rival cut to pieces, shut the gates upon him as he approached the fortress,[1] and refused to take any measures for its defence. The civilian population, however, had no intention of surrendering; they broke open the stores, dragged guns to the ramparts, carried up powder and shot upon their backs, and opened so furious a fire that the French drew off in disgust.

Marlborough, whose recent appointment as Commander-in-Chief of the allied forces had created much ill-will among the Dutch generals, now joined the army, and concentrated 60,000 men, of whom 12,000 were British, in the neighbourhood of Nimeguen. Never was a general more sorely tried by incompetent and jealous subordinates than Marlborough in this campaign. He was comparatively an unknown man; he had never commanded a large army in the field; many of his colleagues distrusted him, and took every opportunity of thwarting his plans; and, above all, his footsteps were dogged by two Dutch civilian officials, styled Field Deputies, who had power to refuse him leave to employ the troops of Holland in operations of which they did not approve. Four times, by rapid marches and skilful strategy, he forced the French into positions where they could only fight at great disadvantage; and four times was victory snatched from him by the obstinacy of the Dutch leaders or the timidity of the Field Deputies. The campaign of

[1] In 1745 the XVIIIth had a somewhat similar experience at Mons. See p. 177.

1702, however, was by no means barren of results, for Marlborough was allowed to recapture various fortresses on the Meuse. The first place to be invested was Venloo: the Germans sat down before the south and east of the town; to the Dutch and the British was allotted the attack on the north and west, and, after three weeks' hard work, the British brigade, of which the XVIIIth formed part, sapped up to the foot of the glacis of Fort St Michael, a strong outwork of the main fortress. Prince Nassau, whom Marlborough had deputed to carry on the siege in his absence, then ordered a lodgment to be made on the top of the glacis as a preliminary to a future attack on the covered way. The whole of the XVIIIth moved into the trenches early in the morning: about midday they were joined by three companies of grenadiers and several hundred men from the other regiments in the brigade; and in the course of the afternoon Lord Cutts called the officers together, and, apparently on his own responsibility, enlarged the orders originally issued. The British were not to be satisfied with making a lodgment, but if they found the French " give way with precipitation, they were to jump into their works and follow them, let the consequence be what it would! 'These were fine orders from a general,' remarks Kane grimly, ' but as inconsiderate as they were, we as inconsiderately and rashly followed them.' "

At four o'clock the explosion of a barrel of powder gave the signal for the assault; the artillery opened a heavy fire, and the British advanced. After a short resistance, the French ran back to the covered way, followed by the Royal Irish, who pursued them into a ravelin, where a captain and sixty men fought gallantly till nearly all were disabled. The survivors rushed towards a small wooden bridge, spanning a wet ditch eight or ten feet deep and a hundred feet in width. The end of this bridge was made of loose planks; and had the French done their duty when they crossed it, they would have tossed these planks into the ditch, and thus made a death-trap, into which the leading British soldiers as they followed them would have been thrust by their comrades in rear. But in their panic the French forgot to take this precaution; the XVIIIth got safely across, and chased the enemy to the foot of the wall of the main fortification. The men were wild with delight at their success, but the senior officers realised that the situation was a desperate one: a few hundred British troops were entangled among the unbreached works of a fort, whose garrison, though undoubtedly surprised, had suffered but little in the attack. To retire was out of the question, but to scale the wall looming high and grim above them appeared impossible, until the fugitives, whom the soldiers were chasing with their bayonets, solved the problem by darting to a part of the wall where much grass grew, and hauling themselves up from tuft to tuft. Where a Frenchman could climb an Irishman could follow, and after a desperate scramble, the red-coats began to mount the ramparts, when the enemy, utterly confounded by the unconventionality of the assault, hastily retired into the body of the fort, threw down their arms, and begged for quarter. Their lives were spared, and the booty given to the troops. This capture cost the British two hundred and ninety-seven killed and wounded.[1] The casualties among the XVIIIth are not recorded.

Two days later the siege came to an end in a very curious way. To celebrate a recent victory in another part of Europe, the Allies paraded all their troops and marched close up to the town to fire a *feu-de-joie* into it with shotted guns and muskets. The inhabitants had suffered much from the bombardment, especially since the cannon of Fort St Michael had been turned against them, and when they saw the movement, feared that the walls were going to be stormed forthwith; some rushed to the Governor to urge him to surrender, while others flocked to the ramparts with white cloths in their hands, crying "Mercy, Mercy, Quarter, Quarter." The Governor asked to be allowed to capitulate, and, says Parker, "as we had other sieges to carry on this season, the Prince allowed them honourable terms."

Nassau next took the fortress of Ruremonde after a nine days' siege, and then joined Marlborough's main army near Liege, an open town commanded by a citadel and a smaller fort. When the French garrison heard that the Allies were advancing, they sorrowfully exchanged their comfortable billets in the houses of the burghers for the casemates of the forts; and as soon as the enemy had left the town, the inhabitants sent a deputation to Marlborough to offer him the city keys in token of submission, and to entreat him to preserve Liege as far as possible from the horrors of war. Cutts, with ten British regiments, was ordered to occupy the town, while the rest of the army began operations against the forts. The siege, which lasted eighteen days, ran its ordinary course: batteries were thrown up, trenches were dug, outworks were captured, and when the gunners had made a practicable breach the assault was delivered. Millner, in his quaint language, tells us that though the French fought very well,

"the Allies after one Hour's very hot and sharp Dispute beat the Enemy from off the Breach, and entered the Fort amongst them with Sword in Hand, killing all before them; and had killed all therein, had not the French instantly thrown down their arms, and earnestly beg'd for Quarter, which our People soon after granted, being always prone to give Mercy, when Need most requires. . . . Much of the Honour of this Action may be attributed to Lord Cutts' good Conduct, in sending up speedily an assistance of Twelve Hundred Men from the ten Battalions in the Town, which suddenly rushed in on the side of the Citadel next to the City, in the very greatest heat of the action, before the Enemy was aware thereof, contrary to their Expectation; the which did very

[1] Millner.

much surprize and daunt the Enemy, and made them quit the Breach much sooner than could otherwise have been expected."

Next day the smaller fort surrendered, and thus, on October 23, 1702, Liege was recovered from the French at a cost of about twelve hundred killed and wounded, of whom nearly half were British. Though none of the regimental historians mention any casualties in the XVIIIth, it by no means follows that there were none among the regiment, for Stearne and Kane, Parker and Millner were all such confirmed fire-eaters that, as a rule, they appeared to consider it beneath their dignity to mention any but very heavy losses. The fall of Liege marked the end of the campaign, and the British contingent marched back to Holland, where the XVIIIth again went into quarters at Huesdon, the town where they had spent the winter of 1701-2.

The year 1703 brought no laurels to the British in Flanders. Dutch incapacity and obstinacy again hampered Marlborough's movements; he failed to bring the French to battle, and accomplished little beyond the retaking of a few small fortresses. At the sieges of two of these places, Huy and Limberg, the XVIIIth was present. The regiment spent the first part of the winter at Breda, then reinforced the garrison of Bergen-op-Zoom, and afterwards returned to Breda, whence it sent a strong detachment to Maestricht.

But if little of importance happened on the shores of the North Sea during this campaign, great events took place in the south of Germany, where the Elector of Bavaria had deserted the coalition and attached himself to the fortunes of Louis XIV. The Gallo-Bavarians, as the troops of the new alliance were called, captured several fortified towns belonging to the Emperor of Austria, and defeated the Imperialists at the battle of Hochstädt.[1] Encouraged by these successes, Louis evolved a plan of campaign almost Napoleonic in its grandeur. Its main object was the capture of Vienna. One army was to force its way from Italy through the Tyrol to Austria; another was to march from Strasburg on the Upper Rhine into South Germany, reinforce the 45,000 Gallo-Bavarians, and join hands with the troops from Italy; while to harass Austria from the rear a strong detachment was to be sent to Hungary to help the inhabitants in their chronic rebellion against the Emperor. In Flanders de Villeroi was to remain on the defensive, while on the Moselle 10,000 troops stood ready to reinforce either flank.

On his side Marlborough had also conceived a daring scheme. As a soldier, he saw clearly that a mere war of sieges would produce no decisive results; as a politician, he saw equally clearly that the coalition would go to

---

[1] The engagement took place virtually on the same ground as the battle of Blenheim in 1704. French military writers always speak of the second battle as Hochstädt, which is confusing to the English student.

pieces unless Austria was delivered from the Gallo-Bavarian peril,—and he
decided that the best way of helping the Emperor was to leave to the
Dutch the defence of the Low Countries, and to carry the war into the heart
of Germany. As he knew that the Dutch would oppose his project to the
uttermost, he took only two or three of his officers into his confidence; he
wrung a reluctant consent from the Dutch Government to the withdrawal
of troops from Holland by pretending that he was about to attack the French
on the Moselle, and for several weeks after he had set his army in motion
the troops had no idea to which part of the Continent they were heading.

On May 19, 1704, Marlborough began his celebrated march; his force
included 16,000 British troops, among whom were the headquarter companies
of the XVIIIth, joined a few days later by the detachment from Maestricht.
Disregarding the protests of the Dutch and of the petty princelings whose
territories were being threatened by the French, he pushed resolutely forward,
and covering from twelve to fifteen miles a-day worked up the right bank of
the Rhine from Coblentz.[1] As each of the French generals formed different
theories to account for Marlborough's unexpected movement, they failed to
combine against him; on the 3rd of June he crossed the Necker, and then
turned south-east towards Donauwörth, a town on the Danube, which he had
decided to make his advanced base for the invasion of Bavaria.

On the 1st of July the Allies encamped at Amerdingen, and at three
o'clock next morning Marlborough marched upon his objective, fifteen miles
off. He rode with the advance-guard—thirty-five squadrons, three regiments
of Austrian grenadiers, and six thousand Continental and British infantry,
among the latter being a detachment of the XVIIIth, about a hundred and
thirty of all ranks.[2] The main body of the army followed two hours later.
Pushing on with an escort of cavalry the Duke began his personal reconnaissance about 9 A.M., and found that the town of Donauwörth lay in a
valley on the north, or left bank of the Danube, and was commanded by a
steep and flat-topped hill. This hill, the Schellenberg, was the key of the
position: the Gallo-Bavarians had connected it with the town by field-works,
and twenty-five hundred horse and ten thousand foot were encamped upon its
summit. During the day Marlborough learned that Louis XIV. had ordered
strong columns from Flanders and the Upper Rhine to move upon South
Germany; and his keen eyes detected on the farther bank of the river
preparations for the immediate reception of a large body of men. He

---

[1] From Parker we learn that the troops used to march off at 3 A.M.; about 9 they reached their
camping ground, where "all manner of necessaries for man and horse awaited them, so that the
soldiers had nothing to do but to pitch their tents, boil their kettles and lie down to rest." This
admirable system, carefully organised by Marlborough, whose care for his soldiers astonished his
foreign colleagues, naturally came to an end after the army had passed out of the territories of the
Allied Powers: once in the enemy's country the British troops had to face many hardships.

[2] The regimental historians do not mention the strength of the detachment. Mr Fortescue states
that the battalions on this occasion were made up of contingents of 130 officers and men from each
British regiment.

accordingly decided to attack the hill at once, without waiting for the whole of his main body to come up: but owing to vile roads and broken bridges it was not until six o'clock that the troops were formed for battle at the foot of the slope, about five hundred yards in length, which led up to the works on the north-west side of the Schellenberg. The infantry of the advance-guard were drawn up in four lines, with the cavalry behind them in two lines; eight battalions were in support, and an equal number were in reserve. During the day the cavalry had made fascines, with which the enemy's ditches were to be filled up, and as soon as these great bundles of faggots had been distributed among the infantry the advance began. Under a cross fire of artillery, the columns breasted the hill without stopping to fire a shot until they were within eighty yards of the entrenchments, when a sudden outburst of grape and musketry made havoc among the crowded ranks. For a moment the men recoiled before this hail of missiles; then recovering themselves, they pushed on until their leaders reached a hollow road, which in the excitement of the moment was mistaken for the ditch in front of the works they were to storm. Before the blunder was discovered the fascines had been thrown in, and consequently when the heads of the columns reached the real ditch they had no means of crossing it, and were exposed to such a hurricane of bullets and hand-grenades that when the enemy made a furious counter-attack with the bayonet some of the troops gave way. Three British regiments saved the situation;[1] they stood like rocks; the partially broken corps rallied on them, and then after a hard struggle drove back their gallant foes into their entrenchments.

A French officer who commanded one of the battalions that fought so stoutly on the 1st of July, 1704, has left a lurid picture of the combat.

"The English infantry led this attack with the greatest intrepidity, right up to our parapet, but they were opposed with a courage at least equal to their own. Rage, fury and desperation were manifested by both sides, with the more obstinacy as the assailants and the assailed were perhaps the bravest soldiers in the world. The little parapet which separated the two forces became the scene of the bloodiest struggle that could be conceived. . . . It would be impossible to describe in words strong enough the carnage that took place during the first attack, which lasted a good hour or more. We were all fighting hand to hand, hurling them back as they clutched at the parapet; men were slaying, or tearing at the muzzles of guns and the bayonets which pierced their entrails; crushing under their feet their own wounded comrades, and even gouging out their opponents' eyes with their nails, when the grip was so close that neither could make use of their weapons. I verily believe that it would have been quite impossible to find a more terrible representation of Hell itself than was shown in the savagery of both sides on this occasion."[2]

[1] These were a battalion of the Guards, Royal Scots, and 23rd.

[2] 'The Chronicles of an Old Campaigner,' by M. de la Colonie (translated by Lieut.-Colonel W. C. Horsley), p. 185.

By dint of drawing men from the parts of the defences unthreatened by the Allies, the Gallo-Bavarians were able to keep the troops on the north-west of the hill at their full strength: and they repulsed the next assault so heavily that it was found necessary to bring a large number of British cavalry into the thick of the fire to support the shaken, though by no means beaten, infantry. Our enemies were beginning to congratulate themselves on their success, when the remainder of Marlborough's main body came into action against the west of the hill, where the works had been almost denuded of their garrisons; they took these works with little loss, repulsed a charge of cavalry, and then struck the Gallo-Bavarians in flank. About this time the Allies made another attempt to carry the entrenchment, and were once more beaten back. So serious did things look that the Scots Greys were ordered to dismount and attack the works on foot; but maddened at the thought that cavalrymen were called in to do the work which foot soldiers had failed to accomplish, the infantry then made one final, desperate effort, and surged triumphantly over the parapet from which they had been repulsed so often. Now at length the French and the Bavarians, exhausted by their magnificent defence, driven from their works in front and hard pressed in flank, gave way; and their retreat soon degenerated into a rout, as they rushed towards the river with all the allied cavalry thundering after them. The victory was very complete: of the twelve thousand men who had watched the Allies form for the assault not more than three thousand rejoined their regiments; the remainder were killed, wounded, captured, or drowned in the waters of the Danube; and thirteen standards, fifteen guns, and all the stores at Donauwörth fell into the victors' hands. But the success was dearly won, for though the engagement lasted less than two hours, it cost the Allies more than five thousand officers and men. The British, as usual, lost very heavily: 33 officers, among whom was a major-general, were killed, and 83 wounded; 420 "sergeants and sentinels" were killed, and 1001 wounded; in all 1537, or "probably more than 33 per cent of the number engaged."[1] To this total the

[1] The British losses given by Millner are practically the same as those adopted by Mr Fortescue (vol. i. p. 427). Sergeant Millner's casualty return is worthy of reproduction.

Corps loss.	Colonels.		Lt.-Colonels.		Majors.		Captains.		Subalterns.		Sentinels.		Total.		Total each K. and W.
	K.	W.	K.	W.	K.	W.	K.	W.	K.	W.	K.	W.	K.	W.	
German (Horse and Foot)	1	2	1	1	1	3	4	10	9	36	268	1130	284	1182	1466
Hollanders	2	1	2	...	...	4	5	19	8	53	361	856	378	953	1311
Hanover	1	...	...	2	1	2	2	10	10	20	189	417	204	451	655
Hessians	...	2	2	...	...	1	2	11	3	14	91	195	97	223	320
Britains (*sic*)	...	2	2	6	1	5	13	12	16	58	420	1001	452	1084	1536
Total	4	7	7	9	3	15	26	62	46	181	1329	3599	1415	3893	5308

Of the above corps there were of the lieutenant-generals killed 6, wounded 5; major-generals killed 2, wounded 2; brigadiers wounded 1.

XVIIIth, out of its detachment of 130 officers and men, contributed 51, or nearly 40 per cent of its numbers. Captain M. Leathes, Ensigns J. Pinsent (or Pensant), S. Gilman, and E. Walsh were wounded; 1 sergeant and 11 men were killed; 3 sergeants and 32 men were wounded.[1]

After the loss of Donauwörth the Gallo-Bavarians fell back upon Augsburg, where they encamped under the guns of the fortress. Marlborough was not strong enough to attack them, and had to content himself with blockading the town while he opened communications with the Elector of Bavaria, to whom he offered tempting terms to abandon Louis and place his excellent troops once more at the disposal of the Allies. The Elector spun out the negotiations until he knew definitely that Marshal de Tallard was coming from the Rhine to his help; then he broke them off suddenly, sending word that he would sooner serve as a private soldier under the King of France than as a general in the Emperor of Austria's army. As Marlborough now learned from Prince Eugene of Savoy, who commanded a detached force on the Danube, that the French were manœuvring to cut off the allied army from its base of supplies, he at once turned northward, and recrossing the Danube joined hands with Eugene near Donauwörth. The situation had become very serious, for though the immediate pressure on the Emperor of Austria was removed, and the French had made no attempt to invade his territories from Italy, it was essential to bring the Gallo-Bavarians to battle and defeat them before further reinforcements had increased their strength, already greater than that of the Allies. It was with much relief, therefore, that on the morning of the 12th of August Marlborough discovered that the French and Bavarians had moved down the left, or northern bank of the Danube, and were then encamped near the village of Hochstädt, a few miles up stream from his own camping-ground.[2] Their right flank was protected by the Danube, here an unfordable river, and by the village of Blenheim, standing two hundred yards from the water's edge. The left rested on Lutzingen, a hamlet at the foot of a chain of broken and thickly wooded hills, which guaranteed it against a turning movement. Between these villages stretched a plateau, white with long lines of tents; and along the whole of its eastern front ran the shallow valley of a tributary of the Danube — the Nebel, a formidable obstacle, for though the stream in itself was insignificant the bogs and marshes through which it flowed were very difficult to cross, and the side of the valley rose so gently towards the camp that it formed a natural glacis, well suited to the movements of all arms. Between Blenheim and Lutzingen were two other villages—Unterglau, on the eastern or far side of the Nebel, was occupied as an advanced post; Oberglau, on the western or near side, was part of the main line of defence. To hold this very strong position, about four miles in length, de Tallard who commanded the Gallo-Bavarians could dispose of an army from 56,000 to 60,000 strong, and sixty guns.

[1] See Appendix 2 (B).   [2] See Map No. 1.

Though de Tallard had risen to be a Marshal of France, he was by no means a clever man, and by his mistakes at Blenheim he played into Marlborough's hands. He failed completely to fathom his adversary's mind: because it was the object of the French to starve the allies out of South Germany rather than to expel them by force of arms, de Tallard did not want to fight a battle, and it did not occur to him that Marlborough, with his inferior force of 52,000 men and 52 guns, might take the offensive. Again, in the disposition of his troops he misinterpreted the military axiom of his period, which warned the chief of an army encamped on ground where it might possibly become engaged, to place his troops in the order in which they would be called upon to fight. In drawing up an army the infantry was usually posted in the centre of the line, with the cavalry on its flanks. To this normal or "sealed-pattern" formation Tallard blindly adhered; but by treating his wings as distinct units and not as part of a great army he produced much confusion; in the centre of the whole line the cavalry of both wings met, but without unity of command; and on each side of this mass of 10,000 horsemen were infantry, with more cavalry on their outer flanks.

As soon as Marlborough had reconnoitred the enemy's position he returned to camp, and settled the outline of the plan of the battle which he intended to force upon the French and Bavarians next day. As their flanks were unassailable he decided to deliver a frontal attack along their whole line: Eugene, with the right wing, was to assail the Elector and Marshal de Marsin, who had made the villages of Lutzingen and Oberglau their respective headquarters; the Duke was to carry Blenheim, where de Tallard had established himself, and break through the enemy's centre between that village and Oberglau. The night was spent in marshalling the troops into their places in the nine columns in which they were to move against the enemy, and at two o'clock on the morning of August 13, 1704, Marlborough began to advance. A thick white mist overhung the valley of the Danube, and though it delayed his march, concealed his movements so effectually that it was six o'clock before the French vedettes discovered that the Allies were upon them; and when an hour later the mist lifted, de Tallard to his astonishment saw a great army preparing to deploy on the far side of the Nebel, the cavalry in the centre, the infantry on the flanks. While Eugene was marching to the ground allotted to him, Marlborough's troops took up their appointed places. Opposite Blenheim, on the extreme left, stood a column under General Cutts, consisting of fourteen British regiments and several German corps: and on Cutts's right was the remainder of the left wing, drawn up in four lines, the first and fourth of cavalry, the second and third of infantry. The Gallo-Bavarians, as soon as they had recovered from their surprise, snatched up their arms and fell in before their tents; and when de Tallard saw a mass of dull red uniforms at the head of the column threatening Blenheim he realised that hard fighting was to be expected near the village, and crowded into it twenty-six regiments of his best infantry, who were so tightly packed that large numbers of the soldiers did not fire a shot throughout the battle. The French rapidly put Blenheim into a state of defence—the walls were loopholed, the garden fences (or palisades as they were called by the historians of the time) were strengthened; the entrances were barricaded with carts, gates, furniture from the houses; while twelve squadrons of cavalry, sent to hold the two hundred yards of ground between the village and the Danube, entrenched themselves behind a "laager" of waggons. Between Blenheim and Oberglau de Tallard drew up his cavalry in two lines, with a third line in support, composed partly of horsemen, partly of nine battalions of infantry whose steadiness was doubtful. Some French writers say that these shaky troops were Piedmontese, taken prisoners in Italy and forced to join Louis XIV.'s service.[1] In the centre de Marsin occupied Oberglau with a strong detachment; behind the hamlet were posted his infantry and that of the Elector, and in front of Lutzingen stood a strong body of cavalry.

While his troops were marching into their places the French Commander-in-Chief added to his many mistakes that of abandoning to the Allies the natural glacis already mentioned, and thus giving them a foothold on which to re-form after they had crossed the Nebel. Parker shall tell the story in his own words. While the Allies were preparing to deploy,

> "the Elector, Tallard and Marsin went to the top of the steeple of Blenheim, from whence they had a fair view of their army: the Elector and Marsin were for drawing the Army, as close to the marshy Ground they had in their Front as possible, and not suffer a man over but on the Points of their Bayonets; but Tallard (a haughty proud Frenchman) was on a different Opinion, and said, that would be no more than making a drawn Battle of it: that the only way to get a compleat Victory would be to draw up their army at some small Distance from the Morass, and suffer us to come over, and the more there came over the more they were sure to kill. Neither the Elector nor Marsin could persuade him out of this Notion; they both were very much dissatisfied, and dreading the consequence, left him, and went to their Posts." [2]

Marlborough had formed for battle long before Eugene was able to do so, for bad roads, broken ground, and many unexpected difficulties greatly retarded the march of the right wing towards the left of the French line.

---

[1] The practice of compelling or inducing prisoners of war to enlist in the army of their captors lasted until the nineteenth century. During the great war with France we had in our pay battalions composed of subjects of every country into which Napoleon had carried his arms. The Emperor had drafted them into his regiments, and when they were taken prisoners they usually preferred to earn pay by enlisting in our army to languishing at Dartmoor or in the hulks. Not unnaturally they showed, as a rule, no great anxiety to meet their former comrades in battle, and usually found their way to the West Indies as garrison troops.

[2] Some French historians, while they admit Tallard's folly in disregarding the opinion of his colleagues, deny that he used the expression attributed to him by Parker, and father it upon St Ruth at Aughrim.

Until Eugene was prepared to attack, Marlborough could not advance without running the risk of being crushed by vastly superior forces; and for several hours his horse and foot were condemned to inactivity while his guns hotly engaged those of the French, which were brought forward towards the Nebel, and fired at every target within their range. The XVIIIth, as usual, must have been well to the front, for Parker mentions that the first cannon-ball "was aimed at our regiment, but it fell short; the second killed one man, which was the first blood drawn that day." After the Duke had carefully inspected his batteries, he ordered the chaplains to read prayers at the head of every regiment, and as soon as the Service was over, to satisfy himself that all was well with his troops and to steady them under the enemy's bombardment, he rode slowly along the whole length of his line, exposing himself with perfect calmness to the projectiles of the French. His extraordinary talents, his charm of manner, his unfailing courtesy, his absolute indifference to danger had already endeared him to the strangely mixed body of soldiery under his command; and when by a miracle he escaped all injury from a cannon - ball which struck the ground between his horse's legs, a great sigh of relief went up from the hearts of Britons and Danes, Germans and Dutch.

It was not until twelve o'clock, four hours after the artillery duel had begun, that an aide-de-camp galloped up to tell Marlborough that Eugene was ready. Then the signal was given, and Cutts, on the extreme left of the line, moved forward to the attack of Blenheim. Under a sharp artillery fire, two of his brigades—one of British, under Row, the other of Hessians— succeeded in crossing the Nebel near the village, and halted under cover to re-form their ranks; then leaving the Hessians in support behind the bank of the stream, Row's five regiments advanced to the assault of a position held by the cream of the French infantry. Until our leading ranks were within thirty paces of the enemy not a shot was fired on either side. The British had been ordered to carry Blenheim with the bayonet if possible, and in no case to burn a cartridge until their General could actually touch the palisades. The French waited till their assailants were so close to them that the worst shot could not fail to bring down his man. Then so tremendous a burst of musketry fell upon the head of the column that the French expected to see the red-coats break and flee; but our men rushed forward through the smoke, cheered on by Row, who succeeded in striking a palisade with his sword before he fell mortally wounded. The British gave one volley, and then attempted to storm—some tried to scale the palisades, others to pull them down, while others again lunged fiercely through the loopholes at the French marksmen, who fired so fast and straight that in a few minutes a third of the brigade was killed or wounded, and the remainder were in retreat, hotly pursued by a body of cavalry. Now followed some wild fighting. The Hessians struck in with great gallantry, and recaptured

Colours which had been lost in the *mêlée*; five British squadrons floundered over the Nebel to the rescue of the infantry, and beat back the French horsemen; but pursuing with more ardour than judgment, they were decoyed under the fire of the infantry in Blenheim and suffered severely. The French followed up their success by bringing up more batteries to sweep the crossing of the Nebel by which the British had advanced; but Cutts soon drove away this audacious artillery and, returning to the charge, delivered a series of desperate but ineffectual assaults upon the village until Marlborough ordered him to make no further efforts to storm it, but to fire volleys into it so continuously that the French would be pinned to their defences, and therefore unable to reinforce their right centre, which he was himself attacking. Parker gives a quaint account of this phase of the battle. After describing a gallant but fruitless assault, he says—

> "The rest of the Foot coming up, they renewed the charge; and those that had been repulsed, having soon rallied, returned to the charge, and drove the enemy from the skirts of the village, into the very heart of it. Here they had thrown up an intrenchment, within which they were pent up in so narrow a compass, that they had not room to draw up in any manner of order, or even to make use of their arms. Thereupon we drew up in great order about 80 paces from them, from which we made several vain attempts to break in upon them, in which many brave men were lost to no purpose; and after all, we were obliged to remain where we first drew up. The enemy also made several attempts to come out upon us: but as they were necessarily thrown into confusion in getting over their trenches, so before they could form into any order for attacking us, we mowed them down with our platoons in such numbers, that they were always obliged to retire with great loss; and it was not possible for them to rush out upon us in a disorderly manner, without running upon the very points of our Bayonets."

While this fierce combat was raging at Blenheim, Marlborough had succeeded, though slowly and with great difficulty, in throwing a considerable number of troops over the Nebel near Oberglau. In the morning the French generals had sneered at the Duke for placing great bodies of infantry between his first and second lines of horse; in the afternoon they discovered that there was method in the Englishman's madness. Foreseeing that the cavalry would arrive on the far side of the stream with their horses blown and their ranks broken, he sent a large number of battalions to lead the way, with orders to push far enough up the enemy's side of the valley to leave room for the allied cavalry to re-form behind their fire. The French horsemen charged down upon the disordered squadrons, but even where momentarily successful they were forced ultimately to retire by the musketry of the infantry, and failed to prevent Marlborough's second line of cavalry from crossing the Nebel. During this stage of the battle, eleven battalions of Hanoverians attempted to capture the village of Oberglau, but were met by a magnificent counter-attack of the Irish Brigade—the men who after the surrender at Limerick had joined the army of the King of France. The Irishmen annihilated two battalions, and smashed through the remainder of the column; but then dashing on too far, were thrown into confusion by a charge of cavalry, and finally driven back with great loss by the fire of three fresh battalions which Marlborough threw against their flank.

On the right, meanwhile, things were not going well for the Allies. The Elector, disregarding de Tallard's order to keep the troops high up on the slope, had moved his infantry right down to the edge of the broken ground near the Nebel, and thus met Eugene's men while they were scattered and exhausted by the difficulties of the crossing; thrice did the Prince of Savoy make a formidable attack upon the Bavarians, and thrice was he beaten back. On the left, however, Cutts was fulfilling his mission admirably, for his rolling musketry detained within the entrenchments of Blenheim the enormous mass of infantry, whose presence on other parts of the field might have turned the scale in favour of the French. But the fate of the battle was to be decided in the centre, where Marlborough had now succeeded in placing eight thousand cavalry in two long lines on the lower slope of the natural glacis which de Tallard had abandoned so unaccountably to his enemy. To meet this danger, the French Commander-in-Chief called up the nine battalions which in the morning he had considered unfit to use in the forefront of the battle, and posted them level with the first line of his cavalry. The Duke met this move by bringing to his front a battery and three battalions of Hanoverians, who engaged the French infantry at short range, and so greatly shook them that they were unable to withstand a charge of cavalry which swept them away, leaving a huge gap in de Tallard's line. That general now had to pay for the vicious dispositions by which the cavalry in his centre had been posted without proper arrangements for combined action. The horsemen of de Marsin's right wing played, not for the safety of the whole French army, but for that of their own commander, and instead of flinging themselves into the breach and presenting an unbroken front to Marlborough, wheeled backwards in order to protect the flank of the column to which they belonged. De Marsin had his hands too full to be able to spare a man to help de Tallard, and before any of the infantry from Blenheim could come to the rescue the Duke's eight thousand troopers were charging up the slope; for a moment the French cavalry stood, then seized with a mad panic they wheeled about and galloped furiously for the river, riding down everything they met in their haste to escape from the German horsemen, who sabred hundreds of them and drove hundreds more into the Danube.

De Marsin and the Elector were in no condition to continue the battle after the rout of Tallard's wing; they retired in fair order, pursued by Eugene's troops. To turn their retreat into a rout Marlborough called off his Germans from the congenial task of cutting their enemies to pieces, and sent them to fall upon de Marsin's flank: but it was now late in the evening; the Germans overtook not de Marsin's column but Eugene's; in the growing darkness each side thought the other was the enemy and halted to prepare to fight, and by the time that the mistake had been discovered and mutual apologies presented and accepted the Gallo-Bavarians' right wing had gained so long a start that further pursuit was hopeless. The battalions in Blenheim were less fortunate, for the Allies blocked every egress with cavalry, and called up infantry to storm the village, when the luckless Frenchmen reluctantly agreed to surrender, and twenty-four battalions of infantry and four regiments of dragoons laid down their arms, and filing through a double line of troops were guarded throughout the night by the British regiments.

History records few defeats more crushing than that of the French and Bavarians at Blenheim. On the morning of the 13th of August Tallard commanded about 60,000 troops, of whom not more than 20,000 ever found their way back to the armies of France or of Bavaria. The carnage in the battle itself was very great, and in the flight large numbers of the French were drowned in the Danube or murdered by the peasants, who, with many old scores to settle, showed no mercy to small parties of disbanded soldiers unable to protect themselves. Among the 11,000 prisoners was Marshal de Tallard; and many guns and mortars, 171 standards, 129 pairs of colours, much bullion, hundreds of pack animals, and the whole of the camp equipage fell into the hands of the conquerors. The victory, however, cost the Allies about 12,500 officers and men, or roughly twenty-four per cent of the force with which Marlborough began the battle. The British casualties, according to Millner's return,[1] amounted to two thousand three hundred and twenty-four of all ranks.

	Corps.	No. of Battalions.	No. of Squadrons.	Colonels.		Lieutenant-Colonels.		Majors.		Captains.		Subalterns.		Sentinels.		Totals.		Total.
				K.	W.	K.	W.	K.	W.	K.	W.	K.	W.	K.	W.	K.	W.	
Britains.	Foot	14	...	1	2	3	4	1	6	17	44	26	74	509	1220	557	1350	1907
	Horse and Dragoons .	...	18	...	...	1	...	2	1	1	3	8	10	101	200	113	214	327
	Total . . .	14	18	1	2	4	4	3	7	18	47	34	84	610	1420	670	1564	2324
Other Allies.	Holland's . . .	14	19	Officers and all stations included . . .												772	1424	2196
	Lunenberg's . .	13	25	Do. do.												824	1580	2404
	Wirtemberg's . .	7	12	Do. do. (Seven squadrons, three of Hesse)												450	674	1124
	Danes	...	22	Do. do.												102	200	302
	Germans . . . (11 batts. Prussian 7 do. Danes).	18	92	Do. do. (of the Empire, K. of Prussia, Circle of Suabia, Wirtemberg, and other places . . .												1724	2500	4224
	Total . . .	66	188	Do. do.												4542	7942	12,484

As a bounty was granted to those who took part in the battle the names of the officers present have been preserved. The Colonel, Frederick Hamilton, was in charge of a brigade, and drew £72. The regiment was commanded by Lieutenant-Colonel R. Stearne, and the Major was Richard Kane : the former received £51, and the latter £90. To each of the Captains— John Moyle, Peter d'Offranville, Jos. Stroud, F. de la Penotière, N. Hussey, Henry Browne, A. Rolleston, and W. Vaughan (or Vauclin), £30 was paid. The Captain-Lieutenant, Thos. Laughlin, and the Lieutenants—George Hall, James Lilly, Robert Parker, Wm. Leathes, Ben. Smith, Wm. Blakeney, W. Weddall (or Weddell), Saml. Roberts, and John Harvey, drew £14 a head ; while £11 was the sum awarded to each of the Ensigns—John Blakeney, Henry Walsh, John Cherry, W. Rolleston, Samuel Smith, R. Tripp, Edward Walsh, and W. Moyle. The Quartermaster, Edm. Arwater, was rated as a lieutenant, and the Adjutant, W. Blakeney, at £2 less ; the Surgeon, R. Weldon, received £12 ; his mate, R. Taylor, was considered only worth £7, 10s. ; and as the Chaplain, the Reverend Henry Reynolds, drew £20, or rather more than the combined bounties of both doctors, it would seem that in Marlborough's army the care of the soul was better paid than that of the body. There were a hundred and sixty-six casualties in the XVIIIth, or about thirty per cent of those present. Among the officers Captains H. Browne and A. Rolleston and Ensign W. Moyle were killed : Captain W. Vaughan (or Vauclin) was mortally wounded : Major R. Kane, Captains F. de la Penotière and N. Hussey, Lieutenants W. Weddall (or Weddell), G. Roberts, J. Harvey, B. Smith, W. Blakeney, and Ensign R. Tripp were wounded. In the other ranks five sergeants were killed and nine wounded ; fifty-two private soldiers were killed and eighty-seven wounded.[1]

The morning after the battle Marlborough marched a few miles up the river, and then encamped for four days to rest his weary troops, to set his hospitals in order, and to dispose of his prisoners, of whom Millner speaks as "a luggage that retarded our progress." During this respite from organised pursuit the French hurried back to the Rhine, whither they were followed by the Allies, who laid siege to the fortress of Landau. The XVIIIth was employed in the covering army, and in the middle of October, a few weeks before the place was taken, all the British infantry were embarked on river boats and floated down the Rhine to Nimeguen, where after a ten days' voyage they disembarked, so greatly reduced by their losses in the campaign that for administrative purposes the fourteen regiments were treated as seven provisional battalions. The troops marched to their winter quarters to enjoy a well-earned rest and to discipline the recruits who joined them from home. While the XVIIIth was at Ruremonde,

[1] See Appendix 2 (B).

where it spent several months, Brigadier Frederick Hamilton retired from the service,[1] and was succeeded as Colonel by Lieutenant-General R. Ingoldsby, from the 23rd regiment of Foot.

The year 1705 afforded the XVIIIth no opportunities of adding to its laurels, for as far as the regiment was concerned the campaign was one of hard marching, great fatigue, and no fighting. Marlborough had planned an invasion of France, and again entrusting to the Dutch the defence of the Low Countries led his British contingent and a large number of their Continental Allies towards the Moselle, whence he hoped to overrun Lorraine and then carry the war into the enemy's country. He expected to be joined by a strong body of Germans under the Prince of Baden, a general from whose jealousy and stupidity he had suffered acutely in the operations of 1704; but after waiting many weeks for reinforcements which never came, Marlborough determined to return to Flanders, where the enemy had begun to show alarming signs of activity. Though Marshal de Villars, one of the best soldiers of France, was watching his movements closely, Marlborough broke up his camp and slipped away unmolested by the French, who were nearly double his strength. With the elaborate politeness of the time, he wrote to de Villars to apologise for retreating without giving battle. "Do me the justice," said he, "to believe that my defeat is entirely owing to the failure of the Prince of Baden, but that my esteem for you is still greater than my resentment for his conduct."[2]

When de Villeroi, who commanded the French in Flanders, heard that Marlborough was coming back from the Moselle, he hastily retired to a series of fortified lines stretching from Namur to Antwerp. These lines the Duke determined to force, and by a series of brilliant manœuvres and rapid marches succeeded in driving de Villeroi from them, with much loss to the French and little to the Allies. But to inflict a decisive blow upon the enemy a great battle was necessary. Marlborough twice placed the French in situations where they would have to fight at a disadvantage, and twice the Dutch generals, in their insane jealousy of the British Commander-in-Chief, forbade the action by refusing to allow their soldiers to engage. The XVIIIth appears to have spent much of the campaign in levelling the captured lines, and when the work was finished, wintered at Worcom, where in January, 1706, Lieutenant-Colonel Stearne received his brevet of Colonel.

The opening of the campaign of 1706 found Marlborough more determined than ever to defeat de Villeroi in a pitched battle; and in order to draw the French general from his fortified lines on the river Dyle, he gave him to understand through a secret agent that, as the Allies realised the Marshal was afraid of them, they were about to besiege Namur, one of the

---

[1] See Appendix 9.   [2] Cust's Annals, vol. i. p. 51.

fortresses of which Louis had repossessed himself by his vigorous action in 1701. The bait took. Stung by this insult, de Villeroi quitted the shelter of his fortifications and marched to Tirlemont, apparently heading for Namur. When Marlborough heard the welcome news, he pushed south-west from Maestricht, with an army little inferior in numbers to de Villeroi's 60,000 troops, and on the 22nd of May encamped at Coswaren, where he learned that de Villeroi was moving upon Judoigne. The Duke decided to attack the French there, and at 1 A.M. on Whitsunday, May 23, 1706, he sent an advance party under his Quartermaster-General, Cadogan, to select a camping-ground near the village of Ramillies, which lies on the eastern edge of the highest table-land in this part of Belgium.[1] Owing to a heavy mist, it was not until eight o'clock that Cadogan discovered that there were hostile troops upon the plateau. Two hours later the sun came out, and revealed to each army the presence of the other, the French moving eastward across the plateau, the Allies advancing from the opposite direction.

The main body of Marlborough's troops had marched two hours after the Quartermaster-General's detachment, but the Duke had overtaken Cadogan early in the day, and began to array his eight columns for battle. De Villeroi, who had the advantage of a thorough knowledge of the ground, took up a defensive position, marked on the right by the village of Taviers, in the centre by Ramillies and Offuz, and on the left by a hamlet known as Autre-Eglise or Anderkirche. A few hundred yards to the south of Taviers the river Mehaigne ran from west to east through bogs and marshes; from Taviers northwards to Ramillies, a distance of about a mile and a half, the soil was firm and well suited for cavalry, but along the remainder of the French line, about a mile and a quarter in length, the Little Geete meandered in a shallow valley through morasses which opposite Autre-Eglise were almost impassable. These villages were strongly held by infantry and artillery, twenty battalions and twenty-four guns being allotted to the defence of Ramillies alone. On the extreme left, between Autre-Eglise and Offuz, were infantry supported by cavalry; from Offuz to Ramillies the line was composed of infantry, while a hundred and twenty squadrons, "interlaced" with a few battalions, were massed between that village and Taviers.

Marlborough decided to attack the French right, between Ramillies and the Mehaigne; and as his reconnaissance showed him that de Villeroi had concentrated the greater part of his force upon this part of his line, he determined, by demonstrating against the Marshal's left, to induce him to send reinforcements to that flank, and thus weaken the remainder of his position. An imposing number of battalions accordingly marched towards the Little Geete, descended into the valley opposite Autre-Eglise and Offuz,

[1] See Map No. 1.

and made ostentatious preparations for throwing pontoon bridges over the stream. On the extreme right of the allied infantry were several British regiments, which the French staff easily identified by their uniforms and their Colours; and when the Marshal heard that the soldiers whom he so greatly feared were facing the left of his line, he drew largely from his right and centre to strengthen the threatened spot. The Duke had successfully "bluffed" de Villeroi; it now remained for him to transfer the greater part of the infantry employed in this demonstration to the points where they were really wanted. On the eastern side of the valley of the Little Geete are hillocks, high enough to conceal the ground beyond them from observers on the plateau; and over these hillocks the leading battalions retired gradually; disappeared, and once out of the enemy's sight, hastened to the centre of the line. The British brought up the rear, but were ordered to halt at the top, turn about and face the enemy: and there throughout the battle several regiments remained, not firing a shot, but by their mere presence immobilising the French left wing, and effectually preventing it from giving the help urgently needed elsewhere.

By one o'clock the Duke's preparations were finished, and after a preliminary cannonade four Dutch battalions were launched against Taviers; twelve battalions of the same nationality attacked Ramillies; while a great body of Dutch cavalry stood waiting to advance when one or other of these villages had fallen into the hands of the infantry. The garrison of Taviers fought well, but owing to the blundering of a French staff officer the reinforcements sent to its support did not arrive in time to prevent its capture, and as soon as the Dutch cavalry saw that their left flank could not be enfiladed from the village they charged the French horse, crashed through the first line, and then were so roughly handled by the second that Marlborough had to bring up many squadrons to their help. But these fresh squadrons did not turn the scale, and before the Dutchmen could be induced to rally, Marlborough — the Commander-in-Chief of the allied army, on whose life depended not only the issue of the battle, but of the whole war—had to plunge into the thick of the *mêlée* and exert his personal influence with the troopers, to all of whom he was well known by sight. But his face and figure were familiar also to the enemy. Some French dragoons broke from their ranks to surround him. He was unhorsed, and would have been killed or captured had not his aide-de-camp mounted him on his own charger. The Dutch then recovered themselves, and the timely arrival of twenty more squadrons turned the tide against the French. While this cavalry fight was in progress, the Danish Horse and the Dutch Guards forced their way through the marshes on the bank of the Mehaigne, turned the French right flank, and fell furiously upon their rear. Encouraged by this good news the main body of Dutch cavalry returned to the charge, and with a final effort shattered the enemy in front of them. Thus assailed on three sides, the cavalry of de Villeroi's right wing lost heart, left the infantry to shift for themselves, and galloped madly off the field.

The battalions who defended the village of Ramillies, mindful of the fate of their comrades at Blenheim, determined to retire before they were completely hemmed in, but as they "could not get out but in great disorder our Horse fell in with them and cut most of them to pieces."[1] The Duke then ordered the brigades of infantry which were massed round Ramillies to bring up their left shoulders and advance against the still unbroken troops at Offuz; but the French did not await their attack; and a couple of British regiments from the extreme right worked through the swamps near Autre-Eglise, and drove the enemy from that hamlet. Though a few of the best French cavalry regiments fought hard to cover the retreat, the greater part of de Villeroi's army was routed and fled in panic, hotly pursued by Marlborough's horsemen, among whom the British squadrons were well to the front.

The French lost in killed, wounded, and prisoners about 11,000 men, 80 standards and colours, 50 guns, and much of the baggage of their army. The Allies on their side lost between 4000 and 5000 men, chiefly among the Dutch and the Danes, to whom the honour of this great victory is mainly due.

There is a curious conflict of evidence as to the part played by the Royal Irish in this battle. According to Kane and Parker, the XVIIIth was among the British regiments which, on the extreme right of the allied line, stood all day on a hill without firing a shot. Stearne, on the other hand, records in his journal that the regiment was "greatly mauled" at the attack on the village of Ramillies; and Millner, at the end of his casualty return (in which the losses of the different nationalities are not given), mentions that "upwards of three hundred of our Horse and Dragoon horses were killed or disabled at the head of the Royal Regiment of Foot of Ireland." If Stearne and Millner are correct, it would appear that the XVIIIth was not only employed in the attack on Ramillies, but was also in close support of the mounted troops during some part of the pursuit.[2]

Marlborough's enemies had blamed him for slackness in not profiting by his victory at Blenheim; but not even his most virulent political opponents could impute want of vigour to him after Ramillies. Although his infantry had paraded before 3 A.M., had marched many miles and had won a great victory, he gave them no rest till 1 A.M. on the 24th, when they were allowed to halt for two hours; then they trudged on "with all the expedition they could without observing any other order than this, that every regiment kept their men as close together as they possibly could, and none of them halted above an hour at a time."[3] Marlborough drove the French back into their own country, and within a fortnight of the battle all the great

---

[1] Kane, p. 69.   [2] See Appendix 2 (B).   [3] Parker, 133.

trading towns had opened their gates to the Allies, while very few fortresses in Flanders remained in the hands of Louis XIV.'s troops. Over the walls of Ostend, Dendermonde, and Menin the French flag still flew, but these towns were attacked and taken in the course of a few weeks.

At the capture of Menin, one of Vauban's masterpieces of fortification, the XVIIIth won much glory. In July the Duke detached 20,000 troops to besiege it; and though the garrison of 5000 men fought admirably and disputed every inch of ground, by the end of the month most of the guns were dismounted, and the approaches of the British brigade had reached the foot of the glacis. The next step was to capture the covered way and counterscarp; and about eight o'clock on the evening of the 7th of August, nine complete battalions, of which the XVIIIth was one, delivered the assault. As Stearne remarks, "this proved warm service," for, as the Allies were swarming up the glacis, two mines were sprung upon them; and when the inevitable confusion was over and the attack was resumed, the French fired venomously at the crest of the glacis, where the British were covering the advance of the working parties bringing wool-packs and fascines with which to throw up entrenchments. The Royal Irish and Lauder's, an unnumbered corps since disbanded, appear to have been at the head of the column, and were so much annoyed by this musketry that without orders they began to reply to it. The flashes of their firelocks gave the French a target, and before the officers could stop the firing the losses in these two regiments had been great. Stearne, who was in command of the XVIIIth, says that the action cost him six officers and more than eighty of the other ranks killed and wounded. Parker, the adjutant of the regiment, mentions that two captains and five subalterns were killed and eight other officers wounded, but is silent about the casualties among the sergeants and private soldiers. Millner agrees with the adjutant about the officers and with the colonel about the men.[1] Notwithstanding their losses, the Allies held the crest of the glacis until eight o'clock next morning, when the working parties had finished the entrenchments; then fresh batteries began to play upon the walls, and in a short time the resistance was fairly beaten down and the garrison surrendered on honourable terms. The siege lasted thirty-one days, and cost the French eleven hundred officers and men, while the Allies' strength was diminished by two thousand six hundred combatants.

In the spring of 1707, the Allies assembled at Bethlehem, where the British contingent was joined by the Royal Irish from their winter quarters at Ghent. Owing to the underhand conduct of the Emperor of Austria, who for his private ends made a secret treaty with Louis XIV. for the neutralisation of Italy, the French were able to withdraw their troops from that country and largely reinforce the Marshal de Vendôme, who had succeeded de Villeroi in com-

[1] See Appendix 2 (B).

mand of their "army of Flanders." But de Vendôme had no wish to fight Marlborough, and a long spell of very bad weather helped him to evade all the Duke's efforts to bring him to battle. Stearne in his journal mentions that "there fell such rain that our men were not able to draw their legs after them, neither could they keep their arms or ammunition dry." On one occasion the Allies were struggling over nine miles of country, along which the French had just retreated, "but what with the enemy marching before us, and our Horse which followed them, and the rain continuing the roads were so deep and miry that the most part of our infantry were not able to reach the camp that night, and it was three or four days before the rear came up, and several of them perished by the way." [1]

In the hope of raising a rebellion in North Britain, Louis XIV. attempted early in 1708 to land the Pretender in Scotland, with a handful of French soldiers to train the partisans who were expected to flock to the standard of the Stuart Prince. The expedition sailed long before the campaign opened on the Continent; to meet it the XVIIIth and nine other regiments were hurriedly shipped off to Shields, where the transports anchored while their escort of men-of-war joined in the chase of the enemy's vessels, which were driven back to France. As soon as the danger was over the troops were sent off to Ostend, where they arrived in full time to rejoin Marlborough's army.

Early in the year it became evident that Louis intended to make a great effort to regain the ground he had lost in Flanders, for he assembled a hundred thousand men behind his frontier fortresses, and placed them under the command of his grandson the Duke of Burgundy, with de Vendôme as his military tutor and adviser. As Marlborough had but eighty thousand troops at his immediate disposal, he arranged that Eugene, the Prince of Savoy, who was in charge of the allied forces on the Rhine, should support him whenever he wanted help. This help was soon required, for the French took the initiative, and at the end of May advanced to the forest of Soignies. While Marlborough concentrated at Hal, de Vendôme rapidly despatched detachments to Bruges and Ghent, where the civil authorities were in his pay; and when Louis' soldiers appeared outside the walls, the gates stood open before them. Having thus secured two very important points in the system of waterways connected with the Lys and the Scheldt, de Vendôme next threatened Brussels; and by forcing Marlborough to move to Asche for its protection, gained time to prepare for the attack on Oudenarde, the capture of which would make him master of the greater part of the Scheldt. He proposed to cover the siege operations from Lessines, a place about thirteen miles south-east of Oudenarde, and hoped to establish his main body there before Marlborough had grasped

---

[1] Other contemporary writers say that a large number of soldiers found a miserable death in the sea of mud through which the army had to struggle.

his plan; but the Duke's secret service agents did not fail him, and when he learned that de Vendôme was to move southwards from his camp at Alost on July 9, he determined to outstrip him by starting from Asche long before dawn on the same day. As the reinforcements from the Rhine had not yet arrived, in point of actual numbers the Allies were considerably weaker than the French; but Eugene, leaving his own troops many marches behind him, had recently joined the English general—and the mere presence of Eugene was in itself worth many thousand men. In a straight line the Allies and the French had about the same distance, twenty miles, to march, but by the roads followed by the Allies the mileage was nearly fifty per cent greater. Almost without a pause, Marlborough's troops tramped steadily from 2 A.M. till noon, when, with fifteen miles to their credit, they halted till the evening, though Cadogan's detachment of eight squadrons and as many battalions was allowed only four hours' rest before starting for Lessines, thirteen miles farther on. Throughout the night the main body pressed forward and reached their destination to find that their exertions had not been thrown away—they had outmarched the French: no enemy was in sight, and Cadogan, who had struggled into Lessines at midnight, had already thrown several pontoon bridges across the river Dender. Not until the Allies had reached their camping ground did the heads of the French columns begin to show on the horizon; and when de Vendôme and the Duke of Burgundy realised that Marlborough lay between them and France, they abandoned all hope of besieging Oudenarde, and fell back on the Scheldt to secure the safety of Bruges.

Marlborough decided to follow them, and Cadogan with eleven thousand troops of all arms, including Sabine's brigade of the 8th, XVIIIth, 23rd, and 37th regiments, quietly left the camp in the small hours of July 11. The duty of this advance-guard was to make all preparations for the crossing from the right bank of the Scheldt to the left by the main body, which was due to arrive at Oudenarde a few hours after Cadogan. Between 10 and 11 A.M. its cavalry scouts had crossed the river a few hundred yards below the town, and were riding up to the thickly enclosed table-land between the principal stream and its northern affluent, the Norken,[1] when they saw to their front a number of French troopers scouring the country for forage. Vendôme had marched down the right bank to Gavre, a few miles below Oudenarde, and was then in process of crossing the Scheldt. These foraging parties were part of the French advance-guard, for de Vendôme, who apparently had taken no steps to watch the movements of the Allies, was so unconscious of danger that many of his men had been allowed to disperse. The French

[1] Owing to the number of villages dotted over the battlefield of Oudenarde it is almost impossible to give a clear description of it in words. Reference to map No. 1 will enable the reader to follow the letterpress without difficulty.

Horse, however, quickly recovered from their surprise at finding Marlborough on their heels, and drove back our scouts, discovering in the course of the pursuit that a body of his cavalry was on the plateau near the village of Eyne, and that some of the bridges over the river near Oudenarde were in his hands.

As soon as de Vendôme realised the situation he decided to form along the slopes overlooking the Scheldt; the line was to stretch from Heurne on his left to Mooregem on his right, and after ordering a detachment of cavalry and seven battalions to occupy Heurne, he rode back to report his dispositions to the Duke of Burgundy, whom he found at breakfast. French writers say that the Prince greatly disliked any interruption at his meals, and the news that the Allies were on the same bank of the river as himself was very unwelcome. There was already great friction between the Prince and his military "bear-leader"; and to vent his spleen upon the Marshal the Duke of Burgundy peremptorily rejected the veteran's plan, and insisted on preparing to give battle, not close to the bank of the Scheldt, where there was a good chance of crushing Marlborough's columns as they came piece-meal into action, but two miles farther back, on the far side of the Norken, with his left at Asper and his right at Wannegem. From that moment things began to go wrong with the French. In the confusion caused by the rejection of the Marshal's scheme no one thought of recalling the cavalry and infantry ordered to Heurne: and these luckless troops marched steadily towards a village which they believed to be Heurne, though it proved to be the hamlet of Eyne, well within the reach of Cadogan's infantry.

While the French generals were laboriously forming their army behind the Norken, Cadogan was throwing pontoon bridges over the Scheldt, and anxiously scanning the horizon for the clouds of dust which would herald the march of the main body of the Allies. But the day was stifling, the roads narrow and bad; it was not until two o'clock in the afternoon that the heads of the columns began to reach the river, and thus set Cadogan free to secure for his chief a good foothold on the left bank. The first thing to be done was to drive the French out of Eyne; and a body of Hanoverian cavalry and three brigades of infantry from the advance-guard were ordered to attack the village. Sabine's brigade of British was in front, and as it was led by the Royal Irish, the XVIIIth was the first regiment under fire at the battle of Oudenarde. Though the garrison of Eyne were conscious that they had been stranded in an impossible position, so far in advance of their main line that they could not hope to be reinforced, they fought well at first; but when they realised that they were heavily outnumbered they lost heart: three battalions surrendered: the others were hustled out of the village at the point of the bayonet, and then fell into the hands of the Hanoverians, who after cutting them to pieces charged the detachment of French cavalry posted near Eyne and chased it into the marshes of the Norken.[1] Cadogan followed up his success by pushing two Prussian regiments towards Groenewald, thus to some extent protecting the right flank of the main body as it crossed the Scheldt.

The French troops who had been powerless to help their comrades at Eyne became clamorous to avenge them, and the Duke of Burgundy, seeing how slowly the Allies defiled over the bridges, determined to take the offensive, and ordered his right and centre to advance. About five o'clock a formidable mass of infantry threatened Groenewald, where the Prussians would have fared badly had they not been reinforced at once by twelve battalions of the advance-guard, who, as they came into action, prolonged the line to the left—*i.e.*, south-wards, towards the hamlet of Schaerken. But as the French continued to gain ground on this part of the field twenty battalions from the main body were flung into the fray, and by continuing to extend to the left as they joined the fighting line, repulsed a dangerous attempt by the enemy to turn the left of the Allies at this point.

In the enclosures round Groenewald every hedge and ditch became a miniature fortress, taken and retaken as the tide of battle ebbed and flowed; and near the village of Schaerken the Allies could hardly keep the enemy in check until the Duke reinforced this part of the line. Then slowly, and with great difficulty, the Dutch and Hanoverians forced the French back a few hundred yards to Diepenbeck; but there they met with so stubborn a resist-ance that they could gain no further ground. Some writers say that the French infantry had fallen back to a belt of abattis prepared earlier in the day; be that as it may, the fact remains that at this point de Vendôme's infantry fought magnificently, and brought Marlborough's foot soldiers to a standstill. Fortunately the Duke had in hand a reserve of some twenty battalions and many squadrons, all of whom had so recently crossed the river that they had not yet come into action; and with these troops he turned the right of the enemy's line, drove in the outer flank of their infantry, and after dispersing a body of de Vendôme's cavalry fell upon the right rear of the French army. About this time, but far too late to influence the issue of the battle, the Duke of Burgundy ordered his left to move forward; but his foot soldiers did nothing, and his horsemen were paralysed by the sight of the British regiments of cavalry, drawn up on the far side of the swamp across which they were called upon to advance. Thus the combat resolved itself into a struggle round the villages of Groenewald and Diepenbeck, and as night fell the flashes of the muskets showed that the French line, ever growing thinner and narrower, was hour by hour more closely hemmed in on front and flank and rear by Marlborough's infantry. Soon it became too dark to distinguish

---

[1] In this cavalry affair the electoral Prince of Hanover, afterwards George II., in charging at the head of a squadron, had a horse shot under him. His rival, the Pretender, served at this battle in the French army.

friend from foe, and after parties from the right and left wings of the Allies had met in rear of the French position and fired into each other, Marlborough ordered his weary troops to break off the battle, to halt where they stood, and be ready to resume the combat at dawn next day. But at daybreak there was no enemy to fight. When the French right flank was turned the Duke of Burgundy again quarrelled fiercely with de Vendôme. The General tried to keep the army together; the Prince insisted on an immediate retreat; the troops lost their discipline, and following the example of Louis XIV.'s grandson, a mass of runaways—generals and private soldiers, horse, foot and artillery—streamed off the field. Not all the French broke, however: by dint of de Vendôme's personal exertions he rallied enough officers and men to form the rear-guard, with which he covered the "stampede" to Ghent.

The French lost about 6000 killed and wounded, and 9000 prisoners;[1] and (according to Millner) we took from them 10 guns, 56 pairs of colours, 52 standards, and 4500 horses. The casualties among the Allies were about 3000 killed or wounded, more than half of which were among the Dutch. The British suffered very little, 53 officers and men being killed and 177 wounded. The Royal Irish, though the first regiment to come in action, were extremely lucky in losing only a lieutenant and 8 private soldiers killed and 12 wounded.[2]

While Marlborough's troops were enjoying forty-eight hours' well-earned rest, an audacious project was forming itself in their great leader's brain. He knew that an expedition was being prepared in England for a descent on the coast of Normandy, and that to meet it many battalions would be drawn off from the centre of France. The Duke of Burgundy's army was reeling under the stroke of Oudenarde, and would take weeks to recover itself. Why should not the Allies profit by this favourable combination of circumstances, and leaving a detachment to watch the garrison of Lille, neglect that great frontier fortress and carry the war into the very heart of France? But the scheme was too daring, even for Eugene, who insisted that Lille must be captured as a preliminary to a serious invasion. So the Duke made up his mind to reduce Lille, and marching across the French frontier formed a camp near Commines, levying large contributions from the neighbouring towns, while he began his preparations for the siege. A single detail will be enough to show how enormous these preparations were—the staff had to collect 16,000 horses to drag the big guns and ammunition over the seventy-five miles of villanous road between Lille and Brussels, where the heavy ordnance was stored.

[1] During the night a large number of French soldiers lost their bearings and strayed into the lines of the Allies. Eugene caught many of them by ordering the drummers to beat the French "retraite," while Huguenot officers shouted out the rallying cries of various regiments. The unlucky soldiers who answered to the call were pounced upon, disarmed, and marched to the rear.

[2] See Appendix 2 (B).

The arrival of the Duke of Berwick[1] with large reinforcements from the Rhine raised the Duke of Burgundy's strength to at least 100,000 combatants. To meet them Marlborough had only 84,000 troops; but when after many weeks' delay his huge convoy started from Brussels, he manœuvred so brilliantly that the enemy was never able to come within striking distance of its cumbrous length. It was not until the 22nd of August that the Allies broke ground before Lille, which every Frenchman regarded as impregnable, for on its fortification Vauban had lavished all his skill, 150 guns and mortars frowned from its works, and Marshal de Boufflers commanded its garrison of 15,000 picked men. The siege was to be carried on by Eugene, while from Helchin on the Scheldt Marlborough covered the operations with the field army. Among Eugene's troops the British were not strongly represented: "only five regiments were detailed for regular work in the trenches"[2]—the 16th, 21st, 23rd, 24th, and as hard knocks were to be expected, it is scarcely necessary to add, the XVIIIth also. The Duke had hardly finished his lines of circumvallation, or, in modern language, the works protecting his own front and Eugene's rear, when he learned that the Duke of Burgundy was advancing to the relief of Lille. For a week the armies lay opposite each other. Marlborough and Eugene were anxious to attack the French, whose position was so bad that Berwick saw nothing but defeat in store for them if they gave battle; but once again the Dutch deputies threw away splendid chances by refusing to allow their troops to fight. The French generals, though under positive orders from Louis to wipe out their disgrace at Oudenarde by winning a great battle near Lille, declined the combat, and withdrew to devote themselves to the safer task of harassing the Allies' line of communication. By taking up and holding strongly positions running along the Scheldt and the Scarpe from Ghent to Douai, they hoped to intercept all convoys from Brussels, at that time the Duke's chief source of supply, but they forgot that in Ostend, which Marlborough had recaptured two years before, he possessed on the open sea a port within easy distance of England. The troops which had just returned from the expedition to Normandy—an expedition as futile as most of our similar enterprises seemed fated to be— were landed at Ostend, where they were employed most usefully in forming a new base.

The chief interest in this part of the campaign is centred in Marlborough's success in keeping the besiegers supplied with food and ammunition, for the French could range at will over the greater part of the country between

---

[1] The Duke of Berwick was a natural son of James II.; he was in the service of France, and greatly distinguished himself at the battle of Almanza in Spain by defeating an army of the Allies, in which were a considerable number of British troops. Almanza has curious points of likeness to Fontenoy, for in both battles the British won a great local success, but being unsupported by their Allies were defeated at the end of the day.

[2] Fortescue, vol. i. p. 504.

Ostend and Lille, and they had possession of the sluices that could inundate the districts through which the convoys had to pass.   After the brilliant little fight at Wynendal, where a valuable convoy fought its way through a very superior force, de Vendôme laid the neighbourhood of Ostend under water; but the Duke organised a service of punts in which, despite the attentions of French gunboats, stores were transported over the deepest part of the flood, and then transferred to vehicles fitted with very high wheels to keep their loads above the level of the water.[1]

The strain upon the Commander-in-Chief at this time must have been indescribable, for in addition to the constant anxiety about his commissariat, things did not always go well at Lille, where de Boufflers defended himself in a masterly manner: Eugene was so badly wounded that for some weeks he could not direct the operations: the engineers made mistakes, and the supply of ammunition was always scanty.   When to these troubles was added the arrival from the Rhine of a large body of the enemy under the Elector of Bavaria, who laid vigorous siege to Brussels, the nerves of most men would have suffered; but with unbroken serenity Marlborough prepared to rescue Brussels from the danger threatening it.   After misleading the French by false reports about his movements, he burst through their line of defences on the Scheldt, and so alarmed the Elector that he hurriedly decamped, leaving behind him his sick, his wounded, and his guns.

The details of the doings of the XVIIIth in the siege of Lille are very scanty; but it is known that in a great, though not very successful assault on September 7, when Eugene lost about 3000 men, his five British regiments between them had 350 casualties, or from a fifth to a sixth of their whole strength.[2]   In a desperate attack on the counterscarp a fortnight later, Eugene was followed by a number of British troops, among whom were some regiments lent for the occasion by the covering army.   In his memoirs he relates that after two assaults had been repulsed with great slaughter, he spoke a few words in English to the brave fellows who rallied round him, and then led them back to the fire, where a musket-ball knocked him senseless. The men thought he was dead; but an intelligent soldier remembered that he was a great friend of the Duke's, and after looking for some conveyance on which to transport him to his quarters, carried him back on a dung cart!   On the 9th of December de Boufflers surrendered on excellent terms, granted him as a proof of Marlborough's admiration for his splendid defence, which had cost France 8000 men, and the Allies about 14,000 in killed and wounded alone. The returns of the British losses are incomplete: Millner states that from the beginning of the siege to October 22, when the French abandoned the town

---

[1] Millner remarks drily that after the French had flooded the country they thought " they had our Army in a Pound, but searching into the depths thereof they at last found themselves most snared therein."   [2] Fortescue, vol. i. p. 506.

and retreated in the citadel, the five British regiments in Eugene's force lost 1600 officers and men; the casualties for the remainder of the siege he was unable to obtain. Stearne briefly dismisses the services of the XVIIIth at Lille in the following words: " Our regiment suffered very much, having two captains and three subalterns killed: our major, with several other officers wounded, and upwards of 200 men killed and wounded." [1]

It would be deeply interesting to know how many of the Royal Irish who watched the garrison of Lille march out with all the honours of war had seen the ceremonial at Namur thirteen years before. Unfortunately it occurred to none of the literary officers of the XVIIIth to record the numbers. The mental attitude of these old warriors is very curious: they seem to have grown tired of writing about battles and sieges, and as the war went on cut their descriptions shorter and shorter, though they were ready to dilate on any departure from the usual routine of warfare. Thus, for example, they all give accounts of a daring attempt to throw reinforcements of powder into Lille. Two thousand cavalrymen started from Douai, carrying large bags of powder behind them, and wearing in their hats " boughs of trees," in imitation of the Germans who always decorated themselves in this way when on an expedition—or as the British soldier would now express it, " when on the job." In the dusk they rode up to the outer barrier of the line of circumvallation, gave over the pass-word, and stating they were a detachment of German Horse with prisoners, were allowed to enter. Then they rode on undetected, until one of the party, to use modern slang, " gave the show away," by remarking in French to a comrade that they had got through the barrier very easily. A watchful sentry overheard him, drew his own conclusions, and by promptly firing at the speaker gave the alarm. The troops, says Millner,

> "instantly turned out of their Tents in only their Shirts and Cartridge Boxes with their Ammunition, and seiz'd their Arms from their Belts, and in a Trice form'd themselves into as good Order as could be expected, and with undaunted Courage, though in the Dark, fired amongst the thickest of the Enemy putting them in great Disorder and Confusion, so that in the Hurly-Burly thereof, several of the Bags of Powder fell off on a Causeway, and was broke; the which by the prancing of the Horses' Feet, took Fire, and thereby blowed up and tore to pieces upwards of one Hundred Men of them, and likewise destroyed a good many of their Horses; but in the interim thereof, a few of them slipt into the City with some Ammunition also; but the major Part was obliged to retire, and that in very great Haste, Disorder and Confusion back again to Tournai. . . . The Besieged made a great Huzzaing that Night because they had got those few in with some Relief of Powder."

While de Boufflers was discussing with Marlborough the terms of capitulation, the other French Generals, thinking that the Duke was as much worn

---

[1] See Appendix 2 (B).

out by the campaign as they were themselves, sent their men into winter quarters and went off to Paris. But they reckoned without their host. Marlborough sprang at Ghent, and invested it, repulsed a great sortie on Christmas Day, and accepted the surrender of the garrison on January 2, 1709. The French troops in Bruges did not wait to be attacked, but abandoned the town and citadel: and then, but not till then, the Allies were allowed to disperse to their winter quarters.

During the greater part of the year 1708 the regiment was deprived of the services of the adjutant, Captain Robert Parker, who was specially selected to act as instructor in discipline and drill to the regiments at that time quartered in Ireland. To any officer the compliment would have been great; but in Parker's case it was especially flattering, because he was a self-made man who had risen from the ranks. His story is an interesting one. His father was a farmer near Kilkenny, where the boy was sent to a school which boasted of a company of cadets (as we should now call them), who were "armed with wooden guns and took great delight in marching and exercising." These cadets must have been a remarkable set of lads, as more than thirty of them obtained commissions, and some indeed became General officers. Parker soon discovered that soldiering was the trade for him, and running away from home, enlisted in an independent company commanded by Captain Frederick Hamilton, the future Colonel of the XVIIIth Regiment. During the Tyrconnel troubles both Hamilton and Parker were disbanded, but April, 1689, found them in Meath's regiment, the one a major, the other a full private. Parker joined with a strong determination to get on in his profession. "I determined to be very circumspect in my behaviour, by which I gained the esteem of my Major and most of the officers of the regiment. I applied myself diligently to the use of arms, and soon became expert in it." Whether he had risen to be a sergeant in the Irish wars is not known: all he tells us about himself at that time is that at Athlone in throwing up an entrenchment he "received a favourable shot on the crown of the head; the ball only grazed on a good thick skull and went off"; and that at the end of the siege he was much injured by a stone dropped on him by the defenders of the castle. He must have been a non-commissioned officer in 1695; desperately wounded at Namur, he found when he returned to duty after seven months in hospital, that he had been gazetted to a commission, with seven ensigns junior to him. Eleven years later he was Captain-Lieutenant and Adjutant, and after receiving at Menin "a contusion on the side of the head which was likely to be fatal," was promoted to be captain of the grenadier company. Parker was so successful in disciplining the infantry in Ireland that, when after two years he returned to duty with the regiment in Flanders, Government made him a present of two hundred pounds.

Though Louis had suffered heavily in 1708, the enormous resources of his kingdom enabled him to send large numbers of fresh troops to the Marshal de Villars, whom early in 1709 he placed in command of the army of Flanders. De Villars' first care had been to secure the safety of Arras, the key to the north-east of France, by throwing up to the east of the town a great line of works which stretched from the Lys to Douai; and from behind these works, known as the lines of La Bassée, he watched the Allies, who owing to the lateness of the season did not take the field till June. Marlborough's first move was to make open, even ostentatious preparations to force the lines; de Villars concentrated to resist them, calling up as reinforcements a large portion of the garrison of Tournai, a fortress some sixteen miles east of Lille. As Tournai was Marlborough's immediate objective, he marched swiftly upon it, and invested it before de Villars discovered how completely he had been outwitted. At the beginning of the siege the XVIIIth took part in an expedition to reduce various small forts in the neighbourhood, and after marching night and day returned "greatly fatigued,"[1] but in time to help to storm the breaches of the ravelin, and to repulse a determined sortie by the garrison, who strove to make up for the weakness of their numbers by the vigour of their defence. Up to the time that the town surrendered and the troops retired into the citadel, the siege had run on normal lines; but when the attack on the citadel began things became very different, for this stronghold was celebrated throughout Europe for its subterranean defences, and the ground outside its walls was honeycombed with casemates, mines, and secret passages. To reach these hidden works the besiegers had to sink deep shafts, and then to drive tunnels fathoms deep under the earth, at any moment liable to be blown sky-high by the explosion of a mine. The desperate work done by the XVIIIth in this phase of the siege is well described by Stearne.

"The enemy and we met several times underground and fought it out with bayonet and pistol, and in twelve days the French sprang sixteen mines, which blew up a great many of our men; and one mine did so much execution that it blew up part of the town wall, two branches of our trenches with a parallel between them, and ruined two of our mines, with a Captain and Lieutenant of our regiment and another officer and forty men, all of which happened on our attack. . . . Our miners discovered the branches of another mine, and as they were busy in finding out the mine itself, they heard the enemy at work in one of their galleries, whereupon a Lieutenant and twenty Grenadiers were ordered to dislodge them, but the Lieutenant being killed at the first onset the Grenadiers retired immediately; after that another officer with a fresh detachment was ordered for that service, but the enemy throwing a great many grenades and making a great smoke with combustible stuff, forced them to retire being suffocated. The next day, the miners being supported by a Lieutenant and sixteen Grenadiers, were at work, to pierce through a gallery they had discovered, but upon their breaking into it,

[1] Stearne.

the enemy threw in upon them a great quantity of straw, hemp, powder and other combustible matter, and being set on fire the Lieutenant and ten of the Grenadiers were stifled. After this manner was this terrible siege carried on, till by degrees we wrought ourselves almost into the ditch. The enemy sprang a mine which was their last effort, with which we had near four hundred men killed, but notwithstanding we lodged ourselves that night on our attack near their palisades, where we raised a prodigious quantity of cannon."

The citadel capitulated on the 3rd of September, after more than 3000 French officers and men had fallen. The besiegers' casualties are given in Millner's return as 1233 killed, 4055 wounded, or a grand total of 5288. Millner is not as clear as usual about the loss of the British, but it seems probable that 178 were killed and 521 wounded, or 699 of all ranks. To what extent the Royal Irish suffered it is impossible to say, but it is probable that in such continuous fighting more officers and men were placed *hors de combat* than are mentioned in Stearne's narrative.[1]

As soon as Marlborough saw that the defence of Tournai was weakening, he marched a large force towards the lines of La Bassée; again demonstrated against de Villars, whom he puzzled completely, and then, after a march of forty-nine miles in fifty-six hours, in pouring rain over roads knee-deep in mud, swooped upon Mons, a town important to the French, though at that time only weakly held. When de Villars slowly realised that the Duke had no intention of wasting his strength in storming highly fortified lines, he advanced with 95,000 men, and entrenched himself at the Trouée d'Aulnoit, one of the few gaps in a belt of woodland which lay a few miles to the south of Mons. He outnumbered the Allies so greatly that they decided not to attack him until the troops left to level the siege-works at Tournai had rejoined headquarters, and thus made Marlborough's numerical strength equal to that of his opponent. These troops, among which were the XVIIIth and several other British regiments, were ordered up at once, but while they were on the march de Villars, by working night and day, rendered his position very formidable. His right rested on the forest of Laignières, half a mile from the village of Malplaquet,[2] which has given its name to the battle of the 11th of September, 1709: his centre ran across the southern end of the gap, which was open, fairly level, and about 2000 yards in width: his left was thrown forward into the continuous series of woods known respectively as those of Taignières, Blangies, and Sart. Across his centre he built long lines of trenches, gun emplacements, chains of abattis, and many strong redans; the woods on his flanks were similarly protected, and when the attackers had forced their way through the abattis which fringed the edges they came under the fire of field-works hidden in the depths of the forest. The weak point of

---

[1] See Appendix 2 (B).   [2] See Map No. 1.

the position was that cavalry could only act offensively on the plain—*i.e.,* the gap between the woods; and as this open ground was covered with defences Villars had to draw up his Horse in rear of the rest of his troops, where they would be unable to come into action unless the Allies broke through some part of the front line.

For the attack of this position, which from the nature of its fortifications had virtually become a fortress, the Duke issued the following orders: The Prince of Orange with thirty-one battalions, most of which were Dutch, was to make a demonstration against the right of the French line; sixty-eight battalions were to assail the northern and eastern faces of the woods of Taignières and Sart; while General Withers, with five British and fourteen foreign battalions, was to strike and turn the extreme left of the enemy's line at the village of La Folie. As the pressure on the French left became intense, the Duke expected (as did actually happen) that de Villars would draw largely from his centre to reinforce the point of danger; then fifteen British battalions and other infantry, till then held back in the centre, were to be launched at the works in the gap, capture them, and thus win a passage for the allied cavalry, which was then to crash through Villars' centre and cut his army in twain. The heavier guns were massed into two great batteries—one playing on the enemy's right, the other on his left.

Though the advanced parties of the hostile armies watched each other throughout the night at little more than a musket's shot distance, nothing happened to disturb the few hours' rest which the Duke allowed his men.[1] Long before daylight the troops were under arms, and when morning service had been read at the head of every regiment, the Duke rode through his army, correcting faulty dispositions and sending to their places in the line of battle the horse and dragoons who during the night had arrived from Tournai. They had left behind them on the road the infantry, who came on as best they could, the last to reach the battlefield being the Royal Irish, whose march was retarded by the slow-moving guns they had to escort.[2] After an hour's artillery duel Marlborough began to carry his plan into effect, and launched his infantry columns against Villars' flanks. At first things went well. His right made some progress, though in the woods of Taignières and Sart the French fought superbly, disputing every inch of ground, and by vigorous counter-attacks often sending their assailants

---

[1] Students of the literature of the Peninsular War will remember frequent mention of the good terms existing between the British and French soldiers when they met on outpost. Things seem to have been much the same in the time of Marlborough, for Millner says that on the night before Malplaquet "several of both sides had frequent and friendly Commerce and Conferences with one another, as if we had been in an alliance together; but at last each man being called to his respective post, our Commerce was turn'd to, and swallowed up in blood, as in the Salutations of the day after appeared."

[2] The Malplaquet roll (Dalton, vol. 6) gives the names of the officers who were at the battle of

reeling back upon their supports; and on his left the Prince of Orange kept the enemy occupied in the forest of Laignières by his feigned attack. Suddenly, in direct defiance of his orders from the Duke, this General took upon himself to attack in real earnest; but the French fell upon his column with such resistless energy that the Dutch, stubborn fighters as they were, were driven back with hideous slaughter. Marlborough received this startling news with composure; he directed the Prince of Orange to content himself with holding the French without again attacking them; and confident of ultimate success, in no way altered his original dispositions.

While the Prince of Orange was being buffeted on the left, Eugene, who commanded on the right flank, was forcing the French backwards through the woods. The process, though slow and very costly, was sure; and when de Villars, who had taken charge of the French left, heard that the red-coats of Withers' column were appearing on his flank at La Folie, he did exactly what Marlborough expected him to do, and weakened his centre to reinforce his left. Three brigades, one of them composed of the Irishmen who had done so well at Blenheim, hurried up to de Villars' help, plunged into the wood, and drove the Allies back on their supports. In this charge the Irish Brigade with reckless valour pursued so far that they lost their formation, and the whole or part of one of its battalions found itself alone in a glade, where it was attacked by the Royal Irish. The XVIIIth had come so late into action that it had been sent off to the extreme right of the whole army, where, in modern phraseology, it seems to have acted "on its own," and according to Parker marched on till it came

"to an open in the wood. It was a small plain, on the opposite side of which we perceived a battalion of the enemy drawn up. Upon this Colonel Kane who was then at the head of the regiment, having drawn us up and formed our Platoons, advanced gently towards them, and the six Platoons of our first fire made ready. When we had advanced within a hundred yards of them, they gave us a fire of one of their ranks, where-

Malplaquet. The asterisks show those who fought at Blenheim, not necessarily in the XVIIIth regiment.

Brevet Lieutenant-Colonel—R. Kane.*

Brevet Majors—M. Leathes* and F. de La Penotière.*

Captains—P. D'Offranville,* N. Hussey,* R. Parker,* W. Weddall,* H. Wingfield, W. Leathes,* Ant. Pujolas,* Jas. Lilly.*

Captain-Lieutenant—R. Tripp.*

Lieutenants—S. Gilman, R. Ingoldsby, Jno. Blakeney,* B. Devenish, John Cherry,* T. Carter, Simon Montford, E. Moyle, R. Reed, Ch. Parker, Jas. Pinsent,* R. Selicke.

Ensigns—Jos. Young, Jas. Smith, Jas. Scott, R. Hawkins, T. Broderick, T. Jennings, A. Forster, G. Halfhide, J. Eyre, J. Hamilton, W. Hopkey, G. Mann.

Adjutant—R. Parker.

Quartermaster—Jacob Berger.

Chaplain—Rev. H. Reynolds.*

Surgeon—Thos. Young.

upon we halted, and returned them the fire of our six Platoons at once; and immediately made ready the six Platoons of our second fire, and advanced upon them again. They then gave us the fire of another rank, and we returned them a second fire, which made them shrink; however they gave us the fire of a third rank after a scattering manner, and then retired into the wood in great disorder, on which we sent our third fire after them, and saw them no more. We advanced cautiously up to the ground which they had quitted and found several of them, killed and wounded; among the latter was one Lieutenant O'Sullivan, who told us the battalion we had engaged was the Royal Regiment of Ireland in the French service."

In this skirmish the XVIIIth, or Royal regiment of Foot of Ireland, had but few casualties; while the Iro-Gallic regiment, as "their opposite number" in Louis' army was termed, is said to have lost several officers and about forty men.[1]

While the Irishmen were settling their quarrel, the climax of the battle was approaching. Eugene had rallied his infantry in the wood of Taignières, and was struggling to hold his own against the fresh troops which de Villars in person led against him. Both generals were wounded—Eugene was struck on the head by a musket-ball, but refused to leave the fighting line to have his injury attended to by a surgeon; de Villars, hard hit in the leg, made a gallant effort to direct the battle from a chair, but swooning from pain was carried away insensible to the nearest village. Though deprived of their leader, the French fought obstinately, and on the right of the allied line the combat raged without any decisive result, neither side knowing that when the three brigades were moved from the centre to the left of de Villars' line, Marlborough had ordered the Dutch forward on his left, and had hurled himself against the heart of the French position. Orkney's fifteen battalions of British infantry, who for many hours had been waiting for their chance, were let loose against the redans across their front, and carrying them after a sharp fight, promptly lined with marksmen the reverse parapets—*i.e.*, those looking backwards into the enemy's second line. On the left, the Dutch infantry atoned for their mistake in the morning by capturing not only the wood of Laignières, but the abattis and trenches connecting it with the works now in the hands of the red-coated battalions, and the Dutch cavalry poured through the openings won by their infantry comrades. But in the scramble over shelter trenches and abattis their ranks became disordered, and before they had time to re-form they were attacked by the Gendarmerie, and forced to take shelter under the muskets of Orkney's battalions, whose steady shooting beat off the French and gained time for Marlborough to come up with the British and Prussian horse. These were

---

[1] Mr Callaghan, the historian of the Irish regiments in the service of France, throws grave doubts on the accuracy of Parker's story, which however is corroborated by other officers of the XVIIIth.

driving the Gendarmerie backwards, when a splendid counter-attack of the
French Household troops crashed through their first line, penetrated the
second, and threw the third into confusion. At that moment Eugene,
dashing up bloodstained from his wound, threw his last squadrons against
the enemy's flank; Louis' Bodyguard wavered and gave way, and de
Boufflers, on whom the command had devolved after de Villars was
wounded, seeing that his centre was pierced, his right dislodged, and his
left beaten though not routed, ordered a retreat.

His retirement was quite unmolested by the Allies, who were too much
exhausted to pursue an enemy who after such a desperate struggle was
still able to retire in good order. Marlborough had begun the engagement
with about 95,000 troops, but by three o'clock in the afternoon twenty
thousand of his men were killed or wounded. Millner's analysis of the
casualties shows that the Germans lost 5321 officers and men; the Prussians,
1694; the Hanoverians, 2219; the Dutch (thanks to the Prince of Orange's
untimely movement), 8680; and the British, 1783. In the British contingent 32 officers were killed and 111 wounded; among the other ranks,
492 were killed and 1073 wounded. Of the XVIIIth, two officers were
wounded, four men killed and six wounded.[1] Though the French lost the
day, only twelve thousand of their men fell; and the only trophies of the
victory left in the hands of the Allies were sixteen guns, five hundred
prisoners, and many standards.

Three days after the battle the Duke resumed the siege of Mons, where
the Royal Irish were among the regiments of the covering force, and when
the fall of the fortress brought the campaign to an end, the XVIIIth returned
to its usual winter quarters in the town of Ghent.

Though no great battle occurred in 1710, the army in Flanders was by no
means idle. As Marlborough failed to induce Villars to try conclusions with
him in the field, he began to prepare for a future invasion of France by the
successive capture of the fortresses of Douai, St Venant, Bethune, and Aire.
The XVIIIth was in the besieging force at Aire, where the small garrison
defended itself gallantly for nearly ten weeks, not surrendering until it had
lost about 1400 men and inflicted nearly five times as many casualties on the
attackers. Nothing is known of the work done in this siege by the XVIIIth;
Stearne and Parker contented themselves with recording that owing to the
capture of a convoy food was very scarce in camp,[2] and that the regiment

[1] See Appendix 2 (B).

[2] Parker, who is corroborated by Stearne, tells a very curious story about the grain rations at Aire.
After saying that the enemy had carried away all the wheat before the beginning of the siege, he
continues, " but we met with a considerable supply, which I fear will scarce be believed by any but
those that saw it. But fact it is, that the soldiers found concealments under ground, which the mice
had laid up for their winter store, and that in such abundance, that it was a great relief to us toward
the end of the Siege. These hoards were from four to six feet under ground, and in many of them
our men found some pecks of corn."

MAP Nº1.

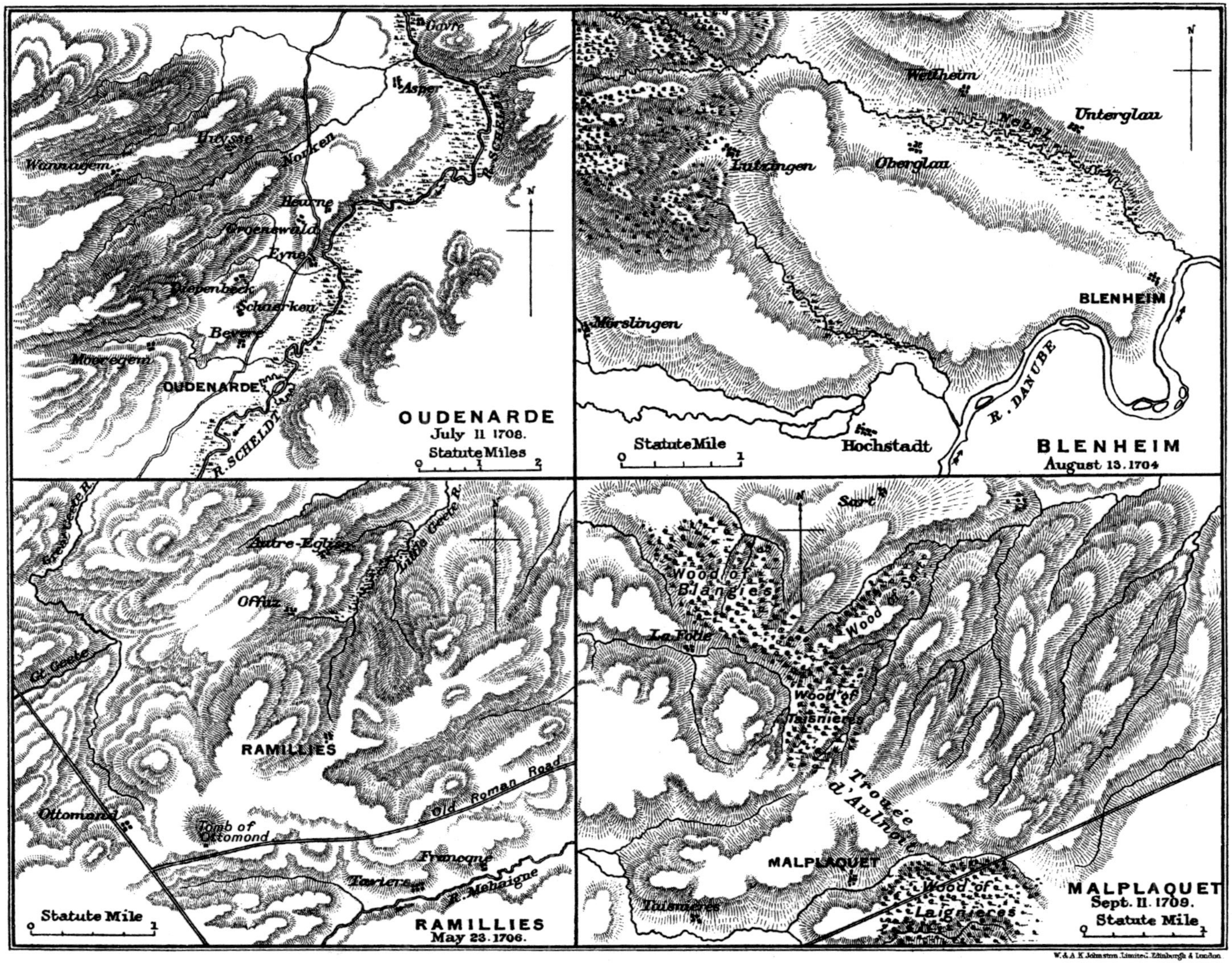

BLENHEIM
August 13. 1704

Unterglau

Nebel

Oberglau

Hochstadt

R. DANUBE

BLENHEIM

Lutzingen

Sonderlingen

Statute Mile
0   1

N

OUDENARDE
July 11. 1708.
Statute Miles
0   1   2

Scheldt

Bevere

Oycke

OUDENARDE

N

MALPLAQUET
Sept. 11. 1709.
Statute Mile
0   1

Sart

Wood of
Blaregnies

La Folie

Wood of
Sars

Trouée
d'Aulnoit

MALPLAQUET

Wood of
Laignies

Thiery

W. & A. K. Johnston, Limited. Edinburgh & London.

RAMILLIES
May 23. 1706.

Old Roman Road

Mehaigne

Taviers

Autre-Eglise

Offiz

Tomb of
Ottomond

Ottomond

RAMILLIES

Statute Mile
0   1

had three officers killed and five wounded, with about eighty casualties among the other ranks.[1]

During the winter of 1710-11 the French made gigantic efforts to protect their country against the threatened invasion, and threw up fresh lines, which ran from Namur to a point on the English Channel a few miles south of Boulogne, using rivers and canals, swamps, and artificial inundations as barriers against the general whom they feared so greatly. Before Marlborough was ready to open the campaign of 1711, his trusted friend and invaluable colleague, Prince Eugene, was recalled to Austria with a large body of troops, but though left with forces greatly inferior in numbers to those of de Villars, he resolved to carry out the first task he had already set himself, the capture of Bouchain. As this fortress was protected by the new lines, which were far too strong to be carried by force, the Duke determined to decoy Marshal de Villars from the opening in the works at Arleux, where he intended to cross. He advanced and retired; threatened first one part of the lines and then another; issued contradictory orders; pretended to be cast down at the loss of a weak detachment intentionally thrown away as a bait to his adversary; simulated alternately rage, dejection, rashness; and deceived not only the French spies in his camp, but also his own army, who began to fear that their beloved "Corporal John" had lost his judgment. By acting apparently like a madman, but really with the profound skill of a great master of war, he lured de Villars forty miles to the westward of Arleux, and on the morning of August 4, ostentatiously reconnoitred the Marshal's position, explaining in unusual detail to the generals who accompanied him the part each was to play in the assault which was to be delivered on the morrow: then he returned to camp and issued orders for the coming battle. At tattoo the word was passed to strike tents and fall in at once, and in an hour the troops were in motion. At first they thought they were merely taking up ground for the attack next day, but when hour after hour they plodded steadily eastward, they were fairly puzzled until, just before dawn, the message ran down the column: "The cavalry have reached Arleux and have passed the lines, and the Duke desires that the infantry will step out." And step out they did! They forgot the fatigue of the fifteen miles they had marched already with heavy muskets on their shoulders and fifty pounds' weight upon their backs, and without a halt for rest or food trudged manfully over an apparently endless plain. When the sun grew hot the work began to tell, and it became a question of the survival of the fittest. The weaker men dropped exhausted on the ground, first by scores, then by hundreds, and later in the day literally by thousands; but without stopping to help their comrades, those soldiers who still had the strength to keep their places in the ranks set their teeth and staggered

[1] See Appendix 2 (B).

on, determined not to be beaten in the race by the French, whose horsemen they could see on the other side of the lines hurrying in the same direction as themselves. Early in the afternoon the leading battalions reached Arleux and reinforced the cavalry, who were already in possession of the entrance to the works. The XVIIIth came up about 4 P.M.; apparently the discipline and the marching powers of the regiment had brought it there fairly intact, but when the men realised that the prize was won and Arleux safe in the Duke's hands, the reaction, inevitable after so prolonged a strain, set in, and half of the Royal Irish collapsed, dead beat and unable to walk another yard. Barely fifty per cent of the infantry had kept up with the army in this forced march, when nearly forty miles was covered in eighteen hours. Numbers of men were found dead from exhaustion, and it was fully three days before all the stragglers had rejoined the Colours.

Marlborough now laid siege to Bouchain, and handled the covering force so well against de Villars' superior numbers that the French failed to interfere with his operations, and on the 13th of September had the mortification of seeing the garrison surrender. The investing force was desperately hard worked during the siege. For thirteen days consecutively the Royal Irish marched and dug trenches all day, and at night stood to their arms, ready to fight at any moment. "This," says Parker, "was the greatest fatigue I ever underwent at any one time of my life." Though the French surrendered before the breach was stormed, they inflicted heavy losses on the besiegers, whose casualties amounted to 4018, of which 1154 were among the fifteen British battalions employed in the siege. The Royal Irish were fortunate: only four officers were wounded, and about forty of the other ranks killed or wounded.[1] It is said that an officer of the XVIIIth, whose courage was as high as his stature was low, was nearly drowned in wading across a deep inundation, so he had himself hoisted on the shoulders of the biggest of the grenadiers of his party, and when safely landed at the foot of the parapet led an assault upon the enemy's works.

The capture of Bouchain was the last service the Duke of Marlborough was allowed to render to his country. Political intrigues had long been directed against him, and when he returned to England in the autumn he was coldly received by Queen Anne, insulted in the House of Lords, prosecuted for peculation by the House of Commons, and deprived of all his offices. Nay, more, to such a height did party pamphleteers rouse popular indignation against him, that the General "who never fought a battle that he did not gain nor sat down before a fortress he did not take" was forced to go to the Continent to escape from the jeers of the London mob. Even before his fall, the Ministers in power had begun secret negotiations with Louis, by which England was to desert her Allies and make a separate

[1] See Appendix 2 (B).

peace with France; and when the Duke of Ormond, his successor in command of the British forces in Flanders, joined the army in the spring of 1712, he understood that he was on no account to cross swords with de Villars.   During several months the British troops were in a very miserable position; for being still, at least in name, part of the allied army, to the supreme command of which Eugene had now succeeded, they followed its operations, but in a novel and humiliating capacity: they were no longer chief actors, but spectators—soldiers whom their Government would not allow to fight; and when Ormond announced to them that the suspension of hostilities between England and France was signed, the news filled them with profound grief. In July they turned their backs upon their former comrades and returned to Ghent and Bruges, after a gloomy march past Douai, Tournai, Bouchain, Lille, and Oudenarde, places which they had helped to take, but to which the Dutch garrisons now contemptuously refused them admittance.

After twenty years of almost uninterrupted fighting, every army requires careful handling at the beginning of peace, but more especially one sore at the ill-treatment of its beloved Chief, sorer still at the loss of its honour by its desertion of its comrades in the time of need.   Ormond did not manage his men well, and neglected their commissariat; the garrison of Ghent lost their discipline, listened to the words of agitators, and formed a mad scheme to rise; loot and burn the town, and then disperse over the Netherlands. The plot was discovered, but two or three thousand men seized part of the town, where they barricaded themselves, holding out until field-guns were brought against them.   Soon after this mutiny was put down the troops were withdrawn to England, but the Royal Irish and another regiment were left to garrison the town until political questions regarding it had been settled.   Their detention at Ghent gave them the opportunity to see Marlborough once more, for when he passed through the town at the end of 1712 the whole garrison was on foot to do him honour.

To many of the officers and men of the XVIIIth Ghent must have been more familiar than their own homes in Ireland, for they had wintered there for many years during the war, and did not finally leave it until the autumn of 1715, when the regiment returned to England.   A few months later it was quartered at Oxford, where "the scholars and the soldiers did not agree," until the officers ordered their men to leave their weapons behind them when they went out at night, taking instead stout cudgels with which to teach the undergraduates good manners.   This stopped the trouble, and all was quiet until, on the Prince of Wales' birthday, the officers lit a bonfire outside the Post Office, and then went to supper.   While they were at table stones began to come in through the window; a number of soldiers rushed to the defence of their officers, and broke the windows of the house from which the supper party had been pelted.   Then arose a furious row: the townsmen turned out; so did the soldiers from their quarters, and headed by a Lieutenant of grenadiers, who "was a little elevated," a mass of Royal Irishmen went through the town breaking every window they could reach that was not illuminated in honour of the Royal birthday. Patrols were sent out to stop the window-breaking, but it is possible they were not very zealous—at any rate, much damage was done before the rioting was stopped. The Dons announced that they would have every officer in the regiment cashiered for this insult to the University, and solemnly complained to the Privy Council, who at once asked for "reasons in writing," or their equivalent at the beginning of the eighteenth century. Then the House of Lords debated the matter at great length, and finally decided in favour of the officers, charging the University with disloyalty for not celebrating properly the Prince of Wales' birthday. Thus the affair ended without detriment to the regiment, and to the great benefit of the Oxford glaziers who had to replace £500 worth of broken glass.

In January, 1712, Lieutenant-General Ingoldsby died. Brigadier-General Richard Stearne, his successor, made over the regiment in 1717 to Colonel William Crosby.[1]

[1] See Appendix 9.

CHAPTER III.

1718-1793.

THE SECOND SIEGE OF GIBRALTAR—THE SIEGE OF OSTEND—
LEXINGTON—BUNKER'S HILL.

LESS than three years after the Royal Irish returned from the Low Countries they found themselves again on foreign service, this time in the south of Europe. During the war of the Spanish Succession there had been much fighting in the Mediterranean, where Gibraltar, and Port Mahon in Minorca, one of the Balearic Islands, had been captured by England, whose possession of these two fortresses was confirmed by the Peace of Utrecht. When this peace was signed every nation hoped that for many years there would be no more wars on the Continent; but very soon relations between Spain and Austria became so strained that the British Government decided to send a squadron to the Mediterranean, to support Austria if Spain attacked her Italian possessions, and to reinforce the garrison of Minorca. Among these reinforcements were the Royal Irish, who, less fortunate than some of the regiments in Minorca, were not selected to serve as marines in our short but successful campaign off the coast of Sicily.

In 1727, the little world of Port Mahon was startled by grave news from the mainland. Spain still smarted under the loss of Gibraltar: every Spaniard looked upon the presence of the red-coats on the Rock as an affront not only to his nation but to himself, and was prepared to risk much to recover the fortress. For the second time since the XVIIIth had been quartered in Minorca, Spain, regardless of the fact that she was not at war with England, was making preparations to recapture Gibraltar. On the first occasion, in 1720, though peace had been restored between the Courts of Madrid and of St James, the Spaniards, under the pretext of reinforcing their garrison at Ceuta, assembled a large number of troops near the fortress, laid violent hands upon a hundred British merchant ships then lying in the ports of southern Spain, and forced their crews to carry warlike stores to the bay of Algeçiras. Gibraltar at that moment was in a deplorable condition—the regiments were weak ; there were only two officers of field rank in the garrison, as the seniors were at home, many of them without leave ; the guns were few in number and bad in quality, and there was only fourteen days' supply of food in store.   The place was in such imminent danger that Colonel Kane, then Governor of Minorca, was ordered to come to the rescue with every man who could be spared from his command.   When he and his reinforcement of five hundred men [1] arrived off the Rock, he found it threatened by three hundred Spanish transports, escorted by six galleys, each manned by 500 slaves, and three 60-gun Maltese war vessels, hired to take part in the attack.   The appearance of the four or five men-of-war with the Minorca contingent frightened away the Maltese, and the Spaniards returned to Ceuta without firing a shot.   Now, seven years later, great preparations for war were again on foot—a fleet of trading vessels was employed in transporting guns, ammunition, and stores from Cadiz to Algeçiras, where as many as forty ships arrived in a day ; large numbers of troops were assembled, and the peasants of Southern Andalusia were swept together to serve as labourers in the siege.   Our Government, however, was under the impression that the Spaniards meditated not a siege but a *coup de main*, and in December, 1726, warned the authorities at Gibraltar to be prepared for " a sudden push on the sea line by scaling ladders, encouraged by the weakness of the garrison." The bearer of this important message was not sent from England by a swift frigate, but was left to make his way to Spain as best he could ; landing at Malaga, he chartered a ship to take him to Gibraltar, but was captured on the voyage by a Spanish man-of-war and thrown into prison.   The despatches, however, were saved and duly reached their destination ; Kane was once more summoned from Minorca, and with a regiment on the point of returning to England reached Gibraltar in February, 1727.   Doubtless the XVIIIth was deeply disgusted at being left behind, but in a few weeks came the turn, not indeed of the whole regiment, but of a portion of it, to share in the honours of the defence.

According to the memoirs of Marshal Keith, a Scottish soldier of fortune, who before he rose to eminence in the service of Russia held a commission in the Spanish army, Kane did not arrive a moment too soon, for there was but a slender guard at the landward gate, and the Spanish soldiers were allowed to come into the town without being searched for arms.   A surprise would have been easy, but the fortress was saved by a strange exhibition of pride. Count de las Torres, who commanded the Spaniards, haughtily said that " would the English give him the town, he would not enter it but by the breach."   In the middle of February his troops, 20,000 strong, took up positions at San Roque, and in order to provoke hostilities began to throw up a

---

[1] It is not known whether any of the XVIIIth were included, but it is probable that Kane brought some of his old regiment with him to the post of danger.

battery on the western beach. General Clayton, who was acting Governor at the time, thereupon wrote to de las Torres in the following terms :—

> "Having observed this morning that your Excellency has opened a trench in order to attack this fortress, which act I hold to be contrary to the treaties existing between our sovereigns, no declaration of war yet having reached my knowledge, I therefore inform your Excellency, that if you do not forthwith order the works to cease I shall be obliged to take necessary measures in consequence. I transmit this to your Excellency by my secretary, to whom I beg a reply may be delivered.
>
> "JASPER CLAYTON.
>
> "GIBRALTAR, *February 22nd 1727.*"

To this letter the Spaniard replied—

> "SIR,—I received your Excellency's letter of to-day's date, and regarding the trench which has been opened as you say to attack the city of Gibraltar, I hereby answer, that what has been done has been on our own ground, to fortify those places where our batteries might be of good service, and as there belongs nothing to that fortress beyond its fortifications, as appears by the very treaties your Excellency alludes to; and your Excellency having taken possession of the towers within our jurisdiction, your Excellency may be fully assured that unless they are immediately abandoned I will act in the manner your Excellency insinuates to *me*, acquainting you at the same time that for besieging the fortress works less distant will be constructed, as you will learn in due time.
>
> "COUNT DAS TORRES.
>
> "CAMPO DE GIBRALTAR, *February 22nd 1727.*"

This truculent answer clearly meant war, and so Clayton understood it; but anxious to do nothing to precipitate hostilities, he contented himself for the moment with firing one shot over the battery as an intimation that work must cease. For an hour he held his hand: then, as the Spaniards wholly disregarded the warning, his guns opened upon them. Thus commenced the second of the series of sieges in which British troops have successfully defended Gibraltar against heavy, sometimes well-nigh overwhelming odds. The first, begun a few months after our capture of the Rock, lasted from October, 1704, to April, 1705; the second continued from the 22nd of February till the 23rd of June, 1727; the third, or Great Siege, lasted nearly four years, from the 16th of July, 1779, to the 5th of February, 1783.

In 1727, the Spaniards attacked from the land side only; their navy took no part in the operations, which were exclusively directed against the North Front and the defences of the Rock from the extremity of the old Mole to Willis's Battery. At the beginning of the siege the garrison had only sixty guns in position, the heaviest being 32-prs., and as "most of the ordnance was old and worn out, more casualties occurred from the bursting of guns than from the enemy's fire."[1] The Spaniards, on the other hand, brought into action ninety-two guns and seventy-two mortars, many of them the best and most modern of their day. De las Torres lost no time in opening his trenches. During the night of February 22nd-23rd five battalions of infantry, a brigade of engineers, and a thousand peasants started work on the first parallel, which ran from the Devil's Tower on the eastern beach along the base of the Rock to the inundation. Next night two thousand of the enemy were moved northwards into ground dead to the guns of the batteries, but not to those of two British men-of-war which, under cover of the darkness, had anchored off the east of the isthmus connecting the fortress with the mainland, or, in other words, the neutral ground. As soon as it was light the sailors brought their guns to bear upon these troops, raking their ranks from end to end, while from the top of the Rock the soldiers hurled down upon the Spaniards live shell, hand-grenades, and stones. The enemy retreated in confusion and with great loss, but de las Torres, after driving away the men-of-war by an overwhelming artillery fire, threw up batteries so completely commanding the anchorage on the east of the isthmus that further flanking attacks of this nature became impossible. Under a heavy cannonade from the garrison, the Spaniards worked without intermission, and in spite of heavy and continuous rain which flooded their trenches and produced much sickness among their men, gradually completed and unmasked many formidable batteries, some of which were within a hundred yards of the Rock.

Throughout the month of March, before further reinforcements began to arrive from England and Minorca, the British troops suffered greatly from fatigue. The guards and piquets were very heavy, absorbing a daily average of 1200 rank and file, and a thousand men were constantly occupied in mounting guns and strengthening the defences. These working parties were commanded by officers of the line, who were struck off all other duty and received half a crown a-day extra pay. The men also drew sixpence a-day extra, and "were assisted by the Jews, who were employed in taking ammunition to the batteries and clearing the ditch of the rubbish beaten down from the upper works by the enemy's shot; these unfortunate Israelites received no pay, and for some time were utterly useless, being paralysed with terror when under fire."[2] Some of them, perhaps to revenge themselves for this forced labour, joined in a conspiracy among the "undesirable" element in the civil population to open the gates to the enemy. The plot was discovered, and punished in the rigorous fashion of the day—two Moors, the chief agents of the Spaniards, were put to death, and after their bodies had been flayed the

---

[1] Sayer's 'History of Gibraltar,' p. 295.

[2] Sayer, p. 197. It would be interesting to know if the staff officer who evolved the idea of thus "employing the unfortunate Israelites" was heavily in debt to them!

skins were nailed to the gates of the fortress as an object lesson on the penalties of unsuccessful treachery.

The elements during the siege were strongly in favour of the British, for such deluges of rain fell in April that the Spaniards' trenches again became untenable and their cover was destroyed. Until the damage could be made good the opening of the great bombardment was necessarily postponed, and during the respite two battalions arrived from home on the 7th of April, and a fortnight later four transports, escorted by the *Sole Bay*, brought five hundred troops, detachments from the corps stationed in Minorca. How many men the Royal Irish contributed is not known; but as Crosby, their colonel, was in command of the whole contingent, it is natural to suppose that the regiment was largely represented. England's command of the sea enabled her to reinforce at will, and in the beginning of May two more battalions reached Gibraltar from home, raising the strength of the garrison to about 5500 non-commissioned officers and men. With them came Lord Portmore, the Governor, who was on leave when the siege began: though quite an old man he had refused to plead his age and infirmities as an excuse for evading his duty, and now returned to take his share in the defence. As soon as the Spaniards had finished their batteries and mounted their guns, they opened a tremendous artillery fire, which was kept up for fourteen days without intermission. During every hour of this time seven hundred projectiles were hurled against our works, and to use the words of an eyewitness, " we seemed to live in flames. . . . Attempts feeble in comparison to the resistless storm of shot and shell that tore over the walls of the fortress, were made to check this murderous fire in vain, guns were everywhere dismounted, and as quickly as they were replaced were again destroyed. In vain the men with dauntless courage threw themselves upon the ramparts and worked to repair the shattered parapets, the heavy shot tore away whole tons of earth and buried the guns beneath the ruins. Butts filled with sand and bound with fascines were heaped together as some covering from the artillery, but they were no sooner in position than they were swept away."[1]

The strain of this bombardment, said to have been greater than any recorded in the previous history of artillery, proved more than the Spanish ordnance could stand. By the 20th of May the brass guns began to droop at the muzzle, the iron guns to burst, and ammunition to run short. Gradually the enemy's fire died down, and when there were but nineteen pieces left in action against them the British restored their shattered works, and mounting thirteen new guns and more than a hundred mortars poured upon the Spaniards a storm of projectiles almost equalling that which had scourged the defenders of the Rock. By dint of tremendous exertions a hundred guns

[1] Sayer, p. 204. This writer mentions that out of the sixty guns in position at the beginning of the bombardment twenty-three were dismounted in seven days.

were placed in position at the beginning of June, and then the tables were turned, for this mass of ordnance opened upon the Spaniards with such a crash that not a single gun was able to reply; the trenches became a heap of ruins; the parapets of the batteries took fire, and the magazines blew up. The first day's cannonade drove the enemy from their forts, and gradually the whole line of works was completely knocked to pieces. On the 23rd of June the news reached Gibraltar that a suspension of hostilities had been arranged between the Governments of England and Spain: all fighting then ceased; the soldiers had played their part, and it was now for the diplomatists to settle the differences between their respective countries. The British losses were remarkably small. Five officers were killed or wounded; in the other ranks 69 were killed; 49 died from wounds or disease, and 207 were wounded. It is not known how many of the XVIIIth were injured, as the casualties of the Minorca contingent are given as a whole. To the Spanish army, on the other hand, the siege proved very costly. Fifteen officers were killed, 42 wounded: of the other ranks 346 were killed, 1119 were wounded, and more than 5000 died of sickness or were permanently invalided by the hardships they had undergone. No less than 875 Spaniards deserted during the siege, some of whom surrendered to our piquets and brought much useful information to the Intelligence officers of the garrison.

When the siege was over, the detachment of the XVIIIth rejoined headquarters at Minorca, where the regiment remained until 1742. Nothing would have been known of the life of the Royal Irish during this period had not copies been preserved of a curious correspondence between Major Gillman, who was in command, and Major-General Armstrong, the Colonel of the regiment.[1] The officers were greatly disturbed at the quality of the recruits received from home, and Gillman in 1729 thus reports on a recently joined draft of sixteen men. "They are the worst I ever saw; two of them the officers would not draw for: one of them wanting above half of his right foot, the other having his backbone and ribs of both sides distorted in a prodigious manner, by which means he is an object of compassion, both of which are to be sent back to England at the expense of the person that recruited them."

Two years later Gillman again entreats that recruiting should be properly conducted.

> "I beg leave to assure you that you have a corps of captains that has the credit of the Regiment entirely at heart and will begrudge no expense in supporting it on all occasions therefore I am thoroughly convinced you will give such necessary orders to the person or persons that are to recruit

---

[1] In 1732 Crosby was succeeded by Sir Charles Hotham, Bart., who on his appointment three years later to a regiment of Guards was replaced by Major-General John Armstrong. See Appendix 9.

the regt. that they receive no bad or old men upon any account whatever. The standard of the regt. is 5′ 7″ without shoes. . . . I entreat your further assistance by getting a few fine fellows at home proper for the Grenadier Company let the expense be ever so great which I'll pay with pleasure, and if two or three beautiful men fit for sergeants *to* said Company could be sent over I'll pay them sergeants' pay until they are provided for because two of the sergeants and the three Corporals are the bane of the Company and not in the least fit to appear under arms but with disgrace."

The next letter (November 20, 1736) recommends that a commission should be granted to Sergeant John Millner, the author of the history of the war in the Low Countries to which frequent reference has been made in Chapter II.

"I beg leave to recommend to your favour on this occasion Sergt. Millner and if it meets with your condescension I am ready to pay down the money for him. I am thoroughly convinced that when so good a man has the honour of being known to you you'll not in the least begrudge any favours that you may be pleased to lay upon him which he will always own in the most grateful manner imaginable.

"As I have mentioned to you in mine of 30th August of the absolute necessity the regiment lies under that it is high time that a Proper Person should be thought of to discharge the duty of Adjutant for the reasons therein mentioned. I assure you I know of no person so proper in the regiment to discharge that duty as Sergeant Millner, who is very willing to do it *gratis*, provided it is for your advantage or any other commands you should be pleased to lay upon him, as you may judge by his journal he wrote of the late war in Flanders to which I find you were pleased to be one of the generous subscribers.

"I should not take the liberty of recommending this poor man to you if I had not sufficient reasons to be thoroughly sensible he is capable of discharging any duty that his superiors are willing to employ him on, and has on all occasions in a very particular manner merited the esteem of all the officers he has had the honour of serving under, as you may see by the generous subscription in his favour, a copy of which I send you enclosed, by which you will plainly see good generous Kane has not forgotten the (illegible ? regiment) always desiring to be a subscriber on the like occasion."

Inclosure—

"We whose names are hereunder written officers of the Royal regiment of Ireland in consideration of the long and faithful service of Sergeant John Millner do hereby desire and empower the agent or paymaster of the said regiment for the time being to stop or cause to be stopped out of respective subsistence or arrears the sum set against our names whenever the colonel of the regiment shall be pleased to recommend the said Millner to his Majesty for a commission in the said regiment."

Anthony Pujola,	.	.	.	£10	0	0
Stephen Gilman,	.	.	.	10	0	0
Charles Hutchinson,	.	.	.	5	0	0
Wm. Sharman,	.	.	.	5	0	0
Anthony (illegible),	.	.	.	5	0	0
Thomas Borrett,	.	.	.	5	0	0
Thomas Dunbar,	.	.	.	5	0	0
Rob Pearson,	.	.	.	5	0	0
James La Tour,	.	.	.	2	10	0
Henry Barrett,	.	.	.	2	10	0
John Coningham,	.	.	.	2	10	0
—— Cotter,	.	.	.	2	10	0
Jonathan Elder,	.	.	.	2	10	0
George Martin,	.	.	.	5	0	0
E. du Conseille,	.	.	.	2	10	0
				£70	0	0
Governor Kane,	.	.	.	10	0	0

In January, 1737, Gillman reports the loss of a subaltern, who can hardly be said to have been cut off in the flower of his youth.

". . . This is to acquaint you with the death of Lieut. John Dalbos of Colonel Pujola's Company who died last night of a tedious and lingering disorder attended with the gout, but in my opinion rather by old age being 75 years. . . ."

The gem of the collection, however, is contained in a letter of introduction given by Major-General Armstrong to Major Gillman, in favour of a young officer just posted to the regiment.

"LONDON, 13*th June* 1737.

"SIR,—The bearer hereof Ensign Stanhope, son of the Right Hon. the Lord Harrington, Principal Secretary of State, a younger brother and very hopeful gentleman, and ambitious to push his fortune in the Military Way, and moreover being desirous of qualifying himself for that purpose, has tendered to do his duty with the regiment. Therefore I earnestly desire you will encourage him in everything that may conduce to his improvement in this way of life.

"As the first thing a youth should learn at his launching out into the World is to know how to live in it, a spirit of economy should be cultivated in him, for which purpose he should be induced to keep a pocket memorandum book wherein he may with other occurrences set down his daily expenses, by perusing of which in his leisure hours he may see how the money goes out and be thereby enabled to proportion his disbursement to his cash, keep out of debt, and thereby avoid the many inconveniences the want of due care draws young men into such in the whole course of their lives they may not without great difficulty be able to extricate themselves.

"And in order thereto as youth is oftentimes moved by the company they keep I must earnestly desire you will introduce him to that of the most discreet and sober gentlemen, and particularly that you will have a watchful eye he keeps company with no sharpers at play, nor with any persons that may induce him to vices destructive of his health. Your due regard to what is above written will very much oblige

"Your most obed^{t.}

most humble servant,

"J. ARMSTRONG."

"*P.S.*—Care must be taken on his arrival to board him with some officer who has a family which I earnestly request you to see done, for much depends on a right beginning."

Armstrong died in 1742, and was succeeded as colonel of the regiment by Colonel Sir John Mordaunt, K.B. On its return home in 1742 the regiment was quartered in the West of England until the spring of 1744, when it was sent to Fareham to guard prisoners taken in the wars we were then waging with the Spanish and the French. In 1739 a trade dispute with Spain had produced a conflict memorable only for our miserable and costly failure to take Cartagena, a flourishing settlement on the Caribbean Sea, in the part of South America then belonging to Spain, and now the Republic of Columbia. Soon afterwards a great war broke out on the Continent of Europe between France and Spain on the one side and Austria on the other. Various German States joined the Franco-Spanish alliance, while England, Hanover, and Holland sent contingents to the help of Austria. At Dettingen George II. gained a victory over the French in 1743, but two years later his son, the Duke of Cumberland, was defeated at Fontenoy,[1] where the magnificent courage and brilliant local success of the British and Hanoverians were nullified by the apathy, cowardice, or jealousy of the Austrians and the Dutch, who after Cumberland had actually forced his way into the French camp sullenly refused to advance and support his column at the moment when victory was within his grasp. Before the news of this glorious, though disastrous day reached England, the Royal Irish had been warned for service abroad, and formed part of a small column which reached Cumberland in the middle of May. Welcome as this reinforcement was, it did not nearly fill the gaps caused by the slaughter at Fontenoy, where the casualties among the British and Hanoverian infantry amounted to 32 per cent, the former losing 3662, the latter 1410 officers and men. With his weakened force Cumberland could not stand up against the French, and as far as most of the English regiments were concerned, the rest of the campaign of 1745 was spent in entrenching defensive positions, and then, under the pressure of the enemy's

[1] See Map No. 2.

manœuvres, abandoning them, only to repeat the experience farther to the rear, while the French, in greatly superior numbers, gradually reduced the fortified towns of Flanders. Some of these places Marshal Saxe, the French Commander-in-Chief, took by force of arms; others capitulated without resistance, and in August he was able to detach a considerable body of troops to attack Ostend, a vital point in Cumberland's lines of communication with England. The garrison was hastily reinforced, the last corps to arrive being the Royal Irish, who on the 9th of August embarked at Antwerp on "billanders," as the boats used for inland navigation were called, and dropping down the Scheldt to Flushing transhipped into sea-going vessels for Ostend. The town was in a wretched condition and quite unfit to stand a siege; the Austrians, to whom it then belonged, had allowed the fortifications to fall into disrepair; the artillery was deficient in guns and stores of every kind, and the three thousand infantry, insufficient for the perimeter they had to guard, were not soldiers of the same nation commanded by generals of their own army, but detachments of British, of Austrians, and of Dutch—men with no common language and dissimilar in discipline, habits, and sentiment. These differences, sufficiently serious in themselves, were accentuated by the undisguised contempt of the English for the Allies who had left them in the lurch at Fontenoy. Nor were these the only difficulties. An essential part in the scheme of defence was the flooding of a large tract of country round the town, but this measure had not been carried into effect, for the Austrians, unwilling to ruin the peasants by inundating the villages and farms, were so slow in issuing the necessary orders that when at length labourers were sent to open the sluices, the French were close at hand and prevented the working parties from accomplishing their task. To have defended Ostend successfully would have taxed the powers of a great leader of men, and none arose to snatch the reins of office from the hands of the governor, a veteran grown old and decrepit in the Austrian service. The General appointed to command the British arrived after the town was invested, and was unable to make his way into Ostend; an Austrian officer of the same rank, de Chanclos, was more fortunate, but though he acted as confidential adviser to the Governor he had not the time, even if he possessed the capacity, to weld the heterogeneous garrison into a good fighting force.

On the same day that the Royal Irish left Antwerp a French General, Löwendahl, appeared before Ostend with 21,000 good troops, a numerous artillery, and 5000 pack horses, laden with fascines for the siege; he finished his first parallel on the 14th of August, and next day threw up batteries on the shore to enfilade the harbour and to keep at a distance the British frigates which hovered about the port. After thus cutting off Ostend from communication with England he pushed on his works with vigour, and on the 18th twenty pieces of artillery and ten or twelve mortars opened a violent cannonade which lasted for four days almost without intermission. The defending troops were greatly overworked; half of them were constantly at the batteries or in the covered way; the remainder had to be ready to turn out at a moment's notice, and as there were no casemates or bomb-proofs, the only shelter for the men when off duty was in barracks and private houses, which rapidly crumbled under the French projectiles. The officers were rather better off, for they shared with the sick and wounded the cellars of the town-hall, made shell-proof with walls of sandbags. All ranks were vilely fed; the officer of the XVIIIth who wrote the anonymous 'Continuation of Stearne's Journal' says "the beef stank, the biscuits were full of maggots." There were not enough artillerymen to man the guns; when the gun carriages were knocked to pieces by round shot there were none in reserve to replace them, and by the end of the siege only seven pieces of ordnance remained fit for use. Three days after the bombardment began de Chanclos wrote gloomily to Cumberland—

"This town is a heap of ruins . . . the great fatigue, and entire absence of quiet, night or day, owing to bomb-shells and cannon-balls, put the garrison into very bad humour, and it is really not saying too much to call it bad. I might even add that one must be an Englishman to put up with what we are suffering here! The enemy is sapping up to the covered way and is attacking on our weakest side. Nearly all our cannon have been dismounted, many artillerymen have been killed and the survivors decline to work the guns."

He thus reported the loss of the town:

"*August* 24.

"On the night of the 22nd a general assault was made on our covered way by fifteen companies of Grenadiers, supported by two battalions. The point chosen was the sea front at low water. We repulsed the enemy more than once, killing and wounding 500 men, and making prisoners of 2 captains, a lieutenant, and 30 odd grenadiers. At day break I assembled my commanding officers to obtain their opinion as to our situation. Everyone agreed that we could not hope to hold out for more than a few days."

As soon as this informal Council of War was over de Chanclos ordered his drummers to beat the *Chamade*; and after obtaining a truce for the burial of his dead he offered to capitulate on condition that the garrison should be allowed to march out of Ostend with all the honours of war, and be escorted safely to Austrian territory.[1] In proposing these terms he forgot to specify

[1] The only mention of British losses at Ostend in the despatches is a casual reference by Cumberland in a letter, where he speaks of the seventy English soldiers taken by the French in the attack on the covered way.

the Austrian fortress to which his troops were to be conveyed, the route by which they were to travel, and the date on which they were to arrive. The French General, however, noticed these omissions, and with suspicious alacrity agreed to Chanclos's terms : the garrison marched out with all due pomp, fully expecting to be escorted at once to the nearest Austrian town ; but soon the troops learned to their deep disgust that the French had discovered the flaws in the articles of capitulation, and were about to send them by a devious route to Mons. This was considered very sharp practice, not at all worthy of an honourable enemy ; but the King of France had every reason for wishing to deprive England as long as possible of the services of the defenders of Ostend, for the young Pretender, Charles Edward, had landed in Scotland ; the rebellion, known in history as "the '45," was rapidly gaining strength ; and Government was clamouring for the return from Belgium of the British troops. After a short halt at Ghent, they were crowded into canal boats for an involuntary "personally conducted" tour through Belgium, and from the description left by an officer of the regiment it is clear that the most ardent sight-seers could have extracted no pleasure from this journey.

> " We were escorted by a party of Horse, and constantly attended by agents of theirs (the French) whose business it was to inveigle away our men, and by large promises (of which these rascals were not sparing) induce them to desert; as our progress was rendered designedly slow we were only drawn by the boors of the country a very few miles a day. A French trooper with his carbine was placed at the head of each billander, who did not fail to threaten the poor wretches with firing at them whenever they did not pull to please them. We continued on board this incommodious embarcation seventeen days, when we arrived in Tournai, where we disembarked."

As Tournai is about thirty-two miles from Mons, the column should have begun its march very early in the morning to have covered the distance in one day, but the escort refused to move till 8 A.M., and consequently it was 7 o'clock in the evening before the British arrived at St Gillain, a fortified village held by the Austrians as an outpost to Mons, a few miles farther on. Alleging that in bringing the garrison of Ostend to this outpost they had fulfilled their undertaking, the French halted, ceremoniously saluted the Colours of each regiment, and then retired. The British officers were at a loss to understand why the French had left the column at St Gillain instead of escorting it to Mons, but in a few minutes they learned the reason from an Austrian general whom Cumberland had sent to meet them. A large body of the enemy's troops were lurking in the neighbourhood, with orders to attack St Gillain if the regiments from Ostend remained there, and if they attempted to reach Mons to capture or exterminate them on the march; the only hope of escape, therefore, was to start at once on the chance that the intercepting force had not already taken up its position. Without a moment's delay the ranks were re-formed, the pans of the muskets re-primed and the bayonets fixed; then in profound silence the weary troops plodded along the causeway leading towards Mons. "As it was a moonlight night we could command a view of the country about us, and as we every moment expected the enemy we continued our march in the greatest order; not a whisper was to be heard; the officers who were present will always remember with pleasure the discipline and good disposition every regiment showed on that occasion. At eleven we arrived at Mons, where owing to some mismanagement we waited two hours before we got admittance."[1] This delay was obviously caused by bad staff work, but the arrangements of the French were no better. The enemy, confident that the Ostend troops would be too tired to push on that night, left no patrols to watch the exits from the village, with the result that 20,000 Frenchmen took up a position astride the causeway an hour after the refugees had found safety within the walls of Mons. For three weeks the Royal Irish were blockaded in this fortress; then thanks to the manœuvres of a relieving force they "slipped out" at dead of night, and in a few days reached the neighbourhood of Brussels.

Affairs in Scotland were now going so badly that nearly every English soldier was recalled from the Continent to defend England against the Jacobite invasion. The XVIIIth landed at Gravesend early in November, and after various changes of quarters embarked for the seat of war in Scotland in the spring of 1746. On the voyage a vexatious incident occurred by which the regiment was prevented from taking any active part in the Scotch campaign. While off the coast of Yorkshire the transports, containing the 12th, 16th, XVIIIth, and 24th regiments, were warned that three French men-of-war were cruising in the neighbourhood; the ships ran for safety into the Humber, where they remained until the report was proved to have no foundation; and owing to this delay the Royal Irish did not reach Leith until the day after the rebels had been finally crushed at the battle of Culloden. For two years the regiment was stationed in Scotland, in the summer making military roads in the Highlands, in the winter quartered at various towns, and when the treaty of Aix-la-Chapelle put an end to the war the XVIIIth was ordered to Ireland, after it had been placed on a peace footing by reductions so sweeping that the establishment of each company was fixed at two sergeants, two corporals, one drummer, and twenty-nine private soldiers.

In 1755, our relations with France were again strained to breaking point: in America the French garrison of Canada and the British garrison of the colonies on the Atlantic coast were waging fierce, though unofficial war in the

[1] Continuation of Stearne.

forests south of the river St Lawrence; and as the conflict seemed likely to spread to Europe, troops were withdrawn from Ireland to Great Britain. Among the regiments hurriedly brought across St George's Channel was the XVIIIth, rapidly recruited up to a strength of seventy-eight men per company. But the "Seven Years' War" brought no laurels to the Royal Irish, who were condemned to inactivity in the United Kingdom, while other corps were winning fame on the Continent and in the West Indies, in Canada and the Philippine Islands. In 1767, four years after peace was declared, the regiment was ordered to Philadelphia, the capital of Pennsylvania, one of the oldest of our American colonies. The beginning of the lamentable quarrel between the mother-country and her English-speaking over-sea provinces found the Royal Irish still quartered at Philadelphia, but in 1774, Boston, the chief town of the colony of Massachusetts, became such a hotbed of disaffection that General Gage, who commanded the troops in British North America, reinforced its garrison with troops drawn from less disloyal centres of population. Among the regiments ordered to Boston was the XVIIIth, at that time very weak in numbers, for hardly any recruits had arrived from home, and those enlisted at Philadelphia were "bounty-jumpers," who deserted at every opportunity.

The causes of the breach between England and the provincials, as the colonists were then called, have been discussed in innumerable histories, and are far too complex to be dealt with in the chronicles of a regiment. It is enough to say here that the dispute began about questions of taxation and trade; the home Government was stupid, slow, and overbearing in its dealings with the provincials, who on their side were petulant, aggressive, and impatient of control. Many of the young Americans believed that as all danger of an attack by France had been removed by the British conquest of Canada, they would be better off as citizens of a republic than as subjects of King George. Both sides were unable to regard the matters at issue from a point of view other than their own: the English Government failed to appreciate the restlessness and desire for expansion natural to young and growing communities of British stock; the provincials were equally unable to realise how slowly new ideas penetrated into the brains of the governing classes at home.

At the beginning of 1775 the whole of Massachusetts was seething with scarcely veiled rebellion, and though the inhabitants of Boston itself were overawed by the presence of Gage's troops, the rural population was so hostile that it was unsafe for officers to go any distance into the country without a strong and well-armed escort. The excitement was increased by the action of the provincial Parliament, which, issuing a proclamation urging all able-bodied men to arm themselves and join the militia, began to collect warlike stores at various places in the colony. One of these depôts was at Concord, a

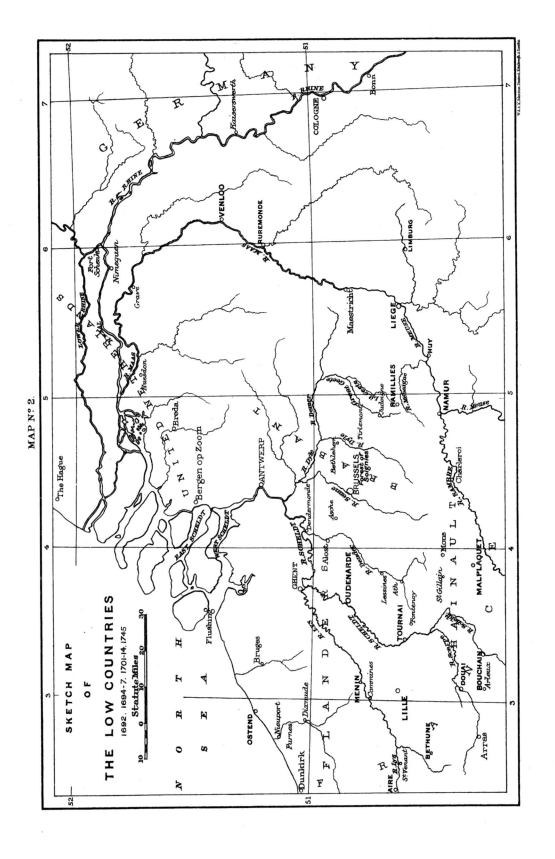

MAP Nº 2.

SKETCH MAP
OF
THE LOW COUNTRIES
1692. 1694-7. 1701-14. 1745
Statute Miles
10   0   10   20   30

village twenty miles from Boston; Gage determined to burn its contents, and on the night of the 18th of April sent a raiding party of eighteen hundred men upon this errand of destruction. Under command of Lieutenant-Colonel Smith the flank companies—*i.e.* the grenadiers and light infantry [1]— of the 5th, 10th, XVIIIth, 23rd, 38th, 43rd, 52nd, and 59th regiments started from Boston before midnight, followed a few hours later by Lord Percy with a supporting body composed of the whole of the 4th and 47th regiments, the battalion companies of the 23rd, and ten companies of marines. As it was known that the provincials' intelligence department was well organised, every precaution was taken to keep the expedition secret; but though the gates of the town had been closed early in the evening and the troops assembled silently at dead of night, their movements were reported by the anti-British faction in Boston, and as they marched through the darkness the ringing of bells and firing of guns warned them that the alarm had been given throughout the countryside. At daybreak the advance-guard ran into a small body of militia at Lexington: there was a parley, followed by a skirmish in which several provincials were hit and the remainder retreated in disorder. Smith lost no time in pushing on to Concord, and while his grenadiers began to demolish the stores some of the light companies guarded the approaches to the village.

So far the raid had been successful, but before describing how rapidly the tables were turned against the troops, the reader must realise with what manner of men Smith's detachment was about to try conclusions. The original settlers in Massachusetts were of picked British stock; the large majority had left the old country to escape from the restraints imposed by the Stuarts upon liberty of conscience, while others had sought in the New World a freer and more adventurous life than England could afford. The mere fact that these men and women had the courage to leave their homes and friends to face the horrors of the unknown, proved them to be above the average in courage and steadfastness of purpose; and the hard life of pioneers; the incessant struggle with nature in a rude climate; fierce fights with the Red Indian savages, who tortured their captives before killing them; long hunting expeditions in vast and trackless forests; life on lonely farms where every man was thrown on his own resources—all had contributed to develop a race of over-sea Britons as formidable to their enemies as they

---

[1] The origin of grenadier companies is mentioned in Chapter I. Light infantry companies were officially recognised soon after the end of the Seven Years' War (1763); they were composed of small, active men, trained to act as skirmishers and in the outpost line. It was the custom to collect the flank companies of different regiments and turn them into provisional battalions: for instance, in the attack on the Terra Nova at Namur the grenadier companies of thirteen battalions were detached from their own corps and brigaded together; and, nearly a hundred years later, both the grenadier and the light infantry companies of the garrison of Boston were used in the same way at Lexington and Bunker's Hill. After the Crimean War flank companies were abolished.

would have been valuable to the Empire if they had been treated with tact, consideration, and justice. It was not in pioneering alone that the New Englanders had found vent for their restless energy; they had taken part in many of our expeditions during the first half of the eighteenth century. In the disastrous failure at Cartagena a considerable number of New Englanders shared in our defeat, and carried home with them a sorry report of the conduct of the army; a contingent of colonists with justice claimed a large share in the glory of the capture of Louisburg, the French Gibraltar at the mouth of the St Lawrence; and in all the interesting, though now forgotten fights between the English and the French in the country round Lake Champlain American volunteers fought side by side with the regular troops. Thus when the provincials determined to take up arms against England, many of the men who later became generals of note in the republican army had served their apprenticeship to war under the Colours of the mother-country. They had studied our drill; they understood our tactics; they knew the merits and demerits of our soldiers, and very soon learned how best to meet our slow and cumbrous movements with their imperfectly trained volunteers, who at the beginning of the War of Independence had many points in common with the Boers of 1899. Both were ardently patriotic; self-reliant to a fault; wholly undisciplined and obeying no order that did not appeal to them as individuals; both fought in bands of friends and neighbours, not infrequently commanded by the local preacher. In one respect, however, the Boers and the American colonists differed widely. In none of their encounters with the British did the burghers ever hold their ground with determination when things had begun to go badly with them, while at Bunker's Hill, the first real battle of the revolutionary war, the provincials "fought to a finish" with such grim tenacity that, had our army been engaged, not with a raw militia, but with European regular troops, its dearly bought success would have been extolled as a feat of arms equal to any in the annals of England.

While Smith's grenadiers were looking for the warlike stores, the light infantry outposts were attacked and driven back into Concord by a very superior force of provincials, who from far and wide had collected to do battle with the red-coats. Boys, full-grown men, greybeards almost tottering to the grave, turned out with splendid enthusiasm from the hamlets of Lincoln, Bedford, Carlisle, and Chelmsford, and surrounding the village like a swarm of bees, set themselves to sting the intruders to death with musketry. Smith determined to retire, and as his column filed out of Concord it became the target of sharpshooters lurking behind houses and log fences and in the woods bordering the rough track that led to Boston. In vain were flanking parties thrown out to keep the enemy at a distance from the main body; the provincials disappeared among the trees and then reappeared farther down the road, using their firearms with deadly effect. The soldiers replied so vigorously that ammunition began to fail them, and as it was impossible to charge a foe who had no formation and whose position was only indicated by isolated puffs of smoke on every side of the column, Smith retreated as fast as possible towards Lexington, losing men at every step. His troops straggled into the village so worn out by hunger and thirst, so demoralised by the biting fire of an almost invisible enemy, that when they saw Lord Percy's detachment drawn up to protect them they flung themselves on the ground, so badly shaken that the supporting troops had to form square round them. For a time there was a lull in the firing; but when more contingents joined the provincials they re-opened such a vigorous fusilade that Percy decided to lose no time in retiring to Boston, fifteen miles away. He handled with much skill the regiments which had accompanied him, falling back from position to position so steadily as to keep his pursuers in some check; and notwithstanding the ever-increasing volume of fire with which reinforcements from Cambridge and Dorchester enabled the colonists to torment him, by nightfall he succeeded in bringing the shattered column safely into Boston. When the casualty returns were prepared, it was found that this disastrous little expedition had cost us in killed, wounded, and prisoners, nineteen officers and two hundred and fifty of the other ranks—a total to which the flank companies of the XVIIIth contributed two private soldiers killed and four wounded,[1] while the losses of the provincials were rather less than a hundred fighting men. The news of the American success spread like wildfire throughout New England; colony after colony threw in its lot with Massachusetts, and in a few days between sixteen and twenty thousand provincials had assembled for the blockade of Boston, then garrisoned by eleven battalions, all under strength, the weakest of all being the Royal Irish, who on the 25th of June could only muster two hundred and fifty-seven of all ranks. Although there was a British fleet at anchor in the bay, Gage could do nothing until more soldiers arrived from England, and by the time the long-expected reinforcements reached him Boston was closely invested by the Americans.

When the first emigrants to Massachusetts decided on the site of their principal town they selected an almost land-locked bay of the Atlantic, where there was good anchorage and shelter from the winter gales. This bay was almost bridged by two peninsulas, which from opposite shores jutted so far towards each other that at the nearest point they were only five hundred yards apart. Boston was built on the southern of these headlands; on the northern, the village of Charlestown nestled at the foot of an under-feature of the semicircle of low hills enveloping the bay. From Bunker's Hill, as the southern end of this underfeature was called, Boston lay within cannon-shot; but neither side attempted to occupy this important position

[1] See Appendix 2 (C).

F

until Gage's reinforcements arrived. Then the British General determined
to seize it, but the Americans, acting either by intuition or on information
from their spies in Boston, forestalled him. On the evening of the 16th of
June twelve hundred men paraded on the common at Cambridge, attended a
prayer-meeting, and then started on an enterprise the object of which was
known only to the most senior of their officers. The column was commanded by Colonel Prescott, who had so greatly distinguished himself at
the capture of Louisburg from the French during the Seven Years' war
that the home Government had offered him a commission in the regular
army. Many of the men in his ranks had seen powder burned in earnest,
and though their muskets were heavy and unwieldy, they had learned to
use them in the pursuit of big game, where an ill-aimed bullet may cost the
hunter his life. By the glimmer of dark lanterns Prescott led his men
across the isthmus connecting the Charlestown peninsula with the mainland,
then crossed Bunker's Hill and halted on a lower ridge, Breed's Hill, where
he quickly traced the lines of a redoubt. To the provincials digging was
no novelty, and they plied pick and shovel so silently and so assiduously
that when the day broke the sailors on board the nearest man-of-war saw
to their amazement an entrenchment, six feet high, standing where over-
night there had been nothing but smooth pasture land. The ships lost no
time in opening fire, and the colonists, unable to reply to our big guns, were
growing unsteady when Prescott hoisted himself on to the parapet where,
under a heavy but ill-directed cannonade he sauntered up and down,
giving directions to his working parties and encouraging those men whose
courage was not as steadfast as his own. With such an example before them
none of the militia flinched; the redoubt grew apace, and was practically
finished before the troops in Boston were ready to attack it. But though
Prescott had every reason to be satisfied with the temper and industry of
his detachment, his situation was a desperate one, and had Gage availed
himself of all the resources at his command, not one of the twelve hundred
adventurers would have made his way back to the provincial camps.
The British had command of the bay; vessels of light draught could sail
close to any part of the peninsula; the isthmus, the only possible line of
retreat for the Americans, was low, sandy, and less than two hundred
yards in width. Gage could have landed behind the entrenchments, and
have attacked the Americans simultaneously in front and rear; he could
have cut off their retreat and starved them into surrender by fortifying
himself upon the isthmus, or by stationing gunboats on either side of it, he
could have made it absolutely impassable by cross fire. These schemes were
suggested to him, but neither he nor any of the British army were in
the mood for scientific fighting, and he decided to regain the prestige lost
at Concord and Lexington by a direct frontal attack upon Breed's

Hill.[1] Four complete battalions and twenty flank companies, including the grenadiers and light infantry of the Royal Irish, were rowed across to the Charlestown peninsula—the right wing under General Pigot was composed of the provisional battalion of light infantry, the 38th and 43rd regiments; in the left wing were the provisional battalion of grenadiers, the 5th and 52nd regiments, commanded by General Howe. While the troops were landing on ground well out of range of the Americans the officers had time to study the position they were to carry. It was a strong one: a gentle slope, covered with long grass and cut up by a series of fences calculated to throw advancing troops into disorder, led up to the redoubt and to a breastwork, which ran for a hundred yards towards the enemy's left. Between the end of this breastwork and the sea was a gap, held by a detachment posted at the foot of Bunker's Hill, where the only cover was a low stone wall, on which hay was piled to give it additional height. The total frontage occupied was about six hundred yards, defended when the fight began by fifteen hundred men and six pieces of artillery.[2] The British brought between two thousand and two thousand five hundred troops into the field, for in addition to the units already mentioned the 47th regiment and a battalion of Marines came into action during the fight.

At three o'clock in the afternoon Howe, who was the senior officer on the Charlestown peninsula, gave the order to advance. At first the movement was covered by the fire of eight pieces—field-guns and howitzers, which had been ferried across from Boston, but soon the supply of cannon-balls ran out, and as the officer in charge of the artillery reported that a marsh prevented his pushing on to within grape-shot range of the enemy, the infantry for a long time were unsupported by the guns. After the regiments had deployed, the light infantry was directed against the enemy's left, while the grenadiers, 5th and 52nd, with the 38th and 43rd in second line, were to storm the breastwork and the redoubt. The day was intensely hot, and the soldiers, burdened with heavy knapsacks, three days' rations, cartouche-boxes, ammunition, bayonets, and muskets weighing fifteen pounds, mounted the hill slowly though in good order. They were allowed to open fire too soon, and their volleys, delivered with perfect precision, were almost ineffective. The provincials wished to reply while their enemies were a long way off, but their leaders knew better than to allow such a waste of ammunition, and while some threatened to cut down the first man who discharged his firelock without orders, others ran along the top of the

[1] The engagement ought strictly to be called that of Breed's Hill, but it has always been known as Bunker's Hill, and will be, as long as the American War of Independence is remembered.

[2] The reinforcements sent to Prescott raised the number of provincials on the peninsula to about 4000, but in Washington's opinion not more than 1500 were engaged at any one time during the day. —Trevelyan's 'American Revolution,' vol. i. p. 363.

parapet kicking the muzzles into the air. It was not until the red-coats were within fifty or sixty yards that the Americans were allowed to shoot, and then their well-aimed musketry was so terrible that the whole British line recoiled before it to the bottom of the hill. Howe re-formed his troops, and again led them up the slope, only to be hurled backwards once more with a loss so heavy that the glacis of Breed's Hill looked more like the breach of a fortress after an assault than an ordinary battlefield. But though they had twice failed to reach the works of the Americans neither Howe nor his men were beaten, and the General had the moral courage to order a third attack, while the soldiers

"had that in them which raised them to the level of a feat of arms to which it is not easy, and perhaps not even possible, to recall a parallel. Awful as was the slaughter of Albuera, the contest was eventually decided by a body, however scanty, of fresh troops. The cavalry which pierced the French centre at Blenheim had been hotly engaged but, for the most part, had not been worsted. But at Bunker's Hill every corps had been broken; every corps had been decimated several times over; and yet the same battalions, or what was left of them, a third time mounted that fatal slope with the intention of staying on the summit. Howe had learned his lesson, and perceived that he was dealing with adversaries whom it required something besides the manœuvres of the parade ground to conquer. And to conquer, then and there, he was steadfastly resolved, in spite of the opposition which respectfully indeed, but quite openly, made itself heard around him. He ordered the men to unbuckle and lay down their knapsacks, to press forward without shooting, and to rely on the bayonet alone until they were on the inner side of the wall. . . . The officers who had remonstrated with him for proposing to send the troops to what they described as downright butchery, when they were informed of his decision, returned quietly to their posts, and showed by their behaviour that in protesting against any further bloodshed they had been speaking for the sake of their soldiers and not of themselves."[1]

Prescott had begun to ask for reinforcements of men and ammunition early in the day, but, as was to be expected in a volunteer army chiefly officered by amateurs, the staff arrangements were so bad that very few troops and no ammunition reached him during the action. Thus when Howe for the third time hurled himself at the redoubt, none of its defenders had more than two rounds left. These last shots were not wasted, for as the troops rushed with fixed bayonets towards the work a venomous fire brought nearly every man in the front rank headlong to the ground; but without a check the ranks in rear surged over the parapet, and falling-to with the cold steel drove the provincials in confusion out of the redoubt. With empty muskets and with few bayonets the Americans could do little at close

[1] Trevelyan, vol. i, pp. 359, 360.

quarters, but many fought stubbornly as they retreated, admirably covered by the men on Bunker's Hill, who, though heavily cannonaded by the fleet, held their ground until their comrades from Breed's Hill had shaken off pursuit. This engagement cost our provincial kinsmen 115 killed and 300 wounded, while of the old-country men 19 officers were killed and 70 wounded; in the other ranks 207 were killed and 758 wounded—a total of 1054 casualties.[1] The enormous proportion of losses among the commissioned ranks was due to the good shooting of picked marksmen, who were kept supplied with loaded weapons by their neighbours. These sharpshooters devoted themselves to picking off the officers, whose glittering gorgets not only revealed their rank, but gave an excellent target at which to aim. Of the part played in the action by the grenadier and light companies of the Royal Irish no particulars have been preserved; nothing is known beyond the fact that three privates were killed and an officer, Lieutenant W. Richardson, and seven privates wounded.[2] Compared to the carnage in some of the flank companies, the losses of the XVIIIth were insignificant, yet the actual percentage was high, for in June, 1775,[3] the companies of the regiment only averaged twenty-six of all ranks, and though the grenadiers and light infantry were usually a little stronger than the battalion companies, it is doubtful whether between them they brought more than sixty-five or seventy men into the field.

Although Gage's dearly-won victory secured to the British the possession of the Charlestown peninsula, and thus guaranteed them against bombardment from Bunker's Hill, it did not improve the situation in other respects. Soon after the battle Washington was elected to the command of the provincial army, and so closely invested Boston that the garrison began to suffer from the want of fresh food. At first the daily ration of salt pork and peas was occasionally varied by fish, but this source of supply was cut off by the American general, who dragged a number of whale-boats overland from the neighbourhood of Cape Cod to the head-waters of one of the rivers flowing into the bay, and manned the flotilla with sailors, of whom there were many in his ranks. With this mosquito fleet he effectually stopped all fishing operations, and under the very guns of our warships

---

[1] Some historians consider that this number should be increased to eleven hundred and fifty.— Fortescue, vol. iii. p. 159.

[2] See Appendix 2 (C).

[3] The following officers are shown by the muster roll as present at Boston on June 25, 1775 :—
Major—I. Hamilton (in command).
Captains—J. Mawby, J. Shee, B. Chapman, J. B. Payne, B. Johnson, R. Hamilton, C. Edmonstone.
Lieutenants—G. Bowes, H. Fermor, John Mawby (adjutant), W. Richardson, W. Blackwood, E. Crossby.
Ensigns—J. Delancey, E. Prideaux, G. Bentricke, T. Serle, F. J. Kelly, C. Hoare, W. Slator.
Quartermaster— —— Batwicke.

captured small craft, and seized the sheep and cattle grazing on the islands in the bay. That such things were possible shows the depths of inefficiency to which our fleet on the American station had sunk in 1775; supine and stupid as were the generals, they seemed models of talent and energy when compared with the admirals with whom they were expected to co-operate. The want of proper food produced much illness, especially among the wounded, whose diet in hospital was the same as that of the men at duty; and the mortality was great. Coal ran so short that wooden houses and churches were pulled down for firewood. Small-pox broke out and claimed many victims. The duties, heavy everywhere, proved particularly trying at the outposts, for the provincials, ignoring the rule of war that piquets are not to be fired upon wantonly, used to amuse themselves by forming parties to stalk and shoot down the sentries as they paced their beats. Beyond these occasional skirmishes there was no fighting; at first the gunners cannonaded the enemy's position, but with so little success that the general decided to waste no more powder in teaching the Americans how to stand fire. As month after month passed in misery and inaction, the soldiers, badly fed, thoroughly dispirited and profoundly bored, grew moody, dirty, careless about their dress, while discipline was only maintained by the stern sentences of the courts-martial which awarded punishments of four hundred, six hundred, and even a thousand lashes.

When the Cabinet realised that Boston was in great want of food they sent out many ships filled with stores of every kind. But the ill-luck which dogged the British throughout the American war prevented the arrival of these vessels. Some were lost at sea; others were blown by a tempest to the West Indies; while others again, laden with cannon and mortars, muskets, flints, and much powder and shot fell into the hands of the Americans, who under Washington's fostering care were rapidly forming a national fleet. These munitions of war were not the only provincial spoils: a daring raid against isolated forts on the Canadian frontier secured a large number of guns, and early in March, 1776, Washington began to bombard Boston with British ordnance, and took possession of high ground to the south of the town, which from want of men neither Gage nor his successor Howe had been able to include within their lines. This position commanded the harbour, and the Admiral warned the General plainly that unless the soldiers could recapture it the men-of-war and transports would be obliged to put to sea. Thereupon Howe, who had long realised that it was impossible to maintain himself in Boston, ordered its evacuation, and on the 17th of March, with the nine thousand troops remaining to him and eleven hundred loyalists who refused to remain behind, he set sail for Halifax in Nova Scotia, in ships so overcrowded that many valuable stores had to be left to fall into Washington's hands, while much of the officers' heavy baggage shared the same fate. The Americans did not hinder the embarkation, for Howe had given out that if the bombardment was resumed he would set fire to the town, and Washington, to whom the threat was reported by his spies, allowed him to depart in peace. The men-of-war, after seeing the troopships safely out to sea, hung about the coast of Massachusetts for a time, but effected nothing, and then were ordered to other parts of the theatre of war.

The XVIIIth had been so worn down by privations and misery at Boston, that it was ordered home to recruit. The men still fit for active service were drafted into other regiments, while the officers, non-commissioned officers, and invalids of the Royal Irish returned to England in the course of the summer of 1776. The XVIIIth was not actively employed during the remainder of this war, which, beginning with our attempt to suppress the rebellion in North America, developed into a struggle for existence against the combined forces of France, Holland, and Spain; for these countries, seeing that our resources were heavily taxed by the struggle in America, and desirous to pay off old scores, took up arms against us. For a time we lost the command of the sea, and could not reinforce Cornwallis when he was besieged at Yorktown by Washington's provincial troops and a large body of French regular soldiers. After a gallant defence, Yorktown fell, and with the lowering of Cornwallis's flag passed away Britain's last hope of re-conquering her rebellious provinces. By the peace of 1783, England was compelled to recognise the independence of the United States, as her revolted colonies now styled themselves; to restore Florida and Minorca to Spain, and to cede to France the West Indian islands of St Lucia and Tobago.

From 1776 to 1783, the Royal Irish were stationed in England and in the Channel Islands, where their officers drilled and disciplined the recruits to such purpose that when the young soldiers were suddenly called upon to perform a most unpleasant duty they were thoroughly equal to the occasion. Early in 1783 the XVIIIth was in Guernsey, where one of the regiments of the garrison had acquired an evil reputation for insubordination. This corps (long since disbanded) suddenly broke out into open mutiny, and after coercing its colonel into promising them privileges entirely subversive of all discipline, apparently settled down; the officers, thinking the trouble was over for the moment, went to their mess-room and sat down to dinner, when a shower of bullets came rattling about their ears. They took cover under the table, but the would-be murderers mounted to windows from which they could pour plunging fire into the mess-room, and were shooting vigor-ously when a sergeant advised the officers to make a dash for the gate of the fort. They did so, and by great luck escaping unhurt by the volley with which their appearance in the barrack-square was greeted, hurried into the town to give the alarm. Two of their number, however, could not run, and found shelter in a coal cellar! As soon as this outbreak was reported, the local militia was turned out, and the XVIIIth ordered to parade forthwith; the fort was surrounded; the drums sounded a "parley"; but the mutineers at first declined to treat, and then demanded that they should be disbanded and sent back to their homes at once. When the Lieutenant-Governor attempted to reason with them, these madmen fired at him and next turned their muskets on the troops. Then more infantry came up, followed by some guns; and there seemed every prospect of a sharp fight, when the mutineers suddenly lost heart, piled arms, and marching quietly out of the fort, surrendered. Happily none of the bullets found its billet among the Royal Irish, who were greatly praised by the military authorities for their good behaviour, and the States (the local parliament) of Guernsey presented a hundred guineas to the non-commissioned officers and privates of the XVIIIth as a tangible proof of gratitude for their services on this occasion.

In the summer of 1783 the regiment sailed for Gibraltar, where it was stationed for the next ten years.

CHAPTER IV.

1793-1817.

THE WAR WITH THE FRENCH REPUBLIC: TOULON—CORSICA—EGYPT.
THE NAPOLEONIC WAR: THE WEST INDIES.

DURING the early phases of the French Revolution the British Government assumed an attitude of strict neutrality in the internal affairs of France, and to this policy it adhered until January, 1793, when the excesses of the Jacobins, culminating in the judicial murder of Louis XVI., compelled England to join the coalition of Continental Powers which had taken up arms to restore order in France, and to safeguard their own dominions, threatened, and in some cases actually invaded by the troops of the Republic. The outbreak of war found the British army in a deplorable condition; it had in no way recovered from its disasters in America, and was "lax in its discipline, entirely without system and very weak in numbers. Each colonel of a regiment managed it according to his notions or neglected it altogether. There was no uniformity of drill or movement; professional pride was rare, professional knowledge still more so. . . . Every department was more or less inefficient. The regimental officers, as well as their men, were hard drinkers, the latter, under a loose discipline were addicted to marauding and to acts of licentious violence." [1] The *physique* was often as defective as the *moral;* some regiments were composed of lads too young to march, while in others the majority of the rank and file were old and worn-out men. A few thousand troops were hurried off to join the forces of the Allies who faced the French in Holland, and a fleet was sent to the Mediterranean under Lord Hood, with orders to co-operate with the adherents of the Monarchy, who were still numerous in the south of France. After Hood passed Gibraltar he bore up for Toulon, then as now one of the principal French naval ports. [2] In its harbour and dockyard lay many warships, commanded by Royalists who hated the Revolution and all its works, and manned by sailors many of whom agreed with the political opinions of their officers. As large numbers of the civilian population in the town shared his views, the Royalist admiral, in the hope of rescuing his

---

[1] Bunbury, 'Narrative of Campaign in North Holland,' pp. 3, 4.   [2] See Map No. 3.

country from the anarchy into which it was plunged, took the extreme step
of entering into negotiations with Hood for the occupation of the port by the
British.   The horror inspired by the Revolution must have been deep indeed
to induce an officer of high rank and unblemished reputation to think of such
an arrangement with a nation regarded by every Frenchman as the hereditary
enemy of his race.   Since the Normans after conquering France had overrun
and subdued England, hostilities between the two countries had been frequent,
almost incessant; we had often raided the French coasts, and for a long time
our kings held as their own the western half of France.   In the hundred
years immediately preceding the outbreak of the Revolution the divergent
policy of their rulers had plunged the two countries into a series of five wars:
their armies had encountered each other on innumerable battlefields in Germany and the Low Countries, in Spain, Canada and the West Indies: their
fleets had met not only in the Mediterranean, the Bay of Biscay, and the
Channel, but in parts of the ocean as remote as the Gulf of Bengal and the
Caribbean Sea; and bands of French adventurers in the service of the native
princes of India had fought with the troops of the East India Company on the
plains of Hindustan.   Very bitter must have been the feelings of the Royalist
officers when they agreed to make over to Hood the forts, the arsenal, the
shipping, the docks, and the town of Toulon itself, on the understanding that
this national property was to be held in trust for the son of Louis XVI., to
whom it was duly to be restored when he ascended the throne.   The French
men-of-war were to be dismantled, but as a concession to sentiment, and to
show that Toulon was not a conquered town but still formed part of the
Kingdom of France, the white flag of the Bourbons was to float over its walls.

On August 27, 1793, Hood, who had been joined by a Spanish squadron,
took possession of the forts.   The landing party consisted of from twelve to
fifteen hundred marines and soldiers who were serving on board the ships.
There was no officer among them of rank higher than a captain; they had no
tents, or stores, or field-guns, and even had they possessed the latter, there
were no engineers or artillerymen to plan a battery or to lay a gun.   Though
the troops met with no active opposition, the attitude of many of the French
sailors was so threatening that Hood decided to get rid of as many of them
as he could, and selecting four of the least serviceable French vessels, he
unshipped their guns and ammunition, and packed into them five thousand of
the most troublesome republican seamen, with " safe conducts " for the French
ports on the Atlantic seaboard.   Having thus disposed of these " undesirables,"
Hood applied to those of the Allied Powers whose territories lay in the basin
of the Mediterranean for help to hold Toulon against the Republicans who
were gathering against him, and by the beginning of November he had collected a very heterogeneous force of about 16,000 men.   When our Ministers
learned that Toulon was in the hands of the Allies they promised to send

Hood large reinforcements; but neither the importance of the place as a base of operations against the Republicans, nor the difficulty of holding its land-locked harbour were adequately appreciated at home; and when more troops were required for our contingent in the Low Countries, for an expedition against the coast of Brittany, and for a raid upon the French islands in the West Indies, the expected reinforcements dwindled to seven hundred and fifty men from Gibraltar, who reached Toulon on the 27th of October. At the beginning of the war the regiments were so weak that this handful of troops included the XVIIIth Royal Irish,[1] the second battalion of the Royals, and detachments of Royal Engineers and Royal Artillery. The exact strength of the XVIIIth is not known, but as on the 25th of June, 1793, there were only two hundred and eighty-three officers and men at the Rock, and as a certain number of sick were left in hospital when the Royal Irish went on active service, the captains must have commanded companies no larger than the sections of the present day. The reinforcements from Gibraltar raised the strength of the British to about 2000 of all ranks; their allies consisted of 6500 Spaniards, 4700 Neapolitans, 1500 Piedmontese, and about the same number of French Royalists.

An army made up of contingents from several nations is necessarily less effective than one formed of soldiers of the same race. Hereditary ill-feeling, professional jealousy, and the want of a common language combine to lessen its value as a fighting machine, unless the General-in-Chief possesses a personality as commanding as that of Marlborough or Wellington. At Toulon none of the senior officers of the Allies were men of genius, and it is doubtful whether even a great soldier, with so curiously composed a force, could have withstood the savage energy that Napoleon, then a young officer of artillery on his first campaign, infused into the Generals commanding the besieging troops. The contingents of the Allies were of very uneven value. The British were excellent, though their courage was not yet thoroughly disciplined; the Piedmontese were very good; the French Royalists, though

---

[1] The muster-roll of the XVIIIth Regiment for the six months ending 25th December, 1793, gives the following list of officers :—

Lieutenant-Colonel—D. D. Wemyss, in command.
Major—J. Mawby (on leave).
Captains—W. Conolly, H. T. Montresor (recruiting), T. S. Sebright (on leave), G. H. Vansittart (on leave), T. Probyn, D. McDonald (on leave), J. Richardson, W. Gammell.
Captain-Lieutenant and Adjutant—R. Powell.
Lieutenants—J. Hope, T. G. Montresor (on leave), W. Morgan, C. Dunlop, Sebright Mawby, H. Wolseley (on leave), W. Byron, T. Mandiville (duty), M. Gamble, T. Holme (on leave), C. Grove, J. Woodcock.
Ensigns—W. Johnston, T. Stuart, W. Iremonger, A. Steuart, W. R. Rainsford (not joined), R. T. Bingham (duty), J. Woodcock, F. Pennyman, G. Minchin.
Quartermaster—W. Musgrove (at Gibraltar for recovery of health).
Surgeon—C. Kennelly.
Mate—T. Jackson.

brave, naturally disliked to fight their republican fellow-countrymen, much as they loathed their political principles; the Spaniards frequently deserted their posts when threatened by a vigorous attack, and the Neapolitans were cowards of the deepest dye. Sir Gilbert Elliot, the diplomatic representative of Britain in the Mediterranean expedition, describes how a party of Neapolitans behaved on outpost. After four of them had been killed in a skirmish, the remainder sent to the officer in charge of the section " to beg to be relieved as they were all *sick !* " With such allies it is not surprising to learn that " no post was considered safe without a proportion of British troops, and they were obliged to be divided and thin-sowed accordingly." [1] Whether from genuine illness, from unfitness for the hardships of active service, or from overwork, the sick list was enormous, and the Generals could never count on more than 11,000 or 12,000 effectives—far too few for the heavy duty they had to perform. To prevent the enemy from planting batteries on the hills commanding the harbour, the Allies were forced to hold a perimeter of fifteen miles, guarded by eight main works with a number of subsidiary connecting posts; and nine thousand men were constantly employed at the outposts, with a reserve of three thousand in the town, to overawe the disaffected part of the population and to reinforce any threatened point.

Up to the time of the arrival of the XVIIIth there had not been much fighting, for the French were engaged in mounting guns, and were not yet in strength to attempt a *coup-de-main.* When the Royal Irish landed they were marched up to the front, but were engaged in no affair of importance until the 30th of November, when they took part in a sortie against a large battery placed by Napoleon himself on the Aresnes heights, from which one of our principal works was commanded. The assaulting column, formed of 400 British, 300 Piedmontese, 600 Neapolitans, 600 Spaniards, and 400 French Royalists, was commanded by General O'Hara, one of the staff at Gibraltar, who had landed at Toulon with the XVIIIth. The instructions he issued were explicit. When the troops reached the plain at the foot of the heights, the column was to break into four detachments, the British on the left, and on reaching the summit they were to capture the battery, occupy the heights, and then stand fast; on no account whatever were they to follow the enemy in pursuit. After making their way, first through a belt of olive-trees intersected by stone walls, and then up a steep mountain cut into terraces of vineyards, the Allies gained the crest, surprised the French, and drove them headlong out of the battery. Had they remembered their orders the success would have been complete, for the guns could have been rolled down the height and carried back to Toulon; but unfortunately the men got out of hand, and dashed madly after the retreating French down a valley and up a hill on the other side, scattering in all directions as they pursued their flying

---

[1] Dundas, ' Summary Account of Proceedings of Army and Navy at Toulon.'

foes. They had lost all vestige of cohesion when they were charged by formed bodies of the enemy, whose counter-stroke changed our victory into a defeat. General O'Hara was wounded and captured; and of the four hundred British engaged, twelve officers and about two hundred other ranks were killed, wounded, or taken prisoner. The survivors fell back to the battery and attempted to hold it, but being unsupported by their Continental comrades had finally to retreat into Toulon, though not before they had spiked six guns.

During the next fortnight the volume of the enemy's fire increased daily; fresh batteries were unmasked in various directions, and everything tended to confirm the reports of spies and deserters that the French, now about 40,000 strong, were preparing for an attack in force. The preliminary bombardment began at 2 A.M. on the 16th of December, when Napoleon concentrated the fire of five batteries upon Fort Mulgrave, one of the most important of the western series of redoubts. It was held by a mixed force: a body of Spaniards occupied the northern half of the work; the southern was in charge of a detachment of British, under Captain W. Conolly, Royal Irish Regiment. By the end of the day the redoubt was in ruins, with half its garrison of seven hundred men disabled; at two o'clock in the morning of the 17th the French advanced against it, but though in overpowering force, for half an hour they made no progress till the Spaniards were seized with panic and left the British in the lurch. The enemy had begun to occupy the northern end of the work, when Conolly, though himself hard pressed, sent a subaltern and thirty-six men to retake it. With splendid courage this handful of soldiers drove back the Republicans, and for a time kept them at bay; but soon the weight of numbers began to tell, the survivors of the detachment were forced backwards, and at four o'clock the "remnants of the XVIIIth" were ousted from Fort Mulgrave. An hour or two later the French, breaking through the line of fortifications at a second point, carried Mont Faron, a hill 1800 feet high, which from the north partly commands the harbour and the town. On the enemy's side of this mountain the slopes are steep and rocky; and as much labour had been expended in increasing their natural difficulties, Faron was considered so impregnable that only four hundred and fifty men were employed to guard its two miles of frontage. At daylight every work upon this hill was attacked and, though none of the British posts were driven in, the French poured through the gaps left by the Spaniards and Neapolitans, and established themselves upon the shoulder of Mont Faron from which Toulon is overlooked.

A disaster such as this had long been foreseen by the senior officers of the British land forces. General O'Hara, and his successor General David Dundas, had frequently represented to Lord Hood the impossibility of making a prolonged defence with so inadequate and so inefficient a garrison as that at his disposal; they had pointed out that if one of the main works should be lost there were no fresh troops with which to recapture it, and that once any part of the line was pierced the harbour and the fleet would be exposed to the enemy's artillery; and they therefore urged that arrangements should be made beforehand for the orderly and systematic evacuation of the place when it became untenable. But Lord Hood was strongly prejudiced against soldiers: throughout his career he had slighted their advice, and he took no steps to prepare for the retreat which the Generals warned him was inevitable, with the result that when all hope of holding the place was gone nothing was in readiness for the retirement, and nearly the whole of the 17th was spent in settling details with the naval and military officers of the different nations. To organise the evacuation was no easy task; not only were there four thousand sick and wounded to be embarked, but room had to be found on the transports or the men-of-war for thousands of Royalists whom it was impossible to abandon to the vengeance of their republican fellow-countrymen; the French ships had to be burned or towed out of harbour, and the arsenal and dockyard to be destroyed. After many hours of weary discussion it was agreed that the embarkation of the troops should begin at 11 P.M. on the 18th; the least important posts were to be withdrawn early, others were to be held to the last moment. The scheme, which required absolute obedience to orders, was nearly wrecked by the Neapolitans, whose misconduct Elliot thus described in a despatch to Government—

" . . . These arrangements were made on the 17th before dinner. Without notice to any person concerned the Neapolitan officers packed up their baggage, and crowded the streets and quays with their preparations for departing on the evening of the 17th. Their baggage was actually sent on board, their general actually embarked that evening, and the troops, quitting every post where they were stationed, continued their embarcation publicly from the quays of the town, from the evening of the 17th to the middle of the next day. Their eagerness, impatience and panic were so great on the 18th, in the forenoon, that the embarcation of the inhabitants was rendered not only difficult but dangerous, the Neapolitan soldiers firing on those boats which they could not get admission to. Many of themselves were drowned in attempting to crowd into the boats, and there was a temporary appearance of confusion and insurrection in the town. The Neapolitan Admiral seems to have been in as great haste as the military. He sailed long before either the British or Spanish squadrons and, without waiting to make any arrangement about either troops or refugees, pushed off for Naples, leaving a good number of Neapolitan troops on board our fleet to find their way home as well as they can." [1]

Until nearly all the allied troops were embarked the British and Piedmontese remained resolutely at their posts, which they did not quit until

---

[1] Minto's 'Life of Elliot,' vol. ii. pp. 205, 206.

recalled into the town to cover the operations of the sailors, who were burning the arsenal and setting fire to the French ships. When the outposts were withdrawn the French crowded into Toulon, and by the light of the flames shot heavily at the blue-jackets, busy at the work of devastation, in which they were helped by a party of the XVIIIth, commanded by Ensign W. Iremonger, one of the two land officers employed on this dangerous duty. For a time a musketry fight raged; then at the appointed hour the soldiers gradually withdrew to their boats, gained their ships, and in two or three hours the whole of the allied fleet was safely out to sea. Though Hood's operations on land utterly failed to advance the cause of the Royalists, and though he did not succeed in destroying the arsenal completely, or in burning all the enemy's ships, he undoubtedly inflicted a serious, though not a crushing blow to the naval power of France in the Mediterranean by his operations at Toulon. When he took possession of the town he found floating in its harbour or building in its dockyard fifty-eight men-of-war of various sizes: thirty-three he annexed or burned to the water's edge, the remaining twenty-five he was obliged to leave behind him, to become the nucleus of a new fleet. The price paid in human flesh and blood for this success cannot be stated, for the losses of the Allies are not to be traced, and the British returns, as far as they were published in despatches, are incomplete, and in the case of the Royal Irish do not agree with the muster-roll made a week after the evacuation. In it appear the names of three sergeants, one corporal, and thirty-four privates who were killed or died during the siege; and one officer, Lieutenant George Minchin, two sergeants, two drummers, one corporal, and thirty-two privates missing.[1] In the unsuccessful sortie of the 30th of November twenty-four rank and file of the regiment were wounded; how many were injured in the daily fighting at the outposts and in the defence of Fort Mulgrave and Mont Faron cannot be ascertained, but it is clear that the Royal Irish played a distinguished part in the operations, and in proportion to their numbers lost very heavily.

As soon as the allied fleet was clear of the harbour of Toulon it dispersed: the Spaniards and the Neapolitans made sail respectively for the Balearic Isles and Naples, while Hood put into the bay of Hyères, a few miles east of Toulon, where he tried to evolve order out of the chaos produced by the hurried embarkation of the troops, and to obtain fresh provisions of which he was in great need. Unwilling to weaken himself by sending British vessels to buy food in the ports of Italy and Spain, he employed upon this service several of the French ships, which, in theory at least, were still under the orders of the Royalist admiral. British infantry were sent on board them as marines, the XVIIIth furnishing a strong detachment under Lieutenant Mawby, who on going on board the *Pompée* found that she was still flying the

---

[1] See Appendix 2 (D).

Royalist flag, and was commanded by French naval officers. The duty was heavy, and the cruise must have been a very unpleasant one, for guards had to be mounted in every part of the vessel to keep her crew from breaking into open mutiny. In one respect, however, Mawby and his companions were better off than their comrades at headquarters, for they escaped the over-crowding caused by the presence of thousands of Royalists in the ships at Hyères. Sir Gilbert Elliot mentions that in the cabin he shared with several naval officers, twenty luckless French refugees, men, women, and children slept huddled together on the floor; and if no better quarters could be provided for the diplomatic representative of England, it is easy to imagine that regimental officers must have been hideously uncomfortable.

At this time England had no possessions in the Mediterranean east of Gibraltar, for Minorca, lost to her in 1782, was not recovered till some years later. Yet to watch Toulon and the southern coast of France, and to encourage the various Italian States to fight for their independence which was already threatened by the armies of the Republic, it was essential that England should possess an advanced naval and military base in the Mediterranean. Such a post awaited us in Corsica, where the inhabitants had profited by the turmoil of the Revolution to rise against their French masters, whom they had driven into the north of the island. The garrison had flung themselves into the fortified coast towns of Bastia and Calvi, and the works fringing the bay of S. Fiorenzo, and the Corsicans soon realised that without professional soldiers, cannon, and munitions of war, they could not hope to take these places, while without a fleet it was impossible to prevent reinforcements from the mainland reaching their enemy. When both parties to a bargain are eager to come to terms negotiations are easy, and the islanders willingly agreed to become subjects of George III., provided that a constitution framed on that of England was granted to them. As soon as the arrangements for the annexation of the island were completed Hood left his anchorage at Hyères, where for five weeks the French had allowed him to remain unmolested, and made for the bay of S. Fiorenzo, at the western base of the great northern promontory of Corsica.[1] Driving the French from their defences, he forced them to fall back on Bastia, their foothold on the eastern coast; then leaving some of the troops at S. Fiorenzo, he sailed for Bastia, already closely blockaded by Nelson's frigates and cut off from communication with the interior by the Corsicans, who excelled in all kinds of partisan warfare. Neither Hood's ships nor the troops accompanying them were at this time in a satisfactory condition: his crews were so weak that he had tried to borrow sailors from the Neapolitan fleet, but without success; and the soldiers numbered little more than two thousand men, who were very ill provided for a campaign, as most of their camp equipage, baggage, and knapsacks had been left behind at Toulon. A

[1] See Map No. 3.

board sat in Corsica to investigate the circumstances in which this loss—a very heavy one to the men—had been incurred, and recommended that £2 should be paid to each sergeant and £1 to each private soldier, adding that though this would not compensate the men for their kit, it was as much as Government could be reasonably expected to give.

Though Hood, as a sailor, was unversed in the military branches of the art of war, he decided after a reconnaissance of Bastia that it would be possible for the troops to carry the defences by a sudden assault from the land side of the town. Dundas, who though cautious by temperament was an educated soldier of much experience, condemned the project as beyond the powers of his small and ill-equipped force, and this difference of opinion at once intensified the friction already existing between the Admiral and the General. Unable to agree on a plan of operations, Hood and Dundas summoned conferences and councils of war, at which no decision was reached ; and their relations became so strained that they ceased to meet, transacting business by means of formal and acrimonious correspondence. Throughout the army the question was hotly debated, and Bastia was reconnoitred by many officers, the large majority of whom became converts to Dundas's opinions. Lieutenant-Colonel Wemyss, who commanded the XVIIIth, was one of the few in favour of an attack, but his views do not appear to have been supported by convincing arguments, for Sir John Moore (then Lieutenant-Colonel Moore, 51st regiment) recorded in his diary that " Wemyss conceives it would be mighty easy to take them " (*i.e.*, the heights commanding the land fortifications), " but cannot explain how, and talks so like a boy that little weight can be given to his opinion." [1] Hood's conduct towards the General and the troops became so intolerable that Dundas took the unjustifiable step of resigning his command and returning to England. Not long after his departure reinforcements reached the officer in temporary command of the army, whose offer to co-operate in the operations was contemptuously rejected by Lord Hood ; and thus, when on May 24th the garrison of 4500 men surrendered, the success was due to the Navy, whose blockading vessels had fairly starved the French into submission, while, with the exception of some artillerymen and the troops serving on the warships as marines, the land forces were hardly employed in the reduction of Bastia.

The only place in Corsica now remaining in the occupation of the French was Calvi, a well-fortified town on the western coast. Lieutenant-General the Hon. Charles Stuart, who on the day of the surrender of Bastia had arrived from England to replace Dundas, lost no time in reorganising his command, and then reconnoitred Calvi, where he was followed by Moore, who had been placed in command of a corps termed "the reserve," and

---

[1] Maurice's ' Diary of Sir John Moore,' vol. i. p. 82.

formed of the flank companies of the Royal Irish, the 50th, 51st, and the remains of the 2nd battalion of the Royals. Calvi was by no means an easy place to besiege, for it was surrounded on three sides by the sea and had good interior fortifications, with outer works of considerable strength. About eight hundred yards west of the town stood the Mozello, a bomb-proof, star-shaped fort, built of solid masonry and mounting ten guns; north of this fort was a smaller battery, flanked by an entrenchment, and to the east rose another battery of three guns. Two thousand yards south-west of the town the fort of Monteciesco commanded the approaches from the southward, which were also swept by the guns of two French frigates anchored in the bay. But though these works were formidable, Stuart considered that the "real strength of the defence lay in the height of the mountains and the rugged, rocky country over which it was necessary to penetrate. It was necessary to abandon regular approaches and to adopt rapid and forward movements." He accordingly decided to bombard Fort Monteciesco with three 26-prs., and under cover of their fire to throw up a heavier battery at night within seven hundred and fifty yards of the Mozello. The labour of moving the guns, ammunition, and stores was immense, for roads had to be cut up the sides of steep hills nine hundred feet in height, and the cannon to be dragged by hand over the cliffs that overhang the landing-place. At the end of June more troops were brought round from Bastia; among them were the Royal Irish, recently reinforced by the return of the *Pompée* detachment, which rejoined in time to share in the fatigues and dangers of the siege.

On the evening of the 6th of July,[1] the Royal Irish were ordered to make a feigned attack on Monteciesco to draw the attention of the enemy from Moore's column, which was preparing to throw up the battery against the Mozello. The ruse was successful; the XVIIIth showed themselves so ostentatiously that the French not only turned all their fire upon them, but reinforced Monteciesco with a body of men who had been posted on the very spot where Moore proposed to place his guns. By dint of great efforts the last of Moore's 26-prs. was dragged into position just before daybreak, thus raising the number of ordnance playing upon Calvi to eleven guns and three mortars, whose fire forced the French to evacuate Monteciesco and move their warships out of range. Stuart then bombarded Mozello assiduously; the French replied with equal vigour; for some days our shot appeared to make little impression on the fort, but on the 18th of July the breach was reported to be practicable, and orders were issued for its assault that night. To conceal the real object of his movements, he arranged that an advance battery should be built in the night in order that the French might think the concentration of troops was merely for

---

[1] The despatch and Moore's diary differ slightly about this date, but they are in substantial agreement about the facts.

the protection of the working party. The task was entrusted to the 50th, who, undiscovered by the enemy, threw up the battery, and then, to quote the words of the despatch, " the Grenadiers, Light Infantry and 2nd Battalion Royals under Lieutenant-Colonel Moore of the 51st Regiment and Major Brereton of the 30th Regiment proceeded with a cool steady confidence and unloaded arms towards the enemy, forced their way through a smart fire of musketry, and regardless of live shells flung from the breach or the additional defence of pikes, stormed the Mozello " . . . while " Lieutenant-Colonel Wemyss, equally regardless of opposition carried the enemy's battery on the left without firing a shot." In Sir John Moore's diary fuller details of this spirited affair are to be found. The various corps assembled at their rendezvous at 1 A.M. on the 19th: the Royal Irish were to attack the half moon (or Fountain) battery on the left, while "the reserve" stormed the Mozello. In ground dead to the fort, though only two or three hundred yards distant from it, Moore formed the grenadiers and light infantry (among whom, it will be remembered, were the flank companies of the XVIIIth) into a column of companies.

"Each grenadier carried a sandbag, and we had a sufficient number of ladders (about fourteen in all). Here we waited for the signal which was to be a gun from the new battery. The General came to me about half-past three. About this time some of the enemy's sentries or piquets fired upon the XVIIIth upon our left, and soon after the signal to advance was given. The General kept for some time at the head of the Grenadiers. A party of artificers a little in our front began to cut the palisades, but we were upon them before they could effect it. Captain McDonald, who commanded the Royal Grenadiers,[1] and I got through the palisades first at an opening made by our shot. The men instantly followed, and giving a cheer, ran up to the bottom of the breach. We were annoyed both by shot, hand-grenades, and live shells, which the enemy had placed on the parapet and rolled over upon us. Luckily neither sand-bags nor ladders were necessary. The Grenadiers advanced with their bayonets with such intrepidity that the French gave way and ran out of the fort—and in a moment the place was filled with the five companies of Grenadiers. Two companies of Light Infantry had been ordered to move quickly round the foot of the fort and get between the enemy and the town, but the Grenadiers stormed so briskly that the Light Infantry could not arrive in time: by this means most of them escaped."

The Royal Irish lost no time in entrenching themselves in the Fountain battery, and worked so well that when at daybreak the enemy opened with grape and round shot the cannonade did them little harm.

[1] The "Royal Grenadiers" may be an abbreviation of the grenadier company of the "Royal Regiment of Ireland," as the XVIIIth was still frequently termed, or of "the Royals." In the 2nd Battalion of the Royals there were at this time two officers called MacDonald, and in the Royal Irish a captain named Donald McDonald. If Moore was accurate in his spelling of the name, an officer of the XVIIIth shared with the future hero of Corunna the honour of being first into the Mozello. In this assault Lieutenant S. Mawby of the regiment is known to have taken part.

Stuart had every reason for wishing to bring the operations to a close, for though his casualties were small, bad food, excessive fatigue, and a pestilential climate had so devastated the camp that by the middle of July two-thirds of his men were in hospital, and the remainder were breaking down at an alarming rate. The large number of sailors who were serving on shore under Nelson were in equally bad case, and the necessity of watching the French at Toulon made it impossible to replace them from the fleet. In the hope that the loss of their principal outworks had shaken the spirit of the French, General Stuart sent word to the garrison that he was prepared to offer them favourable terms; but when Casabianca, their commander, refused to negotiate, he pressed forward his siege-works so fast that on July 31, thirteen heavy guns, four mortars, and three howitzers were in position within six hundred yards of the walls of the town. So effective was their fire that on the 1st of August Casabianca asked for a suspension of hostilities, undertaking to yield in nine days if during that time he was not relieved from France, and as no help arrived the nine hundred men of the garrison surrendered on the 10th. In recognition of their spirited defence of Calvi, which had lasted for fifty-one days, they were granted excellent terms; they marched out with all the honours of war; they retained their side-arms; and they were sent back to France, free to serve against us again as soon as they pleased. The capture of Calvi only cost the British ninety killed and wounded, and the losses of the XVIIIth were proportionately small. Lieutenant W. Byron, whose death assured to his young relative, the future poet, the succession to the peerage, was killed; Lieutenant-Colonel D. D. Wemyss and Lieutenant W. Johnston were wounded; five rank and file were killed, one sergeant and seven rank and file wounded.[1] Yet so greatly had the regiment suffered during the siege from exposure and malarial fever, that when it marched into Calvi its effectives consisted of two officers, four sergeants, and seventy-one rank and file, and though the capitulation brought active operations to an end the losses by disease did not cease. Malaria had taken so firm a hold of the Royal Irish that including those who were killed or died of wounds or sickness during the siege, four officers, nine sergeants, six corporals, and a hundred and fifty-five private soldiers perished during the first nine months the regiment was in Corsica.[2] The mortality was at its height during the month of August, when seventy non-commissioned officers and men died.

Nothing is known of the doings of the XVIIIth during the remainder of our short occupation of Corsica, except that several of the officers were employed on the staff: one of them, Major (afterwards Lieutenant-General Sir H. T.)

[1] The casualties may have been greater, for the losses in the grenadier and light companies cannot be traced. Lieutenant-Colonel Wemyss's wound is not mentioned in the casualty returns.

[2] See Appendix 2 (E).

Montresor, after acting as Governor of Calvi, was placed in command of a battalion of islanders, one of the corps raised for local defence by Sir Gilbert Elliot, who had been appointed Viceroy of Corsica by the Government at home. The lives of the officers left at regimental duty must have been singularly dull, as there was so little communication with England that letters or papers rarely reached the island, and even the Ministry, apparently forgetful of the existence of their new possession, often allowed months to pass without communicating with Elliot. Some amount of cynical amusement, however, was to be derived from studying the mental attitude of the population, who, at first delighted to find themselves British subjects, soon grew weary of the restraints of law and order enforced upon them by their new rulers. The Corsicans watched with ever increasing pride the victories in Italy of their young compatriot, Napoleon Bonaparte; they realised that the English and their Allies made no headway against France on land, and they appreciated the importance of Spain's change of policy, when after deserting the coalition against the Republic she placed her Mediterranean fleet at the disposal of our enemy. They gradually came to the conclusion that in annexing themselves to the British they had joined the losing side, and when the French troops overran Tuscany and seized upon Leghorn, the Corsicans began to give Elliot broad hints that they wished to see the last of him and his garrison of redcoats. The presence of the French in Leghorn, the principal port of Tuscany, was a direct menace to us in Corsica; and as a counterstroke Elliot threw troops into Porto Ferraio, the capital of the little island of Elba, half way between Bastia and Leghorn. To the Duke of Tuscany, part of whose dominions Elliot had thus occupied, the Viceroy justified himself by pointing out that as Tuscany had been unable to defend her territory on the mainland she would have been equally impotent to keep the French out of Elba.

In the autumn of 1796, the British Government, alarmed at the combination of the French and Spanish fleets, determined to recall their forces from the Mediterranean, and the order for the evacuation of Corsica was conveyed to Elliot by a despatch, wherein the abandonment of the island was described in the stilted language of the period as "the withdrawal of the blessing of the British Constitution from the people of Corsica." As a preliminary to the general retirement the troops had to be concentrated at Elba; and the embarkation of the garrison of Bastia, which included some, if not all, of the Royal Irish, was effected in very dramatic circumstances. When Nelson arrived off the port on October 14, he found the town in wild confusion: a committee of virulent Anglophobists had seized the reins of power, and their adherents were virtually masters of the place; British property had been confiscated; British merchant ships were forcibly detained in harbour; a plot was on foot to make the Viceroy a prisoner, and the General, de Burgh, had withdrawn the garrison into the citadel, where they had been followed by large numbers of armed men who insisted on falling-in with the guards and sentries at every post. By threatening to blow the town to pieces, Nelson succeeded in releasing the captured shipping and in saving public and private property valued at two hundred thousand pounds; but though the soldiers and sailors slaved night and day their work was by no means finished when, on the night of the 18th, news arrived that French troops had landed and were marching rapidly on Bastia, while the Spanish fleet was reported to be only sixty miles distant. Even Nelson realised that nothing more could be done: the troops began to move down to the boats, while the guns were spiked by Mawby, an officer of the XVIIIth, who with the grenadier company of the regiment had just been brought back from detachment on the neighbouring islet of Capreja. Though a heavy gale of wind was blowing and the sea was very high every soldier was safely embarked; and not too soon, for as the last boat pushed off from the shore the French advance-guard began to enter the citadel.

The resources of Elba were insufficient to meet the requirements of her suddenly increased population, and at first she drew largely from Piombino, the port of the district known as the Maremma of Tuscany. By garrisoning the town of Piombino and the villages in its neighbourhood, the French so effectually cut off this source of supply that at the beginning of November Elliot and de Burgh determined to make an effort to reopen communication with the mainland of Italy, and sent a column, chiefly composed of the Royal Irish, to drive the enemy from Piombino and the surrounding country.[1] The expedition is briefly mentioned by the Viceroy in a letter of November 6, 1796, where he says, "We take Piombino this evening. This will be the last act of my reign, and in truth the measure of Porto Ferraio was not complete without it. I shall then feel very happy about our supplies."[2] No account of the operations is to be found in the printed bulletins or among the documents at the Record Office; but fortunately some details have been preserved in the Royal Military Calendar, in a précis of the services of General Montresor. Brevet-Colonel D. D. Wemyss, XVIIIth, was in command of the column which was composed of the Royal Irish,[3] under Montresor, then a lieutenant-colonel; two companies of de Roll's Swiss regiment, one of the many corps of continental mercenaries raised at that time by Great Britain, and a detachment of artillery. These troops were embarked on three frigates, which anchored off Piombino early on November 7; Montresor was at once sent on shore to summon the Governor, who after some hesitation agreed to surrender, and without loss of time the soldiers

---

[1] See Map No. 3.   [2] Minto's 'Life of Elliot,' vol. ii. p. 362.

[3] The "proof table" in the muster-roll for Christmas, 1796, shows that the regiment had only three hundred and eighty-seven officers and men "present," while seventy-eight of all ranks were "absent": with the corps, either in the mainland of Italy or in Elba, there were only fourteen officers, while twenty-five were on leave or employed elsewhere.

landed. While Wemyss was taking measures to secure Piombino and to improvise transport for his men his heart must have sunk within him. Outside the walls of the town there were hardly any signs of life; autumnal rains had flooded the country in every direction; a few stone buildings, half farm, half fortress, rose like islands out of the water; thick woods concealed the villages on the neighbouring hills, whither for centuries the inhabitants of the Maremma have betaken themselves at night to avoid sleeping on the fever-stricken plain. After a few hours' hard work Montresor, with a detachment of five hundred men and three field-guns, marched to attack the garrison of Campiglia, a village ten miles off. The country was inundated for three miles, but

> "the hedges and trees on either side of the road being their guide the British waded through, though the buffalos attached to their guns had twice knocked up. On approaching the town the Lieutenant-Colonel sent his light company under Captain Dunlop by another road to cut off the enemy's picquets from the town, and to enter it by the Leghorn road, both of which were executed; after exchanging a few shots with the enemy's outposts, finding the British in their rear, they were compelled to disperse in the woods, which left the town open to complete surprise, inasmuch, that in front of his advance guard, at one o'clock after midnight, Lieut.-Colonel Montresor got into the town with a confidential servant unperceived, and personally seized an orderly French dragoon going with despatches to the garrison of Castiglione from the Commandant of Campiglia to announce the British having landed at Piombino: the entrance to the town was conducted with so much silence and arrangement that the Royal Irish Grenadiers reached the French main guard just as the enemy were turning out under arms, and rushing on them compelled them to lay down their arms, while the Commandant, (whose quarters were over the main guard), escaped by dropping out of his window over the town walls, leaving his supper, (which he had deferred to this late hour) on the table, and which was finished by the British officers when the prisoners were secured and the British patrols and picquets had been placed.
>
> "Colonel Wemyss having proceeded to attack Castiglione, Lieut.-Colonel Montresor secured his post so effectually that during three months the strong garrison of Leghorn never molested them. This little expedition being effectually accomplished, and the troops of Elba having formed their depôts, the British force was ordered back to Elba."

Much had happened while the Royal Irish were on the mainland of Italy. In November the fleet had been obliged to go to Gibraltar for stores, and at the end of the year Nelson had reappeared at Elba with orders from the Admiral, Sir John Jervis (afterwards Lord St Vincent), to embark the naval establishment and rejoin him in the Straits of Gibraltar. Nelson, however, brought no instructions for de Burgh, and when he suggested that as the

Navy had abandoned the Mediterranean it was useless for the troops to remain in Elba, the brave old general, though much perplexed at the situation, decided not to quit his post without orders from his military superiors. Nelson therefore had no option but to abandon de Burgh and his three thousand troops to their fate, and leaving transports enough for the whole of the garrison, and a few vessels with which to keep up communication with the mainland, he rejoined Jervis early in February, 1797. But neither Jervis nor Nelson forgot that a detachment of the British army was marooned in a little island off the coast of Tuscany in imminent danger of capture by the French, and soon after the great naval victory of Cape St Vincent, Nelson dashed back into the Mediterranean, ascertained that de Burgh and his troops were safe, and convoyed them safely to Gibraltar. The Royal Irish landed at the end of April or the beginning of May,[1] and formed part of the garrison of the Rock until, two years later, they again were embarked for active service.

Though the failure of the expedition to Holland in the winter of 1799 had added one more to the list of our unsuccessful enterprises against the French on the continent of Europe, the spring of 1800 found preparations on foot in England for another effort on land against the Republic. Lieutenant-General Sir Ralph Abercromby, with twenty thousand men, was to disembark on the coast of Italy near Genoa, occupy the maritime Alps, and by cutting the lines of communication between Italy and France relieve the pressure on the Austrians, who faced the French on the plains of Lombardy. Owing, however, to the fear of a Franco-Spanish invasion of Portugal and the consequent loss of the Tagus as a friendly port, a large proportion of Abercromby's force was kept back to defend Lisbon in case of need, and when Sir Ralph reached Port Mahon, the capital of Minorca, which since its recapture in 1798 had become our advanced post in the Mediterranean, he had only six thousand men available for active operations. He found despatches awaiting him from General Melas, the Austrian Commander-in-Chief in Italy, begging that British troops might be sent to Genoa, which, after a heroic defence by the French under Massena, had recently surrendered to the Austrians. Melas himself was unable to garrison it adequately: would Abercromby therefore do so? Ordering four thousand men, among whom were the XVIIIth Royal Irish, 571 strong, to follow him, Abercromby sailed at once, but on the voyage

---

[1] The muster-roll of the XVIIIth for Christmas, 1796, was signed at Elba on April 9, 1797. Among the deaths appears the name of Lieutenant George Mallet, who died during our occupation of the island. When the writer of this history visited Elba many years ago, he noticed on the wall of the garden where Napoleon used to walk during his exile in 1814-15, tablets to the memory of two or three British officers. One of these bore the following inscription:—

"Near this place lyeth the remains of Lieutenant George Mallett of the 18th or Royal Regiment of Ireland who departed this life the 13th of January 1797 in the 18th year of his age."

Thanks to the good offices of Mr M. Carmichael, H.M. Consul at Leghorn, and to the kindness of Lieutenant-General Count Simminiatelli, commanding the troops in Tuscany, this tablet has been presented to the regiment, and is now at the depôt at Clonmel.

learned that at Marengo Napoleon had defeated the Austrians, who were retreating all along their line, and had evacuated Genoa. After definitely ascertaining that co-operation with Melas had become impossible, he returned to Minorca, where for many weeks the expedition awaited fresh orders from home. During the halt Abercromby, with the help of Moore who commanded one of his brigades, devoted himself to the improvement of the troops. He strengthened their discipline, made their equipment suitable for active service, and cut down the personal baggage of officers and men to the articles absolutely necessary for a campaign. While he was at Minorca reinforcements gradually reached him, including a body of three thousand eight hundred men who had been on the point of attacking Belle Isle, off the western coast of France, when they were hurriedly diverted to the Mediterranean. Thus, when at the end of August instructions reached him to make a raid against the Spanish port of Cadiz, Abercromby, after providing an adequate garrison for Minorca, was able to embark between ten and eleven thousand men.

A fortnight was spent on the voyage to Gibraltar, where on September 19, he was joined by a large number of troops under Lieutenant-General Sir James Pulteney, the Colonel of the Royal Irish regiment.[1] Pulteney had been sent from England to destroy Ferrol, a naval station on the north-west coast of Spain. He had landed, driven the Spaniards back to the shelter of their works, and then discovered that the Government had sent him on a fool's errand. Ferrol was well armed and fortified, and as he was not nearly strong enough to attack it, he wisely abandoned the enterprise, re-embarked his men, and made sail for the Rock of Gibraltar.[2] Thanks to Pulteney's arrival, Abercromby's command now consisted of about twenty thousand infantry and a thousand cavalry and artillerymen, and in a few days a fleet of a hundred and thirty British men-of-war and troop-ships appeared before Cadiz, the most important naval harbour in the south of Spain. In the conduct of this expedition the General had by no means a free hand, for the Ministry, while ordering him to attack Cadiz, seize the arsenal, and destroy its docks and shipping, emphatically enjoined upon him not to run much risk, and not to land his troops unless he was confident that he could re-embark them safely. Operations conducted on such lines were doomed to failure. After much discussion with the naval authorities, a few thousand troops, including the XVIIIth, were crowded into boats and started for the shore, only to be recalled in a few minutes to their respective vessels, for the Admiral finally declined to guarantee their

---

[1] Pulteney had been known earlier in his career as Murray; he changed his name late in life. See Appendix 9.

[2] This sudden rush of troops to Gibraltar produced great scarcity of food. Eggs were sold at a shilling each, while "moderate-sized turkeys" found eager customers at £3, 10s.

safe return to the ships if once they landed. After a fruitless paper war between Abercromby and his naval colleague the whole fleet made sail, successful only in having covered itself with ridicule. In a few hours a great storm arose: the ships were driven in every direction along the coast of Morocco, where for many days they tossed and rolled in a tempestuous sea until the weather moderated and they reached Gibraltar.

During this storm, and indeed during the whole of the many months that Abercromby's command spent on board ship, the sufferings of the troops were great. The transports were so leaky that when it rained the men were constantly wet; so crowded that there was often not room on the decks for all to lie down at the same time; so ill-provided that the soldiers had no bedding, no covering other than their regimental blankets if, indeed, they were lucky enough to possess such articles. The food was not only indifferent, but inadequate, for an idea prevailed that the ration issued on shore was enough for a man who was taking hard exercise, and therefore on board ship, where the soldier theoretically was a passenger with nothing to do, he required less to eat than on land. In practice the soldier on board a transport had to work as hard as a sailor, and consequently was underfed. His diet of salt pork and biscuit, his ration of water, often scanty and generally tasting strongly of the barrels in which it was stored, and the absence of vegetables all combined to reduce his strength, and he often fell a prey to the scurvy which in those days devastated the fleet.

While the soldiers were still in the Straits of Gibraltar, where, as a sea-sick officer wrote, "the tossing of the ship rendered our situation as landsmen at once inconvenient and ridiculous," Abercromby received despatches of great importance. Dundas, the War Minister of England, had become inspired with a great idea—to abandon the "policy of pin-pricks" by which the conduct of our campaigns in Europe had been hitherto regulated, and strike a blow in defence of the Empire as a whole. The year after we had abandoned Elba Napoleon had embarked in the south of France with forty thousand men, and after seizing Malta made himself master of Egypt and sent emissaries to India, whose intrigues among the native princes complicated our situation in the East.[1] When he returned to France in 1799 he left behind him an army of occupation, whose presence was a continual danger to our power in Hindustan. This army Dundas determined to drive out, and with the reluctant assent of the other members of the Cabinet he now ordered Abercromby to prepare for a campaign in Lower Egypt, while a column, formed of a regiment

---

[1] The conquest of Egypt was no new idea to French statesmen. In the middle of the seventeenth century, while Louis XIV. was revolving in his mind schemes for the aggrandisement of France, he was urged strongly, though unsuccessfully, not to seek expansion in Europe, but to make himself master of Egypt, and by establishing her pre-eminence in the Mediterranean secure for his country the trade of the Levant and of the East. See Mahan's 'Influence of Sea Power on History,' pp. 107, 141, 142.

from Cape Colony[1] and of British and native troops from India, was to land at Kosseir on the Red Sea, strike across the desert to Upper Egypt, descend the Nile, and fall upon the enemy from the rear.[2]

The surrender of the French garrison in Malta on September 5, 1800, placed the island at our disposal, and this, our latest conquest, was fixed as the rendezvous of the fleet, which arrived there in detachments from Gibraltar throughout November. While his troops rested the General strove, though with poor results, to supplement the scanty information about the topography and resources of Egypt vouchsafed to him by Dundas, who had provided him with nothing but an indifferent map of the country and copies of correspondence of doubtful value, intercepted between the French generals at Cairo and their official superiors in Paris. Abercromby, however, learned enough to convince him that without plenty of small craft of light draught he could not land anywhere in Egypt, and on the 20th of December he weighed anchor for the Bay of Marmorice—a deep inlet on the coast of Caramania, one of the provinces of Asia Minor belonging to the Sultan, who was co-operating with England in the Egyptian expedition. Here the General expected to obtain shipping, and the horses with which his cavalry and artillery were still unprovided, but when after a tempestuous voyage he reached his destination on January 2, 1801, he found the Turkish officials so dilatory that he was forced to spend six weeks at Marmorice. Never was time more usefully employed, however, than during this long halt. The troops landed, drilled, collected a great store of firewood for use in Egypt, and prepared gabions and fascines for siege operations. The ships' carpenters were occupied in making small water-kegs and canteens, and light wooden sleighs to be drawn by hand across the desert. Both services were constantly practised in the art of disembarkation, and before the fleet again put to sea the soldiers could swarm down the sides of the transports and take their places in the boats without confusion; while the sailors who rowed the flotilla had learned to keep station and to reach the shore in the prescribed order.

In conceiving the idea of the expedition to Egypt Dundas apparently thought he had done all that could be expected from him, and took no trouble about details. He failed to comply with Abercromby's requisitions for stores and *matériel*. He did not even send him the bullion for which Sir Ralph frequently petitioned, and left him so short of actual cash that for three months the army was unpaid, and the only way by which cavalry horses could be bought at Marmorice was with specie produced by well-to-do officers. It is not surprising, therefore, that Abercromby wrote, "We are now on the point of sailing for the coast of Egypt with very slender means for executing the orders we have received. I never went on any service entertaining greater doubt of success, at the same time with more determination to encounter

[1] Taken in 1795 from the Dutch, then allies of France.   [2] See Map No. 3.

difficulties. . . . The Dutch expedition was walking on velvet compared to this."[1]   On February 22, he put to sea, and after a stormy passage of eight days reached Aboukir Bay—a wide indentation on the western coast of the delta of the Nile, where in August, 1798, Nelson had destroyed the fleet which had convoyed Napoleon's army to Egypt.   Though for several days the waves were too high to admit of disembarkation, small ships were able to reconnoitre the coast closely, and their reports determined Abercromby to land on a narrow promontory which, running north-east from Alexandria for eight or nine miles, separates the waters of the Mediterranean from those of Lake Aboukir, or Lake Madie as it is sometimes called.[2]

Sir Ralph's effective strength consisted of about 16,000 men,[3] including the five hundred cavalry for whom horses had been obtained, and the gunners with sixteen field-pieces.   The infantry were formed into six brigades and a reserve; the latter, a unit double the strength of any of the other brigades, was commanded by Major-General (afterwards Sir John) Moore.   The XVIIIth doubtless wished to serve under the orders of Moore, whose worth they had learned at Calvi, but, with the 8th, 13th, and 90th regiments, found themselves under Major-General Cradock, whose brigade (the second) was composed of battalions of very unequal strength; the 90th had 850 officers and men; the 13th were weaker by a hundred; the 8th had 538 of all ranks, while the roll of the XVIIIth only bore 523 names.[4]   Not all the men in Abercromby's little army were British born.   About 2700 were foreigners: Stuart's Minorca regiment was a collection of ne'er-do-weels from every country in Europe; De Roll's was composed of Swiss; Dillon's of French Royalists; Hompesch's dragoons were Germans, while the Corsican Rangers probably contained some of the men first raised and disciplined by Montresor of the XVIIIth.   To meet this expedition Menou, the French Commander-in-Chief, had under his orders about 21,500 combatants; his cavalry was superb; he possessed sixty-six field-guns; many of his infantry were veterans whom Napoleon had led from victory to victory in the plains of Lombardy. Eleven thousand troops were concentrated at Cairo, 6000 were allotted to the defence of Alexandria and of the coast from that city to Rosetta; 1800 held the country round Damietta; 1000 were absorbed by the garrisons of Suez, Balbeis, and Salalieh; the remainder were stationed in Upper Egypt. The news of Abercromby's appearance off the Delta reached Cairo about the

[1] The expedition of 1799.   Dunfermline's ' Life of Abercromby.'

[2] See Map No. 3.

[3] The historians of this campaign do not agree about the exact strength of Abercromby's army. The figures in the text are summarised from those given in the Life of Abercromby, written by his grandson, James, Lord Dunfermline.

[4] Two field officers, 5 captains, 16 subalterns, 5 staff, 32 sergeants, 14 drummers, 449 rank and file.

same time as a report that a Turkish force was advancing slowly through Syria upon Egypt. Menou, puzzled by the situation, frittered away his strength by sending detachments to unimportant points; he did not at once reinforce Alexandria, and thus when Abercromby disembarked he was met by only two thousand men with fifteen pieces of field artillery.

Until March 7, no landing was possible, but then the weather moderated, and at 2 A.M. on the 8th, a rocket from the Admiral's ship gave the signal to put into execution the scheme which had been repeatedly explained to the officers of both services. The boats were to form up in three lines at a place of assembly, marked by three small craft anchored out of gun-shot from the shore. The first line consisted of large flat-bottom row-boats, each containing fifty soldiers, and of launches carrying field-guns ready for instant use : these boats and launches were to be fifty feet apart, and to keep "interval" and "dressing" accurately. In second line were ships' boats, to help the first line in case of need. Behind them followed the third line—cutters towing launches, full of men of the same regiment as that directly in front of them. These supporting troops were to land in the fifty-feet interval between the boats of the first line. The Reserve, the brigade of Guards, and part of the first brigade were the units named in orders to lead the way, and by 3.30 A.M. they were in the boats; but owing to the extreme shallowness of the water many of the transports were anchored so far from the shore that it was not until 9 o'clock that the last of the troops had reached the rendezvous. Then on the signal of the naval captain in charge the sailors gave way, and in silence, only broken by the regular dip of hundreds of oars into the water, rowed steadily towards the yellow sandhills where the soldiers were to land. Until the first line was well within their range, the French gave no sign of life; then they poured a perfect hurricane of round-shot, grape, and musketry upon the leading boats, several of which were sunk. As soon as the first shot came whistling round their ears, the sailors rowed harder than ever; the soldiers, packed like herrings in a tub, could do nothing but cheer until the bluejackets ran into shallow water, when their turn came; springing overboard, they waded to the shore and fought hand to hand with the French, who lunged fiercely at them with their bayonets as they struggled up the slippery beach. After a short but sharp engagement the French fell back, but not until they had inflicted upon us a loss heavy in comparison to the number of men actually engaged. Among the sailors there were ninety-seven casualties; of the soldiers a hundred and two were killed, five hundred and fifteen wounded, and thirty-five missing, or a total in the two services of seven hundred and forty-nine. The Royal Irish and the remainder of the second brigade had been transferred to small Greek ships of light draft, which moved close inshore to support the advance-guard, but before Cradock could land his troops, the French were in retreat, and thus on this memorable day the XVIIIth did not come into action.[1]

Thanks to the success of this thoughtfully planned, carefully rehearsed, and brilliantly executed stroke, the remainder of the troops disembarked without difficulty, and began to move towards Alexandria. Their progress, however, was very slow, for Abercromby was crippled by want of land transport, and until, by a second victory, he could win the Egyptians to his side and obtain from them camels and oxen, he was forced to rely for his supplies on the service of small craft by which the Navy landed food and stores on the shores of Lake Aboukir, where his left flank rested. The army halted on the 12th in front of a line of sandhills strongly held by the enemy, against whose possible night attack were taken the precautions thus described in Moore's diary: "The 90th and 92nd were put under my command. I divided these two regiments each into three bodies, separated at such distances as to cover the front of the army, and I ordered each body to throw forward one-third of their numbers, with the officers belonging to it, as sentries in front. This formed a strong chain, which was relieved every hour by one of the thirds in reserve. The enemy was so close to us that it was evident that neither army could move without bringing on an action." From this position Abercromby determined to drive the French by a frontal attack combined with a turning movement on their right; and early on the 13th he moved from his bivouac in three huge columns, with the 90th regiment covering the front as advance-guard. The undulations of the ground hid the centre column from the French General, who, thinking that our right and left columns were too far apart to be able to support each other, determined to crush them in detail, and covering his advance by a vigorous and well-aimed artillery fire descended into the plain. Cradock's brigade deployed into line "with great quickness and precision," and pressed on to meet the foe, whose cavalry, after a fruitless attack upon the advance-guard, charged the main body with great determination, but were so hotly received

---

[1] The following officers appear to have landed in Egypt with the regiment :—
Lieutenant-Colonel—H. T. Montresor (in command).
Major—T. Probyn.
Captains—W. Morgue, C. J. Dunlop, H. Snooke.
Captain and Lieutenant—G. Jones.
Lieutenants—J. Jenkinson, P. Hay, J. Hoy, W. Conolly, J. Kennedy, R. Veale, G. Gorrequer, W. Gunn.
Ensigns—F. Hill, H. Bruley, H. W. Beavan, T. Baylis, —— Hutton, W. Brand, A. Deane, J. Smith.
Paymaster—R. Irwin.
Adjutant—T. Gregory.
Quartermaster—M. M'Dermott.
Surgeon—G. B. Waters.
Assistant-Surgeon—W. Maxton.
Major S. Mawby rejoined from sick leave during the campaign.

with well-aimed musketry that they were driven back in confusion. Of the part played by the XVIIIth in this episode the regimental record of service contains a spirited, though somewhat breathless description.

"A strong body of cavalry having meanwhile charged the two regiments supporting the left of the front line, but being repulsed, rode in towards the 2nd brigade under cover of some sand hills; and observing an interval between our regiment and that on its left, immediately advanced to charge through it, in which they must have succeeded had they not been checked by a prompt and well-directed fire from our Light company, for, unfortunately, the left battalion of the brigade having mistaken them, from their green uniforms for Hompesch's Hussars (attached to our army) not only suffered them to ride quietly along their front, but kept calling out to us not to fire upon them; this error having, however, been fortunately discovered when the cavalry were within a hundred paces of us, and in the act of wheeling up to charge, the regiment halted, and opening a steady and rapid platoon fire immediately after that of the Light company, brought down a great number of men and horses, threw them into complete disorder and compelled them to a precipitate retreat, though many of them had even arrived within a few paces of the interval on our left. Had not the Royal Irish so timely opened its fire, the brigade must have been broken through, and the enemy penetrated to the second line, which in firing on them must at the same time have fired upon us. This cavalry, by a strange coincidence, happened to be the 18th regiment of heavy dragoons, and afterwards (when a troop of this corps was taken in the desert) they said, pointing to us, 'had it not been for that regiment it was all over with your expedition.'"

The action raged along nearly the whole line till the French, staggered by the warmth of their reception and overborne by superior numbers, gave way, and retired to the works of Nicopolis, where a series of redoubts stretching across the peninsula barred the way to Alexandria. The enemy covered his retreat with sharpshooters, supported by artillery so mobile and so well-handled that the British were filled with admiration, contrasting its quick movements to those of our field-guns which, from want of horses, had to be dragged laboriously by hand. Abercromby hoped to carry the lines of Nicopolis with a rush, and followed the French across the plain between their first and second positions until he had to halt to make dispositions for the assault. For several hours the troops remained stationary under a murderous fire from the enemy's batteries, waiting to be let loose upon the French; but when a careful reconnaissance had convinced Abercromby that the second position was too strong to be carried until its defenders had been shaken by a heavy bombardment, he reluctantly ordered his little army to retire, and in perfect order it marched back to the ground from which the enemy had been driven in the morning, and settled down into bivouac. The

General was not unmindful of the good work done by Cradock's command; in a general order thanking the troops for "their soldier-like and intrepid conduct, he felt it incumbent on him particularly to express his most perfect satisfaction with the steady and gallant conduct of Major-General Cradock's brigade;" and in his despatch to the Secretary of State for War, when describing the events of the early part of the battle, he stated: "Major-General Cradock immediately formed his brigade to meet the attack made by the enemy; and the troops[1] changed their position with a quickness and precision which did them the greatest honour. The remainder of the army followed so good an example, and immediately were in a situation not only to face but to repel the enemy."

This action cost the lives of six officers and a hundred and fifty of the other ranks; sixty-seven officers and a thousand and two non-commissioned officers and men were wounded; the sailors and marines together lost eighty-four of all ranks; thus the casualties in both services amounted to thirteen hundred and nine killed and wounded. Though the regiments under Cradock's command suffered more than those in the other brigades, losing upwards of five hundred officers and men, the XVIIIth escaped comparatively lightly. Captain George Jones was killed, and three officers, whose names are not mentioned in the despatch, were wounded; among the other ranks a sergeant and forty-five rank and file were wounded.[2] The French did not lose as heavily as we did—not more than five hundred of their troops were put out of action; but they left in our hands four guns and a large quantity of ammunition.

The position that Abercromby now held was about a mile and a half long, stretching from the Mediterranean on the right to Lake Aboukir on the left. In front of the right and centre rose a chain of sandhills; on the left the ground was level. While the heavy artillery and ordnance stores were being slowly moved over the nine miles of sandy track between Aboukir Bay and the bivouac, the General entrenched himself, posting Cradock's brigade on the extreme left of the front line. On the 19th the big guns began to arrive, accompanied by a recently landed detachment of Turks, of such doubtful military value that they were ordered to halt three miles in rear of the British troops. Next day a friendly Arab chief sent word that Alexandria had been largely reinforced, thus confirming the reports from the men on outpost who, through the mists of early morning, had seen long strings of camels moving towards the town. The Arab added that the French proposed to attack us at dawn on the 21st. Though not fully convinced of the truth of this intelligence, Abercromby pressed on his field-works and ordered his troops to stand to arms before dawn—a wise precaution, for the Arab's information proved correct. Menou had accompanied the reinforcements, and after providing an

---

[1] The 8th, 13th, XVIIIth Royal Irish, and 90th regiments.   [2] See Appendix 2 (F).

adequate garrison for Alexandria, could dispose of 10,000 men with whom he proposed to surprise the English before daybreak. A feint was to be made against our left, our centre was to be vigorously engaged, while the full force of the attack was to fall upon the right. As soon as it was crumpled up a general movement along the line was to drive us into the waters of the lake, where we should have to surrender or to drown.

While it was still black night on the 21st, the French began the action by demonstrating against our left, and though the false attack was not pressed home, it was successful in so far that troops, urgently required on other parts of the field, were diverted to the help of Cradock's brigade. In the centre the enemy made no headway against the steady volleys of the regiments facing him; the danger was in his onslaught on our right, where for a long time there raged a series of fierce and confused fights. The piquets were driven in, and the supports surprised by columns suddenly looming out of the murky darkness; reinforcements on either side hurried up, guided by the flash of the muskets and the shouts of the combatants—prisoners and Colours were taken and recaptured, posts lost and regained. At one moment the French slipped unperceived between two corps, which in the very nick of time discovered and routed them with the bayonet: a little later a regiment, while hotly engaged in front, was surrounded by a body of the enemy whose presence was revealed by the sound of a French word of command. The rear rank turned about, and fighting back to back, drove off their foes. Episodes such as these marked the progress of the action until the morning light showed Menou that all his efforts had been unavailing, and that the British line, shattered but unconquered, still held its ground. Mad with rage at his want of success the French General, against the advice of his subordinates, hurled his cavalry, 1200 strong, into the fray. They crashed through a regiment whose formation they broke, though not its spirit, and swept like a torrent over the battlefield until they reached the camp, where the horses stumbled over the tentropes and fell into the burrows, scratched in the sand as sleeping places by a corps whose tents had not arrived. The confusion thus caused was increased by the cross-fire of the infantry who had been left in charge of the baggage, and the French cavalry wheeled about and retired at full speed, leaving the ground behind them covered with their dead. After several more desperate efforts, in which assailants and assailed displayed equal courage, Menou realised that he was defeated, and fell back slowly and in good order. His solid columns offered a splendid target to our artillerymen; but the guns were silent, to the intense surprise of the French who expected to be pursued by a hail of projectiles, and to the mortification of the British infantry, who looked to the gunners to avenge their losses. But the gunners could not fire; they were as short of ammunition as the foot soldiers themselves, many of whom had been forced to rely exclusively on their bayonets in the later phases of

H

the battle. It was not that ammunition was lacking in the camp, but owing to a staff blunder there was no means of getting it up to the fighting line. Had our gunners been able to do their duty the French loss would have been enormous, but they escaped with 2000 casualties.[1] On our side the gallant Abercromby was mortally wounded; and of the 11,500 men engaged, 10 officers and 233 other ranks were killed; 60 officers and 1133 other ranks wounded; 3 officers and 29 men missing. The Royal Irish, who were on the left flank of Cradock's brigade, and therefore far away from the scene of the serious fighting, were almost untouched, only two private soldiers being wounded.

Some days were spent in the work of reorganisation. Stores and ammunition had to be brought up from Aboukir, and arrangements made with the natives for the hire of transport of various kinds. Before the army was ready to move Sir Ralph Abercromby died, deeply regretted by all who had been privileged to serve under him. He was succeeded by a future Colonel of the XVIIIth, Major-General the Hon. John Hely-Hutchinson,[2] who decided to leave Major-General Coote to invest Alexandria with 6000 men, while he himself led the main column to Cairo. As a first step he sent a mixed force of British and Turks across the desert to seize Rosetta, a town important from its position at the mouth of the western branch of the Nile, and a few days later reinforced it with the XVIIIth and the 90th regiments. Rosetta was occupied without trouble; our gunboats entered the Nile; a large amount of river craft was collected, and on May 4, 9500 British and Turkish troops began to move upon Cairo.[3] The march proved a very trying one, for the heat was great, the climate exhausting, and as there were no roads and practically no land transport, the army had to depend for its supplies on the flotilla of boats which accompanied its progress towards the capital of Egypt. Sending a strong detachment to the right bank of the river to connect him with the Turkish contingent from Syria, Hely-Hutchinson worked up the left bank with the main body, gradually capturing or driving away the garrisons of the fortified posts along the Nile. In these small affairs the Royal Irish had no opportunity of distinguishing themselves.

After joining forces with the Turks, the General pushed on towards Cairo, and halting on the 16th of June within a few miles of the city, found the French much more disposed to treat for surrender than to fight. The perimeter of the crumbling fortifications was far too large to be adequately defended by the 9000 effective men to whom the garrison was reduced; outside the walls was encamped an Anglo-Turkish army of 30,000 men, and Baird's

---

[1] If the statements of two of the officers who left accounts of the campaign are correct, this figure must be too low; Walsh in his Journal says that 1160 dead Frenchmen were counted on the ground on the afternoon of the 21st, while another writer states that 1040 of the enemy were buried after the battle.   [2] See Appendix 9.

[3] British—cavalry, 510; infantry, 4800 (among whom were the Royal Irish). Turks—cavalry, 600; infantry, 3600; with the combined force were twenty field-guns.

contingent from India and the Cape might any day bring an important accession to its strength; the civil population was disaffected; the *moral* of the soldiers was shaken by the events of the campaign; all ranks were anxious to return to France, and it was well known that the English were prepared to give them very favourable terms. In such circumstances negotiations proved swift and easy, and on June 27 a convention was signed, by which Hely-Hutchinson undertook to escort the French garrison with its baggage, field-guns and ammunition to Rosetta, and there embark it for the French ports on the Mediterranean. The march from Cairo to the sea, organised and commanded by Moore, was a very delicate operation, brilliantly carried out. It began on July 15: the Turks led the column; then, after a long interval, followed the French infantry and guns, their cavalry abreast of them, but on the left flank, farthest from the river; some distance behind came the British column, with a detachment of dragoons and Turkish cavalry bringing up the rear. Three hundred river craft, filled with sick and baggage, slowly dropped down the Nile under the escort of our gunboats, and kept up constant communication between the French and English columns. The embarkation was completed on the 7th of August, when 13,672 soldiers and 82 civilians sailed for France, in transports convoyed by British men-of-war. Everything passed off smoothly, but of all the British officers at Rosetta none can have been more heartily thankful when the last of our enemies was safely on board ship than Colonel Montresor, who, as governor, was responsible for the safety of the persons and the property of the inhabitants while the French troops were marching through the town.

Hely-Hutchinson now turned his attention to Alexandria, which he had left invested by General Coote when the main body advanced upon Cairo. Thanks to the arrival of large reinforcements from England, he was now able to besiege it in due form, and pushed on his works so fast that on the 31st of August the garrison, 10,528 strong, surrendered on terms identical with those granted at Cairo. The Royal Irish were present at the operations, and with other picked troops their grenadier company, with drums beating and Colours flying, marched into Alexandria to take formal possession of the town. Their triumphal entry marked the end of the Egyptian campaign, in which 500 officers and men were killed and 3058 were wounded: how many died from sickness is not known, but the mortality must have been considerable. In the regiment Captain-Lieutenant G. Jones was killed, and Captain W. Morgue, Ensign H. Bruley, Ensign W. Brand, Quartermaster M. M'Dermott, and fifty-six of the other ranks died from wounds, accident, or disease.[1] During the summer the Royal Irish suffered much from sickness, and in the month of July more than two hundred men were in hospital, chiefly from ophthalmia, which was then raging among the troops.

The thanks of Parliament were voted to both services; the XVIIIth Royal

---

[1] See Appendix 2 (F).

Irish were authorised to carry on the Colours the emblem of a Sphinx and the word "Egypt," and gold medals were presented by the Sultan to all the officers of the regiment. It was not until the year 1847 that a British medal was issued for this campaign, when only three officers—Hill, Beavan, and Deane—were still alive to claim the decoration.

As soon as the last of the French were shipped off to France, Hely-Hutchinson's army was broken up. Some of the troops remained to share with Baird's contingent the duty of holding Egypt for a few months; the remainder returned to various parts of the Mediterranean to await the results of the negotiations for peace then going on between the Governments of England and France. The Royal Irish were sent first to Malta, and then on to Elba, where Montresor was appointed military governor of Porto Ferraio for the second time: and when peace was declared the regiment was ordered home, and landed at Cork at the end of August, 1802.

Though there were many signs that France looked upon the Peace of Amiens more as a truce than as the end of her struggle with Britain, our Government soon began to cut down all military expenditure with unreasoning haste. Wholesale discharges from the army left only 40,000 regular troops in the United Kingdom; the militia, after an embodiment of nine years, were sent to their homes; the "fencible" regiments of horse and foot, raised for purposes of local defence, were disbanded. Thus the renewal of the war in 1803 found us almost disarmed; and when Napoleon collected an army for the invasion of England the Government was hard pressed to raise a garrison sufficient for the needs of the United Kingdom. By paying huge bounties to recruits the numbers of the regular army were increased to 12,000 cavalry and 75,000 infantry; bounties nearly as large attracted 80,000 men to the militia; while to escape a mitigated form of compulsory service, introduced to catch those who would not serve of their own free will, 343,000 men joined corps of Yeomanry or regiments of Volunteers. How far this mass of armed men would have been able to face veterans who had won innumerable victories in western and central Europe is a matter of speculation. Happily for England at the beginning of the nineteenth century, though perhaps unhappily for the British Empire of the present day, the threatened invasion did not take place, and our race had no opportunity to ascertain by practical experience whether Britons, very imperfectly trained to war, are as good fighting men as foreigners who have thoroughly mastered the soldier's trade before they meet their enemy on the battlefield.

Among the steps taken to increase the regular army was the formation of additional battalions of infantry, one or two of which were allotted to existing regiments. The second battalion of the XVIIIth was raised in Ireland in 1803, and, like the first, served in Scotland until the summer of 1804, when both were sent to Barham Downs, one of the many camps in the south of England where large numbers of troops stood ready to march towards the

MAP Nº 3.

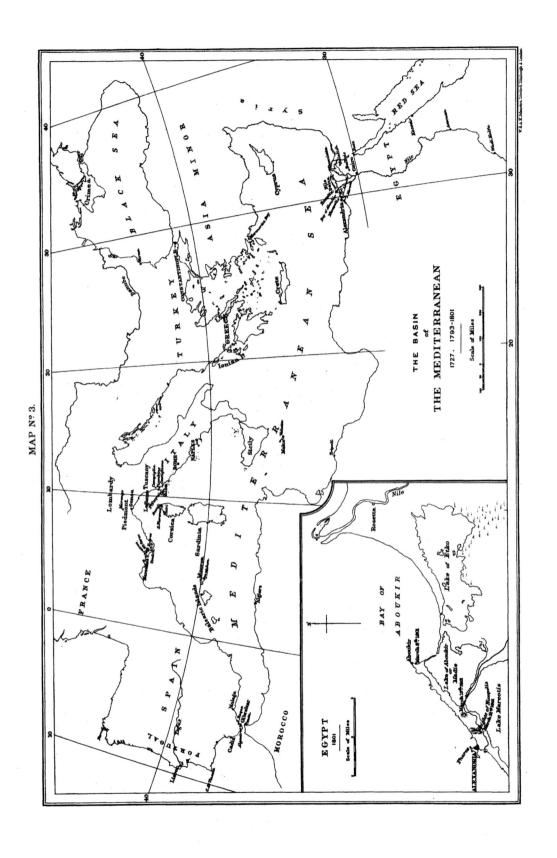

THE BASIN
of
THE MEDITERRANEAN
1727. 1793–1801
Scale of Miles

coast. After a few months the first battalion was ordered to the West Indies, and sailing in January, 1805, with other corps, reached Jamaica at the end of April, 935 strong.[1] The second battalion remained at Barham Downs until the destruction of the Franco-Spanish fleet at Trafalgar put an end to Napoleon's hope of obtaining the temporary command of the Channel necessary to pass his troops across the Straits of Dover. As soon as all danger of invasion was over the encampment was broken up, and the second battalion was sent to garrison Jersey.

When the first battalion of the Royal Irish landed at Kingston, the island was in a fever of anxiety, for the attitude of the black population, who had been thoroughly unsettled by the French Revolution, was disquieting not only in Jamaica but throughout the British West Indies; the coasts were infested by privateers who captured many trading ships; and a great fleet of the enemy's men-of-war was reported to be cruising among the neighbouring islands. These French ships, however, were part of the squadrons sent by Napoleon to decoy Nelson and his brother admirals from their blockade of the seaports on the Mediterranean and the Bay of Biscay: their business was to evade the British fleet, to return to Europe, and joining forces with the remainder of the Franco-Spanish fleet, to sweep all British men-of-war from the Channel before our admirals had discovered that they had quitted the West Indies. Thus Jamaica was not attacked; in a few months the excitement died down, and the Royal Irish fell into the routine of the station where they were destined to spend twelve long and dreary years. Once there seemed a prospect of active service: in 1809 they were ordered to form part of an expedition to the island of San Domingo,[2] where the Spaniards, who had again become our allies, were waging war against the French garrison. Major-General Sir Hugh Carmichael sailed from Jamaica on the 7th of June, and landed three weeks later at Polingue, a port thirty miles from the city of San Domingo, where the Spaniards were besieging the common enemy. As soon as his troops were safe on shore the General hurried up to the front, and after a reconnaissance decided that, as the French had already held out for eight months, the best way to deal with them would be by a sudden and

---

[1] The following officers arrived with the regiment :—
  Majors—R. Campbell (in command) and C. Dunlop.
  Captains—W. Loscombe, H. Snook, G. Reeves, J. Graham, E. Walker, J. E. Inston, D. O'Farrall, R. Smyth, T. Murray, C. O'Gorman.*
  Lieutenants—R. Huson, F. Hill, J. Janns, J. Stotesbury, G. Andrews, A. Baker, R. Wild, P. Scott, R. N. King, R. Hutton, W. Coulson, A. Deane, T. Barflis.
  Ensigns—J. Whitley, J. Strang.
  Adjutant—T. Gregory.
  Quartermaster—J. Atkins.
  Surgeon—G. B. Waters.
  Assistant-Surgeons—F. Micklen and W. Carver.
    * This officer began life as page to the ill-fated Queen Marie Antoinette.

[2] Sometimes called Haiti;

vigorous attack.   At nightfall on the 1st of July his men struggled up from the coast, tired out by heavy marches in pouring rain, over bad roads, through unbridged rivers, and without horses for the guns, which had to be dragged by hand.   Next day the French opened negotiations for surrender, but asked for such impossible terms that Carmichael made his plans to storm the works, and allotted to the Royal Irish an important part in the operations; but before the assault could be delivered the garrison of the town capitulated.   As the tricolor still flew over an outlying fort, Major E. Walker, XVIIIth regiment, was sent to reduce it with the Light companies of his own and two other battalions: but on the approach of the little column, the officer in command laid down his arms, and with the lowering of his flag passed away the last chance of the Royal Irish of distinguishing themselves in the second phase of the great war with France.   The terms of the capitulation were much the same as those granted in Corsica and Egypt: the French were to be sent back to their own country, and after the Royal Irish had seen their enemies safely embarked for France, they returned to Jamaica.   At the taking of San Domingo none of the British were injured, while few if any died of sickness in the island.   In this respect they were infinitely more fortunate than the troops who served in the campaign in San Domingo between 1793 and 1795, when in a few weeks whole regiments were virtually annihilated by yellow fever, which in those three years claimed 40,000 victims from the army and the fleet in West Indian waters.

As the news of Wellington's successive victories in the Peninsula slowly made its way to Jamaica the hearts of the Royal Irish must have sunk very low, when they realised that they were stationed in a part of the world where there was no prospect of adding to the laurels of the regiment.   Yet their lot was common to the greater part of the British army, scattered over the whole face of the globe, in places where the prospect of active service seemed most improbable.   In 1809, England had about 218,000 regular soldiers, of whom only 22,000 were fighting in the Peninsula.   A hundred and eight thousand were locked up in the United Kingdom, to give solidity to the 450,000 Militia and Volunteers then under arms; the Mediterranean fortresses and Sicily absorbed 22,000 ; the West Indies nearly as many ; 8000 guarded the Canadian frontier; the communication with the East was kept open by 900 at Madeira, and nearly 6000 at the Cape ; 4000 held the Island of Ceylon; in India were 24,000 white troops, of whom only 4000 were in the pay of the East India Company, while 1300 were employed in keeping order in the penal settlement of New South Wales.   The corps of artillery and engineers and troops at sea accounted for the remainder of the army.

The second battalion was no more fortunate than the first, for in 1807 it was ordered to a recently acquired British possession in the West Indies, the island of Curaçoa.   In December, 1806, a gallant sailor, Captain Sir Charles Brisbane, was ordered to reconnoitre the island, then belonging to

Holland; converting his reconnaissance into an attack, he led his four frigates into the harbour, and boarded two Dutch men-of-war lying at anchor; then sending landing parties on shore he captured the forts, and made himself master of Curaçoa. The battalion arrived in June, 726 strong,[1] and remained stationary until 1810, when, worn down to a mere skeleton by sickness, and by large drafts to the sister battalion in Jamaica, it was ordered home to recruit. Beyond the fact that in 1808 the officers presented a handsome sword of honour to Brisbane, whom they found installed at Curaçoa as Governor, nothing is known of the doings of the second battalion during its short existence, which ended in 1814, when, like nearly all the other second battalions of the army, it was disbanded. The story of its resuscitation will be found in Chapter IX.

Though neither battalion was on active service in the West Indies, for the expedition to San Domingo cannot be counted as a campaign, the regiment was exposed during this tour of duty in the colonies to dangers greater and far more trying than those of pitched battles. Tropical diseases played havoc among the Royal Irish: between the arrival of the first battalion in the middle of 1805, and its return to England in the spring of 1817, the loss of both battalions from sickness was fifty-two officers and seventeen hundred and seventy - seven non - commissioned officers and men.[2] The heaviest mortality appears to have occurred during the two months ending January 25, 1806, when a hundred and forty names were added to the list of dead. Nor was disease the only peril to which the Royal Irish were exposed. While they were stationed in Jamaica the island was scourged by earthquakes and tidal waves, by fires that destroyed flourishing towns, by floods that laid waste great tracts of cultivated land. There were mutinies among the regiments raised from the slaves; conspiracies among the negroes to murder the white men, and widespread disaffection and unrest throughout all the coloured population. After such grim experiences of West Indian life it was with feelings of great joy that in January, 1817, the regiment bade farewell to the land where so many hundreds of their comrades had perished.

[1] The officers who went out with the second battalion to Curaçoa were :—
  Lieutenant-Colonel—J. W. Graves (in command).
  Captains—J. Hoy, P. Bainbrigge, G. H. Gordon, E. H. Smith, R. Percival, J. O'Connell.
  Lieutenants—J. Aitken, J. S. Owen, J. Cowper, C. Maxwell, R. Delachnois, W. MacDonald, R. Hopley, C. Carleton, F. Munro, J. Aicken.
  Ensigns—L. Hiatt, H. Kennedy, J. E. P. Langharne, E. Stackpoole, T. W. Lowes.
  Adjutant—J. Forrest.
  Quartermaster—D. Cullen.
  Paymaster—H. Salvin.
  Surgeon—B. Cory.
  Assistant-Surgeons—W. Seaman and W. Crofton.

[2] These figures, obtained from returns filed in the Record Office, are considerably lower than those given in Cannon's History of the regiment. The names of the officers who died in the West Indies will be found in Appendix 3.

CHAPTER V.

1817–1848.

THE FIRST WAR WITH CHINA.

THE XVIIIth Royal Irish regiment landed at Portsmouth in March, 1817. Since 1783, the Royal Irish had only served three years in the United Kingdom, and they looked forward to a long tour of duty at home, but the fates were against them. Almost as soon as Napoleon surrendered himself to the captain of the *Bellerophon* the economists in the House of Commons began to demand retrenchment in the army, and with such success that in 1821 only 101,000 men, exclusive of the troops in the East India Company's service, were left to protect the whole of the British possessions throughout the world. The garrison of the United Kingdom absorbed about half the army, the remainder being stationed in India and the colonies, where, it is said, Wellington hid them to be out of sight of the anti-military politicians. Among the regiments ordered abroad was the XVIIIth, which in February, 1821, left Cork for the Mediterranean; it spent three years at Malta and eight in the Ionian Isles,[1] and in March, 1832, returned to England.

In the autumn of 1832, the Royal Irish were quartered in detachments in various towns in Lancashire and Yorkshire; during the general election at the end of the year several companies were called upon to help the civil power in quelling serious riots at Sheffield, Bolton, and Preston, where officers and men won high praise for the combination of forbearance and determination which they showed in dealing with excited mobs. Towards the end of 1833 the regiment was concentrated at Manchester, whence on May 8, 1834, to quote the words in which the Digest of Service records the first train journey of the XVIIIth, it "proceeded by railway conveyance" to Liverpool to embark for Dublin. In September the regiment moved to Cork; a few months later it was at Birr, and early in 1836, while at Athlone, it was warned for foreign service in Ceylon. Throughout their tour of duty in the United Kingdom the Royal Irish received warm commendation from

[1] These islands, acquired by Britain during the Napoleonic war, were ceded by her to Greece in 1864.

all the generals under whom they had served, and these favourable opinions were fully endorsed in a letter from the Adjutant-General, who on December 20, 1834, wrote that "the report of the XVIIIth Royal Irish regiment is considered most satisfactory. The excellent state of its discipline is highly creditable to Colonel Burrell, and Lord Hill cannot be but more disposed to attachment (*sic*) to that officer's exertions when he finds that discipline has been so effectually maintained without having had recourse to corporal punishment for a period exceeding two years."

Two companies under Major Pratt sailed from Cork in the transport *Numa* on November 15, 1836, and arrived at Colombo towards the end of April, 1837. The remainder of the corps, under Colonel Burrell, embarked in the transport *Barossa*, touched at Teneriffe and Rio de Janeiro, and reached its destination at the end of May. After serving for some time at Colombo, where new colours were presented by Lieutenant-General Sir John Wilson, K.C.B., the headquarters and a wing of the regiment were stationed at Trincomalee, where in 1840 welcome news reached them. Trouble had arisen with China, and the regiment was to form part of an expedition against the Celestial Empire. The causes of our quarrel with the Emperor of China, very shortly stated, were that the Chinese had not kept to the treaties of commerce which they had entered into with England; they had attacked and robbed British merchants, fired upon English ships, and grossly insulted the representative of the Queen. The Mandarins, or high officials of Canton, were the chief offenders; to punish them a naval blockade of that port was established; ships of war were ordered up from the Indian station, and a small body of troops was collected to co-operate with the Navy in bringing the Chinese to their senses. The six companies of the Royal Irish in Ceylon sailed eastwards in May and June, 1840, and the three depôt companies, recently landed at Bombay from England, joined headquarters soon after the regiment arrived in China, raising it to a total strength of 667 of all ranks.[1] The other British regiments were the 26th and the

---

[1] Nine companies, consisting of 2 field officers, 7 captains, 16 subalterns, 3 staff, 35 sergeants, 11 drummers, 593 privates—667 all told. The following officers served with the XVIIIth during the whole or part of the China war :—

Field Officers—Colonel G. Burrell; Lieutenant-Colonels H. W. Adams and J. Cowper; Majors R. Hammill, N. R. Tomlinson, W. F. Dillon, J. Grattan, J. J. Sargent, F. Wigston.

Captains—C. J. R. Collinson, W. A. T. Payne, C. A. Edwards, J. P. Mitford, J. C. Kennedy.

Lieutenants—Sir W. Macgregor, Bart., Sir H. Darell, Bart., A. Wilson (adjutant), Hon. C. H. Stratford, G. W. Davis, S. Haly, J. W. Graves, W. A. Gwynne, J. J. Wood, G. Hilliard, A. Murray, F. Swinburne, T. Martin, H. F. Vavasour, D. Edwards, S. Bernard, J. Cockrane, A. W. S. F. Armstrong, J. H. Hewitt, W. P. Cockburn, H. D. Burrell, C. Woodwright, J. P. Mayo, C. Rogers, W. Venour, E. Jodrell, G. F. S. Call, C. Dunbar.

Ensigns—P. Simmons, E. W. Sargent, J. Elliot, M. J. Hayman, L. M. T. Humphreys.

Paymaster—G. J. Call.

49th; the Native army of India contributed detachments of Madras Artillery and Sappers and Miners, a corps known as the Bengal Volunteers, and the 37th regiment of Madras Native Infantry, while the Navy was represented by three line-of-battle ships, two frigates, fourteen smaller men-of-war, four armed steamers, and twenty-seven transports. With this small force England was about to go to war with a country of three hundred and sixty millions of inhabitants, whose seaport towns were defended by forts bristling with ordnance varying in calibre from 68-pr. to 18-pr. guns, and whose army immeasurably exceeded in number the British fighting men. Fortunately for us the Chinese artillerymen, though not wanting in courage, were ill-trained; their forts, though massive, were badly planned; and the infantry, though they often fought well and showed much courage as individuals, were poorly disciplined, badly armed, and as a rule very badly commanded. Though the government of Pekin had spent much money in making cannon on European models, they had neglected to reproduce the muskets with which the troops of the white races were equipped. Thus the Chinese foot soldiers did not possess the equivalent of our flint-lock smooth-bore muskets; their firearms were matchlocks and gingals or portable wall pieces, worked on tripods by a crew of three men, and throwing two-ounce balls. Their other weapons varied; the Tartars, the picked troops of the Empire, used the bow; other corps had spears and swords, while others again carried battle-axes and very unpleasant cutting instruments like bill-hooks, fastened to the end of long poles.

The policy and general conduct of our expedition was entrusted to two Plenipotentiaries. One of these officials soon broke down in health and disappeared from the scene; the other, who was credited with some knowledge of the Chinese character, proved to be amiable and well-intentioned, but vacillating, credulous, and incompetent to meet the wiles of Eastern diplomacy. His gullibility and want of backbone cruelly hampered the movements of the sailors and soldiers until, many months after the beginning of the war, he was replaced by Sir Henry Pottinger, an Indian officer of large experience in dealing with Oriental races.

After assembling at Singapore, the point fixed for the general rendezvous, the fleet sailed for China, and, contrary to the universal expectation, did not stop at the mouth of the Canton river, but followed the coast upwards to the island of Chusan.[1] From its position near the mouth of the Yang-Tse-Kiang

---

Quartermaster—J. Carroll.
Surgeon—D. McKinlay, M.D.   Assistant-Surgeons—C. Cowen, J. Baker, J. Stewart.
Only three of these officers had been on active service. Burrell had served at the capture of Guadaloupe in 1810 and in the war on the Canadian frontier in 1814; Grattan had taken part in the suppression of the rebellion in Canada in 1832; Dillon had been on the staff at the capture of San Domingo in 1809.

[1] See Map No. 4.

river this island was of great strategic importance, and was required as a base of operations. Tinghae, its principal town, was weakly held, but when the Mandarins were summoned to surrender they replied that, though they had no hope of making a successful resistance, they were in honour bound to defend their post. After a short bombardment by the men-of-war on July 5, 1840, the troops were landed, the XVIIIth leading the attack, and the place fell into our hands. Our casualties were very few; the Chinese, on the contrary, lost very heavily, but the climate quickly avenged them. For several months the troops were kept inactive in Chusan, which proved to be a hot-bed of disease. In the hope of conciliating the inhabitants the soldiers at first were ordered to live under canvas, though there were hundreds of houses in which they could have been quartered. The camping grounds were selected without reference to the doctors, who protested in vain when they saw the "tents pitched on low paddy-fields, surrounded by stagnant water, putrid and stinking from quantities of dead animal and vegetable matter. Under a sun hotter than was ever experienced in India," wrote a Madras army surgeon, "the men on duty were buckled up to the throat in their full-dress coatees, and in consequence of there being so few camp followers, fatigue-parties of Europeans were daily detailed to carry provisions and stores from the ships to the tents, and to perform all menial employments, which experience has long taught us they cannot stand in a tropical climate."[1] The troops were fed on rations not only unsuited to the climate but of bad quality; much of the biscuit was bad, and the meat salted in India proved uneatable. Small wonder that in such circumstances intermittent fever, diarrhœa, and dysentery raged among all ranks; and though after a time the troops were moved into the houses of the natives, disease had taken such hold upon all ranks that in November there were not more than five hundred effectives at Chusan. The Royal Irish fared better than the other regiments, as the ships from which they drew most of their supplies were laden with stores prepared not in India, but in England; but still they suffered severely—two officers, Major R. Hammill and Lieutenant H. F. Vavasour, and about fifty of the other ranks died between July 5th and the end of the year.[2] Yet these losses were insignificant compared to those of the 26th, which from nine hundred was reduced to a strength, all told, of two hundred and ninety-one.

In January, 1841, there were combined naval and military operations against the forts at the mouth of the Canton river, in which the Royal Irish took no part as they had been left to garrison Chusan; a few of the regiment, however, were present, probably invalids serving on board ship for change of air. After several batteries had been dismantled and many heavy guns

[1] 'The War in China,' by D. McPherson, M.D., pp. 21, 22.
[2] See Appendix 2 (G).

spiked or otherwise disabled, the Mandarins made a treaty with the Plenipotentiary, by which they agreed to cede to us the island of Hong Kong, to pay a considerable indemnity, and to allow trade to be reopened at Canton, while on our side we undertook to restore Chusan to the Chinese. No time was lost in occupying Hong Kong, of which formal possession was taken on February 26, 1841, two days after the Royal Irish arrived there. Colonel Burrell, XVIIIth, had been the senior military officer throughout the occupation of Chusan, and very thankful must he have been when, after seeing the last of the garrison safely on board ship, he turned his back on the island which proved fatal to such numbers of his men.[1] Very soon after the expedition had been concentrated at Hong Kong it became evident that the treaty was not worth the paper it was written upon. Far from being anxious for peace, the Chinese had only sought to gain time to prepare for war. An army of labourers was strengthening the defences of Canton; an army of soldiers was being collected in the interior of China to man them; large rewards were offered for the capture of British ships and British fighting men; for a battleship a hundred thousand dollars were promised; the Admiral and the Plenipotentiary were worth fifty thousand dollars each; the other officers were rated on a descending scale, while the price of a Madras Sepoy was only fifty dollars. On the 24th of February the fleet bombarded the celebrated Bogue forts in the Canton river; five hundred guns were taken, and everyone hoped that the ships would now be allowed to push up the river and capture Canton, when all movements were temporarily arrested by the announcement that the Plenipotentiary had entered into a truce. As, however, the Chinese did not fulfil its terms, the men-of-war engaged, silenced and destroyed such of the batteries as they had not yet attacked; made their way up the reaches of the river, and anchored close to Canton. The city lay almost defenceless under their guns, when the Plenipotentiary agreed to a suspension of hostilities on condition that the port should be reopened to British trade. This arrangement suited the Chinese admirably: the civil population would be enriched by the money paid by the merchants for the tea crop, then ready for delivery; while the military Mandarins gained time to cast new ordnance, to rebuild their ruined forts, and to reinforce the garrison before again defying the "Barbarians."[2] The troops were ordered back to the harbour of Hong Kong, where Major-General Sir Hugh Gough, who had recently arrived from Madras to take command of the land forces, reorganised his little army, and attempted, though with small success, to infuse his own spirit of determination into the weak-kneed Plenipotentiary, whom Gough in a private letter described as "whimsical as a shuttle-cock."

[1] Half the troops originally landed at Chusan are said to have died there.

[2] The Chinese always described their enemies from the western hemisphere as Barbarians or Foreign Devils.

It was not long before the position of affairs at Canton once more became most serious. The gun factories had been working night and day; the forts had been repaired and re-armed; large numbers of soldiers had arrived; and in May the extermination was decreed of the European merchants, who on the faith of the truce had now returned to their counting-houses. This roused the Plenipotentiary into temporary activity; he arranged with Gough and the senior naval officer for a combined assault on Canton, and warned all Europeans to leave the place forthwith. By the evening of the 23rd of May the navy, after hard work in bombarding the river forts by day and warding off the approach of fire-rafts by night, had prepared the way for the execution of Sir Hugh Gough's plan for the capture of Canton. This city of a million inhabitants was surrounded by walls of great thickness, and from twenty-five to twenty-eight feet in height; its ramparts, bristling with guns, were manned by forty-five thousand regular soldiers and an equal number of militia. To the west, south, and east of the town were large and prosperous suburbs, but on the north this expansion had been checked by a range of heights which, running parallel with the northern wall, completely dominated Canton and its defences. The Chinese had realised that if these heights passed into the hands of the British the town would become untenable: not only had they defended them with four strong forts, armed with forty-two heavy guns, but they had formed a large entrenched camp outside the north-eastern corner of the city, in order further to secure the safety of the heights which they rightly anticipated would be the point of our attack. Such was the position against which Gough, with less than 2800 soldiers, sailors, and marines, was about to try his strength. He divided his little force into two columns of very unequal size.[1] The right, or smaller detachment, was to

---

[1] COMPOSITION OF THE COLUMNS.

		Officers.	Other ranks.	Total.
Right Column.				
Major Pratt, 26th Cameronians	26th Cameronians . . .	15	294	309
	Madras Artillery . . .	1	20	21
	Madras Sappers and Miners .	1	30	31
with one 6-pr., one 5-in. mortar.				
Left Column.				
4th (Left) Brigade, Lieut.-Colonel Morris, 49th Regiment	49th Regiment	28	273	301
	37th Madras Native Infantry .	15	215	230
	1 company Bengal Volunteers .	4	112	116
3rd (Artillery) Brigade, Capt. Knowles, R.A.	Royal Artillery	2	33	35
	Madras Artillery . . .	10	231	241
	Madras Sappers and Miners .	4	137	141
with four 12-pr. howitzers, four 9-pr. and two 6-pr. field-guns, three 5-in. mortars, and 152 32-pr. rockets.				
2nd (Naval) Brigade, Capt. Bourchier, R.N.		27	403	430
1st (Right) Brigade, Major-General Burrell	XVIIIth Royal Irish . .	25	495	520
	Royal Marines . . .	9	372	381
		141	2615	2756

force its way through the western suburb as far as the European settlement, or, as it was locally termed, "the factories"; occupy it, and place it in a state of defence. General Gough took personal command of the left or larger column, which consisted of four so-called brigades, the largest of which had in the ranks less than 900 officers and men. When the left column had been transhipped into all kinds of craft, from smart men-of-war's gigs to lumbering native tea junks, it was towed in a motley procession of about eighty boats for five miles up a creek of the river to Tingpoo, a village about three miles and a half from the western base of the northern heights. Here the fourth brigade landed without opposition, just as the guns of the fleet were thundering out a royal salute in honour of the birthday of Queen Victoria. With the 49th regiment Sir Hugh Gough made a rapid reconnaissance inland, and then, leaving outposts behind him, returned to superintend the disembarkation of the main body.

Daylight on the 25th saw the whole column in motion, slowly threading its way, often in single file, over the densely cultivated rice-fields which lay between Tingpoo and their objective. The XVIIIth was ordered to leave an officer and thirty men at the landing-place to keep open the communications and to protect stores; the duty fell to Lieutenant W. P. Cockburn, who distinguished himself by the skill he displayed a few hours later in beating off an attack by a considerable body of the enemy. Until the infantry were within range of the western pair of forts the Chinese remained silent; then a heavy fire from their guns forced Gough to halt until his artillery could be brought into action. By eight A.M. the gunners had succeeded in dragging two $5\frac{1}{2}$-in. mortars, two 12-pr. howitzers, two 12-pr. field-pieces, and a rocket battery to within 600 yards of the two western forts. These they bombarded vigorously, while the General reconnoitred and issued his orders for the assault: the Naval brigade was to storm the western forts, while the 1st and 4th brigades were to drive the Chinese from the hills close to the eastern forts. Under cover of our guns the troops advanced, exposed to a heavy but fortunately ill-directed fire: with great dash the sailors wrested the western forts from the enemy, who fought with stubbornness though without skill; the infantry swept over the heights with such vigour that the Chinese deserted the eastern forts before the troops had time to close upon them; and the Marines, who had been detached from Burrell to cope with a demonstration against our right flank and rear, disposed of their antagonists with little trouble. In the charge of the XVIIIth upon the forts the grenadier company led in extended order, accompanied by the General, who in his despatch reported that it had seldom fallen to his lot to "witness a more soldier-like and steady advance, or a more animated attack. Every individual steadily and gallantly did his duty. The XVIIIth and 49th were emulous which should first reach the appointed goals; but under the impulse of this feeling they did not lose sight of that discipline which could alone ensure success."

Though the ridge had been won with such ease, the day's work was by no means over. As soon as the Chinese realised that the forts were lost, they opened from the city walls so heavy a fire of guns, gingals, and matchlocks that it became necessary to keep the British troops well under cover, and part of the garrison of the entrenched camp advanced into a village, threatening our left flank. The 49th dislodged them, but later in the day there was such animation in the camp that Gough ordered Burrell to storm it with the Royal Irish, under Lieutenant-Colonel H. Adams, and a company of Marines. Between the foot of the heights held by the British and the enemy's entrenchments stretched a great expanse of rice-fields deep in water; a narrow causeway bridged this inundation, and along it, under a galling fire, the XVIIIth advanced at the double, scattered the enemy in every direction, set fire to the tents, and blew up the magazines. This success was not a bloodless one—three officers were wounded, and there were some casualties in the other ranks. The assault was led by Captain Grattan, whose "spirited conduct" on this occasion led Gough to select him to carry despatches to the Governor-General of India.[1] With the capture of the village the operations ended, for though Gough was burning to assault the northern wall of the town, his heavy guns were not yet in position, and his infantry, out of training from their long detention on board ship, were completely exhausted by the abnormal heat of the day. To this exhaustion the unsuitable dress of the soldiers doubtless contributed not a little. Notwithstanding the protests of the doctors the men still wore tightly buttoned red coatees or shell jackets, stocks, and blue Nankin trousers; and their headgear was a huge shako or a small forage cap, both useless in an almost tropical climate.

Gough's little force bivouacked on the heights they had won, elated at their own success and at that of the right column, which had made good its position in "the factories." Early on the 26th, before our artillery was ready to open fire, the Chinese sent a messenger to say that they desired peace; Gough replied that before entering into any negotiations he must see the Chinese General, and in waiting for this elusive personage, who never appeared, several hours were wasted; then torrents of rain rendered any movements impossible, and Gough had to content himself with completing his preparations for the storming of the city wall on the 27th. But in his plans he had not reckoned with the Plenipotentiary, who, without

---

[1] This distinction won for Grattan a brevet-majority, and incidentally caused him to become the hero of a curious adventure. The ship in which he was returning from Calcutta took fire in the Straits of Formosa. The boat to which Grattan had been told off was fortunate enough to reach the shore, where her crew, passing themselves off as Americans, were claimed by the United States Consul at Macao, and by him sent on to Hong Kong.

consulting the officers commanding the naval and military forces, agreed with the Chinese to accept an indemnity of six millions of dollars, to be paid within six days, when the whole expedition was to retire from the Canton river. Remonstrances were useless, for the Plenipotentiary was supreme, and after several anxious days spent in skirmishing with the local irregular troops, the soldiers re-embarked and the fleet once more returned to Hong Kong, leaving the Chinese more firmly convinced than ever that the English were as easy to hoodwink in diplomacy as they were difficult to fight in battle. These operations cost fourteen killed and ninety-one wounded. The casualties in the Royal Irish were Captain J. J. Sargent, Lieutenants D. Edwardes and G. Hilliard wounded, and five men killed or wounded.[1]

Owing to a combination of adverse circumstances nothing was accomplished by sea or land for some months. The Plenipotentiary, ever engaged in futile negotiations with the Chinese, could not bring himself to accept the active policy pressed upon him by Sir Hugh Gough, who pointed out that the Emperor of China would never respect us until the expedition had forced a passage up the great waterway of the Yang-Tse-Kiang, and struck a vigorous blow at the heart of the Celestial Empire. A great typhoon drove many ships ashore, dismasted others, and blew down part of the settlement at Hong Kong. Malarial fever, caught in the rice grounds around Canton, became so prevalent that at one time two-thirds of the troops were unfit for duty. The Royal Irish did not suffer more than other corps, yet on August 1, six weeks after a draft had raised their strength to 747 all told, 136 of the regiment were in hospital, and three officers died.[2] With the arrival of Sir Henry Pottinger, the new Plenipotentiary, the aspect of affairs changed; and on the 21st of August the regiment formed part of the column embarked for the attack of Amoy—a seaport three hundred miles up the coast towards the mouth of the Yang-Tse-Kiang. The position of Amoy is naturally strong, and since the beginning of the war it had been so greatly fortified that, after it was taken, soldiers and sailors agreed that it would have proved impregnable had it been defended by Europeans. Amoy stands at the head of a bay studded with islands, the most considerable of which, Kulangsu, commands both the city and the strait or channel, only six hundred yards in width, by which the inner harbour is entered. From every island and from every headland guns frowned upon the bay, and, to quote Gough's biographer—

"immediately in front of the outer town stood a succession of batteries, and from these there extended a solid rampart, facing the sea, about

[1] See Appendix 2 (G).

[2] This draft of 2 sergeants and 305 privates joined on June 8, 1841; the next, 152 rank and file, arrived about Christmas of the same year; the third, in June, 1842, was only 43 strong. The officers who died were Lieutenants C. W. Davis, S. Haly, and Lieutenant and Adjutant A. Wilson. The latter was succeeded in his appointment by Lieutenant J. W. Graves.

a mile in length. It was, says an eye-witness, 'well built of granite, faced with earth, extending along the shore nearly up to the suburbs of the city, and designed to command the passage to the harbour. It presented a line of guns, a full mile in length, the embrasures being covered with large slabs of stone protected by earth heaped upon them, and mounting no less than ninety-six guns.' The end of this rampart was connected by a castellated wall with a range of rocky heights running parallel to the beach and the rampart, which was thus protected from a flanking attack. . . . On the island of Kulangsu there were several strong batteries, mounting altogether seventy-six guns, and some of these faced the long stone rampart on the opposite side of the strait, thus exposing the assailants to a cross-fire." [1]

The naval and military commanders decided that the works of Amoy and Kulangsu should be attacked at the same time; the ships were to bombard them in front, while the troops took them in reverse. The morning of the 26th of August saw the plan carried into effect: the batteries at Kulangsu fell easily into our hands: those at Amoy were so strongly built that though two line-of-battle ships poured many thousands of projectiles into them at 400 yards' range, the masonry was practically uninjured. The cannonade, however, served its purpose in preventing the Chinese gunners from sinking the boats in which the XVIIIth and 49th were carried to their appointed landing-place at the foot of the castellated wall. While the Royal Irish, scaling this wall, turned the flank of the works on the sea front, the 49th rushed along the shore and scrambled over the parapet of the great battery; both regiments swept the work from end to end, driving the Chinese before them, and then joined the Marines, who had occupied the heights. Here they commanded the "outer city"; but the "inner city" was protected by a range of hills occupied by a large number of the enemy. Gough ordered the 49th to turn these hills, and sent the XVIIIth straight at the Chinese, up a steep gorge where a few men could have checked a regiment. The Chinese, however, made a very poor resistance; the troops bivouacked on the heights, and next morning occupied the citadel and "inner city" of Amoy. The total British loss was seventeen killed and wounded; among the latter were two men of the Royal Irish. The Chinese suffered severely, and several of their leaders committed suicide rather than accept defeat.

The adventures of the XVIIIth on this occasion are amusingly described by Lieutenant A. Murray, the officer in command of the picked shots of the regiment, who throughout the campaign worked together under his orders—

"We got into boats about 12 o'clock, and were taken in tow by the steamer *Nemesis*,[2] and as we had to go to the different ships

[1] 'Life of Hugh, first Viscount Gough,' by Rait, vol. i. pp. 209, 210.
[2] H.M. Paddleship *Nemesis*.

I

to collect the men, we were towed about the harbour for a long time, at the imminent risk of being capsized, as the string of boats increased every minute, and consequently threading our way through the fleet became more dangerous. I cut one boat adrift to prevent her sinking us, as she was twice our size and was pounding us to pieces, the Colours of the regiment being in the boat with me. . . . The steamer stood pretty closely into the shore, and the boats cast off, the *Nemesis* covering our landing with her guns and rockets. Our Grenadier and Light companies, and marksmen, under the command of Major Tomlinson, were ordered to move to the front to take the flanking wall of the battery, which was done very easily, and they (*i.e.*, the Chinese) only fired a few shots and a volley of rockets. We got over the wall by stepping on each others' backs. On seeing us come over the wall the Chinese, who till then had stood to their guns, . . . now ran in all directions, throwing their large shields over their backs."

After capturing a Mandarin's flag Murray followed the grenadier and light companies along the rear of the batteries, where a number of the enemy came at them boldly; the Chinese were soon dispersed, however, and fell back to a clump of aloe bushes, from which they were driven by a second charge. Of the bivouac Murray writes—

" It was almost night when we reached the summit of the heights and there were ordered to halt for the night. This was rather a pleasant look-out for tired and hungry men, without anything to eat or a house to sleep in, with a bitter cold wind blowing; however there was nothing for it but to choose the softest possible rock, light a cheroot and fancy yourself comfortable for the night. . . . There was great picking and choosing among us for soft rocks; but I believe we all came to the conclusion that one rock is as hard a pillow as another." [1]

After destroying the batteries and securing the five hundred guns captured at Amoy, the expeditionary force put to sea, leaving as garrison of Kulangsu 361 officers and men of the XVIIIth under Major J. Cowper, part of the 26th, and a detachment of artillery—a total of 550 of all ranks. The intention was to attack the towns of Chinhai and Ningpo, and then, in order to efface the bad impression produced by our evacuation of Chusan at the beginning of the year, to re-occupy that island. Bad weather, however, scattered the ships, and, when at length they were reassembled it was decided at once to seize Tinghae, the capital of Chusan, before the Chinese had finished their preparations for its defence. Since we had abandoned it our enemy had fortified the town assiduously. On the sea wall facing the harbour a battery of eighty guns had been thrown up. On the west it ended at the base of an eminence, in our previous occupation known as Pagoda Hill, where cannon were now mounted; to the

---

[1] 'Doings in China,' by Lieutenant A. Murray.

eastward it stretched almost to the foot of a line of heights, entrenched but not yet armed. Gough decided to land at the foot of these heights, and after carrying them to push some of the troops against the town, while others attacked the long battery from flank and rear. The ships were to avoid the fire of the guns on the sea front by taking up their stations on the outer flanks of Pagoda Hill and the eastern heights. The fleet came into action on October 1, 1841, and covered by their bombardment three hundred of the Royal Irish under Lieutenant-Colonel Adams, the newly arrived 55th regiment, and eight guns of the Madras Artillery disembarked under a heavy though ill-aimed fire of matchlocks and gingals. The 55th won the eastern heights, though not without difficulty, for the garrison of Tinghae were soldiers of a better stamp than the defenders of Amoy. The Royal Irish were sent off to the right, marching in quarter column and covered by the flank companies and picked marksmen, who ran into the enemy at an encampment near the long battery. Here the Chinese showed fight, and lost considerably in hand-to-hand work. Murray relates that a " white-buttoned " Mandarin,[1] after wounding one of the marksmen in the chest with a spear, "closed with him and got his forage cap off, another man came up and thrust at him with a bayonet, which he wrenched off, but was shot by a third." While the sharpshooters were thus employed the grenadier company had made its way into the long battery, where there was a sharp skirmish at close quarters round a gun. The Chinese stood bravely, and were not dislodged until another company of the regiment came up at the double, when they fell back, leaving the ground covered with their own wounded and a few of the XVIIIth. In this little fight pistols were used with effect. A Chinaman ran at Murray, sword in hand, but as the hero of the adventure writes, "having no particular confidence in my regulation spit, or perhaps in my own skill as a swordsman, I stuck my sword in the mud beside me, took a steady aim, and shot him." As soon as the Royal Irish had cleared the long battery of the enemy they climbed Pagoda Hill, to find that its garrison had been driven away by the shot and shell of the men-of-war and the artillery. As the Colours of the XVIIIth were raised on the top of the hill, those of the 55th began to float over the walls of Tinghae, and the capital of Chusan once more passed into our hands at the cost of some thirty killed and wounded. In the XVIIIth the casualties were a sergeant and six rank and file wounded. The loss of Chusan greatly annoyed the Chinese, who complained that we had not fought them fairly. Instead of anchoring our ships right under the cannon of the long battery and making a frontal attack by sea and land, as they expected, we had meanly bombarded the extreme ends of

---

[1] The Chinese, like ourselves, have many orders, indicated by the colour of a button, which is worn as we wear the insignia of the C.B., C.M.G., &c.

their line of defence, landed where their guns could not play upon us, and taken the battery in flank. Had cricket been one of the national institutions of China, the beaten troops would doubtless have said that we had not played the game!

Leaving an adequate garrison in Chusan General Gough next attacked Chinhai, a seaport at the mouth of the Ningpo river, twelve miles from the important city of Ningpo. Its fortifications, though strong, were easily turned on the 10th of October, when the place was taken with a total loss of four killed and sixteen wounded. One man in the Royal Irish was killed[1] and four wounded. The Chinese suffered very heavily, for here, as elsewhere in the campaign, their arms were as indifferent as their shooting, and after standing well for a time they broke before a charge, and were then mowed down in every direction. The slaughter of the fugitives was a hideous necessity: we were but a handful in an enormous country, and our enemies were so numerous that we should have been overwhelmed by numbers had we not inflicted severe punishment upon them in every engagement. To the bad marksmanship of the Chinese must be attributed the XVIIIth's good luck on this occasion. As the Royal Irish approached the range of strongly held hills which they were to seize, they found themselves on the bank of an unfordable canal, well under the enemy's fire. This canal was spanned by a bridge, narrow in itself, and made still narrower by an arch across it; the archway was blocked by a large stone, and even after this obstruction had been removed the passage was so small that the men had to take off their great-coats in order to squeeze through it one by one. "We had one or two very stout fellows," wrote one of the officers present, "whom we had great difficulty in pushing through, but when we came to the big drum we *were* in a fix. However, we got a little boat, and put McGiff, the big drummer, and his drum into it, with a pole to shove himself across. The Chinese thought the big drum was some new form of infernal machine, and opened a tremendous fire upon it, much to our amusement, but it was anything but fun for McGiff. He and the drum, however, got over safe and sound, except the drum heads, which were much damaged by bullets."

Three days later Ningpo fell without a shot being fired, and the little army was played into the town by the band of the XVIIIth. Here Gough was obliged to halt: much as he desired to push on to the banks of the Yang-Tse-Kiang he could not do so without troops, and sickness, casualties, and the drain of the garrisons of Hong Kong, Kulangsu, Tinghae, and Chinhai had left him with only about seven hundred and fifty men in hand. With so slender a force he could do nothing but await reinforcements; and for several months the headquarters of the XVIIIth and 49th remained at Ningpo, occasionally

[1] See Appendix 2 (G).

employed in demonstrations to postpone the attack which, as he rightly anticipated, could not be long delayed. Beyond these demonstrations there was little to break the monotony of existence in this Chinese city. The duty was heavy. Nearly five miles of continuous wall, twenty-seven feet high, twenty feet broad, and broken only by six gates, surrounded the town: each of these entrances required a strong guard; the town was patrolled several times during the twenty-four hours; and the field officer and captain of the day, mounted on sure-footed Chinese ponies, rode frequently round the ramparts to visit ground which could not be watched by the sentries on the gates. Once a week the Colours were trooped in the presence of the General, who insisted on the attendance of all officers not otherwise employed. When troops were available there was drill in a large square, to the great delight of a number of little native boys who had attached themselves to the Royal Irish. These children hung about the temple, which had been converted into a barrack, and did odd jobs for the men, helping them to cook and to carry dinners to the guards. In return for these kind offices the soldiers made pets of the boys, and taught them military expressions with such assiduity that in a short time "almost all the young blackguards about the place could swear in very good English." These youngsters proved their friendship with the XVIIIth by confirming the rumours, already current, that during the absence of Sir Hugh Gough, who had been summoned to a conference at Chusan with Sir Henry Pottinger, a great army was about to attack Ningpo; and after warning their soldier friends that next day there was going to be a great fight, they disappeared. This warning was repeated by the traders in the market, who drew their hands across their throats to give their British customers to understand that all the "Barbarians" would soon be killed. In the night of March 9-10, 1842, large bodies of the enemy simultaneously assaulted the south and west gates. The attack on the former was successful; the Chinese forced it open, routed the guard, and were making their way into the centre of the town when they were met by part of the 49th, who drove them through the gate and back into the suburbs with heavy loss. The west gate was held by Lieutenant A. W. S. F. Armstrong and twenty-eight men of the XVIIIth, carefully picked among the best soldiers of the regiment by the adjutant, Lieutenant Graves, who, like every one of the garrison at Ningpo except the officer in temporary command, had realised that there was trouble in the air. Five minutes after the bugles had sounded the alarm the Royal Irish were on parade, and two companies went off at the double to reinforce Armstrong's guard, who, owing to the construction of the parapet, were unable to fire down upon the Tartars as they strove to lever the gate off its hinges with crowbars and axes. Suddenly among the defenders appeared a private, Michael Cushin, described as a first-class soldier with only one failing, who seems to have been the hero of the defence. He had been imprisoned for drunkenness at the west gate, and when the attack began, begged to be released. As soon as his cell was opened, he wrenched the bar off the door and began to use it on the Tartars' heads: next he killed the officer commanding a party of the enemy on the point of clambering over the parapet: then his quick wits solved the problem of the ill-planned rampart. Collecting ten or twelve men, they put their shoulders to the part of it which overhung the gate, and with a few great heaves topped the mass of masonry into the crowd below.[1] Through the gap thus made the guard began to ply their muskets, and when the supports arrived with a light gun, a murderous fire was opened upon the Tartars, who sullenly abandoned the assault and retired, leaving two silk banners as trophies in the hands of the XVIIIth. After the south gate had been re-occupied a handful of British soldiers, among whom were some of the Royal Irish, pushed their way through the town, and near one of the gates found a great number of the enemy drawn up across the street. The infantry reserved their volley until twenty yards from the Tartars, the guns fired canister at fifty yards' range, and a party of the regiment, under Lieutenant Murray, after breaking through a house and fording a canal, occupied the side streets of the thoroughfare down which the enemy was driven, and by their musketry contributed much to his great losses. For six miles the Tartars were hunted, first through the suburb and then in the open country, but there was no fight left in them, and the civilian inhabitants who crowded the streets and roads gave them no help, and appeared to regard the fighting as a spectacle arranged for their own amusement. The attitude of most of the Chinese throughout the campaign, indeed, was one of complete apathy: they looked upon the war as an annoying but unavoidable interruption to their daily life, and finding that their conquerors treated them well, acquiesced in their presence, and made as much money out of them as possible.

The enemy attacked Chinhai about the same time that he attempted to wrest Ningpo from us, but was beaten off with ease by the garrison, largely composed of a detachment of the Royal Irish under Brevet-Major Grattan. A few days after these exciting little episodes, the XVIIIth was present at successful raids against the town of Tze-Ke and other places near Ningpo; but as those of the Royal Irish who were in the column hardly came into action it is unnecessary to describe these skirmishes. About this time Colonel Adams, being invalided home, was succeeded in command by Lieutenant-Colonel N. R. Tomlinson; and in the month of April three companies of the detachment at Kulangsu rejoined headquarters.

---

[1] This account of Cushin's exploits is taken from papers left by General Edwards and Lieutenant-Colonel Graves.

It has already been mentioned that ever since Sir Hugh Gough's arrival he had pointed out that the war would never be brought to a satisfactory conclusion until, abandoning the policy of attacking only the towns on the sea-coast, we pushed our way into the heart of the country, and threatened the Emperor in his palace at Pekin. After much correspondence between the Ministry at home and the Governor-General of India at Calcutta, Gough's strategy was adopted, and in May, 1842, the XVIIIth was afloat again, this time bound for Chapoo, where a naval arsenal was to be destroyed before the fleet entered the river Yang-Tse-Kiang. The place was strongly fortified, but, as usual, the enemy proved unprepared for anything but a frontal attack, and as soon as his works were turned on the 18th of May he was easily routed, except at one point, where the stubborn valour of the Tartar soldiery cost the regiment dear. Finding their retreat cut off, three hundred of these men flung themselves into a large stone house, and determined to take no quarter but to fight to the bitter end. The building was quickly and skilfully prepared for defence. The outer windows were manned by picked shots; the interior passages and the central hall were loopholed; mats were hung to exclude the light, so that if the British succeeded in making their way across the threshold they would plunge into semi-darkness, and not see the loopholes from which they would be shot down by a cross fire. A party of the Royal Irish tried to force their way into this death-trap, but were so warmly received that Lieutenant Murray, who was in command, drew off his men to wait for reinforcements; and after a similar attempt by some of the 49th had been repulsed, the house was surrounded by skirmishers to prevent the escape of any of the enemy. Before long, more companies of the XVIIIth and 49th came on the scene, and the officer in command of the latter corps, who was the senior officer present, decided not to press the attack until the Tartars had been shaken by artillery. The decision was a wise one, but unfortunately Lieutenant-Colonel Tomlinson overheard some expressions which he considered a reflection either upon his regiment or himself, and instantly led a headlong charge towards the entrance of the house. At the door he fell, so desperately injured that in five minutes he had ceased to breathe, while every man who tried to enter with him was killed or wounded. After he was shot down it became almost impossible to prevent the XVIIIth from rushing madly at the building, for the men burned to avenge their Colonel, whom they described as "the best officer who ever said 'Come on' to a grenadier company." In more formal language General Gough recorded the same opinion, saying in his despatch that Tomlinson fell "in full career of renown, honoured by the corps, and lamented by all."

When a few artillerymen came up with a light gun and some rockets they opened on the house, but without result; equally fruitless were the efforts of a party of sailors to set fire to the woodwork of the upper storeys;

then the explosion of a powder-bag made a small breach in a wall through which a few of the Royal Irish tried to force their way, only to be driven back with loss. A second attempt to set fire to the woodwork, however, was more successful, and the explosion of another powder-bag brought down more of the wall, and thus exposed many of the Tartars to our musketry. Soon the whole place was in a blaze, and when at last our men rushed through the doorway from which they had been so often repulsed, they found themselves in a hell on Earth. Three hundred Tartars had defended the building; now all but fifty-three lay dead upon the floor; and of the survivors nearly all were wounded. Many of their wadded cotton uniforms had taken fire, and to the horrors of the reek of blood and the stench of singeing flesh were added the cries of the wounded, as they feebly strove to beat out the sparks which fell from the roof upon their clothing. In the midst of this scene of carnage sat an old Tartar colonel, who, when the red-coats began to show through the smoke, laid down his pipe, snatched up his sword, and cut his throat. This stout old warrior failed to kill himself, and with the rest of the wounded was tended by our doctors, and then released—a chivalrous recognition of their bravery which greatly astonished the prisoners and convinced them that the "foreign devils" were not as black as the Mandarins had painted them. The discovery, unfortunately, came too late to prevent an epidemic of suicide among the population of Chapoo. When our men entered the town it was full of dead: "men, women, and children were found drowned or hanged; whole families seemed to have destroyed themselves, and some, from the positions they were in, must have had difficulty and most desperate resolution to effect their purpose. The wells and every place where they could find water enough were full of bodies."[1]

The Chinese are believed to have fought Gough's little army of 2200 men[2] at Chapoo with 8000 regular troops, 1700 of whom were Tartars. Their losses were, as usual, enormous—from 1200 to 1500—while those of the British were two officers and eleven other ranks killed, six officers and forty-six other ranks wounded. The casualties among the XVIIIth were heavy: Colonel Tomlinson, a sergeant, and three privates were killed;[3] Lieutenants A. Murray and E. Jodrell, a sergeant, a drummer, and twenty-seven rank and file were wounded. One of the pay-sergeants had a very narrow escape: he was in the habit of carrying the company roll in his forage cap, and when at nightfall he wanted to make entries in it he found it cut to pieces by bullets.

As soon as the arsenal, guns, and other munitions of war at Chapoo were destroyed, the expedition made sail for the Yang-Tse-Kiang, where we bom-

---

[1] Murray's 'Doings in China.'

[2] As Gough's reinforcements had not yet joined, he only had with him four British regiments and a small number of gunners and engineers. The XVIIIth were 492 of all ranks.

[3] See Appendix 2 (G).

barded Woosung, a town at the mouth of the river of the same name. Though small, the place was heavily fortified, for the Chinese trusted to its guns for the protection of the lower reaches of the river. In the capture of Woosung the army played no part, for the troopships were aground on mud-banks when the sailors and marines, after knocking the batteries to pieces, landed to take possession of the town. Two days later, on the 19th of June, the Royal Irish formed part of a column which marched fourteen miles inland to Shanghai, destroyed the warlike stores at this great centre of trade, and then returned to Woosung, to find that during their short absence some batteries of Royal Artillery, the 98th, and several Madras regiments had joined the force, and that Major J. Cowper had come up from Kulangsu to take command of the XVIIIth, bringing with him the company which had been left to garrison Chinhai. The fleet remained storm-bound at Woosung until the 7th of July: then the weather moderated, and the Admiral, Sir William Parker, ordered his seventy vessels—men-of-war, transports, and store ships—to weigh anchor for Nankin, now the object of our operations. This enormous city was the commercial capital of China, and the centre of a great network of canals connecting Pekin with the Yang-Tse-Kiang and the southern provinces of the Empire. Once masters of Nankin, we could stop all inland traffic on the canals, and by paralysing the commerce of the country bring irresistible pressure on the Emperor, six hundred miles away in his Court at Pekin. The task before the Navy was a heavy one. In peace time the mere passage of so large a number of ships over a hundred and seventy miles of an almost unknown river would have presented difficulties. Now these difficulties were increased by the necessity of guarding against attack, and by the knowledge that before the guns of the fleet could be trained upon the walls of Nankin we would have to fight the garrison of at least one large town on the banks of the river. The steamers scouted upstream, sounding and surveying as they went: the sailing ships followed in a stately procession many miles in length, watched by crowds of peasants who gazed in wonder at the "war junks" of the Barbarians. On the 20th of July, the rearmost of the fleet reached Chinkiangfu, a walled city fifty miles below Nankin; and next day Gough landed his troops, now numbering 6664 men. The first brigade (Major-General Lord Saltoun) was to clear the enemy from a camp south-west of the town; with the second, Major-General Schoedde was to attack the northern wall of the town; to Bartley's brigade (the third) was entrusted the storming of the western wall. The first brigade did its work easily; the second had hard fighting before its bayonets glittered on the northern wall; the third brigade, and especially the XVIIIth regiment, had exciting adventures in carrying out the duty assigned to them.

The Royal Irish were the last troops to disembark. They did not land till seven A.M., when the heat was already so oppressive that the Adjutant, Lieutenant Graves, persuaded Major Cowper to leave the men's great-coats behind, undertaking to provide the entire regiment with furs from the shops of the pawnbrokers, with whom the wealthy Chinese regularly stored their winter clothing. To go into action without great-coats was quite a new departure, but even more daring was the next order: the men were told to take off their stocks, sling them over the left shoulder, and unfasten three buttons of their jackets and three buttons of their collars! These precautions, though to our ideas not very far-reaching, served their purpose, for while in other corps numbers of men were knocked over by the heat, not a man in the XVIIIth suffered from sunstroke. The regiment was making its way through the suburbs to the western face of the wall, when an A.D.C. arrived with orders for the Royal Irish to come up at the double to the western gate, where the General was anxiously awaiting them. The troops around General Gough were in bad case: many lay senseless from sun apoplexy; the remainder were so exhausted that they could only keep up a feeble fire on its defenders. As soon as the XVIIIth appeared Gough welcomed them with the order "Go on, Royal Irish, and storm." "We halted," writes an officer who was present, "to tell off a storming party of fifty men, and then with arms at the trail and bending low, the stormers made a dash down a cross-street within about twenty yards of the gate, and from the windows of the houses which ran parallel to the wall, we opened fire on the Chinese gunners and soon silenced them. The engineers then advanced and placed a powder-bag against the gate (a very strong one and, as we afterwards found, strengthened by four or five tiers of sand-bags piled against it from inside); we were ordered to lie down; the fuse was lit, and in about ten seconds everything was flying about our heads. This brought us to our feet in a hurry; we gave a cheer and dashed into the archway, which was densely filled with smoke; those who got in first were soon brought to their knees by kicking against the sand-bags which we could not see, but we had to scramble on as quick as possible as there was danger of receiving a poke from a friendly bayonet behind! We got out as black as monkeys, to find ourselves in a sort of yard, surrounded by high walls, with a second gate leading from it into the city. We had just started breaking this second gate down, when we heard a friendly voice behind it shouting 'Hold on, we'll open it for you!'" It turned out that the 55th, after escalading their own wall, had worked round to the western gate, which the Chinese abandoned when they saw their flank in danger.

The Royal Irish were at once sent to drive the Tartars from the western wall. They moved off left in front,[1] and as there was not room on the

---

[1] In the MS. accounts of this engagement, the writers all mention that the regiment marched off "left in front." The XVIIIth must have been very well drilled to be able to do this, for in those days very few regiments could move otherwise than "right in front." This innovation is interesting in connection with the formation of the Royal Irish in the attack on the Dockyard Creek at Sebastopol on June 18, 1855, described in chapter vii.

rampart for four men abreast they marched in threes. The grenadier company were soon dropped to hold a commanding building close to the wall; the
remainder of the regiment pushed on without seeing any of the enemy, until a
keen-eyed officer noticed a large number of Tartars emerging from the shelter
of some houses on the town side of the wall. The commanding officer,
insisting that they were not fighting men but harmless coolies, refused to send
out skirmishers to protect the head and right flank of his straggling
column, and the Tartars were allowed to establish themselves in gardens
surrounded by high walls, which made excellent rests for matchlocks and
gingals. As soon as the regiment was within range they opened a heavy fire
upon the leading company, killing Captain C. J. R. Collinson, wounding
Lieutenant S. Bernard, and causing several casualties in the ranks. The
rampart along which the XVIIIth was marching was so narrow that it was
difficult for messengers to pass rapidly from company to company, and as no
orders were received the men halted for directions: but by the time the
enemy had discharged a second volley, an officer had called upon the Light
company to avenge their captain. Collinson's "Light Bobs" dashed down the
slope of the rampart, scaled the mud walls and, followed by the remainder of
the regiment, fell furiously on the Tartars, who, after a stout resistance, broke
and fled. Not all, however, of the enemy had lost heart. Just as the
regiment had re-formed after the charge, a gigantic Tartar rushed towards the
line, brandishing a sword in each hand; the officers, unwilling to send so
brave a man to his death, made signs to him to retire, but in vain, and he was
almost amongst the men when a well-aimed bullet laid him low. The
grenadier company came in for a full share of the excitements of the day.
Their captain, Wigston, noticed some of the Tartars drawn up across a
narrow street leading to his post, and sent a subaltern, Lieutenant W. Venour,
and twelve men to dislodge them. The Tartars held their fire until the party
of grenadiers were close to them, and then let fly with some effect. Lieutenant
I. H. Hewitt with fourteen men hurried up to reinforce Venour's detachment,
and the street was cleared after sharp hand-to-hand fighting. Hewitt had a
narrow escape: a Tartar cut at him with his sword, and the blow would have
been fatal had not Private M'Carthy "raised his musket and parried it, though
unfortunately with the loss of his thumb, the sword cutting right through
the bone, and also through Hewitt's forage cap, slightly raising the skin of his
head. We left a picket there," continues Lieutenant Murray, "as occasional
shots were still fired from the houses. A short time afterwards a Tartar
soldier rushed in amongst the men and stabbed one of them in the side with
his knife: he was shot instantly. We were obliged to set fire to the houses
to drive the Tartars out of them, for we would not let the men follow them
into the buildings."

Although the troops did their best to stop the frenzy of rage and terror which seized upon the population after we had captured the town, the number of people who committed suicide at Chinkiangfu was as great or even greater than at Chapoo. One instance among hundreds will prove how determined the Tartars were not to survive the disgrace of a defeat. When their General realised that the day was lost he retired to his house, ordered his servants to set fire to the building, and allowed himself to be burned to death. It was fortunate for the success of Gough's little army that the overweening contempt of the Chinese for foreigners had prevented the employment of European adventurers to mould and lead their armies. Had the Tartar troops been trained and disciplined by Continental soldiers of fortune, as were the Sikhs, the enemies whom Gough was to encounter in a few years, a great array of British soldiers would have been required to win on the banks of the Yang-Tse-Kiang victories as decisive as those of Sobraon and Goozerat.[1] In the capture of Chinkiangfu two officers and thirty of the other ranks were killed, eleven officers and ninety-eight other ranks wounded, and three privates missing. The casualties among the small Naval landing party were three killed and twenty-one wounded. The XVIIIth lost one officer, Captain Collinson, and two private soldiers killed; one officer, Lieutenant S. Bernard, two sergeants, and fifteen privates wounded.

While the soldiers were fighting on shore, the sailors were doing invaluable work on their own element by blockading the chief waterways to Pekin; and in a few days the result of the stoppage of trade with the capital was so disastrous to the merchants of China that the Emperor was obliged to sue for peace. But before negotiations had been opened, Pottinger, Gough, and Parker realised that the presence of British troops and British ships at Nankin would greatly stimulate the tardy movements of the Chinese diplomatists, and on August 9, 1842, the whole force, less a small garrison left to hold Chinkiangfu, was ready to assault the walls of the commercial capital of China. But no assault was necessary, as twenty days later a treaty of peace, this time a genuine one on the part of the Chinese, was signed on board a British man-of-war. Its terms were satisfactory: every point on which England had gone to war was ceded by the Emperor; our national honour was vindicated, and the rights of our traders secured. During the negotiations dignified courtesies were exchanged between the Mandarins and the Plenipotentiary. On one of these occasions the grenadier company of the Royal Irish acted as guard of honour to Sir Henry Pottinger while he solemnly dined with the Chinese officials: our late enemies turned out their best soldiers to receive the English guests, but though Lieutenant Murray admits that among them were many tall, fine-looking fellows, he insists that they were

---

[1] How susceptible the Chinese soldiery are to the training of British officers was proved first by the success of Gordon's army in 1860 (see chapter xii.), and later, in 1900, by the good conduct of the Wai-Hai-Wai regiment.

"nothing in appearance to our company, who looked remarkably well, and must have astonished the Chinese much." Though the spectators doubtless admired the physique and martial bearing of the Irishmen who had so often routed the picked troops of China, they must have smiled at the contrast between the comfortable dress of the Tartars, who wore long loose coats and boots coming well up the leg, and the stocks, tightly buttoned shell-jackets and equally tight white trousers of the British army.[1] The spies among the crowd, for the Chinese had many very observant secret service agents in their employ, must have wondered why the infantry who served on board ship were armed with percussion muskets, while those who fought on land carried flint-locks.

No sooner had the treaty of peace been officially ratified by the Emperor of China than the expedition began to descend the Yang-Tse-Kiang with all speed, for the climate had begun to tell heavily upon the health of soldiers and sailors alike. So short-handed from sickness was the crew of H.M.S. *Rattlesnake* that the Royal Irish, by this time nearly as much at home on a ship as in a barrack, helped largely in working her successfully down the river. At the mouth of the Yang-Tse-Kiang the expedition broke up: some of Gough's units sailed for India; others went home, while the corps ordered to remain in Chinese waters proceeded to their several destinations. Among the latter was the XVIIIth, which was sent to Chusan, where its various detachments were assembled by the end of October, 1842. When the casualty returns were prepared it was found that though the losses in action had been small, those caused by dysentery, malaria, and cholera had been very heavy. Lieutenant-Colonel N. R. Tomlinson and Captain C. J. R. Collinson had been killed; Major R. Hammill, Lieutenants H. Vavasour, A. Wilson, F. Swinburn, D. Edwardes, J. Cochrane, G. W. Davis, S. Haly, Hon. C. H. Stratford, Ensign M. Humphreys, and Assistant-Surgeon J. Baker had died from disease; six officers had been wounded but had recovered from their injuries. Among the other ranks nine non-commissioned officers and men had been killed, seventy-seven wounded, and two hundred and fourteen had died from illness, accident, or the effect of wounds.[2] In honour of those who perished a monument was erected in St Patrick's Cathedral. It stands in the north transept—the Walhalla of the regiment, where the old Colours, faded by the sun in many climes and pierced by bullets in many battles, overhang the stately memorials by which the Royal Irish regiment has sought to keep green the memory of its illustrious dead. The numerous monuments are described

[1] Murray tells us that these white trousers were dug up out of store in honour of this ceremonial parade. Throughout the war the XVIIIth wore blue Nankeen trousers.

[2] See Appendix 2 (G). These figures, compiled from documents in the Record Office, are considerably greater than those given in the inscription on the memorial. Probably some of the deaths occurred immediately after peace was made, and were therefore not included among the losses during the war.

fully in Appendix 10, and photographs of them are reproduced in various parts of the book.

At the opening of Parliament in 1843, the House of Lords passed the usual vote of thanks to the troops which had taken part in the campaign. A medal was issued to the officers and men who had served in the Chinese war; leave was granted to the XVIIIth to add to its other battle honours the word "China" and the device of the Dragon, and Colonel G. Burrell, Lieutenant-Colonel W. H. Adams, and Majors J. Cowper and J. Grattan were awarded the C.B.

Very disagreeable orders awaited the regiment on its arrival at Chusan. Four companies were to remain there as part of its garrison until the Chinese had fulfilled all the obligations of the treaty, while headquarters and the greater part of the regiment were to occupy the island of Kulangsu, which our Government also held as a pledge of Chinese good faith. Kulangsu had already acquired the reputation of being one of the most unhealthy stations in China, and the Royal Irish soon discovered that its evil reputation was but too well deserved. According to Lieutenant-Colonel Graves's statement, when the headquarters companies landed they found the detachment of the regiment which had been there for some months in a deplorable condition. There had been many deaths among all ranks; every one of the surviving officers was down with fever,

"and there were not thirty men under command of a sergeant who were fit for duty or could shoulder a firelock. . . . When the Headquarter companies landed from Chusan the men were healthy and well seasoned, but they very soon began to feel the climate, and before long half the men were on the sick list, and we began to bury them very fast. I had been appointed Staff Officer for the island, and at first found much difficulty in getting coffins quick enough, so I ordered twenty at a time to be supplied by a contractor at Amoy. Several of our officers died, and at last I found much difficulty in getting men enough to relieve the guards. I went to our Colonel, Cowper—who was the Commandant of the island—and represented that if we did not get a ship sent up from Hong Kong for the invalids we should very soon have no men for guard. We got a ship and found her of the greatest benefit; she was anchored half a mile out of the harbour, and the invalids sent on board her came back in a week fit for duty.

"A large draft joined from England, about three hundred strong, together with the women and children. This caused a little stir, but it was a short-lived happiness: they went down almost as fast as we could provide coffins for them. We pitched tents and moved our camp daily about the island, but it was no use—cholera and fever still continued. The men began to drink to drown dull care; the officers off the sick list were constantly on Court-Martial duty, and the Colonel received an official letter from Headquarters drawing his attention to the number of Courts-Martial for drunkenness, and directing him to parade the regiment and reprimand the men for their conduct, which was alleged to be the principal cause of the severe mortality. As Staff Officer and adjutant of the regiment I was ordered to read this letter to the men, which I began to do, but I must acknowledge I fairly broke down and had to hand it to another officer to finish. I felt so keenly how our gallant poor fellows were being sacrificed, after their long, hard services, to a climate no one could live in, and *how* they bore it!"

In April 1844, after a hundred and thirty-six officers and men had fallen victims to the climate of Kulangsu,[1] the regiment was reunited at Chusan. The next station was Hong Kong, where the ordinary routine of garrison life in the East was suddenly broken by an urgent and wholly unexpected call to arms. The people of Canton, always overbearing and offensive towards Europeans, had recently insulted and ill-treated British subjects, and their Mandarins had refused to make redress for the outrages. The British Plenipotentiary, Sir John Davis, was a believer in the saying " A word and a blow, and the blow first," and he determined to teach the mob of Canton a lesson they would not soon forget. During the night of the 1st of April, 1847, the Royal Irish, under Lieutenant-Colonel Cowper, with 23 officers and 509 other ranks, and the 42nd regiment of Madras Native Infantry, 399 strong, were packed into a couple of small men-of-war and an armed steamer. Early on the following morning the flotilla was off the entrance to the Canton river; the troops were landed, and driving the Chinese artillerymen from the batteries, spiked the guns. The works higher up the stream were then treated in the same way, but not without vigorous opposition from the enemy, whose aim, however, was much distracted by the steady fire of a party of the Royal Irish, described in the despatches as the " acting gunners of the XVIIIth, who replied to the batteries in a style which would have done credit to experienced artillerymen." As soon as the ships were off Canton the soldiers occupied the "factories"; placed them in a state of defence, and made plans for storming the town. The Royal Irish were looking forward to winning much glory (and much prize money too!) in the capture of Canton, when the Mandarins, greatly perturbed by Sir John Davis's prompt reprisals, hastily made full atonement for their misdeeds, and the expedition returned to Hong Kong. They had done a good week's work: 879 guns, many of great calibre, had been spiked, much ammunition destroyed, and a greatly needed lesson given to the Canton roughs—and all without the loss of a soldier, bluejacket, or marine.

General D'Aguilar, who was in command, mentioned in his despatch the following officers of the regiment, viz., Lieutenant-Colonel Cowper; Captain J. Bruce, A.A.G.; Captain Clark Kennedy, Acting A.Q.M.; Captain J. W. Graves; Captain A. N. Campbell, and Lieutenant E. W. Sargent, Acting A.D.C.

[1] Six officers, 6 sergeants, 6 drummers, and 118 rank and file.

Before the troops left Canton the British merchants asked for an officer to train their newly formed Volunteer corps. Captain J. W. Graves was selected, and with part of the Light company spent two months in "the factories," where between drilling his civilian recruits, drawing up plans for the defence of the settlement against a sudden rush, and eating the good dinners to which the merchants invited him, his time was fully occupied. Soon after this detachment rejoined headquarters the regiment was warned to prepare to sail for India, and on November 20, 1847, embarked for Bengal on the transport ship *Balcarres*. Major W. F. Dillon was in command; with him were 24 officers, 42 sergeants, 15 drummers, and 595 rank and file, and when he arrived at Fort William on January 10, 1848, he found awaiting him drafts from England amounting to 7 officers, 1 drummer, and 334 rank and file. Thus the XVIIIth began its tour of duty in India with a total strength of one thousand and eighteen of all ranks.

CHAPTER VI.

1848-1854.

THE SECOND WAR WITH BURMA.

WHEN the XVIIIth Royal Irish regiment arrived in India the Sikh War appeared to be over, and all chance of winning fresh laurels seemed relegated to the distant future. Further troubles, however, broke out in the Punjab, and for a time the regiment had every hope of again seeing active service under Sir Hugh Gough, as it was ordered up country and incorporated in the "Army of Reserve" on its arrival at Umballa in March, 1849. But Gough's victory at Goozerat[1] had finally crushed the power of our gallant foes; the "Army of Reserve" was not called upon to take the field, and the Royal Irish remained at Umballa till the end of 1849, when they marched to Meerut, where a draft of two hundred and twenty recruits from home awaited them. The two flank companies did not accompany headquarters, as in November they had been sent on an important and interesting duty: they formed the European portion of the escort selected to guard the Marquis of Dalhousie, Governor-General of India, in his progress from Rurki to Lahore, the capital of the great province just added to the British dominions. This detachment of the XVIIIth was commanded by Captain C. A. Edwards, who in a statement prepared for this history mentions that as it was feared fanatics would attempt to murder the Governor-General in his sleep, four picked men of the Royal Irish at night patrolled the space between the inner and outer walls of Lord Dalhousie's tent. These sentries appear to have been abnormally ceremonious in their manners, for the Governor-General, while warmly praising their incessant vigilance, said that he had only one fault to find with them—they *would* salute him when he was in his dressing-gown! It is not clear whether Edwards' party were present at the historic scene of Dhuleep Singh's deposition at Lahore, but they acted nominally as guard of honour, but virtually as escort to this important prisoner on his journey to

---

[1] February 21, 1849.

K

Meerut. In the cold weather of 1850 the regiment was ordered back to Calcutta; from Allahabad the journey was by river, in flats towed by small steamers. On its arrival it was quartered in Fort William, where, when all outlying detachments had been collected, Colonel Reignolds had under his command a magnificent regiment of eleven hundred and five officers and men. As it was generally understood that the Royal Irish would be ordered home in a few months, many officers obtained leave of absence and started for England under the firm impression that for some time there would be no more fighting in the East.[1] But the truth of the saying "You never know your luck" has seldom been better illustrated than in the case of the XVIIIth at the beginning of 1852, when the regiment found itself hurried off to take part in an expedition to Burma.

The causes of this war, the second which the Burmese had forced upon us in the course of thirty years, were almost identical with those which had brought about the conflict with China, described in the preceding chapter. Persistent disregard of treaties and systematic oppression of European traders had culminated in maltreatment of British subjects so flagrant that our Government was compelled to seek redress by arms; and in each theatre of war the prestige of Britain was re-established by the combined efforts of both branches of the Service. The dissensions between England and the King of Ava, as the ruler of Burma was officially described, were brought to a climax by the misconduct of one of his lieutenants, the governor of Rangoon, who wantonly imprisoned the master of a British ship, and exposed him in the stocks to the gibes and insults of an Eastern rabble. When a squadron demanded reparation for this outrage the Burmese temporised, but soon so clearly showed they did not mean to mend their ways that the commodore seized a Burmese ship-of-war and blockaded the port of Rangoon. The truculent governor retaliated by confiscating the property of all British subjects within his reach; and the sailors thereupon towed their prize to sea under a heavy fire from the stockades on the banks of the Rangoon river. When this news reached Calcutta the Indian Government at once ordered a combined naval and military expedition[2] to rendezvous at the mouth of the branch of the Irrawaddy on which Rangoon stands, and on January 19, 1852, Lieutenant-Colonel Reignolds with the headquarters and right wing of the

[1] Some of the officers embarked in the *Buckinghamshire*, an ill-fated ship which was burned at sea on March 3, 1851. They escaped with their lives, but the regimental plate, and the trophies won in many campaigns by the regiment, were lost, with the exception of one piece of plate, a gold snuff-box, saved, according to tradition, by an officer who, when the fire alarm sounded, snatched it off the mess table, thrust it into his trousers' pocket, and brought it safe to land.

[2] The Royal Navy was represented by 6 steamers, 80 guns, 818 officers and men; the Indian Navy by the same number of steamers, 30 guns, 952 officers and men; there were also 7 steamers belonging to the uncovenanted Service, carrying 33 guns, with crews amounting in all to 500. The original land force consisted of 8000 or 9000 troops; later arrivals raised General Godwin's command to a nominal strength of nearly 20,000.

regiment (444 all told) embarked at Calcutta, followed in a few weeks by Lieutenant-Colonel C. J. Coote with the left wing, 518 strong.[1] This was not the first time that the sails of a great British expedition had whitened Burmese waters. In 1824, the King of Ava had invaded the territories of the East India Company, an act of unprovoked aggression punished by the capture of Rangoon, and followed by a long series of operations, in which a very large number of the British troops perished of disease before the Burmese sued for peace, and ceded to us the provinces of Aracan and Tenasserim, long narrow strips of territory washed respectively by the waters of the Bay of Bengal and the Indian Ocean. Rangoon was restored to the King of Ava, and with it two hundred miles of coast-line that lay like a wedge between our new dominions.[2]

In the first phase of the campaign of 1852-53, the operations were chiefly confined to the capture of important towns near the mouths of the great rivers which, rising in the Himalayas, flow through the swamps and forests of Burma on their way to the Indian Ocean. The war-steamers forced their way up the streams and engaged the stockades and other defences on the banks; while the soldiers landed, stormed these works, and then, pushing forward into the jungle, carried the towns by assault. While the operations were confined to the immediate neighbourhood of rivers and navigable creeks no question of land transport arose, but when it became necessary to send

---

[1] The following officers served in the war :—

Lieutenant-Colonel	T. S. Reignolds, C.B. (in command).	Lieutenant .	.	F. H. Suckling.
"	C. J. Coote.	" .	.	H. J. Stephenson.
Brevet-Lieut.-Col.	J. Grattan, C.B.	" .	.	G. A. Elliot.
Major . .	. F. Wigston.	" .	.	J. Canavan.
Captain .	. C. A. Edwards.	" .	.	G. L. W. D. Flamstead.
" .	. A. Gillespie.	" .	.	H. Piercy.
" ,	. G. F. S. Call.	" .	.	H. A. Ward.
"	. A. N. Campbell.	" .	.	J. G. Wilkinson.
"	. W. T. Bruce.	" .	.	F. Willington.
"	. J. J. Wood.	" .	.	F. Eteson.
"	. J. Borrow.	Ensign .	.	T. R. Gibbons.
"	. J. Cormick.	" .	.	T. H. Smith.
"	. A. W. S. F. Armstrong.	" .	.	A. H. Graves.
Lieutenant .	. I. H. Hewitt.	" .	.	G. W. Stackpoole.
" .	. W. P. Cockburn.	" .	.	W. J. Hales.
" .	. C. Woodwright.	" .	.	T. E. Esmond.
" .	. R. Doran (adjt.).	" .	.	G. H. Pocklington.
" .	. E. W. Sargent (adjt.).	" .	.	W. O'B. Taylor.
" .	. M. J. Hayman.	" .	.	J. W. Meurant.
" .	. F. D. Lillie.	Acting Paymaster	Captain A. N. Campbell.
" .	. W. H. Graves.	Quartermaster .	Lieutenant T. Carney.
" .	. G. Swaby.	Surgeon .	J. Stewart.
" .	. C. F. Kelly.	Assist.-Surgeon .	J. H. Dwyer.
" .	. J. Swinburn.	" .	. W. K. Chalmers, M.D.

[2] See Map No. 5.

columns of troops deep into the interior of the country, the innumerable difficulties of fighting in a pathless and tropical jungle at once made themselves felt. The ships could indeed bring stores to the point on the river from which the column struck inland; they could hold a base upon which the troops could fall back in case of need; but there the power of the navy ceased. The wants of the soldiers could only be supplied by bullock-carts or elephants, and the long lines of transport animals had to wind their way through a densely wooded country, admirably suited to the guerilla tactics of surprises and ambuscades. Like the Chinese, the Burmans though brave as individuals were undisciplined as soldiers, and as a rule preferred to fight behind ramparts to meeting their enemy in the field. In China the garrisons of the cities waited our attack behind high stone walls; in Burma the defenders of the towns manned huge timber stockades, in the building of which they were very skilful. A nation of woodsmen, with their sharp square-pointed swords they could hew down forest trees and run up timber barricades with extreme rapidity, and when time was allowed them they could produce really formidable fortifications, such as those awaiting the British at Rangoon. These consisted of a substantial rampart, fourteen or fifteen feet high, about twelve feet wide on the top, and revetted within and without by great teak logs placed vertically, with the lower ends sunk in the ground. The intervening space was filled with well-rammed earth. The logs of the outer revetment stretched up some six feet or more above the level of the parapet, every fourth or fifth log being cut some three feet shorter than the others to form loopholes and embrasures. There were many flanking towers; traverses protected the gates; the ditches were deep, often flooded with water, and protected by thick abattis. Guns, varying in calibre from 32-prs. to wall pieces and gingals, were mounted on the parapets. The infantry were armed with flint-lock muskets, many of them old weapons, worn out and sold as scrap iron by the British military authorities.

When the ships containing the Bengal contingent reached the mouth of the Rangoon river on April 2, 1852, Major-General H. Godwin, who was in command of the troops, sent a vessel under a flag of truce to inquire whether any answer had been received from the King of Ava to the letter containing the British demands for redress. The Burmese replied by firing on the flag of truce, and Godwin, not feeling strong enough to attack Rangoon until the Madras contingent had joined him, sailed for the capital of Tenasserim, Moulmein, at that time threatened by the garrison of the neighbouring Burmese city of Martaban. On the morning of the 5th of April the fleet opened fire upon Martaban, and under cover of the bombardment the right wing of the XVIIIth and part of the 80th landed; a storming party, led by the grenadier companies of these two regiments, scaled the wall, and in a short time the place was in our hands. Thanks to the diary of the late

Colonel G. A. Elliot, then a subaltern in the Royal Irish, interesting particulars have been preserved of this little fight, in which the younger men in the regiment were in action for the first time. Under a heavy but badly directed fire the grenadiers dashed across the twenty yards of ground between the water's edge and the main defence of the city, a thick wall fifteen feet high and about eight hundred yards in length. Here the enemy's bullets began to take effect among the Royal Irish. Colonel Elliot writes that—

"Private Fergusson received three in his left arm, and died of his wounds,[1] John Donovan two in his left hand, Coleman one through his left arm. We ran up and got close under the wall in extended order; the General was seen to take off his hat and give a cheer, which our men returned and then quickly sprung up the wall, (which was overgrown with shrubs) and rushed upon the Burmese, who quickly retired to some jungle, whence they fired, though without much effect. While surmounting the wall one of our officers noticed a man in the regiment get on to the top and look intently into a large bush below him. Still gazing intently, he loosed a brick, flung it down into the bush, raised his musket and shot a Burmese who had been hiding there in cover. We then advanced, and joining part of the 80th, and one of our own companies, skirmished up one of the hills enclosed by the wall, driving the Burmese before us, and charging them whenever they appeared in numbers. The hill was very steep, and obstacles existed in the shape of felled trees with branches pointing downwards. At the top was a Pagoda, surrounded by a wall mounted with gingals, but as there was no resistance, the men rested here for an hour in the shade. We then moved down a lane which led towards the next hill; after advancing about two hundred yards we came to an open space where the bullets began to fly over our heads from the hill in front. The men halted, and Lieutenant-Colonel Reignolds, XVIIIth, who was acting Brigadier, halted for reinforcements: . . . but as soon as the Burmese saw that we had stopped, they began shouting and challenging us to come on, and after a while they poured down the hill towards us. Colonel Reignolds now allowed the men to charge, and with a cheer they dashed forward. The enemy ran back to a wall on the top of the hill and began a badly aimed fire; Glesson, Grenadier Company was struck in the mouth. The enemy evacuated the hill."

After clearing a third hill the detachment whose fortunes Elliot has described joined the main body, and as the enemy were completely routed all marched back to the beach. The casualties in this affair were eight wounded, seven of whom were men of the Royal Irish; but many soldiers were struck down by the sun, a warning, unhappily disregarded, against the folly of wearing in the tropics the same uniform as that in use in the United Kingdom. In the despatch describing the capture of Martaban the following officers of the regiment were mentioned, viz., Lieutenant-Colonel Reignolds;

[1] See Appendix 2 (H). Private Fergusson's name, however, is not among those who died of wounds.

Captain A. N. Campbell, on whom devolved the command of the wing when Reignolds was ordered to act as Brigadier; and Captain A. Gillespie, grenadier company, who was the first man over the enemy's fortifications.

Godwin had now secured the safety of Moulmein; and leaving a small garrison in Martaban, he returned with the greater part of his force to the Rangoon river, where the Madras contingent and reinforcements from Bengal awaited him. Among the latter was the left wing of the Royal Irish, who since its arrival had been employed with the Navy in destroying the stockades at the mouth of the river. On the 10th of April the fleet began to move up-stream, and next morning the steamers were in their appointed positions, ready to bombard the works which defended the landing-places giving access to Rangoon. The Burmese opened fire; the sailors replied with energy, and the cannonade continued till late in the day, when landing parties, among whom were detachments of the XVIIIth, stormed the stockades; and driving away the enemy, cleared the way for the disembarkation of the main body. Though General Godwin had served in the first expedition to Burma, his recollections of the topography of Rangoon would have been misleading had they not been supplemented by information supplied by a British trader, from whom he learned that since the war of 1824-26 part of the town had been abandoned and lay in ruins; a new quarter had sprung up, and the fortifications had been remodelled to meet the fresh conditions. Rangoon was now built in a rough square, with sides about three-quarters of a mile in length, surrounded by deep ditches, and walls sixteen feet high and eight feet thick. In the works was included the Shwe Dagon, turned into a citadel by the mounting of cannon upon the three tiers of huge terraces which support the foundations of this great pagoda. From the landing-places on the river to the gate in the southern wall is about a mile and a quarter; and the Burmese, remembering that in the first war we had marched by that road, concluded that the tactics of 1826 would be repeated in 1852, and concentrated the greater part of their artillery and about ten thousand troops on the southern section of the defences. Godwin, however, completely upset this scheme of defence by declining to attack where he was so obviously expected.

Early on the 12th of April the right column—composed of the XVIIIth, 51st, the 40th Bengal Native Infantry, two guns of the Madras Artillery, and a detachment of the Madras Sappers and Miners—landed, with a day's cooked rations and sixty rounds of ammunition on their persons; by 7 A.M. they were advancing on an outwork, known as the "White House stockade," which obstructed their path through the jungle. The field-guns, escorted by the grenadier and Light companies of the XVIIIth, shelled it till the 51st were ordered to the assault; the other companies of the regiment were following in support, when they were suddenly ordered to halt, and to crowd into the jungle to clear the track for the Madras Sappers and the parties of blue-jackets and European soldiers who carried the scaling ladders, then urgently required at the front. Some of the Royal Irish had been detailed for this duty, which proved a dangerous one, as out of the four men of the regiment told off to the first ladder three were wounded. This delay threw the Royal Irish "out of the hunt," and by the time they reached the stockade the 51st had stormed and occupied it. At this point General Godwin was forced to call a halt: five of the senior officers had been struck down by solar apoplexy, two of them fatally; many of the men lay on the ground senseless from sunstroke; all ranks were worn out by the overpowering heat, and he was forced to bivouac on the ground he had gained. From papers left by Colonel, then Lieutenant, C. Woodwright, XVIIIth, it appears that during the afternoon, while the Royal Irish were slaking their thirst at wells discovered in the jungle, a number of Burmese stalked the covering parties, surprised them by a heavy fire, and occupied a pagoda, from which they directed an annoying fusilade on the watering-place. While other portions of the regiment drove back the enemy's skirmishers, Woodwright's company was ordered to seize the pagoda: this was accomplished successfully, though with the loss of Colour-Sergeant Kelly and several men seriously wounded. Twice in the night the Burmese attempted to rush the bivouac of the Royal Irish, but were driven back by a few rounds of canister from light field-guns.

For more than forty hours General Godwin was unable to advance. His commissariat officers were very slow in issuing rations to replace the one-day's supply carried by the troops; the gunners were equally slow in landing and transporting to the front the four 8-in. howitzers, on which he relied to make a breach in the defences of Rangoon; and it was not until 5 A.M. on the 14th that the column was again in motion. The XVIIIth and the 40th Bengal Native Infantry led, followed by the 51st and the 35th Madras Native Infantry; the 80th were in charge of the guns, and a Madras Native Infantry regiment kept up communication with the ships in the river. Working slowly through jungle so thick that paths had to be cut for the passage of the guns, Godwin avoided the enemy's main stockades; but as his leading troops came within sight of the great pagoda, the guns on its terraces opened fire. Opposite the gate in the eastern wall, by which he proposed to force his way into Rangoon, the ground was so difficult that there was barely room for the XVIIIth and the 80th to form up in quarter columns, while they halted till the guns had made a practicable breach. The Burmese artillery played upon the easy target offered to them, and their skirmishers became so bold that five hundred muskets were required to keep them at a respectful distance from the main body of the infantry. The situation was becoming impossible when it was discovered that the gate had been opened, presumably to afford a safe retreat to the Burmese soldiers who were harassing our flanks. Godwin determined to assault forthwith, and placed Lieutenant-Colonel Coote in command of a storming party, composed of two companies of the Royal Irish, the wing of the 80th, and part of the 40th B.N.I. Under a galling fire, the column moved with great steadiness across a shallow valley, half a mile in width, and swept like a tidal wave over terrace after terrace until the Shwe Dagon was won. Then the Burmese broke and fled in panic, losing heavily in their retreat, especially at a point where part of the grenadier company of the Royal Irish fell upon them in flank with the bayonet, and in a short time Rangoon was in our hands. In the British land forces the casualties between the 11th and the 14th of April were a hundred and forty-five—two officers were killed and fourteen wounded; fifteen of the other ranks were killed, and a hundred and fourteen wounded. Nearly a third of these losses fell upon the Royal Irish: Lieutenant and Adjutant R. Doran, pierced by four bullets, fell mortally wounded at the foot of the pagoda;[1] Lieutenant-Colonel Coote, Captain W. T. Bruce, and Lieutenant G. A. Elliot were wounded; a sergeant and two privates were killed, a sergeant, a drummer, and thirty-seven privates wounded.[2] In his despatch General Godwin mentions four officers of the Royal Irish—Lieutenant-Colonel Reignolds, who was in temporary command of a brigade, Lieutenant-Colonel Coote, Captain G. F. S. Call (Brigade Major), and Captain J. J. Wood, who brought the regiment out of action.

For the next few months the XVIIIth lay sweltering at Rangoon, where General Godwin was obliged to await the arrival of reinforcements before undertaking further operations on a large scale. During this period of enforced inaction life was by no means agreeable: the heat was intense, the labour of hut-building severe, the duties heavy, and there was much sickness among the troops. Two small expeditions pushed out north and west—the first occupied the town of Pegu; the second captured the city of Bassein, important as commanding one of the three navigable mouths of the Irrawaddy. In neither of these enterprises did the Royal Irish play any part. Their only "outing" at this time seems to have been a two-days' hunt after a Burmese official whom the General was anxious to take prisoner. After hard marching they had their quarry almost within their grasp, when he disappeared into the jungle, leaving in their hands a string of carts laden with his numerous wives. In August it became known that the King of Ava, by no means disheartened by the loss of Rangoon and the other towns we had wrested from him, was gathering large forces near Prome, two hundred miles up the Irrawaddy. After a flotilla of gunboats had destroyed the stockades on the banks of the river near that town, Godwin determined to occupy it, to serve as an advanced base in the movement

---

[1] He was succeeded in the Adjutancy by Lieutenant E. W. Sargent.

[2] See Appendix 2 (H).

upon Ava, which he awaited the permission of Government to begin. When the long-expected reinforcements began to arrive, the Royal Irish found themselves in a division commanded by Sir John Cheape. The first brigade was under Lieutenant-Colonel Reignolds, and consisted of the XVIIIth, and the 40th and 67th Native Infantry regiments. Two officers of the Royal Irish were on the staff: Captain G. F. S. Call was Brigade Major to Reignolds' brigade, Captain W. T. Bruce was Assistant Adjutant-General to the first division. This organisation, however, appears to have been merely one on paper, for in September Godwin announced to the troops that he was about to resume active operations, and warned the XVIIIth, the 80th, and the 35th Madras Native Infantry to hold themselves in readiness to embark under command of Brigadier-General Reignolds. These regiments, with some Artillery and Sappers and Miners, disembarked with slight opposition at Prome on the 9th of October, and on marching a short way inland found that the Burmese had disappeared. In the landing there were a few casualties, none of them among the Royal Irish; but that night the young soldiers of the regiment had a stern lesson in outpost duty—one of their comrades, who allowed himself to be surprised on sentry, was killed, and his head sent as a trophy to the King of Ava. While troops were being gradually passed up the river to Prome, the Burmese attacked our garrison in Pegu, and a considerable force had to be sent to the rescue, but the XVIIIth was not employed either in the relief of Pegu, or in the operations of a column sent to clear the jungles round Martaban.

For many months it continued to form part of the garrison of Prome, which was invested by the Burmese, who surrounded the place with stockades, thrown up in the jungle, a mile or two beyond our outposts. In November three companies helped to destroy one of these works, whose defenders had been active in intercepting supplies brought in by friendly natives. Later in the month two companies under Brevet-Major Edwards were sent on a much longer expedition; they formed the British contingent in a small column sent to rid the districts of Khangheim and Padaung of the enemy. Crossing to the right bank they worked up-stream, and at first met with little opposition, though they were "sniped at" by night. "On one occasion the watering-place was surrounded by a small party, and several sepoys who had gone there to fill their drinking-vessels were killed or wounded. The column passed the spot where a few days before the Captain of a native regiment with a small body of his men was surprised by the Burmese, and the place where they were beheaded was still plainly discernible by the blood-stains on the stones. The heads of the Captain and two men had been sent to Ava; their bodies were left on the banks of the river till buried by the English."[1] The senior officer of the

---

[1] General Edwards' statement.

column broke down in health; Edwards succeeded to the command; and from the Digest of Service it appears that after several successful skirmishes he drove the Burmese into a place called Tomah, where he hemmed them in until March, 1853, when reinforcements of all arms enabled him to storm their stockade, and capture their guns, stores, and bullock-carts. During a lull in these operations Major Edwards was sent on a difficult, but interesting piece of work—to lead a small column to the top of the Tonghoo pass over the Yo-Ma range of mountains between Burma and Aracan, and there take charge of a hundred and forty-eight elephants, sent from India by the Governor-General to reinforce the transport of the army. Edwards' command was composed of a hundred of the XVIIIth under Major Borrow, the same number of the 80th, two hundred Sikhs, and a few Madras Sappers and Miners, with three thousand coolies to carry the supplies and drive the slaughter cattle. All went well till the column began to ascend the foothills of the main range, when the coolies, frightened at the steep, jungle-covered slopes, flung down their loads and deserted in a body. As the European troops could carry but a portion of the stores, they soon ran out of tea, biscuit, and spirits, and had to fall back upon beef-on-the-hoof, and for many days had nothing to eat but meat; to the Sikhs, whose religion debared them from animal food, a small quantity of grain was supplied. A day or two after this breakdown of the transport the guides confessed that they had lost their way, so Edwards decided to work upwards, along the course of the streams that furrowed the mountain-side. Slowly but sturdily the troops breasted the hills; by day they hacked paths through the jungle; by night they slept in clothing soaked in many fords and torrents. Yet such was the stamina of the Europeans that during the expedition not one fell ill, and they outmarched the Sikhs, who broke down and had to be left behind. After nineteen days of this tremendous strain Edwards reached the rendezvous; the elephants had not yet come up, but a large supply of rice had already arrived, and his troops, eager for vegetable food, pounced on it with delight. In a few days the elephants lumbered up the pass, loaded with commissariat stores of every kind, on which the men feasted, while the animals rested after their climb. Then the long column of men and beasts crashed downwards through the forest and reached Padaung, on the Irrawaddy, in less than a quarter of the time occupied in the upward march. Official thanks were given to all ranks when the convoy of elephants was handed over to the transport department, and a month's extra batta was granted to those who had taken part in the expedition.

The account of the doings of the XVIIIth at the front must now be broken by Lord Wolseley's description of his first meeting with the regiment of which he is now the honoured Colonel-in-Chief. As a callow subaltern in the 80th, quite new to the practical side of war, he found himself at Rangoon in charge of a piquet, composed in part of very young soldiers of the XVIIIth, who had been left at the base under command of Brevet-Lieutenant-Colonel Grattan. These youngsters were not yet disciplined; they had been greatly amused at the young officer's attempts to march his detachment to its post, and three of them, carried away by their high spirits, took liberties and refused to number off in the way he ordered. Wolseley promptly made prisoners of the culprits, and next morning

"had to appear at the Orderly Room of the Royal Irish detachment. It was a little room in a small teak-built hut, and there Colonel Grattan, C.B., of that historic regiment, daily dispensed justice to his young recruits. He was an old and amusing Irishman, full of quaint stories, and a very pleasant companion. Taken prisoner in the China War, he had been carried about in a cage as a show for the amusement of millions who had never before seen a European. His smiling face and grotesque grimaces always obtained for him a favourable reception. He greeted me pleasantly when I entered the orderly room, where—I may explain for Civilian readers—the Commanding Officer of every regiment and battalion in the Army holds a daily court to administer justice all round. Three prisoners from Tipperary were marched in bare-headed, and were drawn up facing the Colonel, who sat, pen in hand, behind a little table which separated them from him. A Corporal and a file of the guard, with drawn bayonets, stood beside the culprits, an acting Sergeant-Major, standing as all the others were, at "Attention," made up the stage. A solemn silence that somewhat awed me pervaded the scene, and my shyness became greater when the funny-looking colonel addressing me, asked me sternly what complaint I had to make against the prisoners. I told my story as best I could, being extremely impressed by what I believed to be the gravity of the offence. My military reading and study of the Mutiny Act and Articles of War had led me to believe that, next to striking an officer or running away in battle, these prisoners had committed the most heinous offence in absolutely refusing to obey a lawful command when on outpost duty before the enemy. I expected they would be at once sent to trial before a general court martial, and either sentenced to death, or if their lives were spared in consideration of their youth and entire ignorance of a soldier's duty, they would at least be transported.

"When I had finished my awful indictment, the Colonel with his funny little grey eyes, frowned from under his long grey eyebrows, first at me and then in sternness at the boy prisoners before him. There was an awful pause; you could have heard a pin drop if any one there had had such an evidence of civilization ready for the occasion. I held my breath, not knowing what was coming. I looked at the Sergeant-Major; his face was wooden and devoid of all expression as he stolidly looked straight before him into nothing. In a moment a volley of oaths from the Colonel removed the atmospheric pressure. He called the prisoners 'limbs of Satan,' and choking, partly at least I should say because his vituperative vocabulary had come to an end, he jumped to his feet, upsetting the table, with its ink bottle, papers, etc., and rushed upon the prisoners, kicking hard at the nearest, and crying aloud: 'Get out, ye blackguards; never let me see you again.' Whether it was that the prisoners were accustomed to this mode of justice and, being frightened, were anxious to avoid the toes of their Colonel's boots as he lashed out at them or not, they turned round and ran for their lives, the Sergeant-Major after them, with their caps, which he had been holding—according to regulation—whilst this strangely scenic trial was being enacted.

"I was in dismay, and for a moment thought of running too, but seeing the old Colonel burst out laughing, I tried to smile, but it was an unhealthy attempt at hilarity on my part. However, being assured the men would never forget the scene or misbehave again, I went away feeling rather that I had been the culprit, and had only escaped condign punishment through consideration of my youth and complete ignorance of all military customs and laws. I don't know whether these three boys from Tipperary retained a lasting remembrance—as I did—of the curious mode of administering justice, but I am sure their Colonel's conduct was far more in consonance with their views of propriety, and far better suited to the case, than any sentence of imprisonment and trial by court martial would have been. I laugh now as I think of the whole scene, and as I do so, I feel all the more how necessary it is that Irish soldiers should have Irish officers over them, who understand their curiously Eastern character, and who are consequently better able to deal with them than strangers can."[1]

Until the middle of February, 1853, the headquarter companies at Prome had a weary time. Sickness was rampant; in a letter written at the end of November, 1852, an officer of the XVIIIth mentions that the regiment could only turn out 350 men fit to take the field. Ninety men had been buried at Rangoon, where cholera broke out a few hours after the capture of the great Pagoda; for a month the Royal Irish had been dying at the rate of almost one a day; 137 were in hospital; large numbers had broken down and been invalided out of the country. The other regiments were equally unhealthy, and out of the whole garrison of Prome the General could only count on some 900 effectives, whose numbers were daily reduced by the ravages of climate and by the strain of the guards and piquets, which, though cut down as low as safety permitted, told severely upon the troops who remained at duty. The only break in this harassing and monotonous existence was afforded by occasional reconnaissances and night attacks, in which the enemy showed themselves more anxious to murder and decapitate individual men than to close with any formed body of soldiers. Suddenly four companies of the Royal Irish were warned for an expedition to clear the line of communication, which was harassed by Myat Toon, a robber chieftain, who from his lair near Donobyu attacked

[1] Field-Marshal Viscount Wolseley's 'Story of a Soldier's Life,' vol. i. pp. 33-35. See a letter from General C. G. Gordon on the same subject, p. 185.

the native boats in our employ on their way up the Irrawaddy with provisions for the front. The village of Donobyu was about fifty miles above Rangoon; it was connected with the Irrawaddy by a network of creeks, and surrounded by dense jungle, almost impassable from deep nullahs full of water, which cut up the ground in every direction. In this jungle Myat Toon had fortified many positions, formidable in themselves, and most difficult of access to Europeans. The sailors had made several spirited attempts to penetrate into this labyrinth, but their boats were unable to pass the barricades of logs and forest trees with which the waterways had been obstructed; and a combined force of bluejackets and soldiers, acting on land under a post-captain in the navy, was surprised and defeated with the loss of two guns. The army was now to take in hand the punishment of the seven or eight thousand guerillas who followed the fortunes of Myat Toon, and General Godwin selected Sir John Cheape to lead the avenging force, composed of a small body of Irregular Native cavalry, detachments of Madras Sappers and Madras and Bengal Artillery with one 24-pr. howitzer and a 9-pr. field-gun, two hundred of the XVIIIth under Captain A. W. F. S. Armstrong,[1] two hundred of the 51st, two hundred Sikhs, and the 67th Bengal Native Infantry regiment. Major F. Wigston, XVIIIth, was in charge of the right wing of the column, with Lieutenant F. Eteson, XVIIIth, as his staff-officer. Descending the river to within thirty-five miles of Donobyu, Cheape disembarked at Henzada, a village where a number of country bullock-carts awaited him. As he was led to believe that three or four days' march would bring him to Myat Toon's stockades, he decided to fill up his transport with seven or eight days' rations, dash on his enemy, defeat him, and then hasten back to the steamers. Leaving behind him the sick, who, though it was barely a week since he left Prome, were already numerous, he plunged into an unknown country, where his guides proved useless, his information defective and misleading. He could not find the main body of Myat Toon's men, though skirmishing dacoits hung on his flanks, and in four days he was obliged to fall back to the river for supplies. He now transferred his base to Donobyu, which was known to have been evacuated by the enemy, and sending his empty carts there by land under escort of a party of the XVIIIth, he re-embarked with the remainder of his troops for Donobyu, where he remained till the 7th of March, when the native regiment joined him, and with it a draft of recruits for the 80th and a large supply of commissariat stores. After providing for the safety of his base and of another batch of sick men, General Cheape started on his second hunt for Myat Toon, whose entrenchments he was again assured could be reached in three days. Now began

---

[1] According to Colonel Elliot's diary the actual number of Royal Irish who embarked at Prome was nine officers and one hundred and sixty-seven non-commissioned officers and men.

a campaign, short in duration, but harassing beyond measure to the troops engaged in it. The soldiers had to feel their way along narrow paths, often obstructed by trees cut down across the track by foes, who rarely showed themselves by day, though they disturbed the bivouac by sniping shots at night. To bridge the nullahs took much time and labour; the burden of guarding the transport carts was heavy; the heat was steamy, exhausting, and depressing; fog hung over the face of the land until several hours after sunrise; the water was tainted, and cholera broke out among the men. Then rations began to run short, and the column was obliged to halt four days in this pestilential forest while a convoy brought up fresh supplies from Donobyu. After forming an advance base for his spare stores and the sick and wounded, Cheape once more pushed forward, and on the 17th the right wing came upon traces of the enemy, who had blocked the track with a series of abattis and recently felled trees. The Royal Irish were leading, for Wigston, remembering that it was St Patrick's Day and anxious to do honour to the occasion, had detailed them as advance-guard to give them every chance of a fight, if the Burmese would so far oblige them. After they had turned these obstacles, or cut their way through them, they ran against a stockade held by Myat Toon's followers, and with a wild yell dashed at the work, which with the help of the Sikhs they carried "most gallantly" at the point of the bayonet.[1] The defenders did not wait for the cold steel, but after firing up to the last moment bolted into the jungle. One man, however, lingered too long over his parting shot, and was pursued by two subalterns, Hewitt and Eteson, who gave chase down the bed of a dry watercourse. Hewitt slipped and fell; Eteson succeeded in running his quarry down, and was rewarded by obtaining from his prisoner much useful information about the enemy's main position. In this little affair Lieutenant Woodwright and five rank and file were wounded. Next day there was sharp skirmishing before the approach of darkness forced Cheape to halt on a narrow path, leading towards the village reported to be the headquarters of Myat Toon. Very soon after the piquets had been posted and the bivouac formed, the fog fell so heavily as to render reconnaissance very difficult, but when the outposts reported that the enemy was busy felling trees and completing the defences of his position, Lieutenant Eteson, three officers of the Sikhs, and three Sepoys stole forward, ascertained where the enemy was at work, and then returning to the General, described the place with sufficient accuracy to enable the gunners to fire rockets at it with some effect.

At the first glimmer of dawn on the 19th of March, our scouts began to grope their way down a wet nullah close to the bivouac, and followed it to its junction with a large creek, where the sound of voices warned them that the

---

[1] Sir John Cheape's despatch.

Burmese were at hand. Creeping from tree to tree, the reconnoitrers reached the edge of the creek, and peering through the gloom dimly discerned Myat Toon's works on the farther bank. The position was a strong one: the creek served as a moat to a line of cleverly built breastworks, well loopholed, and protected by abattis; the left rested on an impassable swamp; the right ended in a dense thicket. As far as the scouts could see, the enemy's front was about a quarter of a mile long; but its prolongations into the jungle really gave it a length of twelve hundred yards. Cheape would gladly have turned the enemy's right by a flank march; but to do so he would have had to cut a road through thick jungle, and the condition of the troops precluded his imposing so heavy a task upon them, for though their spirit was high, their bodies were enfeebled by the effect of scanty food and bad water, while their numbers had been much reduced by the ravages of dysentery and cholera. There was nothing for it but a frontal attack; slowly and in silence he moved towards the creek, and then under cover of the fog marched along its bank within a hundred yards of the Burmese stockades. For a time this processional movement was not discovered, for Myat Toon, convinced that the British would not leave their bivouac till the sun had dispelled the fog, had taken no precautions against surprise; then suddenly a rolling fire burst from the whole face of the works; to meet it, the Sikhs were extended along our bank of the nullah, while the remainder of the troops fell back into the jungle to form for battle. Thus began an engagement as confused as the ground on which it was fought. At first a musketry duel raged across the creek; then scouting parties, or, as we should now call them, battle patrols, ascertained that opposite the enemy's right of the line of stockades the creek ran dry, and was crossed by a track, which proved to have been prepared for defence: large forest trees had been felled across it; it was swept with grape from the two guns captured from the navy, flanked by a detached work, and pitted with *trous-de-loup*. A storming party was hastily organised; and the detachment of the 80th attempted to force its way across to the other side of the creek, but being inadequately supported, failed in its object. Then the Royal Irish and the Sikhs tried to push through the dense belt of jungle on the right of the Burmese line, but could not pass the abattis and detached breastworks hidden in its thickets. Finally, the General decided that at all costs the track must be won and the stockades near it carried at the point of the bayonet. The troops, as may well be imagined, were by this time greatly scattered, and while the buglers were rallying the infantry, the Bengal artillerymen, with the help of stragglers from the British detachments, dragged their 24-pr. howitzer into action only twenty-five yards from the enemy, and covered the concentration of the foot soldiers by a destructive storm of canister. In this episode Private —— Connors, Royal Irish, greatly distinguished himself. Early in the fight a Burmese bullet had broken his left arm; he made his way to the doctor, had the broken limb temporarily bound up, and then under heavy fire helped to run the howitzer up to the front, tugging at the spokes of a wheel with his right arm. At length a number of men from the XVIIIth, 51st, and 80th were collected, and, guided by Ensign Wolseley, charged down the track yelling at their enemies, who manned the parapets and shouted defiantly, " Come on, Come on ! " to them in Burmese. This is not the place to describe how Wolseley led his mixed command, nor how he was struck down, hard hit, at the moment of victory; his personal adventures in this charge, the second he led during the engagement, are narrated in the first volume of his Autobiography. It is enough to say that the troops advanced with determination, swept over the works, and killed and wounded large numbers of the four thousand men opposed to them. Those of the Royal Irish who took part in the final rush were well to the front : Lieutenant W. F. Cockburn fell desperately wounded as he scaled a stockade; Lieutenant Eteson was one of the first into the main work; and a party, led by Lieutenant Woodwright, recaptured the two naval guns, and marked the number of the regiment upon them with a rusty nail.

Cheape's success would have been complete if he had been able to secure Myat Toon; but the Chief escaped with his life, though with little else, for he was compelled to abandon all his supplies and munitions of war. To follow him farther into the jungle was impossible, for the health of the column was so bad that the General was obliged to return to Donobyu, and thence to Prome where his steamers anchored on April 2. The operations against Myat Toon had been costly; the losses in action were one hundred and thirty, while cholera alone caused more than a hundred deaths. Most of the casualties occurred on the 19th of March, when eleven men were killed and eighty-four officers and men wounded. In the Royal Irish regiment Lieutenant W. F. Cockburn died of his injuries; Major F. Wigston was severely wounded; a corporal and eight men were killed; a sergeant and twenty-six men wounded; three colour-sergeants and eleven men died of cholera;[1] and the health of the whole detachment was so much affected that on landing at Prome only twenty-two officers and men remained fit for duty. Major F. Wigston, Captain A. W. F. S. Armstrong, and Captain W. T. Bruce were mentioned in despatches.

The regiment was not again in action during the Burmese war, as negotiations for peace put a stop to all further operations in the field. The province of Pegu was annexed to England, and as soon as the new territory settled down, the XVIIIth was ordered to Calcutta, arrived there at the end of November 1853, and a few weeks later embarked for home.

In recognition of their services Majors F. Wigston and C. A. Edwards were awarded brevet-lieutenant-colonelcies, and Captains A. N. Campbell and

[1] Appendix 2 (H).

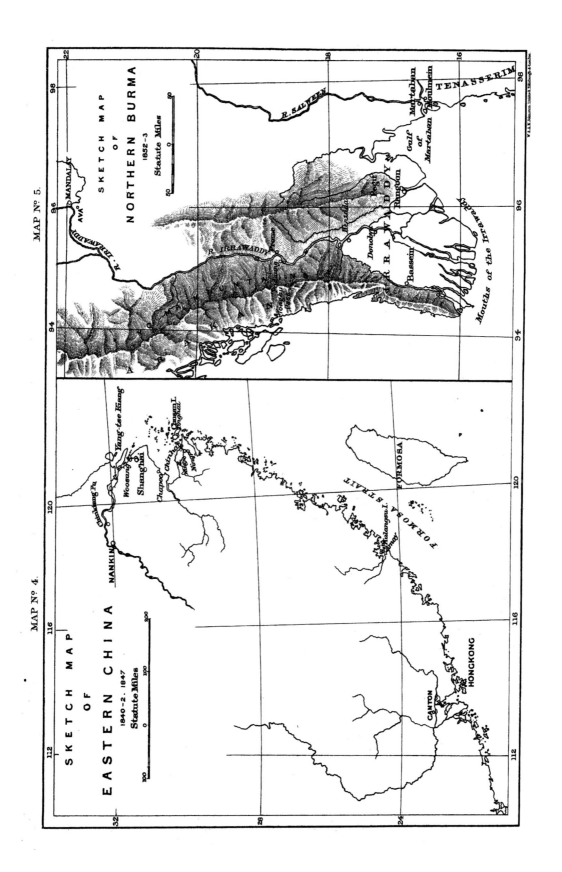

MAP Nº 5.

SKETCH MAP
OF
NORTHERN BURMA
1852-3
Statute Miles
50   0   50

MAP Nº 4.

SKETCH MAP
OF
EASTERN CHINA
1840-2. 1847
Statute Miles
100   0   100   200   300

W. T. Bruce brevet majorities. A medal and clasp was issued to all ranks, and the word "Pegu" was added to the battle honours of the regiment. The losses of the Royal Irish in this campaign were enormous. When they returned to India their roll had been reduced by three hundred and sixty-five officers and men, of whom but few had been killed in action or died of wounds; the remainder had fallen victims to the diseases which rendered the swamps and jungles of Burma fatal to Europeans.[1] The names of the officers who perished in Burma are recorded on the memorial at St Patrick's Cathedral.

[1] See Appendix 2 (H).

L

CHAPTER VII.

1854-1856.

THE WAR IN THE CRIMEA.

WHEN the Royal Irish reached England in June, 1854, after a six months' voyage from Calcutta, they were greeted by the news that for the first time since Waterloo Britain had become embroiled in a European war, and in alliance with France had sent troops to protect Turkey against the Russians, who had invaded the part of the Sultan's dominions then known as the Danubian principalities. The Czar had long cast covetous eyes on Turkey, whose European provinces on the Ægean and the Sea of Marmora prevented the expansion of Russia towards the Mediterranean, and thus limited her seaboard to the Baltic and the Black Sea. In the middle of the nineteenth century Turkey appeared to be so decadent a country that its ruler was commonly described as "the sick man"; the Czar actually threw out suggestions to England that she should divide with him "the sick man's heritage," and on her indignant refusal he determined to bide his time and pick a quarrel with the Sultan on the first opportunity. A pretext soon presented itself in a dispute between the Greek and Latin branches of the Christian faith concerning their respective rights in the Holy Places of Jerusalem: the Czar hotly espoused the cause of the Greek Church, while the Emperor Napoleon III., reviving the historic claim of France to represent the Latin Church in Palestine, vigorously supported the views of the Roman Catholics. The Sultan, profoundly indifferent to the rivalries of those whom his religion taught him to regard as infidel dogs, attempted to propitiate both sides, but with such conspicuous ill-success that the Czar declared war against him in October, 1853, and invaded the Turkish provinces on the Danube. To defend Turkey against this wanton and unprovoked attack, England and France in the spring of 1854 landed a considerable number of troops at Varna, a Bulgarian port on the Black Sea. It was from no love of the Turks that England thus plunged into war with Russia: she took up arms in pursuance of the foreign policy which for centuries she has followed on the Continent, and sided with the weaker state—not on altruistic grounds but solely to preserve the balance of power in Europe, and to prevent the Czar from possessing himself of Constantinople, and thus obtaining direct access to the Mediterranean Sea.

The Anglo-French troops were still at Varna when, in the interests of peace, Austria brought such pressure upon the Czar that he recalled his armies from Turkish soil. But though the immediate danger to Constantinople was averted by this intervention, the governments of England and France agreed that there would be no safety for Turkey, and therefore no tranquillity in European politics, until the Russian fleet in the Black Sea had been captured or destroyed, and its base at Sebastopol levelled to the ground. When the demolition of this great naval station was thus determined on, the allies knew little of Sebastopol,[1] except that it was a fortress in the south of the Crimea, a peninsula jutting into the Black Sea from the mainland of Russia: and no soldier in western Europe had any conception of the difficulties awaiting the Anglo-French Expedition when it put to sea from Varna on September 7, 1854. Exclusive of the crews of the great fleet of warships by which the transports were escorted, the fighting men numbered about 63,000, of whom 28,000 were French, 7000 Turks, and 28,000 British. The French were under Marshal St Arnaud; Lord Raglan, who had served on Wellington's staff in the Peninsular war, commanded the British troops. Neither of these officers lived to see the end of the campaign: St Arnaud died in September, 1854, and was succeeded by General Canrobert who, after a few months, resigned his post to General Pelissier: Lord Raglan fell a victim to cholera at the end of June, 1855, and was replaced by General Simpson. The Turks were commanded by Omar Pasha.

The effort to collect and equip for war the comparatively small body of men forming the British quota of the combined forces had greatly taxed the military resources of England. After the fall of the great Napoleon had restored peace to Europe, enormous reductions had been made in our military expenditure;[2] not only was the *personnel* of the army cut down, but the *matériel* was allowed to fall into decay. For more than thirty years every arm and every department of the service was systematically starved, with results well summed up by Lord Palmerston, who in 1846 bluntly informed his colleagues in the Cabinet that our military weakness was such that England existed "only by sufferance and by the forbearance of other Powers." This opinion was endorsed by the highest authority in the British army, for Wellington himself acknowledged that our supply of guns, arms, ammunition, and all kinds of stores was inadequate. Nor were these grievous shortcomings atoned for by any high standard of efficiency amongst the troops, for though the drill and discipline of the army were alike excellent, neither the soldiers nor the departments vital to their existence in the field were

[1] See Map No. 6.   [2] See chapter v. p. 120.

trained in the slightest degree for active service; indeed, until 1853, when a few thousand men spent some weeks under canvas, no camp of exercise had been formed in England since the end of the Great War with France. Marksmanship was almost a lost art; and although the deadly volleys of the British infantry in the Peninsula had won for our troops the reputation of the best shots in Europe, musketry was so entirely neglected during the dead period after Waterloo, that the injunction " Fire low, and hit 'em in the legs, boys," was the only instruction given to recruits. Even in the Foot Guards the men were considered to be masters of their weapon if, once in every three years, they fired thirty rounds of ball cartridge. The military education of the officers was no better than that of the rank and file; there was no attempt to teach them anything beyond barrack-square drill; the vast majority grew up ignorant of every detail of their profession, and as the Staff College at Camberley was not then in existence, the officers selected for employment on the staff proved in the majority of cases to be blind leaders of the blind. The few veterans of the Peninsula who were still to be found among the Generals had seen war on a grand scale; the officers who had served in eastern and colonial campaigns had acquired much useful knowledge in these distant operations, but with these exceptions the Staff and regimental officers were as untrained in the practice, as they were unversed in the theory of war.

When the Royal Irish reached England they were quartered at Chatham and Canterbury. At first there seemed no likelihood of their being actively employed, for when the regiment had left India many men had volunteered into other corps, and the climate of Burma had told so heavily on those who still remained with the Colours that a large number of them were unfit for active service. Fortune, however, befriended the XVIIIth; in October the flank companies under Brevet-Lieutenant-Colonel Edwards were ordered to Windsor, to strengthen the militia battalion which had replaced the regiment of Foot Guards at the Royal Castle. Her Majesty, Queen Victoria was much impressed by the bronzed and soldierly appearance of the detachment, and learning from Colonel Edwards that the regiment was most anxious to serve in the war, she was pleased to direct that the XVIIIth should proceed forthwith to the Crimea, where reinforcements were urgently required. As the result of the medical examination proved that less than four hundred men were fit for the campaign, volunteers were invited from other regiments: four hundred joined from the 94th, a hundred and fifty from the 51st, and smaller contingents from other corps. On December 8, 1854, the regiment, eight hundred and forty-eight strong,[1] embarked at Portsmouth in the s.s. *Magdalene*,

---

[1] The officers were—
  Colonel—T. S. Reignolds, C.B. (in command).
  Major and Brevet-Lieutenant-Colonel—C. A. Edwards.

and reached the Crimea at the end of the year, about three months and a half after the Allies had made good their footing on Russian soil.

To enable the reader to understand the condition of the British Expeditionary Force when the *Magdalene* steamed into the harbour of Balaclava, it is necessary to give a very short account of the main events of the war up to the end of 1854. Between the 14th and 18th of September the Allies[1] were engaged in landing at Kalamita Bay, about thirty miles north of Sebastopol; two days after their disembarkation was completed they forced the passage of the river Alma, defeating the Russians so completely that they were allowed to march southward without molestation, and to form bases on the coast within a few miles of Sebastopol, the British establishing themselves at Balaclava, a little port eight miles to the south, the French at Kamiesch Bay, six miles to the south-west of the fortress. The Russian stronghold lies on the shores of a harbour, in shape not unlike a T: the top of the letter is represented by an arm of the sea running eastward from the Euxine for about four miles, and varying in width from a thousand to twelve hundred yards, while the leg is formed by a narrow creek which from the south runs into the main inlet, about two miles from the entrance to the open sea. On these deep and sheltered waters the whole of the Russian fleet could ride in safety, protected by a ring of forts from attack by land or sea, and the labours of successive generations of engineers had converted the western shore of the creek, or inner harbour, into a vast arsenal and dockyard, round which a thriving and populous city had sprung up. The Generals of the

Majors—J. C. Kennedy and G. F. S. Call.
Captains—J. Cormick, M. J. Hayman, A. W. S. F. Armstrong, J. Laurie, R. Inglis, H. F. Stephenson, C. F. Kelly, and J. Swinburn.
Lieutenants—J. G. Wilkinson (adjutant), T. E. Esmonde, G. W. Stackpole, W. O'B. Taylor, R. H. Jex-Blake, J. R. Blacker, E. H. Wilton, W. J. Hales, and A. T. Frederick.
Ensigns—J. T. Ring, J. R. Wolseley, C. J. Coote, T. D. Baker, W. Kemp, F. Fearnley, A. L. Dillon, and C. Hotham.
Quartermaster—M. T. Carney.
Surgeon—W. K. Chalmers, M.D.
Assistant-Surgeons—T. Crawford, —— Ryatt, —— Phillip.
Between January and September 1855 the following joined the regiment in the trenches before Sebastopol :—
Captains—H. A. Ward and G. A. Elliot.
Lieutenants—G. H. Pocklington, J. W. Meurant, J. S. Theobald, R. J. Adamson, A. Cottee, and M. T. Cunningham.
Ensigns—C. N. Fry and H. Shaw.
Joined after September 1855—
Major—A. N. Campbell.
Captains—E. W. Sargent, J. Borrow, and A. H. Graves.
Lieutenants—J. F. Bryant, R. W. E. Dawson, T. M'G. M'Gill, C. G. D. Annesley, E. Wilford, S. Darvell, E. D. Ricard, W. B. Burke, R. Bell, and H. Hutchins.
[1] The allied forces at this time consisted of the English, French, and Turkish troops; the Sardinian contingent of 18,000 men under General La Marmora did not reach the Crimea till May, 1855.

Anglo-French forces soon ascertained by reconnaissance that they had not nearly men enough to invest the whole perimeter of the fortress, and at the same time to repel the attacks to be expected from the enemy's field troops. All they could hope to accomplish was to pour upon one portion of the defences a fire so heavy as to become insupportable ; and as the real power of the defence was obviously concentrated in the arsenals, stores, and barracks round the inner harbour, the Allies selected the southern works, those protecting the heart of the fortress, as the object of their first attack, and took up positions on the plateau between Balaclava and Sebastopol. Bounded on the north by the harbour, on the west and south by the sea, and on the east by the valley of the Tchernaya, the surface of this plateau, or "Upland" as the British termed it, was seamed by ravines which, beginning as mere depressions in the ground, grew deeper as they approached the fortress, finally becoming precipitous gorges, difficult for troops to cross. Close to the harbour the ground between these gorges rose into gentle elevations, crowned by works which, as soon as the Russians realised that the southern side of the fortress was threatened, were heavily armed and greatly strengthened. The largest of these ravines, dividing the plain from south to north, descended to the head of the inner harbour, and served as the boundary between the British on the right, and the French on the left of the besiegers' line.

Owing to the inability of the Allies to invest the fortress completely, communication continued uninterrupted between the northern part of Sebastopol and the interior of the Crimea ; early in October the civilian population quitted the town, and thus relieved the troops of the burden of feeding thousands of useless non-combatants. The forethought of the Russians had collected in the magazines of Sebastopol enormous supplies of guns, ammunition, and warlike stores ; the commissariat was well provided ; the garrison consisted of 38,000 men—soldiers, military workmen already partially trained to arms, and sailors from the men-of-war which, at the approach of the Allies, had been sunk to block the mouth of the outer harbour. Among the regular troops was an officer in himself worth an army—Todleben, an engineer who had already made his mark in the fighting on the Danube. When it became known that the Allies were sailing for the Crimea he was sent to Sebastopol, where he became the mainspring of the defence. His courage and genius, his versatility and resource, his boundless energy, his power of inspiring enthusiasm and devotion among his men won for him the deepest respect of his enemies, and the fervent admiration of his fellow countrymen, who with good reason claim for him a high place among great military engineers. He soon had an opportunity of displaying his talents. In the middle of October the Allies opened fire upon the fortress, and at the close of the bombardment had reason to be satisfied with the result, for the works were reduced to shapeless heaps, the batteries ruined, the guns disabled. But next morning the assailants discovered that in Todleben they had to meet a master-mind: during the night he had rebuilt the parapets, repaired the batteries, and replaced the damaged guns from the almost boundless supply of cannon at his command. On the 25th, the Russian Field army, which after its defeat at the Alma had retired into the interior of the Crimea to await reinforcements, made an unsuccessful attempt to break the line of communication between the British camps on the Upland and Balaclava. A few days later the Allies determined to assault the fortress, but their project was discovered by the enemy. At dawn on the 4th of November, the garrison and the field army together attacked the British right; and though after a desperate battle, to which the name of Inkerman has been given, the victory remained to the Allies, it was dearly bought: the British casualties were 597 killed and 1760 wounded, while those of the French were 143 killed and 786 wounded. The Russians on their side lost more than 12,000 men, of whom a very large proportion were left dead upon the field.

So far our army had not fared badly in the campaign: the hardships had not been greater than were to be expected on active service, and reinforcements had filled the gaps caused by casualties and disease. Cholera, indeed, hung about the camp, and the men were undoubtedly overworked, for when the Anglo-French generals drew up their plans for the siege, the share in the operations which Lord Raglan undertook was greater than his troops could accomplish without undue fatigue. But despite sickness and overstrain the health of the army was fairly good, and when, a few days after Inkerman, it was officially announced that the Allies would spend the winter in the Crimea, men looked forward to the prospect without great apprehension, for the weather was fine, and the Indian summer, bright, mild, and dry, gave no hint of the rigours of the coming winter. Suddenly a terrific storm of rain and wind burst upon the Crimea, levelled whole camps and blew the tents, and all that the tents contained, far and wide over the Upland; the supplies of food and forage at the front were destroyed, and communication with Balaclava was temporarily cut off by the force of the hurricane. Had the fleet of store-ships then at anchor at Balaclava, or lying off the port, escaped destruction, the damage, in great measure at least, could have been repaired; but twenty-one vessels were dashed to pieces, and eight more disabled. The ships that went to the bottom contained forage, ammunition, war-like stores of every kind, drugs and surgical appliances, warm flannel shirts and drawers, woollen stockings, boots and watch-coats—everything that the army most urgently required. When fresh supplies arrived at Balaclava from England the means of conveying them to the Upland was utterly inadequate, for we had landed without a transport corps, depending for land carriage on such horses and vehicles as could be seized in the Crimea. The animals thus obtained died fast from want of forage, and in January, 1855, the Commissariat department could only muster 333 horses and mules and 12 camels, while the divisional transport consisted of a few ponies, dying from starvation and overwork. Though horses in plenty were to be bought in the countries near the Crimea, and many transports were available to bring them to Balaclava, it was useless to import animals until forage arrived to feed them, and forage unhappily was an article of which the Treasury had neglected to make an adequate provision. Consequently upon the troops fell the whole labour of carrying on their shoulders from the port to the camps everything that was required, not only for their own support, but for the conduct of the siege. As was to be expected, the men broke down terribly fast; in November there were nearly 17,000 on the sick list; in December there were more than 19,000 ineffectives, and in January, 1855, no less than 23,076 men filled the hospitals. The horrors of this period of the war are well described by Field-Marshal Sir Evelyn Wood, who served on shore as a midshipman in one of the Naval brigades.

"In the early part of the winter the battalions at the front were generally on duty two nights out of three, and later, every alternate night. The life of the rank and file was thus spent :—The men were mustered carrying great-coat and blanket, just before dusk, and marched through a sea of mud into the trenches. These were cut up by deep holes from which boulders and stones had been taken, and into these holes on dark nights, the men often fell. When the soldier reached his position, he had to sit with his back to the parapet, and his feet drawn up close under his body to allow others to pass along the four-feet-wide trench. If he was not detailed for a working party, nor for piquet in the trenches or in advance of them, he might lie down, resting as best he could, in a wet ditch. Assuming that the soldier was not on piquet, and that there was no alarm—and these were of frequent occurrence—he could, after the working parties and their reliefs had ceased to move about the trenches, repose till daylight, when he marched back to camp, and after a few hours' rest had to carry a load of some kind.

"The comparative repose enjoyed by those men who were required only as a guard, or reserve in the trenches, was very different to the condition of those who were employed from 200 to 300 yards in advance of our works, often within conversational distance of the opposing sentries. The reliefs for the sentries could snatch a dog's sleep for four hours out of six, hoping their comrades would by remaining on the alert give them time to jump up ere the enemy was on them ; but for the two hours that each man was out near the enemy, the strain on the nervous system would have been great even to a robust, well-fed man. These sentries had necessarily to stand absolutely still, silent and watchful, and as the severity of the weather became more and more marked, numbers of men whose frames were weakened by want of adequate nutritious food, were found in the morning frost-bitten and unable to move. One battalion which landed nearly 900 strong early in November, was actually in the trenches six nights out of seven, and then became so reduced, not only in numbers,[1] but also in the men's bodily strength, that it was unable for some time to go there again.

"When the soldier got back to camp, he used to lie, often in a puddle, which chilled his bones, under a worn-out tent, through which the rain beat. The less robust would fall asleep, completely worn out, to awake shivering, and in many cases to be carried to a hospital tent scarcely more comfortable than the tent which they had left, and thence to a grave in two or three days. Those who were stronger, went out to collect roots of brushwood, or of vines, and roasted the green coffee ration in the lid of the canteen, afterwards pounding it in a fragment of shell with a stone, ere they boiled it for use. Others, unequal to this laborious process, would drink their rum, and eating a piece of biscuit, lie down again in the great-coat and blanket which they had brought, often wet through from the trenches.

"In the afternoon the soldier was sent on 'fatigue' duty from five to seven miles, according to the position of his camp, usually to Balaclava, to bring up rations. On his return he had again to gather fuel in order to boil the salt beef or salt pork in his mess tin, which did not hold water enough to abstract the salt. A portion of the meat therefore only was consumed, and it was necessary from time to time to tell off men to bury the quantities thrown away. Salt pork which was issued two days out of seven, was frequently eaten by the men in its raw state, from the difficulties of finding fuel to cook it.

"Shortly before dusk the soldier either marched back to the trenches, or lay down to sleep if he was not on piquet in front of the camp. Many men disliking to report themselves sick, were carried back from the trenches in the morning, and died a few hours afterwards. Those who were reported sick were taken to hospital, in many cases merely a bell tent; here the men lay, often in mud on the ground, and in many instances their diet was only salt meat and biscuit.[2] They were moreover so crowded together that the doctors could scarcely pass between the patients.

"The Regimental Medical officers unable to provide comforts, medicine or proper housing, were eager to send down their patients, even in storm and rain, to Balaclava, as the best chance of saving their lives. As we had no ambulances, and the French could not always lend us mule litter-transport, many were necessarily carried on cavalry horses, which slipping upon the hill outside Balaclava, often caused further injury or the death of the patient.

.   .   .   .

"The small schoolhouse at Balaclava, which we used as a hospital, held only between 300-400 men, thus the great majority of the sick and wounded were necessarily laid on the beach, exposed to all weathers, while awaiting their turn for embarcation in the transports. On the steamer running between Balaclava and the Bosphorus—a voyage of 36 to 48 hours—the soldier seldom got anything but tea and biscuit, sometimes

---

[1] In February, to 290 all ranks.

[2] Note by the author—This was no improvement on the Peninsula, where the patients suffering from typhus and dysentery were fed in the same way.

only water.   During this short but terribly trying passage, from 8 to 9 % succumbed and were thrown overboard.   Once on shore there was often a further painful wait on the beach before they were carried up to the hospital.

.   .   .   .

"We who saw the 'old soldier' die without a murmur may well be excused dilating on his virtues, when we endeavour to describe what he suffered for our country, the ministry of which, having given him a task far beyond his strength, failed to supply him with clothes and food.   It is impossible to overpraise the disciplined silence of men under privations, which in a few weeks reduced one battalion from nearly 1000 effectives to a strength of 30 rank and file." [1]

This misery was at its height when the Royal Irish disembarked at Balaclava on December 30, 1854; casualties, hardships, and disease had so thinned the British ranks that in January, 1855, to meet all requirements of the siege Lord Raglan had only 11,000 men at duty on the Upland, many of whom were only fit to be in hospital: one day, indeed, after providing fatigues to bring up the necessaries of life from Balaclava, he could only turn out two hundred and ninety officers and men to guard his trenches —about one-twentieth part of the garrisons of the forts opposite his works, against which at any moment the Russians might have directed a sortie.   The regiments upon which the war had told most heavily had almost ceased to exist: one battalion paraded for duty with a few officers, a sergeant, and seven rank and file.   With his army in such a condition, it was impossible for Lord Raglan to continue responsible for the whole of the ground allotted to him at the beginning of the siege, and the French, who had been very largely reinforced, and whose sufferings, though great, were in comparison with ours but insignificant, relieved him on the extreme right of his line.   The material result of this necessary but deplorable admission of weakness was to "sandwich" the British between two wings of the French army, while morally it reduced us to the position of a mere contingent in the forces of Napoleon III. By England's persistent neglect of all things military she had sown the storm, and her unhappy soldiers in the Crimea reaped the whirlwind; and it was not for many months, after thousands of lives had been wasted [2] and money spent like water, that her army was once more able to take its proper place in the forces of the alliance against Russia.

The Royal Irish were not at once sent up to the front, but for nearly a fortnight were employed on fatigues about the port.   Thanks to this delay they were able to see their baggage and camp equipage safe on shore, and thus, when ordered to the Upland, they began the campaign well prepared to

---

[1] 'The Crimea in 1854 and 1894,' by Field-Marshal Sir Evelyn Wood, pp. 204 *et seq.*

[2] Between November, 1854, and February, 1855, there were 9000 deaths in hospital : at the end of February there were no less than 13,600 officers and men in hospital : and though during that month large drafts raised our strength on paper to 44,000, only 18,000 were "present and fit for duty."

face the hardships that awaited them. In this respect they were far better off than the regiments which first landed in the Crimea. The original expedition had disembarked with hardly any vehicles; the men were so much enfeebled by the climate of Varna that they could not bear the weight of their knapsacks, which with the rest of the baggage were left on board the transports; and when these vessels ultimately reached Balaclava, knapsacks, stores, and regimental property of every kind were lost in the confusion which for many months reigned supreme at our base of operations. The miseries undergone by the troops who landed at the beginning of the war have already been described; and the ragged, jaded starvelings who dragged themselves from the camps on the Upland to the port of Balaclava on the daily quest for food were in pitiable contrast to the well-fed, well-clothed, well-shod men of the XVIIIth. These material advantages doubtless contributed largely towards the comparative immunity from sickness enjoyed by the regiment during the siege, but an even more important factor in its wellbeing was the presence in its ranks of a large number of soldiers who had been on active service, and of many officers who had learned in two long wars not only to take care of themselves, but also of the men under their command.

On January 12, 1855, the Royal Irish received orders to join Major-General Sir William Eyre's brigade, then composed of the 4th, 38th, and 50th regiments, which formed part of the third division under Lieutenant-General Sir Richard England; and leaving a guard over such of their property as they could not carry with them, they started for the Upland. Their introduction to campaigning in the Crimea was a rude one; a blizzard raged as they floundered through deep snow along a track, marked by the bodies of transport animals killed by starvation and overwork; and when late in the afternoon they reached Eyre's camp, they were told off by companies to find shelter in the lines of other corps, for their own tents had been left standing at Balaclava from want of transport to move them. When the Royal Irish succeeded in bringing up their tents from Balaclava, they settled down in camp with the handiness of seasoned troops. Most of the officers dug out the earth inside their tents to a depth of eighteen inches, piling the soil on the curtains to keep out the wind. There was no means of draining the inside of these habitations, "holes in the ground, roofed over with canvas," as they were well described, but as the camp of the third division was pitched on dry and porous ground the XVIIIth were not troubled with water inside their tents, nor outside had they the miseries of mud and standing pools which made the camps on low ground so wretched. As for " warming the tents," continues Captain Kemp's [1] statement,

[1] Captain W. Kemp, probably the last surviving officer of the XVIIIth who served in the Crimea, has supplied the author with much valuable information. When a subaltern of six months' standing, Captain Kemp was appointed acting adjutant of the regiment.

" in mine we improvised a stove out of an old square biscuit-tin ; we let part of it into the earthen wall of the dug-out tent, and made a chimney-pipe out of round meat tins, slipped one inside the other.   This chimney passing through the soil, came out clear of the canvas and was then turned upwards for a couple of feet.   It answered well, though we were at times half smothered with the smoke.   Wood for fuel was very scarce. A small quantity was served out for the soldiers' cooking places, but the men had to carry it into camp on their shoulders for a distance of two miles or more.   Their cooking was done in the usual trench in the open, but in very severe weather—rain, wind or snow—it was impossible to keep the fires going : this was one of the great hardships of the campaign. The cooking for the officers was done close to their tents, in holes or trenches dug by the servants, who used to throw the earth round the kitchen, and cover it with any bits of canvas they could find.   Our servants had to forage for firewood, and generally brought back nothing but the wet roots of vines which they had grubbed up."

Each officer took out with him to the war a canteen containing cooking utensils, plates, dishes, and cups, but the wear and tear of camp life soon made havoc of this kit.   At a farewell dinner given in March by the XVIIIth to Colonel Reignolds when, completely broken down by hardships, he made over the regiment to Brevet-Lieutenant-Colonel Edwards and went home invalided, each of the officers had to cook some part of the feast in his own kitchen, and brought the remnants of his plates, knives and forks, and the articles of food he had provided to the dinner, where empty jam pots took the place of soup plates and champagne glasses.

As soon as the Royal Irish joined Eyre's brigade they began to do duty in the trenches, where parties were sent for twelve hours at a time to guard the works, make good with sand-bags the damage done to the parapets by the enemy's projectiles, and improve the drainage.   In March, when the weather began to moderate, the tour of duty was increased to twenty-four hours, much to the men's satisfaction, as those who were not wanted by day for guards or working parties snatched some hours' sleep in the dry caves of the great ravine which, as has already been mentioned, marked the left of the British front.   The duty, heavy for all, was particularly hard on the officers, who were often in the trenches for seventy-two hours in the week.   By day they had to direct the men at their labours, by night to be prepared to meet an attack from the fortress.   Thanks to their incessant care in seeing that the men were always ready for any emergency, and to half-hourly visits to the sentries, the officers of the XVIIIth were never surprised, and whenever the regiment was in the trenches the Russians received so unfriendly a welcome that they never attempted to push home, though on several occasions they crossed bayonets with the outlying sentries.   These local attacks were not the only dangers of night work during the siege.   If the wind served, and the Russians heard a party at work, they threw fireballs, which on striking the ground burst into a great flare; then, guided by the light, they poured grape upon the labourers, who used to throw themselves for shelter behind the parapet of the trench until the cannonade ceased. Things began to brighten on the Upland in March: a great burst of indignation at home against the archaic methods by which the army was administered had roused the officials of the War Office and the Treasury to a tardy sense of their shortcomings: a gang of navvies from England had almost finished a railway from Balaclava to the camps; a transport corps had been organised and was doing good service,[1] and the troops, once more properly clothed, discarded the weird garments with which they had covered their nakedness during the winter months, and began to resume the bearing of British soldiers. So marked was the improvement in the appearance of the men that some martinets considered that only one thing was required to bring the army up to its old level—the resumption of the stock, which by general consent had been discarded at the beginning of the war: but this relic of barbarism was not taken into use for many months, and then only on the ceremonial parades at the end of the war. In justice to the XVIIIth it should be said that throughout the siege all ranks managed to turn out respectably attired. The officers wore their red shell-jackets or blue frocks under the regimental great-coat; and they were also provided with a non-regulation garment, much like the "coat-warm-British" of the present day, made of serge, lined with rabbit-skin, and reaching almost to the knee. The great-coats of the men looked decent, and concealed the blankets below them, converted into loosely fitting under-coats by the simple expedient of cutting holes in them for the men's arms to come through. All ranks had fur caps, the envy of the whole army. About this time the Minié rifles, with which the army were then supposed to be armed, were issued to the Royal Irish, who had been hurried off to the war equipped with Brown-Bess percussion muskets, the same weapons that they had used in Burma.

Even in the worst part of the winter the Allies never wholly discontinued their siege operations, and as the weather became less severe their parallels were pushed forward steadily towards Sebastopol. The Russians on their side had not been idle: large reinforcements from the field army so abundantly made good the losses of the garrison that Todleben could command the services of 6000, and even on occasions of 10,000 men in carrying out his

---

[1] An extract from Hamley's 'War in the Crimea,' p. 208, will show the inability of the Treasury to realise the needs of the army in the Crimea. The Land Transport Corps was formed by an able and energetic officer, Colonel McMurdo, "who had so well used his opportunities that horses, trained drivers, escorts and vehicles were being rapidly assembled and organised. All this demanded a great outlay, insomuch that on one of the Colonel's many requisitions, the Secretary to the Treasury, Sir George Trevelyan, had written, 'Colonel McMurdo must limit his expenditure.' When the paper returned to the Colonel with these words, he wrote below them: 'When Sir George Trevelyan limits the war, I will limit my expenditure!'"

improvements of the defences. He seized and fortified fresh ground over-looking some of the works of the Allies, and devised a successful method of harassing the men on duty in the trenches. Under cover of darkness he dug numbers of shallow rifle-pits within musketry range of our lines, posting in each a marksman whose duty it was to shoot at every living target he could see. These pits were gradually connected by continuous trenches, and became a source of much annoyance to the Anglo-French troops, who found them difficult to deal with: to turn the sharpshooters out with the bayonet was costly, while to shell so small a mark as they presented was very difficult, and therefore little sandbag forts were run up at intervals on the parapets of the trenches, manned by soldiers detailed to keep down the skirmishers' fire. In spite, however, of Todleben's efforts the Allies succeeded in arming their batteries with an imposing number of heavy guns, and early in April finished their preparations for a vigorous bombardment, the prelude (as it was universally believed) to the storming of Sebastopol. The French could bring to bear 378 pieces of ordnance; the British had only 123 guns and mortars available, but as for the most part they were much more powerful than those of the French, the difference in weight of metal was not great. The cannonade began on the 9th of April, and raged for ten days and nights, for though the guns did not fire after the sun was down, the mortars continued to play upon the fortress throughout the night. Though mitigated by Todleben's genius for rapid repairs, the effect of the bombardment was very great, and all ranks were awaiting orders for the attack when Canrobert, who on the death of St Arnaud had succeeded to the command of the French, decreed that the assault was to be postponed.[1] The fire of the guns was gradually allowed to die down: the digging parties resumed work upon the approaches: and the Russians were allowed to carry out the restoration of their works without interruption other than that of occasional shots from our batteries. This bombardment cost the enemy 6000 men: in the ranks of the Allies the casualties were far smaller, amounting among the French to 1585, among the British to 265 of all ranks.

Up to the middle of June the record of the XVIIIth is one of exceedingly hard work, unbroken by the excitement of any important engagement. The Royal Irish were employed in many different ways. They toiled along the track, first from Balaclava, and then from railhead to the camps on the Upland, laden, to use the soldiers' expression, "like commissariat mules," with stores; they were on fatigues of every kind, from digging parallels and throwing up batteries to making gabions and fascines; and they took their

---

[1] The influence of Napoleon III.'s personal ambition on the conduct of the siege and the effect of the rivalries of his Generals are well described in Hamley's 'Crimea,' wherein the student may learn how difficult, if not impossible, it is for the chiefs of two allied powers, engaged in the same operation of war, to see eye to eye, even on the most important occasions.

turn in the trenches, where, though they demanded and often obtained the dangerous privilege of guarding the approaches nearest to the enemy, their losses were small. Between the 6th of February, when their first casualty occurred, and the 17th of June, only six men were killed and thirty-six wounded. Of these injuries, however, many were of the gravest nature: on one occasion a shell from a Russian mortar burst among a detachment on its way to the trenches and struck down ten of the party. To save the lives of the wounded the surgeons had to perform amputations upon each of them, and seven men lost a leg apiece, two an arm each, while the least hurt escaped with the loss of a hand. This comparative immunity from casualties, however, was not to last, for the regiment was now to be called upon to undergo an ordeal nearly as severe as those in its campaigns under William III. and Marlborough. At the beginning of June the immediate object of the Allies was the capture of three outlying fortifications, outposts which covered the left of the line of Russian defences. The trenches of the French right attack were faced by the White Works and a hill called "the Mamelon," the latter of which barred the way to the Malakoff redoubt, one of the keys of the main position; the British sap led to "the Quarries," where a number of works covered the Redan, a fort as formidable and as important as the Malakoff itself. On the 6th of June another great bombardment began; five hundred and forty-four pieces of heavy ordnance hurled shot and shell into the Russian works, and though answered by almost an equal number inflicted great injury: many cannon were dismounted and earth-works ruined before darkness imposed silence upon our guns, though not upon our howitzers, which continued to fire throughout the night. Thanks to the boundless energy of Todleben and the dogged industry of his men, much of the damage was made good before dawn; the cannon were remounted and the parapets rebuilt; but early in the morning the English and French re-opened fire with such terrible effect that in two hours the *moral* of the defenders was seriously affected. Then the infantry of the Allies was let loose, and after heavy fighting succeeded in taking the points assailed. In these achievements the XVIIIth had no part, as the third division was not employed in the capture of the Quarries.

As soon as these three outlying works had been taken, the Allies began to prepare for an attack on the Malakoff and the Redan, and on the 17th of June the batteries concentrated a furious fire on the Russian fortifications, with results so destructive to the enemy's artillery that everything appeared to promise success for the assault on the morrow. Lord Raglan and Marshal Pélissier, who had recently been placed in command of the French army, had already agreed upon their plans; remembering how rapidly during the night of the 6th-7th of June the Russians had re-fitted their batteries, the Generals decided that the cannonade should be resumed at daylight for two hours, when it was calculated that the enemy's guns would be silenced and the repairs of the night destroyed. The infantry was then to come into action, the French against the Malakoff, the British against the Redan. Barnard's brigade of the third division was to support the storming columns, while on the extreme left Eyre, with the other brigade of the same division, was to threaten the fortifications on the Russian right of the Redan and in front of the Dockyard Creek, and to convert his demonstration into a serious attack if the assault on the Redan proved successful. Raglan's preparations for the execution of his part of this scheme were completed, when suddenly, late on the night of the 17th, Pélissier informed the British Commander-in-Chief that he had resolved to dispense with the preliminary bombardment, and to storm the Malakoff at daybreak. Against his own judgment, and in an evil hour for the Allied armies, Raglan consented to this all-important change of plan; the infantry attacks on the Malakoff and the Redan were delivered without adequate artillery preparation; Todleben, who had done wonders during the night, was ready at every point, and the combined assault was beaten back with heavy loss. The only troops on whom Fortune smiled this day were those of Eyre's brigade, who fought magnificently, and worthily sustained the honour of the British army. The brigade was at this time composed of the 9th, XVIIIth, 28th, 38th, and 44th regiments, but so heavily had the campaign told upon them that, when in the small hours of the 18th of June Eyre mustered these five battalions, there were but two thousand men in their depleted ranks. Covered by an advance-guard of a hundred and fifty sharpshooters — volunteers from each company in his command — the General left his camp while it was still black night, and marched down the great ravine towards the Dockyard Creek. At daybreak, just as the troops detailed for the assault on the Redan were swarming out of the trenches in which they had been assembled, Eyre's advance-guard reached a cemetery, surprised the occupants of the rifle pits by which it was defended, and captured it without much trouble. This cemetery marked one flank of the enemy's line, the other rested on a mamelon;[1] and to quote the words of Eyre's report, the intervening ground "was intersected, and the road barricaded with stone walls, which our men were obliged to pull down under fire before they could advance. In rear of this position, towards the fortress, the enemy occupied several houses, there were bodies of the enemy seen in rear, but in what strength I could not say. This position, under cover of the walls of the fortress, was strong." Well might General Eyre describe the position as "strong." The suburb, of which these houses formed part, consisted of villas standing in gardens, planted with peach-trees in full blossom, and surrounded with

---

[1] A small rounded hillock, not to be confused with "the Mamelon," the outwork to the Malakoff.

low stone walls, thickly overgrown with vines. From several points it was commanded by the Russian artillery; to our "half-left" was the Garden Wall battery; in front rose the Creek battery, built at the head of the inner harbour of Sebastopol; on our right was the Barrack battery, and hidden behind the Redan were field-guns, which after the assault on that work had failed turned their fire upon Eyre's regiments.

Before describing the doings of the XVIIIth in detail it will be well to give a short account of the work done by the brigade as a whole. Such an account is to be found in the letter to 'The Times'[1] by Sir William Russell, the celebrated war correspondent, who, writing only two days after the battle, seems to have obtained his facts from the reports supplied to Eyre by the officers commanding his units. As Russell's letter is in substantial agreement with Eyre's report to his divisional general, its evidence appears valuable. After mentioning that the advance-guard occupied the cemetery with small loss, he says—

"the moment the enemy retreated, their batteries opened a heavy fire on the place from the left of the Redan and from the Barrack battery. Four companies of the XVIIIth at once rushed on out of the cemetery towards the town, and actually succeeded in getting possession of the suburb. Captain Hayman was gallantly leading on his company when he was shot through the knee. Captain Esmonde followed, and the men, once established, prepared to defend the houses they occupied.[2] As they drove the Russians out, they were pelted with large stones by the latter on their way up to the battery, which quite overhangs the suburb. The Russians could not depress their guns sufficiently to fire down on our men, but they directed a severe flanking fire on them from an angle of the Redan works. There was nothing for it but to keep up a vigorous fire from the houses, and to delude the enemy into the belief that the occupiers were more numerous than they were. Meanwhile the Russians did their best to blow down the houses with shot and shell, and fired grape incessantly, but the soldiers kept close, though they lost men occasionally, and they were most materially aided by the fire of the regiments in the cemetery behind them, which was directed at the Russian embrasures; so that the enemy could not get out to fire on the troops below. The 9th regiment succeeded in effecting a lodgment in the houses in two or three different places, and held their position as well as the XVIIIth. . . . While these portions of the 9th and XVIIIth, and parties of the 44th and 28th were in the houses, the detachments of the same regiments and of the 38th kept up a hot fire from the cemetery on the Russians in the battery and on the sharpshooters, all the time being exposed to a tremendous shower of bullets, grape, round-shot, shell. The loss

---

[1] Russell's 'The War,' vol. i. pp. 490 *et seq.*

[2] According to a tradition in the regiment, the men found the breakfast-tables laid for the Russians whom they had so rudely dispossessed, and promptly availed themselves of the hospitality of their enemies !

M

of the brigade under such circumstances, could not but be extremely severe. One part of it, separated from the other, was exposed to a destructive fire in houses, the upper portion of which crumbled into pieces or fell in under fire, and it was only by keeping in the lower storey, which was vaulted and well built, that they were enabled to hold their own. The other parts of it, far advanced from our batteries, were almost unprotected, and were under a constant mitraille and bombardment from guns which our batteries had failed to touch."

Though the repulse of the main British column left Eyre in a situation of hourly increasing peril, he resolutely continued to hold the points which the dash and bravery of his troops had gained. At first he hoped that the Redan might yet be stormed, when his brigade would be ready to follow up the victory; and when it became clear that the attack was not to be renewed he declined to fall back, until an authority higher than his own had decided how much of the ground that his brigade had won was to be retained. Though Eyre was wounded comparatively early in the day, it was not until late in the afternoon that, after giving orders for the gradual withdrawal of the troops from the houses nearest to the enemy, he made over his command to the next senior officer and quitted the battlefield. The process of withdrawal took several hours, and it was not until 9 P.M. that the Royal Irish, the last regiment of the brigade to retire, began its march back to the camp of the third division.

How the XVIIIth fared must now be told, as far as possible, in the words of the officers who had the honour to be present. Late on the 17th, the rumour had run through the lines of the Royal Irish that the town was to be assaulted next day. The men were wild with joy at the prospect of taking part in the attack, and talked and sang in their tents so incessantly that the officers could get no rest during the few hours allowed the regiment for sleep. At 1 A.M. on the 18th of June, a date ever memorable in the annals of the regiment, six hundred and sixty-nine officers and men paraded in front of the camp of the 9th regiment, where the brigade was formed, the XVIIIth in front, the 44th, 38th, 28th, and 9th regiments following in the order named. On the march down the great ravine occurred an interesting instance of the rigidity of the drill which, in the middle of the nineteenth century, fettered the movements of the British army. It has been mentioned that every infantry regiment then had two flank companies of picked men: those of the right, or grenadier company, were chosen for height and strength; those of the left, or Light company, were selected for activity and intelligence. On the parade ground the rule was that all battalion movements should be made from the right, and consequently that in column the grenadier company should always lead. Colonel Edwards had learned in the school of the Chinese and Burmese wars that all drill is but the means to one end, the successful attack on an enemy; and thinking that on this occasion the quick-moving "Light Bobs" were the men first to be employed, marched off "left in front." This daring innovation did not long pass unnoticed, and almost within sight of the enemy he was ordered to halt, and countermarch his regiment in order to bring the grenadier company to the head of the column. In 1855, the countermarch was an evolution slow and ponderous in broad daylight, and doubly difficult of execution in semi-darkness, at a time when the pulses of all ranks were throbbing with the excitement of a night march and an impending battle. After the manœuvre was carried out, the brigade once more advanced, forming into a mass of close columns whenever the ground permitted. Though it was now almost day the Russians had not yet detected the presence of Eyre's troops, and the General took an opportunity of addressing the Royal Irish, telling them he knew they would prove themselves good soldiers and "this day do something that will ring in every cabin in Ireland." Then he added, "Now, men, above all things you must be quiet or you'll get peppered!" In answer to this very reasonable appeal a shout arose from the ranks, "All right, your Honour, we'll get in. Three cheers for the General!" Before the officers could stop them the men had given three lusty cheers. Eyre remonstrated, but the Royal Irish were far too eager for the fray to be sensible, and in response to his reiterated entreaties for silence they burst out into stentorian cheering, this time for Old Ireland. "Let them go in and attack," cried the General in despair; "they will only draw fire upon us!"

From a letter written by Colonel Edwards two days after the battle, it appears that while the advance-guard was driving the Russians from the cemetery at the point of the bayonet, the XVIIIth

> "halted in the open ready for action. Just here the first round-shot danced among us, and as the advance party had extended and were under such cover as they could find, we met the intruder. That peculiar thud (once heard, never forgotten) denoted that the round-shot had told, two men being killed. But we were compelled to wait a little longer, and then the Grenadier company moved off in skirmishing order, soon followed by Nos. 1 and 2 companies. These three companies occupied the ruined houses on the Woronzoff road."

As the grenadiers, led by Captain Armstrong, were pressing forward they found their way obstructed by one of the stone walls mentioned in General Eyre's report. Two subalterns raced for the wall, and leapt it at the same moment: Lieutenant Taylor landed safely on the other side, but Lieutenant Meurant was shot dead as he rose at the jump. Soon afterwards the remainder of the regiment in column of sections was moved forward in support, along a lane leading towards the suburb from the great ravine, the rocky cliffs of which gave the XVIIIth some cover from cannon shot.   The Russian riflemen, however, speedily found the range, " and the men," says Colonel Edwards,

"commenced to fall fast.   The General had given me orders to stand there, but the casualties were then so great that I put the men behind the houses and walls, which saved them much.   I did not see the General again; he was wounded across the head.

"All this time the men were coming back from the front, hopping or crouching according to the nature of the wound, amongst them my friend Captain Hayman, supported by two men, shot through the knee, but with a cheerful smile on his face.   Seeing that the advance was much weakened I supported them with two other companies, sending Major Kennedy to the front; he was shortly after slightly hit on the side of the head, but not compelled to return.   The enemy knew well the position of the houses they were in, and threw the shell amongst them.   Fancy one of these visitors falling within ten feet of you— down you must lie, and close too, and wait for its bursting, when you are fortunate if you have nothing worse than dust to complain of !   They not only gave shells, but rifle-balls and grape, and many a poor fellow who went out to help a wounded comrade was obliged in his turn to be carried in desperately wounded.

"Again the front calls out for ammunition and more men.   'Up, my boys, catch hold of that barrel of ammunition, and rush through the whizzing balls, the tearing grape!'   Away they go with a cheer!   About 12 o'clock the last company but one went out and other companies, returning, dreadfully thinned, formed the support.   Shortly after one, more men were wanted; I sent out the last company and went myself. Away we hop from stone to stone or bush: 'ping-ping' passes the rifle-bullet crashing around you; you feel the grape; never mind, on you must go!   I found the advanced parties in a row of houses under the battery, regularly enclosed by a screen of projectiles; you could only creep about.   In the morning these houses had been occupied by the Russians; by the time I got there, everything was broken:—pier glasses in shivers; the piano (or as a man called it, the music-box) torn open; beds, tables and wardrobes in jumbles of masses.   The enemy did not like our being there, nor did they like that the houses gave us cover; they therefore set fire to them with shells.   About 3 o'clock I received an order to retire, which I could not comply with as there were eighteen wounded men to bring away, which could not be done till dark."

According to Colonel Edwards, the three companies of the XVIIIth in the ruined houses on the Woronzoff road and the other battalions of the brigade also received this order, and gradually drew back, leaving the greater part of the Royal Irish in a most dangerous situation.

"Every moment our small party was decreasing.   What weary hours they seemed from three till eight, and just before it was time to move, the enemy brought field-pieces to bear upon the houses, and they commenced knocking them down about our heads. At last I heard with joy 'The last wounded man has been carried off, Sir.' 'Well, then, go away by twos and threes: keep up a warm fire. When across the open, bugler, sound the Regimental Call and the Retire.'

"The work is done, but out of 669 men who left the camp, 250 of the Royal Irish had suffered more or less. We did not get home till ten o'clock, wearied and exhausted. The remainder of the brigade acted on our right, and the 44th lost nearly as many in proportion as we did. Our brigade was more than successful, and have received great praise, especially the Royal Irish regiment."

In so broken and disjointed a combat it is always difficult for the General to select officers and men for special commendation. Eyre appears to have found it impossible to do so, and after stating in his report that every one in his brigade "most nobly performed his duty," and that "the conduct of all was so exemplary that he could scarcely with justice particularize individuals," he contented himself with mentioning the names of his staff and the officers commanding the advance-guard and the five regiments of the brigade. Colonel Edwards' report on the part played by the XVIIIth doubtless recorded some of the deeds of valour performed by the Royal Irish; but unhappily no copy of this document has been preserved in the archives of the regiment. His letter, vivid and deeply interesting as it is, was written, it is believed, for the information of Her Majesty, Queen Victoria, and aims obviously at giving a general account of the engagement, without any unnecessary detail. The "Digest of Service" should have contained every particular of the doings of the regiment, but unfortunately it was compiled by an officer who recorded the adventures of the XVIIIth in the Crimea in two or three loosely-written pages of foolscap, from which everything of historical value was omitted. Thus the only accounts of the exploits of the Royal Irish on the 18th of June are to be found in a few statements, contributed by officers many years after the war was over, and in the dry official words announcing the bestowal of decorations. Every soldier knows that for one specially brave deed reported after an engagement, scores pass unnoticed or are forgotten, and therefore the instances now given can be regarded only as specimens of the conduct of the regiment as a whole.

Captain Thomas Esmonde was awarded the Victoria Cross [1] for two acts of bravery, the first of which was performed on the 18th of June. The Gazette runs as follows: "for having, after being engaged in the attack on the Redan, [2] repeatedly assisted at great personal risk under a heavy fire of

---

[1] The Victoria Cross was instituted in 1856. Before that time the only way in which a non-commissioned officer or private soldier was rewarded for conduct meriting higher recognition than a medal for meritorious conduct in the field was by a dole of money. For officers there was no decoration to commemorate a deed of remarkable courage.

[2] Eyre's capture of the cemetery and suburb was officially included in the attack on the Redan.

shell and grape, in rescuing wounded men from exposed situations; and also, while in command of a covering party two days after, for having rushed with the most prompt and daring gallantry to a spot where a fire-ball from the enemy had just been lodged, which he effectually extinguished before it had betrayed the position of the working party under his protection, thus saving it from a murderous fire of shell and grape, which was immediately opened upon the spot where the fire-ball had fallen."

Captain Dillon volunteered to rescue from under a heavy fire of grape and musketry seven wounded men, who were lying in the houses nearest to the Russian works, and succeeded in doing so.

Sergeant John Grant belonged to one of the companies in the houses nearest to the Russian battery, and brought a message from his captain to Colonel Edwards. When Colonel Edwards saw that Sergeant Grant was bleeding from two severe wounds he desired him to fall back out of harm's way, but Grant so earnestly begged to be allowed to return to his officer that Colonel Edwards permitted him once more to risk his life in crossing the fire-swept belt of ground between the supports and his own company. Grant lived for many years to enjoy an annuity of £20, which accompanied the medal for meritorious service in the field, awarded to him for this act of bravery.

Lieutenant T. D. Baker displayed great gallantry throughout the day, as did Sergeant John Gleeson, Corporal Niel O'Donnell, and privates J. Weir, E. Loughton, and J. Byrne.

As an instance of the spirit shown by the wounded who were left upon the field, this story is quoted from Russell's account of the battle. During the armistice of the 19th for the collection of the wounded and the burial of the dead, Major-General Eyre came to the part of the cemetery where a sergeant of the Royal Irish lay, with both his legs broken by a round-shot. "General," exclaimed the non-commissioned officer, "thank God, *we* did *our* work, anyway. Had I another pair of legs, the country and you would be welcome to them!"

The operations of the 17th and 18th cost the French 3500 men, the British 1500, the Russians 5400, and of the six generals and commanders, French and English, who led the attacks on the 18th, four were killed and one disabled. When Eyre's casualty returns were made up, it was found that his brigade had lost 562 killed and wounded. To this total the Royal Irish contributed no less than 259, almost 39 per cent of the regiment as it went into action. Among the officers, Lieutenant J. W. Meurant was killed, and ten were wounded, several being dangerously or severely injured. They were— Major J. C. Kennedy; Captains J. Cormick, A. W. S. F. Armstong, M. Hayman, H. F. Stephenson, and J. G. Wilkinson; Lieutenants W. O'B. Taylor, W. Kemp, F. Fearnley, and C. Hotham. Of the other ranks 57 were killed or mortally wounded, 16 were dangerously and 87 severely wounded, and 88 more slightly injured.[1] The wounded were gradually carried back to the camp of the IIIrd brigade, which they soon filled to overflowing. To our modern ideas the preparations for their reception were singularly rough. "So many of us had been hit," writes Captain Kemp, who himself had been struck by a bullet in the knee, "that the orderly room and mess huts and every other available place was appropriated for our use. At first my leg was doomed to come off, and I was laid on the amputation table for the purpose, but as I was too weak then it was left on till the morrow. Next day I was allowed to retain it by the decision of one of the staff surgeons, who said, most luckily for me, 'Let us give the poor lad a chance,' but I became very ill from fever and the intense heat of the tent,[2] and shortly afterwards was ordered home. I was moved to Balaclava in one of the 'carrying chairs' slung on the side of a mule, and fainted nearly all the way from sun and weakness."

After their double repulse at the Malakoff and the Redan the Allies lost no time in resuming the ordinary operations of the siege: their approaches were steadily pushed forward, and their guns kept up a heavy fire upon the fortress. In July the average daily loss in Sebastopol was two hundred and fifty, while each day in August saw the strength of the garrison diminished by eight or nine hundred officers and men. The Russians, magnificently stubborn fighters as they were, began to realise that the place was becoming untenable. The parapets were crumbling under the projectiles of the Anglo-French artillery; many guns were disabled or worn out, and though there was still a large reserve of cannon in the arsenal, the fire of our mortars made it impossible to mount them on the shattered batteries. Round the disabled guns the dead lay in great heaps, while the wounded could not be moved till darkness brought some respite to the harassed garrison. Barracks, arsenals, and store-houses were all more or less in ruins; and the hospitals, overflowing into the streets and squares of the town, were rapidly emptied into a cemetery, grimly termed "the grave of the Hundred Thousand." Towards the end of August the Russians determined to abandon Sebastopol; they began to build a bridge across the outer harbour, strong enough to carry guns and waggons upon its sixteen feet of roadway; threw up barricades across the streets of the town, and laid great mines under the forts and magazines. On the 5th of September, the Allies once more brought all their guns into action, and bombarded the fortress, almost without intermission, for three days and nights, and on the 8th, the French once more assaulted the Malakoff, and the British the Redan. As the third division was in the reserve

[1] See Appendix 2 (I).

[2] Early in 1855 the Government realised that tents were unsuitable quarters for the besieging army: and wooden huts were sent off to the Crimea, not of one, but of several sizes and patterns. This want of uniformity in design caused great confusion, and the XVIIIth had not received its full complement of huts at the time of the attack on the Redan.

and did not come into action, the XVIIIth regiment was not engaged, and therefore all that need be said about the result is that we failed to take the Redan, while the French carried the Malakoff, and succeeded in holding it against the strenuous efforts of the enemy to recapture it.   These attacks were made by the Russian rear-guard to gain time for the retreat of the main body from the southern shores of the harbour, and were so far successful that when the French General heard that the head of the enemy's column was marching over the bridge, he was still too uncertain of ultimate success to attempt any interference with the retirement.   During the night the Russians successfully exploded many of their mines; destroyed their few remaining warships; set fire to the town in many places, and called in the troops from the forts; and by daybreak on the 9th the whole of the garrison, carrying with them most of the wounded, had crossed the bridge, broken it behind them, and found safety on the heights to the north of the harbour of Sebastopol.   The losses on both sides in this, the last important episode in the Crimean War, were very heavy.   Our defeat at the Redan cost us 2271 officers and men, among whom were three generals, wounded: the French casualties amounted to 7567 of all ranks, including five generals killed and four wounded: the Russians lost nine generals and 12,906 other officers and men.

With the fall of the fortress the war in the Crimea came virtually to an end.   The Allies had accomplished their self-imposed task of destroying Sebastopol and the Black Sea fleet; there was no immediate object to be gained by a pitched battle with the Russian Field army; disagreements on questions of future policy caused a considerable amount of friction between the Ministers of Queen Victoria and the Emperor Napoleon III., and fettered the movements of the Generals, who engaged in no further operations except two comparatively unimportant raids against the towns of Eupatoria and Kilburn, in neither of which the XVIIIth regiment took part.   The French, indeed, were not anxious, if indeed they were able, to continue the war; but the English had atoned, though very tardily, for their previous neglect of their army, by preparing so energetically for another campaign, that in November there were in the Crimea 51,000 British troops, a contingent of 20,000 Turks, raised, trained, and officered by Englishmen, and a German legion of ten thousand men.[1]   The good health of this large body of soldiery showed how excellent our system of administration had become at the seat of war; at home recruits were forthcoming in great numbers; the militia had relieved

---

[1] Since the Russian War no subjects of a foreign power have been enlisted in a body to serve under the British flag.   At the end of the Crimean War a considerable number of the German legion were sent at their own request to South Africa as settlers, where they became useful members of the white population.   During the last war with the Boers, the author met in a Free State town an old German cobbler, who, after proudly dilating on his services in the Legion, explained that though he was too old again to shoulder a rifle with the British, he would be proud to mend their boots !

the troops in the United Kingdom and the Mediterranean of much garrison duty; Malta was full of trained soldiers, eager to be employed on active service; in short, the Army, purified by the ordeal it had passed through, had become once more a first-rate fighting machine. But the troops arriving after the fall of the fortress had no opportunity of distinguishing themselves, for though the enemy annoyed us by cannonading Sebastopol from the northern shore of the harbour, he made no offensive movement against the camps on the Upland. Thus the second winter in the Crimea was a time of comparative rest for the greater part of the army, though not for the regiments placed at the disposal of the Royal Engineers to complete the destruction of the forts, arsenals, and dockyards of the fortress. To the Royal Irish fell a very heavy task, the demolition of the docks in the inner harbour. As Colonel Edwards was senior to the engineer officer in charge of the work, the headquarters of the XVIIIth remained outside the town, and Major Call was placed in command of the working parties, which practically consisted of the whole of the Royal Irish. The labour of preparing the docks for destruction was very great, and the hardships of the men extreme: to quote the words of the general order of February 7, 1856, praising the zeal and perseverance of all ranks, and thanking Major Call, among other officers, for his valuable services, "the work was carried out in the depth of winter; the docks occasionally flooded, the shafts filled with water, the pumps choked with frost; but all ranks united to overcome difficulties, and the mass of ruins is a proof of the success attending the cheerful performance of a laborious duty."

This official record is not the only testimony to the good behaviour of the Royal Irish while they worked like navvies in the docks. General C. G. Gordon, who as a young officer of Royal Engineers had served in the Crimea, replied to a request for information about the doings of the XVIIIth at the siege of Sebastopol in a characteristic letter :—

"PORT LOUIS, 3/3/82.

"MY DEAR MAJOR SAVILE,—Thanks for your note received to-day. I am afraid I cannot write anything which would be of value about the 18th Royal Irish, as it is now 28 years ago or nearly so, since the Crimea. I know that they were a favourite regiment with the R.E. for work, both in the trenches and in the destruction of the docks, from the energy and pluck of the officers and men, and it was then that I formed my opinion of Irishmen being of a different nature than other Britishers inasmuch as they required a certain management and consideration, which, if given them, would enable you, so to speak, to hold their lives in your hand. The officers liked the men and the men liked the officers; they were a jovial lot altogether, but they would do anything if you spoke and treated them as if you liked them, which I certainly did. You know what great hardships they went through in the Docks in working at the shafts which, 30 feet deep, were often full of water, if left, unpumped out, for 12 hours. Poor devils! wet, draggled, in their low ammunition boots, I used to feel much for them, for the Generals used to be down on them because they were troublesome, which they were when people did not know how to manage them.

"Kindest regards to General Edwards, a fine, clever old officer who had all our respect.

"I am sorry I can write you no details.—Believe me, yours sincerely,

"C. G. GORDON."

It will be noticed that neither in the official expression of thanks nor in Gordon's letter is there any reference to the fact that the Russians frequently shelled the working parties at the docks. The troops were so used to being under fire that they looked upon it as an everyday occurrence, and a few casualties were considered unworthy of notice. Thanks, however, to Colonel Elliot's diary, we know that rheumatic fever and frost-bite were not the only dangers to which the Royal Irish were exposed. On December 3, 1855, the Russians fired two hundred and fifty shells, wounding four men of the regiment; on the 21st they dropped three shells into a barrack-room, luckily without hitting any one, but smashing beds, knapsacks, and rifles in every direction; on the last day of the year a shell carried away the arm of a private,—Fitzgerald.

While with immense difficulty the English and French engineers were levelling the naval and military buildings to the ground, and shattering the docks beyond all hope of restoration, the diplomatists of Europe were doing their utmost to bring hostilities to an end; late in February an armistice was arranged, and on the 30th of March, 1856, the world was gladdened by the news that peace had been proclaimed. The effort to save Constantinople from the Russians, though successful, had cost England dear, as these grim figures show—

	Killed.	Died of Wounds.	Died of Disease.	Wounded.	Total.
Officers	157	86	147	515	905
Non-Commissioned Officers .	161	85	574	579	1,399
Privates	2,437	1,848	15,320	10,782	30,387
	2,755	2,019	16,041	11,876	32,691

Though our Allies also suffered severely, the losses of the Western Powers and of the Ottoman Empire pale into insignificance before those of the Russians. During the last six months of the siege 81,000 soldiers were killed or wounded in or around Sebastopol; the whole campaign in the Crimea cost the Czar 153,000 troops; while the reinforcements from the interior of Russia endured such terrible hardships on the march to the Black Sea that hundreds of thousands of men broke down on the way. It is believed that Russia's total loss during the war was not less than half a million of men.

The casualties in the XVIIIth Royal Irish regiment were—

Officers—

Killed . .	.	Lieutenant J. W. Meurant.
Died of disease	.	Lieutenant E. D. Ricard.
Wounded	.	Major J. C. Kennedy.
		Captains J. Cormick, A. W. S. F. Armstrong, M. Hayman, H. F. Stephenson, J. Wilkinson.
		Lieutenants W. O'B. Taylor, W. Kemp, F. Fearnley, C. Hotham.

In the other ranks, 41 were killed, 44 died of wounds, 70 died from accident or disease, and 275 were wounded. Their names will be found in Appendix 2 (I).[1]

During the first nine months of its service in the Crimea, the regiment was reinforced by 289 non-commissioned officers and men, who arrived in drafts from home, and later from Malta where the four reserve companies were stationed; and on September 9, although between 140 and 150 men had been killed or died in hospital, and 219 had been invalided or become ineffective from various causes, there remained, exclusive of officers, no less than 724 effectives present with the Colours.[2] The XVIIIth regiment was among the last to leave the Crimea; it was not until June 20, that it embarked on H.M.S. *Majestic*, an eighty-gun ship, fitted with an auxiliary screw. Though the crew received their soldier passengers most hospitably, the voyage was not an agreeable one. The subalterns were berthed in the cockpit, where, as one of them recorded in his diary, "there was no room to wash, or dress, or put our baggage; sentries and reliefs passed through our sleeping-place all night long, shaking us out of our hammocks; then at a certain hour ruthless sailors came and packed away the hammocks, whether you wanted to get up or not; and finally, there was no place to be sick, for the bulwarks were so high that you could not see over them!" On the 18th of July the Royal Irish landed at Portsmouth, entrained for Farnborough, and were marching thence to Alder-

---

[1] These numbers, which are taken from official documents in the Record Office, do not agree completely with those on the Crimean "Memorial" in St Patrick's.

[2] One of the drafts had a narrow escape from shipwreck in the Sea of Marmora. Their transport, the s.s. *Cleopatra*, in the middle of the night of August 15th was in collision with another steamer, the *Simla*, which was so badly injured that her captain ran her ashore to prevent her from sinking in deep water; the *Cleopatra* was cut down to the water's edge, but managed to reach the Golden Horn, where the troops were at once transhipped and sent on to Balaclava.

shot when they were ordered to quicken their pace as Queen Victoria was waiting to welcome the regiment. Colonel Edwards thus describes Her Majesty's inspection of the soldiers who had fought her battles in China, Burma, and the Crimea: " When formed in line the appearance of the regiment showed signs of service, the old clothing, long beards, and the dust of the march giving the men but a sorry aspect. Her Majesty, passing down the line on foot, requested me to point out men most deserving of her notice. My answer was, ' Were I to do so, the whole regiment would step to the front." However, several of the wounded officers and men were presented. When the Queen arrived in front of the Colours, I respectfuly submitted to Her Majesty that the regimental badge of the Harp and Crown had been removed from the uniforms of the men, and the Queen most graciously gave orders that they should be restored."

For their services in the Crimea many officers, non-commissioned officers, and men received promotion or reward. Lieutenant-Colonels C. A. Edwards and J. C. Kennedy were appointed to be Companions of the Order of the Bath; Edwards also was made a Brevet-Colonel; Major G. F. S. Call, Captains J. Cormick, A. W. S. F. Armstrong, J. Laurie, and M. J. Hayman each received a step in brevet rank. Captain T. Esmonde was one of the first to receive the Victoria Cross, and the newly instituted medal for distinguished conduct in the field was awarded to Sergeant H. Morton, Corporals M. Egan and T. Murphy, and the following private soldiers, viz., R. Baglin, E. Erwin, T. Flannery, H. Forrestall, R. Marshall, W. Major, J. M. Guinness, N. O'Neill, J. Sessman, 2830 P. Whelan, 3521 P. Whelan.[1] In the matter of foreign decorations the XVIIIth fared well, as each of our Allies presented orders or medals to specially deserving officers and men. Brevet-Colonel Edwards, Brevet-Majors Armstrong and Hayman, Sergeant-Major T. Watt, and Sergeant J. Grant were created members of the French Legion of Honour by Napoleon III., who also bestowed war medals on Colour-Sergeant E. Dunne, Sergeant J. Harvey, Sergeant J. Gleeson, Corporal N. O'Donnell, and Privates J. Cox, E. Laughton, and J. Byrne. Victor Emmanuel gave the Sardinian war medal to Lieutenant-Colonel J. C. Kennedy, Brevet Lieutenant-Colonel Call, Lieutenant T. D. Baker, and Private J. Weir. The Turkish Order of the Medjidie was awarded to Colonel Edwards, Lieutenant-Colonel J. C. Kennedy, Brevet-Major Cormick, and Lieutenants C. Hotham, O'B. Taylor, W. Kemp, and C. J. Coote. The British medal for the Crimea and clasp for Sebastopol and the Turkish medal were awarded to all who had taken part in the siege, and the word "Sebastopol" added to the battle honours of the regiment.

A stained-glass window has been placed in the north transept of St Patrick's Cathedral in honour of those who fell in the war with Russia.

[1] See Appendix 4.

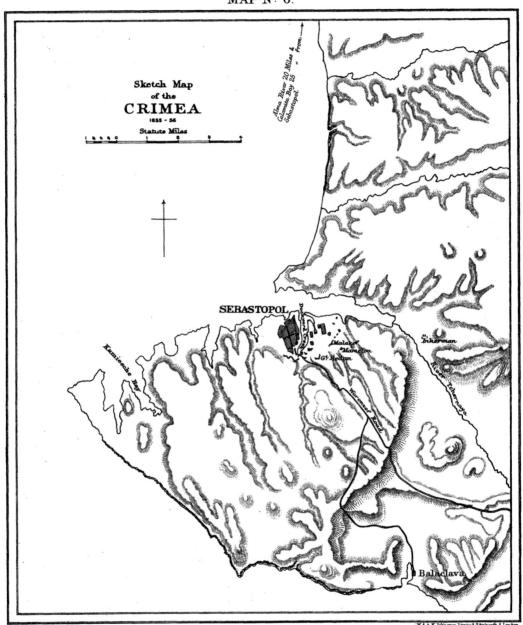

Sketch Map
of the
CRIMEA
1855 - 56
Statute Miles

Alma River 20 Miles &
Catcatca Bay 25 " from "
Sebastopol.

SERASTOPOL

Inkerman

Kamiesche Bay

Malakof
Mamelon
Gt Redan

Woronzof Road

River Tchernaya

Balaclava

CHAPTER VIII.

1856-1859.

OPERATIONS DURING THE MUTINY IN INDIA.

FOUR days after the Queen had inspected the regiment it moved to Dublin, where the arrival of the reserve companies from Malta and the depôt from Preston brought up the numbers at headquarters to seventeen hundred and sixty-nine of all ranks. On the 25th of August, new Colours were presented by the Earl of Carlisle, Lord Lieutenant of Ireland, the old Colours finding a fitting resting-place in St Patrick's Cathedral, where they hang over the monuments to the Royal Irishmen who laid down their lives for their country in the swamps of China, in the jungles of Burma, and on the blood-stained glacis of the fortress of Sebastopol. A few months later the regiment was warned for foreign service, this time at the Cape of Good Hope, but the order was cancelled when the news reached England that the native army of Bengal had mutinied, and the XVIIIth remained in Ireland, very indignant at not being sent at once to help quell the rising in India. It was not until the autumn of 1857 that the War Office determined to employ the Royal Irish in the East: an advance party of three companies (in all, 208 officers and men) embarked on September 24, followed in two months by headquarters and the remainder of the XVIIIth (666 of all ranks), who reached Bombay early in February, 1858.[1] They landed, hoping to

[1] From the muster roll of June 25, 1858, it appears that the officers in India at that date were—
Colonel—C. A. Edwards (in command).
Lieutenant-Colonel—G. F. S. Call.
Majors—J. Borrow, A. N. Campbell, E. W. Sargent.
Captains—C. G. D. Annesley, J. Canavan, G. A. Elliot, W. F. G. Forster, W. H. Graves, H. M. Havelock, C. F. Kelly, G. H. Pocklington, J. Swinburn, W. O'B. Taylor, R. H. J. Black, R. P. Bishopp.
Lieutenants—R. J. Adamson, T. D. Baker, J. R. Blacker, J. F. Bryant, W. B. Burke, S. Darvell, C. Hotham, W. Kemp (adjutant), J. T. Ring, H. Shaw, J. S. Theobald, F. Fearnley, E. L. Dillon, E. A. Noblett, H. Adams, R. H. Daniel, E. Hall, I. Wiley.
Ensigns—J. F. Daubeny, W. T. Le Brunn, T. Watt.
Surgeon—T. Crawford, M.D.
Assistant-Surgeons—F. Ffolliott, R. A. Hyde, C. E. Porteous, M.D.
Quartermaster—T. Carney.
Paymaster—C. E. Preston.

be in time to take an active part in the campaign, and their disappointment was bitter when they were ordered to Poona, a great city in the Bombay
Presidency. The Royal Irish found much heavy work awaiting them, for
the place was then, as it still is, a hot-bed of sedition, ready to revolt at any
moment; and the troops were constantly under arms to prevent an outbreak.
But as the accounts of successive British victories in northern and central
India reached the malcontents, the danger diminished, and in April, 1858, the
local situation had sufficiently improved to warrant the withdrawal of part
of the British garrison from Poona. On the Royal Irish was thrown the
duty of providing detachments in various places in western India, to watch
native regiments of doubtful loyalty, and help the civil power in re-establishing law and order round their posts. With the dispersal of the regiment
disappeared its chances of service as a complete unit, but each company
commander still hoped to have to deal individually with a body of rebels, or
with one of the bands of marauders called into existence by the mutiny.
Fate, however, was not kind to the Royal Irish in 1858-59: the strenuous
work of the detachments was unrelieved by a single fight, and even when
three or four companies were brought together for some combined movement they had no luck; in extreme heat they made forced marches,
cut roads through jungle, forded rivers, but all to no purpose: wherever
they went the enemy disappeared, to fall into the hands of some column
operating many miles away.

In a letter from Dr Ffolliott, one of the regimental assistant-surgeons,
are preserved a few details of the experiences of one of the detachments.
Captain J. Canavan started from Poona on April 23, 1858, with two subalterns and a hundred and twenty of the Royal Irish, a company of Bombay
native infantry, camel transport, and dhoolies for the sick and wounded, and
at the end of a month's hard marching brought his column to Asseerghur
without a casualty and with no sick men. According to Ffolliott, who was
in medical charge, this immunity from disease was due to the care taken
to keep the men's clothing dry at the numerous fords through which the
road ran: the troops were allowed ample time to undress before going into
the water, and to put their clothes on again before the march was resumed.
Asseerghur was an old native fortress, perched on the top of an almost
perpendicular rock rising nearly eight hundred feet out of the plain. As it
had never been occupied by European troops, there were no barracks; the
men were quartered in an old mosque; while the officers occupied a large
bungalow, where they used to entertain a few European ladies who had
taken refuge in Asseerghur while their husbands were in the field. Every
week there was a dinner-party, followed by a dance to the drums and fifes of
the detachment.

On his way to take up the command of a brigade at Mhow, Colonel

Edwards was present at one of these entertainments, where he must have been pleased at the determination of his officers to keep up their spirits under the bitter disappointment of finding themselves thus completely " side-tracked." In November, Asseerghur was greatly excited at the report that Tantia Tope was in the neighbourhood. Tantia was one of the few native leaders who had shown good military qualities; he had fought well against Lord Strathnairn (then Sir Hugh Rose) in central India, and when after many defeats he had betaken himself to the country north of the Nerbudda, he had evaded the columns threatening him from many directions. The net, however, was now closing in upon him; it was believed he would try to break southwards into the Deccan, and as Asseerghur commanded one of the approaches to this part of India it became a place of temporary importance. One evening the Fort Adjutant bustled into the quarters of the XVIIIth with great news: in a few hours Tantia Tope, with eight or nine thousand men, was going to attack Burhanpore, a rich and populous town not many miles away; Canavan with fifty men of the Royal Irish was to throw himself into the city, and Ffolliott was to accompany him. While Canavan was issuing his orders, Ffolliott went off to make medical arrangements at the hospital, where, to use his own words, " I found every sick man in war paint. My acting hospital sergeant said there was not much the matter with them; they had heard there was to be a fight that night, and wanted to join the party going, so I discharged them out of hospital. Canavan made no distinction; the first fifty for duty were ordered to fall out, and in two hours from the time we were warned we were on the march." As Canavan and his party were considered to be going on a forlorn hope, every European not on duty was on the parade ground to wish the Royal Irish " good luck " as they moved off, and the ladies were in tears, until their grief was changed to mirth at the discovery that the doctor had filled his pouch, not with medical appliances, but with revolver cartridges. Many of the garrison sat up till dawn, listening anxiously for the burst of fire with which it was feared the detachment would be overwhelmed. But no crash of musketry broke the stillness of the night, and before Canavan reached Burhanpore he learned the place had been reinforced by a larger column, with whose movements the Commandant of Asseerghur was unacquainted, and that Tantia Tope had disappeared. As no fighting was expected, Canavan was ordered to return to his own post without delay—another instance of bad luck, for in a day or two there was a sharp skirmish near Burhanpore, in which his company would certainly have taken part.

In January, 1859, the greater part of the regiment was brought together under Lieutenant-Colonel Call, and made many marches through the district of Jaulna, vainly pursuing Rohilla freebooters who had no intention of standing up to fight. As soon as these robber bands dispersed, the XVIIIth went back to garrison duty at detached posts, and in three or four months, when the country had begun to settle down, most of the companies joined headquarters at Sholapur, and then marched to Hyderabad in the Deccan, which they reached on June 21, 1859. The muster roll shows that three officers, Captain W. F. G. Forster, Lieutenant T. Watt, and Assistant-Surgeon C. E. Porteous, and twenty-seven of the rank and file died of disease during the Indian Mutiny campaign.[1]

[1] See Appendix 2 (J).

CHAPTER IX.

1858-1882.

RAISING OF THE SECOND BATTALION: THE WAR IN NEW ZEALAND.

AFTER the Indian Mutiny a considerable increase in the strength of the army was sanctioned by Parliament, for the reasons stated in chapter x., and additional units of infantry were raised, not as new regiments but as second battalions of existing organisations. The XVIIIth was one of the regiments selected for this augmentation, and on March 25, 1858, forty-four years after the original second battalion had been disbanded,[1] the nucleus of a new second battalion was formed at Enniskillen by the transfer from the first battalion of a hundred seasoned soldiers.[2] A hundred and fifty men joined from the Dublin City militia; other militia regiments contributed volunteers, and recruits came in fast from the north of Ireland. For the first few months of its existence the new battalion was in charge of Major A. W. S. F. Armstrong; then Lieutenant-Colonel A. N. Campbell, on promotion from the first battalion, assumed the command which he continued to hold until October, 1859, when he exchanged with Lieutenant-Colonel A. A. Chapman, 48th regiment. In the same month the battalion was sent to England, and two years later to the Channel Isles, where the detachment at Alderney did good service in fighting a great fire which threatened to devastate the island. Though the greater part of the rank and file was composed of growing lads, "the ready and willing spirit displayed by all and their coolness under such circumstances"[3] greatly impressed the local authorities. This incident proved, if proof had been necessary, that the task of converting a mass of recruits into trained and disciplined soldiers had been entrusted to good hands; and early in 1863, the second battalion was considered to be fit for foreign service,

---

[1] See p. 119.

[2] Drummer Joseph Timmins sounded the first "Fall-in" for the second battalion. After long service with the Colours, he was appointed to the permanent staff of the third battalion at Wexford. He was discharged about 1890, and died a few years later.

[3] Letter of thanks to the regiment from P. B. Le Bin, Lieutenant-Judge of Alderney, 1st November, 1862.

and was selected to relieve one of the regiments then garrisoning New Zealand. When the various detachments from Jersey, Guernsey, and Alderney had concentrated at Parkhurst in the Isle of Wight, they were inspected by Major-General Lord William Paulet, who in a complimentary speech commented with pleasure on the great increase in the height of the men since he had last seen the battalion eighteen months before.

On April 2, 1863, the headquarters and eight companies under command of Lieutenant-Colonel Chapman sailed from Portsmouth in the ship *Elizabeth Anne Bright*, followed on the 12th by the two service companies under Brevet-Colonel G. J. Carey in the ship *Norwood*.[1] The depôt companies were stationed at Buttevant. After a prosperous and, for a sailing-ship, a rapid voyage of ninety-one days, the *Elizabeth Anne Bright* on the 4th of July reached Auckland, where three weeks later the *Norwood* arrived also. When the leading ship dropped anchor, the Royal Irish learned that war had broken out with the natives, and that the battalion was to take the field at once. Before describing the part played by the XVIIIth in the campaign a short account must be given of the Maoris, the enemy at whose hands the second battalion was to receive its baptism of fire. According to native traditions, New Zealand was peopled many centuries ago by an adventurous race (said by ethnologists to be of Malay stock) who, swarming off from the Melanesian archipelago, crossed the Southern Pacific in war canoes and landed in New Zealand, which they named the Land of the Long White Cloud. Either the country was uninhabited or the aborigines were easily conquered, for no trace of their presence is found in Maori folklore. The newcomers first occupied the coasts, and then gradually spread over the whole of the North and South islands, forming clans which recognised no central authority and held all land within their borders as the property not of individuals but of the tribe. Between the tribes there was incessant strife, which hardened the Maoris into

---

[1] The following officers left England with the battalion, or joined during the New Zealand war :—

Lieutenant-Colonel—A. A. Chapman, in command.

Major and Brevet-Colonel—G. J. Carey.

Major—J. H. Rocke.

Captains—Sir H. M. Havelock, V.C. (who later assumed the name of Havelock-Allan), J. Inman, W. D. Chapman, R. P. Bishopp, E. A. Anderson, J. T. Ring, T. D. Baker, W. Kemp, F. Fearnley, E. L. Dillon, E. A. Noblett, H. Shaw, J. F. Daubeny.

Lieutenants—R. W. E. Dawson (adjutant), T. C. Wray, E. Hall, J. A. J. Briggs, S. T. Corrie, W. F. Thacker, E. A. Marsland, G. A. Nicolls, C. G. Minnitt, W. T. Croft, J. J. R. Russell, F. P. Leonard, O. R. Lawson.

Ensigns—J. B. Jackson, C. Dawson, A. J. A. Jackson, J. G. Butts, B. G. Haines, C. G. Phillips, F. J. S. Pringle, H. D. Bicknell, W. E. Chapman, H. Jones, D. R. Macqueen, G. B. Jenkins, J. C. Fife, A. R. H. Swindley, E. C. Milner.

Adjutant—Lieutenant R. W. E. Dawson.

Quartermaster—J. Stainforth.

Surgeon—G. W. Peake, M.D.

Assistant-Surgeon W. I. Spencer.

Paymaster—C. F. Heatly.

a nation of fighting men, skilled not only in every wile of savage warfare but also, as we shall see, in the art of fortifying their strongholds.

The existence of the Maoris and the very position of the country they inhabited remained unknown to Europeans until 1642, when Tasman, the great Dutch navigator, sighted the Land of the Long White Cloud. His government kept the information to themselves; and Captain Cook, a British explorer even more celebrated than his Dutch forerunner, rediscovered New Zealand in 1769, established friendly relations with the natives, and took formal possession of the country for his sovereign, George III. But neither at that time nor for many years later was England in the mood to develop her new acquisition. Her conflict with the American colonists, her struggle with the European coalition which supported their rebellion, and her gigantic efforts to save the Continent of Europe from the domination of Napoleon, had taxed her resources to the utmost; and it was not until seventy years after Cook had annexed the country that definite official steps were taken to assert British authority in New Zealand. But long before our Government decided to occupy the islands, adventurous Britons had established themselves among the Maoris. The penal settlement, formed towards the close of the eighteenth century at Sydney, provided a port from which New Zealand became accessible from the mainland of Australia, and a brisk trade gradually sprang up between the natives and ship's captains in timber, potatoes, and native flax. Nor were these the only articles of commerce. Collectors of curiosities in Europe were eager to possess specimens of the tattooing or face ornamentation for which the Maoris were celebrated, and the heads of warriors, defeated and slain in battle and preserved as trophies in the villages of the victors, were eagerly exchanged for the muskets with which the white strangers were armed. By degrees little settlements of Europeans grew up at various points along the coast—each an Alsatia to which escaped convicts, deserters from the garrison of Sydney, run-away sailors, riff-raff of every kind, sought a refuge from the trammels of civilisation. Many of these wanderers threw in their lot with the natives: some perished miserably; others were well treated and lived with the Maoris for many years. A few of the survivors were men of some education, and from their reminiscences, and those of the missionaries and pioneers who arrived from England in the early "forties," it is possible to form an idea of the Maoris before they became tamed by British influence. Their character as a nation was very complex. Though cannibals, and bloodthirsty to a degree, their sense of honour was high, and their word once pledged was considered inviolable. They were by no means devoid of chivalry; their language was full of poetry; their manners were dignified; their laws were well defined, and the tenure of land and the ownership of movable property were regulated by customs, enforced by the power of the whole clan.

In the course of years the condition of the European settlements became a serious scandal; law and order were unknown, and there were constant collisions between the natives and the Europeans, in which the white men appear to have been frequently the aggressors. The Governor of New South Wales, who was supposed to exercise a shadowy authority over the British in New Zealand, reported strongly to the Colonial Office on the subject, and the missionaries loudly complained that their efforts among the Maoris were hampered by the presence of a considerable number of Europeans, .whose conduct was unrestrained by any form of government. In 1840, England yielded to the pressure of public opinion and formally annexed New Zealand. This step, ostensibly taken solely for the benefit of the Maoris, was also influenced by political considerations, for the French had long desired to establish themselves in the Southern Pacific: ever since the time of Cook their ships had occasionally visited New Zealand, and it was known that France was preparing to found a colony in the South island. An English frigate, the *Druid*, sailed with the newly-appointed Governor about the same time as *L'Aube*, a French man-of-war started in charge of a transport full of emigrants for New Zealand. Our ship outstripped the French vessels, and when *L'Aube* reached the South island her captain, to his bitter mortification, found that the Union Jack had been hoisted forty-eight hours before!

The terms upon which New Zealand passed into the hands of the Crown were almost unique in the history of England. Our possessions in the East have been won by the sword in wars forced upon us by the lawlessness of the neighbouring States. In America the presence of a large French garrison in Canada and at the mouth of the St Lawrence was a thunder cloud constantly overhanging the New England colonies until we captured Quebec in the Seven Years' War. In the southern hemisphere Australia was a no-man's land —a wilderness inhabited only by a few tribes of degraded savages. The necessity of defending the colonists in South Africa against the attacks of marauding Kaffirs has caused the gradual extension of British rule from Cape Town on the Atlantic to Zululand on the Indian Ocean. But in New Zealand the chiefs were treated as our equals when, at the solemn treaty of Waitanga in 1840, they ceded on behalf of their clans the sovereignty of their territories to Queen Victoria, and accepted her protection, and with it all the rights and privileges of British subjects.

For several years after this treaty was made the country seemed thoroughly quiet: large numbers of emigrants arrived from England and prospered greatly in their new homes; and the majority of Maoris appeared to acquiesce in our presence. Some of the clans were glad to be saved from internecine strife; others appreciated the increased demand for their staple productions of flax and timber, which was one of the results of the European influx; but others again, especially the tribes in the centre of the North island, grew dissatisfied with the new order of things, and elected a king to rule over them, who established a capital at Ngaruawahia, a strategic point at the junction of the Waikato and Waipa rivers.[1] From a mistaken policy of non-intervention this movement was not put down, and it rapidly degenerated into openly expressed antagonism towards the settlers. In 1862, to quote the words of one of the Ministers of the Crown, it "presented the following features :—

"An elected king, a very young man of no force of character, surrounded by a few ambitious chiefs who formed a little mock court, and by a body-guard who kept him from all vulgar contact and from even the inspection of Europeans, except on humiliating terms ; entirely powerless to enforce among his subjects the decisions of his magistrates ; an army, if it might be called so, of 5000 to 10,000 followers scattered over the country, but organised so that large numbers could be concentrated at any one point on short notice ; large accumulated supplies of food, of arms and ammunition ; a position in the centre of the island from which a descent could be made in a few hours on any of the European settlements ; roads prohibited to be made through two-thirds of the island ; the large rivers barred against steamers so that nine-tenths of the country was closed against the ordinary means of travel and transport ; the Queen's law set at utter defiance ; her magistrates treated with supercilious contempt ; her writs torn to pieces and trampled under foot ; Europeans who had married native women driven out of the King's districts, while their wives and children were taken from them, unless they would recognise and pay an annual tribute to the King ; all this accompanied by an exhibition of the utmost arrogance and undisguised contempt for the power of the Queen, the Governor and the Europeans."[2]

The safety of the colony was threatened seriously by these sullenly rebellious tribes ; and when in 1863, a body of the King's followers intervened in a dispute between Maoris and Europeans in the south-west of the North island, war became inevitable. The King's party, which was largely composed of the Waikato tribe, planned to open the campaign by raiding Auckland and exterminating its white inhabitants. Lieutenant-General Sir Duncan A. Cameron, who was in command of the Imperial troops in New Zealand, and Sir George Grey, the Governor of the colony, decided to anticipate the Maoris by advancing upon their strongholds in the wild country south of the Waikato. This river rises in the centre of the North island and winds its way northwards from its source to within forty miles of Auckland, when it turns sharply to the south-west at the native village of Te Ta. Here a tributary, the Mangatawhari creek, joins it from the north-east, and the two streams marked the northern limit of the district held by the followers of the King. Civilisation had spread about twenty-five miles to the south of Auck-

[1] See Map No. 7.
[2] 'The War in New Zealand,' by W. Fox, late Colonial Secretary and native Minister of the Colony, pp. 30-32.

land, and a metalled road ran past scores of prosperous farms, tangible proofs
of the success which had attended the colonists in this part of New Zealand.
At the village of Drury the good road was replaced by a rough and narrow
track, which winding through a broad belt of bush known as the Hunua
forest, crossed very undulating country much cut up by deep ravines, half
buried in ferns and scrub. This dense forest, which a series of almost
impenetrable thickets rendered ideal for Maori offensive tactics, was to be
the scene of many skirmishes in which detachments of the XVIIIth greatly
distinguished themselves.

The arrival of the Royal Irish brought up the number of regular battalions
in New Zealand to seven;[1] but by no means all of these were available for
the front. It was necessary to keep up the strength of the detachments in
various parts of both islands; the line of communication absorbed a great
quantity of fighting men, and garrisons had to be provided for the settlers in
lonely hamlets and isolated farms. Though at one time during the war the
armed whites in the colony reached the respectable total of 15,000 men,
the greatest force of regular and volunteer troops actually under the hand
of the General at any time appears never to have exceeded two thousand five
hundred. To form an accurate estimate of the numbers against us is impossible, for many tribes remained neutral, others were on our side, while
others again took but a fitful part in the operations and preferred to plunder
settlers rather than to meet soldiers in the field. One point, however, seems
quite clear; on every occasion when there was serious fighting we greatly
out-numbered our savage but very gallant foes.

As soon as the Royal Irish landed they were sent to Otahuhu, a camp
a little to the south of Auckland, where General Cameron was concentrating
his troops. Here the battalion received their campaigning kit: officers and
men were provided with blue serge "jumpers," haversacks, water-bottles and
pannikins: all ranks carried a blanket and waterpoof sheet, rolled, and slung
over the left shoulder; the men were armed with Enfield rifles and bayonets.
Five days later the column marched through Drury to the Queen's redoubt,
a work which commanded the crossing of the Waikato at Te Ta. A detachment of two hundred of the XVIIIth, under Captain Inman, was dropped at
Drury to hold that post on the line of communication, and a few days later
the whole of the battalion appears to have been echeloned along the bush track
between Drury and the Queen's redoubt. On hearing that Cameron was
in motion the Maoris divided their forces: one column was to hold the
British at the Waikato while the other was to turn Cameron's left, harass his

[1] 1st battalion, 12th, and 2nd battalions, 14th and XVIIIth regiments, and the 40th, 57th, 65th,
and 70th regiments, which were still one-battalion corps. There were detachments of Royal Artillery
and Royal Engineers, a Military Train, a Naval brigade, and various Colonial corps, including a contingent of friendly natives. The 43rd, 50th, and 68th regiments, and a considerable number of
volunteers enlisted in Australia, reached New Zealand later in the war.

communications, and if possible swoop upon Auckland. It was with the enemy's right wing that the Royal Irish were chiefly engaged for the first few months of the war, but before giving an account of their doings it is necessary to sketch very briefly the operations south of the Waikato.

On July 12, 1863, Cameron crossed the river and dislodged the enemy from the heights of Koheroa above the Mangatawhari creek. He was, however, unable to follow up this initial success; for nearly three months difficulties of land transport, the want of steamers of sufficiently light draught for river work, and the activity of the Maoris on his rear prevented further movements against the series of works which at various points commanded the right bank of the Waikato. The military genius of the Maoris and its limitations were alike revealed in these fortifications, in which the system of defence evolved by a long series of inter-tribal conflicts had been cleverly adapted to new conditions of war. Before firearms were introduced into New Zealand, the

"Maoris' *pahs*, or stockaded and entrenched villages, usually perched on cliffs and jutting points overhanging river or sea, were defended by a double palisade, the outer fence of stout stakes, the inner of high solid trunks. Between them was a shallow ditch. Platforms as much as forty feet high supplied coigns of vantage for the look-out. Thence, too, darts and stones could be hurled at the besiegers. With the help of a throwing stick, or rather whip, wooden spears could be thrown in the sieges more than a hundred yards. Ignorant of the bow and arrow, and the boomerang, the Maoris knew and used the sling; with it red-hot stones would be hurled over the palisades among the rush-thatched huts of an assaulted village, a stratagem all the more difficult to cope with as Maori *pahs* seldom contained wells or springs of water." [1]

In the series of skirmishes dignified by the name of the Maori war of 1860-61 the natives had carefully studied our tactics and our weapons; and in the war of 1863-66, in order to bring into play the muskets and double-barrelled guns with which they were armed, and to minimise the effect of our rifle and shell fire, they selected positions open in front, with flanks resting on rivers, swamps, or impenetrable bush. They made great use of earthworks and of redoubts, square or oblong in shape, flanked at opposite angles by bastions and surrounded by ditches, in some cases twelve feet wide and measuring eighteen feet from the bottom of the ditch to the top of the parapet. Pushed out to the front and flanks were two or three tiers of rifle-pits or short trenches, connected by sunk roads with each other and with the main work. The marksmen in these pits were often protected by head cover, made of trunks of trees or of hurdles thatched with fern and covered deep with earth; and to break the force of a bayonet charge, stout palisades were sometimes built in front of the rifle-pits with spaces left for grazing fire to sweep over the glacis. Yet though this system of fortification showed that to

---

[1] Pember Reeves, 'The Long White Cloud,' pp. 48, 49.

their natural cleverness the Maoris added the power of rapidly absorbing new ideas, their intelligence failed them in one essential particular. In the selection of a position they never realised the importance of a good water-supply, and when an attack was threatened they neglected to store their works with water, trusting to their young men to bring in by night the quantity required for the next day's consumption. Thus after a close invest-ment of a few days they had no alternative but to cut their way out or to surrender.

While General Cameron was waiting for his river steamers, a rumour reached the Maoris at Meri-Meri, the position nearest to Cameron's encamp-ment, that the General and his soldiers were short of food. Under a flag of truce the Chiefs sent down the river a little fleet of canoes laden with potatoes and milch-goats as a present to the British troops. This was by no means an isolated instance of native chivalry, for, to use the slang of the present day, the Maoris were "sportsmen," and always said that there was no glory in fighting hungry men. When at length the arrival of river craft enabled Cameron to move, he threatened the front of the works of Meri-Meri with five hundred men, among whom were a detachment of Royal Irish, while a turning party of rather greater strength, in barges mounted with Armstrong guns, was towed to a landing-place in rear of the enemy's works. The Maoris did not await the attack, but fled southwards across country which recent rains had made impassable for Europeans. Cameron occupied their position, which the detachment of the XVIIIth fortified under the direction of the Royal Engineers. In November the General took an important step towards freeing the line of communication from the natives who harassed his convoys in the Hunua forest and ravaged the farms in the neighbourhood of Auckland. Many of these guerillas came from the country round the estuary of the Thames river, and thither he sent an expedition under Brevet-Colonel Carey, XVIIIth regiment, to overawe the district and establish a line of blockhouses between the Thames and the Waikato. While Carey was carrying out his mission successfully Cameron pushed up the river, and on November 20th, attacked the formidable works at Rangiriri, the Maoris' second position on the Waikato. Before the enemy had been thoroughly shaken by artillery the order was given for the assault, and though repeated and gallant charges were delivered, the troops that day achieved but a partial success, bought at the cost of 132 casualties. Under cover of the night several hundred of the enemy escaped; the remainder, 183 in number, surrendered at daybreak and were made prisoners of war. In this engagement the Royal Irish were represented only by one officer, Captain and Brevet-Lieutenant-Colonel Sir H. Havelock, V.C.,[1] then serving on the headquarter staff as D.A.Q.M.G., and a

---

[1] Brevet-Colonel Carey, Lieutenant-Colonel Havelock, afterwards Havelock-Allan, V.C., D.A.Q.M.G., and Captain T. D. Baker, A.M.S., were so constantly mentioned in despatches through-out the war that it is unnecessary to record the fact after each affair in which they were engaged.

few men. The losses at Rangiriri greatly dispirited the enemy, who allowed Cameron to march unmolested up the right bank of the Waikato, and on December 9, 1863, to occupy Ngaruawahia, the capital of the rebellious country.

The Royal Irish were hard at work on the line of communication during this time. Tracks had to be cut through virgin forest and garrisons provided for settlers' farms; convoys needed large escorts, while the road along which the waggons lumbered had to be strongly piquetted and constantly patrolled. In these duties detachments of the XVIIIth met with many exciting adventures; they alternately rescued parties of other regiments from imminent danger or were themselves saved from destruction by the timely arrival of reinforcements. Many laurels were won in these skirmishes, of which the details, as far as they have been preserved, are here recorded.[1] Six days after the headquarters of the battalion had reached the Queen's redoubt Captain Ring, with Ensign Bicknell, two sergeants, and forty-seven rank and file, was sent in charge of a convoy to Drury. The track passed through a forest, thus described by an officer of great experience of campaigning in the forests of many parts of the British Empire: "The bush of New Zealand is wonderfully dense and entangled. A European going into it about twenty yards and turning round three times is quite at a loss to find his way out again unless he is somewhat of an Indian path-finder and can judge of the points of the compass by the bark of the trees, the sun, &c. Trying to run through the bush one is tripped up by the supplejack and other creepers." [2] While on the march Ring fell into an ambuscade of about 140 Maoris; fire was opened by invisible enemies upon his advance-guard, his right flank, and his rear; a driver and two horses in the centre of the convoy fell wounded; the line of waggons was thrown into confusion, and the Maoris attacked his left flank. He retired immediately with as many men as he could concentrate, and, in skirmishing order, kept the enemy at bay for some time; then seeing himself nearly surrounded he retreated into a settler's farm, which he held until some of Inman's detachment at Drury extricated him from his dangerous situation. In this affair four men were killed and ten wounded.[3]

Soon after this affair Ring found himself in charge of a mixed body of troops at Keri-Keri, on the road which runs north-east from Drury through the Wairoa country to the coast. With him were five officers and about two hundred rank and file of the battalion, and two officers and a hundred men of a New Zealand militia regiment. In the morning of the 22nd of July he learned that a number of natives had murderously attacked two settlers,

---

[1] The regimental records of the New Zealand War are far from complete, for the battalion was constantly broken up into small detachments, buried in stockades in the depths of the bush. Between these detachments and headquarters communication was most difficult, and for weeks, and even months, the various portions of the regiment knew nothing of each other's proceedings.

[2] 'Bush Fighting: The Maori War,' by Major-General Sir J. E. Alexander, p. 59.

[3] See Appendix 2 (K).

and immediately afterwards heard heavy firing about two miles off near Pukekewereke, where sixteen volunteers were defending themselves against very heavy odds. Leaving the militia and two officers and a hundred of his own men to hold the post, he hurried to the rescue with Lieutenant Wray, Ensigns Jackson and Butts, and the remainder of the Royal Irish. On reaching the scene of the skirmish Ring opened fire, and, to use the words of his report, "the natives retreated to my former entrenchment above the *wharé*[1] at Keri-Keri; the fire of the skirmishers drove them down the side of the hill into the brushwood; the leading skirmishers on the right, under Lieutenant Wray, took possession of the hill and kept up fire on them; I, with another body of skirmishers, proceeding to take that on the right flank, but found that the natives, who mustered a strong force, nearly surrounded me; here I lost a man killed, whose rifle and bayonet were taken possession of by the natives, though not without serious loss to them. I then concentrated my men on the entrenchment, and having heard from a Royal Artillery officer who rode up to my position that the 65th regiment was in my immediate vicinity, I requested that he would inform the officer commanding the 65th that there was a track in the enemy's rear, and that if an attack were made in that direction it would be of great service. As it was quite impossible for me to follow so strong a force of the enemy into the bush with my small force, I remained in the entrenched position until close on sunset, keeping a steady fire on the enemy, who were endeavouring to obtain the body of the private who was killed and whom I would not leave. I repeatedly tried to obtain possession of the body by sending out volunteers of the man's company, but desisted, finding it would entail greater loss. I was about to retire, leaving a rear-guard in the entrenchment, when the mounted artillery arrived." The gunners were closely followed by a party of the 65th, who threw themselves into the fray with great spirit. On the appearance of these fresh troops the natives drew off into bush so thick that no pursuit was possible, and after the body of the dead soldier had been recovered the whole force returned to their entrenchments. This affair cost the battalion one man killed and four wounded.[2] For Ring's conduct and good judgment on this occasion General Cameron recommended him for a brevet-majority, to which he had been gazetted in England before he fell mortally wounded at the engagement of Orakau on March 31, 1864. The detachment was commended for the firmness with which they had held their ground against superior numbers.

The next time any of the XVIIIth were in action seems to have been on the 25th of August. The attack on Ring's convoy had shown how easily traffic could be stopped in the Hunua forest. To make communication safer through this belt of bush the Government of New Zealand set a large number of men to cut down the scrub on either side of the road. Soldiers as well as

---

[1] Native house or hut. [2] See Appendix 2 (K).

civilians were employed on the work; among the former were a party of a corps which appears not only to have been ignorant of the first principles of warfare, but grossly disobedient to orders. General Cameron had officially reminded the troops that axe-men should always be protected by a covering party; but the detachment disregarded this order and, far from taking precautions for their safety, piled arms near the road under charge of a single sentry. The Maoris crawled through the bush, rushed the sentry, and before the detachment could regain their rifles nearly all the arms had fallen into the enemy's hands. Several of the — were hit; the remainder, defenceless without their rifles, had fallen back for shelter into the forest, when the guard of a convoy, chiefly composed of a company of the Royal Irish, under Captain R. P. Bishopp, appeared on the scene, and after an hour's sharp skirmishing succeeded in driving away the enemy. In this affair one man of the XVIIIth was wounded.[1] Early in September the headquarters of the Royal Irish were moved to Drury, leaving two companies under Captain Noblett to man the Queen's redoubt. During the month three detachments of the battalion had brushes with the enemy. Half a mile from the village of Pokeno, near the Queen's redoubt, a party of 62 non-commissioned officers and men, under Ensign C. Dawson, were attacked by a body of natives, who fired into them from the rear. A bayonet charge drove the enemy into a gully, down which the Royal Irish pursued them for half a mile, when a burst of war-whoops and yells from the village warned Dawson to collect his men to meet a fresh danger. Making his way back to Pokeno, he was received by a volley from Maoris hidden among the stumps and logs of timber in a clearing in front of the village, and from another party on his left flank. Dawson had his men well in hand, kept them in skirmishing order, and maintained a steady fire from all available cover, until he was extricated from this unpleasant situation by the arrival of a party of the 40th, and later by a further reinforcement, the escort to a convoy commanded by Captain Noblett, XVIIIth regiment. The Maoris fled before the levelled bayonets of the combined detachments and took refuge in the bush, into which the soldiers could not follow. A few days later, a convoy in charge of a body of volunteers broke down at Pukekohe, near Drury; some of the Royal Irish, under Captain Inman, were sent to its assistance, and found the waggons stuck in deep mud, while the Maoris were attacking the stockade which contained the garrison of the post. Inman's party rescued the convoy; then, reinforced by the volunteers, they went in with the cold steel, and received praise from General Cameron for " the gallant manner in which they charged the enemy, driving him back into the bush with severe loss from the position he had taken up near the stockade." For his

---

[1] See Appendix 2 (K). It was not until the bush had been cleared for two hundred yards on each side of the track that waggons could move through the forest of Hunua with safety.

services on this and other occasions Captain Inman received a Brevet-Majority.

About the same time another party of the XVIIIth were in action on the Wairoa road, along which various blockhouses had been built to cover the approach to Auckland. One of these works, the Galloway redoubt, was in charge of Major Lyon, an ex-Imperial officer, under whose orders some of the battalion were placed. On the 15th of September the Maoris attacked the redoubt, but were beaten off, after an affair in which the steadiness of the Royal Irish was conspicuous. Two days later Lyon, who had been reinforced by another party of the XVIIIth under Lieutenant Russell, took the offensive, and under cover of darkness led his troops towards Otau, a native village occupied by local insurgents. It was found to be on the far side of a river, and while Lyon searched for a ford, he engaged the enemy with musketry—according to a well-known historian, with unexpectedly important results—

"Across the stream at early dawn a detachment of the XVIIIth regiment poured concentrated fire upon the *wharés* [huts]. They did not know that within them was a band of Maoris, who had come to join the fighting, and who, under the volleys poured upon the huts, fell like sheep. The troops, unable to cross the stream, withdrew, unconscious of what they had done. Major Lyon, who made a circuit by a bridge, found the settlement deserted. 'The *wharés*,' he said, 'were riddled with shot, blood in profusion both inside and out. They were unmistakably taken by surprise.' In after years a Maori who was present told how extensive was the slaughter unwittingly inflicted by the XVIIIth, who exercised themselves by firing at the huts without knowing how they were occupied. As the wounded and dead were carried away before Major Lyon reached the spot, he also was ignorant of the severity of the blow inflicted." [1]

In October, the battalion were again fortunate enough to rescue a party of New Zealand volunteers from a dangerous situation. An officer of the irregulars while reconnoitring a large body of natives near his post at Manku, was drawn into an engagement, forced back into his stockade, and closely surrounded. The news reached Drury in the evening, and a strong party of the XVIIIth under Captain Noblett was at once sent, with some of the 70th, to the relief of the volunteers. Pushing on throughout the night the troops early in the morning reached Manku, from which the Maoris decamped promptly, thus depriving the Royal Irish of the excitement of a skirmish. They at once returned to Drury, where they arrived after twenty-two hours' continuous marching. At the end of the month two companies in charge of Captain Noblett reinforced Ring's post in the Wairoa country; and in

[1] G. W. Rusden, 'History of New Zealand,' vol. ii. p. 45. In another passage (p. 173) this author considers that the destruction of this war party signally foiled the Maoris' scheme of attack on Cameron's left and rear.

November an expedition, largely composed of the Royal Irish, was sent to avenge outrages committed on the settlers in this district. The marauders had stockaded themselves in a position surrounded by dense bush, swamps, and precipitous ravines, but after a skirmish the *pah* was captured and destroyed.

In war opportunities of distinction do not come to every officer, and such in a marked degree was the case in New Zealand, where much good work was done by some of the officers of the XVIIIth whose names do not appear in General Cameron's reports. Though the vigorous action of the troops on the line of communication and in the Wairoa country prevented the Maoris from raiding Auckland itself, it was impossible for Cameron with the small number of men at his disposal to carry the war into the enemy's country, and at the same time protect all the outlying farms cleared in the bush by enterprising settlers. In most cases the colonists abandoned their farms, sent their women and children to Auckland, and turned themselves into a militia, which proved a valuable asset in the British force. Occasionally, however, the entire population of a settlement held its ground, and required help from the troops. Thus, in September, Captain Kemp[1] with 150 of the Royal Irish was sent to the relief of one of these outposts of civilisation; a forced march through virgin forest, past many farms which the Maoris had looted and burned to the ground, brought him to his destination, where he found the colonists had thrown up stockades round their tiny church, in peaceful times used by various denominations as a place of worship, but now turned into the keep of the primitive fortress. Leaving these brave pioneers a supply of provisions and cartridges, and a small party of troops to give backbone to the defence, he returned to Drury, where his next duty was to form a post at a deserted farm on the line of communication. With his own company and fifty men under Lieutenant Briggs he cut down tree ferns, and with their trunks, lashed together with wild vines (locally known as supplejack), built a strong palisade, eight feet in height, enclosing not only the farm buildings but also space enough for the tents of his detachment. As soon as the farm had been placed in a state of defence, the British instinct of cleanliness asserted itself, and the house and outbuildings were thoroughly cleansed; then parties of men were sent out to "round up" the farmer's cattle which had strayed into the forest, while others improved the defences and escorted the convoys to the next post on the way to the front. Encouraged by the presence of the detachment the farmer returned with his family to his house, which can hardly be described as a peaceful home, for, to quote Captain Kemp's diary, "Our nights were disturbed by seeing lights in the bush. I burned all the low scrub (near the farm), and twice a-week

---

[1] Captain Kemp and Captain Briggs have supplied the author with valuable information—the former by sending extracts from his diary, the latter by recording his reminiscences of the campaign.

took out a skirmishing party and scoured the forest: we saw a few natives but they always escaped us in the thick undergrowth. However we were not further molested." Kemp's diary then briefly records a succession of escorts to convoys and to prisoners taken at the fight of Rangariri; much road-making, and marches knee-deep in swamps.

In January, 1864, the Royal Irish were employed in various ways.[1] Part of the battalion was sent to guard the line of communication from the Queen's redoubt southward to Ngaruawahia; the remainder formed the garrisons of the chain of works which Brevet-Colonel Carey had established between the Waikato and the estuary of the Thames. Thanks to Captain Kemp, we know something of the hard work done by those of the XVIIIth who were in charge of these posts. On the 7th of January, with two hundred men, he

"marched to the Surrey redoubt; it was very hot as we skirted the swamps and many men fainted from the heat. We placed a detachment in the redoubt, slept in the open outside it, and marched at 5.30 A.M. next day eight miles to the Esk redoubt on high ground in open fern-covered country. Here I left Briggs and a detachment and took my company down to the Miranda redoubt, four miles farther on, situated at the edge of a steep cliff overlooking the estuary of the Thames and defended by a small river on the north side. Here I had command of two hundred men, one half being Waikato militia. We enlarged the redoubt and made a road down to the landing-place (previously all stores were dragged up the face of the cliff and the Commissariat suffered heavy losses). We made a floating bridge over the small river, sunk a well for drinking water, and built a small redoubt on the approach from the south in which a strong piquet was posted at night. Boats being unable to come in at low water we made a causeway across the mud flats to a deep-water landing-place. . . . We were annoyed at first by spies and small parties of the enemy at night, so I sent out scouring parties and destroyed their villages, bringing in large quantities of beautiful peaches, potatoes, and other vegetables."

At the end of January, General Cameron had accumulated enough stores at Ngaruawahia to warrant his advancing farther to the southward. He therefore worked up the right bank of the Waipa, building and garrisoning redoubts as he advanced, and in a few days reached the village of Te Rore, where for nearly three weeks he was brought to a halt—not by the enemy, but by the eternal difficulty of supply and transport. Shoals in the rivers made water-carriage uncertain, and though the crews of the little steamers, the flat-bottomed row-boats, and the other craft specially built for the expedition did their best, this mode of transport was always liable to break

[1] The strength on December 1, 1863, of the ten companies of the second battalion of the XVIIIth was 2 field officers, 9 captains, 20 subalterns, 5 staff, 47 sergeants, 22 drummers, 763 rank and file fit for duty, and 24 sick, or a total of 892 of all ranks.

down. By land things were no better. In the plain between the Waikato and Waipa rivers there were hardly any roads, and the native paths, winding through forests of tree ferns, were so narrow that men could only march in single file. These paths crossed innumerable creeks running in deep water-courses, impassable for guns or waggons till roads had been cut down the steep banks and bridges thrown over the streams. The difficulty of keeping supplied even the small number of men—less than 2500—who were concentrated at Te Rore was enormous, for though Cameron's headquarters were only eighty miles from his base at Auckland, every box of " stores had to be shifted twelve or fourteen times on account of changes of land and water carriage." [1] To relieve this strain Cameron cut a road through the bush to Raglan, a port twenty miles distant on the west coast, and thus gained a second or subsidiary base, but as a set-off to this advantage a considerable number of men were necessarily withdrawn from active operations to guard the new line of communication.

While the advance depôt at Te Rore was being gradually filled up, the Maoris threw up a formidable chain of works to bar farther advance into their country; but after a few skirmishes they were manœuvred from these positions and disappeared into the mountains in the centre of the island. To prevent their return down the Waikato river, a post was formed on its left bank at Pukerima, and manned by the headquarter companies of the XVIIIth from Ngaruawahia. The stay of the battalion at the Maori capital had been uneventful, though to celebrate the temporary reunion of most of the companies pony races and sports for the men were organised, and made a welcome break in the monotony of the campaign, for in the long intervals between active operations amusements for all ranks were not to be obtained. An officer writes: "There were very few opportunities during the war for gymkhanas and that sort of thing, and a 'sing-song' over the camp-fire was as much as could be attempted. Occasionally a little duck-shooting from canoes was obtainable if we were stationed near a river, or more rarely a raid on the semi-wild boar sometimes to be met with in the bush. Pigeon-shooting was sometimes to be had, but this was about all."

Not all the companies went with headquarters to the new post; some held the works on the lower reaches of the river, and a detachment of four companies under Captain Ring was at Te Awamutu, where Colonel Carey, recently promoted to be Brigadier-General and second-in-command of the forces in New Zealand, was throwing up strong redoubts. Here everything appeared to be quiet until a scouting party of colonists discovered that a number of Maoris had slipped back to the Waikato plain, and were vigorously entrenching themselves a few miles off near the native village of Orakau. Carey at once reconnoitred the *pah*, and decided to

[1] Alexander, p. 129.

move on the enemy's position during the night; the main column was to advance on Orakau,[1] while smaller parties were to place themselves by forced marches on the enemy's flank and rear. Like a good soldier, Carey did not issue his orders till the last moment, and it was not till after dark on the 30th of March that the officers of the detachment of the XVIIIth heard the news, which reached them in a very dramatic manner. They were sitting at mess in a native hut, dimly lighted by a few camp lanterns, when the voice of a staff officer was heard calling for Ring, who in a few minutes returned, looking pale and depressed. Waiting until the soldier servants had left the hut to reply to his comrades' inquiries as to the cause of his sudden gloom, he explained that the detachment was to march that night to attack the *pah*, and he added in confidence that he had a presentiment that his last hour was close at hand. "I have taken part in many affairs of this kind," he said, "but I have never felt as I do now." When his friends "chaffed" him and tried to cheer him up, he answered, "Oh! never fear. I'll do my duty." After issuing the necessary orders to the detachment he wrote his farewell letters, hastily put his affairs in order, and then marched off with the advance-guard, which he had the honour on this occasion to command.

The column reached Orakau at dawn on March 31. The Maoris, though evidently taken by surprise, opened fire on the advance-guard, composed of 120 Royal Irish and a party of 20 men of an irregular corps, known as the Forest Rangers. Ring extended his men into skirmishing order, and, supported by a company of the 40th, led them to the attack. The position, which apparently had not been reconnoitred adequately, proved very formidable. On a swelling down the Maoris had thrown up an "earthwork with good flank defences, deep ditches, with posts and rails outside, and nearly covered from view by flax-bushes, peach-trees, and high fern."[2] Though repulsed by the fire of their unseen enemies Ring's men re-formed quickly, and reinforced by a second company of the 40th, made another but equally futile effort to storm the works, being again beaten back with the loss of several officers and men, among whom was Brevet-Major Ring, mortally wounded. When Captain Baker, XVIIIth, D.A.A.G., saw that Ring was down, he flung himself off his horse, and calling for volunteers led a third assault. This failed also, but though these three attacks were unsuccessful, they served their purpose by so completely occupying the attention of the enemy that he did not realise that the British troops were hemming him in on every side; and though the cordon was at first but slender it sufficed to prevent reinforcements from throwing themselves into the *pah*. At mid-

---

[1] This column was composed of 728 of all ranks; among them was a detachment of the Royal Irish—1 captain, 3 subalterns, 1 staff, 5 sergeants, 3 drummers, and 140 rank and file. The smaller columns were 250 and 100 strong.   [2] Carey's despatch.

day a large party of Maoris tried to break through our lines from the outside, but a few shells and the musketry of the outposts kept them at a respectful distance, unable to do more than excite their besieged comrades to further resistance by shouts and war dances.   As soon as the detached columns detailed to surround the *pah* were in their places, Carey began to sap up to the works, covering his movements with artillery fire.   In defending themselves against this bombardment the Maoris showed great resource. "Long bundles of fern were cut and bound with strips of green flax until an enormous mass of yielding fern received the harmless cannon-balls and guarded the earthworks."[1]

Throughout the afternoon and night the besieged kept up a heavy fire upon the troops, who "dug themselves in" so effectually with their bayonets that the casualties were few.   The sap was pushed on vigorously, and on the 1st of April various small reinforcements, snatched up from the line of communication, reached Carey.   Among them was a party of the XVIIIth under Captain Inman, composed of 1 captain, 2 subalterns, 8 sergeants, 2 drummers, and 110 rank and file, and 70 officers and men of the 70th; after marching all night, they were sent at once into the trenches and rifle-pits with which the *pah* was being rapidly encircled.   Though the enemy kept up a heavy fire upon the men digging in the sap, the work went on without intermission until the morning of the 2nd, when Lieutenant-Colonel Havelock brought into camp a quantity of hand-grenades, which a brave artilleryman, at the risk of his life, hurled into the enemy's rifle-pits.   Under cover of the confusion produced by these missiles Carey ran into the sap a 6-pr. Armstrong gun, whose fire breached the palisades, and beat down the musketry directed upon the working-parties.   The situation had improved so much that he was preparing to assault, when General Cameron ordered him to stay his hand.   The General had recently arrived on the scene, but not wishing to deprive Carey of his command announced that he was present as a spectator only; learning, however, that many women and children were in the *pah*, he desired that the garrison should be given the chance to surrender before the attack was pressed home.   The condition of the Maoris was now desperate.   When surprised by our sudden swoop on Orakau, they had little or no water in the *pah;* our line of outposts and rifle-pits proved impenetrable to the parties who sought for water in the night; their only food was raw potatoes; their losses in fighting men had been considerable, and their supply of bullets was almost exhausted.   Yet they disdained to yield, and when an interpreter addressed them, saying, "Hear the word of the General: you have done enough to show that you are brave men; your case is hopeless; surrender, and your lives will be spared;" they haughtily replied, "This is the word of the Maori: we will fight for ever and ever and ever."   They were then

[1] Rusden, vol. ii. p. 205.

invited to send away the women, and answered, "The women will fight as well as we."

After this abortive negotiation fire was reopened on both sides, and some of the troops appear to have lost their heads and attempted to storm the *pah* without orders.[1] One of these unauthorised assaults was led by a soldier in the XVIIIth, Private Hannon, who, throwing his forage cap over a partially breached spot in the defences, dashed after it with some twenty men, for the most part belonging to New Zealand corps. After clambering over a stout fence they dropped into a ditch, where Hannon and nine other brave men were mown down by a volley fired at point-blank range. But though a similar attack by a party of regulars and volunteers also failed to carry another weak spot in the fortifications, every hour saw the Maoris less able to face the storm of grape-shot, hand-grenades, and rifle-bullets poured upon them on every side. Suddenly Rewi, their war chief, decided to cut his way out or to perish in the attempt. While his followers mustered among the huts round which their works were built, they sang one of the hymns taught them by the missionaries, and then, remembering the old days before white men had settled in New Zealand, chanted invocations to their ancient gods.

> "Their voices," says Rusden, "were heard by the wondering English, who were to marvel still more at their daring. At the rear a double line of the investing troops had been thrown back under cover to enable a gun to open fire. Through that opening, about four o'clock in the broad day, chanting their appeal to the God of battles and moving steadily as in scorn of their foes, the Maoris marched towards the narrow neck of swamp between the ridge and mound. Carey (in his official report) said they rushed. Mr Fox writes that an eye-witness told him 'they were in a great column, the women, the children, and the great chiefs in the centre, and they marched out as cool and steady as if they had been going to Church.' Rewi ordered that no shot should be fired. The little ammunition left was needed for defence in the desperate course through the swamp. . . . Some accounts state that as if to deceive the troops and gain time for the fugitives, a Maori, while his countrymen departed, sprang up with a white flag on the parapet and was riddled by bullets. One chief, more successful, diverted the English for a few moments; he walked coolly towards the troops and surrendered."[2]

The regiment (not the XVIIIth) charged with the defence of the ground across which the Maori column was moving, was disposed in two lines, the foremost lying under a bank which, while it covered the men from fire from the *pah*, prevented their watching the ground in front of them. The Maoris

---

[1] Some of the historians of the New Zealand War assert that these assaults were ordered by General Carey: others hold that they were unauthorised: the balance of evidence is in favour of the latter opinion.

[2] Rusden, vol. ii. pp. 207, 208.

marched towards this bank, and, incredible as it seems, passed through these two lines of British regular troops, apparently without opposition. It was rumoured at the time that before the men in the first line discovered that the natives were out of their trenches, the Maoris had actually jumped over their heads and were well on their way towards the second line! Thanks to the energy of the General and his staff and the zeal of the remainder of the troops, the natives did not escape in a body, but were headed off by a handful of mounted men, who punished them severely in a pursuit which lasted until nightfall. Thirty-three prisoners fell into our hands; more than a hundred bodies were found on the field; it was known that at least twenty men had been buried in the *pah*, while traces in the bush proved that a considerable number of killed and wounded had been carried away after the troops had been recalled to camp. The natives themselves acknowledged to a loss of two hundred, out of a strength considered by General Cameron not to exceed three hundred fighting men. Well might the British General in his despatch say that it was impossible not to admire the heroic courage and devotion of the Maoris in defending themselves so long against overwhelming numbers.[1]

When the Royal Irish were let loose, the men were wild to avenge the death of Captain Ring, who was deservedly respected and admired by all ranks in the regiment. Though the officers did all they could to prevent unnecessary slaughter, more than one Maori was slain in the belief that it was he who had fired the shot which laid Ring low. When a fugitive was overtaken the cry arose, "That's the man that killed the Captain!"—then came a wild yell, a bayonet thrust, and all was over. Not all the XVIIIth, however, were believers in such stern methods: two instances of clemency are recorded, one of which unhappily ended fatally to the poor Irishman. A soldier overtook and seized a Maori and spared his life; the prisoner was lying on the ground exhausted and apparently harmless, and his captor had turned away for a moment, when the native seized a rifle and shot him dead. The savage's triumph was short-lived, however, for other men of the XVIIIth were on the spot and silenced him for ever. In the other case there was no such tragedy. Early in the pursuit a Maori was taken prisoner and placed in the charge of two privates, who, as they heard the shouts of their comrades dying away in the distance, cursed their bad luck in being obliged to remain

[1] Two anecdotes will show how stern was the courage of the Maori warriors. General Alexander describes how an officer was standing at the head of the sap, watching his opportunity to enter the *pah*. The head of a fierce-looking Maori appeared above the parapet, but the Englishman was a quick shot and the head disappeared. When the troops got into the works the officer looked for the man he had hit. The Maori had dropped with a bullet through his brain, but this death-wound was not his only injury. Some time during the siege his leg had been broken and roughly bound up with flax and a tent-peg, to enable him to go on fighting. In the retreat a native for some time escorted a party of women and children. "As his pursuers approached," says Mr Rusden, "he turned and knelt down to take deliberate aim. Time after time, without firing a shot, he thus arrested the pursuit while the women fled. At last he himself was shot, and it was found that his gun was not loaded."

behind. An officer came up when their impatience reached its climax, and overheard this conversation. "Shall we kill him, Barney?" Barney thought for a moment, and then shook his head. "I couldn't kill the craytur in cold blood, Pat, but I wish we were quit of him." "Kick him and let him go," was the ready response. No sooner said than done; the prisoner disappeared into the bush, while Pat and Barney hurried after the regiment!

The British losses were sixteen killed and fifty-two wounded. The casualties among the Royal Irish were one officer (Brevet-Major Ring) and eight of the other ranks killed or mortally wounded, nine non-commissioned officers and men wounded.[1] In his official report Brigadier-General Carey, after expressing his deep regret at the death of Brevet-Major Ring, brought the services of Captain Inman to the notice of the General Officer commanding in New Zealand.

After the capture of Orakau the enemy retired again into the mountains, whither Cameron did not deem it prudent to follow him; and when the disaffected tribes in other parts of the North island heard how inconclusively the campaign on the Waikato had ended, there was an insurrection in the east, chiefly memorable for our defeat at the Gate *pah*, while in the south-west (the Taranaki country) there were frequent skirmishes between the troops and hostile natives.[2] To neither of these scenes of action were the Royal Irish summoned; after occupying Ngaruawahia for three months the regiment marched to Otahuhu camp, where it formed part of the garrison of Auckland during the remainder of the year.

At the beginning of 1865, the Royal Irish were sent to the south-west coast of the North island, to reinforce the small number of regular troops holding the Taranaki (or New Plymouth) district, where since the war began the British had been able to do little more than to hold redoubts round a few settlements, and to send occasional punitive expeditions into the enemy's country. In the beginning of the campaign the rebel tribes, the adherents of the King, had fought us solely on political grounds; they objected to our presence and wished to drive us out of New Zealand, but no question of religion entered into the quarrel. Many of the Maoris had embraced Christianity, and had become such strict Sabbatarians that on one occasion the garrison of a besieged *pah* left their works on a Sunday morning to attend chapel, with results disastrous to themselves. But early in 1864, the British

---

[1] See Appendix 2 (K).

[2] General Alexander tells an interesting anecdote about the fighting in the Taranaki district in 1864. In a skirmish the son of a chief was made a prisoner, badly wounded in the leg. To save his life the surgeons amputated the limb, and when the young man was fit to be moved a message was sent to his father that he might take the lad back to his village. The chief was very grateful for the kindness his son had received at our hands; he presented the General with a cartload of potatoes, and assured him that in future he would not kill any wounded soldiers who fell into his hands, but would only cut off one of their legs and send the men back to camp!

learned that a set of fanatics had arisen, named Hau-Haus, whose tenets, appealing to all that was worst in the Maori character, were a weird mixture of cannibalism, paganism, and Christianity.[1] In April 1864, a detachment of the 57th was badly cut up near New Plymouth; an officer, Captain Lloyd, and six men were killed by the Hau-Haus, who cut off their heads and drank their blood. A few days later, according to the native accounts, the Angel Gabriel appeared and ordered Lloyd's head to be exhumed and carried throughout New Zealand, to serve as the medium of Jehovah's communication with man. As soon as the head was disinterred it appointed priests, and announced that thanks to the protection of Gabriel and his angels the followers of the new religion would be invulnerable: the Virgin Mary would be constantly present with them: the religion of England was false and its scriptures must be burned; men and women were to live together promiscuously; the priests would obtain victories by shouting the word "Hau,"[2] and could invoke the help of legions of angels for the extermination of the whites. As soon as New Zealand had rid itself of the English, men would arrive from heaven to teach the Maoris all the arts and sciences known to Europeans. This extraordinary creed is believed to have been evolved by educated and unscrupulous natives, who realised that the Maoris had been shaken in their allegiance to the "King movement" by the result of the Waikato campaign, and that a stronger bond of union was required than a purely political organisation, the fortunes of which were not then in the ascendant.

Though in several affairs with the 57th the Hau-Haus learned by bitter experience that they were by no means invulnerable to Enfield bullets, the new religion found many converts. The tribes in the south-west of the North island had always been turbulent and hostile. They had committed grave and unprovoked outrages, such as the murder of a party of soldiers in 1863, which heralded the outbreak of the war. They were now in a state of open hostility, and almost the only part of the district which acknowledged the Queen's rule was the ground enclosed by the redoubts round the settlements of Taranaki and Wanganui. The Government of New Zealand decided that there could be no peace until the tribesmen had been chastised, their power broken, and their country opened up. To accomplish these objects General Cameron had about five thousand troops, a thousand white volunteers, and a thousand native auxiliaries. His plan of campaign was that two columns, one based on Taranaki, the other on Wanganui, should force their way along the coast until they joined hands on the road between these two settlements.

On January 2, 1865, a detachment of seven companies (about 500 of all ranks) of the Royal Irish, under Major J. H. Rocke, embarked for Wanganui

[1] Fox, pp. 126, 139, 140.
[2] Hence the name "Hau-Haus," by which these fanatics were generally known.

in H.M.S. *Falcon* and *Eclipse*, the remainder of the battalion being left under Lieutenant-Colonel Chapman at Otahuhu camp. On the voyage the *Eclipse* ran ashore on a sandbank, but the soldiers were transhipped to another vessel, and on reaching their destination took their place in a column commanded by Colonel Waddy, 50th, consisting of the Royal Irish; 50th; detachments of Royal Artillery and Royal Engineers, and a small party of extemporised cavalry, in all 963 officers and men. On January 24, Waddy moved up the coast towards the Waitotara river. The route first led past settlers' farms, well-planted and rich in clover-fields, and then skirted native villages, deserted by the Maoris, who had left their peach-groves and patches of tobacco, Indian corn, and water-melons to the mercy of the troops. Next came a weary stretch of steep sandhills, and it was late in the afternoon when Waddy halted near a lake close to the Maori village of Nukumaru. During the march no enemies had shown themselves, and from Colonel Waddy's report it appears that the camp was formed before the outposts were in position. When the tents were pitched piquets were sent out; among them was a party of the Royal Irish, under Captain Hugh Shaw, with orders to take up ground half a mile to the north of the camp. Shaw moved off in skirmishing order and cautiously approached a patch of bush close to the village, which it was necessary to occupy. It was not until he was within thirty yards of this bush that a large number of Maoris, lurking in the thicket, disclosed their presence by a heavy fire. Though surprised, Shaw kept his head, and remembering that he had just passed a small ditch with a fence in front of it, rallied his party behind this meagre cover, which was but sixty yards from the Maoris' position. As soon as he had set his rifles to work he counted his men, and found that one was missing, lying hard hit half-way between the piquet and the natives in the bush. Shaw was in a dilemma. To leave the man where he was would condemn him to certain death, for at nightfall he would inevitably be tomahawked by the Maoris: to order a few of the piquet to bring him in was to expose the rescue party to very great danger, nor did Shaw wish to send men on a forlorn hope unless he himself led them. Yet, if he did head a rescue party, he was technically abandoning his post, and, during his absence, throwing upon his subordinates the responsibility not only for the lives of the piquet but for the safety of the whole camp. Shaw decided to face this risk—a very grave one, as the events of the next day proved—and called for volunteers to help him save the wounded man. Four private soldiers, Brandon, Brien, Kearnes, and Clampitt sprang to their feet and dashed headlong after their officer. In a few moments these five gallant men were bending over their comrade, whom they found still living. The air around them seemed alive with bullets, for the piquet was firing viciously at the puffs of smoke which marked the lairs of the Maori sharpshooters, while the enemy concentrated his musketry upon the rescuers. There was no time to consult how best to move the wounded man : Shaw caused him to be hoisted upon his own back, and, staggering under the weight, carried him back in triumph to the piquet. Incredible as it may seem, neither Shaw nor any of his companions were hit in this adventure. Shaw was awarded the Victoria Cross, while privates James Kearnes, George Clampitt, and John Brandon were presented with the silver medal for distinguished conduct in the field.[1]

The sound of the firing brought up Major Rocke with a hundred men of the battalion, and thanks to this reinforcement the piquet was able to maintain so hot a fusilade that the enemy did not attempt either to surround, or to close in upon them. For some hours the fire-fight raged, the natives returning shot for shot; then the musketry died down, and the Maoris stole away to the shelter of a neighbouring *pah*. Early on the morning of the 25th, the piquet was relieved by Captain Noblett with seventy-five of his own men, and twenty-five of the 50th regiment. On the right he posted his party of the XVIIIth near the village, while on the left his detachment of the 50th watched a deep watercourse, with banks covered by a thick growth of wild flax. On the far side of this watercourse was another piquet, also of the 50th, but not under Noblett's command. During the forenoon not an enemy was seen; the bush seemed absolutely deserted, but it was the lull before the storm. In the middle of the day the Maoris suddenly abandoned their traditional policy of standing on the defensive in carefully fortified positions, and two columns, in all about 600 men, falling simultaneously on the flanks of Noblett's piquet swept it before them, and pushed forward so vigorously through the breach thus made in the outpost line that for a time the safety of the camp was seriously imperilled. From the scanty details preserved of this interesting fight it appears that about two P.M. Captain Noblett heard firing on his left, where Enfield bullets were falling among his detachment of the 50th. On hurrying to the point of danger, he discovered that these badly directed bullets came from the far side of the watercourse, where the distant piquet of the 50th was trying to stem a Maori rush. After making necessary dispositions he ran back to the right of his ground, to find that there also the natives were attacking in strength; they had set fire to the bush, and under

[1] The official description of the act of bravery for which Captain Shaw was awarded the Victoria Cross is as follows : " For his gallant conduct at the skirmish near Nukumaru in New Zealand, in proceeding under a heavy fire with four privates of the regiment who volunteered to accompany him to within thirty yards of the bush occupied by the rebels, in order to carry off a comrade who was badly wounded. On the afternoon of that day Captain Shaw was ordered to occupy a position about half a mile from the camp. He advanced in skirmishing order, and, when about thirty yards from the bush, he deemed it prudent to retire to a palisade about sixty yards from the bush, as two of his party had been wounded. Finding that one of them was unable to move, he called for volunteers to advance to the front to carry the man to the rear, and the four privates referred to accompanied him, under a heavy fire, to the place where the wounded man was lying, and they succeeded in bringing him to the rear."

cover of the smoke were pushing fast through the village, and driving the piquet of the XVIIIth backwards towards the camp. When the alarm was given all the troops not on outpost fell in and hurried up to the front. The first party ready to move was Captain Daubeny's company of the XVIIIth; in a short time they met Captain Noblett's piquet in full retreat; Noblett rallied his men upon the reinforcement, and then the two detachments, extending into skirmishing order, by their steady front and well-sustained fire effectively checked the enemy. Elsewhere, however, things did not go so well, and the natives were almost in the camp before the combined effect of a charge of mounted men and the shells of 6-pr. Armstrong guns drove them back into the bush. In their retreat the Maoris abandoned twenty-two killed and two wounded, and succeeded in carrying away about seventy dead or injured warriors. In the two days' fighting the British casualties were—officers, one killed and two wounded; other ranks, fifteen killed and thirty wounded. The losses of the XVIIIth were three private soldiers killed and twelve wounded, one mortally.[1] The General in his report favourably mentioned the names of Major Rocke, Captain Shaw, and Captain Dawson.

After this repulse the Maoris retired to a *pah* close by at Wereroa, a position which they deemed impregnable. This opinion General Cameron appeared to share, for he did not attack, but, hoping to entice the enemy out of his works, moved slowly up the coast. At the mouth of the Waitotara river Major Rocke and four companies of the Royal Irish were left to guard a bridge of casks, while the remainder of the battalion, recently joined by the three headquarter companies under Lieutenant-Colonel Chapman, marched with the rest of the column to Patea. Here they remained for many months in charge of a line of posts on the road between Wanganui and Taranaki, sharing in only one of the few operations which took place in this part of the country in 1865.[2]

The state of affairs in New Zealand at this time was very unfortunate. General Cameron, who commanded the Queen's troops, was at daggers drawn with Sir George Grey, the Governor of the colony. The New Zealand ministry was wrangling fiercely with the Cabinet at home, for at the very time that Cameron announced he could not carry out Grey's policy without considerable reinforcements of regular troops, the Colonial Office intimated that the War Office was about to withdraw five battalions from New Zealand.[3] The General was already worn out by physical fatigue and mental anxiety:

---

[1] See Appendix 2 (K).

[2] The only event recorded of the stay of the XVIIIth at Patea is the death of two young officers, Lieutenants Lawson and Jenkins, who, unable to swim, were carried by the tide out of their depth and drowned.

[3] The unavowed but well-understood object of this reduction in the regular forces in New Zealand was to throw upon the colonists the chief burden and expense of the war, of which the Home Government was thoroughly weary.

the threatened withdrawal of the troops was the last straw on the camel's back; on the ground of ill-health Cameron asked to be relieved of his command, and in August, 1865, was succeeded by Major-General Trevor Chute. About a month before the new Commander-in-Chief arrived, Sir George Grey, who had in vain urged Cameron to attack the *pah* at Wereroa, remembered that before entering the service of the Colonial Office he had been a captain in the army, and determined to prove to the Maoris that their vaunted stronghold was not impregnable. On the morning of July 20, he assembled a small column, consisting of a hundred of the 14th regiment, an equal number of the Royal Irish under Captain Noblett, and about four hundred and seventy colonists and friendly natives. In his plan of attack Grey allotted a duty to the regular troops which required great discipline and steadiness: they were to demonstrate, and threaten an attack upon the front, the best defended face of the fortification, while the colonists and "friendlies," by a long and circuitous march, established themselves on ground from which the rear of the Maori works could be commanded. The two hundred regular troops pitched their tents well within view of the natives, threw out posts, marched and countermarched, and successfully "bluffed" the enemy into the belief that a large body of soldiers were preparing for an assault. The irregulars succeeded in placing themselves unseen in rear of the *pah*; there was some work with the rifle, and then the Maoris, seized with panic, swarmed down a steep cliff and abandoned their fortress, almost without firing a shot in its defence. A reinforcement of fifty of the XVIIIth were brought up from the line of communication by Major Rocke, who was now in command of the regiment,[1] but they took no part in the affair. The enemy lost fifty men and many stores: in Sir George Grey's column there appear to have been no casualties.

For the rest of the year 1865 the headquarters of the battalion remained at Patea, with detachments along the coast. In December, General Chute was directed by the Governor to prepare an expedition against the Hau-Haus who infested the country between Taranaki and Wanganui. He drew a hundred officers and men under Major Rocke from the posts held by the Royal Irish; 139 of all ranks from the 14th regiment; about 100 from the 50th, and with 45 of the Forest Rangers and 300 native auxiliaries, took the field at the beginning of January, 1866. After making himself master of the strongly palisaded village of Otahuhu,[2] he led his column on a more difficult enterprise, the capture of the Putahi *pah*, which stood in a clearing on the top of a hill, 500 feet in height, with sides rough with spurs, seamed in every direction by watercourses, and covered with dense jungle. Only one path led from the plain to the summit through this labyrinth, difficult in itself and rendered

---

[1] Lieutenant-Colonel Chapman was invalided home in June. As Brevet-Colonel G. J. Carey was an acting Brigadier-General, Rocke, as the next senior officer, assumed the command of the battalion.

[2] Not to be confounded with the camp near Auckland.

almost impassable by the stockades and other defences with which it was known to bristle. Chute decided to avoid this death-trap by attacking the *pah* from the rear. Long before dawn on the 7th of January, 1866, his troops had begun a march, which in his despatch he described as "one continued struggle through a dense primeval forest and bush, over ravines and gullies which could in most cases only be ascended and descended by the aid of supple jack, and then only with great difficulty. The distance to be traversed could not have exceeded four miles, but the obstacles and obstructions opposed to us made it a severe task for four hours." General Chute's method of attacking the Maori works was rough but effective. "There was usually," writes General Alexander, "an open plateau in front of the *pahs;* he brought his men there to the edge of the bush, and when his line and supports and natives in reserve were all ready he made his bugler sound a single G; the men advanced from under cover, and on the double G being given a rush was made at the *pah,* hatchets were drawn from the belts of the men, the withes of the outer fence were suddenly cut, the palisading broken through, and the *pah* stormed with cheering in the smoke." Such was his plan at the capture of Putahi. As soon as the Forest Rangers reached the plateau they opened out into skirmishing order, lying down within 400 yards of the enemy to cover the formation of the remainder of the troops, who as they emerged gradually from the bush were extended—the detachment of the XVIIIth on the right, the 14th in the centre, and the 50th on the left, with the native contingent in reserve. It was more than an hour before the soldiers at the rear of the column, breathless from their exertions in scaling precipices, had found their places in the ranks. During that time the Hau-Hau garrison, about two hundred strong, had first performed a war dance to keep up their spirits, and then fired, but with little effect, upon the troops. When Chute's line was in order he gave the word to advance. Under a heavy but almost harmless fusilade the soldiers moved forward, as steadily as on an ordinary parade; when they were within eighty yards of the enemy the double G was sounded; they charged and burst into the *pah,* driving the enemy before them headlong into the bush. A general pursuit followed, in which the Hau-Haus are said to have lost considerably; then the troops were called off; the *pah* was destroyed and the column marched back to camp. In this affair the British casualties were two men killed and ten wounded, none of them belonging to the XVIIIth.

In the course of the next few days General Chute captured several more of the Hau-Hau strongholds, and wound up his punitive expedition by marching round the east of Mount Egmont to Taranaki, by a track believed to be impracticable for civilised troops. In these successes, however, the XVIIIth had no share, for Rocke's party was ordered back to Patea the day after the Putahi *pah* was captured. With Chute's march the war, as far as

most of the regular army was concerned, came to an end. The British
Government decided that the Imperial forces should no longer be actively
employed, as it considered that the Maoris had been sufficiently weakened for
the colonists to finish the struggle without further help from the mother
country.[1] Nearly all the troops were accordingly withdrawn from the neighbourhood of Wanganui; the Royal Irish, however, remained in their old posts
in the Patea-Wanganui district, which continued to be much harassed by
rebellious tribes. Communication along the coast road was interrupted;
small parties of colonists were frequently surprised and murdered; and the
local forces were twice rudely handled in operations in the bush. Occasionally
the garrisons of the posts made sorties against the insurgents, but nothing of
importance occurred until October, 1866, when the Governor arrived at Patea
and called upon Major Rocke for the help of his regiment in quelling dis-
turbances in the country round Wanganui. Major Rocke was in the happy
position of being his own commanding-officer, with no senior present to whom
the question had to be referred. He joyfully responded to Sir George Grey's
appeal by organising a mobile column of three hundred Royal Irish and an
equal number of New Zealand militia, and led the combined force to Wain-
gongoro, where the Governor at an interview with the rebel leaders failed to
persuade them to lay down their arms. Sir George Grey at once moved
towards Papoia, a native village buried in the heart of the forest, believed to
be strongly fortified, and known to be approachable only by difficult paths.
He determined to surprise this village by an attack at dawn, and Rocke accordingly paraded his men at midnight on the 17th-18th of October. The Royal
Irish led the march, preceded by a storming party under Lieutenant Pringle, who
had volunteered for this dangerous duty. Silently, and with every precaution
to avoid giving the alarm to their watchful enemy, the Royal Irish slowly
followed the friendly natives who guided them along a steep and narrow
track. At daybreak the men at the head of the column noticed that the path
was leading into a glen, and a few minutes later discovered that across this
glen the Hau-Haus had thrown a huge barricade, nine feet in height, made of
the trunks of trees and crowned with a stiff "post and rails" fence. At this
moment a number of natives, hidden in the bush, opened a heavy fire upon the
storming party, but Pringle disregarded this flank attack, and with his men
rushed at the barricade, breached it with axes, and drove the defenders into
the bush. The rest of the column poured through the gap and swarmed into
the village, which the Maoris hastily abandoned, leaving several dead behind
them. This success, obtained without loss to the XVIIIth, was quickly
followed up by Rocke, who, making his way across country hitherto believed
to be impassable to Europeans, raided several hostile villages, which the Hau-

---

[1] It was not till 1870 that the last embers of the rebellion were completely stamped out by the
local forces of New Zealand.

Haus, cowed by the capture of Papoia, abandoned without resistance.   At the conclusion of this three weeks' campaign, the gallantry of Lieutenant Pringle in his charge on the barricade was brought to the notice of the officer commanding the troops in New Zealand ; and two of the men who accompanied him, privates Acton and Hennigan, were awarded the medal for distinguished conduct in the field.[1]   It may here be mentioned that although this affair was the last in which regular soldiers took part, it was not until 1869 that the issue of a medal for the New Zealand war was sanctioned, while not until 1870 was leave given to the regiments which had been engaged in the war to add the words "New Zealand" to the battle honours on their Colours.   For their services Brevet-Colonel G. J. Carey and Brevet-Lieutenant-Colonel Sir H. M. Havelock, Bart., V.C., were created Companions of the Order of the Bath ; Major J. H. Rocke received a Brevet-Lieutenant-Colonelcy ; and Captains J. Inman and T. D. Baker were promoted to Brevet-majorities.

During the time the Royal Irish were engaged in active operations against the Maoris their casualties were—

Officers—

Died of wounds, . . .	Brevet-Major J. T. Ring.
Died from accident or disease,	Lieutenants F. P. Leonard and O. R. Lawson.
	Ensign G. B. Jenkins.

Other ranks—

Killed or died of wounds, 17 ; died from accident or disease, 39 ; wounded, 36.[2]

Until March 1867, the regiment continued to hold the line of posts between Patea and Wanganui ; then the condition of the country warranted the concentration of the Royal Irish at the latter place, where they remained till December, when headquarters and six companies were sent to Auckland, with two detachments, each of two companies, at Napier and Taranaki.   When the headquarter companies reached Auckland the command of the battalion was assumed by Lieutenant-Colonel G. A. Elliot, who had arrived from England on promotion from the first battalion, *vice* Colonel Chapman, retired on half-pay.   At this time the effective strength of the battalion was 861, all told.[3]

There is little of interest to chronicle in the doings of the battalion during the year 1868.   The headquarters remained at Auckland, with detachments in various parts of the colony.   The armament of the Royal Irish was modernised by the issue of Snider breech-loading rifles to replace the muzzle-loading Enfields with which the men had hitherto been provided. In December

[1] See Appendix 4.

[2] See Appendix 2 (K).   The rivers in New Zealand took heavy toll from the Royal Irish, eight of whom were drowned in fording streams.

[3] Three Field-Officers, 8 Captains, 12 Lieutenants, 5 Ensigns, 1 Surgeon, 1 Assistant-Surgeon, 1 Paymaster, 1 Quartermaster, 49 Sergeants, 21 drummers, 759 rank and file.

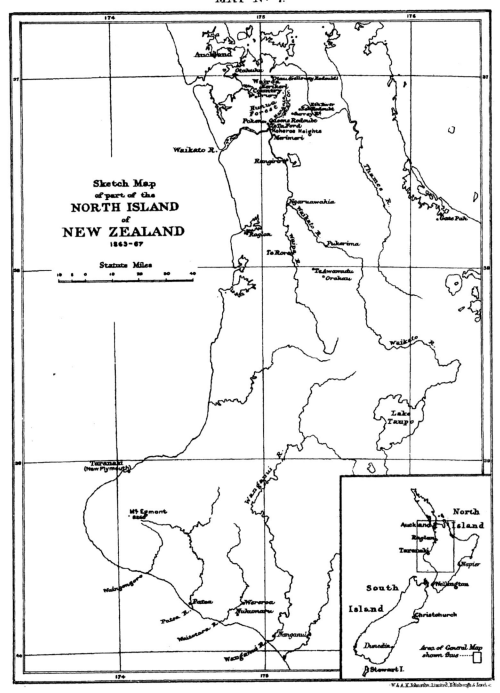

Sketch Map
of part of the
NORTH ISLAND
of
NEW ZEALAND
1863-67

Statute Miles

W. & A. K. Johnston Limited, Edinburgh & London.

Colonel Beatson, the officer who for a year and a half had commanded the troops in New Zealand, left the colony; before sailing he issued farewell orders in which he expressed his "unqualified satisfaction with the correct and soldierly conduct of the 2nd battalion, XVIIIth Royal Irish regiment, which reflects credit not only on themselves alone but also on the British army of which they are now almost the only representatives in this distant colony." Early in 1869, the battalion was warned to be in readiness to relieve the 50th in Australia. The European population, however, strongly opposed the departure of the Royal Irish : officers and men were alike popular with all classes of society, and while on personal grounds the colonists wished to retain the regiment among them, from the political point of view they deprecated the withdrawal of the XVIIIth, who were the rear-guard of the British army in New Zealand. As a concession the Ministry at home reluctantly postponed the departure of the battalion, but after a few months again ordered it to Australia. The Government of New Zealand remonstrated warmly against this decision, and offered to guarantee for five years any annual payment which the War Office might fix as the price of the retention of the XVIIIth. But as the Imperial Government had decided to throw upon the settlers the responsibility for the defence of the colony, it decided that no regular troops should remain in New Zealand, and at the beginning of 1870 the battalion embarked, the headquarters and four companies for Sydney, and detachments of two companies each for Melbourne, Adelaide, and Hobart.

How highly the Royal Irish were appreciated in New Zealand will be seen by the following extracts from official documents, newspaper articles, and farewell speeches on the subject of their departure. Sir George Bowen, who succeeded Sir George Grey as Governor of the colony, recorded his "sense of the important service rendered by the 2nd battalion, XVIIIth Royal Irish during the present rebellion, and also of the admirable conduct of the officers and men, who have invariably maintained the most cordial relations with their fellow-subjects. Their approaching departure is viewed with deep and general regret both on public and on personal grounds." [1]

In a speech made by Sir George Arney, Chief Justice of the Colony, on the 16th of February 1870, the following passage occurs :—

"I believe that every inhabitant of New Zealand has heard often of the 18th Royal Irish—has heard not only of that gallant and distinguished regiment, but also of the society of gentlemen who have won the affections, I believe, and certainly have commanded the respect, of the whole colony. And that which I have said of the Officers, I may in some degree also say of the men. As the head of one special department, I can say that during my long sojourn here, I have known no other

[1] Governor Sir G. Bowen to Colonial Office, 9th March 1869.

regiment which has been so distinguished by its freedom from crime; and the men of this regiment have themselves thus become respected, not only by those of their immediate class, but by all classes of society in the Colony. That circumstance must be taken as due not only to the efficient command of the Officer at the head of the regiment, but also to the temper and discretion with which his orders have been carried out by the Officers of the regiment. I will say but little on the fact that this Colony is now losing the presence of this gallant regiment; it is a subject which, I believe, is a painful one to the hearts of the whole of the colonists in New Zealand. I believe that the 18th will be universally regretted, as they are now universally respected."

The Ministers of the New Zealand government also gave their testimony to the good conduct of the regiment in a communication to the Governor.

"Memorandum for His Excellency.

"Ministers cannot permit the last detachment of Her Majesty's 18th regiment to leave the Colony without expressing the regret which they feel at the departure of the regiment, and bearing testimony of the uniform good conduct of the force under the command of Lieutenant-Colonel Elliot, during the period of its service in the Colony; the sentiment which the Government thus places on record is that of the whole community.

"The Government also desires to express the feeling which it entertains of the readiness which Lieutenant-Colonel Elliot, and the Officers commanding detachments under him, have always displayed to aid the Colony as far as lay in their power.

"The Government also desires to record its appreciation of the uniform courtesy and consideration which they have experienced on the part of Lieutenant-Colonel Elliot in their communications with him through His Excellency the Governor.

"(Signed)   William Fox,
"*Premier.*"

By the beginning of March, 1870, the various detachments of the regiment had settled down in their new stations, but they were not destined long to enjoy the pleasures of life in the capitals of the Australian colonies,[1] for very soon came orders for the regiment to return to England. The policy of withdrawing all Imperial troops from New Zealand had been carried out. It was now Australia's turn to be denuded of her garrison, and in August 1870, after hundreds of men had taken their discharges in order to settle in Australasia, the Royal Irish embarked for Plymouth. The sailing ship *Silver Eagle* left Sydney on the 21st of August with the four headquarter companies; Lieutenant-Colonel Elliot was in command, and with him were one captain, four subalterns, two surgeons, and one hundred and thirty-five other ranks. On board the sailing ship *Corona*, which left Melbourne about the same time, were

---

[1] Now "colonies" no longer, but "States" of the Australian Commonwealth.

Brevet-Lieutenant-Colonel Rocke and two other field-officers, five captains, nine subalterns, and two hundred and forty-six other ranks. The *Corona* arrived at Plymouth on November 16; the *Silver Eagle* made so long a voyage round Cape Horn that before she reached port on December 5th, it was currently reported that she had been lost at sea.

The Australians were profoundly moved when the Royal Irish left their shores. The XVIIIth was already very popular, and apart from this personal feeling, the settlers were deeply wounded at the removal of this, the last British regiment of the garrison of Australasia. While all men regarded this step as the breaking of one of the few visible links between the mother country and her offshoots in the southern hemisphere, many pessimists hinted that the policy of the Home government was intended to force all the colonies into a declaration of independence. When the *Corona* sailed from Melbourne fifty thousand people crowded to the beach to wave a sad farewell to the XVIIIth, gloomily comparing the departure of the regiment with the abandonment of Britain by the Roman legions. Happily these prophets of evil were mistaken. The loyalty of the colonies to the Empire is unimpaired, and the tie of sentiment has been strengthened by the presence in three African campaigns of large bodies of volunteers from Canada, Australia, and New Zealand, who fought shoulder to shoulder with Imperial troops in quarrels with which the colonists were concerned solely as members of the British race. Though the offer of two thousand Australasian militia and volunteers to serve against the Boers in the war of 1881 was refused by Mr Gladstone's government, four years later eight hundred men from New South Wales were fighting at Suakim, and four hundred Canadian *voyageurs* were steering whale-boats upon the Nile in the expedition towards Khartoum: while in the recent struggle with the Boers for the possession of South Africa, nearly thirty thousand men from Greater Britain represented the oversea provinces of the Empire in the army of the old country.

When the second battalion landed in England, it was quartered at Devonport, where the energies of the officers and non-commissioned officers were devoted to welding into shape the recruits enlisted to fill its depleted ranks. These youths were of poor physique and small stature, and only three hundred were finally accepted as suitable for the Service, but good food and systematic training did wonders for them: in a year their average height had increased an inch, while they had grown two inches wider round the chest. The burden of drilling and disciplining this mass of raw material fell upon the adjutant, Lieutenant H. B. Moore; his success was so conspicuous that when he left the army in 1873, Lieutenant-Colonel S. Wilson, who in

1871 had succeeded Colonel Elliot in command, warmly thanked him for his work in a regimental order. During the six years spent by the battalion at various garrison towns in England nothing of interest occurred, except that the Royal Irish were represented in the Ashantee war by Major T. D. Baker and Lieutenant I. W. Graves, both of whom were mentioned in despatches.[1] In June, 1876, the retirement of Colonel Wilson placed Lieutenant-Colonel R. H. Daniel in command ; and in the following month began a tour of duty in Ireland, as barren of events as had been that in England. The battalion was at Kilkenny in the spring of 1878, when in anticipation of a possible war with Russia part of the reserve was called out, and four hundred men from the Kilkenny and Wexford militia were poured into the ranks of the Royal Irish, whose officers led a strenuous life during the three months of the embodiment. On the death of Colonel Daniel in May, 1882, Lieutenant-Colonel C. F. Gregorie arranged an exchange with Lieutenant-Colonel M. J. R. M'Gregor, first battalion, and was gazetted to the command of the second battalion on September 14, 1878. After passing three years in Ireland, the home battalion of the Royal Irish spent two years at Aldershot, and then was moved to Chatham where the marching-in state showed a strength of 15 officers, 37 sergeants, 12 drummers and 356 rank and file. Here it remained until August, 1882, when it embarked for Egypt on active service.

[1] Among the other officers mentioned was Lieutenant H. S. F. Bolton, who enlisted in the army in 1859 : obtained his commission in the West India regiment ; was a special service officer in Ashantee, and finished his career as a major in the Royal Irish regiment.   He is now one of the military Knights of Windsor.

CHAPTER X.

THE FIRST BATTALION.

1865-1884.

CHANGES IN ARMY ORGANISATION : THE SECOND AFGHAN WAR.

WHILE the second battalion of the Royal Irish regiment was winning its spurs in New Zealand, the first was quartered in southern India. At the end of 1865 it was ordered home ; volunteering into other corps was permitted, and 381 non-commissioned officers and men elected to finish their service in the East, while 29 officers [1] and 450 other ranks, with 44 women and 72 children, embarked in February, 1866, at Bombay in two ships, the slower of which did not reach England until the end of June. Two years later the battalion was sent to Ireland, and in August, 1871, was warned for another tour of foreign service. This order filled all ranks with dismay, for if any corps in the British army had the right to expect a long rest at home it was the first battalion of the XVIIIth. Since 1692, when it first landed on the Continent, it had spent a hundred and nineteen years out of the United Kingdom, and between 1837, when it sailed for Ceylon, and its return from India in 1866, it had served abroad with one short break of less than six months' duration ; it had fought with distinction in China, in Burma, and in the Crimea, and had shared in the suppression of the Indian Mutiny. To explain why the War Office sent the first battalion on foreign service again so quickly, it becomes necessary to allude briefly to the long series of changes in the organisation of the army which began to take effect in 1870.

The strain thrown on the military resources of Britain by the Crimean War and the Indian Mutiny had convinced even the most determined economists in the House of Commons not only that the army was

---

[1] As Lieutenant-Colonel G. F. S. Call had already started on his homeward voyage, Major E. W. Sargent was in command ; the other officers with him were Captains C. J. Coote, J. F. Bryant, and R. I. Adamson ; Lieutenants J. W. Home, T. B. Meredith, J. F. Mosse, W. Sherlock, and T. N. R. Burton ; Ensigns G. A. Macdonnell, H. B. Moore, G. C. Irving, T. H. S. Sewell, G. W. N. Rogers ; Adjutant W. H. Herbert ; Paymaster R. B. Farwell ; Quartermaster M. Hackett ; Surgeon J. H. Lewis ; Assistant-Surgeons H. A. Coglan and W. Orr.

too small, but that it was utterly lacking in power of rapid expansion in case of need. To increase its numbers in time of peace was comparatively easy, and by the addition in 1858-59 of second battalions to the twenty - five senior regiments of the line, the infantry was materially strengthened. But to render the army more elastic, more fit to meet a sudden national emergency, was a far more difficult matter. The process by which the XVIIIth was brought up to war strength for the Crimea[1] was the only method then known for making a regiment ready to take the field, for as there were no reservists to replace men too weakly or too young for a campaign, the ranks of a corps ordered on active service could only be filled by the depletion of other units, which by this process of " robbing Peter to pay Paul " were reduced to impotence, until they in turn had obtained recruits and trained the raw material into soldiers. Of the various attempts to form an adequate reserve one only was successful — the " militia reserve," composed of the best men in the constitutional force, who for a small annual retaining fee undertook in case of need to serve as regular soldiers in any part of the world. But this was only a reversion to the methods of the Crimean days, for it called away the pick of the militia at the moment when they were required, if not for active service, at least for garrison duty at home and in the Mediterranean ; and at best it could produce but a limited supply of men who were obviously very inferior in quality to well-trained ex-regular soldiers. The problem of how to create an adequate reserve remained virtually unsolved for many years, though numberless committees were appointed to consider the question in all its bearings. The subject was, indeed, most complex. The army at home had to be prepared to defend the British Isles, to embark on expeditions beyond the limits of the United Kingdom, and to replace the waste caused by death, by invaliding, and by the discharge of " time-expired " men among the troops abroad, of whom 70,000 were quartered in India, while nearly 50,000 more were scattered in garrisons among our fortresses and colonies in other parts of the world. Gradually the opinion gained ground that it was hopeless to expect the army to discharge these varied duties, unless there was behind it a large body of highly-trained and disciplined men who, when a war was imminent, could be counted upon to reinforce the troops at home ; and the brilliant success of the Prussians in " the Seven Weeks' War " of 1866, determined our government to adopt a modification of the German principle of short service with the Colours, followed by a period of service in the Reserve. To devise a system suitable to an army recruited by voluntary enlistment, and of which a very large proportion is normally stationed abroad, required years of preparation, and it was not until 1870 that Mr Cardwell, then Secretary of State for War,

[1] See chapter vii.

began to introduce the great innovations which modernised the British army. By the abolition of "purchase," rich men were no longer able to buy their steps, and by the power of the purse obtain promotion over the heads of their poorer comrades; the ages were fixed at which officers of various ranks were to retire, so that a reasonable flow of promotion was obtained; the garrisons of the tropical colonies were reduced, while those of the great oversea provinces were gradually withdrawn; recruits were enlisted for twelve years—the first six to be passed with the Colours, and the remainder in the Reserve; while to provide for an adequate and systematic flow of trained men to India and our other outlying possessions, regiments were linked together in pairs—one serving at home, the other abroad. One of the functions of the "home" battalion was to impart to the recruits the ground-work of military training, and, when the young soldiers were fit to serve out of the United Kingdom, to send them in drafts to the "foreign" battalion, where they remained for the rest of their service with the Colours, and then on their return to the United Kingdom were transferred to the Reserve. In the first twenty-five regiments, which already possessed two battalions, the process of "linking" was effected without the difficulty and friction which frequently occurred in cases where two corps, strangers to each other in tradition and sentiment, were suddenly brought into the intimate relation of virtual partnership; and when in 1882, regiments ceased to be designated by numbers, and the identity of the original units was merged into that of the territorial regiment, the XVIIIth became the Royal Irish regiment with no regret beyond that of the loss of the number under which it had won distinctions in every part of the world.

As the second battalion had only just returned from New Zealand and Australia, it was the turn of the first battalion, under the newly introduced system, to go abroad; and on January 18, 1872, Lieutenant-Colonel G. H. Pocklington, with 26 officers and 606 other ranks, embarked for Malta. After three years the first battalion, 917 strong, sailed for India under command of Lieutenant-Colonel E. L. Dillon, and early in December reached Bareilly, where it was quartered for nearly four years. While it was at this station His Majesty King Edward VII., then Prince of Wales, made a Royal progress through the Eastern Empire that would one day be his, and on the 6th of March, 1876, stopped at Bareilly on his way from the Terai to Allahabad: His Royal Highness was received by a guard of honour of the Royal Irish, while the remainder of the battalion lined the avenue through which he passed on his way to the palace of the Nawab of Rampore. In the evening the Prince did the battalion the honour of dining with the officers, and gave to the mess portraits of the Princess of Wales and himself as a memento of his visit, and a few days later two large steel engravings of the Prince and Princess of Wales were sent by His Royal Highness as a present to the sergeants' mess. A year later the death occurred of Field-Marshal Sir John Forster Fitzgerald, G.C.B.,[1] who since 1850, when he succeeded Lord Aylmer, had been the Colonel of the XVIIIth, Royal Irish regiment. This veteran, whose age had earned for him the title of "the father of the British Army," was born in Ireland in 1786, before the abolition of the iniquitous system by which wealthy men were allowed to buy commissions for infants prattling in the nursery. At the mature age of eight Fitzgerald was a captain in the regular army, at seventeen he was a major, and he obtained his lieutenant-colonelcy when only twenty-four years of age. He served in the Peninsula, commanding a brigade in the battle of the Pyrenees in 1813; in 1854 he became General, and in 1875 received a Field-Marshal's bâton. He died in March, 1877, at Tours, and by the special order of Marshal Macmahon, then President of the French Republic, the whole of the garrison attended the funeral to pay to the British officer the honours accorded to Frenchmen of his exalted military rank. He was succeeded as Colonel of the XVIIIth by Lieutenant-General Clement A. Edwards, C.B.[2]

The first battalion changed stations from Bareilly to Ferozepore in February, 1878, and just after Lieutenant-Colonel M. MacGregor succeeded to the command on September 13, 1878, two companies were detached to Mooltan, while a third was sent to Dera Ismail Khan, one of the posts guarding the north-west frontier of India. For a few days there seemed to be a chance of "blooding" some of the young soldiers of the XVIIIth, for the Mahsood Waziris raided into our country and burned the town of Tank some thirty miles from Dera Ismail Khan. The native cavalry of the garrison were at once sent to the scene of the outrage, and fell heavily upon the freebooters, many of whom were killed and wounded, while the remainder fled to the neighbouring hills, where they threw up sangars and challenged us to attack them. But the officer in command of the British column was not disposed to squander the lives of his troops by assaulting stone breast-works without a preliminary bombardment; and remembering that some of the Royal Irish had been taught gun-drill at Dera Ismail Khan, he ordered up a couple of pieces, manned by soldiers of the XVIIIth under an officer of the regiment, Lieutenant H. Shuldham-Lye. The amateur gunners, "spoiling for a fight," pushed on to Tank at speed, but when the tribesmen heard that guns were to be used against them they suddenly dispersed, and the little campaign came to an end. For its services the detachment was officially thanked by the officer in command of the operations.

A few months after the Royal Irish arrived at Ferozepore Russian intrigues involved Britain in war with Afghanistan, an independent State whose mountains overhang part of the north-west frontier of India. As

[1] & [2] See Appendix 9.

early as 1837, England and Russia were contending for the privilege of directing the foreign policy of the Amir of Afghanistan, upon whose borders the rival European Powers were advancing by giant strides in the course of their Asiatic conquests; and when the Amir, Dost Mahomed, cordially welcomed a Russian officer, who brought from the Czar proposals for an alliance against England, our government determined to depose Dost Mahomed and to replace him with a nominee of their own. The attempt to carry this scheme into execution produced the first Afghan war, in which the Czar made no effort to help the Amir, being satisfied at having involved his great rival in an expensive and disastrous campaign with the country he proposed some day to use as a stepping-stone in the invasion of India. At the end of the Crimean war Russia, foiled in her projects against Turkey, devoted her energies to the subjugation of Central Asia, where vast territories fell into her hands; and by the conquest of Khiva in 1873, she advanced her outposts to within four hundred miles of our Indian frontier, establishing herself within easy striking distance of Afghanistan. Shere Ali, the Amir, trembling for his independence, offered his friendship to England if she would give him a specific promise of help against Muscovite aggression, but as our government refused any such guarantee he decided to throw in his lot with Russia. In 1877, there was war between the Sultan and the Czar, and as it seemed probable that England would again intervene by force of arms to save Turkey from annihilation, the Russians intrigued more vigorously than ever with Afghanistan, sending a military envoy to the Amir, who received him with every mark of distinction. To counteract the effect produced in every village in India by the knowledge that a Russian envoy had been officially welcomed at Kabul, the Viceroy decided that a British mission should visit Shere Ali, who was informed that Sir Neville Chamberlain was coming to discuss matters of importance with him in a friendly spirit. In due time the mission set forth from Peshawar, but in the Khyber Pass, just within the Amir's boundary, its members were turned back by Afghan troops, who under orders from Kabul refused to allow them to advance farther into Afghanistan. As Shere Ali declined to apologise for this insult, war became inevitable, and after our ultimatum had been rejected British troops invaded his country from various points.

It is not proposed to describe the operations of the second Afghan war, for the first battalion of the Royal Irish, upon whom fortune had frowned during the Mutiny, were still pursued by ill luck, and played but the smallest part in the campaign. Though the war began in November 1878, it was not until the beginning of the following year that the first battalion was ordered up from Ferozepore to join the reserve division of the Northern Afghanistan field force at Peshawar. A few weeks later this division was broken up; the battalion was transferred to the Khyber Line force; and on May 2, 1879, eight hundred and four stalwart Royal Irishmen found themselves at the foot of the great wall of rock which forbids access to Afghanistan from the plains of India.[1] This natural rampart is pierced by the Khyber Pass—a dark and gloomy gorge, winding its way between high mountains which so nearly approach each other that in places their rugged sides are only ten or twelve feet apart. Through this defile, one of the most difficult in the world, runs the track which for centuries has been the highway of commerce between Central Asia and Hindustan. In the middle of the pass the mountains, suddenly receding, form a plain, where the battalion spent the next ten months in discharging the useful but unattractive duties which fall to the lot of line of communication troops. They had to hold Lundi Kotal and Ali Musjid; to provide escorts for convoys through the pass, and to piquet the neighbouring hills. The guards were numerous, for the local tribesmen were expert thieves, to whom every British rifle was worth its weight in rupees; and notwithstanding the vigilance of the sentries in the sangars round the camp, Afridi robbers succeeded in abstracting a few firearms from the tents in which the men were sleeping. A good many non-commissioned officers and privates were lucky enough to escape from the drudgery of this existence by obtaining employment as signallers on the Kabul-Peshawar line, where from constant practice they became experts with flag and heliograph. During the summer there was a sharp outbreak of cholera in the battalion, which cost the lives of Quartermaster R. Barrett and sixty of the other ranks.[2] "It came up from India in the most curious way, right along the signallers' posts. We heard of it first at Jumrood; a few days afterwards a man in the first post was taken ill; a few days more and the second post was attacked, though there appeared to be no communication possible (except by heliograph) between the posts, and it gradually kept on till it reached the regiment. We knew it was coming; we could not move, and I think," writes an officer, "that it showed the

[1] The following officers of the regiment served in the Afghan War :—
  Lieutenant-Colonel—M. J. R. MacGregor.
  Majors—R. I. Adamson and H. Shaw, V.C.
  Captains—A. J. A. Jackson, J. G. Butts, J. Blair, H. F. S. Bolton, W. W. Lawrence, St G. A. Smith, E. Tufnell, and J. W. Graves.
  Lieutenants—S. Phillips, J. B. Forster, J. H. A. Spyer, P. A. Morshead, H. S. Lye (adjutant till promoted captain), S. S. Parkyn, C. E. Le Quesne, H. M. Hatchell, Hon. M. H. H. McDonnell, and P. B. Lindsell.
  Second Lieutenants—N. A. Francis (adjutant), R. M. Maxwell, A. I. Wilson, D. M. Thompson, B. J. C. Doran, E. B. W. J. Fraser, S. Moore, H. F. Loch, and H. E. Richardson.
  Quartermaster—R. Barrett, succeeded by Sergeant-Major W. Jamieson.
  Paymaster—Captain J. Forbes-Mosse.
[2] The names will be found in Appendix 2 (L). A memorial to those who lost their lives in Afghanistan, in Egypt in 1882, and the Nile campaign of 1884-85 is in the barrack square of the depôt at Clonmel.

THE AFGHANISTAN, EGYPT (1882) AND NILE CROSS AT CLONMEL.

staunchness of the Royal Irish that they never went to pieces at all." To keep up the spirits of the men and give them some amusement the officers rigged up a gymnasium and laid out a polo-ground and racecourse, where regimental gymkhanas were often held.

Although the first battalion was not actively engaged in the Afghan war, the officers and men who served in the Khyber Pass received the medal, and the regiment was permitted to add the words "Afghanistan 1879-80" to its battle honours. At the end of the campaign in 1881 the Royal Irish returned to India, and for the next two years and a half oscillated between the great cantonment of Rawal Pindi and the hill station of Kuldurrah. On May 23, 1882, when Lieutenant-Colonel M. MacGregor's term of command expired, he was succeeded by Lieutenant-Colonel H. Shaw, V.C., and in July of the same year the death of Lieutenant-General Edwards broke one of the few links still connecting the XVIIIth with its campaigns in the middle of the nineteenth century. He died full of years and honours, respected and admired not only by the regiment with which he had passed the best years of his life, but by every officer and man with whom he had served during his long career.[1] Lieutenant-General and Honorary General Sir Alexander Macdonnell, K.C.B., was appointed to replace him as Colonel.[2] A few weeks after the Royal Irish lost their Colonel, the second battalion sailed from England for Egypt to take part in the campaign described in the next chapter. The first battalion continued to serve in India until August, 1884, when in its turn it was summoned to Egypt as one of the corps selected for the attempt to rescue General Gordon from the dangers besetting him at Khartoum. The account of the doings of the first battalion in the Nile Expedition will be found in chapter xii.

[1] & [2] See Appendix 9.

CHAPTER XI.

THE SECOND BATTALION.

1882-1883.

THE WAR IN EGYPT.

IN Chapter iv. the campaign of 1801 is described, in which the Royal Irish regiment played a distinguished part in the expulsion of the French from Egypt. To explain why, more than eighty years later, it became necessary for British troops again to take the field in the valley of the Nile, a few words of historical retrospect are necessary. Our short occupation of Egypt in 1801 was purely military and in no way interfered with the status of the country, which for many years continued nominally to be a province of the Ottoman Empire. In the first half of the nineteenth century an adventurer named Mahomed Ali, who started in life as a small government official in Turkish employ, made himself master of Egypt and conquered the Soudan, a vast no-man's land, which from Wadi-Halfa, the southern boundary of Egypt proper, stretched for 1300 miles up the valley of the Nile. For thirty years he waged an intermittent war with the Sublime Porte, occupying Syria and threatening the safety of the Sultan in Constantinople itself, until the great Powers of Europe, which in 1827 had combined to destroy the Turkish fleet at Navarino, united in 1840 to save the Ottoman Empire from disruption, and sent a joint naval expedition against Mahomed's garrisons on the Syrian seaboard. Next year the Sultan made peace with his rebellious vassal, who restored Syria to his overlord as the price of the hereditary viceroyalty of Egypt, which was then conferred upon him. A few years later the opening of the "overland route," by which mails and passengers for the East were carried between Alexandria and Suez, began to bring Egypt closely within the sphere of British politics; and the completion in 1869 of the Suez canal by a French company, whose moving spirit was M. de Lesseps, the engineer, made the safety of the new waterway, and the good government of the country through which it ran a matter of paramount importance to the British

Empire.[1] Yet England by no means desired to add the possession of Egypt to her other burdens. Her attitude is well described by Lord Cromer:

"The general political interest of England was clear. England did not want to possess Egypt, but it was essential to British interests that the country should not fall into the hands of any other European Power. British policy, in respect to Egypt, had for years past been based on this principle. In 1857 the Emperor Napoleon III. made overtures to the British Government with a view to the partition of the northern portions of Africa. Morocco was to fall to France, Tunis to Sardinia, and Egypt to England. On this proposal being submitted to Lord Palmerston, he stated his views in a letter to Lord Clarendon. 'It is very possible,' he said, 'that many parts of the world would be better governed by France, England, and Sardinia than they now are. . . . We do not want to have Egypt. What we wish about Egypt is that it should continue to be attached to the Turkish Empire, which is a security against its belonging to any European Power. We want to trade with Egypt and to travel through Egypt, but we do not want the burden of governing Egypt. . . . Let us try and improve all these countries by the general influence of our commerce, but let us abstain from a crusade of conquest which would call down upon us the condemnation of all other civilised nations.' On another occasion Lord Palmerston used the following homely but apt illustration. 'We do not want Egypt or wish for it ourselves any more than any rational man with an estate in the north of England and a residence in the south would have wished to possess the inns on the north road. All he could want would have been that the inns should be well kept, always accessible, and furnishing him when he came with mutton chops and post-horses.'"[2]

Unfortunately Egypt was anything but well governed. A thin veneer of European civilisation barely concealed the barbaric methods of the East, and the corruption and extravagance of her rulers were almost incredible. In 1863, her public debt was about three millions and a quarter sterling.[3] Thirteen years later, under the rule of Ismail, it had increased to sixty-eight millions, with a floating or unfunded debt of twenty-six millions more, or ninety-four millions in all. As the funded debt had been contracted in Europe, chiefly in the money markets of London and Paris, and as a large portion of the floating debt was due to European creditors, the English and French Cabinets wrung from the Khedive a reluctant consent that European men of business should be appointed to investigate the financial condition of his country. In 1878, the Anglo-French committee of enquiry discovered that the finances of Egypt were rotten to the core. For the debt of ninety-four millions there was practically nothing to show, except the Suez canal, towards the building of which the Government of Egypt had contributed sixteen

[1] See Map No. 8.
[2] Cromer's 'Modern Egypt,' vol. i. pp. 91, 92.
[3] The figures quoted are all in British currency.

millions.[1] There was no money to pay the interest on the bonds, and the old method of raising a fresh loan to pay the interest on those already in existence was obviously no longer possible.

In the hope that the influence of high-principled European men of business would improve the government, the Powers insisted that the Khedive should employ ministers of their selection. He did so, but by resolutely obstructing the officials thus imposed upon him, he reduced the administration to such a state of chaos that in June, 1879, the patience of England and France was exhausted, and with the concurrence of the other Powers and the reluctant consent of the Sultan, the Khedive was deposed in favour of his son, Prince Tewfik. The change of viceroy did not, however, produce the result anticipated. Affairs did not improve under Tewfik's rule; by the end of 1881 the population was in a ferment; a strong anti-European feeling had arisen among the people, while the army was mutinous, and regarded not Tewfik but Arabi, a clever and intriguing Egyptian colonel, as its master. With the object of strengthening the Khedive's position, England and France in January, 1882, addressed to Tewfik a "dual note," stating that they considered his maintenance on the throne as the sole guarantee of good order and prosperity in Egypt. This note, however, in no way impressed the population; the condition of the country daily grew more unsatisfactory, and by May a series of military demonstrations had made Arabi the virtual dictator of Egypt, though Tewfik continued in name to be its ruler. Massacres of Christians in various parts of the country caused an enormous exodus of the European population,[2] trade was completely dislocated, and the safety of the Suez canal appeared imperilled.

The Egyptian army, exclusive of the garrison of the Soudan, consisted of about 9000 men actually serving with the Colours, but more than 50,000 men had passed through the ranks into the reserve, and in the Bedouins, the dwellers in the desert, Arabi had a further reserve, though of very doubtful value. His artillery was powerful; exclusive of heavy guns there were forty-eight batteries of field-artillery, not, however, fully horsed. When war broke out the reserve men were recalled, and 40,000 recruits enlisted, who after a few days' drill were thrust, virtually untrained, into the ranks. Egypt was rich in horses and camels, and in addition to the horses required for the artillery, eleven thousand transport animals were obtained from the population. Nominally, these beasts were the free-will offerings of their owners, but there is reason to believe that the generosity of their donors was greatly stimulated by the use of the *courbash*.

---

[1] The British Government in 1875 suddenly bought up four millions' worth of Suez Canal shares, owned by the Khedive, which he was about to put upon the market. This stroke of policy made England a large shareholder in the Canal Company, and therefore gave her an important position in the commercial management of its affairs.

[2] About 90,000 Europeans, chiefly English and French, carried on business in Egypt at this time.

During 1881, and the first part of 1882, many communications on the subject of Egypt had passed between the governments of England and France and the other European Powers.[1] All were agreed that order should be restored on the banks of the Nile, but, save England and France, none seemed disposed to undertake the task. At first France was much more inclined to a military intervention than Britain, for England in 1882 no more desired to annex Egypt than in 1857, when she rejected the French Emperor's schemes for the partition of northern Africa. But she remembered that, even before the time of the great Napoleon, France had cast covetous eyes upon Egypt, and as it was impossible for England to allow Egypt to be occupied by any Continental nation, her obvious policy was to co-operate with France, and by re-establishing order and good government in the country to render the Egyptians capable of managing their own affairs without European guidance. To this policy England loyally adhered until France refused to advance further in the matter. As tangible evidence that the Western Powers really intended to support the Khedive, an Anglo-French squadron was sent to Alexandria, where it lay for several weeks, until our Admiral, Lord Alcester (then Sir Beauchamp Seymour), discovered that in direct defiance of the Khedive's orders, Arabi was preparing to make good his threat to attack any European troops landing in Egypt. Not only was he mounting guns on the fortifications, but he was also attempting to prevent the British fleet from leaving the port by secretly throwing great blocks of stone into the entrance of the harbour. Through Lord Alcester, the British government informed Arabi that unless he at once desisted the forts would be shelled. Arabi promised compliance, but when the search-lights from the ships were turned on, it was seen that under cover of night the work was being pressed forward.[2] The danger to the fleet soon grew too serious to be ignored, and after repeated but equally fruitless warnings, notice was given to Arabi that on the 11th of July the forts would be bombarded. Thereupon the French Admiral announced that his instructions did not permit him to take part in such an operation, and on the 10th he steamed out of Alexandria, leaving his British colleague in the lurch. The forts were bombarded with complete success, and Arabi, retiring inland for a few miles, threatened Alexandria from a position at Kafr-el-Dauar, astride the railway to Cairo. To save the town from pillage by its mob, and to defend it against attack by the Egyptian army, a large number of British sailors and soldiers were landed. The troops

---

[1] Lord Cromer's 'Modern Egypt,' vol. i., gives an excellent account of the European diplomacy of this period.

[2] A quaint report by an Egyptian officer in charge of a battery "complained of the very improper conduct of the English fleet in that, whilst his men were at work on the battery at night, suddenly a blaze of electric light was thrown upon them, so that what they were doing could be seen as if it were day—a proceeding which, as the officer avers, was distinctly discourteous on the part of the English."—Maurice, 'Military History of the Campaign of 1882 in Egypt.'

had just arrived from Cyprus, where, under Lieutenant-General Sir A. Alison, a brigade, supplied by the Mediterranean garrisons, had been assembled with secret orders to seize and protect the Suez canal against Arabi, who had openly expressed his determination to destroy it.

Meanwhile preparations for an expedition were on foot in England. An army corps drawn from the United Kingdom, the Mediterranean garrisons, and India was to be sent to Egypt under command of Lord Wolseley (then Lieutenant-General Sir Garnet Wolseley) with the temporary rank of General. It consisted of a cavalry division, two infantry divisions, artillery, engineers, and a strong contingent of British and native soldiers from India. In the first division, under Lieutenant-General G. H. S. Willis, were the 1st, or brigade of Guards, commanded by H.R.H. the Duke of Connaught, and the 2nd brigade (in which was the 2nd battalion of the Royal Irish), under Major-General G. Graham. The second division, commanded by Lieutenant-General Sir E. Hamley, was composed of the brigades of Major-General Sir A. Alison and Major-General Sir E. Wood. The Indian contingent, which was to join Lord Wolseley in Egypt, was led by Major-General Sir H. T. Macpherson. The total number of troops who embarked as part of the original army corps were 25,309.[1] The units selected for the war were mobilised; the reserve, or to be strictly accurate, those of its members who had left the Colours within two years were called out; transports were engaged and fitted up for troops, and the House of Commons voted the necessary money. Suddenly the policy of France completely veered round, and on the 29th of July, only nine days after the French Ministry had formally engaged to take part in the expedition, the Chamber by an enormous majority refused to spend a penny upon the restoration of law and order in Egypt. This remarkable change of front, which not only threw the whole expense, but the whole conduct of the expedition upon the British, was doubtless annoying to our statesmen, but agreeable to our generals, many of whom knew from personal experience in China and the Crimea how difficult co-operation with our French allies had proved in those campaigns. The defection of the French caused no alteration in Lord Wolseley's plans. To crush the Khedive's mutinous army and to restore order among his subjects it was essential that Cairo, the hot-bed of disaffection, should be occupied as speedily as possible by British troops, and this he proposed to do by landing, not at Alexandria, but at Ismailia, a town on the canal half-way between Suez and Port Said. From Ismailia to Cairo is about seventy-five miles, while from Alexandria to the capital is nearly double that distance. By the former route the track would lie alongside a canal of drinkable water, over hard sand which made a fair surface for marching. In the latter route, *i.e.* through the Delta of the Nile, there were

---

[1] Reinforcements of many thousands more were on their way to Egypt when the collapse of Arabi's rebellion rendered their presence at the front unnecessary.

practically no roads fit for wheeled vehicles, the local traffic being carried on by railway, by pack animals, and by boats on the innumerable canals by which the country is irrigated. Moreover, during the months of August, September, and October—the time of "high Nile," which was rapidly approaching—the whole of the Delta is under water. Thus, of the two lines of advance, that through the desert was obviously the better one, and it possessed the additional advantage that the preparations for undertaking it served to protect the Suez canal from attack, and to secure possession of the canals by which Suez, Ismailia, and Port Said are supplied with drinking water. It was of the first importance that Arabi should remain in complete ignorance of the British plans; and thus the bombardment of Alexandria and the landing of Alison's brigade, neither of which had formed part of Lord Wolseley's original scheme, turned to our advantage, for the arrival of Alison's troops confirmed the Egyptian General in his opinion that the invading army would disembark at Alexandria. Wolseley seized every opportunity to strengthen him in this belief; Alison was ordered to keep Arabi constantly in fear of an attack, and succeeded in doing so by a series of demonstrations against the works which the rebel army had thrown up.

By the end of July the troops began to leave the United Kingdom: and the second battalion of the Royal Irish regiment, almost the last corps to sail, embarked on August 8, 1882, at Plymouth, bound, as was then believed by all on board, for Alexandria. To enable the reader to appreciate the situation when the battalion reached the seat of war, it is necessary to give a short account of the events which took place while it was still at sea. On the 15th of August Lord Wolseley arrived at Alexandria, and with his naval colleague, Admiral Lord Alcester, settled the details of the combined operation by which the sailors in the men-of-war already stationed in the Suez canal were to seize and hold the towns upon its banks, until the soldiers could begin to land at Ismailia. A considerable portion of the expedition had already disembarked at Alexandria, and transports were daily, almost hourly, arriving from England. The question of how these troops were to be re-embarked and despatched to the canal without giving Arabi any clue to their destination now had to be solved. Throughout his career as a soldier, Wolseley had urged the necessity of deceiving your enemy in war: now he had a great opportunity to give the British army an object lesson in the art of mystifying an opponent, and right well did he avail himself of it. A strong believer in the truth of the axiom that whatever is rumoured in your camp to-day will be known to-morrow to the enemy, he determined to mislead, not only Arabi but the whole of the British army as to his intentions. Orders were accordingly issued for a combined naval and military attack from the sea upon the forts at Aboukir Bay, supported by the troops left to garrison Alexandria. Not even General Hamley, who was in command at Alexandria, was in the secret; and with the help of his brigadiers, Alison and Wood, he worked out elaborate details for co-operation in the advance of the main body after it had landed at Aboukir Bay; the scheme was submitted to Wolseley and gravely approved! At noon on the 19th of August all the troops, except those left to hold Alexandria, were on board their ships, and eight ironclads and seventeen transports steamed away towards Aboukir. Before his departure the Commander-in-Chief handed a sealed packet containing his real plan to General Hamley, with strict orders not to open it till early on the morning of the 20th. The fleet reached Aboukir in four hours, and anchored till nightfall, when the gunboats and other small naval craft stood inshore and engaged the forts, while the big ships slipped away unobserved and arrived at Port Said early next morning, to find that the navy had carried out their instructions admirably. The sailors had surprised the detachments of the enemy watching Port Said, Ismailia, and Suez; these places were in their hands. They were in possession of the whole of the Suez canal. They had prevented any vessels from entering it and, to clear the way for the transports, had ordered all steamers then in the canal to tie up at the *gares* or shunting-places, familiar to every soldier whose service has taken him east of Suez. The merchant ships complied with three exceptions. A French mail-boat claimed the right to pass, and was allowed to do so as a matter of international courtesy: two English master mariners of the baser sort disobeyed, and when the British gunboat that regulated the traffic was out of sight they followed in the Frenchman's wake. This incident considerably delayed the entrance of the British fleet into the Canal, but by the evening of the 23rd, the day before the Royal Irish reached Lake Timsah, 9000 men and a few stores had been landed at Ismailia; the fresh-water canal and the whole line of railway between Suez and Ismailia had fallen into our hands, and communication by land had thus been secured with the Indian contingent, which had begun to disembark at Suez on the 20th. Thanks to Lord Wolseley's *ruse de guerre*, these successes had been obtained almost without bloodshed.

The report that Aboukir was to be bombarded duly reached Arabi, who sent large reinforcements to the threatened forts. The Egyptians believed that the Delta was the object of the British attack, and consequently had concentrated the greater part of their army at the mouths of the Nile, with a body of 12,000 men at Tel-el-Kebir, a post in the eastern desert thirty-three miles to the westward of Ismailia. To this flank guard was allotted the duty of defending the Delta against an enemy based on the canal, and of guarding Zag-a-zig, the most important junction in the railway system of Egypt. By his successful feint upon Aboukir, Wolseley prevented the despatch of reinforcements from the Delta to Tel-el-Kebir, and thanks to the rapidity with which the naval landing-parties had seized the telegraph lines, news of the occupation of the Suez canal did not reach the garrison of Tel-el-Kebir in time to enable them to oppose our disembarkation at Ismailia. Very shortly after Arabi heard that Wolseley had landed on the bank of the canal he transferred his Headquarters to Tel-el-Kebir, where his Intelligence department must have been singularly inefficient, for, "strange as it may appear, it now seems to be certain that the great transfer of force on the 19th of August from Alexandria to Ismailia remained unknown to Arabi till he heard of it with evident astonishment about a year later in Ceylon,"[1] where, after the war was over, he was detained as a political prisoner. But though the British General had thus stolen a march upon his enemy, many difficulties still confronted him, well described in the following extract from the official history of the campaign.

"There was only one small pier at Ismailia. Ships did not at first anchor nearer than about half a mile from the shore. Every man, every horse and every gun, as well as all the ammunition and stores for the supply of the army, had first to be transhipped from the transports into barges and small boats, rowed or tugged to shore, and then landed on the small pier. . . . In no sense were the conditions for the rapid landing of a large number of troops and of a vast quantity of stores in existence at Ismailia. It is true that this state of things could be ultimately changed by our engineers. But this would also be a question of time. Every tool, every scrap of material, all the bridging stores and all the means of constructing other piers, for laying down tramways and increasing the pier accommodation must, by an inexorable necessity, be first landed under the conditions actually existing. Materials for all these purposes, including landing-stages expressly made for Ismailia, had been prepared in England before the expedition sailed, but it would not be possible to send them forward in the most advanced vessels of the fleet, for those ships must be otherwise filled. In order to secure the all-important lines of communication—the railway and Sweet-water canal—for the advance from Ismailia, it was essential that the first vessels of the fleet should be occupied by the troops which would be sent forward to seize them. These troops, once sent forward, must be supplied with food and ammunition, so that a considerable force, with all its guns and equipment, tons of supplies, ordnance stores and ammunition and the means of local transport . . . must be sent on in the most advanced ships before any engineering material for the improvement of the means of landing . . . could be put on shore."[2]

The Egyptians had dammed the "Sweet-water" canal at Magfar, a few miles west of Ismailia, and the water, the only supply for the towns on the Suez canal and for the army when it moved into the desert, was falling rapidly. While keeping every available man at work at Ismailia, Lord Wolseley sent Graham with a small force of all arms to Magfar, and after two days' skirmishing, not only occupied that place, but Kassasin also, where

---

[1] Maurice, p. 41.   [2] Maurice, pp. 25, 26.

an important lock, twenty miles up the canal from Ismailia, fell into our hands. Here Wolseley determined to establish an advanced base, where, under the protection of a comparatively small force, supplies could be accumulated in readiness for the campaign in the desert. Graham was left in charge of this post; among his troops were two of the units of his brigade (the 2nd), viz.: a battalion of Royal Marine Light Infantry and the 2nd battalion, York and Lancaster regiment; the remainder of his command, the 2nd battalion of the Royal Irish regiment and the 1st battalion of the Royal Irish Fusiliers, though they landed on the night of the 24th, did not take part in these preliminary operations, being detained at Ismailia to help in unloading the store-ships and transports.

The Royal Irish arrived from England with a total strength of seven hundred and seventy-one, including a hundred and fifty non-commissioned officers and men from the reserve.[1] Among their fellow-passengers was a newspaper correspondent, Major Terry, a half-pay officer, who found the XVIIIth such good comrades that he attached himself to the battalion throughout the war. From his account the voyage was a pleasant one, the ship comfortable, and the troops well fed. The time passed quickly, for in addition to the ordinary routine of life on board a transport, the officers were hard at work reading the books on Egypt with which Colonel Gregorie had provided himself, and lecturing to the men about the country in which they were going to fight. The correspondent described the rank and file as "rather under height, but a very broad-shouldered and robust body of men, with quiet manners and pleasant to talk to. Intensely Irish, they easily brighten into excitement in their amusements, and when their own stirring national airs are played by the band." At Malta the XVIIIth heard many rumours about Lord Wolseley's plans, but the only definite information they received was the order to paint their helmets and belts mud-colour, and to dull the brass-work on their uniforms. To our modern ideas the red serge jumpers and blue serge trousers in which the expedition took the field was a kit singularly ill adapted for a campaign in Egypt. Spine-pads and spectacles with blue glasses were served out, but many men did not understand the value of these novel articles of equipment, and lost them, much to their sorrow when a few days later they found themselves in the desert exposed to

---

[1] The officers who went out to Egypt with the battalion were Brevet-Colonel C. F. Gregorie (in command); Majors J. M. Toppin and G. W. N. Rogers; Captains J. H. Daubeney, C. E. Dixon, C. E. G. Burr, H. S. Lye, C. E. Le Quesne, and H. M. Hatchell; Lieutenants E. J. Grant, A. G. Chichester, J. H. Chawner, G. H. Symonds (Adjutant), D. G. Gregorie, A. S. Orr, W. R. B. Doran, A. T. Ward, H. D. Daly; Quartermaster and Honorary Captain T. Hamilton; Surgeon J. Prendergast, A.M.D.; Paymaster P. A. Robinson. Attached to the battalion were Captains C. N. Jones (Connaught Rangers) and H. H. Edwards (Royal Welsh Fusiliers); Lieutenants G. P. Hatch (Wiltshire regiment), N. L. Pearse (Derbyshire regiment), H. H. Drummond-Wolff (Royal Fusiliers), and E. M. Barttelot (Royal Fusiliers).

the full blaze of a semi-tropical sun.   On the 22nd the *City of Paris* reached Alexandria, and was immediately ordered on to Port Said, where the battalion found the navy in possession of the town, apparently quite as much at home there as in Portsmouth harbour.   As the ship was steaming slowly along the canal, the Royal Irish were much entertained by a party of blue-jackets, stationed at Kantara to protect the floating bridge.   The guard of sailors turned out and presented arms in the most orthodox fashion; and then produced a concertina and played "Rule Britannia," dancing on the sand and swinging their cutlasses round their heads with immense energy.

On August 24, the *City of Paris* arrived at Lake Timsah, and anchored in the midst of a great fleet of warships and transports, the latter surrounded by steam-launches, tugs, and lighters, all busily employed in landing at Ismailia the *personnel* and *matériel* of the expedition.   This town, a creation of M. de Lesseps, is on the western shore of the lake, where, half-hidden in groves of palm and plane trees, it lies like a green oasis in a desert of yellow sand.   Here the Royal Irish remained for the next four days, earning golden opinions by the sustained energy which they displayed in carrying out the irksome duty of moving stores from the water-side to the railway station. Then came the welcome order to join their brigade at Kassasin.   They moved in detachments, constantly halting to help repair the railway and to clear obstructions from the Sweet-water canal.   The march was a singularly unpleasant one : the heat was very great, the dust and flies were exasperating to a degree, the tents had gone astray, and the only water to be had was from the canal, which belied its name, as it was polluted by the dead bodies of Egyptian soldiers.   Several of the stations on the railway showed traces of the recent presence of Arabi's troops, who in their flight had abandoned their rifles and ammunition, and left their dead unburied behind them.   There was so much work to be done on the line that it was not until late on the 8th of September that the last companies of the Royal Irish reached Kassasin.

Arabi had been misled by the lying reports of his Bedouin scouts, who informed him that they had cut the communication between Ismailia and Kassasin, and that the latter was held by a small force, whereas as a matter of fact the railway from Ismailia to the front was in working order ; Kassasin was occupied by about 8000 men under General Willis, and the brigade of Guards, a battery, and a regiment of cavalry were all within reinforcing distance.   Acting on this false information, he determined to take the offensive, and at dawn on the 9th he put his troops in motion and pushed from Tel-el-Kebir towards Kassasin with several squadrons of cavalry, thirty or thirty-one guns, and seventeen battalions of infantry.   His cavalry advance-guard greatly outnumbered our mounted troops, who however succeeded in holding back the Egyptian horsemen, until the infantry had taken up a position astride the canal to meet the attack now threatening from the west and north.   Covered by a vigorous but comparatively harmless cannonade, the enemy's infantry, a large part of which had been brought by train, advanced towards the camp, the uniforms of the regular soldiers contrasting strongly with the white robes of the Bedouins as they moved over the low sandy hummocks of the desert.   For a time General Willis stood on the defensive, and the Royal Irish were detailed as the escort to the field-guns.   Then he gave orders for a general advance, and the battalion was placed in echelon on the right rear of the first line of Graham's brigade, ready to form front to the right, and face the flank attack which for a moment was anticipated.   At first the battalion moved in quarter column, and then in line; at no time during the 9th was it extended for attack, for the British guns played so rapidly upon the Egyptians that they fell back in disorder, giving Graham's brigade no opportunity to close with them; and by half-past ten the enemy had retired to his works at Tel-el-Kebir, leaving four field-pieces in our hands.   From his entrenchments Arabi opened an angry but harmless artillery fire upon the troops, who by General Willis's directions halted out of range.   In ceasing his pursuit at a moment when it seemed that a vigorous, though necessarily costly attack might have made him master of the entrenchments, General Willis was acting in perfect accord with the spirit of Lord Wolseley's strategy, for Alison's brigade of infantry had only just arrived from Alexandria at Kassasin, and the Commander-in-Chief was not yet ready to advance across the desert.   Had the Egyptians been attacked and beaten on the 9th, Wolseley could not have followed up the victory, and therefore their defeat would not have been the absolutely crushing blow that he hoped to inflict (and did actually inflict) upon them a few days later.   The British troops remained facing Tel-el-Kebir for about three hours, and thus secured time for a careful reconnaissance of Arabi's position; then they were ordered back to camp. The Egyptian losses were severe, but the British casualties were only three men killed, two officers and seventy-five other ranks wounded.   Among the wounded were Captain H. H. Edwards, Royal Welsh Fusiliers (attached to the XVIIIth) and two private soldiers of the battalion.[1]   A subaltern in the Royal Irish thus recorded the experiences of the second battalion on this occasion : "Just as we were sitting down to breakfast the bugles sounded for us to fall in, and a minute or two later the enemy had got so close that they began lodging shell in our camp and made it so hot that the —— had to clear out sharp.   We were out pretty quick, and were alongside some guns which opened on the enemy and of course drew their fire on us.   For about an hour we were in a pretty warm corner; shells burst thickly around us, but

[1] See Appendix 2 (M).

no one was touched except two men slightly wounded. After a time we got the order to advance, and in doing so we got a few rifle-shots among us which did not do us any harm. Our men did not fire a shot. As we advanced the enemy retreated. We were left to cover the retirement of the battalions who had been in the firing line and were relieved at four o'clock in the afternoon."

In a short time the Commander-in-Chief's preparations were completed; the whole of the troops selected for the march across the desert were concentrated at Kassasin, and those appointed to hold the lines of communication were at their posts. Lord Wolseley had already formed his plan of attack, which he thus described in his despatch of the 16th of September—

"The enemy's position was a strong one; there was no cover of any kind in the desert lying between my camp at Kassasin and the enemy's works north of the Canal. These works extended from a point on the Canal 1½ miles east of the railway station at Tel-el-Kebir for a distance almost due north of about 3½ miles. The general character of the ground which forms the northern boundary of the valley through which the Ismailia [1] Canal and railway run is that of gently undulating and rounded slopes, which rise gradually to a fine open plateau from 90 to 100 feet above the valley. The southern extremity of this plateau is about a mile from the railway and is nearly parallel to it. To have marched over this plateau upon the enemy's position by daylight our troops would have had to advance over a glacis-like slope in full view of the enemy and under the fire of his well-served artillery for about five miles. Such an operation would have entailed enormous losses from an enemy with men and guns well-protected by entrenchments from any artillery fire we could have brought to bear upon them. To have turned the enemy's position either by the right or left was an operation that would have entailed a very wide turning movement, and therefore a long, difficult and fatiguing march, and what is of more importance, it would not have accomplished the object I had in view, namely to grapple with the enemy at such close quarters that he should not be able to shake himself free from our clutches except by a general fight of all his army. I wished to make the battle a final one; whereas a wide turning movement would probably have only forced him to retreat, and would have left him free to have moved his troops in good order to some other position farther back. My desire was to fight him decisively where he was, in the open desert, before he could take up fresh positions more difficult of access in the cultivated country in his rear. That cultivated country is practically impassable to a regular army, being irrigated and cut up in every direction by deep canals. I had ascertained by frequent reconnaissance that the enemy did not push his outposts far beyond his works at night, and I had good reasons for believing that he then kept a very bad look-out. These circumstances, and the very great reliance I had in the steadiness of our splendid infantry, determined me to resort to the extremely difficult operation of a night march, to be followed by an attack before daybreak on the enemy's position."

[1] Otherwise known as the Sweet-water Canal.

The field-works at Tel-el-Kebir were not of uniform strength, for Arabi, believing that the British would advance along the Sweet-water canal, had devoted himself to the fortification of the right of his line, where for more than two miles stretched an unbroken series of breastworks, with parapets five or six feet high, and ditches varying from eight to twelve feet in width, and from five to nine feet in depth. Behind these defences about two miles of interior works had been thrown up, connected with those in front by rifle-pits and trenches, and from redoubts built at numerous salients, cross-fire could be poured in every direction. Towards the left the works dwindled in size, and at the extreme northern end of the line, that which, as we shall see, was attacked by the Royal Irish, they were but a mere collection of shelter trenches. Arabi had twenty-five thousand soldiers, six thousand Bedouin irregulars, and about sixty guns with which to defend these fortifications against the eleven thousand infantry, two thousand cavalry, and sixty-one guns that the British Commander-in-Chief could bring against him. The remainder of Wolseley's command was absorbed by the garrisons of Alexandria, Port Said, Ismailia, Suez, and other points on the Suez canal, and the posts on the line of communication between Kassasin and the base at Ismailia.

Though the British advance was to be astride the Sweet-water canal, the main attack was to be delivered on the works to the north of it, where the first division was to assault the left, the second division the right of the entrenchments. The cavalry division, with its batteries of Royal Horse artillery, was to circle round the left of the Egyptian position, threaten its defenders from the rear, and pursue them when the infantry had driven them from their entrenchments. On the south of the canal the Indian brigade and the naval contingent were to clear the country, capture the villages which had been placed in a state of defence, and seize the important railway junction of Zag-a-zig. To the field batteries an interesting *rôle* was assigned. It was obvious that in a night march they could not discharge the ordinary duty of artillery, that of keeping in check the enemy's fire so as to render it possible for the attacking infantry to advance. But it was almost equally obvious that, if the forty-two field-guns could be brought up to the entrenchments of Tel-el-Kebir by early dawn, they would be able to pour a crushing short-range fire upon the defenders: if either division required support the guns would be at hand to give assistance, and should either of the infantry attacks fail, the artillery would be ready to beat the enemy down behind his works until the attackers were able to renew the assault. The seven field batteries therefore were ordered to march in the interval between the infantry divisions, keeping level with them.

The first and second divisions and the field artillery were assembled after dark on September 12, on the rising ground known to the Staff as Ninth Hill, which lay about four miles to the east of Arabi's position. To give the enemy's scouts and spies no clue to the intended movements the tents were not struck till sunset, when all bugle calls ceased. Then the troops were set in motion, the men marching light with a hundred rounds of ammunition, rations, and water-bottles.[1] As soon as the sun went down the Royal Engineers began to set up on Ninth Hill long lines of posts, running many hundred yards into the desert, to serve as guides towards the enemy's entrenchments. The night was unusually dark, the posts were hard to find, and it was not till eleven P.M. that all the units had reached their proper places. Graham's brigade was on the right of the line, with its battalions standing in the following order from the right, Royal Irish, York and Lancaster, Royal Marine Light Infantry, Royal Irish Fusiliers: in the centre were the field-guns: on the left was Alison's brigade. H.R.H. the Duke of Connaught's brigade of Guards supported Graham, while in rear of Alison was a small brigade of two battalions under Colonel Ashburnham, King's Royal Rifle Corps.

At 1 A.M. on the 13th of September, Graham called together the officers commanding the battalions of his brigade and in a low voice gave them instructions, briefly and to the point: the works of Tel-el-Kebir were to be surprised; the troops were to close upon them at earliest dawn, and carry them at the point of the bayonet. The soldiers were then roused; the orders were explained to them, and in half an hour the greater part of the army was on the march to attack an enemy of nearly double its numbers, and holding fortifications about which, except their strength, little definite was known. The Indian brigade did not leave its resting-place, south of the Canal, until 2.30 A.M., as to have moved earlier would have run the risk of giving the alarm to the inhabitants of the belt of cultivated land through which Macpherson had to march. Throughout the night telegraphic communication was kept up between the Indian brigade and a detachment of Royal Marine artillery, who followed behind the second division. It was many years since a British general had attempted operations at night upon so large a scale. In the Peninsula Wellington's troops had been thoroughly accustomed to marching and manœuvring in darkness, but the art was now almost a lost one, and Wolseley wisely gave great latitude to his divisional generals in the choice of the formations in which their commands were to advance; he wished the brigades to be so marshalled that no manœuvring would be necessary to pass them from the order in which they marched into that in which they were to attack, and he suggested, though without positively commanding, that each brigade should move in line of columns of half battalions at deploying intervals. Neither Alison nor Graham adopted the suggestion in its entirety.

[1] The orders directed that the water-bottles should, if possible, contain cold tea, the beverage which Lord Wolseley constantly recommended on active service.

Alison drew up his men in line of half battalion columns of double companies, and not only marched but attacked in this formation; Graham first moved in columns of half battalions at deploying intervals, but found it necessary to make several changes in formation before he finally closed with the enemy. Nothing but the perfect discipline of the troops enabled Lord Wolseley and his generals to move this great mass of men and guns at dead of night, across nearly four miles of ground which it had not been possible thoroughly to reconnoitre, and to bring it to within a few hundred yards of the fortifications before it was detected by the enemy. No smoking was allowed; the men were as silent as the grave; the few orders issued were passed along the ranks in a whisper. In the blackness of the night Staff officers riding from flank to flank found it impossible to see a column, when two hundred yards away from it; yet when their ears had grown attuned to the silence, which at first appeared crushing and unnatural, they became aware of a low dull noise, that sound of human feet, of horses' hoofs, of jingling harness, which no forethought could prevent. Fortunately throughout the night a little breeze blew from west to east, and thus Arabi's men, being up-wind, would have heard nothing if their watch had been vigilant, instead of extremely negligent.

In the 2nd brigade the precaution of extending a chain of connecting links between the half battalions did not ensure perfect leading by the guides. Sometimes the half battalions would open out, and at others close unduly upon each other. These mistakes had to be corrected, and each correction took time. At an hour variously estimated between 3 and 4 A.M.[1] General Willis considered that the 2nd brigade had come within range of the Egyptian works. He wished to rest his men for a moment, and accordingly, after forming line, ordered a short halt. With the priceless trust of British soldiers in their officers, the men immediately dropped on the sand and fell fast asleep during the few minutes' repose which they were allowed. About the same time the Highland brigade was halted to refresh the men. As all orders were passed in a low tone from company to company and from battalion to battalion, this order was not at once received by the troops on the outer flanks; they continued to advance, but as they remained in touch with the centre they lost direction and by the time the command reached them they had wheeled inwards, though quite unconsciously. Thus the brigade halted not in line, but in a crescent-shaped formation. When the order was given to resume the march the flank battalions, quite unaware that they had lost direction, moved straight to their front, and soon almost crashed into each other. Each thought the other was the enemy, but by a triumph of discipline, every man waited for orders to fire, and thus gave time for the officers to discover the mistake. The brigade was halted, the companies of direction placed on the true line of advance, and the remainder of the Highlanders,

---

[1] It was forbidden to strike matches, so watches could not be consulted.

gradually and successively drawing back, re-formed upon the proper alignment. This mistake, which took about twenty-five minutes to correct, is a good example of the difficulty of night operations and the necessity of implicit obedience to orders.

After a short rest Graham's brigade again advanced, this time in line, but the formation was found unsuitable, and was changed to an advance by fours from the right of companies. To keep in the proper direction was no easy matter, especially as the mass of artillery on the left was steering a few degrees too far to the northward, and thus continually elbowed the 2nd brigade off the right path: to correct this pressure frequent turns half-left and half-right had to be made. Suddenly, at about 4.45 A.M., "far away to the left was heard a tremendous rattle of musketry, mingled with the firing of big guns, succeeded by ringing and sustained cheers, and "—to quote the special correspondent who, as already mentioned, had attached himself to the Royal Irish—"we felt sure that the Highland brigade had found its quest and run into it." At this moment it became necessary again to correct a mistake in direction, and "a halt and change of front a quarter circle to the left were at once ordered. . . . A rattling fire of small arms now opened on us from the works, distant about 600 yards.[1] It was still dusk, but the blackness of night had given place to a pale darkness, through which the flashes of fire sparkled with ceaseless rapidity."

By this time, owing to the difficulty of marching at night over the featureless desert with nothing to steer by but the stars, Lord Wolseley's force was no longer in line but in echelon from the left, and when the Highlanders struck the enemy's works the head of Graham's brigade was probably more than 800 yards from the Egyptians' entrenchments. As soon as the brigade had formed line the Royal Irish pushed forward, and were rapidly nearing the position when the brigade-major, suddenly appearing on the scene, told Colonel Gregorie it was General Graham's wish that he should form the Royal Irish for attack. Though it was obvious that the battalion was too close to the trenches for the evolution to be carried out accurately, the necessary orders were given, and C and D companies extended, with B and E in support, and the remainder in reserve. Then the leading companies swept onwards under a heavy but fortunately ill-directed fusilade; the supports and reserves closed upon the firing-line, and with wild yells and almost without firing a shot, the Royal Irish swarmed over the shelter trenches at the extreme end of Arabi's line, driving before them at the point of the bayonet the Egyptians, who slowly and in good order fell back to a second line of works in rear. The Royal Irish were now enfiladed by a redoubt on their left flank, but taking no notice of its fire they pressed onwards until, after driving the Egyptians from the second line of entrench-

[1] This distance is understated; it was probably more than 800 yards.

ments, they were peremptorily halted and ordered to re-form their ranks. While this second charge was being delivered, Lieutenant Chichester made a gallant effort to storm the redoubt with a few men; but he and two or three of his followers fell wounded, and it remained in the hands of the enemy until the York and Lancaster carried it with a rush. The Marines and the Royal Irish Fusiliers gradually made themselves masters of the works in front of them, and the Egyptians, falling into confusion, and to a large extent abandoned by their officers who were among the first to fly, retired in disorder. When they discovered that the British cavalry had swung round the left of their position and were directly threatening them from the rear, their retreat became a rout. Yet there were many among the rank and file, especially in the regiments composed of Nubians, who had shown bravery in the battle, and at the time it was thought that had these men been well led they would have been formidable enemies. The justice of this opinion has been proved by the services of the modern Egyptian troops in the Soudan, where regiments of Egyptian peasants and Soudanese blacks, trained and officered by men of the regular British army, have on many occasions acquitted themselves excellently.

Some interesting episodes have been recorded of the part played by the Royal Irish in this phase of the engagement. The special correspondent relates that as the battalion was advancing towards the first line of trenches two men, mad with excitement, dashed out of the ranks and rushed towards the enemy. For a moment they disappeared, but

> "presently they were seen by themselves, beyond the first works, and in front of the big redoubt, in the very midst of the foe. These gallant two! One was on his knee facing south-west; apparently he is conscious of having gone beyond support. The Egyptians in their trenches and ditches are in front, to right and to left of him. He glances back towards where kneels, a few yards behind him, his brave companion. But who can save you now, rash, gallant young Irishmen! You have turned from the front of your regiment and are cut off from all aid. My position on horseback enabled me to see the men, who, kneeling, were hid by the trenches from their own regiment. I saw an Egyptian officer move up behind the left of the leading man, and seizing his arm, strike him over the head or shoulder with his sword. A struggle ensued, but the smoke of battle hid them from further view. After the fight Colonel Gregorie found two dead bodies of his men among the others of his regiment in the place described: their names were Corporal Devine and Private Milligan."

The good conduct of other soldiers is thus described by Colonel (then Lieutenant) Chichester—

> "They stood back to back, tackled six Nubians, and accounted for them all. I now forget their names, but I was going to recommend

them for reward, but afterwards heard that they had been killed later in the battle. A very brave reservist in my company was badly wounded and lay on the ground close to where I had fallen. He had eight bullet holes in his body, yet he only died the day that our transport full of wounded arrived at Plymouth. When the men came to attend him on the battlefield, he said, ' Don't mind me; look after others, worse hurt.' "

In sharp contrast to the gallant behaviour of this Irishman was the treachery of an Egyptian officer who lay injured on ground occupied by the XVIIIth. One of the men offered him water; he drank it, and then suddenly rolled over, snatched up a rifle and shot down one of the soldiers who were tending him. Prompt steps were taken to prevent this ruffian from doing more mischief!

After pursuing for some distance, Graham halted to re-form his brigade in readiness for further action. He had every reason to be proud of his command, for, as he reported to Lord Wolseley, "the steadiness of the advance of the 2nd brigade under what appeared to be an overwhelming fire of musketry and artillery will remain a proud remembrance." As he rode from battalion to battalion he was greeted with many cheers, a tribute to the leader who, though a stern disciplinarian, had ever proved himself mindful of the comfort of his men, watchful of their safety, and who had now led them to decisive victory. By the time the second brigade had re-formed its ranks the troops on the left had also finished their work. The task set to Alison's command had proved much harder than that allotted to Graham's battalions. Not only were the fortifications which faced the Highland brigade far stronger than those attacked by the second division, but when the Highlanders had surmounted them they came under a very heavy fire from the inner works. But thanks to the timely aid of the guns, which pushed right into the entrenchments, the enemy was driven back in wild confusion, and in less than an hour Arabi's army was shattered as completely as it had been surprised.

Lord Wolseley lost no time in reaping the fruits of his victory. As soon as the enemy's works were in his hands the cavalry were ordered to continue their pursuit, and to strain every nerve to reach Cairo before Arabi had been able to burn it, as he had threatened to do if he was defeated; while the Indian brigade, which had completely driven the enemy from the cultivated country on the southern bank of the canal, was to push on to Zag-a-zig, and by occupying it, prevent the various detachments of Arabi's troops in the Delta from coming to his assistance. Both enterprises were successful. At four o'clock on September 14, the cavalry after a magnificent forced march began to appear before the gates of Cairo, where Arabi, who was one of the first to quit the entrenchments of Tel-el-Kebir, had taken refuge. Without attempting to fight, or to carry out his plan for the destruction of the city, he surrendered at once, and with him the garrison of ten thousand men. The Indian brigade made itself master of Zag-a-zig, capturing much rolling stock, in which a great portion of the infantry was moved up to Cairo. With their arrival the war was over, and in ten days' time every garrison in Egypt had been disarmed, and the men set free to resume the avocations of peace.

Not all the British infantry, however, went on at once to Cairo. Among the regiments left at Tel-el-Kebir was the second battalion of the Royal Irish, who thus had plenty of opportunity to admire the fifty-eight guns which had been taken on the 13th. In the engagement the Egyptians are believed to have lost about two thousand killed;[1] of the number of their wounded there is no record, but several hundred were tended by our army doctors, while many uninjured prisoners were taken, disarmed, and turned adrift. The British casualties were nine officers killed and twenty-seven wounded; of the other ranks forty-eight were killed, three hundred and fifty-five wounded, and thirty missing — in all, four hundred and sixty-nine.

In the Royal Irish the losses were:

Killed . . . Captain C. M. Jones (attached from the Connaught Rangers) and three other ranks.

Mortally Wounded . Four private soldiers.

Wounded . . . Lieutenant A. G. Chichester and Lieutenant H. H. Drummond - Wolff (attached from the Royal Fusiliers) and fourteen other ranks.[2]

After a week at Tel-el-Kebir the Royal Irish were moved by train to Cairo, where they were quartered in a barrack, the filth of which was so great that to this day the remembrance stinks in the nostrils of those who occupied it. The duty was heavy; there was much sickness among all ranks, and beyond ceremonial parades in honour of the return of the Khedive to the capital in which he had been reinstated by British bayonets, nothing of interest occurred during the three weeks the battalion spent in Cairo except a great fire, in the suppression of which it was employed. Lieutenant W. R. B. Doran (now Colonel Doran, C.B., D.S.O.), in a letter written at the time, thus described the part played on this occasion by the

---

[1] A delightful story is told of one of the XVIIIth who was asked on his return home how many of the enemy had fallen. He replied, "I don't just know, but I killed devil a one less than five hundred with my own bayonet!"

[2] The names will be found in Appendix 2 (M). There is a memorial to those who died in this campaign in the barrack square of the depôt at Clonmel.

Royal Irish, who were fortunate to escape without any of the casualties which occurred among other corps—

"On the 29th of September we were startled by a tremendous bang, followed by what sounded like a succession of cannon-shots. After an interval there was another great explosion, more cannon-shots, and then a rattle of musketry. We thought at first it was some kind of plot. It turned out that a lot of trucks full of powder, unexploded shells, and small-arm ammunition had been set on fire by another train containing hay. How the hay was set on fire no one has yet found out. About 6.30 P.M. we were turned out in a great hurry, and went to the railway station, to stop all traffic in the streets in the neighbourhood, and to prevent the scum from beginning to loot; they had just begun, but they got such 'toco' from the 'Tommies' that they soon stopped their little games. We remained guarding the streets till nearly 1 A.M., when we were relieved and began, as we thought, to march home, but were grievously disappointed, as before we had gone half a mile we were halted in a square and told to lie down and go to sleep in the road. I was rather hungry, as I had not quite finished my dinner when the order to fall in came, so I managed to get a sort of penny bun from one of our captains, half of which I ate; the other half I put under my head and went to sleep on the hardest bed and strangest pillow I have ever had!"

The battalion was sent to Alexandria[1] on October 11, and a month later Lieutenant-Colonel Gregorie, after serving his full time in command, was succeeded by Lieutenant-Colonel R. W. E. Dawson. On February 1, 1883, the medals with clasps for Tel-el-Kebir were presented to the Royal Irish on the racecourse of Alexandria by a veteran soldier, Field-Marshal Lord Napier of Magdala, G.C.B., and a few days later the battalion, which to the great satisfaction of all ranks was not included in the 10,000 troops left to hold Egypt for the Khedive, sailed for Malta, and after remaining there for three months, landed at Plymouth at the end of May, 1883.

The regiment received permission to add to its battle honours the words "Egypt 1882" and "Tel-el-Kebir."

Lieutenant-Colonel C. F. Gregorie was appointed a Companion of the Order of the Bath; Major G. W. N. Rogers and Captain J. H. Daubeney each received a step in brevet rank; Quartermaster and Honorary Captain T. Hamilton was made an Honorary Major; Lieutenant A. G. Chichester and Sergeant E. O'Donnell were mentioned in despatches. The following officers

---

[1] The mosquitos at Alexandria appear to have made a great impression, not only on the bodies, but also on the imaginations of the young officers of the Royal Irish. One subaltern stated that these pests had bitten his foot through the sole of a shooting boot, while another asserted that the mosquitos were so intelligent and so strong that three of them used to combine to lift up his mosquito-net to allow their friends to feast upon his hot Irish blood.

were permitted to accept and wear decorations awarded by the Sultan, viz.: Lieutenant-Colonel Gregorie, the Medjidie (3rd class); Major Rogers, the Osmanieh (4th class); Captain Daubeney, Medjidie (4th class); and Lieutenant Chichester, Medjidie (5th class), and all ranks were presented by the Egyptian government with a decoration known as the Khedive's Star.

Two officers attached to the second battalion—Captain H. H. Edwards, Royal Welsh Fusiliers, and Lieutenant H. H. Drummond-Wolff, Royal Fusiliers, were also mentioned in despatches.

CHAPTER XII.

THE FIRST BATTALION.

1884-1885.

THE NILE EXPEDITION.

AT the time of England's armed intervention in Egypt in 1882, the Khedive's authority extended nominally far beyond the limits of the province which Mahomet Ali had wrested from the Sublime Porte. The founder of the Egyptian dynasty, not satisfied with fighting his Suzerain the Sultan in Syria, had pushed armies up the Nile into the heart of the Soudan, or country of the Blacks, a no-man's land which stretched from Wadi Halfa, the southern boundary of Egypt, to the Great Lakes far beyond the equator. This region had no form of government; its inhabitants were oppressed by Arab slave-hunters; its condition was pitiable in the extreme. Mahomet Ali gradually conquered every tribe in the Nile valley up to the junction of the White and Blue Niles, where he built Khartoum, and thrust forward outposts in every direction from the capital of his new dominions, which was about a thousand miles south of Cairo. The country thus annexed became known as the Egyptian Soudan, and extended from the shore of the Red Sea to the western frontier of Kordofan; it was about the size of France and Germany put together, and its population in 1883 was estimated at fourteen millions of mixed breed, the descendants of the aboriginal negroes and the Arabs who overran the country early in the Mohammedan era. This blend had produced a race possessing the outward characteristics and mental attributes of the Arab, combined with the endurance and brute courage of the Negro.[1] After anarchy such as had prevailed in the Soudan, almost any form of government might have been expected to improve the condition of the country; but in this respect Egyptian rule completely failed. Taxation was heavy; extortion was the rule, rather than the exception, and slave-hunting, with all its attendant horrors, was not suppressed; indeed, thanks to the connivance of the officials, who were virtually in partnership with the slave-dealers, it so

[1] Colvile, 'History of the Soudan Campaign' (official), p. 1.

greatly increased that the country was rapidly becoming depopulated, when in 1869, the pressure of British public opinion compelled the Khedive to institute reforms in the administration, and to appoint an Englishman, Sir Samuel Baker, as Governor-General of the Equatorial provinces, which stretched from Khartoum to the Great Lakes. Five years later Baker was succeeded by General (then Colonel) Charles George Gordon, who held the post till 1879. Though both accomplished much towards the establishment of better government and the suppression of slave-hunting, their efforts were cramped and thwarted by the officials at Cairo and at Khartoum, who were naturally disinclined to lose the enormous profits they derived from the trade in slaves. A country so mercilessly treated only needed a leader to turn upon its oppressors, and in 1881, such a leader arose in the Soudan. A prophecy had long been current among Mohammedans that about this time a "Mahdi" would appear and convert the whole world to the true faith, and of this prophecy a religious adventurer, named Mohammed Ahmed, availed himself to the uttermost. He proclaimed himself the Mahdi whose advent had been predicted, and announced that as soon as the Soudan had joined his cause he would march on Egypt, destroying all who opposed him, and convert the whole world to Islam. Such was the spiritual part of his programme, carefully prepared to rouse the fanaticism latent in every Mohammedan; the temporal advantages he offered to his followers were universal equality and community of goods. Although denounced as an impostor by the educated Mussulmans, who probably regarded his socialistic propaganda with misgivings, he rapidly gained a great following, and obtained several successes over the Egyptian garrisons, which were at this time in a wretched condition. The troops had not been paid for many months, in some cases even for years: the soldiers were undrilled, their officers incompetent to drill them: the loyalty of all ranks was as doubtful as their courage. To stiffen this unpromising material, several Englishmen in the service of Egypt were sent to Khartoum; among them was Hicks Pasha, at one time an officer in the Indian army, now the newly appointed Commander-in-Chief of the Khedive's troops in the Soudan.

In September, 1883, Hicks, acting under the orders of the Egyptian government, led an expedition into the depths of Kordofan, where the Mahdi had retired to organise the tribesmen, from thirty to sixty thousand strong, whom his recent victories had attracted to his standard. Hicks commanded about 11,000 weakly and ill-fed men, of whom many were so unwilling to be soldiers that to prevent desertion they had to be sent up the Nile in chains. His artillery consisted of thirty-six Krupp, Nordenfelt, and mountain guns, and his transport was supplied by six thousand horses and camels. The whole of the Egyptian troops were thoroughly out of heart; they were aware that they were about to march into a country of which little was known except that it was almost waterless, and that they would encounter hordes of desperate and ruthless fanatics. As the men filed out of Khartoum they were in floods of tears. The fate of such an army may easily be imagined: on the 5th of November it was surprised by the Mahdi with 40,000 of his followers, and cut to pieces, near El Obeid in Kordofan.[1] Hicks and the other Europeans died fighting dauntlessly to the last; the Egyptians allowed themselves to be butchered almost without resistance: three hundred were given quarter, only to become the slaves of the victors, into whose hands passed the guns, much ammunition, thousands of rifles, and all the transport animals. One man alone escaped to bring the news to Khartoum. Yet so little was the importance of the Mahdist movement appreciated by the English government that at the very time Hicks's column was being destroyed in Kordofan, Mr Gladstone was urging the reduction of the British army of occupation in Egypt. When Hicks's fate became known in Cairo the situation grew very complicated. The Cabinet in London, afraid of being drawn into armed intervention in the Soudan, had persistently assumed an attitude of aloofness on the subject of Hicks's operations, and, affecting to ignore the fact that Britain was virtually, though not officially, mistress in Egypt, and that a word from her representative at Cairo, Lord Cromer (then Sir Evelyn Baring), would have stopped the expedition, declined all responsibility on the ground that it had been undertaken solely on the authority of the Egyptian government. The annihilation of Hicks's army had placed Khartoum in a position of great danger: only two thousand troops were left to man the four miles of earthworks by which the town was ringed, and its communications with Cairo and Suakim were seriously threatened. The generals in command of the British army at Cairo admitted that, if the Mahdi advanced on Khartoum, it would be impossible to hold it in its existing condition, and that in all probability the whole valley of the Nile, as far south as Wadi Halfa, would be lost to Egypt. Alarmed at the crushing blow which had befallen him, and at the consequences likely to follow it, the Khedive begged that British troops might be sent to the Soudan, or, if these should not be forthcoming, that a contingent of Turks might be imported to hold Khartoum. Our government refused to move a single soldier to the Soudan, but had no objection to the employment of a Turkish force to garrison Khartoum, provided that no expense was thereby thrown upon the Egyptian Treasury. They, however, advised Tewfik to abandon all territory south of Assouan, softening the blow by the promise that England would defend not only Egypt proper, but also the ports of the Red Sea against the Mahdists. To this wholesale dismemberment of his dominions the Khedive demurred, and again suggested a Turkish occupation of the Soudan, whereupon England sternly replied that if the Egyptian ministers would not carry out the evacuation of the Soudan they would have

[1] See Map No. 9.

to make room for Englishmen, ready to enforce her policy. The Khedive thereupon withdrew his opposition, and agreed that the whole of the Soudan, except the port of Suakim, should be abandoned to its fate. During these negotiations the situation at Khartoum had become so serious that the senior European officer there, in reporting that it would be impossible to hold the town against the whole population of the Soudan, which had now thrown in its lot with the Mahdi, urged that immediate orders should be given for a withdrawal down the river. The question next arose—who was to effect the withdrawal, not only of the troops, but also of the officials, traders, and other members of the civil army of occupation in the Soudan ?

The English ministers then bethought themselves of General Gordon, one of the most remarkable characters of the nineteenth century. His career had been a strange and eventful one. After serving with distinction as a Royal Engineer in the Crimea, the chances of war carried him to the Far East where he played his part in the Anglo-French expedition to China. When the object of the campaign was accomplished, peace was signed with the Emperor of China, but the end of the war found some of the most fertile provinces of the Celestial Empire in the hands of great hordes of in-surgents, with whom the Chinese authorities were wholly unable to cope. Gordon was lent to the Emperor to command a force of Chinamen, raised by himself and officered by adventurers of mixed nationality. With a rare combination of military talent and personal courage, readiness to assume responsibility, power of influencing his subordinates, and complete absence of self-seeking, he welded his unpromising material into good soldiers, with whom he stormed many walled towns and won battles innumerable against vastly superior numbers. After a long struggle, in which his men earned the title of "the ever-victorious army," he completely crushed the rebels; and then, disbanding the troops who had learned to look upon him as invincible, he returned to Europe with the justly earned reputation of a born leader of men. During his five years' sojourn in the Soudan Gordon had acquired great influence over its inhabitants. The fighting men had learned to follow, the slave-hunters to fear him : the traders respected his stern and evenhanded justice : all classes knew that his word, once pledged, was never broken, and that his orders must be obeyed to the letter. At a few hours' notice, Gordon was sent to Egypt to secure the retreat of the garrison of Khartoum and of the thousands of civilians who would probably wish to accompany it, and also to effect the evacuation of the remainder of the Soudan. For this enormous task he was allowed one Staff officer, Colonel D. Stewart,[1] 11th Hussars, with whom he reached Khartoum on February 18, 1884.

---

[1] Colonel Stewart had already been to Khartoum, where he was sent on a tour of inspection soon after the European officers had demanded large reinforcements to enable them to make head against the Mahdi.

While Gordon was on his way up the Nile, the tide of war was setting strongly against the Egyptians in the eastern Soudan, where a wing of the Mahdi's army was commanded by Osman Digna, an ex-slave dealer who had been ruined by the capture of his *dhows* by British cruisers. Osman Digna had stormed several fortified towns and villages, held by the Khedive as outposts round Suakim, and had cut to pieces columns of Egyptian troops sent at various times to the relief of the garrisons scattered throughout the district. Suakim itself was threatened, and the ships of war then lying off the port landed bluejackets and Marines for its protection, while Major-General Sir Gerald Graham was sent from Cairo to reinforce them with 4000 British troops. There were two sharp engagements at El-Teb (February 29) and Tamai (March 13), in which Osman Digna fought with magnificent courage, but sustained such heavy losses that his power for evil appeared sufficiently diminished to warrant the withdrawal of the British soldiers from the eastern Soudan.

While these events were taking place round Suakim, things were going badly with Gordon at Khartoum, and though direct telegraphic communication with him was cut off about a month after his arrival, the news which reached Cairo showed that his position was becoming one of considerable danger. In April, the Secretary of State for War began to realise that it might become necessary to send an expedition to rescue Gordon, and called upon Lord Wolseley for a plan of campaign. In his reply Wolseley showed that Khartoum could only be approached by the caravan roads converging on Berber from the Red Sea or by the valley of the Nile, and strongly advocated the latter route. He proposed to move the dismounted troops up the river in boats, and after pointing out that Gordon's supplies would not permit him to hold Khartoum later than the 15th of November, urged that immediate preparations should be made to meet possible contingencies. For several months government took little action beyond making inquiries about the track across the desert from Suakim to Berber, and sending naval officers up the Nile to report whether Lord Wolseley's scheme was practicable. These officers reported against it, and Sir F. C. A. Stephenson, the General commanding the British troops in Egypt, agreed with their views. On the other hand, a committee composed of three officers who had taken part in the Red River expedition in Canada emphatically expressed their opinion that Wolseley's plan was perfectly feasible, and pointed out that the naval objections to it were based on the assumption that steamers of considerable size, and boats up to 40 tons burden would be required, whereas the army only asked for whale-boats, which could be used at any state of the Nile.

While these discussions were going on, the tide of Mahdism steadily flowed northwards. To meet a possible attack upon Egypt proper, the bulk

R

of the Khedive's army, then in process of reorganisation by British officers, was hurried to Assouan, where it was strengthened by English battalions; the Nile was patrolled by steamers manned by the navy; and irregular levies of Bedouins, also commanded by British officers, were pushed up the river into Dongola, the most southern portion of the Egyptian dominions in which the authority of the Khedive was still recognised. Dongola was ruled by a Mudir who, though originally in sympathy with the Mahdi, had been won back by golden arguments to the cause of his Suzerain. In the course of the summer his territory was attacked; it was considered necessary to help him with British bayonets, and the 1st battalion of the Royal Sussex regiment was moved southwards from Assouan. On the 8th of August, only eight days before the Royal Sussex reached the town of Dongola, a vote of credit was obtained from the House of Commons to cover the expense of sending troops to the assistance of the Mudir; but though by this vote government definitely committed itself to the Nile route, and therefore to the use of small boats, it was not until the 12th that official sanction was given for the construction of these craft. Four hundred were then ordered, and in a few days the number was doubled. The boats were to carry twelve men with their equipment, ammunition, and rations; to be suitable alike for rowing, sailing before a wind, and tracking (*i.e.*, being hauled up stream from the bank), for ascending and descending rapids, and for passing over shallow and rocky places in the river: to be as light as possible, yet strong enough to be dragged over short stretches of ground to avoid cataracts; and to be 32 feet in length, 6 feet 9 inches in breadth, and only 2 feet 6 inches in depth. The first consignment reached Alexandria on September 22, the last on October 18, 1884.

It had not been proposed to employ Lord Wolseley in the expedition, but on August 26, he was appointed to command the troops upon the Nile. He reached Cairo on September 9, when there were actually in Egypt, or on their way thither, a regiment of cavalry, one battery of Royal Horse artillery, one of Royal Field artillery, one camel battery of mountain guns, and two garrison batteries; four companies of Royal Engineers, one of which was at Suakim; a battalion of mounted infantry, 423 strong; and thirteen and a half battalions of infantry—in all, nearly 11,000 officers and men, among whom were the first battalion of the Royal Irish regiment. Not all these troops, however, were available for the actual operations at Khartoum when that far-distant goal should be approached. The garrisons of Cairo and Alexandria absorbed four and a half battalions of infantry, a squadron of cavalry, and all the artillery except the mountain guns. Though the Egyptian army held the line of communication from Cairo to Hannek, it was considered necessary to strengthen this section with a British battalion, while to secure the Nile between Hannek and Berber, at least five battalions would be required. Lord Wolseley aimed at placing about 5400 men in line at Shendi, a place on the river about 100 miles south of Berber, and the same distance to the northward of Khartoum, and after making allowance for the inevitable wastage of troops in an expedition such as he was to conduct, and for the possibility that he might have to send part of his column on a sudden dash across the desert, he asked the War Office to supply him with eleven hundred more men, volunteers from regular regiments at home, to be turned into "camelry"—*i.e.,* infantry mounted upon camels. The request was granted, and these reinforcements arrived in time to reap a large share of the honours of the campaign.

Before any troops could be moved to Shendi, through a country from which little or no food could be obtained, it was necessary to form an advanced base as high up the river as possible, where stores of all kinds were to be collected before the main body began to arrive from Cairo. It was also necessary to establish along the line of communication on the river a chain of intermediate depôts, from which the troops would draw rations and thus preserve intact the cargo of stores with which each whale-boat was to be freighted. Korti was selected for the advanced base, and there, when the first thousand miles of its journey from the sea was accomplished, the expeditionary force was to effect its preliminary concentration.[1] As far as Wadi Halfa, about 750 miles above Cairo, the navigation of the Nile presents no great difficulties, and every available river steamer and river boat was pressed into the service. But above Wadi Halfa a formidable series of cataracts, or rapids as they should more accurately be termed, proved fatal to so many of the native craft that the transport of stores to the higher reaches had almost entirely to be carried out by the whale-boats. It was not until the 1st of November that a sufficient quantity of supplies had been sent up the river to warrant Lord Wolseley in moving the main body of his infantry. Then as speedily as possible each corps was despatched in turn on its journey southward. Towards the end of December the first battalion of infantry reached Korti, where the camelry, who had marched along the banks of the Nile, were beginning to assemble; in about four weeks more the last regiments arrived, and by the end of January the preliminary concentration had been successfully accomplished.

While the second battalion was winning fresh honours for the regiment at Tel-el-Kebir, the first battalion was in India. It was stationed at Meerut

---

[1] The junior ranks of the British army are so used to receiving their rations with regularity on active service that they appear to think the Army Service Corps can feed them as the ravens fed Elijah. They do not realise the enormous amount of thought and calculation which have been lavished on the subject for months before the opening of a campaign. It is not within the scope of a regimental history to describe in detail the process by which Lord Wolseley succeeded in feeding his column in a country the principal products of which are water and sand. Those who wish to study the subject will find full information in Colvile's 'History of the Soudan Campaign,' and Butler's 'Campaign of the Cataracts.'

in August, 1884, when the welcome order was received to start for Egypt forthwith on active service. In high spirits at the prospect of a campaign, all ranks worked with a will; by the 20th the preparations were finished, and the Royal Irish, after a very hot railway journey, embarked at Bombay on the 29th, and three weeks later arrived at Cairo in magnificent order. They are described by an officer who was then serving with the regiment—

"When the 1st battalion Royal Irish landed in Egypt in 1884, it was, bar none, the finest battalion I have ever seen, both in physique and in general appearance. Under Colonel M. MacGregor they were considered to be the best dressed regiment in India, and since his departure they had lived up to their reputation. In this respect they presented a very marked contrast to many of the battalions in Egypt, who were dressed in a very hideous grey serge very similar to that worn by convicts, which was worn apparently exactly as it had been issued from store. Their physique was equally distinguishable from the Corps who had lately arrived from home. The average service was (if I remember right) about seven years, and the average height, taken from the annual return prepared at Wady Halfa, was 5.7¾, and the chest measurement was 38″. While we were at Cairo a gymkhana was held at Gezireh, where one of the events was a tug-of-war open to all troops in garrison. The Royal Garrison artillery for some time past had invariably won this contest: so invincible were they considered that no infantry regiments would compete against them, and they used to take the prize on every occasion with a 'walk-over.' On the arrival of the Royal Irish, we determined to enter our team, which had been practically unbeaten in India. On the day of the gymkhana the R.G.A. expected to have another 'walk over,' when to their surprise and to that of the spectators (we had kept the fact dark that we intended to enter a team), ten strapping Royal Irishmen, in jerseys of the regimental colours, stepped out on to the ground. The gunners were so unprepared for this that they hadn't even taken the trouble to be suitably dressed for a tug-of-war. So confident were they of beating all comers that instead of the usual line they had arranged an open ditch filled with water, across which the opposing teams had to pull. It was not many minutes before the two leading gunners were in the water, and the rest, to save themselves a ducking, had to let go the rope!"

The Royal Irish were almost the last troops to leave lower Egypt; but at length the long-expected order reached them, and on the evening of November 12, 1884, they entrained for Assiut, the farthest point to which the railway ran up the Nile. The marching-out state showed a strength of seven hundred and forty-six officers and men.[1]

[1] Lieutenant-Colonels—H. Shaw, V.C. (in command), T. C. Wray (second in command).
Majors—A. W. Simpson, E. Tufnell, C. E. Dixon.
Captains—J. H. A. Spyer, J. B. Forster, H. W. N. Guinness, W. J. F. Morgan, A. M. Boisragon.
Lieutenants—C. M. Stevens, A. I. Wilson, B. J. C. Doran, S. Moore (adjutant), K. P. Apthorp,

Next morning, after a journey of 229 miles, the Royal Irish arrived at Assiut, and at once exchanged the train for the barges in which they were to be towed 318 miles to Assouan, at the foot of the First Cataract. The men were packed into four barges, in each of which a subaltern was on duty for twenty-four hours at a time; the remainder of the officers were divided among the steamers and a *dahabiah*. "That night the halt was not sounded till 10 o'clock, when," wrote a young officer of the Royal Irish, "a nice job we had of it. Our steamers did not keep together, so that we had to go along the bank for about a mile in the dark, and draw rations for the next day, and very ticklish work it was, as the path was quite close to the river and bits of the bank were continually falling in." Progress was slow, for both barges and tugs occasionally ran on to sandbanks, and it was not until November 24, that the flotilla, which had been joined by the 2nd battalion, Royal West Kent regiment, reached its destination. As the barges could not pass the rapids the Royal Irish landed, and spent an unhappy day in the belief that they were to remain at Assouan. They had been ordered to encamp, and some of the officers were on their way to select the ground, when a tremendous roar of cheers and Irish yells told them the battalion had received good news; shortly afterwards a staff-officer informed them that they were to proceed up the river forthwith, and after a short journey in the railway turning the rapids, the Royal Irish re-embarked at Shellal, this time in the sailing-boats or *dahabiahs* in which the traffic of the Nile from time immemorial has been carried on. The next stage (210 miles) in the voyage was to Wadi Halfa, the frontier town of Egypt, and the most southern point which Roman legions had occupied in the valley of the Nile. Here a long stretch of rapids called the Second Cataract barred the passage of all local craft at that time of year, and the troops landed and went into camp, where owing to a block on the line of communication the battalion was detained for more than a fortnight. This halt was by no means a restful one, for the fatigues were incessant, but some of the officers found time to reconnoitre the nearest of the rapids through which they were about to pass, and reported that a task awaited the XVIIIth as arduous in its way as any that had fallen to the lot of the regiment during the two centuries of its existence. The Second Cataract, like that at Assouan, is turned by a line of railway thirty-three miles in length, which ended at Gemai, where, in an improvised dockyard, the whale-boats lay waiting for the Royal Irish. By December 16, the line of communication was again clear, and the first detachment—B and E

E. F. Rickman, L. C. Koe, and W. R. B. Doran. Lieutenant H. J. Jones joined at Wadi Halfa on December 8.

Quartermaster and Honorary Lieutenant—W. Jamieson.

Paymaster and Honorary Major—J. Forbes-Mosse (attached; before joining the pay department this officer had been in the XVIIIth).

Surgeon—Captain G. B. Hickson, Medical Staff.

companies under command of Lieutenant - Colonel Wray — were sent by rail to Gemai, where they took possession of their "whalers," and many stores. When these were packed the flotilla started in single file, and some- times sailing, sometimes rowing (with many different strokes and styles), worked up a smooth stretch of river till nightfall, when the boats were tied up to the bank, and the crews disembarked and pitched their camps. Next morning the detachment reached Sarras, where the remainder of the stores were issued. Each whaler carried the arms, ammunition, tents, and camp equipage of her crew, materials for repairing any damage she might sustain on the voyage, and cases containing a hundred days' rations for twelve men. These cases were not to be opened, but were to be delivered intact at the point of concentration, the supplies for current use being drawn at the various posts on the line of communication. By the time the whole of the freight (about four tons) was on board the boats, the load of boxes at stem and stern rose so high above the gunwales that the men at the oars were half-hidden behind the high-piled cargoes.

Lord Wolseley had always attributed much of the success of the little Red River expedition to the skill of the boatmen, or *voyageurs* who navigated his canoes over the waterways of Canada. With some difficulty he induced the British government to sanction the enrolment of a corps of Canadian boatmen for the much larger expedition of 1884 ; nearly four hundred officers and men were raised, many of whom proved themselves as valuable on the Nile as their predecessors had been on the rivers of Ontario and Manitoba. These *voyageurs* joined the whalers at Sarras : they were placed in charge of the actual handling of the boats, but, except as watermen, they had no authority. The flotilla as a whole was in charge of the regimental officers, who were distributed among the whalers, but in every company many boats were necessarily commanded by sergeants and even by corporals. In most cases the non-commissioned officers were as ignorant of boat work as their men, and with their crews had to learn by experience the use of oars and sails, the employment of poles to prevent the whalers from being dashed against the rocks, and the art of tracking. Even the best of the *voyageurs*, though experts in other branches of boatmanship, knew nothing of sails, which were not used in the navigation of the rivers with which they were familiar. In the forenoon of December 18, B and E companies pushed off from Sarras, followed by the remainder of the battalion, less G company, which next day brought up the rear. Thus the whole battalion was now afloat, engaged in a ceaseless struggle with the rapids of the Nile, and greatly handicapped by want of *voyageurs*, of whom the supply had run so short that instead of a couple of Canadians being posted to each boat, as had been the case with the corps first up the river, only two could now be allotted to each company of the Royal Irish. The difficulties encountered, as will be seen, were enormous, but the first battalion of the Royal Irish overcame them with brilliant success, and made the passage up the river faster than any other corps in the expeditionary force. In order to "get the last ounce" of work out of his troops, Lord Wolseley appealed to both the sporting and the patriotic instincts of his soldiers by offering a prize of £100 to the non-commissioned officers and men of the battalion which made the fastest run with the fewest accidents from Sarras to Debbeh, and by promising that the winning corps should be selected for the post of honour in the farther advance towards Khartoum. The money prize was awarded to the Royal Irish, who thus won the right to share in the hardships of the march across the desert to Metemmeh. Before that march is described, some account must be given of the portion of the Nile up which the Royal Irish had to force their way before they could hope to strike a blow for the relief of Gordon. For eighty miles above Sarras the river runs through a wild and barren region known as Batn-el-Hájar or the Womb of Rocks, of which the official historian gives the following description :—

"After leaving Sarras the first serious obstacle to navigation is the cataract of Semneh, the foot of which is reached after an eleven miles' pull against a smooth, swift current running between high rocky banks. Then come ten miles of swifter-flowing water, against which, however, with the help of a moderate breeze, it is possible to proceed with the help of the track lines. At the head of this rapid is the great 'Gate of Semneh,' a narrow gorge, between two rocky cliffs, partly blocked by two islands about equi-distant from the shores and from each other. Through the three passages thus formed the whole pent-up volume of the Nile rushes as through a sluice-gate. Here the boats have to be unloaded, and their cargoes, package by package, carried for half a mile over the rocks and deposited near smooth water above the cataract. Then the track lines are passed round the rocks, and two or three boats' crews manning one line, each boat is in turn hauled by main force up the water slide and run in opposite its cargo on the beach.

"For the next sixteen miles the course of the river is unimpeded by any serious obstacle, still for every yard the current runs as strong as the Thames in flood, on every side the basalt mountains radiate their heat, and everywhere the sunken rocks lie in wait for the unwary steersman. At the end of this distance the cataract of Ambako is reached, a very different piece of water to that of Semneh. At the latter spot an obstacle to navigation was formed by the volume of the Nile being pent into a narrow gorge ; at Ambako the same effect is produced by a broad expanse of river being choked by an innumerable mass of reefs and islets. At full high Nile, when the lower rocks are buried deep beneath the surface, the cataract is not a formidable one ; but as the river falls and reef after reef makes its appearance, the difficulties of navigation increase, until at low Nile the cataract has become impassable for the larger native craft, and is a grave source of difficulty even to the buoyant English whalers.

"Here every means of propulsion has to be employed. At one moment the whalers, under the lee of some islet, may be paddled gently up a narrow lane of almost stagnant water. Then, as the shelter of the rock is lost, though its crew pull for dear life, it is carried back some hundreds of yards until a point of vantage is reached near the shore. Next the track line is got out, and step by step the boat is hauled round a projecting point by a treble boat's crew. Now a fresh breeze and a clear reach of moderate water make it just possible to gain a few hundred yards by making the very most of sails and oars; then a bit of shelving shore is met with, along which good progress may be made by half the crew tracking, while the remainder stay on board and use their punt-poles. At length, by dint of perseverance, the five miles of rapid are surmounted in twice as many hours of incessant labour, and another eight miles of open water are entered on."[1]

Though no two cataracts are exactly alike, their general features are much the same, and therefore it is enough merely to mention the others passed by the XVIIIth. Above the rapids of Ambako came the cataract of Tanjur, which, though only two miles and a half long, usually took the boats a whole day to ascend, and fifteen miles higher up was another rapid, nearly as troublesome as that of Semneh. This was succeeded by ten miles of smooth water running between hills crowned with ruins, relics of a nation so ancient that its very name has been forgotten. Then followed the cataract of Dal, round which stores had to be carried for three or four miles by hand; these rapids once passed, the boats entered a long reach of calm but swift-running water 100 miles in length, at the head of which two more cataracts, those of Kaiber[2] and Hannek, had to be surmounted. From Hannek to Korti the navigation of the Nile was fairly easy.

The record of the forty days spent by the battalion between Sarras and Korti is one of unceasing toil. The Royal Irish worked like galley slaves. From dawn to dark, in burning and daily increasing heat, they rowed, and poled, and hauled the boats by ropes through the easier portions of the rapids. In the more difficult places it became necessary to lighten the whalers, and the crews had to unload them partially or entirely and to transport the cargo across the rocks, work the boats through the broken water, and then carefully repack them, with the knowledge, acquired by bitter experience, that an hour or two later the performance would have to be repeated. Occasionally, to avoid some especially bad piece of river, the boats had to be emptied, lifted out of the water, and hauled across country on the rollers provided for the purpose. Sometimes a boat missed the narrow passage among the rocks which barred her way, and was whirled backwards down the current until

[1] Colvile's 'History of the Soudan Campaign,' vol. i. pp. 117-119.

[2] The cataract of Kaiber is termed the Third. It should really be numbered the Eighth. Butler, 'Campaign of the Cataracts,' p. 200.

the men on the banks, hanging on to the drag ropes with their arms almost wrenched from the sockets, succeeded in hauling her into slack water. Occasionally a whaler was wrecked ; nearly every day and sometimes several times in the day one or more were injured by striking against submerged rocks, and in default of professional boat-builders the officers had to repair the damage themselves. Major-General (then Captain) Burton Forster's diary contains many references to his labours as a shipwright, and a few are quoted almost at random, to show what "handy men" the officers of the XVIIIth became in the expedition of 1884-85. "Found Sergeant Evans's boat again broken at a small rapid. Stopped, and put in a plank about nine feet long, as the original one was cracked all that distance." . . . "Got all the ten boats of my Company up rapids by dark and beached them for repairs." . . . "Four-fifths of the keel torn off Corporal ——'s boat, mended her." The work went on for seven days a-week ; there was no rest on Sundays, or even on Christmas day, the entry for which runs—" Divine service for Roman Catholics, then drew boats up main rapids, kept moving, and unloaded in the evening." In less arduous circumstances the voyage up the Nile would have proved a pleasant experience, for the scenery possesses a weird beauty of its own, wholly unlike that of any other part of the world; the climate is glorious, and the endless series of ruins which line the banks interesting in the extreme. But the officers of the Royal Irish had no time to admire scenery, or to study the archæology of the ancient Egyptians. They had suddenly been turned into fresh-water sailors; they had become jacks-of-all-trades— shipwrights, doctors, dock labourers ; they had to maintain discipline, to keep up *moral*, and to cheer the men when under the strain of unceasing toil even their buoyant spirits for a moment flagged.

An officer of the regiment thus records his reminiscences of the boat work on the Nile—

"Greatcoats and nothing else was the favourite kit with the men of my boat, who prided themselves on their dress and were anxious to save one good suit of khaki in which, they said, they would march into Khartoum. It was a handy costume when you stuck on a sandbank or struck upon a rock, as you could be overboard in a second to shove the boat off. Very often my men used to row in their 'birth-day suits'! Just before we started up the Nile I had been transferred to a new company, and my skipper[1] left the detailing of the crews of the boats to the Colour-Sergeant, who took advantage of my youth and innocence (?) to put into my boat ten of the biggest blackguards in the company, and a really good corporal of the old stamp (Corporal George M'Kee). Though I was new to the company, my future boat's crew were well known to me by name and sight as being constant attenders at the

---

[1] For the benefit of the civilian reader it must be explained that "Skipper" is army slang for the officer commanding a company.

Orderly Room, so I thought a 'few kind words' would do them no harm, and consequently informed them that I knew them well, but that we were going to have no d——d nonsense in my boat, or out of it they would go to sink or swim! A grin of amusement was all the answer I got to my short speech.

"When we started off the Corporal and I were the only two men who had ever handled an oar in their lives, Luckily the Corporal was a good tough nut, and had been stroke in the regimental boat some years previously when we were in Malta. That first day's row is still a nightmare to me. We left Sarras at 12 noon, the Corporal and I doing the rowing, while the remainder did their best to imitate us, but only succeeded for the most part in 'catching crabs.' The current for the Nile was slight—but except quite close in-shore it ran at about 3 miles an hour. Unfortunately our Cox, never having handled a tiller before, kept alternately running us out into the stream or into the banks. The distance from Sarras to Gemai was only 12 or 14 miles, but we did not get there till 8 P.M., and I thought we should never get there. I was more dead-beat than I have ever been before or since, and once I had thrown myself on to the sand when we eventually reached Gemai, I could not have gone another yard. However, youth and a sound sleep worked wonders, and next morning I was as fit as a fiddle, and started loading up the food stuff—a job requiring a lot of time and care, as each box had to be fitted into its place like blocks in a Chinese puzzle. With the stores, we also took in one or two Canadian *voyageurs* per company. My company had two. Regiments who had preceded us had had a *voyageur* for each boat, but a good many of them had become 'fed up' and had gone home or to Hospital, and by the time the Royal Irish went up the river, the supply only ran to about one or two for every 10 or 12 boats.

"I was given a French Canadian, and the company tool chest, and told to bring up the rear—a pleasant task which meant I had to go to the assistance of any boat in difficulties on a rock or sandbank, come last into the night's halting-place, and when there sit up most of the night mending the 'lame ducks' of the fleet. The actual mending did not take so long, as we soon learnt to patch up holes and tears, but the repairs usually involved the unloading of the boat, and fitting together the 'Chinese puzzle' of boxes in the dark was an operation that took two or three hours.

"My Canadian was a very fine specimen of his class, and had a flow of bad language—both French and English—that I have seldom heard surpassed or even equalled. Owing to my being able to talk a certain amount of French, we became very good friends, and under his instruction I became an expert *voyageur* both at the helm and with the pole in the bows, and could have taken a boat up any of the rapids. Though we were such good friends, it did not prevent him 'doing me in the eye.' Each boat had a box labelled 'Medical comforts,' which was on no account to be opened. Very foolishly the authorities had a printed label on the box showing its contents, which in addition to beef-tea, arrow-root, &c., also consisted of 2 bottles of brandy and two of port wine. It had been reported that no box of medical comforts had reached its destination intact. I determined that my boat should be the exception, so the box was put in the stern of the boat, so that I could keep my eye on it during the day while I pulled stroke, and at night I slept on it in the boat. Never did it go out of my sight except at the portages, when my friend George, the Canadian, volunteered to carry it for safety's (?) sake. I drew the line at carrying boxes at portages, and trusted George. When, however, my box was examined on arrival at Korti, though it appeared quite untouched, the liquor was all gone, the arrowroot, &c., were, however, quite complete; George had no use for *them!*

"It was marvellous how quickly the men took to rowing. In a few days they were pulling powerful if not stylish oars, and they certainly put their hearts and their backs into it. My crew of blackguards were simply splendid, and we never had any difference of opinion. On one occasion we came to a very stiff bit of water, and I turned round and said, 'Now, boys, we'll have to pull here,' and the man behind—one of the biggest and sturdiest scamps in the battalion, said, 'Begorra, sir, we'll pull to hell wid you,' and a voice from the bows added, 'and out the other side, sir.'

"The Nile sores were the things that troubled us most; any scratches or in many cases ordinary rowing blisters, turned into festering sores which nothing could cure so long as we remained on the river. I took the skin off my ankle shoving the boat off a rock, and tho' I kept it perfectly clean, and put vaseline on it, it would not heal. The strange thing was that once we got into the desert, tho' we could not wash, these sores all began to heal at once.

"Other regiments suffered terribly from lice, but so far as I know we had none in the Royal Irish. I certainly had none in my company. I attribute this to the fact that our men were always in the water to shove the boat off if she stuck on a sandbank or rock, while I noticed other regiments seemed to dislike getting into the water, and used to try to shove off a boat that stuck with poles and oars, and much bad language. The day's work did not vary much: we awoke at the first streak of dawn—had some tea or coffee and biscuit—bully beef if you cared for it, and then used to sail if the wind was really strong—which to us seemed very seldom,—to sail and row, if the wind was only moderate. If there was no wind, or an adverse one, it was a case of rowing, or towing if the bank was favourable, the latter being a quicker mode of progression than rowing against the strong current. If we had a really good sailing breeze, we didn't like to waste it, and had cold bully beef and biscuit at about midday as we sailed along, but if we had had a tough morning's row or two, we used to halt for about an hour to have a hot meal. At about sunset the leading boat of the company would halt for the night at some suitable spot, and the others if possible closed up. This often was not possible, owing to the numerous mishaps that were always taking place from bumps on rocks and sandbanks. The boats, when the Royal Irish took them over, had done several trips already, and were for the most part in a pretty rotten condition, and the materials for repairing them had run out, so that we had to use any expedients such as biscuit tins, &c., to patch them up. I thought myself lucky if

a

on arrival at the night halting-place there was no damaged boat to mend, and that in consequence I could get a full night's sleep—such a splendid sleep it was, too, under the clear sky of the Soudan winter! The ordinary monotony of the journey was broken at places like Dal, where one had to pull for four solid hours up a gigantic mill-stream, sometimes only gaining a few feet after half an hour's pull, when one's muscles felt as if they would crack. At Dal we took out the rifles and ammunition and a few of the boxes out of each boat, took a picked crew of eight men, and had two half-breed Indians in the boat, one at the helm, the other in the bows with a pole. It was most exciting work, and at first the task looked an impossible one, but the skill with which the *voyageurs* took advantage of every back water, and shot past the most dangerous-looking places was perfectly marvellous. Most of us officers learnt the trick before we reached Korti, and could have qualified as *voyageurs*. Amongst the *voyageurs* I should tell you, there were some who had not much claim to the title, and hardly knew the stern of a boat from the bow. They had come out for a picnic, but when they saw the Cataracts they 'went sick'! One of the so-called *voyageurs* was a man who had been in the Royal Irish a short time before we went to Egypt. He was a smart, plucky fellow, who soon learnt the tricks of the trade, and by the time the regiment came up he was quite an expert, and went by the name of 'Dare-Devil Dick.' Some of the *voyageurs* were an insubordinate lot, and gave a good deal of trouble—especially in wanting to halt, and as they were not subject to military law it was difficult to know what to do with them on these occasions. One gentleman, however, met his match, after he had been particularly abusive to an officer who was well known in the service for his handiness with his fists. The *voyageur*, amongst other things, said that he was not going to obey any one's orders, and that he was as good a man as any officer, so the officer told his men to row ashore, which they did; he then took off his coat and said, 'You said you were as good a man as I am, take off your coat and I'll show you whether you are or not.' The Canadian looked at him for a moment, and then said, quite quietly, 'No, boss, I guess not.' 'All right,' said the officer, 'you will obey my orders in future, or out of the boat you go, neck and crop.' After that there was no further trouble.

"Pipes, or rather a lack of pipes, were soon a matter of great difficulty. The old soldier had not acquired the modern habit of cigarette smoking, and clay pipes were practically the only kind the men ever smoked. In the rough work of the Nile boat the supply of these soon gave out, and in my boat after about a week there was only one stump of a 'dhudheen' left amongst the twelve of us. This was passed round, each man getting 'two or three draws and a spit' out of it. I had started with three or four briar pipes, but they all disappeared—appropriated, I regret to say, by officers. As I did not care to share the dirty little stump that did duty for a pipe in my boat, I had to devise something as a substitute for my beloved briars. A broken oar-handle for the bowl, a boat's auger, and a hollow reed for the stem soon provided me with the means of making quite a serviceable article. As the ash of the oar got very charred, the bowl had to be lined with a bit of biscuit tin. My patent was soon copied, and in a few days, as far as my crew was concerned, it was a case of 'one man one pipe.' My pipe did me yeoman's service till after the return of the battalion from Metemmeh, when, amongst other luxuries in the shape of jam and sardines, an enterprising Greek brought up a store of wooden pipes which he sold at fabulous prices."

The only amusement on the voyage was to watch the wild geese and pelicans which abounded in some parts of the river, to look for traces of the hippopotami, much disturbed by the long procession of whale-boats through the upper part of the river, and to take "pot-shots" at the crocodiles. The old ones were wary, and offered but indifferent targets for the officers' revolvers; the young ones, less used to the ways of mankind, were slower in taking to the water. One, indeed, remained so long on an overhanging bank that when a party of the Royal Irish approached him his only means of escape was by taking a header into the water, right over a man who was standing on the edge of the river.

On the 23rd of January the leading boats reached Korti, where by the 27th the whole regiment was assembled, but not in the same strength as it left Cairo. The hardships and fatigues of the unaccustomed life had taken toll, and many men had been dropped at various hospitals on the line of communication.[1] One soldier had been drowned in the Nile, a fate which Lieutenant-Colonel Hugh Shaw, V.C., nearly shared. His boat was working close in-shore when a sudden fall of earth and stones from the bank struck her gunwale, and threw him into the swiftly running river. As soon as the dust had cleared away he was seen struggling in the stream; instantly Orderly-Room Sergeant Hanrahan and Colour-Sergeant Moylan plunged into the water, swam to him, and held him up until all three were rescued. For this gallant action the bronze medals of the Royal Humane Society were awarded to these non-commissioned officers. The Royal Irish won great praise not only for the short time in which they made the passage from Sarras, but also for the excellent care they had taken of the stores with which their boats were freighted, and Lord Wolseley's thanks were officially conveyed to them in a special general order dated the 4th of February, 1885.

"The following battalions in the order given have completed the journey from Sarras to Debbeh in the quickest time :—

1. The 1st Battalion Royal Irish.
2. The 1st Battalion Gordon Highlanders.
3. The 1st Battalion Royal West Kent.

---

[1] Captain Forster's marching-out state at Sarras showed a total of ninety-two in his company; his marching-in state at Korti only seventy-seven of all ranks.

The 2nd Division Naval Brigade, the Royal Irish, and the Royal West Kent have distinguished themselves by the care they have taken of their boats. The division of the Naval Brigade and Captain Forster's Company of the Royal Irish handed in their supplies at Korti complete, no case or package being either damaged or missing. General Lord Wolseley congratulates the men of the Royal Irish most heartily upon having won the small prize which he offered to mark his personal appreciation of the battalion which should accomplish the difficult journey of about 370 miles in the shortest time. As they have been first on the river, so he hopes they may be amongst the first to enter Khartoum, and he feels assured that he can wish this old and distinguished regiment nothing more thoroughly in accordance with its own desires.

"It has been most gratifying to watch the manner in which all the battalions have striven to reach at the earliest date this point where the army was to concentrate, and Lord Wolseley warmly thanks both officers and soldiers for the untiring spirit shown by them in overcoming the many and serious obstacles to navigation presented by the cataracts and rapids of the great river. All alike have worked well and cheerfully under conditions entailing considerable privation and continuous labour.

"The conduct of all ranks has been most creditable to the army, and Lord Wolseley will not fail to bring the energy and discipline that have been shown to the notice of Her Majesty the Queen.

"EVELYN WOOD,
"*Chief of Staff.*"

In forwarding his cheque for £100 Lord Wolseley wrote as follows :—

"CAMP KORTI, THE SOUDAN,
11*th March* 1885.

"DEAR COLONEL SHAW,—It is with the greatest pleasure that I send you the enclosed cheque for £100, the prize won by your splendid Battalion by having come up the Nile to Debbeh in boats in less time than any other Regiment. Being an Irishman myself it is very gratifying to feel that my small prize has been carried off by my own countrymen.—Believe me to be, dear Col. Shaw, very truly yours, WOLSELEY."

The general situation, as far as it was known when the XVIIIth reached Korti, was very gloomy. Khartoum was besieged on three sides, and on Gordon now rested the entire burden of its defence. In August he had sent his only fellow-countrymen, Lieutenant-Colonel D. Stewart and Mr Power, the correspondent of 'The Times,' on a mission down the river; their steamer had been wrecked, and they had been treacherously murdered by Arabs who had offered them hospitality. Thus with no officer whom he could trust, no friend in whom he could confide, he was left alone to face the hordes of fanatics by whom he was surrounded, while his men were suffering much from physical privations, and from the mental depression produced by waiting in vain for the British troops who, as their General had repeatedly assured them, were coming to their help. The tone of Gordon's latest messages, brought by native runners to Lord Wolseley, showed that his position was growing so desperate that the time for which Khartoum could hold out must no longer be reckoned in months and weeks, but in days and hours. A modification of the plan of campaign had therefore become necessary. In the original scheme the point for the second concentration of the relieving force was fixed at Shendi, a town on the right bank of the Nile, faced on the opposite shore by the villages of Metemmeh and Gubat. But the passage of a column of boats over the four hundred miles of river between Korti and Shendi would inevitably take several weeks. Hitherto the troops had only been called upon to overcome natural difficulties: now they would be in the enemy's country, and while working up rapids at least as troublesome as those already ascended, they would be exposed at any moment to attack and consequent delay. Even if unmolested on the lower reaches, they were committed to one serious military operation, the capture of Berber, a town on the Nile a hundred miles below Shendi; it commanded the river, and therefore must be seized and occupied before the expedition could pass it on the voyage up stream. From these various causes the column must necessarily move so slowly that long before the first whaler could be expected to appear off Shendi, Gordon might be overwhelmed, yet the Nile was the only route by which a large body of troops with adequate supplies could be placed within striking distance of Khartoum. For smaller detachments, however, the river was not the only possible line of advance. A glance at the map will show that the Nile in its windings between Shendi and Korti forms two sides of a huge triangle, the third side of which is marked by the camel track, 173 miles in length, linking Korti with Metemmeh. This road crosses the Bayuda desert, a barren waste of sand, dotted at rare intervals with wells for the most part inadequate for the needs of any considerable number of animals and men—yet in a dash across this desert lay the only hope of saving Gordon.

Lord Wolseley determined to divide the force which remained available for active operations after the safety of his line of communication had been secured. To Major-General Earle he entrusted the "river column," a strong brigade of all arms, which, after capturing Berber, was to establish an advanced base near Shendi. The camel corps and various other troops were placed under the orders of Brigadier-General Sir Herbert Stewart, who was to lead the "desert column" across country to Metemmeh, and there establish an advanced base. If the information he received there convinced him that Khartoum was at the last gasp, he was to push forward at once with the "camelry" to Gordon's rescue, but if the danger did not seem immediate he was to stand fast, and co-operate with Earle when the river column had won its way to Shendi.   If Stewart halted at Metemmeh, his Intelligence officer, Colonel Sir Charles Wilson, was to embark with a few picked men on the Egyptian steamers which were known to be waiting on that part of the Nile to establish touch with the British, push on towards Khartoum, and, if possible, communicate with Gordon.

Though Lord Wolseley was intensely anxious to place Stewart's column within reach of Gordon, it was not until the end of December that the preparations for the movement were completed.   Among the innumerable difficulties which confronted the commander of the expedition two stood out pre-eminently.   One was the probability, almost the certainty, that at Metemmeh the desert column would find neither food for themselves nor forage for their camels, and that a large amount of bulky supplies must therefore accompany the troops.   The other was the fact that, although camels were the only means by which stores could be carried across the desert, the number of these animals at his disposal was inadequate, and could not be supplemented from local sources, as the Mudir of Dongola had failed in his promise to obtain a large quantity of them from his tribesmen.   As enough camels could not be collected to carry to Metemmeh in one trip the *personnel* and supplies of the column, Wolseley decided to cross the Bayuda desert by stages.   To carry out this plan it was necessary, as a first measure, to form a depôt between Korti and Metemmeh; and Gakdul,[1] 98 miles from Korti, was selected, as it was known that its two or three natural reservoirs yielded a good supply of drinking water.   In addition to the stores which were to be left at Gakdul, and the supplies for the march there and back, the camels had to carry not only their own food, for the desert yielded but scanty grazing, but also water for the whole column, as it was known that the wells between Korti and Gakdul could not be depended upon.   As the XVIIIth a month later followed the track of this convoy, the details of the march of Stewart's "camelry" will show how remarkable were the performances of the first battalion, when it crossed the desert on foot.   At 3 P.M. on December 30, 1884, the first convoy of 2206 camels started, with an escort of about 1100 troops, the mounted infantry on camels, the XIXth Hussars on their horses.   With an interval of two hours the column marched till 7.30 A.M. on the 31st, rested for eight hours, then pushed on again, stopping at 8 P.M. for a short time at the wells of Hambok, where a small quantity of very indifferent water was obtained, and halted at 1.15 A.M. on January 1, 1885, at the well of El Howeiya, which yielded no better water than that of Hambok.   At 8.30 A.M. the convoy was again in motion, and plodded on till 1 P.M., rested for two hours and a half, and then pushed on throughout the night and early morning until at 6.45 A.M. on the 2nd it reached Gakdul, where there

[1] This name is spelt Jakdul in some maps.

proved to be abundance of good water. The ninety - eight miles from Korti had been covered in 63¾ hours, 32¼ hours of which had been spent in actual marching; but weary as the troops were, no rest could be allowed them. The stores with which the camels were loaded had to be unpacked and arranged in proper order; the camels to be watered—a process which occupied the whole day, and the post to be prepared for defence, for though from the absence of formed bodies of the enemy it was clear that the march across the desert had taken the Mahdists by surprise, their scouts had been seen hovering in the distance.

Before the next stage in the advance to Metemmeh could be undertaken the intermediate base had to be completely filled up with supplies, and to bring these, Stewart started on the return journey to Korti less than four- teen hours after he had reached Gakdul. He left behind him a garrison of 422 officers and men to guard the wells, and improve the arrangements for watering the troops and the camels; and he dropped small parties at the minor water-holes to clean them to the best of their ability. By noon on the 5th Stewart was back at Korti; but though his men had not suffered from their exertions, his camels had felt the strain. Tired by their long march up the Nile, the animals were in poor condition when they left Korti; they had been on short rations of food and water on the journey to and from Gakdul, and though every effort had been made to bring more camels from lower Egypt, the supply of fresh animals was quite inadequate, and the rest of the work in the desert had to be done by beasts whose strength and endurance was rapidly diminishing. On the 7th a second convoy of 1000 camels left Korti: 100 were laden with small-arm ammunition, 80 with medical stores, 30 with artillery stores, the remainder with food supplies. This column reached Gakdul in safety, and on its return passed Stewart, who on the 8th marched from Korti with 1600 troops, about 300 natives (chiefly camel-drivers from Aden), 2228 camels, and 155 horses.

The second phase of the desert march began on January 14, when Stewart pushed southwards from Gakdul with 1802 officers and men, three light pieces of artillery and a "Gardner" gun, 155 horses belonging to the XIXth Hussars, 1700 riding and 1188 transport camels. Two days later the XIXth Hussars came into contact with the enemy near the wells of Abu Klea, where on the 17th the Mahdists, after a very desperate fight, were defeated with a loss of about a thousand killed. Our casualties were 9 officers and 65 other ranks killed, 9 officers and 85 other ranks wounded. Struggling onwards towards Metemmeh, the desert column again met the enemy on the 19th, this time at Abu Kru, close to the river. The Arabs fought with as much gallantry as at Abu Klea, but were again heavily defeated, and fled leaving the ground covered with their dead. To us the cost of this engagement was 1 officer and 22 other ranks killed, 8 officers

s

and 90 other ranks wounded; among the latter was Sir Herbert Stewart, who eventually succumbed to his injuries. When he fell, Colonel Sir Charles Wilson succeeded to the command of the troops, though Captain Lord Charles Beresford, R.N., in charge of the small Naval contingent which accompanied the column, was actually the senior officer present.

On the 20th, Wilson occupied the village of Gubat, which is within half a mile of the river; next day he threatened Metemmeh, two miles farther inland, but before his attack had developed several Egyptian steamers came in sight, and some hundreds of Gordon's Soudanese soldiers landed, bringing the news that a considerable body of Mahdists were advancing. Wilson recalled his troops; fortified himself at Gubat; reconnoitred in various directions, and after many delays owing to the worn - out machinery of the river-boats, embarked on the 24th with a handful of the Royal Sussex and a considerable number of the Soudanese on his mission to Khartoum. It was not until this date that he was able to send off a despatch to Lord Wolseley describing the battle of the 19th and the movements which followed it. This report reached Korti in the early morning of January 28, and Wolseley at once decided to send Sir Redvers Buller to take command of the desert column, and to reinforce it with infantry, who were not to be carried on camels but to march on foot. Mindful of his promise that the battalion which won his prize on the river should have every opportunity of distinguishing itself on land, Lord Wolseley selected the Royal Irish to accompany Sir Redvers, and ordered them to move in detachments, the headquarters with A, B, and C companies starting that evening, the remainder following as soon as possible. In the afternoon of January 28, 1885, the battalion paraded for Lord Wolseley's inspection, dressed in the fighting kit devised for them by a former commanding officer, Colonel M. J. R. MacGregor. It consisted of a khaki-coloured frock and trousers of cotton drill, a helmet covered with the same material, grey woollen putties, a woollen shirt, socks, and ammunition boots; spine protectors, cholera belts, and drawers had been issued, but were not in general use among the rank and file; all hands carried haversacks, wooden water-bottles, and rolled greatcoats. The officers wore "Sam Browne" belts, which supported their swords and field-glasses, revolvers and cartridge-pouches; the non-commissioned officers and men were equipped with braces and waist-belts, pouches containing seventy rounds of ammunition, three-edged bayonets (longer than those in use at the present day), and Martini-Henry rifles. As in previous campaigns it had been discovered that when these rifles were fired fast, the barrels became so hot that it was almost impossible to grasp them, they were fitted with leather hand-guards, tightly laced round the stock and barrel behind the back-sight, to enable the men to get a firm grip of their weapons. The remainder of the campaigning kit was carried on transport camels; to every ten men was allotted one animal, which was loaded with their camp kettles, a blanket and a waterproof sheet apiece, and one or two sea-kit bags, each of which contained sets of the following articles, viz. : one flannel shirt, two pairs of socks, a tin of grease, a canteen, a towel, soap, and a hold-all, complete. The troops were allowed no tents.

When Lord Wolseley rode on to the parade ground he was saluted by as fine a body of soldiers as he had ever seen. By a process of natural selection the weakly men had been weeded out in the voyage up the river, and only those of perfect constitution had reached Korti. Thanks to the varied forms of exercise they had taken since they left Cairo, the soldiers drawn up before him were in rude health and fit to go anywhere and do anything. After he had warmly praised their appearance, which he described as "hard, lean, and long-legged," and informed them that to the regiment would probably be awarded the prize for the race from Sarras to Debbeh, he warned the Royal Irish that very hard work awaited them in the Bayuda desert. Before they could reach Gakdul they would have to make six marches, each sixteen miles long, in a country so dry that they must not count on receiving more than half a gallon of water a-day, a ration which they must make do for drinking, cooking, and washing! He wound up his speech by telling the XVIIIth that he trusted soon to join it on the other side of the desert, a hope, however, doomed to be frustrated by specific orders from home desiring him to remain at Korti, the better to direct the movements both of the desert and the river columns, the latter of which had been set in motion on the 24th of January.

When the inspection was over the headquarter companies returned to their preparations for the march. The skins containing water for the journey were filled, rations drawn, camels taken down to the river to drink and then loaded, and just after nightfall on January 28, 1885, the column started — as all ranks hoped and believed for Khartoum. The first two or three stages of the journey across the desert were by no means agreeable. The men of the XVIIIth had not only to look after their own regimental camels and those of the large convoy they were escorting to Gakdul, but to watch over the safety of a number of slaughter cattle and to prevent the camel-drivers from tapping the water-skins, which were not to be opened unless by order of high authority. Though the Royal Irish had mastered the ways of a whale-boat in the rapids, they were new to the tricks of the camel-drivers, who, from idleness or dishonesty, often fastened the loads so insecurely that in the night everything slipped off the saddles and fell in a cascade upon the sand. The soldiers had to pick up the boxes of stores and baggage which littered the desert and re-pack them firmly; they had also to halt frequently to enable weakly or lazy animals to keep up in their proper places; but when, after two or three rude experiences, they had learned how to cope with the camels and the natives who drove them, these initial difficulties were overcome and the troops pushed sturdily on towards Gakdul. For the greater part of the way the track ran over great plains of yellow sand, which played havoc with the men's boots, already partly worn out by the *portages* on the Nile; but occasionally it crossed low round-topped ridges of black rock, belts of coarse dark-green grass, and thick growths of low acacia and mimosa trees. As the column marched at night and rested by day, the officers were able to get some sport; a gazelle was bagged and many sand-grouse were seen, though not hit, for the Martini-Henry rifle hardly lends itself to shooting birds on the wing! The rations consisted of a pound of ship's biscuit and the same amount of preserved salt beef, an ounce of tea and three of sugar, an ounce of preserved vegetables, a quarter of an ounce of salt, and $\frac{1}{320}$ of a gallon of lime juice. The thirst produced by the combined effect of the salt beef and the dry heat of the desert was great, and the regular allowance of half a gallon of water was hardly sufficient to quench it. General Forster's diary records the joy with which all hands greeted the occasional issue of a larger supply; an additional quart rendered it possible to do a little cooking, while an extra half gallon brought some form of washing within the range of practical politics! On the half gallon issue the men could only spare enough water to make tea; as their salt beef had been well cooked before it was hermetically sealed in tin, they ate it cold; if water enough could be obtained, the preserved vegetables were soaked and boiled in the lid of a canteen.[1] To rest the camels, now breaking down fast from the combined effects of too much work and too little food and water, the convoy halted at the wells of El Howeyat for twenty-four hours and then marched on to Gakdul. The headquarters of the Royal Irish reached this post early on the 4th of February, and next day were joined by four more companies (D, E, F, and G) of the battalion under Lieutenant-Colonel Wray. Unencumbered by the charge of a large convoy, this detachment had covered the ninety-eight miles between Korti and Gakdul in a hundred and eight hours—a very fine performance for men who, though in perfect all-round training, had done no marching for many weeks.

The journey across the desert had so far been uneventful. The only exciting incident was the escapade of a lance-corporal, who temporarily losing his reason, wandered into the desert, and was not rescued till he

[1] The Maconochie ration, so much appreciated during the war of 1899-1902, was not then in use.

had strayed twelve miles from the bivouac. A few tribesmen, captured by the irregulars who guarded the lines of communication, were the only enemies seen; they were wild-looking savages, short but wiry, with fierce eyes gleaming under shocks of matted hair, and armed with formidable spears more than five feet in length. They did not form part of the Mahdi's regular army, but were local freebooters, more disposed to plunder than to fight. When the Royal Irish were a few miles north of Gakdul they met messengers hurrying to Korti with the news that Khartoum had fallen. On the 5th they had comparative rest, but on the 6th they were kept hard at work filling water-skins at the wells, ready for the next stage in their advance—Gakdul to Abu Klea, a distance of fifty-two miles. While thus employed they were joined by H company, which had been detained at Korti when the second detachment moved forward. In their anxiety to lose no chance of distinguishing themselves the company had made a great march, winding up by covering twenty-eight miles on the last day. Sir Redvers Buller, who had ridden part of the way from Korti with the headquarter companies, did not allow H company to start with the rest of the battalion when it marched on the 7th, but, mounting them on camels, sent them on a day or two later. How the men liked this new form of locomotion is not recorded, but it is probable that many agreed with the sailor who, after his first ride, remarked, "My camel is a queer beast. He's been playing cup and ball with me all the afternoon and only missed me twice!"

Hitherto only the precautions usual in ordinary warfare had been taken on the march and in the bivouac, but now that the Royal Irish were well in the enemy's country and liable to attack at any moment, the formation was adopted which recent experience had proved to be best suited for fighting in the Soudan. Under the immediate escort of one company, successive lines of camels, about forty abreast, lumbered along in a loose column which, if necessary, could be closed up into a solid mass. At one of the front angles of the column of camels were four companies; at the opposite rear angle was the remainder of the battalion, both marching in column or half-column of companies, ready to form square at a moment's notice. The animals laden with the reserve of ammunition moved behind the leading companies into whose square they were to be received in case of danger; those bearing the rations and the water-skins followed the companies in rear, who were charged with their defence. If the enemy attacked, each square could support the other with flanking fire, and both could rake the ground over which spearmen would have to pass in order to close on the camels with the cold steel. At every halt square was formed, and at night the bivouacs were surrounded with *zaribas*—walls of stone, boxes of stores, saddles or mimosa bushes, anything, in short, which would serve to break a sudden rush of the Mahdi's followers.

The column, however, was not attacked, and notwithstanding the cumbrous formation in which the Royal Irish moved they got over the ground fast, and on one occasion marched twenty-four miles in twenty-five hours and a quarter, coming in fairly fresh, alert, and fit for outpost duty. They reached Abu Klea on the morning of the 12th, passing close to the battle-field of January 17, still covered with dead bodies, for though the Mahdists had buried their chiefs, the rank and file remained where they had fallen. Two companies, C and E, were dropped at the wells to strengthen the garrison of the post; the remainder of the battalion, after a few hours' rest, started for Gubat, where they arrived next day after a march of twenty-one miles, "swinging into bivouac," as Sir Redvers Buller reported, "as cheerily as if they had been going to a field-day at Aldershot." The troops of the desert column received the XVIIIth with great enthusiasm, turning out to a man to cheer it into camp. Among them were the soldiers who had accompanied Wilson in his abortive attempt to rescue Gordon from Khartoum, and who had just struggled back to Gubat after a series of adventures, remarkable even in the annals of the British army. In two tiny steamers, manned by natives of very doubtful loyalty, they had laboriously passed through the long and dangerous series of rapids known as the Sixth Cataract, and after running the gauntlet of the enemy's guns and rifles, had arrived off Khartoum—to find that barely thirty-six hours earlier the town had been captured by the Mahdi, into whose hands Gordon, if he was still alive, had undoubtedly fallen. Wilson realised that his mission had failed, and with a heavy heart ordered his steamers to retire down the river. The retreat was conducted in circumstances as unpropitious as can be imagined; the native crews, excited at the defeat of the Christian General, were almost mutinous; the Soudanese, by far the majority of the fighting men on board, were stupefied by the knowledge that their wives and children were in the Mahdi's clutches; every hour the dangers of navigation increased, for the Nile was sinking fast, and in one night dropped no less than three feet. But in spite of all difficulties Wilson made good progress down stream until his steamers, one after the other, were wrecked by the treachery of the Arab pilots. Landing his troops on an island he entrenched himself, and succeeded in informing the British at Gubat of his desperate plight. The sailors at once manned one of the river boats and fought their way up the Nile in time to save Wilson and his comrades from the destruction which threatened to overwhelm them.

On his way to Gubat, Buller had received a despatch from Lord Wolseley written after the news of the fall of Khartoum had reached headquarters, but before the rescue of Wilson's detachment had been reported at Korti. His orders were to ensure the safety of Wilson and his men; to send all sick and wounded back to Korti; to make every preparation for the evacuation of Gubat, and if he considered it necessary, to fall back to Abu Klea or even to Gakdul. When Buller reached Gubat the situation was full of difficulty. Wilson indeed was safe, but within two miles of the bivouac was the strongly built village of Metemmeh, which we had threatened but not seriously attacked. It was held by two thousand of the enemy, almost delirious with joy at their victory at Khartoum; the Intelligence officers had ascertained that three or four thousand Mahdists, well provided with rifles, guns, and ammunition would shortly reinforce Metemmeh, and as there was nothing now to detain the Mahdi before Khartoum, his main army might also have to be reckoned with. The supplies of the desert column were running short: at Gubat there were only rations for twelve days, and the depôt at Abu Klea contained but a similar quantity. Worse than all, the transport was breaking down rapidly; "the camels," Buller reported, "are emaciated, and their carrying power small. Indeed I do not think we have camels enough to get this force out at one go." After a few hours' deliberation he reluctantly decided to retire, and began his preparations, fortunately unhindered by the enemy who circled round the bivouac without attempting to close in upon it. Early on the morning of the 13th of February the sick and wounded were sent off, the convalescents on camels, the worst cases on stretchers carried by Gordon's Soudanese. The convoy was escorted by part of the camel corps and three companies of the Royal Irish, and when all danger of an attack seemed over, the detachment was ordered to rejoin the main body of the battalion. Just as the three companies reached the bivouac a Hussar orderly dashed into the lines to report that eight or nine miles off the convoy was surrounded by a large number of the enemy, and was in great peril. Colonel Shaw and half a battalion of the XVIIIth hurried off to the rescue, but to their deep disgust did not come into action. The Mahdists had surrounded the convoy on three sides and were pouring in a fairly well directed fire when a detachment of camelry, on the way from Abu Klea to Gubat, suddenly struck the enemy on the flank just as the Royal Irish began to come in sight. The Arabs did not await Shaw's attack and retired, leaving the convoy free to go on to Abu Klea, which it reached without further incident. Shaw's half battalion did not accompany the sick, but was ordered back to Gubat, where the troops spent the night in destroying stores which could not be carried away and throwing into the Nile boxes of ammunition for which there was no transport. As day broke on the 14th, the column, 1700 strong, was set in motion. With the exception of a few of the XIXth

Hussars whose horses were still serviceable, all arms and all ranks trudged over the desert on foot. The post of honour, the command of the rear-guard, was entrusted to Colonel Shaw, who covered the retreat with the Royal Irish, two guns, a detachment of the XIXth Hussars, and three hundred of Gordon's Soudanese. A few of the enemy followed, but when Buller halted and offered battle the Mahdists drew off, and by midday on the 15th the column was in bivouac at Abu Klea. The men had not suffered much on the march, though the boots were beginning to fall off their feet, but so many animals had dropped from exhaustion that General Buller was forced to admit that any active operations were entirely out of the question, until the mounted corps were supplied with fresh camels, the transport camels replaced, and the XIXth Hussars completely remounted. There was not forage enough for the surviving animals, and it was evident that the wells could not be relied upon to supply the whole of the troops now concentrated around them. Buller accordingly decided to send back to Gakdul most of the camelry, all spare camels, and nearly all the XIXth Hussars, while with the remainder of his command he awaited instructions at Abu Klea.

The two companies of the XVIIIth detached to garrison the post of Abu Klea now rejoined headquarters, bringing with them a record of excellent service performed in clearing the bush which surrounded the wells, building *zaribas*, and similar useful though unshowy work. Early on the 16th, the battalion was directed to entrench one of the low hills which encircle the wells; just as the shelter trenches were finished and occupied, and the men were eating a well-earned meal, large numbers of the enemy appeared on ground commanding the defences of the Royal Irish, and opened fire at about 1100 yards' range. To meet this attack, which enfiladed some of the trenches, fresh works had to be thrown up under continuous and sometimes very heavy musketry. "The Gardner and the screw-guns gave the enemy a little physic," wrote an officer in his diary, "but the rebels kept it up all night, and we expected an attack at any time. Next morning they began in a desultory sort of way, but a few shells and a strong infantry fire made them lie close. Finally a field-piece of theirs came into action, but its shells fell short and dead. Two of our 7-pounders went out and fired a round or two, and the Mahdists then disappeared. We had an easy night on the 17th, and only regretted two things: one that we had not had a slap at them, the other that we had not received the half pound of bread that was due to us as a ration!" During this prolonged skirmish, in which there were many "close shaves" from the flat-trajectoried Remington rifles used by the enemy, Quartermaster and Honorary Lieutenant Jamieson and thirteen other ranks were wounded.[1] In the column the total casualties

[1] See Appendix 2 (N).

were three men killed, four officers and twenty-three other ranks wounded. For the next few days the regiment was very busy cutting down scrub and building redoubts — work with which the enemy's fire did not materially interfere, as it was delivered from a very respectful distance.

When the untoward news of the fall of Khartoum reached England, the country was profoundly moved. A great cry for vengeance arose, and amidst a whirlwind of telegrams from the Cabinet, Lord Wolseley recast his plans, and proposed that the towns of Abu Hamed and Berber should be captured, and held during the summer as posts to cover an advance in strength up the river in the cool season. Government accepted the idea, and sent an expedition to Suakim to draw off to the shores of the Red Sea part of the enemy who might otherwise attack the troops echeloned along the Nile. But by the middle of February it become evident that Wolseley's scheme was too ambitious. The river column, though successful in an engagement at Kirbekan, was making slow progress up stream owing to the abnormally "low Nile." To enable this column to arrive at Berber with its cargo of stores intact, the original plan had provided that it should be fed by convoys across the desert of Korosko, but recent events at Khartoum had roused the fanaticism of the tribesmen to such an extent that it was very improbable this route would long remain open. A large quantity of Earle's biscuit had proved uneatable; the remainder would only carry the column to Berber and back to Korti, and therefore none could be left to ration the garrison of Berber when that place had been taken. Wolseley thereupon proposed that the Royal Irish and part of the camel corps should strike across the Bayuda desert and fall upon Berber from the westward, but he was forced to abandon this idea when he realised that the transport, without which it was impossible to undertake the expedition to Berber, had completely given out, and that the marching power of the troops was seriously crippled by the condition of their boots.

> "In view of all these conditions the Commander-in-Chief felt that he was no longer justified in persevering with the combined movement of the Desert and River columns on Berber, and he was forced, reluctantly, to abandon all hope of taking that place before the autumn. The intention to take Berber being given up, the capture of Abu Hamed became unnecessary; it would only have led to a useless waste of life, and have unnecessarily prolonged the line of river to be defended during the summer months. The retention of the Desert column in its exposed position in the desert was equally without object. A concentration on the Nile became the only course open to Lord Wolseley. Orders were accordingly sent on the 20th February, directing the river column to return . . . and at the same time Sir Redvers Buller was directed to return to Korti."[1]

[1] Colvile's 'History of the Soudan Campaign,' vol. ii. p. 73.

In obedience to this order the one thousand seven hundred and forty effectives,[1] left to General Buller, made ready to march on the evening of the 23rd of February after an exciting day. About 11 A.M. Captain Morgan, Royal Irish Regiment, from his outpost to the south-east of the bivouac had signalled that masses of the enemy were advancing towards Abu Klea. Later it was reported that the Mahdists, between five and eight thousand strong, had halted two or three miles from the wells. The situation was a serious one, but neither the General nor his men were disturbed at the news: the packing was carefully finished, the convoy of wounded sent off under a strong escort, the wells filled up with thorny scrub and the many saddles for which there were no camels left, and soon after sunset the troops filed away in good order, leaving the Royal Irish to bring up the rear. The camp fires were made up, the usual bugle calls were sounded, and then in groups of twos and threes the men of the XVIIIth silently collected at the appointed place and were formed into a rear-guard. Whether the evacuation of the wells was unnoticed by the enemy, or whether the Mahdists thought it wiser not to attack the retiring column, is not known, but the fact remains that Buller was not seriously molested in his retreat, of which Major-General Burton Forster's diary gives interesting details. "During the night of the 23rd-24th many camels fell down and were left behind. Halts were numerous, and we had a very hard and awkward march in the dim moonlight through the grass and scrub till 11.30 P.M. The *rouse* sounded at 4 A.M. (24th) and we started at 5, having come about 9 miles from Abu Klea. We marched till about 9.30, seeing only a few of the enemy's scouts in the afternoon, and halted about 18 miles

[1] Marching-out state from Abu Klea, 23rd February 1885 :—

Corps.	OFFICERS.			OTHER RANKS.			Camels.	Horses.	Natives.
	Available.	Sick.	Total.	Available.	Sick.	Total.			
Naval Brigade, . . .	11	...	11	102	2	104			
XIXth Hussars, . .	1	...	1	13	1	14			
Light Camel Regiment, .	13	1	14	196	6	202			
Mounted Infantry Camel Regiment, }	20	1	21	311	5	316			
Royal Artillery, . . .	6	...	6	75	2	77			
Royal Engineers, . .	2	...	2	24	...	24			
Royal Irish Regiment, .	21	1	22	596	13	609			
Royal Sussex do., .	7	...	7	217	7	224			
Royal West Kent do., .	1	...	1	21	...	21			
Commissariat and Transport Corps, }	6	...	6	38	...	38			
Medical Staff Corps, . .	5	1	6	43	...	43			
Headquarter Staff, . .	6	...	6	4	...	4			
Army Chaplain, . .	1	..	1						
	100	4	104	1640	36	1676	1180	30	386

from Abu Klea. The vedettes fired at them and they disappeared. We started again at 5 P.M., and marched on till midnight, rested on the 25th till 5 P.M., when we started again, halting at 9.30 P.M. after doing 13 miles. Next morning we started at 6 A.M. and reached Gakdul about noon. . . . The work has been stiff and hot, especially on a daily ration of three-quarters of a gallon of water! . . . I think the march of 56 miles in 64 hours is very creditable to Buller's column. . . . The men have been in their clothes without changing or washing from the 16th to the 26th, and it has told on them: they are not as fit about the feet as we could wish. Some of the officers succeeded in changing their socks once during the ten days, and were more comfortable in consequence."

An interesting account of the retreat is given in a letter written from Gakdul on February 27, 1885, by Colonel B. J. C. Doran, C.B., then a subaltern in the first battalion, Royal Irish regiment.

"You will see by the address that we have commenced retracing our steps towards Korti, we arrived here yesterday morning and very thankful we all were to get in. The march back has been so far anything but comfortable, and our march going up was child's play compared with this retreat, for of course then the regiment was by itself in two detachments and could consequently move pretty quickly having only a small amount of transport to hamper it, but marching with the "Desert Column" as it is called, is quite another thing, besides having a large Hospital of sick and wounded to take care of. We left Abu Klea on the 23rd in two parties; the first consisting of the Hospitals and the whole of the baggage, rations, &c., for the column escorted by some mounted infantry started at 2 P.M. I went with this lot, as I am acting Quartermaster now to the regiment. The second party consisted of all the troops and did not start till 7 P.M.: they had no baggage or transport to hinder them, so of course when they started were able to catch us up, as they did about 8 or 9 miles out of Abu Klea where we halted and where a depot of water had been left; they got in about 1 A.M. We started off again at daylight and marched till about 10 A.M., when the whole column halted, pretty well done up; the water question all along has been a very difficult affair. We were to rest here until 4 P.M., when we were again to start off, however just as everyone had made themselves as comfortable as is possible on these occasions under a blanket to keep off the sun and were just getting a few winks of sleep, we were startled at hearing heavy firing going on in our rear; it was at some distance but the sound of cannon being fired was quite distinct, everyone was up like a shot, and orders were given to get all baggage loaded ready to move off at once. However, after half an hour's excitement we desisted, as it was discovered to be only about two men and a boy (natives) amusing themselves—we presume to frighten us—with some gunpowder in cases. To understand the cause of all this alarm, you must know that ever since the night we were potted at the natives still hovered around Abu Klea, and we only moved out just in time.

Had we stayed there another day, we should have had a good fight, for just as the column I was with was about to start, from one of the outlying posts on the neighbouring hills it was signalled down that the enemy were seen advancing from Metemmeh direction in thousands; this caused a good deal of excitement; however, after coming within about 2 miles of our advanced posts, they all halted and settled down for the night. Meanwhile the column with sick and wounded got away and were well clear of all the hills and in a fine open desert by the time it was dark, and where we halted, as I said before, we were joined by all the remainder of the garrison that night, they having sneaked out under cover of the dusk. All the wells we filled up and left fires burning so as to deceive the enemy. I don't suppose they found out we had gone until next morning, and then pretty late, as they would not have approached the place except very cautiously. It was a very nasty place to get out of, as for about six miles the road or track runs in a valley with commanding hills on both sides, and had the enemy made any attempt to hold the ground at the head, where it emerges into the desert, very few of us would have got out without scratches. Once in the desert we did not mind how many came on us, so now you can understand the commotion caused by the firing of cannon, as we thought they must have found out and were following us. This of course was almost impossible, as where they were encamped they had only one or two wells which they must have dug, and they must have wanted water, as they could not have got any since they left the river at Metemmeh, and it would have taken them quite a day to clear out the wells we had filled in at Abu Klea. In the first 24 hours after leaving Abu Klea we had done about 30 miles, not bad going for a column on an allowance of water, in the desert in fact. Everyone had to walk, except the sick and wounded, because all the camels belonging to the camel corps and mounted infantry had to be used for transport and baggage animals. There were only just sufficient to bring us away, and nearly all of them were completely played out before they commenced the march. However, we struggled on somehow, and arrived here more dead than alive. Thank goodness we are getting a day's rest here, which will enable the men to pull themselves together, get some decent food and plenty of water to drink, and that good. If I had been told a month ago that I should drink as filthy water as I have done, day after day, and been very thankful to get it, I should have laughed! The thickness of pea-soup was considered *good*: sometimes, if it was thicker, then it might be a little bad, but not to be thrown away. Considering all things, the desert march has been *the* most trying thing known in a campaign for years. By the time we arrive at Korti, we shall have been away five weeks or more. We shall not have so many difficulties to contend with henceforward, as the next half will be much easier and I doubt the enemy following us beyond this. Everything about movements is kept a State secret here, and we don't know what is going to happen, except we move out of this to-morrow or next day—they say to Merawi, to help the column gone up the River, but I have my own idea that we are going straight to Korti, though the Colonel told the officers on parade yesterday that after a day's rest here, we were to move towards Merawi.

It will be getting very hot here soon, and if we are to summer out here, it would be advisable to try and build ourselves some sort of shelter. However, I suppose when we get to Korti we shall probably then know what government has settled to do about the Soudan. I am sure if they only saw it, they would have no desire ever to keep such a country!"

At Gakdul the Royal Irish had a comparatively pleasant rest. A quantity of stores had recently arrived from Korti, and as there was no means of carrying them back, the Commissariat distributed them among the troops, who were regaled on jam, cheese, fresh bread, fresh meat, vegetables, and other long-forgotten delicacies. The men had time to change their clothes, there was enough water for washing, and better than all, a great budget of letters from home awaited the regiment. Some of the units of the column started at once for Korti, but it was not until the 2nd of March that the battalion was warned to start next day, an order which was very welcome, for the wells had begun to give out, and "the water had become filled with living animals, smelt, and was as fit to drink as a dirty duck pool!" From the 5th to the 8th the Royal Irish halted at the wells of Megara, where a successful foray of desert robbers upon the slaughter cattle considerably reduced their rations of meat. Then they once more pushed northward, this time in detachments, the last of which reached Korti on the 14th. As Lord Wolseley rode out to welcome them he saw men whom a civilian would have derided as tramps and scarecrows, but in whom a soldier's eye recognised troops of the finest quality. Their uniforms hung in rags, patched where patching was possible with any material that had come to hand. Their boots were a nightmare. Their skins were the colour of mahogany, their faces seamed with the lines which hunger and thirst, exposure to heat and cold, want of sleep, and prolonged exertion stamp upon every soldier in a campaign. Their stern eyes, their hard-set mouths, their steady march and proud carriage all showed that their spirit and discipline were as high as ever, and that the great fatigues of their marches in the desert had in no way impaired the efficiency of the Royal Irish. On the 16th Lord Wolseley inspected the battalion, warmly thanked all ranks for the work they had done, and informed them that General Buller had reported on them in the most favourable terms.

Among those who had done much towards keeping the *moral* of the XVIIIth at the high standard maintained throughout the Nile campaign was the Roman Catholic chaplain, the Reverend Father Brindle, D.S.O., now Bishop of Nottingham, whose name even now is one to conjure with in the Royal Irish regiment. After serving with the second battalion in the war of 1882, he accompanied the first battalion throughout the whole of the expedition up the Nile. His genial personality, his devotion to duty, his coolness in danger, his indifference to hardship, combined to give him a remarkable influence over the men, which he exerted invariably in the highest interests of the Service.

The Royal Irish thoroughly enjoyed the comparative civilisation of the headquarters camp. They were once more under canvas; they had an inexhaustible supply of water; and they feasted their eyes, weary from the glare of the Bayuda desert, upon the palms and acacias growing on the narrow strip of cultivation which fringes both banks of the Nile. But they were not allowed to rest there long. When the rear-guard of the desert column returned to Korti, the British government were still determined to avenge Gordon and to crush the Mahdi's power at Khartoum; and Lord Wolseley arranged to concentrate the expeditionary force for the summer in cantonments along the Nile near Korti. The XVIIIth was assigned to a movable column, commanded by Brigadier-General Brackenbury, whose headquarters were at Debbeh, with detachments in the neighbouring villages, one of which, Kurot, was occupied by the Royal Irish, where they settled down, as they thought for many months. Some of their huts were made of logs, grass mats, and similar materials, bought from the natives and issued to the troops; others were built of bricks, made out of the soil on the banks of the river and dried in the sun. "The battalion," writes an officer who was present, "excelled at making the moulds for these bricks, and a sergeant, Kelly, was the crack moulder." The want of straw, however, proved as serious a hindrance to the brick-making of Wolseley's troops as to the Israelites of old, for many thousand bricks cracked and were wasted. But only a fortnight after the last unit had reached its allotted post, Wolseley was warned by the Cabinet that owing to the possibility of England being embroiled in war elsewhere, the expedition to Khartoum might be abandoned, and on the 11th of May he received orders to withdraw from the Soudan. He obeyed; but as the General-in-Chief in Egypt, who had been studying the local situation for many months, he strongly protested against the new policy, pointing out that if we retreated the Mahdi's power would greatly increase, and that the British government would not only have to reinforce the garrison of Egypt, but to fight for the protection of that country. The difficulty of carrying out the evacuation was greatly increased by the necessity of bringing back about thirteen thousand natives, who, having thrown in their lot with us, could not be abandoned to the tender mercies of the Mahdists; but by dint of careful organisation and hard work the task was accomplished. General Brackenbury's command started on the 1st of June in whale-boats for Abu Fatmeh, where three hundred men of the XVIIIth, under Lieutenant-Colonel Wray, were landed, and after marching some distance down the Nile rejoined the remainder of the battalion. Though the difficulties were light compared to those of the upward voyage, they were by no means insignificant, for the *voyageurs* had gone back to Canada, and the Royal Irish, who acted as

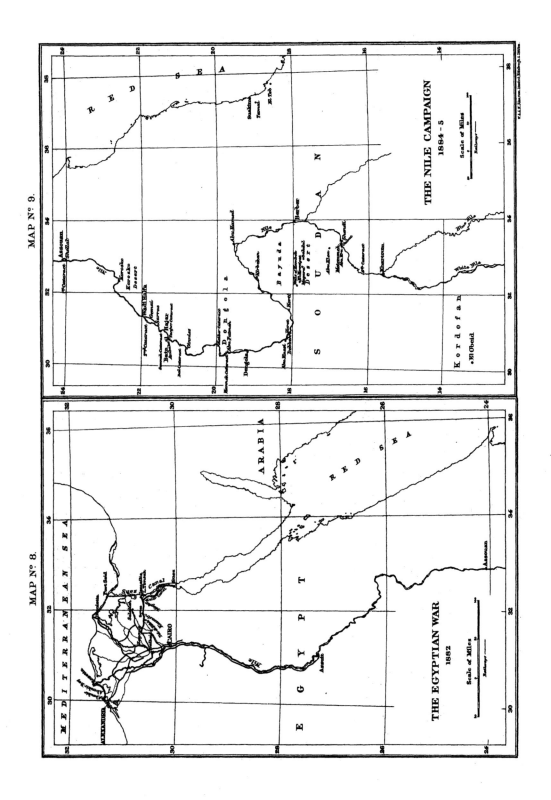

MAP Nº 9.

THE NILE CAMPAIGN
1884 - 5

Scale of Miles

MAP Nº 8.

THE EGYPTIAN WAR
1882

Scale of Miles

rear and baggage guard to the column, had much work in towing and mending whale-boats, wrecked or damaged in shooting the rapids. When the battalion reached Alexandria, it was joined by a strong draft: a hundred and seventy-nine non-commissioned officers and men from the second battalion at Malta had landed in January, of whom fifty-eight had been fortunate enough to be sent to Suakim, where they served as mounted infantry in the eastern Soudan. Thus by a curious chance the Royal Irish were represented in the campaign of 1884-85 not only on the Nile, but also on the shores of the Red Sea, where a young officer of the regiment, Lieutenant D. G. Gregorie, who had already greatly distinguished himself while serving in the Egyptian army, was awarded the fourth class of the order of the Osmanieh.

As a matter of historical interest it may be mentioned that Lord Wolseley's predictions proved singularly correct. Within six months of our withdrawal from Dongola a large body of the enemy attempted the invasion of Egypt, besieged for forty days a fort held by British troops, and did not retire southwards until on December 30, 1885, they had been defeated at the battle of Ginniss. To meet this incursion it was found necessary to hurry nearly seven thousand British troops up the Nile, and to increase the garrison of Lower Egypt by about three thousand men.

In despatches Lord Wolseley mentioned the following officers of the Royal Irish: Lieutenant-Colonel Shaw, V.C.; Captain Guinness, and Lieutenant B. J. C. Doran. Lieutenant-Colonel Shaw was awarded the C.B.; Captain Guinness was promoted to a Brevet-Majority, and Lieutenant B. J. C. Doran was noted for a Brevet-Majority on his attaining the rank of Captain. The Egyptian medal and clasp for the Nile, 1884-85, and the Khedive's Star were issued to all ranks. In 1886, the regiment was permitted to add to its battle honours the words, "Nile 1884-5," in commemoration of the ascent of the River and the operations in the Bayuda desert.

The first battalion, Royal Irish regiment embarked at Alexandria on August 24, 1885, in the s.s. *Stirling Castle*, and arrived at Plymouth on September 9.

CHAPTER XIII.

THE SECOND BATTALION.

1883-1902.

THE BLACK MOUNTAIN EXPEDITION: THE TIRAH CAMPAIGN.

EARLY in 1884, the second battalion of the Royal Irish regiment began a long tour of foreign service. Its first station was at Malta, where drafts from home brought up its numbers to a total of nine hundred and sixty-seven of all ranks.[1] While at Malta, the battalion heard that the expedition, described in Chapter xii., was to be sent to the relief of Gordon at Khartoum, and hoped to be included in it, but the War Office decided otherwise; and though the Royal Irish were represented in the Nile column, the honour, as we have seen, fell to the first, not to the second battalion, which remained stationary till January 7, 1885, when leaving a large detachment as a reinforcement for the first battalion in Egypt, it sailed for Bombay, and early in February reached Umballa with a strength of six hundred and fifty-two of all ranks.

A month later the battalion was ordered up to Rawal Pindi to increase the number of British regiments at a *durbar*, which the Amir of Afghanistan was to attend. On the journey the Royal Irish were in a very alarming railway accident: part of the troop train ran off the line—three bandsmen, Moore, Tod, and Frost, were killed; Lieutenant-Colonel Dawson was seriously injured; Major Hamilton, Lieutenant Symonds, Surgeon-Major Pratt, Bandsman Hayes, and Drummer Brennan were also hurt. As soon as the *durbar* was over the battalion proceeded to Subathu, where, with a detachment at Jutogh, it remained until November, 1887, when it changed stations for Nowshera, with detachments at Fort Attock and Cherat. While on the march the Royal Irish were annoyed by thieves, who hung about the outskirts of the camp in the hope of stealing modern firearms, for which there was a constant demand among the hillmen beyond the frontier. To keep their rifles safe, the soldiers before going to sleep at night used to tie or strap them to their legs, but even this precaution sometimes failed. On one occasion a small detachment

---

[1] 25 officers, 3 warrant officers, 33 sergeants, 15 drummers, 891 rank and file.

secured their firearms in the usual way when they turned into their " E. P." tent; but one of the party was not well, and to let him rest comfortably a comrade slept with both his own and his friend's rifle fastened to him. In the middle of the night the Good Samaritan woke, feeling that some one was stealthily touching him; he instantly raised an alarm, when down fell the tent, and before the men could crawl from beneath the heavy folds of canvas, the thieves made off with a rifle. On investigation it was found that the robbers had noiselessly undone all the tent ropes with the exception of the four corner ones, which, when their presence in camp was discovered, they had cut through to cover their retreat. The Royal Irish took such stern measures to prevent further thefts that the thieves for a considerable time avoided a battalion which they described as a *"Shaitan ki pultan aur Sahiblog bahut zaberdust."* This may be translated freely—The Devil's own regiment with very high-handed officers !

During the time the second battalion was at Nowshera, one of its subalterns, Lieutenant W. Gloster, did a very daring piece of work. He had become noted for his good military sketching, and was specially selected to do reconnaissance work across the border beyond our frontier post at Hoti Maidan. His instructions were those which many officers before and since have received when sent on similar enterprises: he was told that though it was most desirable that the work should be done, the government would not be responsible for him: and that on no account was he to cause trouble on the border: if he liked to apply to the Guides at Hoti Maidan for an escort he might do so, but in all probability his request would be refused. The commandant at Hoti Maidan declined to help him, saying that if an escort of the Guides showed themselves beyond our frontier the whole of the country might break into a flame. Nothing daunted, Gloster in some mysterious way made friends with several of the Headmen along the border. "How he did it," writes the officer who describes the adventure, " I don't know, as he couldn't speak a word of any language but English, and his only mode of conversation with his Pathan pals was a tremendous slap on the back, and 'How are you, old cock ? ' One night he was taken across the frontier by one of his new friends, made his sketch in the early hours of the morning, and was back on British territory just as his presence was discovered and the tribesmen were assembling to cut him off."

On July 22, 1888, Lieutenant-Colonel T. C. Wray, who had been in command since January 9, 1887, died suddenly of heart disease, and was succeeded by Lieutenant-Colonel G. W. N. Rogers.

The second battalion in September, 1888, was called upon to take part in a punitive expedition beyond the north-west frontier of India. Hazara, a wild and rugged district on the left bank of the river Indus, about eighty miles east of Peshawar, had long been disturbed by the lawless conduct of

T

some of the tribes of mountaineers inhabiting the no-man's land beyond our border. The Akazais, the Khan Khel of the Hassanzais and the Alaiwals raided into our country, looted the villages, and killed peaceful British subjects; and though punished by the infliction of fines and by being "block-aded"—*i.e.*, debarred from bringing their produce into British territory, they did not mend their ways. Growing bolder from comparative immunity, they brought matters to a head by attacking and killing a party of officers and men who were surveying a part of the Black mountain, within the Queen's dominions. To avenge these two Englishmen and the Gurkha soldiers who were murdered with them; to maintain our prestige in India, and to prevent an outbreak on other parts of the north-west frontier, a considerable force was mobilised and placed under the command of Brigadier-General J. W. M'Queen, C.B., A.D.C. It consisted of three mountain batteries (two British and one native), a company of Sappers and Miners, the 1st battalion of the Suffolk, and the second battalions of the Northumberland Fusiliers, Royal Irish, and Royal Sussex regiments, eight battalions of native infantry, and a native pioneer battalion. These troops were organised in two brigades, commanded respectively by Brigadier - Generals C. N. Channer, V.C., and W. Galbraith; and to meet the requirements of mountain warfare, in which it is impossible for one man to supervise the movements of a large body of soldiers, the brigades were subdivided into two columns, to each of which a British battalion, 600 strong, and two native regiments were allotted. A native cavalry regiment, the second battalion of the Seaforth Highlanders, and a native infantry regiment formed the reserve. The Royal Irish, whom Major Brereton commanded until Lieutenant-Colonel Rogers returned from leave at home, were in the fourth column,[1] the other units of which were part of a British mountain battery, three companies of the 34th Pioneers, the 4th and 29th Punjab Native infantry, with a field hospital and a detachment of military telegraphists. The whole force, including some Kashmiri troops and three hundred of the Khyber rifles, numbered 272 officers and 12,282 non-commissioned officers and men; the strength of the fourth column was 51 officers and 2414 of the other ranks.

The immediate object of the expedition was the punishment of the Khan Khel and the Akazais, whose watch-towers and villages were perched among the crags and precipices of the range which, in some places rising

---

[1] The following officers of the Royal Irish regiment served in the Hazara campaign :—
  Lieutenant-Colonel and Brevet-Colonel—G. W. N. Rogers.
  Major—R. K. Brereton.
  Captains—W. J. F. Morgan, F. J. Gavin, A. N. Lysaght, Brevet-Major—B. J. C. Doran.
  Lieutenants—K. P. Apthorp, A. S. Orr, W. R. B. Doran, A. T. Ward, P. de S. Bass,
      H. J. Downing, A. B. King, L. C. Koe, J. E. Cullinan, C. W. Garraway, T. L. Segrave,
      G. O. R. Wynne, C. W. Walker, W. Gloster, R. O. Kellett.
  Paymaster—Honorary Captain P. A. Robinson.
  Quartermaster—Honorary Major T. Hamilton.

to a height of more than 9000 feet, cuts off the valley of Agror from the left bank of the Indus. It was decided to penetrate into this maze of mountains from two directions: three columns of the Hazara Field force, after concentrating at Ughi, the chief British outpost in the Agror valley, were to cross the range from east to west, while the fourth column, commanded by Colonel A. C. W. Crookshank, was to assemble fifteen miles to the south-west of Ughi at Derband, our frontier village on the Indus, and push northwards up the left bank of the river.[1] As this detachment could not be expected to join hands with the main body for several days, it was accompanied by General Galbraith, who, while leaving to Colonel Crookshank the actual handling of the troops, took charge of the general operations. Though there was little definite information concerning the prospective theatre of war, it was known that the roads were impracticable for any but mule transport; so baggage was reduced to a minimum; no tents were taken, and regimental officers were cut down to fifty, the lower ranks to sixteen pounds weight of kit. The main body had with it five days' supplies and a hundred rounds of ammunition per man, seventy on the person of the soldier, thirty on mule-back. As the fourth column to some extent was acting independently, its supply was increased to seven days, and the number of rounds carried by mules was doubled. A general reserve of a hundred rounds per man was formed at the base.

The fourth column had finished its concentration on October 1, and on the morning of the 2nd, Galbraith advanced seven miles into the enemy's country and bivouacked at Chamb, on a site he had reconnoitred while awaiting the arrival of his troops. Here he was informed by telegraph that owing to delays in bringing up stores to Ughi he was to make no forward movement for twenty-four hours, so after his mountain guns, escorted by four companies of the Royal Irish, had driven the enemy from the neighbouring hills, he improved the track leading from his bivouac into the valley of the Indus. Before dawn on the 4th, he had secured his right flank by crowning the heights with a detachment of native infantry, and as soon as it was light the advance-guard — two companies of the Royal Irish under Captain Lysaght — began to descend into the gorge of the river.[2] At 8 A.M. the advance-guard had reached comparatively open ground, where Lysaght halted to allow the remainder of the troops to come up; then he pushed on again, and an hour later a few of

---

[1] The distances are only approximate.

[2] The column marched in the following formation. The advance-guard of two companies of the Royal Irish was followed in succession by brigade headquarters, two guns, and three companies of Native infantry. Then came the headquarters of the column, the remainder of the Royal Irish, two more guns and some Gatlings, five companies of native infantry, the regimental reserve ammunition, a company of native infantry, the Field hospital, and a detachment of Royal Engineer telegraphists. In rear was the whole of the baggage, including the seven days' supply, escorted by four companies of native infantry.

the enemy opened fire from the village of Shingri. The Royal Irish extended to the left of the hamlet, two companies of native infantry made a similar movement to the right, and with little difficulty and small loss the outpost was routed and dispersed. For another mile nothing was seen of the enemy, but when the advance-guard approached the next village, Towara, the hillmen were found awaiting our attack. Across the valley, here about twelve hundred yards in width, stretched their first line : the right rested on a patch of jungle growing amidst the boulders on the river bank ; the left was posted on the crags of the lowest tier of the bare and arid mountains which form the eastern wall of the gorge of the Indus. Rather less than a mile above Towara the valley was completely closed by a steep spur or under-feature, on the far end of which the village of Kotkai, built on a huge mass of broken rocks, commanded not only the spur itself, but also the bed of the river, the hillmen's line of retreat and the only track by which the British could continue to force their way northward up the left bank. On this spur the enemy, whose total strength was computed at 4000 fighting men,[1] had established his second line in well-built sangars ; and on the eastern hills lurked about a thousand sharpshooters, armed with rifle and matchlocks, whose fire upon the valley below them would cross with that of a detachment of equal strength, posted in breastworks on the heights overhanging the western bank. Against the hillmen who held this formidable position General Galbraith could bring into action only his mountain guns, a couple of Gatlings, and about fourteen hundred foot soldiers, as the remainder of his men were employed in guarding the baggage and in crowning the hills in rear of the column.

Galbraith's first care was to rid his flanks of the enemy. Covered by the fire of the guns and the steady and well-directed volleys of the Royal Irish, the 34th Pioneers drove the hillmen from the jungle on the left, while the 4th Punjab infantry scaled the precipitous heights on the right, pushing the foe before them in confusion. But the process took time, and it was not until 1 P.M. that the Royal Irish were allowed to move towards the enemy in the plain, where many flags showed that the tribesmen were assembled in large numbers. When the battalion had gained six hundred yards it was halted behind a low stone wall, and ordered to open upon the foe in front of them, while the guns shelled the defenders of the Kotkai ridge. By this time, the flanking detachments had done their work and were once more level with the troops in the centre, and Galbraith, considering that the hillmen were sufficiently shaken to warrant his assaulting their first position, ordered a general advance. With perfect steadiness

---

[1] These are the official figures. In the opinion of some of the officers who were present they are too high.

the Royal Irish moved forward with sloped arms towards a clump of trees three or four hundred yards distant; the mountaineers who held this part of the line were beginning to fall back, when the word "Charge" was shouted by some unauthorised person whose identity has never been discovered; the call was sounded by a bugler, and with a wild yell the battalion dashed forward. They had covered some fifty yards of ground, when from a nullah about eighty yards off emerged a horde of swordsmen, Hindustani fanatics, each of whom had sworn to gain Heaven that day by slaying at least one of the Unbelievers. The suddenness of their appearance, their demoniacal yells and headlong rush might have startled any troops, but the Royal Irish were staunch; after an instant of surprised inaction the company commanders ordered their men to fire independently, and then to meet the rush with the bayonet. An officer thus described the affair in his diary: "We got the word to charge; the men went at them with a will, bayoneting or shooting every Ghazi within reach. The swordsmen then wheeled away as if they did not quite relish us, and went towards the 34th Pioneers, who fell back a bit at first but then pulled themselves together. Our men wheeled up of their own accord and followed the Ghazis, and I don't think many got away. We killed or wounded about a hundred.[1] In the pursuit Gloster with one or two dare-devils of his company dashed after one of the enemy who was carrying a standard, shot him down, and brought back the flag in triumph."[2]

After the main body of the enemy had been dispersed, several incidents occurred characteristic of warfare on the north - west frontier of India. When the fighting appeared to be over, a medical officer, seeing a sepoy lying hard hit on the plain, went off alone to dress his wounds, and suddenly found himself surrounded by five Ghazis; one he brought down with his revolver; the others circled round him, waiting their chance to dash in and hack him to pieces. The Royal Irish at that moment were re-forming their ranks; a patrol of an officer and four men hurried to the doctor's rescue, and shot three of the fanatics; the fourth came on most pluckily, and was only ten yards from our men when one of them shot him, and then pinned him to the ground with his bayonet. These hillmen are wonderfully tenacious of life, and although the Ghazi had a Martini bullet through his chest and a bayonet wound in his stomach he strove up to his last gasp to kill his hated foes. A little later in the day General Galbraith was the hero of an adventure in which the good marksmanship of the battalion undoubtedly saved his life. While the Royal Irish were

[1] As the official account states that eighty-eight dead bodies were found on the ground over which the swordsmen attempted to charge, it is clear that the Royal Irish used their weapons to good purpose.
[2] This trophy, pierced with more than one bullet, hangs in the Officers' Mess of the second battalion.

sitting on the ground in quarter-column, waiting for orders, the General on foot, unarmed, and with no escort but his aide-de-camp who was mounted, walked over the battlefield to ascertain from two friendly hillmen who accompanied him if any of the dead belonged to tribes which were nominally neutral.

> "Suddenly [writes an officer] we heard some shots fired, and looking up we saw about two or three hundred yards off the General running as hard as he could towards us, closely followed by some Ghazis. The A.D.C.'s pony had became unmanageable so he could not fire, and the Ghazis were catching the General up; we accordingly ordered two or three picked shots to fire—risky work, for the fanatics were within a few yards of the General and he almost masked our fire. Still the risk had to be taken, and (luckily perhaps) as we fired, the General stumbled and fell, and the whole of the Ghazis were shot. We heard afterwards that when the General was examining the corpses, two of the supposed 'deaders' had jumped up and gone for him, and being unarmed, he could do nothing but run. The 'friendlies,' seeing the General's plight, had gone for the Ghazis, and as they were all dressed alike, we were unable to tell friend from foe, and had shot all four of them."

In the course of the afternoon a hospital was established in a clump of trees, among which stood a shrine packed with the furniture and other belongings of some of the tribesmen with whom we were at war. From one of these trees a Ghazi was dislodged by a bullet; the sound of the shot brought up a couple of our men who, suspecting that more fanatics were in hiding, began to rummage among the lumber in the shrine, where two more Ghazis were discovered to whom very short shrift was allowed. When the advance was resumed, half the battalion was ordered to keep down the fire from the sangars on the right bank of the river, while the other companies and part of the 29th Punjab infantry climbed the ridge and moved upon Kotkai. They entered it without opposition, for the enemy, already shaken by the shells of the mountain battery, retired before them to Kunhar, a village two or three miles higher up the river. By the time we were in possession of the Kotkai position the day was so far spent that pursuit had become impossible, and the wing of the Royal Irish was sent down to bivouac in the plain, while the native regiment remained to hold the village as an advanced post.

The next few days were full of varied occupations. The battalion marched with convoys of sick to Chamb, carried stores over rocks that the mules could not face, escorted the General up precipitous mountains when he visited tribes of doubtful loyalty to arrange the terms on which their neutrality was to be secured, and for more than one day carried on a long musketry fight with the hillmen, who had now flocked to the farther side of the river, whence they maintained a harassing fire upon our working parties. Under the steady shooting of the Royal Irish, the enemy gradually melted away, and when the British brought river craft up the Indus to replace the ferry-boats which had been destroyed, the mountaineers realised that the river was no longer an impassable barrier and disappeared, leaving the road-makers unmolested in their heavy task of converting mere goat-tracks on the side of a cliff into roads wide enough for the passage of heavily laden mules in single file. On the 11th the whole column reached Kunhar, though the road was still so rough that over the greater part of it the baggage had to be passed by hand. The 12th was spent in improving the path to Gazikot, a mile or two higher up the river; and on the 13th, Galbraith transported the Royal Irish and part of his native infantry across the river in boats, marched through various deserted villages, and blew up a hill fortress at Maidan. The tribesmen watched his proceedings from the neighbouring heights, and when he began to retire attacked his rear-guard, but were driven back, and the column regained the left bank without difficulty. After the destruction of Maidan the enemy began to lose heart, and though the troops in the fourth column made several raids into the mountains on each side of the Indus, occupying villages so filthy that the Europeans could not sleep in the houses and had to bivouac upon the roofs, they did not again come under hostile fire. On all these operations the Royal Irish were employed, and in their spare time Galbraith found plenty of occupation for them in the unexciting but very arduous work of improving the communications with the frontier of India.

While the fourth column was forcing its way up the Indus the other columns pushed eastwards from the Agror valley. They climbed mountains, made roads, destroyed watch-towers, and burned hostile villages with small loss, for they met with no opposition such as that which had awaited Galbraith at Kotkai, and their casualties were mainly caused by the "snipers" who harassed their bivouacs at night. Thus taken between two fires, the Hassanzais and Akazais learned that though slow to rouse, the Government of India when it begins to strike, does so with effect. Astonished to find that the fastnesses of the country could be reached by regular troops, dismayed at the loss of several hundred of their fighting men, and realising that the longer they deferred their submission, the heavier would be their punishment, these clans decided to surrender; paid the heavy fines imposed upon them, and promised amendment for the future. During the negotiations there was an episode in which Lieutenant Gloster played an amusing part, thus described by one of his brother officers—

"When the hillmen with whom we had been fighting came to the conclusion that for the time being they had had enough of it, they began to send Jirgahs or deputations of headmen to interview General Galbraith, who had very little knowledge of the manners and customs of the Border tribes. Presuming on his ignorance of frontier etiquette, they used to behave towards him with gross impertinence: they would walk into his hut and greet his Pathan orderlies, who acted as interpreters, with great respect, but take no notice of the General himself; then sit down without being asked, and finally spit on the floor—a particularly gross form of insult throughout the East. Gloster who since the engagement at Kotkai had been orderly officer to the General, was present at these interviews and used to boil with rage, but as his chief took no notice he had to swallow his wrath as best he could. But Gloster's chance came when Colonel . . . , an officer of long experience on the frontier, joined the column and took over the conduct of the negotiations for peace. On the morning after Colonel . . .'s arrival the tribesmen walked into the new-comer's hut with their usual swagger and went through their customary insulting performances—but not for long, as Colonel . . . turned upon them, first with a volley of abuse in Hindustani and Pushtu, and then with his stick and boots. In amazement they made for the door, and then as each astonished Pathan passed out, he got a blow on the side of the head from a huge fist, followed by a hearty kick from a long and powerful leg. A very chastened and exceedingly polite deputation returned to make terms next day!"

As soon as the Hassanzais and Akazais had made their peace with the Indian government, a portion of General M'Queen's command moved northwards to punish other recalcitrant tribes; but as the fourth column played no part in these operations it is not necessary to describe them. As far as the Royal Irish are concerned, the only incident during the remainder of the Black Mountain campaign was the visit of the Commander-in-Chief in India, General Sir Frederick Roberts, who on the 28th of October inspected the second battalion at Palosi, and complimented all ranks on their behaviour during this little mountain war. Early in November the expedition had finished its work; the columns marched back across the British frontier, and the Royal Irish, passing through Durband, arrived at their old station of Nowshera on the 23rd of the month.[1]

General Galbraith in a farewell order thanked all ranks of the fourth column for the admirable manner in which they had performed their duties, adding that their exemplary behaviour and unvarying good discipline had not been less conspicuous than their conduct in the field. His official report on the operations of the river column mentioned Major R. K. Brereton and Lieutenant W. Gloster, Royal Irish regiment, and the Roman Catholic chaplain attached to the battalion, Father Francis Van Mansfeld, who during the fighting on October 4, distinguished himself by carrying water to the wounded under a heavy fire. The losses of the Hazara Field force during this short campaign were small: the total casualties, including two officers mortally wounded, were

[1] While the regiment was at the front Mr Rudyard Kipling in a ballad made the immortal

less than a hundred. In the second battalion of the Royal Irish two men were killed and three wounded in action, while two were fatally injured by falling down a precipice.[1]

Mulvaney predict the result of sending an Irish corps on a campaign where field canteens were not allowed. Thanks to the kind permission of Mr Kipling the ballad is reproduced.

"THE WAY AV UT !"

"The Black Mountain Expedition is apparently to be a tetotal affair."—*Vide* 'Civil and Military Gazette,' October 5, 1888.

"A charge of Ghazis was met by the Royal Irish, who accounted for the whole of them. . . . The Royal Irish then carried the position."—'Pioneer.'

"I met with ould Mulvaney and he tuk me by the hand,
  Sez he : 'Fwhat *kubber*' from the front, and will the Paythans stand ?"
"O Terence, dear, in all Clonmel such things were never seen,
  They've sent a rigimint to war widout a fiel' canteen !

"'Tis not a Highland rigimint, for they wud niver care,
  Their Corp'rils carry hymn-books an' they open fire wid prayer—
  'Tis not an English rigimint that burns a blue light flame,
  'Tis the Eighteenth Royal Irish, man ! as thirsty as they're game !'

"An' Terence bit upon his poipe, an' shpat behin' the door—
  ' 'Tis Bobs,' sez he, 'that knows the thrick av making bloody war.
  Ye say they go widout their dhrink ?" "and that's the trut,'" sez I !
"Thin Heaven help the Muddy Khels they call an Akazai !

"I lay wid them in Dublin wanst, an' we was Oirish tu,
  We passed the time av day, an' thin the belts wint '*whirraru*,'
  I misremember fwhat occurred, but, followin' the shtorm,
  A 'Freeman's Journal' Supplemint was all my uniform !

"They're rocks upon parade, but oh ! in barricks they are hard—
  They're ragin,' tearin' divils whin there's ructions on the kyard—
  An' onless they've changed their bullswools for a baby's sock, I think
  They'd rake all Hell for grandeur—an' I *know* they wud for dhrink !

"An' Bobs has sent them out to war widout a dhrop or dhrain ?
  'Tis he will put the '*jildy*' in this dissolute campaign.
  They'd fight for frolic half the year, but now their liquor's cut,
  The wurrd 'l go : 'Don't waste your time ! the bay'net and the butt !'

"Six hundher' stiflin' throats in front—tu hundher' lef' behind
  To suk the pickins av the cask whiniver they've a mind !
  I would *not* be the Paythan man forninst the '*Sungar*' wall
  Whin those six hundher gintlemen projuce the long bradawl !

"They will be dhry—tremenjus dhry—an' not a dhram to toss—
  Divils of Ballydaval, Holy Saints av Holy Cross !
  An' Holy Cross they all will be from Carrick to Clogheen,
  Thrapesin' after naygur-*log* widout a fiel' canteen.

"Will they be long among the hills ? my troth, they will not so—
  They're cramming down their fightin' now to have ut done, an' go—
  For Bobs, the Timp'rance Shtrategist, has whipped them on the nail.
  'Tis cruel on the Oirish, but—'tis murther on the Kheyl !"

[1] See Appendix 2 (O).

The Indian Medal with a clasp for "Hazara 1888" was granted to the troops who took part in this expedition.

Until December, 1889, the second battalion remained at Nowshera; then it was stationed for a short time at Peshawar, and in April, 1890, headquarters and four companies were moved to Cherat, where the medals for the Hazara campaign were presented on parade by Mrs Rogers, the wife of the officer who then commanded the battalion. The year 1890 was memorable in the sporting annals of the regiment. After having been in the final tie for the Infantry polo tournament for three years running, the officers of the second battalion won it at Umballa with a team composed of Captain Apthorp, Lieutenants Cullinan, Kellett, Wynne, and Garraway—the last mentioned taking the place of Wynne, who met with an accident during the game. The non-commissioned officers and men also had a triumph in winning the Calcutta football tournament. The month of December found the second battalion on the way to Lucknow, where they remained till November, 1894, when a five weeks' march brought them to Jubbulpore, an excellent centre for big game shooting. The officers lost no opportunity of going after tiger, and Lieutenant J. B. S. Alderson had a very exciting adventure in which his life was saved by the coolness of Lieutenant-Colonel Lawrence, then in command of the battalion. In the Chitri jungle Alderson was following up a wounded tiger on foot, when the beast charged and seized him by the arm. Colonel Lawrence rushed to the rescue, and with three steady shots killed it, but not without much difficulty, for as the huge brute lay upon Alderson mauling his arm, the bullets had to be placed so that they would strike the animal without doing his victim any harm. When Alderson was brought into hospital, he was so weak from shock, fatigue, and loss of blood that it was pronounced unsafe to put him under chloroform, and it was nearly midnight before all his numerous wounds were dressed. Though suffering agonies he never uttered a word, except from time to time to ask one of his brother officers, who were standing round his bed, to fill and light the pipe, which he did not allow to go out during the operation. His right arm had been bitten through, but neither the bones nor arteries were injured, and he recovered—to meet a soldier's death a few years later in the South African war.

During the cold weather of 1896-97 the second battalion was inspected by the Lieutenant-General commanding in Bengal, who pronounced it to be "in first-rate order, in a very efficient condition, and quite fit for active service." The Commander-in-Chief in India considered this "a very satis-factory report on the battalion, which appears to be very well commanded by Colonel Lawrence." A few months after this inspection matters began to go badly on the frontier, where for some time past fanatical priests had been preaching "a Holy War" against the English. The first tangible symptom of unrest was a treacherous attack by the hillmen of the Tochi valley upon a

British officer and his escort; then followed an outbreak in the Swat valley, where the tribes suddenly fell in thousands upon our post at Malakand. The garrison fought gallantly, and in spite of enormous odds held their ground for several days until the enemy were dispersed by a relieving column. The Mohmands were the next to rise, and finally the Afridis and Orakzais took up arms against us. To meet this formidable though fortunately ill-combined attack, troops were hurried to the frontier; among them were the Royal Irish, who on August 13, 1897, received the order to mobilise for active service. The news was welcomed by the battalion with wild enthusiasm, and proved so good a tonic to the large number of non-commissioned officers and men who, though apparently recovered from the malarial fever prevalent at Jubbulpore, still had the seeds of the disease lurking in their system, that eight hundred and twenty-seven of all ranks were passed by the doctors.[1] In two days everything was in readiness, and on August 15, the Royal Irish entrained for Rawal Pindi. The journey, at that time of year always an exhausting one, was made doubly trying by the result of a railway accident; the troop trains, timed to reach Pindi early in the morning, did not arrive there till nearly midnight, and by some departmental blunder the battalion was left all day without food or shelter from the sun. At Khasalghur, where the rail ended, the Royal Irish had very heavy work, loading and reloading stores in extreme heat. Then followed several forced marches, in the first of which they escorted a convoy four or five miles in length for twenty-six miles over a very rugged country, drained by two rivers passable only at deep fords. When they joined Major-General Yeatman-Biggs in the Miranzai valley, they found his column at Hangu, a village at the base of the foot hills of the great Samana ridge, where the camp, pitched on fields from which

---

[1] The following officers took part in the Tirah Campaign :—
Lieutenant-Colonel—W. W. Lawrence (in command).
Majors—J. B. Forster, H. S. Lye, F. J. Gavin, E. Lindesay.
Captain and Brevet-Major—B. J. C. Doran (served on the staff throughout the operations and was mentioned in despatches).
Captains—A. S. Orr, A. B. King, D. H. Davis (adjutant), G. F. R. Forbes, R. G. S. L. Moriarty, H. N. Kelly.
Lieutenants—J. B. S. Alderson, C. E. Galway, F. L. Fosbery, E. F. Milner, E. H. E. Daniell, W. H. White, F. M. Watkins, F. S. Lillie.
2nd Lieutenants—C. de J. Luxmore, T. J. Willans, L. J. Lipsett, H. W. R. Potter, G. W. P. Haslam, T. C. FitzHugh, M. Furber, J. G. Lawrence, D. Barton.
Quartermaster and Hon. Lieutenant—J. J. Fox.
Surgeon—Major C. R. Bartlett, R.A.M.S.
The following officers were attached to the battalion :—
Captain—G. L. Hobbs, the Connaught Rangers.
Lieutenants—H. E. Tizard, Royal Munster Fusiliers ; B. C. W. Williams, Yorkshire regiment ; A. J. B. Church, the Connaught Rangers ; F. A. D'O. Goddard, Royal Munster Fusiliers ; H. R. G. Deacon and F. J. Byrne, both of the Connaught Rangers ; G. A. Ellis and M. L. Pears, both of the Cameronians (Scottish Rifles).
Second Lieutenant—H. W. Gough, the Connaught Rangers.

the crops had just been reaped, stood on ground saturated by the heavy rain of the monsoon. In a previous campaign on the frontier, an imperfectly entrenched British force had been attacked at night by a horde of hillmen, whose determined rush was not repelled without great difficulty and hard fighting. Mindful of this episode, Yeatman-Biggs had ringed his camp with works, which were occupied by the troops at night, when, to avoid offering a target to "snipers," the tents were struck. As the weather was very wet and steamy, it was impossible for the men ever to get their clothes thoroughly dried, and during the fortnight that the headquarters of the battalion remained at Hangu there was much fever among those who were unlucky enough to be left in camp,[1] but the companies sent on detachment kept in good health and accomplished the remarkable marches mentioned in Colonel Lawrence's order, quoted in appendix 5.

On the evening of September 12, General Yeatman-Biggs issued orders for his column to march forthwith to the rescue of a party of the 36th Sikhs, who were hard pressed in Fort Gulistan, an advanced post on the Samana ridge. At that moment the battalion was so reduced by detachments and by sickness that only two hundred and ninety-five Royal Irishmen were present to take part in the arduous operations by which the Gulistan garrison was relieved on the 13th. After this success Yeatman-Biggs was ordered to remain on the Samana; the sick of the battalion were sent up from the hospitals below, and in the pure air of the mountains rapidly regained their health. In addition to the ordinary camp guards, duties, and fatigues the battalion was employed in road-making and in reconnaissances among the hills; and in high spirits and absolutely unaware that they had been reported upon unfavourably, all ranks anxiously awaited orders for a farther advance into the enemy's country, when a telegram reached Colonel Lawrence from a civilian friend at Rawal Pindi, telling him of a rumour that the Royal Irish were to be ordered back from the front for garrison duty in India. Colonel Lawrence at once went to the General, who said it was true that the battalion was to go back, as the doctors reported it to be saturated with malaria. At the Colonel's request a medical board was assembled, whose members were instructed to be very thorough and searching in their examination, and to pass no one who was not thoroughly fit for the hard work of active service. The doctors did not see the whole of the battalion, as a hundred and fifty officers and men were absent on detachment, but out of those whom they inspected, five hundred and twenty-three were passed as absolutely fit, and above the average physique of the army. With this favourable report in his hand, Colonel Lawrence made every effort to obtain the recision of the order

---

[1] During the short time the battalion was at the front no less than 455 of the Royal Irish fell ill and were admitted into hospital.

but without success; and on September 30, appeared the following paragraph in Major-General Yeatman-Biggs' Field Force orders : " under instructions from Army Headquarters, Simla, the 2nd battalion, Royal Irish regiment, is to proceed to Rawul Pindi for garrison duty, on relief by the 2nd Derbyshire regiment."

It will be observed that no reason was given for the removal of the battalion from the fighting line; and soon after the Royal Irish reached Rawal Pindi rumours, most injurious to their character as soldiers, became current in civilian circles and found their way first into the Indian and then into the British newspapers. Major-General Sir Henry Havelock-Allan, the Colonel of the regiment, was in England when these rumours were repeated by the London press; and stirred to the heart by the aspersions on the fair fame of the corps with which he had so long and honourable a connection, he hurried to India to investigate the truth of these stories. Shortly after the second battalion returned to Rawal Pindi Colonel Lawrence was appointed to the command of the XVIIIth regimental district; but before leaving India he went to Simla to ascertain if possible why the battalion had been so unjustly treated. He was unable to obtain an interview with the Commander-in-Chief, but from the Adjutant-General he learned that, several days before the medical board had been convened, General Yeatman-Biggs had reported that the Royal Irish were so saturated with malaria that they could not keep up with the rest of the column. As General Havelock-Allan and Colonel Lawrence crossed on the voyage without meeting in any port, the former landed at Bombay with an unbiassed mind; without stopping to see the battalion at Rawal Pindi he hastened to the frontier, and after the fullest inquiries in every direction was able to assert proudly that the Royal Irish had behaved like good soldiers in the Tirah campaign. By his tragic death in the Khyber Pass at the end of December, the regiment apparently lost its only influential friend in the East, and when, shortly afterwards, the authorities at Simla refused to grant the board of inquiry for which Lieutenant-Colonel Forster had applied in order to refute the libels on his battalion, the spirits of all ranks sank very low. The dignified attitude of the officers under misfortune won universal respect and admiration at Pindi; and it speaks well for the discipline of the battalion that in such distressing circumstances there was no sign of angry feeling among the men, and that all ranks, knowing that there was no grounds for the aspersions made against them in the press, possessed their souls in patience until their conduct should be investigated by an authority even higher than that of Simla.

While Havelock-Allan was on the frontier he had laid the grievances of the Royal Irish before General Sir William Lockhart, who was in command of all the troops engaged in the Tirah campaign; and after Lockhart had seen the battalion at Havelock-Allan's funeral at Pindi, he exerted himself so vigorously on its behalf that, after being closely inspected by the chief army doctor in India, it was ordered back to the front, and on February 9, 1898, joined the third brigade, under Colonel (now Lieutenant-General Sir Ian) Hamilton, in the Bara valley. Thence it moved up to Barkai, where the expeditionary force received the Royal Irish with open arms. "The fuss that has been made over us is wonderful," wrote an officer of the XVIIIth. "Every general within fifteen miles of Barkai rode over to congratulate the regiment in the names of their respective commands, and the officers were inundated with shoals of complimentary telegrams." Unfortunately, as far as Hamilton's brigade was concerned, all fighting was over when the battalion was allowed to return to the front, and thus it had no opportunity of again meeting the enemy; but still it had been sent back to the fighting line, and thus from the military point of view its honour was completely vindicated. One thing, however, was still needed to re-establish the second battalion in the eyes of civilians—a letter from Army headquarters at Simla clearing it from the charges made against it in the newspapers. Such a letter arrived on the 17th of February, but being marked "confidential" could not be sent to the public press for publication. When Colonel Lawrence received from the second battalion a copy of this confidential letter, he rightly considered that for the complete exoneration of the Royal Irish he should be permitted to make its contents known to the world; he accordingly asked leave of Colonel Gough, Secretary to Lord Wolseley, then Commander-in-Chief of the British Army, to publish it to the brigade of regular and militia battalions of the Royal Irish territorial regiment, about to assemble at Kilworth under his orders. In reply "as an exceptional case and in view of his proceeding to Kilworth where other battalions of the regiment are stationed" he received an extract from a letter from the Adjutant-General to the Commander-in-Chief, India, which runs as follows :—

"I am directed by the Secretary of State to inform you that a perusal of the papers connected with the withdrawal of the 2nd battalion, Royal Irish regiment from the field force on the North-West frontier has satisfied the Commander-in-Chief that a grave injustice was done to the 2nd battalion, Royal Irish regiment when it was recalled from field service."

Colonel Lawrence immediately published this complete exoneration in an order to the troops at Kilworth (see appendix 5).

In order that the public should realise how completely the charges against the Royal Irish had been refuted, it was suggested that some signal honour should be conferred upon the regiment. Her Majesty Queen Victoria, always remembering the XVIIIth when they guarded her at Windsor, had been much concerned at the libels on her Irish soldiers; she at once appreciated the importance of proving to the world that the rumours about the second battalion were absolutely without foundation, and by her command Lord Wolseley was appointed to be the first Colonel-in-Chief of the Royal Irish regiment. This mark of the Queen's favour closed the Tirah incident, the most painful episode in the long history of the regiment.

As the second battalion was not one of the corps fortunate enough to be sent from India to South Africa for the Boer war, the record of its service during the remainder of the period embraced by this history is almost barren of interest. In February, 1900, the Royal Irish distinguished themselves at Mhow in putting out a dangerous fire, and were specially thanked by Major-General Nicholson, C.B., who commanded the district—

> "The General Officer Commanding wishes to convey to the troops in garrison, his thanks for the excellent work done by them during the last few days in endeavouring to extinguish the recent fire in the Commissariat stack-yard. The promptitude with which Officers and men of the Royal Irish regiment turned out on the first alarm undoubtedly saved the remainder of the stacks at the time, and the zeal evinced and arduous work done by all the troops in garrison on that and subsequent days has been fully appreciated by the General Officer Commanding, and he will have much pleasure in bringing the same to the notice of the Lieutenant-General Commanding, Bombay Command."

A month later the battalion learned from Army Orders that to commemorate the gallantry of the Irish regiments in the recent battles in South Africa, the Queen had ordered that in future all ranks of these corps should wear on St Patrick's Day a sprig of shamrock in their head-dresses—a recognition of national sentiment which caused great satisfaction to both battalions of the XVIIIth, and to every other Irish regiment in Her Majesty's army.

In the ordinary course of Indian reliefs the second battalion was due to turn its face homewards in the autumn of 1900, but owing to the war in South Africa all such arrangements were cancelled, and the Royal Irish were ordered to remain at Mhow, where they were still quartered when in July, 1901, Lieutenant-Colonel J. Burton-Forster, relinquishing the command on appointment to the Staff, was succeeded by Lieutenant-Colonel H. S. Shuldham-Lye. The dislocation of reliefs was not the only effect produced on the second battalion by the South African war. As every recruit, as soon as he was fit for active service, was sent to join the first battalion, there was great danger that the second battalion would become dangerously weak if the time-expired men left India at the end of their engagement to serve with the Colours. As every battalion in India was in a similar plight the government offered liberal terms to men willing to re-engage, viz.—a bounty of £10 with a two months' furlough at home, or an additional bounty of £16 in lieu of furlough to all ranks below the rank of sergeant, who had completed six years and three months' colonial service, and who had not entered upon the twelfth year of such service. The men who accepted these terms were to engage to extend their service so as to complete twelve years with the Colours. Twenty-two of the Royal Irish accepted the £10 bounty with furlough; two hundred and ninety-seven preferred to have £26 paid into their hands, and did not take a holiday at home.

WINDOW COMMEMORATIVE OF SOUTH AFRICAN WAR, 1899-1902.
St Patrick's Cathedral, Dublin.

CHAPTER XIV.

1885-1900.

·THE FIRST BATTALION.

MOUNTED INFANTRY IN MASHONALAND : THE WAR IN SOUTH AFRICA :
COLESBERG AND BETHLEHEM.

For nearly four years after the return of the first battalion to England in 1885 it was quartered alternately at Plymouth and Devonport. During this time only three events of importance occurred in its history. In February, 1886, General Sir Richard Dennis Kelly, K.C.B.,[1] from the Prince of Wales's Leinster Regiment (Royal Canadians), was appointed Colonel of the Royal Irish regiment, *vice* Lieutenant-General and Honorary General Sir Alexander MacDonell, K.C.B., transferred to the Rifle Brigade. New Colours were presented to the battalion on September 7, 1886, at Devonport, by the Lady Albertha Edgcumbe, daughter of the Earl of Mount Edgcumbe, at a ceremony marked by a departure from precedent; hitherto the Colours of the Royal Irish had always been consecrated by a clergyman of the Church of England, but on this occasion the service was performed by a Roman Catholic priest in recognition of the fact that the large majority of the rank and file were members of the Church of Rome. In the Gazette of March 9, 1889, Sir Richard Kelly was transferred to the command of the Border regiment, and was succeeded by Lieutenant-General and Honorary General George Frederick Stephenson Call, C.B.[2] From Plymouth the battalion, six hundred and ninety-nine of all ranks, under Lieutenant-Colonel A. J. A. Jackson, was ordered in May, 1889, to Colchester, where it was inspected by its new Colonel, General Call, who after serving in the XVIIIth in China, Burma, and the Crimea, had commanded it in India. While at Colchester two serious misfortunes happened. In the autumn of 1889 the sergeants' mess was burned down, and in it were lost several cups and trophies, and worse than all, the two engravings given by the late King Edward VII. to the non-commissioned officers during his visit to India while he was Prince of Wales.

[1] & [2] See Appendix 9.

U

Nearly two years later, on July 31, 1891, the officers' mess hut met with a similar fate. A little past midnight, after the mess had been closed, an officer discovered that the building was on fire. The alarm was at once given; not only the Royal Irish, but the whole of the garrison turned out, but their united efforts, coupled with those of the town fire-brigade, failed to master the flames, and the hut and nearly all it contained was destroyed. There were several gallant but fruitless attempts to save the Colours; and it was only at great personal risk that Private W. O'Neill succeeded in bringing away the silver model of a whale-boat, the trophy commemorating the battalion's success in the race up the Nile. Among the few things rescued was the snuff-box, which, as already mentioned on page 146, was the only piece of regimental plate saved from the wreck of the *Buckinghamshire* in 1851.

Late in the autumn of 1891 the battalion was ordered to Ireland, and arrived at the Curragh in November under Lieutenant-Colonel J. D. Edge, whose marching-in state showed a strength of 697 officers and men. Next year, on November 14, new Colours were presented by Lady Wolseley, to replace those lost in the fire at Colchester. At the end of the ceremony Lord Wolseley addressed the Royal Irish, and after reminding his audience that throughout his military career he had been intimately associated with the regiment, he continued as follows :—

" I served side by side with it in Burma when I was very young. I met it again in the Crimea, and I can well remember what pride I felt as an Irishman in its gallant conduct on the 18th June, 1855. It also served in India whilst I was there during the Mutiny, and it must be in the remembrance of many of those who are now on parade that we were comrades together during the war in Egypt in 1882. I remember well, in the first streak of dawn on the desert of Tel-el-Kebir, seeing the Royal Irish among the first to cross the entrenchments, and again, two years later, we met on the Nile, in which expedition they played a distinguished part. I felt proud that they should have been the winners of a prize which was offered to the battalion which made the journey up the river in the shortest time. I have a very much prized trophy of the expedition which was given me by one for whom I have the greatest respect—one of the very best men and best soldiers I ever knew—I refer to Father Brindle, your former chaplain, who accompanied you from Cairo up the river, and then across the Desert to Gubat. The trophy is the flag of the boat in which he made the voyage up the Nile; it is marked ' H Company, Royal Irish.' Yours is one of the oldest regiments in the army. When first raised it was named ' The regiment of Ireland.' That name was changed by William III. to the Royal Irish regiment, as a reward, a distinction for your gallant services at the taking of Namur. If I were to enter into detailed history of the regiment it would be to give a history of the British army, for the history of one may be said to be the history of the other. I chanced to read an old book the other day, describing the wars of the early part of the last century, in which it was stated that the discipline, system of drill, and fighting, training of the army then had been copied from the discipline and military system long established in the Royal Irish regiment.   As you know from the names of the battles on your Colours you shared in all the glories of the Duke of Marlborough, and although hereafter I have no doubt you will add many names to these Colours—for we shall have wars as long as the world lasts—no greater victory than that of Blenheim or Ramillies can ever be shared in by any regiment.   Now, what is the value of all this glory to a regiment, or to the army of which it is a part?   It is this, it intensifies the pride of the regiment, and the pride of that Empire to which we all belong; it is an incentive to those who come after us to imitate, and, if possible, to excel the deeds of their forefathers.   May God bless these Colours and prosper this fine old distinguished regiment."

After three years at the Curragh the battalion was ordered to Limerick, where it arrived early in November, 1894.   The Royal Irish had hardly settled down in their new quarters when they lost their Lieutenant-Colonel, J. D. Edge, who died in Dublin on the 15th of December, and less than a month later General Call followed him to the grave.   Lieutenant-Colonel J. H. A. Spyer succeeded to the command of the battalion: General Call was replaced by Lieutenant-General and Honorary General R. W. M'L. Fraser, on whose transfer to the Royal Warwickshire regiment less than a year later, Major-General and Honorary Lieutenant-General Sir Henry Havelock-Allan, V.C., a former officer of the XVIIIth, was appointed to fill the vacancy on November 22, 1895.

In the spring of 1896 news reached England of a dangerous native rising in Rhodesia, a huge territory lately added to the possessions of Britain, and bounded to the north by the Zambesi river, to the east by Portuguese East Africa, and to the south by the Transvaal.   The distances in the theatre of war were so enormous, and the mobility of the enemy so great, that the War Office determined to reinforce the troops in South Africa with foot soldiers who could ride, and the battalions at home were called upon to furnish detachments of officers and men who had been trained to act as mounted infantry.   Lieutenant S. G. French was selected to command the contingent from the Royal Irish, and with thirty non-commissioned officers and men, formed part of a composite unit known as the Irish Company, mounted infantry.   They embarked on May 2, 1896; landed at Cape Town, and after remaining some time encamped at Wynberg, sailed to Beira, the harbour in Portuguese territory from which Rhodesia could be approached most easily by sea.   Thanks to the courtesy of the Government at Lisbon, our troops were allowed to make use of the port, and to pass through the belt of coast land between the ocean and the frontier of Rhodesia.   Once arrived at Salisbury, the principal British settlement in our new territory, the handful of Royal Irish were allotted to a column under Lieutenant-Colonel E. A. H. Alderson, and were employed in pacifying northern Mashonaland. This is not the place to describe the expedition: it is enough to say that the representatives of the regiment did well on every occasion when they were engaged.[1] In Colonel Alderson's report of November 25, 1897, he stated that "the detachment under Lieutenant French did their work excellently in every way, especially when on active service in Mashonaland. After the action at Makia's Kraal on August 30, 1896, I had much pleasure in reporting them to Sir Frederick Carrington, K.C.B., K.C.M.G., commanding the forces in Rhodesia, as follows: 'I should like to mention the ready way in which the Royal Irish section of the Irish Company, Mounted Infantry, followed Lieutenant French across a considerable piece of open ground under a brisk fire.'" When Lieutenant French and his detachment returned to England they rejoined headquarters where the medal, issued to all who took part in the campaign, was presented to them in due course.

The Royal Irish were so popular in Limerick that, when it became known that the first battalion was to move to Dublin in the autumn, the townspeople petitioned the Government to allow it to remain for another year. When the request was granted the Corporation took the opportunity of presenting the commanding officer, Lieutenant-Colonel Spyer, with a very complimentary address, containing many references to the uniformly good conduct of the regiment, and to the high esteem with which it was regarded by all creeds and classes of the population. The Royal Irish were still quartered in Limerick at the time of the Jubilee celebrating the completion of the sixtieth year of Her Majesty Queen Victoria's reign. Certain disloyalists attempted to mar the rejoicings by hoisting a black flag upon one of the islands of the Shannon; the local authorities were most anxious to remove this emblem of treason, but the owners of the river boats, intimidated by the rabble, refused the large sum of money offered for the use of their craft, and there appeared no means of reaching the obnoxious flag, when Private —— Cullen, Royal Irish regiment, came to the rescue, and, to quote from the account of his gallant feat which appeared in the London 'Globe' of July 5, 1897,

> "lowering himself by a rope from the barracks, which overhang the river, he plunged in, and struck out for the rock. Crowds congregated on the opposite bank, and some at least—for there are many in Limerick too loyal and too sensible to be the playthings of vindictive agitators— watched his progress through the fierce current in mental trepidation. He reached the rock, tore up the pole and flag, and not daring to return in the teeth of the stream, swam with his capture to the bank. It was only after a long and hard struggle that he was able to make land, where

[1] For casualties see Appendix 1 (P).

a strong body of police met and escorted him back to barracks. Had it not been for the police, serious if not fatal injuries would have been done him, as a great crowd of women were prepared to stone him as he approached."

At the end of 1897, the Royal Irish regiment heard with deep regret of the death of their Colonel, Sir Henry Havelock-Allan, V.C., who, while in India to disprove the charges brought against the second battalion, was killed in the Khyber Pass on December 31, 1897. He was succeeded by Major-General C. F. Gregorie, C.B.,[1] who had commanded the second battalion at Tel-el-Kebir. In the summer of 1898, as has been already mentioned, Her Majesty Queen Victoria paid the regiment the very high honour of directing that Field-Marshal the Right Honourable Garnet, Viscount Wolseley, K.P., G.C.B., G.C.M.G., Colonel Royal Horse Guards, Commander-in-Chief, should be appointed Colonel-in-Chief of the Royal Irish regiment.[2]

In August, 1898, the first battalion moved to Buttevant with many regrets, for officers and men alike had found Limerick an ideal station. The racing was good, the hunting excellent,[3] the inhabitants were hospitable and thoroughly appreciated the good qualities of the Royal Irish, whom they had grown to look upon as personal friends. In the autumn of 1898, the bronze medal of the Royal Humane Society was presented to Lieutenant E. M. Panter-Downes by Colonel W. W. Lawrence, commanding the XVIIIth regimental district; the circumstances in which this decoration was won are set out in the following extract from Colonel Lawrence's speech on parade, when he pinned the medal on to the recipient's breast:—

"I have a very pleasing duty to perform this morning, and that is to present to Mr Panter-Downes, of the 1st battalion, the Royal Humane Society's medal for risking his life to save that of a gentleman at Kilkee, Co. Clare, in August last. Captain Vigors and Mr Panter-Downes went to bathe that morning. There was a very heavy sea running, and the waves were breaking over the rocks. They noticed a man's clothes on the cliff, but saw nothing of him at the time. Shortly after they saw him in the water, in a very exhausted condition, almost at the last gasp. Mr Panter-Downes at once jumped in and swam thirty or forty yards through the surf to the drowning man. He secured him, and with him swam back to the iron ladder used by bathers, where Captain

---

[1] See Appendix 9.

[2] Gazette of July 19, 1898. See chapter xiii. and Appendix 9.

[3] While out with the hounds at Clonmel one of the officers of the first battalion made a sensational jump, thus described in the sporting papers: "Mr Vigors, of the Royal Irish Regiment, now stationed at Clonmel, was riding a cob he had purchased a short time previously from Mr Burke, and racing at the road fence (a low wall on the inside, but very treacherous on the roadway, as it had been cut away 9 feet to level a hill) the cob jumped clean on to the road, with a fall outside of 11 feet. The horse never fell, but Mr Vigors fell on the cob's neck, and slipped off at the far side of the road, luckily unhurt."

Vigors met him, and between the two of them they got the man in safely. When they were on the ladder the waves were washing over them, and they were in danger of being carried away."

On Colonel W. W. Lawrence's retirement from the service he was succeeded in command of the 18th regimental district by Colonel J. H. A. Spyer, who was promoted Colonel on the 16th of January, 1899. In the same Gazette Major H. W. N. Guinness was promoted to be Lieutenant-Colonel. The autumn of 1899 found the battalion still quartered in Ireland, with the eyes of all ranks turned upon South Africa, where the course of political events showed with ever-increasing clearness that the South African republics were determined to force a war upon Great Britain. The causes of the quarrel are too complex to be discussed in a regimental history; from the soldier's point of view the all-important question was whether England was to continue the paramount power in South Africa or to be ousted by the Dutch republics, and the earnest hope of every man in the regiment was that the XVIIIth would be allowed to take part in the struggle in which this great question was to be decided. For a time this hope seemed destined not to be fulfilled, for though Captain S. E. St Leger was appointed to command a company of mounted infantry, of which a section was provided by the Royal Irish,[1] the first battalion was not among the troops selected for the "Expeditionary Force" despatched to the seat of war in October and November. The officers made every effort to induce the War Office to send the battalion to South Africa, but failed to obtain anything more definite than a promise that if more troops were required, every attention would be paid to the desire of the Royal Irish to be actively employed. When it was decided to strengthen the expeditionary force with another division, the 5th, the battalion hoped to find a place in one of its brigades, but it was not included in General Warren's command, and until the beginning of December there seemed no prospect that it would take part in the Boer war. The Royal Irish were then at Aldershot, where they had arrived on November 24, to join the second battalions of the Bedfordshire, Worcestershire, and Wiltshire regiments in the 12th infantry brigade, commanded by Colonel, afterwards Major-General R. A. P. Clements. They had not yet thoroughly settled down in their new quarters when they were roused to the highest pitch of enthusiasm by the news that the 12th brigade was to mobilise forthwith, and to start in a few days for South Africa as part of Lieutenant-General Kelly-Kenny's newly formed division, the 6th. Then began a rush so tremendous that those who went through it now look back on the time between the 2nd of December, when the orders were received, and the 16th, when the battalion sailed, as a nightmare; there was an enormous amount of work to be done; the days

[1] See page 361.

were very short; the barracks were badly lighted; everyone was at fever heat with excitement; and the strain upon the officers and non-commissioned officers was quite indescribable. All men over twenty years of age had to be medically examined to see if they were fit for active service; clothing and equipment for the field had to be drawn and fitted, and arrangements made for the well-being of the women and children of the battalion, whether "on" or "off" the strength; the reserve men had to be brought over from Clonmel, armed, clothed, and fitted out in every way.[1] Lectures on the value of inoculation against enteric were given to induce men to submit themselves voluntarily to the operation; soldiers whose marksmanship was below the average received additional instruction in musketry, and preparations were made for the disposal of those men who were too young or not physically fit for the campaign. In the midst of all this bustle, three officers and sixty-seven of the other ranks were sent off to the mounted infantry at Shorncliffe,[2] and the reservists — three sergeants, seven corporals, and two hundred and seventy privates — arrived, who, from their age, their long service, and the experience which many of them had gained on the north-west frontier of India, proved invaluable in the South African war.

The Royal Irish, who shared the s.s. *Gascon* with the Wiltshire regiment, embarked at Southampton with thirteen officers, one warrant officer, and 672 non-commissioned officers and men, or a total of 686 of all ranks, under the command of Lieutenant-Colonel W. H. N. Guinness.[3] To understand why so small a number of officers started with headquarters for South Africa, the reader must remember that before the battalion left Ireland it had furnished a draft of men trained to mounted infantry work, who were accompanied by three officers; during the weary weeks when it seemed probable that the Royal Irish would remain at home as part of the garrison of the

---

[1] For the details of the kit and equipment with which the soldiers sailed for South Africa, see Appendix 6.

[2] See page 365.

[3] The following officers went to the war with the battalion; followed it to South Africa; served on the staff, or with mounted infantry. (The ranks are those held at the beginning of the war):—

Lieutenant-Colonel—H. W. N. Guinness (in command).

Major—H. M. Hatchell.

Majors—F. J. Gavin, A. N. Lysaght, K. P. Apthorp.

Captains—A. S. Orr, H. J. Downing (Adjutant), W. Gloster, W. E. S. Burch, J. B. S. Alderson, G. M. Grogan, F. L. Fosbery, E. F. Milner, E. H. E. Daniell, R. L. Owens, R. G. L. Crumpe.

Lieutenants—W. H. White, M. H. E. Welch, A. W. Brush, L. L. Farmer, E. M. Panter-Downes, J. A. M. J. P. Kelly, G. A. Elliot, T. C. Fitz Hugh, H. T. A. S. Boyce, G. W. P. Haslam.

Second Lieutenants—G. H. Holland, J. L. O. Mansergh, H. Anderson, W. M. Acton, C. E. Dease, J. L. Cotter, G. A. O'Callaghan, L. W. M. Lloyd (seconded from 4th battalion), H. G. Gregorie (from Imperial Light Infantry), Hon. H. R. T. G. Fitzmaurice-Deane-Morgan (3rd battalion), W. A. Senior (nominated by the authorities of Public Schools), S. Hutchins (9th battalion K.R.R.C.), R. B. S. Dunlop (Channel Islands Militia), F.

United Kingdom, several officers had obtained staff appointments in South Africa, or had been attached to regiments already at the seat of war, and, as has been already mentioned, three more joined the mounted infantry while the battalion was at Aldershot.

The XVIIIth sailed from England under all the depressing influences of the "Black Week"—the disastrous seven days in which three considerable bodies of British troops sustained severe reverses at the hands of the Boers.   General Sir Redvers Buller, then in supreme command in South Africa, had been defeated at Colenso in his attempt to extricate the defenders of Ladysmith from the grip of the burghers whose commandos hemmed them in on every side.   Lieutenant-General Gatacre had been heavily repulsed at Stormberg in his attack upon one of the columns that had invaded the north-east of Cape Colony.   Lieutenant-General Lord Methuen, after three successes in his march from the Orange river towards Kimberley, had failed with heavy loss to dislodge Cronje from the kopjes of Magersfontein.   But though the country was profoundly depressed at the news of these successive defeats, the spirits of the Royal Irish were as high as ever, and even had their buoyant temperaments been influenced by the national gloom at the time of their departure, life on board the *Gascon* was too full of occupation to allow time for thinking of unpleasant things. As the reservists had not joined in time to be equipped fully before they left Aldershot, their field service kit was issued to them on the voyage; and as many of them had not been trained to the use of the Lee-Metford rifle, they were put through a course of musketry at sea.   All hands were daily exercised in physical drill; ammunition carriers and company scouts were selected and given theoretical instruction in their duties; identity cards were prepared and sewn into the men's clothing, and wire cutters served out.   To provide healthy amusement for the troops the officers organised "tugs-of-war" and other forms of athletics in the afternoons, while concerts and "sing-songs" filled up the evening hours.

Call, T. B. Vandaleur (Local Military Forces of Cape of Good Hope), F. J. R. Hughes (3rd battalion), A. C. S. Fletcher, R. Palmer (3rd battalion West Riding regiment).

Quartermaster and Honorary Captain—F. P. Reger.

Surgeon—Lieutenant J. Matthews, R.A.M.C. (during the greater part of the war).

The officers who served extra regimentally were—

On the Staff—

Majors—A. G. Chichester, B. J. C. Doran, Brevet-Major W. R. B. Doran.

With Mounted Infantry—

Captains—R. A. Smyth, S. G. French, R. R. Arbuthnot, S. E. St Leger.

Lieutenants—P. U. Vigors, E. C. Lloyd, S. H. L. Galbraith.

The following officers of the 5th (Irish) Volunteer battalion, King's (Liverpool regiment) were attached at various times :—

Captain—T. Warwick Williams.

Lieutenants—J. Goffey, J. H. Grindley, J. L. L. Ferris, W. G. Lindsey, H. M. Bayer, D. R. Grindley.

When the *Gascon* reached Cape Town on the 6th of January, 1900, the Royal Irish and the Wiltshire were ordered not to disembark, as the destination of Clements' brigade was still uncertain. For three days the battalion remained inactive, with little to do but to gaze on the lovely scenery of Table Bay; to admire the great fleet of transports and store-ships floating on its waters, and to form some idea of the general situation at the front. This was no easy matter, for the censorship over the South African press was severe, and the papers in Cape Town gave much less news of the war than those published in the United Kingdom. Gradually the Royal Irish ascertained that the Boer leaders had not known how to profit by their victories. The state of affairs had not altered materially since the *Gascon* left England, and the Union Jack still waved over the three towns to which the burghers were laying siege. The reports from Mafeking were satisfactory, and showed a spirit of hopeful resolution, contrasting favourably with the attitude of part of the civilian population of Kimberley. This great mining centre was held by a force of improvised volunteers, stiffened by half a battalion of regular infantry and a few gunners. Its townspeople had been greatly discouraged by Methuen's defeat at Magersfontein; they were now beginning to feel the privations of the siege, or rather of the investment, for in the true sense of the word Kimberley was not besieged; and every native runner who made his way through the enemy's lines brought urgent appeals for immediate relief, not only from politicians and merchants, but also from Mr Rhodes, whose influence at the diamond fields was so commanding that he was virtually dictator of Kimberley. In Natal the garrison of Ladysmith had just repulsed a vigorous assault upon their southern defences; but supplies were beginning to run short, enteric and dysentery were rampant, and privations and overwork were beginning to tell heavily upon the *physique* of Sir George White's troops, whose *moral*, however, hardship and fatigue had in no wise impaired. In the field the enemy had made no more progress than in his siege operations. No Boer commando had crossed the Tugela to harass Sir Redvers Buller as he lay echeloned along the railway from Chieveley to the coast, and thus he had been unmolested while preparing for his second attempt to relieve Ladysmith—the effort which beginning on the 10th of January, 1900, ended in failure twenty-eight days later at Vaal Kranz. In Cape Colony the Boers had been as slothful as in Natal. Gatacre's opponents were still concentrated round Stormberg; the commandos which had raided across the Orange river by the Norval's Pont bridge were so stoutly opposed by Lieutenant-General French that they could advance no farther than Colesberg: Cronje, who since his victory on December 11, 1899, had remained inactive at Magersfontein, was confronted by Methuen's entrenchments at the junction of the Riet and Modder rivers, and the railway between Methuen's camp to the bridge over the Orange river was adequately guarded. Thus the invaders had not gained ground, and as even the most disaffected of the Cape Dutch had no intention of breaking into open rebellion until commandos of Transvaalers or Free Staters appeared among them, no general rising throughout the colony had taken place; and the safety of the railways running from the coast to our various advanced posts was not seriously imperilled, though the protection of those lines of communication immobilised a large number of troops.

Four days after the *Gascon* steamed into Table Bay, Field-Marshal Lord Roberts arrived at Cape Town to take command of the army in South Africa. For political reasons the disembarkation of the headquarter staff was made the occasion for a military display; troops lined the streets, and a company of the Royal Irish was sent on shore to form a guard of honour at the landing-stage. A few hours later the *Gascon* sailed for Port Elizabeth, where on January 12, 1900, the battalion landed, and was ordered to a camp three miles from the harbour. It was so long since the XVIIIth had been on active service that among the rank and file only the reservists, and indeed not all of them, knew how varied and how arduous are the fatigue duties which troops are called upon to perform in a campaign, and the first day's work in South Africa proved very trying to men just out from England: in burning heat they had first to take their part in unloading the ship, then to pack the stores and baggage on a train which stopped a mile short of their destination; next to "off-load" the goods, and finally to carry them by hand into the camp and there arrange them in proper order. Before many weeks were over the young soldiers, partly by experience and partly by the teaching of their older comrades, had learned that in war for every day spent in fighting fifty are occupied in marching, in making entrenchments or breast-works, in mending roads, in building bridges, in digging waggons out of deep mud-holes, and in dragging guns up the sides of precipitous mountains. Early on the 13th, the battalion was ordered up country to reinforce General French, who with a column of all arms was defending the western portion of the De Aar-Naauwpoort-Stormberg railway which, running roughly parallel with the Orange river, links together the various lines from the coast to the interior of the sub-continent. The eastern part of this cross-country railway was in the hands of the enemy, and one of the most important points left to us was Naauwpoort junction, only thirty-three miles south of Colesberg, the little town where Schoeman, the leader of the invaders, had taken up his quarters. He had intended to drive the British garrison out of Naauwpoort, break up the line connecting Cape Town with Kimberley, and then raise the standard of revolt in the central provinces of Cape Colony; but by a series of brilliant and audacious manœuvres French had gradually edged him back into the network of kopjes encircling Colesberg. Now, in the middle of January, our infantry watched the southern and western faces of this natural fortress, while our mounted troops, widely thrust out on either flank, sought opportunities to harass Schoeman's communications with the Orange Free State. The railway from Port Elizabeth to Bloemfontein, the capital of the Free State, had been recovered to within ten miles of Colesberg; and railhead was at Rensberg siding, where the battalion arrived on the 15th after a journey full of novel experiences. Owing to want of rolling stock the soldiers were conveyed, not in ordinary passenger carriages, but in open goods trucks. If a company was lucky it travelled in empty trucks, but if there were no "empties" available, the men had to perch on the top of loads of coal or stores, and to cling on for dear life as the train swayed violently in rounding sharp turnings in the line. Every bridge and every important culvert was held by detachments of local volunteers, who as the train approached their post emerged from their improvised shelters to beg for newspapers, and to report that all was well. Every station was guarded by irregular troops, and on the platforms were loyalist ladies, who enthusiastically greeted the Royal Irish, pressing fruit, flowers, and tobacco upon them, and begging for regimental buttons or badges as mementos of the meeting. At every siding stood long trains, shunted to give passage to the troops—some composed of "empties" going back to the base to refill, others laden with supplies of every kind for the front. At long intervals there were halts at stations to give the men time to eat the meals, for which preparations had been made in advance by the Railway staff officers in charge of the line; and as the troop-train gradually neared railhead it passed several villages where French had met and beaten back the enemy while the battalion was still upon the sea.

When the Royal Irish reached Rensberg they heard that they were to reinforce the extreme right of French's main line, then resting on Slingersfontein, a farm ten miles south-east of Colesberg. The burghers, discovering that this post was weakly manned, were becoming aggressive; and only a few hours before, a detachment of New Zealand Mounted Rifles under Captain Madock, R.A., with a handful of the Yorkshire regiment, had found very great difficulty in beating back a determined attack upon two hills, which, rising about four hundred feet above the plain between Slingersfontein and the Boer positions round Colesberg, were held as outworks to the farm. General Clements was placed in command of the Slingersfontein area, and when on the 16th the battalion, now provided with transport waggons and mules, arrived at his headquarters, he ordered Colonel Guinness to occupy these kopjes as permanent detached posts. Three companies marched off to

"Madock's" and "New Zealand hills," as the scenes of the previous day's fighting were now called; the rest of the Royal Irish went on picket; and though the strain of work slightly diminished as the remainder of the 12th brigade successively joined its headquarters, for the next few weeks the battalion was on outpost for two nights out of three. As soon as Slingersfontein was fairly safe, French used it as a pivot for the mounted troops with whom he was trying to find and turn the enemy's left flank, but as to the east and south-east of Colesberg he was checked by commandos in superior and apparently ever-increasing strength, he sought at the other end of his line for opportunities to manœuvre the enemy still farther backwards towards the Orange river. Before he was able to profit by the information gained in his reconnaissances to the north of the village, he was summoned to Cape Town by Lord Roberts, who desired to explain to him personally the part allotted to the cavalry division in the plan of campaign, elaborated by the Commander-in-Chief and three or four of his most trusted advisers since their arrival in South Africa. In a regimental history it would be out of place to describe how the main army was assembled within striking distance of the western frontier of the Orange Free State: it is enough to say that, thanks to the absolute secrecy maintained by the few officers who were in Lord Roberts' confidence, the long and difficult process was effected with remarkable success. The troops were entrained without an idea where they were going; the military railway officials despatched the trains in obedience to orders they did not understand; contradictory and misleading reports were spread broadcast over the colony in order to deceive the enemy's spies and sympathisers. This policy produced the desired result. The burghers, completely puzzled by the information that reached them, failed to penetrate the object of Lord Roberts' movements, and beyond reinforcing the commandos at Colesberg, made no important changes in their dispositions.

As the cavalry division was now required to cover the concentration of the main army, French returned to Rensberg to superintend its transfer to the Orange-River–Kimberley line; and on the 6th of February, after seeing the last of his own troops quietly disappear from the neighbourhood of Colesberg, he made over the command of the district to Clements, whom Lord Roberts had appointed to continue the work hitherto performed by the cavalry commander. The duty entrusted to Clements was no easy one. The detachment left with him was weak in numbers, weaker still in mobility; it consisted of two squadrons of regular cavalry; about 650 Australian volunteers, many of whom had arrived in South Africa as foot soldiers; 450 regular infantry, of whom a considerable proportion were by no means good riders; one battery of Horse, one of Field artillery, and two howitzers; the 12th brigade of infantry and half a battalion of the Royal Berkshire regiment. With this small force he had to maintain himself on a front twenty-five miles in length against a foe whose numbers were now estimated to be between 11,000 and 12,000 men, well armed and mounted, and whose artillery, a 40-pr., five field-guns, and five pom-poms, was by no means to be despised. Clements carried on the system of defence devised by French. Companies or larger detachments of infantry were posted on important points, a mile or more apart, in rough forts built of the stones and boulders with which the hills were strewn. Every opportunity was taken to make these works more secure, and as the Royal Irish plied pick and shovel and crowbar to improve their defences, careful observation was kept on the enemy's big gun, and whenever the 40-pr. was turned in their direction a signal warned them to take cover instantly. Thanks to the vigilance of their look-out men, the Royal Irish, though frequently shelled, were able always "to go to earth" in time, and suffered no losses from the cannonade. The front and flanks of the positions were watched by groups of sentries, concealed from the enemy's view and fire by sangars—the dry-stone breastworks, of which constant use was made throughout the war. Very soon after French's troops had been withdrawn, the burghers discovered that the British facing them had perceptibly diminished in strength, and at once began a series of attempts to turn Clements' flanks and cut off his communications with the rest of the army. Between the 6th and the 11th there was fighting on various parts of the line, and so many shells fell among the tents of the Royal Irish and the Worcester that the camps were removed to less exposed positions.[1] On the 12th, both flanks were severely bombarded and then attacked by riflemen, who succeeded in ousting the defenders of Hobkirk's farm, the post marking our extreme left. At the other end of the line the half battalion of the Worcestershire, which was holding a group of kopjes to the east of Slingersfontein, was hotly shelled, and then exposed to a rifle-fire so heavy that after considerable loss it was unable to retain the whole of the ground entrusted to it, though the greater part was stubbornly and successfully defended till nightfall.

Clements had been obliged to throw every available man into his fighting line, and thus, when his left was turned and his right in serious danger, he had no reserves in hand with which to recapture the lost positions. He decided therefore to retire, and while the troops on the flanks were still able to hold the Boers in some degree in check, he made his preparations to fall back on Rensberg. From details which have been preserved of the way in which the troops were withdrawn from the right of the line, we learn that each of the detachments, scattered over the many miles of country comprised in the Slingersfontein area, received orders to leave its post at

---

[1] One of the shells fell in the tent occupied by the Roman Catholic chaplain, Father Alexander—happily when he was not at home! At Bloemfontein he was succeeded by Father Rawlinson, who was attached to the battalion for many months. The Anglican chaplain was the Reverend —— Wright.

an hour timed to bring it into camp thirty minutes before the column was to march. At about 8 P.M., after all the Kaffirs employed as bullock-drivers had been "rounded up and placed under guard to prevent their bolting," the oxen were inspanned with as little noise as possible, and as each waggon was ready it was sent off to the unit to which it was allotted. The tents were then struck, each corps leaving a few standing to deceive the enemy, and finally the telegraph and signalling stations were dismantled and packed up.[1] While the carts and waggons were returning to the rendezvous of the baggage, a company of the Royal Irish was sent to reinforce a detachment of the battalion in guarding a defile through which the column was about to retire, and when the troops were assembled the march began. Part of the XVIIIth, preceded by a few mounted scouts, formed the advance-guard; then came two guns of the Royal Horse artillery, followed by the whole of the transport vehicles and the remainder of the guns, under escort of dis-mounted troops. The convoy was flanked by infantry, with supports dis-tributed at intervals throughout its length. The rear-guard was composed of the rest of the foot soldiers in column of half companies at column distance, followed by a company in extended order, and covered by the whole of the mounted troops, widely extended. Thanks to the brilliancy of the moonlight and to the fact that the burghers made no attempt to harass the retreat, Clements arrived early on the 13th at Rensberg, where to his annoyance he found that the Boers had anticipated his movements by occupying a range of kopjes, which from the east commanded the railway from Rensberg to Arundel, the next station southward on the line towards Naauwpoort Junction. As the presence of the enemy among these kopjes made it impossible for him to remain at Rensberg, the General determined to fall back on Arundel, which he reached at 5 A.M. on the 14th of February.

Here for a few days he stood on the defensive, his infantry holding positions on the hills, his mounted men demonstrating vigorously on either flank. During this time the *rôle* of the Royal Irish was much the same as that assigned to them at Slingersfontein: four companies held a large kopje to the left rear of the village, and the remainder of the battalion was con-stantly employed on outpost and on fatigues of every kind. The enemy was by no means inactive, and on the 20th attacked Clements in front and on both flanks, but without success; and the good fortune which had attended the XVIIIth throughout the operations at Colesberg continued at Arundel, for though at both places it was frequently shelled and often exposed to the fire of long-range snipers, no casualties occurred while it was serving south of the Orange river. In a short time Clements was reinforced by two field-batteries, two 5-in. guns, a battalion of British militia, and a considerable number of mounted volunteers, chiefly from Cape Colony and Australia;

---

[1] Lieutenant E. M. Panter-Downes, Royal Irish, was in charge of the signallers, and received much praise for his work in the Colesberg-Arundel operations.

and after driving away the detachment of the enemy which was threatening his left rear, he gradually recovered the ground he had abandoned, shelling the Boers out of successive positions, the flanks of which he threatened with his mounted troops. At that moment it was not part of the Commander-in-Chief's plan to strike hard for the Norval's Pont bridge, so Clements' movements were comparatively slow, but on the 28th of February he re-occupied Colesberg without opposition, for as the Boers had heard of Cronje's surrender at Paardeberg,[1] they were now falling back on the Orange river, doing as much damage as possible to the railway in their retreat. Clements followed them, repairing the line as he advanced; and on the 8th of March the head of his column stood on the left bank of the river, facing a considerable number of burghers, who from the other side of the stream exulted in the destruction of the Norval's Pont bridge, the three central spans of which they had blown up. It was impossible to attempt to force the passage of the Orange, as floods rendered it impassable for several days; the pontoon troop did not arrive as soon as it was expected; when it did come up several of the pontoons proved unserviceable, and it was not until the 15th that the river was bridged by a structure, 260 yards in length, supported partly on pontoons and partly on piers extemporised from casks. Large numbers of the labourers employed in its construction were supplied from the ranks of the Royal Irish. As soon as the bridge was practicable, a considerable body of troops crossed at once and established themselves unmolested on the soil of the Free State.

To those who judge of the importance of a military operation by the length of the casualty lists, the work done by the Royal Irish and the other units of the 12th brigade since they landed in South Africa will appear insignificant, as between the 6th of February and the 15th of March the total losses in Clements' whole command only amounted to 327 killed, wounded, and missing. Soldiers, however, will appreciate the value of the part played in this stage of the campaign by General Clements, who, in the words of the official historian, "had to detain the Boers at Colesberg and prevent them from swooping upon the lines of communication south of the Orange—a movement which, if successful, would have caused an outbreak of active disloyalty in large districts of Cape Colony hitherto sullenly quiescent. By maintaining himself between Rensberg and Arundel he fulfilled his chief function, as well as the hardly less important duties of guarding the right rear of the main army, of securing the safety of the important railway junction of Naauwpoort, and incidentally of keeping under his fire a body of the enemy who might otherwise have joined in the opposition to Lord Roberts' march."[2]

---

[1] The mounted infantry of the Royal Irish were present at the relief of Kimberley, and at Cronje's surrender on February 27.

[2] 'Official History of the War in South Africa,' vol. ii. p. 250.

The history of the battalion for the next two months is almost devoid of interest. The Royal Irish formed part of the column which Clements led from the Orange river to Bloemfontein, over a vast and gently undulating plain, dotted at rare intervals with villages whose inhabitants, professing to be tired of the war, readily handed over to the troops a few hundred rifles, some of modern pattern, others so obsolete as to be fit for nothing but a museum of antiquities. On the 4th of April, the 12th brigade reached the capital of the Free State, where it remained stationary for several weeks, fully, though by no means agreeably, occupied in the drudgery which fell to the lot of every soldier fated to garrison any of the towns wrested from the enemy. There was much wood cutting: many fatigues at the railway station: heavy guards and outposts, and frequent route marches. For men whose drill was not perfect there were parades; and when drafts began to arrive from home, courses of musketry and judging distance were carried out for the benefit of the new-comers. The use of the rifle was not the only part of a soldier's trade in which the youngsters required training. As they were ignorant of the art of making themselves comfortable on active service their comrades, who had learned much since they landed at Port Elizabeth, took this branch of their education in hand, and taught the recruits to live together in groups of three men, dividing the work among them: one collected fuel—*e.g.*, cow-dung or scraps of wood; the second looked after the fire and cooked; while the third pitched the bivouac and acted as orderly man to the little mess.

In May the battalion was in great strength, for although exposure, hardships, and enteric fever had begun to take toll, the drafts had more than made good the waste of the campaign. The deficiency of officers was a thing of the past, for many had found their way out to South Africa within two or three weeks of the landing of the battalion at Port Elizabeth, and others had brought out drafts from home. In March six officers and a hundred and ninety-six other ranks joined near Arundel; in April two officers and ninety six men (chiefly from the militia reserve) reached Bloemfontein; and on May 8, two large parties reported themselves to Colonel Guinness: the first consisted of two officers and ninety-six men from the depôt; the second was a company of volunteers—three officers and a hundred and nine other ranks from the 5th (Irish) battalion of the King's (Liverpool regiment). In no war ever waged by Britain has the stream of reinforcements been so abundant, so evenly distributed, and so well maintained as in the long struggle with the Boer republics. The Royal Irish were not more favoured than other corps, yet from the time the battalion landed until peace was declared no less than 1180 non-commissioned officers and men joined headquarters. The second battalion provided 150 seasoned men from India, and eight drafts, 443 in all, were sent out from home by the officer commanding details: the militia battalions of the Royal Irish territorial regiment contributed 423 (exclusive of three officers),[1] and the Irish volunteers in Liverpool furnished a contingent of 164 (also exclusive of five officers).

In years to come, when the nation has realised that for its own safety every male citizen must be trained to arms, students of regimental history will wonder how so many partially instructed troops found their way into the ranks of the Royal Irish. Neither the militia nor the volunteers were liable to serve abroad in case of war, but as has been said in Chapter x., in the militia a reserve of men had been established, picked for physique and character, who in return for a small annual retaining fee had assumed the liability to serve in time of war as regular soldiers in any part of the world. As soon as the reserve of the regular army was called out, these men were summoned to the depôt of their territorial regiments, and gradually sent out to the battalions in South Africa. The militia reservists joining the Royal Irish were for the most part hardy, though not highly trained peasants who after a short experience in the field became very valuable soldiers. When the United Kingdom began to understand that the campaign in South Africa was developing into the most difficult and arduous war she had waged for nearly a century, all branches of the Auxiliary Forces volunteered for active service. The regiments of Yeomanry became the nucleus of the mounted force sent to South Africa under the name of Imperial Yeomanry : many militia battalions went out as complete units, and volunteer battalions were permitted to form from their ranks companies of picked officers and men, whose function it was to reinforce the infantry of the line at the seat of war. The Royal Irish were fortunate in their volunteer company, which was well officered and composed of men mostly Irish by descent, whose trades as engineers, boiler-makers, fitters, carpenters, and bricklayers had developed both their muscles and their brains. The company landed on March 11, but on its way up country, to use the slang of the South African war, it was "snaffled on the L. of C.," or in other words, detained at various posts on the lines of communication, where all ranks learned so much of their duty in the field that a week after they joined at Bloemfontein they were considered fit to take their turn at the outposts : and in the forcing-house of active service they speedily developed into a very useful body of men.

When the militia reservists and the volunteers reached Bloemfontein it was anything but a cheerful place, for enteric still raged in the hospitals, and the road to the cemetery was daily trodden by long processions of soldiers, bearing on their shoulders stretchers whereon rested the bodies of the comrades whom they were carrying to the grave. To counteract these

					Officers.	Other ranks.
[1] 3rd battalion Royal Irish regiment (formerly Wexford militia),				. .	2	136
4th	,,	,,	,,	(formerly North Tipperary militia), .	1	127
5th	,,	,,	,,	(formerly Kilkenny militia), . .	...	160

X

depressing influences the officers organised rifle meetings, inter-company football matches, and athletic sports of various kinds. The effect of these amusements was good, but better still was the news that the brigade was once more to take the field, when on the 17th of May General Clements was ordered to entrain his command to Winburg, a little town about sixty-five miles north-east of Bloemfontein.

Since the battalion had landed at Port Elizabeth the military situation had improved marvellously. Ladysmith, Kimberley, and Mafeking had been relieved. Lord Roberts had forced his way across the south-east of the Free State, captured Cronje with 4000 burgers at Paardeberg on February 27, and entered Bloemfontein on March 13, to find that the enemy had scattered northwards before him in panic. When the burghers who faced Gatacre and Clements in the north of Cape Colony heard of Cronje's surrender, they fell back into the east of the Free State, leaving rear-guards to watch the Orange river, and if possible prevent the British from crossing it at Bethulie and Norval's Pont. Lord Roberts' first care on reaching the capital of the Free State was to join hands with Gatacre and Clements; to make himself master of the railway from Bloemfontein to the Orange, and to secure the waterworks on which the troops were dependent for pure water. From the country west of the railway no serious attack was anticipated, but as there was danger that the large number of Boers who had betaken themselves to the mountainous regions in the east of the Free State might rally, destroy the waterworks, and cut the railway — the line of communication with the coast—the Commander-in-Chief sent a strong mounted flank-guard into the hills east of the waterworks, while with smaller detachments he covered the right or eastern side of the railway. At the end of March and beginning of April these flank-guards were overtaken by a series of misfortunes: the largest and most important was defeated with heavy loss at the waterworks in an engagement known as Sannah's Post; the second was captured at Reddersberg; a third narrowly escaped a similar fate by a hasty and exhausting retreat;[1] at Wepener only did we still hold our ground. Yet, though these reverses were annoying, their effect was very transitory, for the Boers failed to seize the opportunity of falling upon the railway, and by frittering away their strength in an unsuccessful siege of Wepener allowed an uninterrupted stream of supplies to reach the army at Bloemfontein. Strengthened by large reinforcements from England and from Natal, Lord Roberts then began a series of manœuvres by which he succeeded in pushing the enemy backwards towards their eastern fastnesses, and at the end of April the danger to the line of communication was so greatly diminished that he was free to resume the main object of the campaign.

[1] According to the Official History, one part of this detachment marched 45 miles in 36 hours; the other covered 73 miles in 52 hours.

The Commander-in-Chief's plan was as vast as it was simple. Upon Pretoria, the capital of the Transvaal, were to converge several columns working on a front nearly three hundred miles in length. On the extreme right of the line, General Buller was to sweep the Boers out of the mountains of northern Natal, where they had established themselves after they had been obliged to abandon the siege of Ladysmith. Far away on the extreme left, a force, based on Kimberley and commanded by Lieutenant-General Hunter, was to relieve Mafeking and invade the Transvaal from the west. Lord Roberts was to lead the main army along the railway from Bloemfontein to Pretoria, with his left covered to some extent by Lieutenant-General Lord Methuen, who was to move northwards through the west of the Free State; his right was to be guarded by two strong columns under Lieutenant-Generals Ian Hamilton and Colvile,[1] while to Lieutenant-General Rundle, who commanded the recently landed 8th division and the body of South Africans styled the Colonial division, was entrusted the duty of preventing raids upon the railway between Bloemfontein and the Orange river by commandos from the hilly country east of the line. The area which Rundle had to watch has been described as "the granary and the manœuvre ground of the Orange Free State, a region dotted with towns and villages, wealthy in crops, and abounding in the water-courses, ridges, and kopjes on which the Boers had fashioned their favourite tactics. Here men could both hide in safety and subsist in ease; the harvest of the past year had been too rich for its owners to be willing to desert their stores. The region, in short, formed an irresistible attraction both to farmers and fighting men; and it flanked the British communications from end to end."[2] In a series of successful skirmishes Rundle gradually pushed the enemy before him, and by the middle of May his line stretched from Clocolan to Winburg. Lord Roberts had entered Kroonstad on the 12th, and so satisfactory did the situation in the south-east of the Free State then appear that a redistribution of the forces was sanctioned, in the course of which the 12th brigade was ordered from Bloemfontein to Winburg.

For a few days after its arrival the battalion was employed in building sangars at various points round the town, and as no enemy appeared to test these works many a young soldier thought that his labour had been wasted; but this was not the case, for when at the end of August the place was suddenly attacked, the fortifications thrown up by Clements proved of great value in the defence, in which some of the mounted infantry of the regiment took part. On May 26, the battalion started for the town of Senekal, now

---

[1] A large party of the Royal Irish mounted infantry served in Hamilton's column.

[2] Official History, vol. iii. p. 105. This part of the Orange Free State had been the scene of a long series of wars with the Basutos, whom the original Vortrekers (the pioneers of the Dutch emigration from Cape Colony) had gradually driven back into the mountains of Basutoland.

the advance base in the eastern Free State, and during a three days' "trek" realised the truth of the camp saying that the march of a British column in South Africa could be traced by "bully-beef" tins and dead animals, for the dreary, dusty, khaki-coloured plain was littered with empty rations cases, and with the carcases of mules and oxen abandoned by the troops as they pressed forward to the front. With this very uninviting piece of country the Royal Irish were destined to make further acquaintance, as during the month of June they furnished several strong escorts to convoys over the forty miles of road between Senekal and the railhead at Winburg. The 12th brigade remained nearly a month at Senekal, where the Royal Irish, who spent two nights a-week shivering in the works round the town, became painfully aware that though the winter days on the veld are glorious the nights are abominably cold.

While the battalion was at Senekal the Free State burghers under Christian De Wet had taken the initiative in the eastern part of their republic: they had made prisoners of considerable detachments, captured large and valuable convoys, and by breaking up the railway at several points to the north of Bloemfontein had interrupted the line of communication with Pretoria, where Lord Roberts, after occupying Johannesburg, had hoisted the British flag on the 5th of June. Among the measures at once taken by the Commander-in-Chief for the pacification of the Orange Free State was the formation of strong flying columns to penetrate into the districts in which the burghers were still in arms. One of these columns was to be commanded by Clements, who, with his own brigade and that of Major-General A. H. Paget (the 20th), was to march upon Bethlehem where a considerable number of the enemy were known to be assembled. With nearly 5000 men[1] Clements left Senekal on June 28, bound in the first place for Lindley, a village forty miles to the north-east, where he

---

[1] Composition of Clements' column on June 28, 1900 (from Clements' Staff Diary):—

2nd Bedford regiment	854
2nd Worcester　,,	846
1st Royal Irish　,,	892
2nd Wiltshire　,,	903
8th Battery R.F.A.	136
2 guns 5-in. 6th Co. R.G.A.	63
1 section ammunition column	17
1 section 38th Co. R.E.	32
2nd Brabant's Horse and 2 companies Yeomanry	696
16th Imperial Yeomanry	237
Malta M.I.	133
Royal Scots M.I.	67
12th brigade Field Hospital	38
12th brigade Bearer Company	33
12th brigade Supply Depôt	9
	4961

was to join hands with Paget before moving towards Bethlehem. The column marched in what the troops called "the picture-frame formation": half battalions in very extended order formed the front, sides, and rear of a vast hollow square, covering two or three miles of ground, while the mounted troops scouted widely in every direction. At Klipplaat Drift, three miles from Senekal, the Boers opened fire upon the advance-guard with four guns, a pom-pom, and a maxim, and made so stout an opposition that Clements had only gained seven miles when the approach of night obliged him to bivouac, with the enemy still in strength on his front and flanks. Though most of the work fell on the mounted troops, part of the Royal Irish regiment was engaged during the afternoon. A young officer who had recently brought out a number of recruits to the battalion thus describes his experiences in this, his first engagement: "The regiment was the left flank-guard. It was the first time that many of us had been in action, and we realised the truth of the saying that 'it takes a ton of lead to kill a man,' for though for several hours we were under a hot rifle fire from invisible enemies at more or less effective range, with shells falling among us, I don't think we lost more than one man killed.[1] Our militia reservists were splendid in their ignorance of danger. As the bullets were whistling over their heads one of them was heard to ask his comrade whether 'it was the birds making that noise!' He must have been brother to the man who, when ordered to set his sights at a prescribed range, explained his failure to do so by saying that he 'didn't know figures.'"

Before daylight next morning the mounted troops dashed upon a ridge about a mile and a half from the bivouac, forestalling the burghers in its occupation. The Boers thereupon fell back in the direction of Bethlehem, leaving a rear-guard who first harassed the troops by long-range "sniping," and then disputed the passage of a drift at the Zand river. In the course of this day's skirmishing a private in the battalion was wounded.[2] After Paget and Clements joined hands they turned towards Bethlehem, thirty miles to the south-east of Lindley, and pushed through bodies of the enemy who, though they appeared unwilling to commit themselves to anything but a feeble skirmish, watched every movement with the eyes of a lynx, determined to lose no opportunity of punishing any carelessness on our part. Thanks to Clements' vigilance, his column was very little harassed on the march, but a strong flank-guard on Paget's left was very roughly handled: a battery was rushed, and for several minutes the guns passed into the hands of the burghers, from whom they were rescued only after a sharp fight.

Clements bivouacked on the 5th of July at Bontjeskraal, about eight miles north-west of Bethlehem, and with a column greatly reduced in

[1] & [2] See Appendix 2 (Q).

numbers by the absence of the Malta mounted infantry [1] and the Bedfordshire, who by the order of the Commander-in-Chief had been sent back to
garrison the village of Lindley, he advanced early next morning through
scenery thoroughly characteristic of this part of South Africa.   A broad
valley, bounded by flat-topped, square-sided kopjes bare of vegetation and
forbidding of aspect, descended by a gentle slope towards the belt of rolling
downs by which Bethlehem is encircled and commanded on every side.
As the Royal Irish, who were in advance-guard, cautiously made their way
down this valley, they caught distant glimpses of the trees and scattered
houses of the settlement, standing like an oasis of civilisation in a wilderness of veld, while far to the south the horizon was bounded by the
mountains of the Brandwater Basin — range upon range of fantastically-
shaped peaks white with freshly fallen snow, as yet unmelted by the morning
sun.   The troops had little time, however, to admire the weird beauty of
the scene, for the burghers had revealed their presence by shelling the
outposts at dawn, and as the advance-guard began to debouch it came
under fire from the position, strong by nature and improved by fortification, where five thousand men with seven pieces of artillery awaited our
attack.   From Vogelsfontein, a farm three miles north-east of the town,
their line curved outwards along the western rim of the depression in
which Bethlehem stands, and then turning sharply to the east ended at
Volhuter's Kop, a grim pile of rocks dominating all the approaches from
the south.   Before Clements allowed the advance-guard to become seriously
engaged, he sent a flag of truce to the officer in command of the burghers
to demand the instant surrender of the town, but after receiving a laconic
refusal from Christian De Wet [2] he began to carry out the scheme already
concerted with General Paget.   The enemy's flanks were first to be turned by
the mounted troops and then assaulted by the infantry; the 20th brigade

[1] So called because the officers and men belonged to regiments stationed at Malta at the beginning
of the war.

[2] The correspondence was as follows :—

"I, Ralph Clements, Major-General, having full power from Field-Marshal Lord Roberts, G.C.B.,
&c., Commander-in-Chief of Her Britannic Majesty's forces now in South Africa, hereby demand the
surrender of the town of Bethlehem to me by 10 A.M. this day, Friday, July 6, 1900—failing which I
shall bombard the town.

"The inhabitants are hereby informed that should the town surrender, and subsequent to its
surrender any firing takes place at the troops under my command when occupying it, the town will be
shelled and burned.   R. CLEMENTS."

"To well-respected Sir R. CLEMENTS.

"RESPECTED SIR,—In connection with the missive you have addressed dated 6th July to the village
of Bethlehem I have, your Excellency, herewith to state that no reply can be given.

"The responsibility will rest on you for the blood of innocent women and children in case you should
bombard the town.—I have the honour to be, Sir, &c.,

"C. R. DE WET,
Chief Commandant."

was to carry Volhuter's Kop on the south; the 12th brigade to make itself master of Vogelsfontein farm on the north. The plan was a simple one, but it miscarried, as owing to the great length of De Wet's position, the difficulties of the ground, and the failure of the mounted men on our extreme left to make their way over a rocky watercourse, the movements of the infantry were greatly delayed, and though late in the afternoon Paget won a little ground, the 12th brigade made no material progress, and when night put an end to the engagement neither of the enemy's flanks had been turned, or even threatened seriously.

When the 12th brigade deployed, the Royal Irish were on the right, the Worcestershire on the left, the Wiltshire in support. About 1 P.M. the XVIIIth advanced in column of double companies, widely extended, the leading companies each formed in two lines of skirmishers with ten paces interval between the men and two hundred yards' distance between the lines. Very soon shells from guns scattered along a ridge about five thousand yards to the eastward began to fall among them, and for a time our artillery gave no great help, until a field-battery dashed through the ranks, caught up half a company to serve as escort, and pushed on to a ridge where it came into action. The burghers at once turned their pieces against the audacious battery, and thanks to this diversion the battalion had been able to move forward to within rifle-shot of the enemy's trenches, when an order brought it to a halt. For the rest of the day the Royal Irish remained stationary, skirmishing with the enemy in their front, annoyed by marksmen concealed in the houses of the town, and enfiladed by rifle and maxim fire from a hill upon their right. So biting indeed was the musketry from this hill that to escape it one of the companies was forced to take cover in a donga, where it remained till nightfall, when the XVIIIth was ordered to withdraw and bivouac at a farm out of range of the enemy's rifles. In the opinion of the rank and file the only good point in this weary day's work was that though the battalion had been engaged for several hours it had only two men wounded, but the General knew that the time had not been wasted, for he had seen so much of De Wet's position that he was able to recast his plans, and had now determined, while not relaxing his efforts to turn the flanks, to deliver a crushing blow at the centre of the Boer line, where it rested on a hill half a mile to the north-west of Bethlehem.

Long before daybreak on the 7th the troops began to take their places for the renewed attack; and the Royal Irish stumbled over the uneven surface of the veld until they were halted at daybreak by Colonel Guinness, who pointed out to his officers the dim outline of a kopje, just visible in the uncertain light. This hill, he said, General Clements considered the key of the position: it was to be taken at all cost; the Royal Irish had been selected to deliver the assault, and three companies of the Wiltshire regiment were to support them in second line. As the mists of dawn gradually cleared away the officers realised that their objective was the very hill from which their right had been harassed by musketry on the afternoon of the 6th; they knew that it was strongly held, for a patrol from one of their outposts, reconnoitring it during the night, had heard the voices of many burghers talking in the trenches; and they could see that a long slope, bare of cover and exposed throughout to the enemy's fire, led up to its crest, where two guns had been posted within the last few hours. If our gunners succeeded in beating down the defence, the hill would be comparatively easy to carry; but if the stress of battle compelled them to turn their projectiles in another direction, many a good soldier would fall before the day was won. As soon as it was light enough for the artillerymen to see, the field and 5-in. guns opened a slow, well-aimed cross-fire upon the hill, and the Royal Irish prepared for the attack. Colonel Guinness formed his battalion in three lines: the first consisted of B company; the second (the supports) was composed of H, G, and C, in the order named from right to left; in the third (the reserve) were F, E, and D companies. One company, A, which had been on outpost all night, did not rejoin till the position was nearly won. The supports and reserve were in lines of columns of half companies, whose extensions were not to exceed three paces. Before 7 A.M. the scouts of B company became warmly engaged with the burghers, who could be seen in strength upon the hill; Captain Daniell reinforced them with half his company (H), and then for a long time a fierce fire-fight raged, the Boers trying to crush B company with musketry and shrapnel, while Daniell's men kept up a vigorous fusilade to cover the supporting companies, which were gradually making their way into the front line. D company ranged up on the left, the volunteers on the right; while still farther to the right G company came into action, firing heavy volleys. The expenditure of cartridges was great, and during this phase of the combat the pouches of D company were replenished at least four times by the ammunition carriers, who, to quote from Captain Daniell's diary, "walked about, backwards and forwards, up and down the firing line without the slightest fear. I specially noticed a lad named Hanrehan and Lance-Corporal Ryan, the company tailor." Whenever the officer commanding a company considered it was possible to push on, the subaltern or sergeant in charge of each section selected two soldiers, who dashed forward for about thirty yards, and then dropping on the ground covered the advance of their comrades with their shots. Then followed another pair, and yet another, until the whole of the section was in its new position, when its commander, who had superintended the movement, in his turn dashed over the bullet-swept ground. Troops less highly trained, less perfectly disciplined than the Royal Irish, would have required an officer to head them in these rushes, but the men of the

XVIIIth could be trusted to advance and to carry out their orders without such leading; the difficulty was not to get them to go on, but to prevent their going on too fast and too far. Whenever the ground was favourable the companies were "pulled together" and steadied, to prepare them for the next rush. A sergeant in the Royal Irish thus describes his impressions of

> "the first fair stand - up fight the regiment had been in during the war. We advanced to a real attack such as you read about in text-books, over comparatively level ground affording scarcely any cover, and with due attention to intervals between individuals and firing line, supports, and so forth. A very frosty morning, bright and bracing; a steady controlled fire to greet us as we deployed for attack; a G.O.C. implicitly believed in by every man in the battalion; a C.O. who possessed every one's confidence; and officers in front (too much so indeed) to lead the way—such were our surroundings. In the ranks one cannot see much in a general engagement, but I have a distinct recollection of there being a total lack of confusion during the action: signals, words of command, were quickly responded to; the passing of orders was rapidly carried out; volunteers for every purpose were numerous; wounded men were instantly cared for and taken back to the dressing-station by the stretcher-bearers."

The battalion gained ground, but not rapidly, for the opposition was considerable and the firing line had been again reinforced, when just as the leading men had reached a belt of burned grass, on which their khaki clothing was unpleasantly conspicuous, they were brought to a sudden halt by a donga—a natural moat protecting the part of the hill on which the enemy's guns were posted. As this donga was impassable, the only thing to do was to turn it; and each company successively moved off to the right in perfect order, circled round the head of the obstacle, and then re-formed in the required direction as steadily as though on parade in a barrack square. At this moment our bombardment swelled into a violent cannonade. Our musketry had already made itself felt among the defenders of the hill, and when the shells began to rain upon them, the burghers, who, in the words of an artillery officer, "had hitherto stuck to their work like men," lost heart, and gradually quitted their trenches, leaving to a few of their gunners the task of saving the guns. These gallant fellows succeeded in getting one away in safety, and did not cease their efforts to remove the other until a mass of Royal Irish, yelling like demons and with bayonets fixed, were within a couple of hundred yards of them. Then they turned and fled for their lives, and the gun, one of the 15-prs. lost by the 77th battery at Stormberg, once more passed into the hands of its lawful owners. While part of the battalion established itself on the crest of the hill, where a long line of trenches, cut deep into the rock, showed how diligently the Boers had fortified this part of the position, the remainder was held in readiness to push forward into the town. But with the capture of the hill the engagement virtually ended; Paget, with the help of two companies of the Royal Irish, made himself master of Volhuter's Kop almost without loss: Vogelsfontein was occupied without resistance, and the burghers streamed away in full retreat, followed only by the shells of the artillery, for the mounted troops (chiefly Imperial Yeomen and Australian Rifles) were still too new to their work to be launched in pursuit of an enemy who never proved more formidable than in a rear-guard action. The comparative ease with which the Boers were driven out of Bethlehem was owing to the fact that De Wet had learned that a column of British under General Hunter was moving down on him from the north;[1] as he felt unable to make head against this reinforcement, he had only fought to gain time for his main body to join the large number of Free Staters, who from behind the Wittebergen range faced General Rundle and the 8th division. To this is due the small number of casualties on the 6th and 7th of July, together amounting only to a hundred and six killed and wounded—a total to which the Royal Irish contributed almost half. Among the officers Captain J. B. S. Alderson was mortally, and Captain T. Warwick-Williams (volunteer company) slightly, wounded; of the other ranks, two were killed, four died of their injuries, and forty-seven were wounded.[2]

As soon as the engagement was over the troops were allowed to fall out and cook their food; fires sprang up everywhere, and while some of the men made porridge from meal found in a neighbouring farm, others tried to convert the burghers' pigs into pork. An officer thus describes the scene: "One of the volunteers pursued a very old beast with a field-telegraph pole poised above his head; when he got within striking distance he brought it down with a crash, but of course by the time it reached the ground the pig was well away. Then up galloped one of Brabant's Horse, who with bayonet fixed tried to use his rifle as a hog-spear; he lunged at the pig, missed it, buried his bayonet in the ground, and came a lovely cropper off his horse. This old pig was a wary brute, and after running many risks, escaped unhurt." In the course of the afternoon some of the officers of the battalion were allowed to visit Bethlehem, which they found no better and no worse than the other towns in the Free State. In this part of South Africa every settlement had the same general characteristics. In the middle of an unpaved, undrained, and evil-smelling market square was a large church, built at the expense of the congregation by an architect who apparently took a barn as his model of ecclesiastical architecture. The square was fringed with the most important buildings in the place—the government offices, the bank, the

---

[1] The greater part of the Royal Irish mounted infantry were in this column, see p. 367.

[2] See Appendix 2 (Q).

stores, and the hotels—not standing side by side, but apparently dropped down from the sky at random, with great gaps between them, where loose cattle roamed at will. The dwelling-houses were scattered along the roads leading from the church to the open veld. Those belonging to British traders and to burghers who had acquired a veneer of European civilisation stood in pretty gardens, gay with flowers and planted with trees, and looked like small "villa residences" transported from a London suburb to the wilds of South Africa. The abodes of the old-fashioned Boers, on the other hand, were nothing but cottages built of sun-dried bricks, without a tree, a flower, or a blade of grass to mitigate their hideousness.

A few hours after the occupation of Bethlehem General Clements issued this general order:—

"The G.O.C. wishes to congratulate the force under his command on the way in which it has acquitted itself during a trying time since it marched from Senekal. The mounted troops had very hard work, and have seen a good deal of fighting. The artillery have performed most excellent work and made excellent practice. The infantry have had hard work, continuous marching, and done excellently while in contact with the enemy. The Royal Irish regiment particularly distinguished itself to-day. To one and all the thanks of the G.O.C. are due, and he has the utmost confidence that the 12th brigade force as now constituted will continue to maintain the high reputation it has already won."

CHAPTER XV.

THE FIRST BATTALION.

1900-1902.

SOUTH AFRICA (*continued*).

SLABBERT'S NEK: THE BRANDWATER BASIN: BERGENDAL: MONUMENT HILL:
LYDENBURG: THE MOUNTED INFANTRY OF THE ROYAL IRISH REGIMENT.

Two days after Bethlehem was taken, General Hunter's column entered the
town, and Clements fell back towards Senekal to obtain the supplies of
which his men were much in need. After a week's halt at Biddulphs-
berg, the 12th brigade was recalled by General Hunter, now in command
of the whole of the troops in the eastern Free State, to take part in a
great combined movement against the burghers who had retired into the
hilly region drained by the river Brandwater, and locally known as the
Brandwater Basin. It is bounded on the south by the river Caledon, the
frontier of the native state of Basutoland, whose savage warriors, longing
for a pretext to attack their hereditary enemies the Boers, stood ready to
resist any violation of their territory, and thus forbade the passage of the
stream. To the west, north, and east the basin is enclosed by high, almost
continuous ranges, which, springing from the right bank of the Caledon,
form a huge horse-shoe, whose northern foot-hills sink into the plain a few
miles south of Bethlehem. This mountain wall is about seventy miles in
perimeter, and is crossed at five places by roads fit for wheeled traffic: the
western face (the Wittebergen) is pierced by Commando Nek, the northern
by Slabbert's and Retief's Neks, the eastern (the Roodebergen) by Naauwpoort
Nek and the Golden Gate. Very soon after Hunter arrived at Bethlehem, he
decided to fight his way with part of his force into the Brandwater Basin
from the north and west, and to drive the burghers into the arms of detachments posted at the mouths of Naauwpoort Nek and Golden Gate: but
before this plan could be carried into effect he had to wait for supplies of
food and ammunition, and it was not until a fortnight after the occupation of

Bethlehem that his troops were ready to begin work. On July 21st, his army was thus distributed: Rundle with the 8th and Colonial divisions stretched from Ficksburg to Senekal; the brigades of Clements and Paget lay at Wit Kop and Witnek, a few miles north-west of Slabbert's Nek; the Highland brigade (the 3rd, under Major-General MacDonald), stood at Bethlehem ready to march on Retief's Nek; and Major-General Bruce-Hamilton with the 12th brigade, to which part of the Royal Irish mounted infantry had been attached, commanded the exit from Naauwpoort Nek. Next day orders were issued for a general attack along the whole of the western and northern line; Rundle was to bombard Commando Nek, while Clements and MacDonald assaulted Slabbert's Nek and Retief's Nek respectively. Clements advanced on the 22nd to Bester's Kop, the enemy's outposts retiring before him towards Slabbert's Nek. He had only two of his four battalions at that moment with him, for the Worcestershire had been temporarily detached, and the Bedfordshire had not rejoined from Lindley.

During the night, the draft of ninety-eight non-commissioned officers and men, with whom Major Lysaght had joined the battalion on the 18th, had a rough introduction to the joys of campaigning in South Africa: there was a great storm; rain fell in torrents; many of the horses broke loose and stampeded in every direction, and when the Royal Irish fell in after a hurried meal of sodden biscuit and bully beef, they were wet to the skin, and longed for the excitement of a fight to get their blood once more in circulation. But the General's plans had been kept secret, and the Royal Irish, who were in advance-guard, had no idea that an action was imminent, and trudged wearily over the rough surface of the rolling down, scarcely glancing at the curious line of isolated kopjes which, at intervals of a mile or more, rose like watch towers across their path. Suddenly distant firing was heard; at the sound of the guns the XVIIIth stepped out vigorously, and soon discovered that Brabant's Horse, the cavalry screen to the column, were being shelled by the defenders of Slabbert's Nek. As Clements reconnoitred this formidable position, he found that its difficulties had not been exaggerated by his guides—loyal Britons settled in the Free State, who at the outbreak of the war had placed their local knowledge at the disposal of the Intelligence department. The Nek, or pass, ran through a defile about half a mile in width, overhung by steep, almost precipitous mountains, and its entrance was partially barred by a low rounded knoll, with smooth glacis-like sides, seamed with trenches which swept the ground to the front and flanks. To the left of the defile, as he looked at it, was a long square-topped kopje, with cliff-like walls that only a goat could climb: to the right stretched another kopje, higher, longer, and more irregular in shape, with five great spurs projecting from its rugged flank. Above these spurs rose a series of ledges, like the steps of a gigantic staircase; the hillside was strewn with boulders and honeycombed with caves, and the topmost peak raised its snowy crest nearly two thousand feet above the plain. The greater part of this kopje was held by the left wing of the enemy, and Clements realised that until he had taken it he could not hope to force the pass ; therefore, as soon as his flanks were covered by mounted troops, and his artillery had begun to shell the trenches on the Nek, he directed Lieutenant-Colonel Grenfell, with part of his corps (the 1st Brabant's Horse) and a few Imperial Yeomanry, to seize one of the projecting spurs. This mission the irregulars fulfilled, but when they began to scale the ledges they were brought to a standstill by a furious burst of musketry ; the General at once ordered two companies of the Wiltshire to occupy a spur on the right of that ascended by Brabant's Horse, and directed the Colonel of the Royal Irish, who were then about five thousand yards from Grenfell's spur, to send two companies to reinforce the dismounted troopers. The choice fell on G (Captain Gloster) and H (Captain Daniell), the former being in command of the whole detachment.

After a stiff climb, H company joined Grenfell on one of the ledges or steps in the kopje, where they found Brabant's Horse hotly engaged with the burghers, who held two tiers of rocks, the lower four or five hundred yards up the hillside, the higher about two hundred yards farther off ; another body of the enemy enfiladed the ledge from a donga. In an hour or two Gloster joined Daniell, prolonging the line to the left, where, to quote from a letter of Lieutenant Kelly, a subaltern in G company, "we fired wildly at where we thought the enemy were, for we could not see a man, but had a good idea, as they were shooting uncommonly straight. Brabant's were on the same ledge with us, and a real cheery lot they were—quite delighted with everything and full of jokes." Just after the Royal Irish had snatched a mouthful of food, a message arrived from the General, "as soon as you have occupied the spur, send two companies to the top of the hill." Gloster and Daniell reconnoitred the ground, and decided to "rush" the next belt of rocks, Gloster working up to them from the right, while Daniell made a dash across the open. After sending for ammunition and filling the men's pouches, Gloster moved forward with half his company, leaving Kelly with the remainder of G company to support his advance with musketry. Following the plan made by the two captains, Daniell gave Gloster about ten minutes' start, and then pushed on from both flanks, but though Kelly kept up a vigorous fusilade upon the ridge of rocks, the immediate object of the combined attack, the enemy was unshaken, and the bullets fell like hail among the men of H company as they ran up the slope. Suddenly Gloster's half company began to appear on the right, moving in such a way as to come under the musketry of Kelly's party, who from their position could not see Gloster's men ; the danger was so imminent that Daniell himself ran back across the fire-swept zone and ordered Kelly to follow him to the ridge, now held by the leading troops. When they reached the front line they found that Gloster, mortally wounded, was sinking rapidly. Again to quote his subaltern: "he had reached the top quite under cover, and in his usual dashing manner was pushing forward in front. He climbed up and looked over a rock; and seeing some Dutchmen quite close, raised his rifle, and as he did so was shot, as was another man in exactly the same way. The bullet passed through the right fore-arm and chest. He was a really gallant fellow, and died nobly." When Daniell thus succeeded to the command of the detachment, the situation was very unpleasant. The ledge upon which the men crouched was so commanded by the enemy's fire that every time a soldier peered over it he drew a storm of bullets: and on the left front the burghers seemed to be in force within twenty or thirty yards of our position. The men were anxious to avenge Gloster's death with the bayonet, but a charge was impossible, for it could only have been delivered on a very narrow front and under converging fire. There was nothing for it but to lie under the crest of the ridge, to keep the men on the alert by shooting at the rocks behind which the Boers were ensconced, and to report by signal that any farther advance would be attended by very serious risk. Fortunately, cartridges never ran short, as the ammunition carriers were able to reach the firing line under cover from the left rear, where Lieutenant Panter-Downes with a few men showed so determined a front that he kept the burghers at a respectful distance, and prevented them from enfilading Daniell's party.

While Gloster's detachment was struggling for foothold on the hill the battalion marched towards the foot of Grenfell's spur; on the way two companies (D under Captain Milner and F under Captain White) were diverted to the left front to watch the burghers in the trenches on the pass. The plain that these companies had to cross looked perfectly level from a distance, but in reality was a series of undulations over which without a landmark it was difficult to move in the right direction. Such a landmark was found in a cluster of Kaffir huts, but the Boers had taken the range accurately, and when D company passed between the kraals it was greeted by a storm of bullets, by one of which Captain Milner was dangerously wounded. Neither company halted until it was about nine hundred yards from the works on Slabbert's Nek, with whose defenders for the rest of the day they exchanged a slow but steady fire; and from the right of D's line the Boers who were facing Gloster's party could be plainly seen; "but," writes an eye-witness, "we did not dare to shoot much at them, as they were too much mixed up with our men."

As two companies were acting as escort to the guns, the main body of the XVIIIth was now reduced to two companies of regular soldiers and one of volunteers. This skeleton battalion was finally halted about eighteen hundred yards to the left rear of Grenfell's spur, and in widely extended lines, lay for many hours exposed to the shots of marksmen, who were so well concealed that they offered a very poor target in return. The headquarter companies of the Royal Irish had nothing to do except to fire an occasional round in the direction from which the enemy's bullets came; to listen to the bursts of musketry from the hill, and to wonder how long the shells of a pom-pom playing on them from the Nek would continue to fall among the regiment without doing any harm. Happily only one of these horrible little projectiles found a billet: it shattered the big drum, greatly to the amusement of every one, except the drummer, who was fast asleep beside it. The damage to the drum was soon avenged by a 5-in. shell, which smashed the pom-pom and blew several Boer gunners to pieces.

When darkness put an end to the combat, the result of the day's operations seemed meagre in the extreme. Brabant's Horse and Gloster's detachment of the Royal Irish had doubtless made a lodgment on the hill to the right of the pass; but they could do no more than hold their ground, and could expect no help from the two companies of the Wiltshire, who had failed to establish themselves on the spur which they had been ordered to seize. The works on the Nek had been vigorously bombarded, but their defenders appeared to be unshaken by the shells of the artillery and the threatening presence of Paget's brigade on the left of the guns. But the General was in no way dispirited, for excellent news had reached him in the afternoon. An officer of Brabant's Horse, who with a small party of mounted men was watching the outer flank of the big kopje, heard that Grenfell and Gloster were "held-up" on the ledges, and determined to ascertain if there was no other way to the top of the hill. By "a most daring and successful reconnaissance" on foot, he discovered a track leading to the summit, running well to the right of the ledges, through ground apparently unoccupied by the enemy. When Clements received this report he saw that once he had gained possession of the top, he could outflank the burghers facing Brabant's Horse and the Royal Irish, drive them before him into the Nek, and then rake its defences with rifle-fire. As it was then too late to attempt any important movement, he ordered a squadron of Brabant's (dismounted) to be at the summit by daybreak next morning, promising them the support of four companies of the Royal Irish and two of the Wiltshire regiment, who were not to follow the path discovered by the officer of Brabant's, but to ascend by a ridge still farther to the right. While most of the infantry bivouacked on the ground they stood on, four companies of the Royal Irish were assembled, and moved to the farmhouse fixed as the rendezvous of the little column. At 4 A.M. on the 24th Lieutenant-Colonel Guinness, who commanded the combined force, began to ascend the kopje, described by General Clements as "an almost unclimbable hill"; four hours' desperate scrambling brought the Royal Irish, breathless and exhausted, to its highest crest, where they found the dismounted troopers of Brabant's Horse, who moving by a shorter and easier route had gained the summit some little time before their comrades of the XVIIIth. Hitherto the march had been unopposed, but now a few shots were fired by burghers who appeared more anxious to retire than to fight. Part of the infantry then joined hands with G and H companies whose adventures during the night will be told later; the remainder drove the enemy before them, turned the works upon the Nek, and swept them with musketry from the left rear. A great burst of cheering greeted the appearance of the Royal Irish on the top of the hill; a general advance was ordered; the Boer resistance suddenly collapsed, and by 11 A.M. Clements was master of Slabbert's Nek.

An officer has supplied the author with a very spirited account of the proceedings of the headquarter companies, from which the following extracts have been taken:—

"We arrived at the farm about 7 or 8 P.M. on the 23rd, without transport, and consequently without blankets or food, on the coldest night I remember having spent during the war. After seeing the men settled and giving them leave to break open their emergency rations, we went into the farm building. Here the Wiltshire officers who had arrived before us, had already made themselves comfortable before a fire in the kitchen, and had a chicken roasting for their breakfast. There were six of us, and we had had nothing inside us since dawn—hence lowering of the moral sense and theft! We had only two emergency rations among us: we ate them: they were excellent, but not enough, and we eyed that bird hungrily until the Wilts nodded: then some one suggested the eating of that chicken. We needed very little persuasion to tear it limb from limb, and we devoured it hastily, like house-breakers at supper in a burgled house! The anger of the Wilts was great when a couple of hours later they awoke; they did not suspect us at the time, thinking we had been all asleep, and their wrath was directed against the men. So warped had our sense of right and wrong become that it was not until we had dined them next day in camp that we gave ourselves away. . . . After a few hours' sleep we — *i.e.*, A, D, F, and the volunteers, and two companies of the Wiltshire, started on our night march, led by Colonel Guinness and a guide, and a more miserable time we never had. It was bitterly cold, with a Scotch mist blowing sharply down from the hill above us. The necessity for secrecy forbade our smoking, and the effort to keep from coughing, kicking down stones, and otherwise making a noise was very trying. The track lay up a 'razor-edge' sort of ridge, very slippery and strewn with boulders. The higher we climbed the more difficult it became, until finally we were 'clawing up' on hands and knees, and the last bit, just as there was a glimmer of light, was the worst of all: we had to pull each other up by our rifles, yet, with precipitous ground all around us, we lost not a man."

The column had now reached the shoulder of the kopje, and rested on the snow-covered ground for a short time while Colonel Guinness and the guide

Y

looked for a path towards the top.   The path, when found, proved to be a mere goat-track, on a narrow ledge with a wall of rock on the right hand and a precipice on the left.   On this track there was only room to walk in Indian file, and

"we were about half-way across this bit when the fog lifted a little and showed us what a giddy path we were following.   It also showed us a few slouch-hatted figures on a spur below us.   I can tell you we company officers were fairly alarmed, caught as we were in a place where move-ment of any sort, except fore or aft, was impossible, so it was to our great relief that we discovered these men to be a handful of Brabant's scouts.   A few shots were fired at us at about 8 A.M. when we got to the real top of the hill, by a few Boers, some on a knoll below us and others to our front, but these men soon cleared out.   The fog was now lifting rapidly and the sun came out as we advanced down into position on the knoll overlooking the Nek itself and the Boer line of retreat.   Heavy firing had been going on since dawn, down where the rest of the brigade was, and across the valley where Paget's brigade was also trying to force the pass.   For some time we saw nothing, then a few small mounted parties of Boers were seen riding off towards Fouriesberg.   We opened fire, the range I think being about a thousand yards.   This was the signal for a regular bolt of the whole Boer force.   We fired rapidly on them, but I don't know if we did much execution firing at such a steep angle downwards.   Our right was hurried forward down the hill, but the steepness and difficulty of the ground prevented our getting much closer. By the time we had got well down, practically all the Boers had cleared out.   It was wonderful to see how the men bucked up.   Before the firing began they were moving about like a lot of cripples, 'dead to the world,' and anxious only to get a few minutes to sit down and sleep in.   The moment they realised what was going on, all this was thrown off and they were as happy and as energetic as a parcel of schoolboys."

While the headquarter companies of the battalion were doing this fine piece of rock climbing, G and H were clinging to their ground with the utmost determination.   As soon as it became dark Daniell had posted the men with him, about a hundred of all ranks, along the ridge in little detachments of three or four; in front of each post lay a sentry, flat on his stomach, peering over the rocks to watch the movements of the enemy.   Up to mid-night the Boers "sniped" assiduously; then the fire died away, and Daniell and Kelly moved constantly up and down the line to make sure that the soldiers, lulled by the sudden silence and exhausted by hunger and fatigue, had not fallen asleep.   About 4 A.M. on the 24th, Panter-Downes brought up the remainder of H company: while this welcome reinforcement was being posted there was an alarm, caused by the approach of a number of Kaffirs whom the Boers had sent to reconnoitre the position: the men promptly lined the top of the ridge, and speedily gave the burghers to understand that the Royal Irish were quite ready to receive them! When day broke, says one of the officers who was present—

> " we quickly found out that the enemy were still there, but they had left the rocks on our left, so we occupied them. They ' hotted ' us for a bit, but as soon as the companies appeared on the top of the mountain they began to disperse. The guns kept up a hot bombardment, and very soon we could see the enemy beating a retreat all round. We sent down for water and food, made ourselves comfortable, and watched the enemy retire. Brabant's brought up our gun and the Hotchkiss, and made some splendid practice among the Boers as they left a hill, and we saw a good many of them knocked over. . . . We received tremendous congratulations for our part in the battle, especially the charge up the hill. . . . We buried poor Gloster and five men by a tree at the foot of the hill." [1]

The capture of Slabbert's Nek cost only forty-four casualties, of which many occurred among the Royal Irish. Captain W. Gloster was killed; Captain E. F. Milner was dangerously wounded; six of the other ranks were killed, and ten wounded, three of whom died of their injuries. [2]

In General Clements' report of July 26, he gave high praise to the 1st battalion, Royal Irish regiment, in these terms—

> "Lieutenant-Colonel H. W. N. Guinness has again proved himself a commanding officer of the first class. His battalion has throughout proved itself to be all that could be desired on service. His leading of a force on the 24th of July over an almost unclimbable hill, and by this means turning the enemy's position at Slabbert's Nek, is deserving of special mention.
>
> "Captain W. Gloster, who I regret to say was killed while leading his company at Slabbert's Nek on the 23rd of July, was an officer of great promise. By his death the Service loses a most valuable company leader.
>
> "Captain E. H. Daniell has proved himself a first-rate company leader in difficult circumstances by the handling of his men on the 23rd and 24th of July, on both of which dates he showed great gallantry.
>
> "Lieutenant J. A. M. J. P. Kelly did particularly good service on the night of the 23rd of July, in leading his men over an open space, 300 yards wide, swept by a heavy cross-fire, and maintaining his position all night at close quarters (20 yards) from the enemy who were holding the rocks and caves in his front."

In the same report General Clements stated that Major K. P. Apthorp, who was temporarily employed as an intelligence officer on his staff, had afforded him " very great help until taken prisoner on June 6."

---

[1] When the author visited Slabbert's Nek in 1907 he found the grave well kept, and marked by handsome cross of white marble. The graves at Bethlehem were also in good order.

[2] See Appendix 2 (Q).

The following non-commissioned officers and private soldiers were also mentioned :—

No. 4512, Lance-Corporal P. Doyle;[1] No. 4248, Lance-Corporal M. Tytherleigh; No. 4868, Lance-Corporal J. Rathbone; No. 1408, Private —— Baker; No. 4129, Private —— Ryan; and No. 5024, Private P. Dumphy, particularly distinguished themselves on the night of July 23. No. 4506, Private J. Kavanagh, who showed remarkable courage and coolness on the same occasion, was wounded while carrying a message across ground heavily swept by fire.

As soon as General Clements learned that the Highland brigade had driven the Boers from Retief's Nek, he marched two or three miles along the road to Fouriesburg, the chief town in the Brandwater Basin, and then encamped. The halt was very welcome; an officer writes, "we were all very much done up, especially those who had been in Colonel Guinness's night march, and after a good 'square' meal and a double issue of rum (Reger, our Quartermaster, surpassed himself on this occasion) there were few of us awake that afternoon." Next day the whole of Hunter's army was in motion. MacDonald was sent to help Bruce Hamilton in the task of sealing the mouths of Naauwpoort Nek and the Golden Gate, the passes by which the Boers might dash eastward into the open country round Harrismith, the principal town in that part of the Free State. Clements and Paget marched through a fertile country, well watered and full of prosperous farms, towards Fouriesburg, whither Rundle, who had dislodged the burghers from Commando Nek, was also hastening. As the advance-guard of the 8th division was the first to reach the goal, Clements' and Paget's brigades were halted a few miles from Fouriesburg, and did not move again until the 27th, when they entered the place after a feeble opposition from a few snipers dropped by the main body of the enemy who, still ignorant that British troops awaited them at the eastern passes, were retreating at speed towards Naauwpoort Nek and the Golden Gate. But though most of the burghers were hurrying eastward, it was necessary to ensure that no detachments should break out through Slabbert's, Retief's, or Commando Neks, and so heavy was the call upon the infantry to garrison these defiles that Hunter could only muster five battalions to drive the Boers into the net spread by MacDonald and Bruce Hamilton. One of these was the 1st battalion, Royal Irish regiment, which with part of the Wiltshire formed the advance-guard under Clements on the 28th, when the burghers fought a rear-guard action near Slaap Kranz ridge with great tenacity and cunning. The position proved to be a very strong one, and Clements was unable to oust the enemy from it, though his artillery and infantry were engaged throughout the day. Colonel Guinness was

---

[1] Lance-Corporal Doyle was promoted to be corporal on July 26, 1900.

anxious to be allowed to seize a commanding knoll in front of the left of the Boer line, which seemed to offer a good base for an assault upon the pass itself, but General Clements considered that the Royal Irish had done enough for the day, and ordered a battalion of the Scots Guards, recently arrived on the field, to occupy it. At midnight they advanced on the main position and found it undefended, for the Boers, after checking the whole column for many hours, had silently disappeared when they saw that the odds had become too heavy for them to face. The casualties of the day amounted to thirty-four killed and wounded, the Royal Irish losing one man killed and five wounded.[1]

With the encounter at Slaap Kranz the campaign in the Brandwater Basin came to an end. De Wet had always opposed the policy of retreating into the mountains of Fouriesburg, but his views had been over-ridden, and, as mentioned on page 330, he had fought Clements at Bethlehem to gain time for the main body to complete its concentration in the valley of the Brandwater. When he arrived there with his rear-guard, he set himself to convince the members of his very unruly army that the fastnesses to which they had betaken themselves would prove not a sanctuary but a trap, and urged them to follow him in a bold dash into the open veld. His rough eloquence appeared to convince the majority; his scheme for breaking out of the mountains was accepted, and on the night of July 15, he made his way with two thousand six hundred men across Slabbert's Nek, and headed northwards, in the full belief that within twenty-four hours the remainder of the burghers would follow him. But as soon as De Wet's commanding personality was removed the Free Staters fell into confusion; instead of carrying out the plan to which they had agreed they began to quarrel among themselves; they lost precious days in wrangling over the choice of another leader, and by the time that Hunter's columns were advancing upon the passes they had become demoralised, suspicious of their chiefs and of each other. Dry rot spread so rapidly among them that on the 30th, Prinsloo, who claimed to have been elected General-in-Chief, surrendered with 4140 men, three guns (two of which had been lost by the Royal Horse artillery at Sannah's Post), 4000 horses and ponies, many waggons, a large number of rifles, and a million rounds of small-arm ammunition.

The Royal Irish saw enough of the prisoners to form an idea of the manner of men with whom they had been fighting since the beginning of the year. The first impression was one of utter astonishment. Was it possible that this motley crowd of civilians formed part of the burgher levies which for many months had constantly opposed and frequently defeated the British army? Some were old men with long white beards; others

[1] See Appendix 2 (Q).

were in the prime of life; others, again, were lads not half-way through their teens; none wore a vestige of uniform, and the majority were dressed in clothes so badly cut that no self-respecting peasant in Europe would have condescended to wear them. Yet among the captives every grade of society in the Free State republic was represented: there were land-owners, who possessed tens of thousands of acres and great wealth of flocks and herds; members of Parliament; civil servants; merchants; lawyers; doctors; and last, but by no means least in numbers, "bywohners," or poor Boers, who, as they had no land of their own, were allowed to squat on the estates of their richer neighbours. The land-owning class, as a rule, were magnificent men, well-grown, sturdy, and inured to hardships; constant hunting on their farms had made them good rifle shots and excellent judges of distance,[1] and, as has already been mentioned, many of them had served in campaigns against the Kaffirs. In character they much resembled the British yeomen of two hundred years ago, for although brave, patriotic, and hospitable, they were ignorant, obstinate, and deeply distrustful of new men and new ideas. A certain number of the professional classes had been sent in their youth to Europe to complete their education; their travels had greatly widened their intellectual horizon, and as they did not stay away long enough to lose their sporting tastes or their hereditary instinct for irregular warfare, they proved a valuable asset in the Boer army. In dress as well as education these younger men presented a curious contrast to their fellow-citizens, who were still as uncouth in speech and manners as the original pioneers of the Free State, while the Europeanised burghers were dressed in well-cut Norfolk jackets, boots, and breeches, and spoke English admirably with accents acquired at the Universities of Oxford, Edinburgh, or Glasgow. The very baggage owned by the prisoners when they surrendered showed how wide a difference there was between the old school and the new. The old-fashioned burghers, however rich they were, had gone on active service with their few belongings packed in old and shapeless carpet-bags; the youngsters took the field with kit-bags or suit-cases imported from England.

General Hunter's success in the Brandwater Basin, to which the Royal Irish contributed not a little, was far-reaching in its results; in the words of the official historian "it removed in a moment the possibility of attack in force from the west, which had kept Sir Redvers Buller's army chained fast to the railway from Heidelberg down to Ladysmith. True, De Wet, Olivier, and other guerillas were still at large, but, vagrant and weakened,

---

[1] In South Africa every estate in the country is called a farm, but this is a misnomer, for no Boer landowner (at least before the war) thought of working his estate as a farm in the European sense of the word. He was indifferent to agriculture, and devoted his land to the raising of stock. By Australians the Boer farms would be called runs; by Canadians from the north-west of the Dominion they would be described as ranches.

they were unlikely seriously to raid Natal across the Drakensberg, an eventuality which had never been absent, and with reason, from Sir R. Buller's mind. None had known better than he how vulnerable still that many-gated colony was to incursions which would have undone in a few hours the heavy work of months." [1] Now General Buller was able to organise a mobile force to march northwards against the Pretoria-Komati Poort railway in order to co-operate with Lord Roberts in the invasion of the Eastern Transvaal, where the remnants of the Boer army still kept the field. In this great movement the Royal Irish were destined to play their part, for on the 1st of August Clements' brigade left Hunter's army; on the 9th it marched into Kroonstad, and after many halts and delays on the railway reached Pretoria on the 18th. It was one of the peculiarities of the war in South Africa that no General could hope to keep his brigade intact for any length of time; so far Clements had been fortunate, but now his turn for dismemberment arrived, and after bidding farewell to the commander whom they admired and respected deeply, the Royal Irish were sent off to Belfast, a station on the Komati Poort line, where they joined Major-General Smith-Dorrien's brigade (the 19th) in a column commanded by Lieutenant-General Ian Hamilton. [2]

The battalion was not actively engaged on the 27th of August in the battle of Bergendal, though some of the companies on outpost came under long-range artillery fire from the formidable position astride of the railway, which Lord Roberts and Sir Redvers Buller attacked respectively in front and flank. When the Boers fell back from their carefully prepared entrenchments they retired at first along the railway; but under the dis-

[1] Official History, vol. iii. p. 380.

[2] In Hamilton's Force were soldiers from all parts of the British Empire. The Divisional troops were Brabant's Horse (South African volunteers); two batteries of Royal Field artillery; four guns of a Canadian volunteer battery; the "Elswick battery," manned by artisans, volunteers from the north of England; two 5-in. guns, and a section of pom-poms.

Mahon's Force was composed of a battery of Royal Horse artillery; a section of pom-poms; the Imperial Light Horse (South African volunteers); Lumsden's Horse (volunteers from India, largely recruited from planters in Behar); a battalion of Imperial Yeomanry (volunteers from the Old Country); a squadron of Hussars, and mounted volunteers from Queensland and New Zealand.

Infantry brigades—Smith-Dorrien's: the first battalions of the Royal Scots, Royal Irish, and Gordon Highlanders, and the mounted infantry of the City Imperial volunteers; Cunningham's: 1st battalion King's Own Scottish Borderers, 2nd battalion Royal Berkshire regiment, 1st battalion Argyll and Sutherland Highlanders.

The Engineers, Ammunition and Supply Park, Hospitals, and Bearer Companies were all supplied by the regular army.

The strength of Smith-Dorrien's Infantry units was as follows :—

	Fit for duty.		Sick at headquarters or on detachment.	Total.
	At headquarters.	On detachment.		
1st Royal Scots	1206	61	121	1388
1st Royal Irish	868	239	199	1306
1st Gordon Highlanders .	741	236	153	1130

spiriting influences of this, its latest defeat, the burgher army soon began to fall to pieces. One column struck southward; a second hurried eastward towards the Portuguese frontier; while a third, commanded by General L. Botha, turned northwards and headed for the maze of hills by which the town of Lydenburg is surrounded. This detachment made so firm a stand at Badfontein that Sir Redvers Buller, who had been entrusted with its pursuit, asked for reinforcements, and General Ian Hamilton was sent to his help with the greater part of his column. Starting from Belfast on September 3, Hamilton, after two days' hard marching and continuous skirmishing, succeeded in placing himself on the right rear of Botha's entrenched line at Badfontein; the Boers thereupon drew off eastward to Paardeplaatz, a huge mountain within distant cannon-shot of Lydenburg. As a preliminary to dislodging the burghers from this new position, the British troops occupied Lydenburg during the morning of the 7th; in the afternoon, after the bivouacs had been formed, the soldiers were allowed to bathe in the creeks; they were splashing about in the water, when suddenly two 6-in. guns began to fire from Paardeplaatz, ten or eleven thousand yards off, and an unlucky shell killed two men of the battalion and dangerously wounded another.[1] The Royal Irish were at once moved to a place of safety, and for the rest of the day had the satisfaction of watching the Boer gunners waste invaluable ammunition upon the empty shelters of the bivouac. Next day (the 8th) Paardeplaatz was carried by the British troops. The Boers held a precipitous hill, 1500 feet in height, and shaped exactly like a horse-shoe: the only track ran to the farthest point of the shoe up an ever-narrowing ridge, cleft asunder in various places by deep dongas, almost impassable even by infantry. Two 6-in. guns commanded the path, and lighter guns and pom-poms were posted on various points along the crest. Hamilton was ordered to attack in front and to turn the left flank, while Buller worked round the right of Botha's line. Although the turning movements involved several hours of hard marching and scrambling, the frontal and flank attacks were delivered simultaneously, and carried the position with a rush. A wing of the Royal Irish (F, G, H companies, and the volunteers) under Major Hatchell were the first troops to reach the topmost ridge, which commanded the enemy's only line of retreat, a natural causeway a few yards wide, with deep precipices on either side of it. This road was crowded with Boers, who, after saving their guns, were now in full retreat; the mass presented a splendid target for musketry, but just as the men were bringing their rifles into play down fell a mountain mist, completely veiling the burghers from their view. To pursue amidst the precipices in such a fog was impossible; the only thing left to do was to fire volleys in the direction

[1] See Appendix 2 (Q).

taken by the enemy, who is said to have suffered some loss from these unaimed bullets. The British casualties were small; and in the Royal Irish only one man was wounded.[1]

Hamilton now returned to the railway, and then moved eastwards towards Komati Poort, over country in places so difficult as to be almost impassable. For instance, part of his route lay over hills so steep that in the ten miles between Godwaan station and Kaapsche Hoop the track rose 2200 feet. To lighten the loads, the wooden cases enclosing the biscuit tins were removed, and the soldiers were made to carry their second blankets, usually transported in the waggons. As the column toiled up the steep inclines, the troops hauled the vehicles after them by main force, and when the descent began, each waggon was held back by ten men, who steadied it with drag-ropes down the worst places on the road. Though Hamilton encountered none of the enemy, the march was in many ways an exciting one. A company of the battalion was crossing a railway bridge only wide enough to carry a train, when the sound of an engine was heard in a cutting hard by, and an officer who was present wrote—

"I know my hair stood on end. A scramble ensued, which is rather amusing to *look back upon.* Some of us just slipped over the edge and hung on by the sleepers, with the torrent, thirty or forty feet below, to fall into, and rocks to land on if you missed the water. The train was, however, pulled up before getting on to the bridge, and all got safely over. I believe the rear-guard saw a lion on the last march down the Kaap valley into Kaapmuiden. One of the men in my company woke up one fine morning to find a snake asleep beside him. It was with some difficulty he was able to persuade his fellows he was not a de Rougemont, and when at last they carefully pulled off the blankets—the wretched fellow was sweating at every pore with fright —they discovered a particularly venomous-looking puff adder coiled up between his legs! The snake was duly killed, but I imagine that man will never forget the horrible five minutes he must have spent before persuading those around he was not blarneying them."

On September 25, Hamilton caught up the advance-guard of the army at Komati Poort, where an amazing amount of stores and railway plant had been found, but no enemy. On the approach of the British the burghers had broken into small bands and disappeared along the Portuguese frontier; some returned to their homes and either took no further part in the war or joined our side; others, to whom all honour as brave and determined enemies is due, reassembled to form the guerilla bands which kept the war alive for twenty-one weary months after the Boer army had ceased to exist as a formed and organised body of men.

[1] See Appendix 2 (Q).

The troops composing Hamilton's column received his thanks for their exertions in a general order, dated October 1, 1900—

"General Ian Hamilton wishes to congratulate his force on the fine work which has been performed by them since they marched out of Belfast on September 3rd, 1900. During this period they have driven the enemy out of his most formidable selected positions—first on the main Lydenburg road, where they barred the progress of the Natal arms; and secondly, on the height overlooking Lydenburg itself. They have also encountered and overcome every sort of natural obstacle, and have carried the British flag through tracts of waterless bush, and over ranges of lofty mountains to the most remote frontier of the enemy. All this has been done with so much spirit, and so cheerfully, as to excite the G.O.C.'s greatest admiration, who will take the first opportunity of informing Lord Roberts of the splendid work done by all ranks under his command."

In an unofficial letter, written after the war was over, General Smith-Dorrien stated that of all the troops which came under his orders in South Africa, "none served me more loyally or gave me less trouble than the Royal Irish; I have nothing but pleasant associations to remember with regard to the time I had the honour of having the battalion under my command."

The Royal Irish spent a few days in clearing the railway and in attending a review of the British troops, held in honour of the birthday of the King of Portugal, and then were ordered to entrain for Belfast; the journey, by no means an uneventful one, is vividly described by Captain Dease.

"The regiment returned from Komati Poort in several trains, as there was an excess of rolling stock on the line which wanted moving up towards Pretoria. The Boers had made quite a mess of things on the railway. They had fired great numbers of trucks and disabled a good many engines. The big bridge across the Kaap at Kaapmuiden had also been destroyed, and rather cleverly too. They had blown down the upper part of one of the piers, got steam up in one of the heavier "Free State Railway" engines, set it going from Kaapmuiden station, and succeeded in absolutely smashing up the damaged pier, as well as the spans on either side. The volunteers and C company did most of the work on the building of a deviation and temporary bridge, which was taken in hand immediately. We left Kaapmuiden at about 5 P.M. on the 30th September. As I had had some mechanical training as a boy, I took on the driving of the second train, in which were most of our officers. The first train was given five minutes' grace before I was told to start. My fireman was a corporal in the Royal Scots, I think, who had 'been on' a traction engine at home, while the second man was also a soldier from some other regiment, with an equal recommendation for his present job! I myself had a fair knowledge of locomotive work, but (at that time) little of the vacuum brake: anyway, I certainly had not sufficient knowledge of the work for the job in hand. All went well till we got to the deviation and bridge we had made over the Kaap. Here the fun began. The road up the other side was at so steep a gradient that I couldn't get my train up it. We stopped and rolled back over the bridge. A second try met with as little success. It then occurred to my fireman and myself that if we 'backed' up the grade behind the bridge, and then rushed forward down on to the bridge the momentum would carry us over. This it did, but the train must have had a narrow escape of wrecking that frail, temporary structure. After this we proceeded 'with caution,' going not more than about 10 miles an hour. Darkness fell about three or four miles beyond the Kaap bridge. The 'road' here runs along the sides of hills, with a steep slope to the Krokodil Valley, a couple of hundred feet below. Naturally the curves are very sharp, and cuttings numerous. I was very 'jumpy' at the time, not knowing the road and uncertain of myself as a driver, and kept the speed down. It was fortunate I did so, for as we rounded a corner a group of men on the hillside shouted to me to 'stop,' 'danger,' &c. I jammed down the air-brake hard and shut off steam, bringing the train up with a terrific jerk, to find the buffer of my engine within a few yards of the rear of the train in front. The sudden pull up had caused quite an upset in the trucks behind, as the jerk was hard enough to roll everyone and everything in the trucks over. We found that the driver of the first train's engine (also an amateur like myself) had allowed the water to run too low in his boiler, melting the plug over his fire-box, and rendering the engine totally useless. We were still talking about our narrow escape when suddenly round the curve behind us were seen the front lights of a third train. We happened to have no 'tail lights,' and before warning could be given our train had been run into with a terrific smash from behind. For a few minutes the confusion was indescribable. Then things straightened themselves out. A piquet was sent some distance down the line to prevent another train colliding with the third train, and parties went to work extricating the injured. The extraordinary thing was that although quite a number of trucks had been 'piled up' in our train, nobody was killed, and only about thirty or forty hurt. One of the latter was Deane-Morgan : he had been standing on the edge of a culvert when the crash came, and, without thinking, he involuntarily took a step backwards, and dropped about thirty feet or so into the bed of a nullah. He hurt his knee badly, but no bones were broken—another extraordinary escape.

"We spent that night and part of the next morning clearing away the wreck, and at last arrived at Krokodil Poort, the next station, in the afternoon. The journey thence to Waterval Onder was exciting only to me on the engine, as it was performed through the night, but peaceful to everyone else."

After these adventures the Royal Irish reached Belfast on the 4th of October, and at once relieved the troops then holding the outposts round the town, where the duty was so heavy that when the Commander-in-Chief ordered the battalion to Pretoria to represent Ireland at the formal annexation of the Transvaal to the British Crown, only three companies could be spared to take part in the ceremony. Along the whole of the Pretoria-Komati Poort railway, as indeed on all the lines throughout the theatre of war, every station was held as a fortress; every train was guarded by soldiers;[1] every bridge and almost every culvert absorbed a detachment, great or small, for its defence; while flying columns were often required to disperse the guerilla bands which threatened weak points on the line of communication. Until December, the Boers in the eastern Transvaal occupied themselves chiefly in train-wrecking; but on the 28th of that month they stormed a strongly entrenched post at Helvetia, captured a large number of men, and carried away in triumph a 4.7-in. gun. Encouraged by this success, they determined to attack the posts along eighty miles of railway; the stations at Pan, Wildfontein, Wonderfontein, Belfast, Dalmanutha, Machadodorp, and Nooitgedacht were to be assailed simultaneously, though the main effort was to be against Belfast, where a great depôt of stores and much ammunition formed a prize worth striving for. Though the headquarters of three battalions were stationed at Belfast, the Colonels of the Royal Irish, the Shropshire Light Infantry, and the Gordon Highlanders could muster between them no more than 1300 men — a small number of foot soldiers with which to furnish outposts, guard the town and guns, and reinforce threatened points on the enormous perimeter of fifteen miles rendered necessary by the formation of the ground around the place. The remainder of the garrison consisted of two hundred and eighty of the 5th Lancers, a hundred and eighty mounted infantry, a battery of field artillery, and two 4.7-in. guns.

Belfast was defended by three main groups of works, more of the nature of detached posts than of outposts in the ordinary acceptation of the term. South of the railway the Gordon Highlanders were in charge of a long stretch of rising ground; on the other side of the line the Shropshire Light Infantry held Colliery Hill, to the north-west of the town; while the Royal Irish were responsible for Monument Hill, a kopje two miles north-east of the centre of Belfast, and for one of the 4.7-in. guns, which was posted upon it. These hills, three miles apart, were linked by a party of mounted infantry at a drift half-way between them. Early on the 7th of January, 1901, Major Orr's detachment at Monument Hill was relieved by Captain Fosbery, who was in command of his own company, A, and of D company (Captain Milner); Lieutenant Dease was the only subaltern with the party, which consisted of ninety-three officers, non-commissioned officers and men. Fosbery at once began to improve and complete the partially finished defences he had taken over from his predecessor, but the number of workers at his disposal was not great, for D company had just returned

---

[1] The experience gained after some months of escorting trains is epitomised in the instructions issued by the Chief of the General Staff, which will be found in Appendix 7.

from an exhausting spell of train-escort duty, and as he wished to allow Captain Milner's men time to rest, he kept them in reserve and gave them little to do. By sundown, however, much had been accomplished, and when General Smith-Dorrien came to visit the post he was satisfied with the progress made, though he disapproved of the loopholes, which he directed should be altered, but owing to the darkness it became impossible to carry out this order, and its execution was postponed till the morrow.

The top of the hill is a plateau about eight hundred yards long, and less than a quarter of a mile in width: at the northern end a rough stone sangar, four feet high, enclosed the 4.7-in. gun: farther to the south a semicircular trench partly surrounded the tents occupied by D company: a short way down the south-western slope of the hill a blockhouse of stone and sods was virtually completed, and scattered along the perimeter of the plateau were eight small trenches, two of which were not yet fit for use. By the scheme of fortification the whole of the post should have been ringed with a strong barbed-wire fence, but at nightfall this portion of the defences was not completely finished. After Fosbery had sent two sections to a subsidiary post connecting Monument Hill with the left of the Gordon Highlanders, there remained in hand six sections, which he thus disposed for the night. Two sections of A company were to man the perimeter trenches, with a sentry posted a few yards in front of each; the remaining section of A with the maxim was to act as a support in the sangar, from which, as will be seen, the 4.7-in. gun had been withdrawn; the three sections of D company were to sleep in their tents, but to be ready at a moment's notice to line the trench near their little camp. In the course of the evening a mist settled down upon the country round Belfast, so heavy that in the town itself the range of vision was limited to twenty yards; on Monument Hill it was like a London fog, and effectually prevented patrolling to the north-east, east, and south-east, where the precipitous sides of the kopje fell into broken ground, difficult even by day to search with any degree of thoroughness. Thus the safety of the post was entirely dependent on the vigilance and sharp hearing of the sentries in front of the trenches.

Nothing occurred to disturb the garrison of Belfast until midnight, when heavy firing, beginning at Monument Hill, then spreading to Colliery Hill, and finally raging at the Gordons' posts, showed that the burghers had surrounded the town and were assailing it vigorously on every side. From information obtained by the British officers captured during the engagement, it is known that General L. Botha, who had under him about two thousand men, had allotted to the Ermelo commando the task of driving the Gordon Highlanders from the southern works: the Middelburg commando was to engage the Shropshire Light Infantry at the Colliery, but not to press home the attack until General B. Viljoen, with seven hundred and fifty of the

Johannesburg and Bocksburg commandos, had made himself master of
Monument Hill—a post which was to be carried at all cost, not only on
account of its tactical importance, but also because the burghers were determined to capture the big gun which they thought was left at night on
the top of the kopje. Fortunately, during the 7th, General Smith-Dorrien had
decided that it should be dragged down the hill and back into the artillery
lines at nightfall; and thus the gun was preserved from the fate which
overtook the defenders of the sangar in which the Boers expected to find the
piece of ordnance they coveted so earnestly.

Owing to the fact that of the three officers on Monument Hill one was
killed and the others wounded and carried away by the enemy, the official
report of the part played by the Royal Irish is necessarily somewhat
meagre. But, thanks to a narrative prepared by Captain Dease, and to
information supplied by others who were present, it is possible to form some
idea of the desperate struggle for the possession of the hill. The night
piquets were posted at dusk, and the officers of A company divided the duty
between them, Fosbery taking the watch till 2 A.M., when Dease was to
relieve him. Everything was quiet till about a quarter to twelve, when
Dease, who was in a shelter near the tents of the reserve, heard a distant
challenge, followed almost immediately by the report of a rifle. Nothing
happened, and as nervous sentries often fired at imaginary enemies, no one
was disturbed by the single shot, though, as it turned out, it was fired not by a
British soldier but by a burgher, who when the sentry at the north-east trench
challenged, shot him dead. Dease was trying to go to sleep again, when
two more rifles rang out; he dashed out of his shelter, and with Fosbery,
whom he met in the fog, hurried to the centre of the plateau to ascertain the
cause of the firing. On the way they came under a sudden fusilade from a
party of Boers who, after scaling the northern and north-eastern slopes of the
kopje, had surprised and carried a couple of the trenches, thus establishing
themselves inside our line of works. The two officers rushed forward and
reached the gun sangar just as the burghers were advancing upon it.

"The fog," writes Captain Dease, "at this time was extremely dense,
and the position of the enemy could only be distinguished by the flashes
of the rifles. The Boers at first concentrated on the maxim gun, and a
tremendous hand-to-hand combat took place. Our men used their
bayonets with effect, and some of the machine gunners (who had slung
their rifles in an abortive effort to get the gun to work) set-to with
picks, axes, and anything they could lay hands on. In short, as the men
said, 'it was the father and the mother av a fight!' The enemy suffered
so severely that they ceased trying to get over the sangar wall, but
remained a yard or two on the far side, pouring in a terrific rapid fire
at the crest line of the sangar. It is difficult to be clear about the
sequence of events, but I think that among the eighteen men originally

in the sangar there were only one or two casualties during the hand-to-hand part of the fight; but during the next phase, when the Boers contented themselves with sweeping the crest, we lost very heavily, for our fellows, the lust of battle on them after the hand-to-hand fight near the machine gun, exposed themselves in a most reckless manner, and were with difficulty prevented from getting out of the sangar and charging into the enemy. The action had continued for about half an hour, when the Boers made a second rush on the gun, and being met at that point by a mere remnant, forced us back. At this moment, as we were gradually drawing back towards the entrance to the sangar, 3733 Private J. Barry,[1] who was nearest the maxim, picked up a pickaxe lying near it. As he forced his way to the gun through the Boers, efforts were made to stop him, and he had just time to drive in the point of the pick into the junction of the barrel and breech-casing before he was literally swept down by a hail of bullets from the enemy round him.[2] As he was shot at by about a dozen burghers within five yards' distance and from all sides, I fancy they must have played havoc in their own ranks! Fosbery now realised that the position in the sangar was untenable, and shouting out to us to 'charge through the entrance and make for the blockhouse,' led the way. The Boers were there in great force, and we were met with a very hot but unaimed fire. Only Fosbery, Corporal Gorman, and myself took part in this charge; all the rest of us were either killed or wounded. About ten yards from the entrance Fosbery, in trying to club down a Boer with the butt of his carbine, was wounded in two places: I got a few yards farther, and while occupied with a couple of the enemy in front was hit on the head by a butt-ended rifle, and temporarily stunned: Corporal Gorman, I think, surrendered, but of this I am uncertain, as I was too busy to notice what he was doing, as he was behind me. When I recovered consciousness about ten, perhaps twenty, minutes later, I searched for and found Fosbery, who was still alive. I did what I could in the way of first aid, but he was hopelessly hit and had already lost a great deal of blood. The Boers were so close to him when they shot him down that his clothing was scorched all round the wounds. A little after this I suddenly ran into a group of wandering Boers, and having lost my carbine when I was knocked over, was easily collared and put under escort. But of this and all subsequent proceedings I can remember nothing. I had been singularly unfortunate in the fight in jamming my revolver (a Service Webley) as I reloaded it. It was no good to me, and I can remember using it as a missile during the charge—I hope with effect! A carbine that night was a useless weapon for officers. We had no bayonets, and the short length of the stock and barrel placed us at a great disadvantage in the hand-to-hand *mêlée*."

While the support was fighting desperately in the gun sangar against overwhelming odds, most of the piquets on the perimeter were swamped by sheer weight of numbers. Their trenches were of a type found very useful

---

[1] Barry had served with the 2nd battalion in the campaigns on the north-west frontier of India.

[2] The machine gun was recaptured a few months later by the Royal Irish, and was presented to the regiment by the Secretary of State for War in 1904.

by the battalion in actions where it had been exposed to continuous bombardment, such as those in the Colesburg campaign—narrow slits in the ground, 2 feet 6 inches wide, nearly 5 feet deep, loopholed with a parapet 2 feet in height and at least 3 feet in width. But excellent as this pattern had proved elsewhere, it was not a success in very close fighting at night, for the trench was so deep that its occupants could not see over the parapet, and the loopholes were ill adapted for firing on an enemy at a few yards' range. Around these works parties of Boers, from twenty to two hundred strong, suddenly loomed up out of the fog and closed rapidly from all sides upon the defenders, whom they covered with their rifles, demanding instant surrender. Though thus caught in an absolute death-trap, most of these little groups of four or five soldiers showed fight, not laying down their arms until one or more of their number had been killed or wounded. Here Lance-Corporal Dowie, a veteran who had served in the Egyptian war of 1882, met a glorious death. He was in command of a small trench, which he succeeded in holding during the first assault: he refused to surrender, though he must have realised that resistance was hopeless, and with his men continued to fight on desperately until a number of burghers, rushing in from behind, overwhelmed the party and left Dowie dead in the work he had defended so gallantly.

The reserve fared no better than the piquets or the support. When awakened by the sound of battle, the men of D company manned the broad and shallow trench by which, as it has been said, their tents were enclosed, though very incompletely. At first the attack came from their front and right, but after the capture of the sangar had made the Boers masters of the northern end of the hill, a fresh body of the enemy fell upon them from the left rear. There was a short, wild struggle; then the burghers surged forward, and hemmed in the men of D so closely that many of them could not use their bayonets, and while the Boers in front seized the muzzles and pointed them in the air, those behind knocked our men down with the butts of their Mauser rifles. By this time Captain Milner was severely wounded: and those of his company who were not killed, wounded, or prisoners ceased to be a formed body of troops. Singly or in small groups they tried to make their way towards Belfast, but in the fog they stumbled across large parties of the enemy, into whose hands they fell. Out of the ninety-three officers and men of the Royal Irish on the hill only seven escaped; the remainder were killed, wounded, or captives in the hands of the enemy. Little more than half an hour after the first shot was fired the defence had been beaten down completely, and the only sounds to be heard on Monument Hill were the groans of the wounded, and the hoarse shouts of the burghers as they collected the rifles and ammunition and sought vainly for the 4.7-in. gun, which they hoped to turn upon the garrison of the town.

When the attack began General Smith-Dorrien had only two companies—

(one of the Royal Irish and one of the Shropshire Light Infantry) available as reinforcements for the posts north of the line. Both companies turned out, stood to their arms, and awaited orders, while Lieutenant-Colonel Spens, Shropshire Light Infantry, at once reconnoitred towards Monument Hill, and before the firing had quite died down, met a soldier who gave him the grim news that Fosbery's detachment had been cut to pieces. Halting his party, Spens went forward with two or three men to ascertain for himself the real position of affairs, and, undetected by the enemy, worked his way up the kopje until he reached a wire fence from which he could see the burghers swarming over the camp which they were looting. Then, convinced that the post was lost indeed, he withdrew, taking with him the men of two small outlying piquets whom the enemy had not discovered, but who, in his opinion, would inevitably be captured as soon as the fog lifted. This daring reconnaissance was equalled by that of a corporal in the 5th Lancers, who volunteered to find out what had happened to the Royal Irish. He thus described the scene upon the hill—

"I left the road and struck across the veld, and by running, creeping, crawling, and rolling I managed to get up to the wire entanglements which encircled the post. The difficulty now was to get through the wire. I could hear shouts and groans, and there was some shooting going on, but whether Briton or Boer was in possession I could not tell. I dared not go round the entanglement to the entrances, as I knew they would be guarded, and so by a series of wriggles soon found myself inside the post. What was to be done now? I knew if I were seen I should be shot, whoever held the hill, so I continued to wriggle and roll on my stomach. I soon came across the effects of the fight, the dead bodies of the infantry and Boers, and the tents which had been cut down on top of the Irishmen. Some one was calling 'Water, for God's sake give me water,' and suddenly a dog barked a few yards to my right, and I could just distinguish a man. I immediately covered him with my rifle, but apparently he had not seen me. I remained where I was for some time, and then slowly crawled back a little and worked my way to where I heard the shouts for water coming from. I soon found two of the Irishmen badly wounded, and asked them in a whisper what had happened, but the only reply was a piteous appeal for water. I then crawled some fifty yards to the cook-house and found a camp kettle with some water in it, and slowly wriggled back to the two wounded men, and filling my cap with water gave them a good drink. They then told me that the Boers had rushed the sentries in the fog, cutting down the tents on their occupants, and shooting and clubbing the men as they rushed out, and although the garrison had made a gallant fight they were overpowered and the post captured. There was a lot of shouting going on by the Boers, and I quietly crawled towards it, and then there was a shot. Beyond a man standing on the monument I could see nothing, and so gradually crawled back to the wire entanglements; as soon as

z

I was clear of these ran back to the horses, where I found Sergeant Evans and Aldridge safe, and we rode back to camp and made our report." [1]

Along the rest of the line of outworks the enemy pressed home the attack with great gallantry and determination, but was repulsed at all important points. The Gordon Highlanders beat back Botha's burghers, though with the loss of a small isolated post, and the Shropshire Light Infantry maintained their hold on the vital part of their position, though also with the loss of a small outlying detachment. Only at Monument Hill were the Boers successful, and this success, obtained solely by overwhelming numbers, they failed to turn to account. Whether they were dispirited by their losses, bewildered by the fog, or crippled by the want of trained staff officers to direct their movements and carry out Botha's plans, it is impossible to say, but the fact remains that beyond capturing some scores of rifles, a few tents, and much ammunition from the Royal Irish, the burghers accomplished nothing, and retired so hastily with their prisoners and booty that when Spens returned in the early morning to Monument Hill he found it occupied only by the dead and wounded.

It will be remembered that Botha's scheme provided for the simultaneous attack on seven posts along the railway. These attacks were duly made, but in most cases they were not serious, and in none were they successful. The returns prove that Belfast was the real objective of the burghers, for out of 179 casualties sustained in the defence of these seven places, 143 fell upon the troops in Belfast. The Royal Irish were by far the greatest sufferers; of the three officers on Monument Hill, Captain Fosbery was killed, Captain Milner was severely wounded, Lieutenant Dease injured, and both were taken prisoners; while among the ninety non-commissioned officers and privates eight were killed outright, five died of their wounds, twenty-two were wounded in varying degrees of severity, and fifty-one were taken prisoner.[2] The Boers on their side also lost heavily: in the attack on Belfast fifty-eight burghers were killed, of whom fourteen fell at Monument Hill.

General Smith-Dorrien, in his report on the events of the 7th-8th of January, stated that the heavy loss in killed and wounded among the Royal Irish was "sufficient evidence that their defence was a fine one." He specially mentioned Captain Fosbery for his "splendid work in command of the post," adding that from all sides he heard how well this officer had behaved until he was shot down. In Force Orders, dated the 12th of January, 1901, he expressed his

---

[1] For his conduct on this occasion No. 4216 Corporal H. N. Forbes was awarded the medal for Distinguished Conduct in the Field.

[2] See Appendix 2 (Q).

"appreciation of the steadiness of the troops on the morning of the 8th. He would specially mention the fine defence of the Royal Irish piquet at the monument under that gallant officer, Captain Fosbery, whose death he deplores, until overwhelmed by vastly superior numbers after a hard fight. . . . He regrets the heavy losses, but does not consider them heavy, considering the determined nature of the attack. He also considers that had it not been for the fog the attack would have been much more easily repulsed."

The General also wrote as follows of Private John Barry :—

"I would especially call attention to the heroic conduct of No. 3733 Private J. Barry, Royal Irish, who seeing the machine gun surrounded by Boers seized a pick and began to smash the action, which he completed in spite of the threats of the Boers. I regret to say that the Boers in retaliation shot him dead, or I would have recommended him for a V.C."

The War Office decided to award this honourable decoration to Barry, although he was not alive to wear it, and it was presented to his widow to be held as a treasured heirloom in Barry's family. Thus, for the third time since the Order of the Victoria Cross was instituted, did a member of the Royal Irish regiment win this, the highest prize for valour in the British army.

For several days the garrison of Belfast toiled continuously to make good the weak points in the defences revealed by the night attack, and then settled down into the old routine of occasional raids into the neighbouring country and frequent skirmishes on the line of communication. A party of the Royal Irish under Captain Grogan had an extraordinary escape while escorting a train about this time; the burghers had mined the railway with dynamite and expected to see the train and its guard of soldiers blown sky-high, but their hopes were disappointed; a couple of heavily laden trucks in front of the engine met the full force of the explosion and were hurled off the rails; none of the escort were hurt, and the greater part of the train was uninjured.

On February 22, F, G, and H companies under Major Orr were sent to Helvetia, where they spent a fortnight in remodelling the defences, and then moved on to Lydenburg as escort to a convoy of supplies for the troops holding that distant post. Though unopposed by the enemy the march was very trying, for the rain fell in torrents, and the road, deep in mud, led across three rivers where the water reached to the waists of the soldiers as they struggled through the fords. Very soon after the convoy reached its destination Lieutenant-Colonel C. W. Park, Devonshire regiment, who at that moment was senior officer at Lydenburg, learned that a small commando of about seventy Boers had established itself in a valley near Krugerspost, twelve or fourteen miles north of the British camp. He determined to capture the laager, and on the 13th of March issued orders for the night march by which the burghers were to be encircled and surprised. The infantry selected for the enterprise were three companies of the Rifle Brigade, three of the Devonshire, and the detachment of the Royal Irish, now under command of Captain W. H. White, *vice* Major Orr, who had been obliged to go into hospital. They were to be carried in ox waggons for six miles; then after dismounting they were to make a long sweep across the veld to avoid a Boer piquet, the position of which had been ascertained, and on reaching a specified point break into three small columns, and crown the hills commanding the laager. The operation was by no means easy, for its success demanded not only that the troops should accomplish the various stages of the march within the time allowed by the calculations of the staff, but also that the guides should lead the detachments quickly and unerringly to the appointed places.

As soon as the column left the road its troubles began: the surface of the veld was seamed with spruits, pitted with bogs, and covered with high grass; it was impossible to move in close formation, and once the companies had been opened out, it became so difficult to maintain connection between the various units that when the troops reached the spot where the encircling movement was to begin, they were half an hour "behind scheduled time." The Royal Irish detachment was now handed over to a guide, who led it along a ravine which every moment grew narrower and steeper. At first the man seemed confident in himself; then suddenly he lost his head, and confessed he was doubtful about the exact position of the laager. The situation was serious, for if the Royal Irish did not succeed in making their way to the ground allotted to them in the scheme of attack, there would be a gap in the enveloping line through which the Boers might easily escape. Captain White accordingly sent Lieutenant Panter-Downes with H company up the ravine with orders to push on and connect with the left of the Devons, while he himself moved the remainder of the detachment farther to the left to feel for the Rifle Brigade. Just as the first glimmer of dawn was showing in the east a message from Panter-Downes arrived to report that he had discovered the laager, which was not visible from the slope up which White was climbing. While F and G companies linked up with the Riflemen and gained a crest commanding the Boer camp, H strove to get into touch with the Devons, but before Panter-Downes could make his way across a very difficult piece of broken ground the Boers took the alarm, discovered the gap in our line, and hurled themselves upon it, not without success, for though they left thirty-seven of their number in our hands, the remainder of the commando escaped. Some of them owed their liberty to the chivalry of the Royal Irish; in the words of the Record of Service they "would have been shot down had they not worn long night-drawers and so been mistaken for women." Though about half the *personnel* of the commando got away, all its *matériel*—tents, waggons, horses, and much grain—fell into Colonel Park's hands at a cost of only five casualties, all among the Royal Irish.[1]

In a few days the detachment returned to the railway and rejoined the battalion, which now had been withdrawn from the garrison of Belfast to take part in active operations in the northern Transvaal. Early in the year the Intelligence department had become aware that the repeated attacks upon the railway were intended to divert attention from the preparations for a great raid to the southward, by which General Botha hoped to restore the shattered fortunes of the republican armies. Lord Kitchener, who on Lord Roberts' departure for England in December, 1900, had succeeded to the supreme command of the British forces in South Africa, first sent General French with 22,000 combatants to harry Botha's commandos south of the Pretoria-Delagoa Bay line, and then organised a body of nearly 10,000 men with whom Lieutenant-General Sir B. Blood was to sweep a huge piece of country, bounded on the south by the same railway, on the north by the 25th degree of latitude, on the east by the Stenkamps Berg, and on the west by the Oliphant river. The principal settlement in this district was Roos Senekal, on which Blood's troops were to converge from various points. Three of the columns were commanded by Major-General F. W. Kitchener, the remainder by Major-General R. S. R. Fetherstonhaugh; the Royal Irish were allotted to that under the immediate orders of Colonel Park, who was one of Kitchener's subordinate commanders. Leaving the railway on March 27, the battalion reached Lydenburg on April 11, where began six months of work as arduous, monotonous, and disagreeable as ever British soldiers were called upon to perform. On some occasions the Royal Irish formed part of an outer ring of troops whose business it was to block every Nek and every drift by which a commando could break from the net that was closing upon it; at other times, as part of the striking column, they made forced marches by day and night, too often to find that the burghers had taken the alarm and had fled, leaving behind them their womenkind, who they knew would be well treated by the British. They had to "round-up" great mobs of cattle, to remove women and children from farms used as headquarters by the local guerillas, to escort convoys, and to march incessantly "in a most difficult country over almost impossible roads." For weeks together they never bivouacked twice in the same place, and whenever they found themselves for a few days at Lydenburg or at a station on the line, instead of resting, they had to build blockhouses. On one of these brief visits to the comparative civilisation of the railway the battalion was joined by Lieutenant

[1] See Appendix 2 (Q).

W. G. Lindsey and thirty non-commissioned officers and men of the 5th (Irish volunteer battalion, the King's (Liverpool) regiment, who on May 20, 1901 arrived to replace the volunteer company which on October 8, 1900, had started on its journey back to England.

A detailed account of the work of the regiment between April and October, 1901, would contain so little beyond a list of bivouacs at places with uncouth and unknown names, that no attempt will be made to follow the wanderings of the Royal Irish : the reader who desires to know their exact position on every day throughout this period will find the information in Appendix 8. At the end of September the battalion, to use the South African expression, " came off trek," and as soon as it had been refitted, relieved the Manchester regiment at Lydenburg. An idea of the straits to which the men had been reduced by hard marching will be gathered from a report dated September 1 : " many have no shirts at all, and others have no boots. All the boots and trousers are in a bad state and will not hold together much longer."

Colonel Park took the opportunity of thanking the officers and men for their services in a farewell order dated October 1, 1901—

> " It is with the greatest regret that the Officer Commanding the column has now to part with the first battalion, the Royal Irish regiment, the last remaining unit of the original force which started from Lydenburg under his command five and a half months ago.
> " The splendid fighting qualities of the Royal Irish are well known to all, and their magnificent marching powers and the good spirit of all ranks under the hardships and privations of active service have been the admiration of the O.C. column, and of all ranks who have served with him. Colonel Park wishes them the best of good luck, and trusts that at some future time he may have again the honour of serving with this gallant and distinguished regiment."

Though the war had already lasted for two years, the strenuous exertions of Botha, De Wet, and a few other Boer leaders prolonged the struggle, hopeless though it was, for nine months longer. During this time the battalion remained at Lydenburg, taking its share of duty in garrisoning the town, in escorting convoys, and in manning the fifty-five blockhouses by which the place was linked with the railway at Machadodorp, forty-five miles away. From the regimental point of view only two incidents worthy of record occurred in this phase of the war : the capture of B. Viljoen, the Boer general who had inflicted so heavy a loss upon the Royal Irish at Monument Hill, and the destruction by dynamite of a blockhouse held by a party of the Royal Irish.

At the beginning of the year 1902, Schalk Burger, the acting President of the Transvaal Republic, was in hiding near Dulstroom with the few adherents who formed his so-called government. Viljoen, the commander of the remnants of the commandos raised in the districts north of the Pretoria-Delagoa Bay railway, had been driven to Pilgrim's Rest, whence Burger summoned him to a conference to arrange for the transfer of the "government" to the comparative safety of that remote settlement. The preliminaries being settled, Viljoen preceded Burger on the journey over the fifty miles of country between Dulstroom and Pilgrim's Rest. This ride, writes the author of the Official History, "proved to be the last of the Boer leader's many adventures. The British Intelligence Department was keenly watching the vagrant legislature; and ambuscades lay in many a likely spruit-bed and rail and river crossing. Into one of these traps—laid by a party of the Royal Irish regiment, sent out under Major A. S. Orr by Lieut.-Colonel H. Guinness —fell Viljoen as, having stolen past the outposts of Lydenburg, he made to ford the Spekboom river." The details of the capture were as follows: at about 7 P.M. on January 25, 1902, Major Orr with five officers and a hundred and twenty of the other ranks was suddenly ordered to hasten to two drifts, where it was reported that a party of burghers would attempt to cross during the night.[1] Captain Farmer was sent with a detachment to block one of these drifts; near the other Major Orr hid the remainder of his force, posting twenty men in a ruined farmhouse a few hundred yards to his flank.

By 10 o'clock at night the trap was set, and the soldiers were resting after their long march over heavy mealie-fields and through spruits swollen by recent rain, when the detachment in the farm opened a sharp fusilade on a small number of Boers approaching from the south-west, and drove them towards the drift where Orr had established himself. So perfectly in hand were the Royal Irish that, though they could hear horses galloping towards them, they remained silent and motionless until the leading horsemen, who rode in pairs, were almost under the muzzles of their rifles. Then Colour-Sergeant J. Boulger, who was nearest the road, shouted "Hands up." Disregarding this summons the Boers galloped on: Boulger realising that they meant to dash through the drift, opened fire on the horses of the two Boers in front: his men followed his example, and the animals, one pierced by nine, the other by three bullets, dropped dead, in their fall pinning to the ground their riders, Viljoen and Bester, one of the General's staff. Then there was a short confused skirmish, in which Nel, another of Viljoen's staff, and a Cape

[1] According to regimental tradition the information reached Captain White, Royal Irish, the local Intelligence officer, in a curious way. Viljoen had in his service a Kaffir, whose father was employed by us at Lydenburg. The younger Kaffir overheard Viljoen mention in conversation that he meant to return to Pilgrim's Rest on a certain day; and obtaining leave of absence, passed the news on to his father, who in his turn reported it to the Intelligence department. It seems almost incredible that Viljoen should have been guilty of such an indiscretion as to talk of his intended movements within earshot of a Kaffir: but if the account is accurate, it affords another illustration of the truth of the saying—"What is rumoured in your camp to-day will be known to-morrow by the enemy."

Boer lost their lives; the remainder of the party, which numbered ten in all, escaped, though not across the drift. As soon as Viljoen and Bester had been drawn from beneath their horses, they were recognised by one of the civilian scouts, who told Major Orr the names of the prisoners. Between men who have frequently faced each other in battle arises a curious feeling of quasi-friendship, and the Royal Irish and the commandos led by Viljoen had frequently met on many a hard-fought field: moreover, after Monument Hill Viljoen had treated his prisoners, both officers and men, with great kindness: therefore, as Orr hurried his captives to Lydenburg he assured them that they had fallen into good hands, and during the few days that Viljoen remained at Lydenburg awaiting an escort to the railway the regiment did its best to make his captivity agreeable. The burghers were very anxious to rescue him; and one night, writes an officer, "two or three of them stole into the town to see if it was possible to dig him out, but finding a sentry at his door and another at his window gave up the attempt, leaving behind them a clever cartoon of Lord Kitchener sitting in a zariba of barbed wire, surrounded by surrendered burghers whom he was imploring to go out and persuade the others to come in, while floating above him was the spirit of Joe Chamberlain! The drawing was signed, 'Phil Jung, with apologies to Phil May.'" In his report Colonel Guinness specially mentioned Major Orr, to whose good dispositions of the force at his command was due the successful issue of the affair, and Colour-Sergeant Boulger,[1] who had been very favourably reported upon by Major Orr.

The dynamite episode occurred two months later. Among the block-houses held by the Royal Irish was one, named by the troops Ben Tor, which stood on a kopje so thickly covered with big boulders that the sentries could not watch all the approaches to it. The building was of stone, roofed with sheets of galvanised iron; and on the night of the 18th of March it was held by a non-commissioned officer — Sergeant M'Grath — and nine private soldiers. About two o'clock in the morning of the 19th, the two men on sentry outside the blockhouse heard sounds which they rightly interpreted to be those of approaching feet. While one remained on the look-out, the other crawled into the blockhouse and reported to Sergeant M'Grath, who immediately stood to arms and manned his loopholes, but almost before the men were in their places a bomb was hurled on the roof, which unfortunately being flat, not sloping, afforded the missile a secure lodgment. In a second there was a tremendous explosion: the blockhouse was wrecked; one of the walls was thrown down, and every man of the garrison dangerously or severely wounded, except the sentry outside who escaped all injury. After capturing this man the Boers waited for some minutes to see if any one was still on foot; then, satisfied that no resistance was to be expected,

---

[1] Afterwards Sergeant-Major, 2nd battalion, Royal Irish regiment.

they rapidly looted the blockhouse and decamped, fortunately without finding the boxes of reserve ammunition hidden under the sheets of galvanised iron which formed the beds of the garrison. Beyond stripping some of the wounded, the burghers did their victims no harm, and sent off the uninjured soldier to summon medical aid from Lydenburg. By dawn a detachment of troops, a doctor, and an ambulance were on the way to Ben Tor, where, says one of the officers, "the place was like a shambles—too horrible to describe." As soon as the wounded men had been removed,[1] the blockhouse was rebuilt and greatly strengthened.

Nothing of note occurred in the battalion during the remainder of the campaign, which was brought to an end by the declaration of peace on May 31, 1902. This is not the place to discuss the terms upon which the Boer guerillas were allowed to surrender their arms and return to their homes; to enumerate the enormous sums spent by the Imperial Treasury in rebuilding and restocking the burghers' farms, or to speculate on what may be the ultimate effect on South Africa and the Empire of the policy by which, little more than five years after the last shot was fired in the war, all the rights and privileges of self-government were granted to our former enemies. Whatever the future may have in store for England, the Royal Irish regiment will always have the satisfaction of remembering that throughout the long struggle with the Boer republics, all ranks worthily maintained the honour of their corps.

The doings of the officers and men who served in the mounted infantry are in no degree less interesting than those of the first battalion, but, unfortunately, want of space renders it impossible to describe in detail the many engagements and operations of importance in which they took part. All that can be attempted is a bare outline of their work, with a few instances of the many exploits which the independent nature of their employment gave them the opportunity to perform. Though for a time the two contingents were in the same brigade, they were employed together so seldom that their movements are chronicled separately.

When the first battalion was called upon to provide a section for Captain St Leger's Cork company of the 1st regiment of mounted infantry, commanded by Colonel E. A. H. Alderson, the choice fell upon Second Lieutenant P. U. Vigors and thirty-seven non-commissioned officers and men, who landing at Cape Town early in November, 1899, were sent up country to De Aar, a place important as a great railway junction and an advanced base, where large quantities of stores had been accumulated. Here they spent

[1] See Appendix 2 (Q).

nearly three months, chiefly on detached duties, such as guarding the railway bridge at Hanover Road, outposts, and patrols, one of which once pushed out as far as Prieska in the north-west of Cape Colony. Early in February, 1900, the 1st regiment of mounted infantry was allotted to the 1st brigade of mounted infantry, a newly-formed body under Colonel O. C. Hannay, and composed of the 1st, 3rd, 5th, and 7th regiments of mounted infantry (all regular soldiers) and several corps of Australian and South African volunteers. In the 5th regiment the Royal Irish were well represented; it was commanded by Major Hatchell, an officer of the XVIIIth; and one company, or a quarter of its total strength, had been contributed by the first battalion.

The Royal Irish section of the Cork company of the 1st mounted infantry charged with the cavalry at Klip Drift, and took part in the relief of Kimberley; reached Paardeberg some days before Cronje surrendered, and shared in the actions of Poplar Grove and Driefontein. In the operations outside Bloemfontein on March 12, the Cork company succeeded in forestalling the Boers in the occupation of an important kopje, just north of the Leper hospital. At the disastrous affair at Sannah's Post on the 31st of March, where the section served in the rear-guard covering the retreat of our broken force, all did well, and an officer and a lance-corporal especially distinguished themselves. As Captain St Leger was superintending the retirement of the rear section of the Cork company he saw a big man, dismounted, running after the horsemen. St Leger called him, and ascertained that he was Corporal Parker, 1st Life Guards, who after escaping from the trap in the Korn spruit had attached himself to the mounted infantry. While the corporal was speaking he was shot through the right shoulder, and at that moment St Leger's orderly, Drummer Radford, noticed that his officer was staying behind and rode back to him. Thinking he could manage the Life Guardsman alone, St Leger ordered Radford to return to the company, but when he tried to get the trooper on to his (St Leger's) horse, failed to do so, for the man's wound had made him incapable of helping himself, and he was too heavy to be lifted into the saddle. There was no time to be lost, so with his right arm round the trooper's waist, he half supported, half dragged him in the direction in which the Cork company had retired. With his left hand St Leger led his horse, which grew very restive under the pitiless hail of bullets that literally tore up the ground under the animal's belly. As the Boers followed up the little group, now completely isolated and a long way behind the last of the rear-guard, the outlook seemed almost hopeless. Suddenly St Leger realised that if he could succeed in getting his wounded man a few hundred yards farther on, they would not only find temporary cover in some low-lying and broken ground, but would also be protected by the fire of a party of Roberts' Horse who, some distance off, were holding back the enemy on this part of the battlefield. The burghers came on fast, and three of them galloped up to within a hundred yards of the fugitives, and emptied their magazines at them as they disappeared into cover. As the Boers fired from the saddle none of their bullets took effect. Bad as the situation was, it grew worse when the section of Roberts' Horse turned about, and galloped to a position farther to the rear. Happily St Leger managed to attract the attention of one of them—a gallant man, who raced back to him with a led horse, on which they managed to hoist the Life Guardsman, who, though faint from his wound, was still able to ride once he was in the saddle. Then they galloped hard, scattering in order to offer a smaller target to the shower of Mauser bullets by which they were pursued. Corporal Parker recovered from his wound completely; and neither the trooper in Roberts' Horse nor Captain St Leger was hit; indeed, good luck followed the latter throughout the day, for thanks to the resolution of his groom, Private Ward, his favourite pony was saved from the general wreck of the column. Private Ward was riding with the waggons when they fell into the ambush; when called upon to surrender, he refused to do so, and though his own horse was hit, succeeded in escaping with St Leger's pony, in whose saddle-bags were sixty sovereigns, just received for the men's pay. Lance-Corporal Hall distinguished himself by two acts of signal bravery under very heavy fire. Noticing a wounded gunner staggering along in the retreat he rode back to him, and placed him upon his own horse: later in the day, when the Boers were pressing hard upon the mounted infantry, he saw a trooper of Roberts' Horse whose pony had been killed and who was in imminent danger of being shot or captured. He dashed after a stray horse, caught it, and brought off the irregular in safety. Hall escaped unhurt; only three of the Royal Irish were wounded in this engagement.[1]

The section formed part of the army which invaded the Transvaal, and was at the passage of the Reit and the Zand rivers, the action of Johannesburg, the capture of Pretoria, and the battle of Diamond Hill (11th and 12th of June). For the next few weeks it remained in the neighbourhood of Pretoria, chiefly engaged in outpost duty, sometimes of a very exciting nature. Thus at Reitvlei, on July 15, a piquet of sixteen men was saved from capture or destruction by the intelligence of Sergeant Connolly who, discovering that a party of two hundred burghers with three guns was threatening the post, reported so clearly and so promptly that his officer was able to signal for reinforcements, which fortunately arrived in time. When Lord Roberts began to advance towards Komati Poort the Cork company pushed on with the remainder of the mounted infantry; a few of the Royal Irish

---

[1] See Appendix 2 (Q). Captain St Leger's exploit would have remained unknown had not Corporal Parker written to his own commanding officer to report the matter. Unfortunately the non-commissioned officer's letter did not reach the War Office until the list of rewards for South Africa was finally closed.

section were fortunate enough to be engaged at Bergendal, but none reached
Komati Poort, the company remaining at Kaapsche Hoop until November,
when it was ordered back to Pretoria and thence to the northern frontier of
Cape Colony.

Since the beginning of June, De Wet had kept the Free State in a blaze,
and although after his failure in various minor enterprises he was chased up
and down the country, and very roughly handled at Bothaville on November
6, he rallied enough burghers around him to be able to swoop upon the
British garrison of Dewetsdorp, which surrendered to him on the 23rd of
November, 1900. The fall of this place seemed to remove one of the chief
obstacles to the raid into Cape Colony which for months had been discussed
round the camp fires of every Free State commando,[1] and De Wet pushed
towards the Orange river, believing that once he gained its southern bank
the Dutch population in the colony would welcome him with enthusiasm.
As soon as his plan was discovered, troops were hurried from all parts of the
theatre of war towards the Orange river, among them the column to which
the Cork company was attached. After a long and weary journey by train
from Pretoria to Bethulie, it shared in the operations in December by which
De Wet was prevented from crossing the river, and driven backwards into the
eastern Free State, where though harried incessantly by our troops he never
abandoned his scheme for a second invasion of British territory. The Cork
company was soon called away from the pursuit of De Wet to that of two of
his lieutenants, Kritzinger and Hertzog, who succeeded in passing across the
river and waged guerilla warfare in many districts of Cape Colony. Early
in February, 1901, De Wet, with extraordinary skill and equally extraordinary
good fortune, threaded his way through the troops closing round him, and
dashed across the Orange at an unguarded drift, but there his lucky star
failed him, and the British mounted troops, though almost spent by their
unending pursuit of Kritzinger and Hertzog's raiders, who had now joined
the commandos of their leader, drove the invaders back into the Free State
at the end of February, 1901.

Between March and November 1901, the section was in the south of the
Free State, occupied in clearing the country and similar uncongenial duties,
the monotony of which was relieved by occasional skirmishes. In one of
these affairs two soldiers distinguished themselves. Private W. Sweeney found
himself surrounded by four mounted Boers who, covering him with their
rifles, called upon him to surrender; though they were all within fifty yards
of him he refused to do so, and firing at them from the saddle succeeded in

---

[1] As early as May, 1900, the author ascertained from Boer prisoners that in the commandos it was
commonly said that if the burghers were driven out of Pretoria they would break back through the
east of the Free State and burst into Cape Colony by the drifts over the Orange river near Aliwal
North.

making his escape. His name was specially mentioned to the General commanding the column for his gallantry on this occasion.[1] Private Radford, while carrying a message for Lieutenant Vigors, was wounded and his horse was hit under him; nevertheless he delivered his message and then made his way back to report that he had done so. The next two months were spent at Winburg, and in January, 1902, the section began to take part in the "drives" which marked the final phase of the war in the north-east of the Free State. In addition to the non-commissioned officer and men already mentioned, Lieutenant Vigors, in the statement he prepared for the regimental records, gives praise to the good conduct throughout the war of Sergeants Kennedy and Colthorpe, Lance-Corporals Mackay and Griffin, Privates Tobin and (5914) Power.

It was said on page 311 that just before the battalion sailed from England Captain R. A. Smyth, Lieutenants S. H. L. Galbraith and E. Lloyd, with sixty-seven of the other ranks went to the mounted infantry at Shorncliffe. From this nucleus developed a company, composed of the same officers and a hundred and thirty-six non-commissioned officers and men, who landed at Cape Town on January 31, 1900, and formed part of the 5th regiment of mounted infantry. The company received its baptism of fire on February 11, 1900, while reinforcing the flank-guard of a convoy in difficulties between Ramah and Roodipan. In this affair Private M. Maher greatly distinguished himself by volunteering to carry a written order to a detachment, separated from the main body by a broad stretch of ground completely swept by the enemy's fire. He set an excellent example by walking, not running, across the danger zone; delivered the note, and then, refusing to remain with the detachment which was under cover, coolly returned to report that the order had duly reached the officer to whom it was addressed. Maher was not hit; in this affair there were only two casualties among the Royal Irish, neither fatal.[2] The company was at a skirmish near Jacobsdal, where Major Hatchell was wounded; and after a long night march arrived at Klip drift on the Modder river on the 15th, too late to take part in Lieutenant-General French's charge through the Boer position, though in time to see the cavalry division re-form and start on its final advance upon Kimberley. The Royal Irish were sent on outpost at once, and remained on piquet until dawn, when they were ordered to work eastward down the river to Klipkraal drift, one of the fords by which it was expected that Cronje, now in full retreat from the kopjes of Magersfontein, would attempt

---

[1] This man's death was a sad one: he fell down a well, 45 feet deep, at Needspan, and his body was not discovered for several days. An officer writes of him: "he was one of the best soldiers and the cheeriest of men whom I have ever met; and his behaviour both in camp and field was excellent."

[2] See Appendix 2 (Q).

to cross the stream.   The company was engaged all day with the Boer rear-guard, and several men were wounded, among whom was Sergeant Peebles, whose experiences were singularly unpleasant;[1] while on patrol he was shot through the thighs, and falling helpless on the ground was stripped naked by marauding Boers, and left for dead, until late in the evening he was rescued by a party of his comrades.   After spending the night in guarding a battery of artillery, the company at daybreak on the 17th was sent to ascertain if the burghers still held the ground they had occupied when darkness put an end to the combat.   As soon as the Royal Irish reported that the position had been evacuated, the column was set in motion, but the Boers had gained a long start; their rear-guard again fought stoutly, and it was not until late in the evening of the 17th that the mounted infantry bivouacked two miles south of Paardeberg drift, near the laager which Cronje had formed a few hours sooner, when to his dismay he found that he had been "headed off" by French, who with a weak brigade of cavalry and two batteries of Royal Horse artillery from Kimberley had thrown himself boldly across the Boer general's path.   At 4 A.M. on the 18th, Hannay's brigade marched eastwards to form the right of the line of troops with which Lord Kitchener proposed to attack the enemy's position on every side.   The Royal Irish company was engaged all day, and in the ill-fated charge led by Colonel Hannay against the north-east face of the laager was represented by Captain Smyth, Lieutenant Lloyd, and thirteen or fourteen non-commissioned officers and men, of whom several privates were wounded.[2]   During the remainder of the operations, ending in Cronje's surrender on February 27, the company was employed in scouting and patrolling the country south-east of Paardeberg; and after taking part in the action of Poplar Grove it marched into Bloemfontein with Lieutenant-General Tucker's column on March 16th.

During the next five weeks the 5th regiment of mounted infantry was not employed in any important operation, but at the end of April it joined a force under Lieutenant-General Ian Hamilton, which forced its way through the defile of Israel's Poort, and after co-operating in driving the Boers from Thabanchu, marched northwards as right flank-guard to the main column in Lord Roberts' advance from Bloemfontein to the Transvaal.   Between the 23rd of April, when the Royal Irish company left Bloemfontein, and the 4th of June, when it entered Pretoria, there were few days when it was not under fire, and it was present at nearly all the actions in which the enemy was driven from one fortified position after another.   Considering how constantly the company was engaged its casualties were not heavy: at Thabanchu, Captain Smyth and a private soldier were wounded; at Welkom, Private Murphy was killed by a shell, which striking him on the back of the head, hurled him ten feet out of the saddle;

[1] & [2] See Appendix 2 (Q).

and in a fight between Heilbron and Lindley on May 20, Lieutenant M. H. E. Welch and several men were wounded by the burghers, who after driving in the rear-guard succeeded in getting between the main column and the right flank-guard, of which the Royal Irish company formed part.[1] In this skirmish, where Britons and Boers were fighting in a confused mass, Captain Smyth had a narrow escape: he had given up his horse to a wounded Royal Irishman when a mounted burgher tried to ride him down, but Smyth "dodged" the charge, and then laid his enemy low by a well-aimed shot. Though the company was exposed to heavy artillery fire at the battle of Diamond Hill, none of the officers and men were hit; and the same good fortune attended them for many weeks, for though as part of Hamilton's (afterwards Hunter's) Force, the 5th M.I. fought their way from Heidelberg to the Brandwater Basin, there were no casualties among them until July 28, when at Naauwpoort Nek Corporal Hogan was blown to pieces by a shell, and a private soldier was wounded. After Prinsloo's surrender the company helped to escort two thousand prisoners to the railway, reaching Winburg on August 12, and in less than a fortnight was again "on trek," this time in a column hurriedly despatched to the help of a detachment which, while reconnoitring in the Doornberg range, a few miles from Winburg, had been surrounded by a body of Boers five times its strength. This detachment, composed of South African volunteers and a handful of British militia, was hard pressed, and had lost nearly fifteen per cent of its numbers when the Boers retired on the approach of the relieving column. The only casualty among the Royal Irish was Captain Smyth, who was so severely hurt by a fall that he was obliged to go into hospital. Captain Brush replaced him in command of the company, at that moment only about thirty strong, the remainder of the men being either in hospital or stranded in various parts of South Africa waiting for remounts.

A few hours after the return of the troops to Winburg on the 27th of August, the town was attacked by the Boers, who finding it too strong to take, drew off and sent a portion of their force against Ladybrand. The 5th mounted infantry and all other available troops were at once concentrated at Bloemfontein, and after relieving Ladybrand hunted the commandos up and down the Orange Free State for many weeks. As a rule the burghers succeeded in eluding their pursuers, but on November 6, 1900, C. De Wet with a strong body of men was surprised near Bothaville by the 5th mounted infantry under Major K. E. Lean, Royal Warwickshire regiment, who when Major Hatchell was wounded at Jacobsdal had succeeded him in command. The fight began at dawn and lasted till midday, when the timely arrival of reinforcements broke down the enemy's resistance; De Wet and the greater part of his followers retired in confusion, leaving behind them a detachment of brave men, who fought stubbornly until,

[1] See Appendix 2 (Q).

threatened by a charge of bayonets, they hoisted the white flag. Our spoils of war included a 12-pr. Horse Artillery gun, taken by the Boers at Sannah's Post, and one of the 15-prs. lost by us at Colenso; four Krupps, a pom-pom, a machine gun, much artillery and rifle ammunition, many horses and carts, and a hundred and thirty prisoners. The Boers lost twenty-five men killed and thirty wounded; our casualties were thirteen killed and thirty-three wounded, among whom were three of the Royal Irish.[1] Most of the company were hotly engaged on the right of the line throughout the action, often at very close range; while a few were attached to the guns, where three privates of the Royal Irish greatly distinguished themselves. One of the gun detachments was reduced to a single man, who served his piece alone; while Privates Radigan and Maher by their steady and well-aimed shooting kept back a party of the enemy who threatened to take the gun in flank. In another part of the field Private Murphy was conspicuous by his bravery in dragging a wounded officer from under a deadly fire. Two or three days later Major-General Knox thanked the whole of the company for their services at Bothaville, and gave especial praise to these three men for their behaviour during the fight.

Soon after the 5th regiment of mounted infantry had refitted at Kroonstad important news reached them: De Wet had recovered from his losses at Bothaville, and had appeared in the south-east of the Free State, where he was attacking Dewetsdorp, whose defenders were hard pressed. The regiment was sent off by rail to Edenburg, where it joined the relieving column, which unfortunately did not arrive in time to prevent the surrender of the garrison. The company for the next two months marched almost incessantly in the eastern half of the Free State, chasing De Wet, who, like the rainbow, was always " in the next field." They had a couple of days' rest at Christmas, when they bivouacked at a farm near Ficksburg, where, according to the diary of one of the officers, "the only liquid available for our dinner was of so substantial a nature that a mugful evaporated would leave enough solid matter to make a good-sized brick! We shared the only dam in the place with the horses, mules, and oxen. Tea was an impossibility, and the coffee we swallowed with our eyes shut." Towards the end of January, 1901, it was discovered that De Wet was secretly concentrating his burghers for another attempt to raid into Cape Colony. Many columns, including that in which the 5th M.I. were serving, were directed against him and caught up his rear-guard at the Tabaksberg, where on the 29th of January the Boers fought a delaying action, in the course of which a handful of the Royal Irish earned praise first for their dash in "rushing" a kopje, and then for holding it against very heavy odds. The 5th were now ordered to Bloemfontein, and after a slow railway journey detrained at Bethulie to take part in the move-

[1] See Appendix 2 (Q).

ments by which De Wet and his guerilla bands were to be expelled from Cape Colony. They were sent off to the north-west, and so hard was the marching that when the Royal Irish company reached Hopetown at the end of February, it had lost sixty out of the eighty horses it possessed a month before. In the course of the trek Private Maher again came to the fore by volunteering to cross a drift, in order to ascertain if the farther bank of the river was occupied by the enemy.

From Hopetown the company worked its way back to the east of the Free State, on one occasion bivouacking near Ramah, where it had smelt powder for the first time, on another halting at Hout Nek, where under Hamilton it had fought at the beginning of May, 1900. During the remainder of the war the 5th regiment of mounted infantry was chiefly employed in patrolling, escorting convoys, and clearing farms, duties which entailed incessant and monotonous work. The process of clearing a farm of food and forage was by no means easy, especially when it had to be done very quickly by a flank-guard under stringent orders to keep its proper place in the column. After a harassing day's work, an officer in the regiment wrote in his diary that "to tell a flank-guard to clear farms on its march is all very well in theory, but when it comes to getting sacks of wheat or tons of loose mealies [*i.e.*, Indian corn] out of a back room through several narrow doors or narrower windows, the flank-guard often finds itself left behind the rear-guard. Some people seem to think that in clearing a farm you have only to blow a whistle, and all the animals commit suicide and all the grain jumps into the nearest dam." It must not be imagined that these duties were carried on unopposed. There were frequent skirmishes; in one of these affairs (October 17, 1901) a detachment of the Royal Irish company, finding itself surrounded by an overwhelming force of burghers in a place from which there was no possibility of fighting its way out, was compelled to lay down its arms after the officer in command and three soldiers had been wounded.

The British losses in South Africa were by no means heavy, considering that the war lasted two years and eight months, and that during a great part of the time more than a quarter of a million of troops were in the field. The casualties were—

	Officers (exclusive of staff).	Other ranks.	Total.
Killed	518	5,256	5,774
Died of wounds, disease, or from accident . .	554	15,614	16,168
Wounded	1851	20,978	22,829

2 A

The casualties in the Royal Irish regiment were as follows:[1]—

Officers—

Killed	. . .	Captains S. G. French, W. Gloster, and F. L. Fosbery.
Died of wounds .	.	Captains J. B. S. Alderson, R. R. Arbuthnot, and Sir John Power, Bart. (5th battalion).
Died of disease .	.	Captain G. A. Ashfordby-Trenchard (5th battalion) and 2nd Lieutenant A. C. S. Fletcher.
Wounded .	. .	Majors H. M. Hatchell and B. J. C. Doran; Captains E. F. Milner, R. A. Smyth, and T. Warwick-Williams (volunteer company); Lieutenants M. H. E. Welch and J. A. M. J. P. Kelly.
Severely injured	.	Captain G. Hearn (4th battalion).

Other ranks—

Killed.	Died of wounds.	Died from accidents.	Died from disease.	Total.
27	15	6	61	109

Wounded, 128; severely injured, 2.

In recognition of the services of the Royal Irish regiment the words "South Africa 1900-02" were added to the battle honours on the Colours, and the following officers, non-commissioned officers, and private soldiers were mentioned in despatches and received special rewards for their services:—

To be Companion of the Order of the Bath—Lieutenant-Colonel H. W. N. Guinness.

To be Companions of the Distinguished Service Order—
Major H. M. Hatchell, Major A. S. Orr, Major and Brevet-Lieutenant-Colonel W. R. B. Doran, Major H. J. Downing, Captain E. H. E. Daniell, Lieutenant J. A. M. J. P. Kelly.

Promotions by brevet—
Major A. G. Chichester, Major A. N. Lysaght, and Major B. J. C. Doran to be Brevet-Lieutenant-Colonels.
Captain R. A. Smyth (mounted infantry) and Captain E. M. Panter-Downes to be Brevet-Majors.

To be Honorary Major—
Quartermaster and Honorary Captain F. P. Reger.

Mentioned in Despatches—
Major K. P. Apthorp, Captain E. F. Milner, Captain A. W. Brush,

[1] See Appendix 2 (Q).

Lieutenants S. H. L. Galbraith, P. U. Vigors, E. C. Lloyd, and H. G. Gregorie (while serving in the Imperial Light Infantry before he joined the Royal Irish regiment).

The Victoria Cross was awarded to No. 3733 Private John Barry.

The Distinguished Conduct Medal was awarded to the following non-commissioned officers and men who were also mentioned in despatches :—

Sergeant-Major J. Bergin. *Sergeants* J. O'Connor, H. Loney, T. Connolly. *Lance-Corporals* P. Doyle, E. Lovely, P. Dumphy, W. Tytherleigh. *Privates* T. Baker, W. Sweeney, M. Maher, J. Murphy, J. Radigan.

Mentioned in Despatches—

Colour-Sergeants : T. Mahoney, J. Reddan, E. Murray.

Sergeants : H. Hall, T. McHale. *Lance-Sergeants :* C. Kennedy and T. Kelly.

Corporals : M. Kelly, J. Chaffey. *Lance-Corporals :* J. Moran, M. Tobin, J. Rathbone, C. Beresford.

Privates : J. Kavanagh, J. Kennedy, J. O'Neill, J. Ryan, J. McCullough, W. Patterson, M. Healey, H. Densmore (volunteer company).

Special promotions—

Corporal Wallace was appointed Lance-Sergeant for good service during the campaign, and Private P. Doyle was promoted to be Corporal to reward his excellent behaviour at the action of Slabbert's Nek.

In the militia battalions affiliated to the Royal Irish the following were mentioned in despatches :—

Captain C. Langford, 4th battalion, serving with Imperial Yeomanry.

Captain A. B. Crabbe, 5th battalion, with Imperial Yeomanry.

Lance-Corporal J. Mahood, 5th battalion, while on railway patrol on May 16, 1901, "was suddenly fired at by a party of Boers who were mining the line. Though mortally wounded he continued to fire as long as he could hold his rifle."

To all who served in South Africa one, and in many cases two medals were granted. Towards the end of 1900, it was believed officially in England that the war was virtually at an end, and a medal was struck, bearing the effigy of Queen Victoria, for issue to those who had taken part in the campaign. But after the war had dragged on for more than a year longer, it was decided to prepare a second medal with the effigy of King Edward VII., which was to be given to all who had served in the war for eighteen months and who had been in South Africa on January 1, 1902. Clasps were granted for various battles, sieges, and series of operations, and for service in certain specified areas during the years 1899-1900; and also for service in any part of South Africa during the years 1901-1902. The battle clasps obtained by the first battalion were for Wittebergen (*i.e.*, Bethlehem, Slabbert's Nek, Brandwater Basin), and Bergendal; the Royal Irish section of the 1st mounted infantry received clasps for the Relief of Kimberley, Paardeberg, Driefontein, Johannesburg, Diamond Hill, and Bergendal, and the Royal Irish company of the 5th mounted infantry for the Relief of Kimberley, Paardeberg, Johannesburg, Diamond Hill, and Wittebergen.

During the war the militia battalions of the regiment were embodied, and formed part of the garrison of the United Kingdom.[1]

In memory of the members of the regular or militia battalions who died in South Africa two memorials have been erected, one in St Patrick's Cathedral, the other in the barracks at Clonmel. Both are described in Appendix 10.

It has been decided that this history should end with the close of the South African war, and therefore nothing will be said about the doings of the regiment since May, 1902. And indeed, a detailed record would show little beyond that unceasing training for active service for which the army and the nation have to thank the campaign in South Africa. During this period there have been only two incidents of note. In December, 1905, the first battalion had the honour of sending three officers and a hundred men to guard His Majesty George V. when, during his tour in India as Prince of Wales, he was encamped at Kala-Ki-Serai. Three years later the same battalion was mobilized for active service in the expedition against the Mohmands on the north-west frontier of India; but unfortunately for the Royal Irish, this hill campaign was brought to so speedy and successful a conclusion that they were not called up to the front.

During the two hundred and twenty-seven years of its existence the XVIIIth regiment has served in nearly all the important wars in which England has been engaged, and has earned undying laurels whenever it has had an opportunity of distinguishing itself. The roll of battle honours, long as it is, by no means commemorates all the achievements of the regiment: in the Low Countries the Royal Irish took a leading part in the storming, not only of Namur, but of many other fortresses; in the capture of the Schellenberg, in the engagement at Bunker's Hill, in the defence of Toulon, and in the fighting in Corsica the regiment won great praise, but the names of none of

---

[1] The names of most of the militia officers who were seconded in these battalions for service in South Africa have been mentioned already; among the others who did duty either with mounted infantry or with other infantry corps at the seat of war were: Captains G. H. P. Colley, J. O. Johnson, A. J. Fox, and Lieutenant E. H. B. Thompson.

these operations are emblazoned on its Colours.   Early in its career, the regiment earned the reputation of being second to none in the British army. This reputation it has maintained to the present day; and the author is convinced that when in years to come, his successor writes the continuation of this history, it will be seen that the future generations of officers and men of the Royal Irish regiment have carried on the glorious traditions of the XVIIIth, and have rivalled, though they could not surpass the brilliant feats of arms which have been described in these pages.

THE SOUTH AFRICAN WAR MONUMENT AT CLONMEL.

APPENDIX 1.

THE MOVEMENTS OF THE XVIIITH ROYAL IRISH REGIMENT
FROM THE TIME OF ITS FORMATION IN 1684 TO THE END
OF THE WAR IN SOUTH AFRICA IN 1902, AND THE PLACES
WHERE IT HAS BEEN QUARTERED IN TIME OF PEACE.

1685 . . Sailed for England ; quartered at Chester, and then returned to Ireland.

1687 . . At the Curragh during the summer.

1688 . . At the Curragh during the summer : then sailed for England, and marched to London, thence to Salisbury ; returned to Colnbrook near London, and in the winter quartered in Hertfordshire.

1689. April . Hertfordshire to Chester ; thence to Wales.

1689. August . Ordered to Ireland on active service. (See Chapter I.)

1689 to 1691 . On active service in Ireland. (See Chapter I.)

1691. December At Waterford and Youghal.

1692 . . Embarked at Waterford for Bristol; marched to Portsmouth and sailed to the Low Countries on active service, returning in the autumn to Bristol.

1693. May . Bristol to Portsmouth where the regiment was embarked on men-of-war to serve as Marines ; in the autumn it was landed, and after a short time at Norwich, returned to the Low Countries on active service. (See Chapter I.)

1694 to 1697 . On active service in the Low Countries until the end of 1697, when the regiment was sent to Cork. (See Chapter I.)

1698 . . Moved from Cork to Waterford.

1699 . . Moved from Waterford to Dublin.

1700 . . Moved from Dublin to Kinsale.

1701 . . Ordered to Low Countries in anticipation of active service.

1702 to 1712 . On active service in the Low Countries and Germany. (See Chapter II.)

1713-14 . . In garrison at Ghent.

1715 . . In the autumn part of the regiment returned to England, and was quartered at Gloucester.

1716. February The remainder arrived at Gloucester ; later in the year the whole regiment moved from Gloucester to Oxford.

1717. May . Moved to Portsmouth.

1718 . . Embarked at Portsmouth for Minorca.

1727 . . A detachment was sent from Minorca to reinforce the garrison of Gibraltar during the siege of 1727. (See Chapter III.)

1727 to 1741	.	At Minorca.

1727 to 1741 . At Minorca.

1742 . . Embarked at Minorca for Portsmouth ; quartered on arrival in and around Taunton.

1743 . . Taunton to Exeter and Plymouth.

1744 . . Exeter and Plymouth to the neighbourhood of Hounslow and thence to Fareham.

1745 . . To the Low Countries on active service (see Chapter III.) ; returned to England in the autumn and quartered at Dartford.

1746. March . Dartford to Gravesend, where the regiment embarked for Scotland, but arrived too late to take part in the suppression of the Jacobite rising. Leith to Nairn, Inverness, and Elgin.

1747 . . Concentrated for the summer at Fort Augustus ; during the winter quartered at Edinburgh and Stirling.

1748 . . Edinburgh and Stirling to Berwick, Newcastle, and Carlisle, and thence to Glasgow.

1749. February Glasgow to Ireland ; stationed at Enniskillen and Ballyshannon.

1750 . . At Kinsale.

1751 . . At Cork.

1752 . . At Waterford.

1753 . . At Dublin.

1754 . . At Londonderry and Ballyshannon.

1755. April . Embarked for Liverpool ; marched to Berwick, in October to Edinburgh.

1756. May . Edinburgh to Fort William, with detachments in the Highlands.

1757 . . Returned to Ireland.

1758 to 1766 . In Ireland.

1767 . . Ireland to Philadelphia, North America.

1775 . . On active service in North America. (See Chapter III.)

1776 . . North America to England ; quartered at Dover.

1777 . . At Dover.

1778 . . At Coxheath encampment.

1779 . . At Warley encampment.

1780 . . At the encampments at Finchley, and "Hyde Park in London."

1782 . . England to Jersey and Guernsey.

1783. July . Guernsey to Portsmouth, and in October to Gibraltar.

1784 to 1792 . At Gibraltar.

1793 . . Embarked at Gibraltar for active service at Toulon. (See Chapter IV.)

1794 to 1797 . On active service in the Mediterranean.

1798-1799 . At Gibraltar.

1800-1801 . On active service in the Mediterranean. (See Chapter IV.)

1802 . . In the summer embarked at Elba for Cork, where they landed on August 29th ; quartered at Armagh.

1803 . . In the summer ordered from Armagh to Newry, where a second battalion was raised. Both battalions were quartered in Scotland during the autumn of 1803, at Edinburgh, Haddington, and Dunbar.

1804 . . In the summer both battalions sent to the camp on Barham Downs near Canterbury ; the *second battalion* sent later in the year to Jersey.

1805. January . *First battalion* embarked for Jamaica, where it arrived at the end of April or beginning of May.

1806 . . *First battalion* in Jamaica ; *second battalion* in Jersey.

1807 . . *First battalion* in Jamaica : *second battalion* embarked for West Indies and was stationed at the island of Curaçoa.

1808 . . No change of stations.

1809. June 7th   *First battalion* from Jamaica to the Island of San Domingo (see Chapter IV.) on active service and back to Jamaica ; *second battalion* at Curaçoa.

1810   . . *First battalion* at Jamaica : *second battalion* returned to England.

1811   . . *First battalion* at Jamaica : *second battalion* ordered to Jersey.

1812 to 1813 . No change of stations.

1814   . . *First battalion* at Jamaica : *second battalion* disbanded.

1815-16 . . The regiment at Jamaica.

1817   . . Returned to England, landing in March, and was stationed at Brighton, Chatham, Sheerness, and finally at Hilsea Barracks.

1818   . . Hilsea Barracks to Haslar and Gosport ; in December returned to Ireland, landing at Cork, and was stationed at Fermoy.

1819. January . Fermoy to Waterford, Wexford, Carlow, Duncannon Fort, Kilkenny.

1820. July   . Ordered to Cork.

1821. February Cork to Malta.

1824. May-June Malta to Ionian Isles.

1825 to 1831 . In the Ionian Isles.

1832. February 6 Embarked for Portsmouth ; landed on March 7th, and marched to Weedon, whence a Wing was sent in July to Tynemouth and Sheffield ; the remainder of the regiment followed soon afterwards to Ashton. Later in the year the regiment sent detachments to Wigan, Chester, and Mold.

1833. August . Headquarters ordered to Salford Barracks, Manchester, where the detachments rejoined.

1834. May 8 . Manchester to Dublin.

„   October . Dublin to Limerick, with detachments at Newcastle, Killaloe, Tipperary, Tarbert Fort, Carrick Island, and New Port.

„   August . Limerick to Birr.

1836. March . Birr to Athlone, with detachments at Roscommon and Shannon Bridge.

„   Nov. 15 . Detachment of the regiment embarked at Cork for Ceylon.

1837 to 1840

„   Jan. 10 . Headquarters and remainder of regiment embarked at Cork for Ceylon.

„   April 10. The detachment arrived in Ceylon.

„   May 31 . Headquarters and remainder of regiment arrived in Ceylon ; regiment stationed at Colombo with detachment at Point de Galle ; later headquarters moved to Trincomalee.

1840. May 1 . Headquarters and part of regiment embarked for the China war, followed shortly by the remainder of the XVIIIth. (See Chapter V.) On active service.

1841   . . On active service.

1842   . . On active service till peace signed : then quartered at Chusan and Kulangsu.

1845. May   . Concentrated at Hong Kong.

1846   . . At Hong Kong.

1847   . . At Hong Kong, and for a few days on active service in the Canton river.

„   Nov. 20 . Embarked for Calcutta.

1848. January 10 Landed at Calcutta and quartered at Fort William, with a detachment at Dum-Dum.

„   Dec. 19 . Headquarters and the greater part of regiment embarked on river steamers for Allahabad, whither they had been preceded by a detachment.

1849. Jan. 22 . Headquarters arrived at Allahabad ; ordered to Umballa.

„   March 24 Arrived at Umballa.

„   Dec. 25 . Began the march to Meerut.

1850. Jan. 4 . Arrived at Meerut ; detachment sent to Cawnpore.

1850. Oct. 14 . Began the march to Allahabad.

„ Nov. 21 . Arrived at Allahabad.

„ Nov. 22 . A wing of the regiment embarked at Allahabad for Calcutta.

„ Dec. 14 . Arrived at Calcutta.

1851. January 22 Headquarters and the other wing embarked at Allahabad for Calcutta.

„ Feb. 15 . Arrived at Calcutta.

1852. Jan. 19 . Headquarters and a wing of the regiment embarked for Burma on active service. (See Chapter VI.)

„ March 14 The remainder of the regiment followed.

1853 . . On active service in Burma ; returned in November to Calcutta.

„ Dec. 27 . Embarked in four transports for England.

1854. May-June Arrived in England : stationed at Chatham with a detachment at Canterbury, and for a short time also at Windsor Castle and Wellington Barracks, London.

„ Dec. 8 . Embarked for active service in the Crimea. (See Chapter VII.)

„ „ 30 . Landed at Balaclava.

1855 . . On active service in the Crimea.

1856 . . On active service in the Crimea till the declaration of peace.

„ July 10 . Landed at Portsmouth, and after a few days at Aldershot, proceeded to Kingstown for Dublin.

„ Aug. 27 . Dublin to the Curragh.

1857. March to } A detachment sent from the Curragh to Kilkenny on duty during the
April election.

„ Sept. 24 . A detachment embarked at Cork for Bombay on active service against the mutineers of the Bengal army.

1857. Nov. 12 . The detachment was followed from the Curragh by headquarters and the remainder of the regiment, which embarked at Cork.

„ Dec. 3 . The detachment arrived at Bombay, and was sent to Poona. (See Chapter VIII.)

1858. Feb. 6 . Headquarters and remainder of the regiment arrived at Bombay, and were sent to Poona.

For the next twelve months the regiment was split up into many detachments, which frequently changed their stations. Among other places they were temporarily quartered at Colaba (Bombay), Mahableshwar, Poona, Singhur, Malligaum, Nassick, Ahmednagar, Jaulnah, Sattara, Asseerghur, Sholapore, and Adjunta.

„ March to } *A second battalion* was raised at Enniskillen, in Ireland.
April

„ Aug. 30 . Enniskillen to Londonderry.

First Battalion.

1859. May 26 . Headquarters and five companies left Sholapore for Secunderabad.

„ June 21 . Arrived at Secunderabad, where they were gradually joined by the detachments, the last of which did not reach headquarters till the spring of 1860.

Second Battalion.

„ March 29 Londonderry to the Curragh.

„ Oct. 17 . The Curragh to Aldershot.

First Battalion.

1860 . . At Secunderabad.

Second Battalion.

„ October . Aldershot to Shorncliffe.

FIRST BATTALION.

1861. . . At Secunderabad.

SECOND BATTALION.

,, Aug. 21 . Shorncliffe to Portsmouth.

FIRST BATTALION.

1862. . . At Secunderabad.

SECOND BATTALION.

,, May 28 . Portsmouth to Jersey with a detachment at Alderney.

FIRST BATTALION.

1863. . . At Secunderabad.

SECOND BATTALION.

,, Feb. 21 . Jersey and Alderney to Parkhurst.
,, April 1 . Headquarter and eight Companies embarked at Portsmouth for New Zealand.
,, ,, 12 . The remainder of the battalion followed.
,, July 2 . Headquarters reached Auckland, New Zealand ; the second ship arrived somewhat later. The battalion was at once employed on active service. (See Chapter IX.)

FIRST BATTALION.

1864. . . At Secunderabad.

SECOND BATTALION.

On active service in New Zealand.

1865. . . The same.

FIRST BATTALION.

1866. Jan. 16 . Marched from Secunderabad to Sholapore, arriving on February 8 : train to Poona and on to Bombay, where it embarked on two ships, the slower of which did not reach England till June 30th. The battalion was quartered at Shorncliffe.
,, Dec. 13 . Shorncliffe to Aldershot.

SECOND BATTALION.

On active service in New Zealand.

FIRST BATTALION.

1867. Aug. 19 . Aldershot to Chester, with detachments at Weedon, Bradford, and Liverpool.

SECOND BATTALION.

In New Zealand ; headquarters at Auckland, with detachments at Taranaki and Napier.

FIRST BATTALION.

1868. May 21 . Chester to Edinburgh with detachment at Greenlaw.
,, Oct. 14 . Edinburgh to the Curragh.
,, November Detachments were sent during the elections to Dublin and Naas.

SECOND BATTALION.

In New Zealand : the headquarters and detachments as in 1867, with a company at Wellington.

FIRST BATTALION.

1869. Oct. 26 . The Curragh to Belfast ; detachments sent at various times to Londonderry, Carrickfergus, Newry, Monaghan, Armagh, Galway, Gort, Portumna, Oughterard, and Birr.

SECOND BATTALION.

In New Zealand : stations as in 1868.

FIRST BATTALION.

1870. June 21 . Belfast to Birr.
   „   July 12 . Birr to the Curragh.

SECOND BATTALION.

From New Zealand to Sydney (New South Wales), with detachments at Melbourne (Victoria), Adelaide (South Australia), and Hobart (Tasmania).

   „   August . The battalion embarked at Sydney and Melbourne in two ships, the slower of which arrived at Plymouth on December 4th.

FIRST BATTALION.

1871. May 22 . The Curragh to Cork, with a detachment at Camden Fort.
   „   Aug. 26 . Cork to Fermoy.

SECOND BATTALION.

At Devonport.

FIRST BATTALION.

1872. Jan. 18 . Embarked at Cork for Malta.
   „   Jan. 30 . Landed at Malta.

SECOND BATTALION.

   „   July   . Devonport to Aldershot.

FIRST BATTALION.

1873 .   .   . At Malta.

SECOND BATTALION.

   „   August . Aldershot to Gosport.

FIRST BATTALION.

1874. Oct. 20 . Embarked at Malta for Bombay.
   „   Nov. 15 . Landed at Bombay.
   „   „   25 . Arrived at Bareilly ; detachment at Moradabad.

SECOND BATTALION.

   „   May   . Gosport to Shorncliffe.

FIRST BATTALION.

1875 .   .   . At Bareilly.

SECOND BATTALION.

   „   June-July Shorncliffe to Aldershot for summer drills and then to Colchester.

FIRST BATTALION.

1876 .   .   . At Bareilly.

SECOND BATTALION.

   „   July   . Colchester to Fermoy, with detachments at Hardbowline, Rocky Island, Tralee, Clonmel, and Mitchelstown.

FIRST BATTALION.

1877. . . At Bareilly.

SECOND BATTALION.

Fermoy to the Curragh for summer drills and then to Kilkenny, with detachments at Waterford, Clonmel, Duncannon Fort, Carrick-on-Suir.

FIRST BATTALION.

1878. Feb. 13 . Bareilly to Loodianah by train, marching on to Ferozepore.
„   Feb. 24 . Arrived at Ferozepore.
„   Sept. 29 . Detachments sent to Multan and Dera Ismail Khan.

SECOND BATTALION.

„   May 1 . Kilkenny to the Curragh.
„   Aug. 9 . The Curragh to Dublin.

FIRST BATTALION.

1879. . . At Ferozepore.

SECOND BATTALION.

„   May 19 . Dublin to Aldershot.

FIRST BATTALION.

1880. Jan. 4-25 On march to Peshawar.
„   April 30 . Marched to Lundi Kotal on active service in the Afghan war. (See Chapter X.)

SECOND BATTALION.

At Aldershot.

FIRST BATTALION.

1881. Mar. 18-19 Returned to Peshawar.
„   April 11 . Arrived at Rawal Pindi.
„   „ 24 . Marched to Kuldanah in the Murree Hills with detachments at Chungla gully and Bara gully.
„   Nov. 6 . Kuldanah to Rawal Pindi with a detachment at Ghariat.

SECOND BATTALION.

„   Oct. 19 . Aldershot to Chatham.

FIRST BATTALION.

1882. . . At Rawal Pindi.

SECOND BATTALION.

„   Aug. 11 . Chatham to Portsmouth, for Egypt on active service. (See Chapter XI.)
    After the Tel-el-Kebir campaign was over, the battalion was quartered in Cairo from September 20 to October 11, when it was sent to Alexandria.

FIRST BATTALION.

1883. May 4 . Rawal Pindi to Kuldanah, with detachments as before.
„   Oct. 11 . Kuldanah to Rawal Pindi, and on to Meerut.
„   Dec. 11 . Arrived at Meerut ; detachment at Fategarh.

SECOND BATTALION.

„   February Alexandria to Malta.
„   May 17 . Malta to Portsmouth.
„   „ 27 . Portsmouth to Aldershot.

First Battalion.

1884. Aug. 20 . Meerut to Bombay.
„ „ 29 . Sailed for Egypt.
„ Sept. 29 . Reached Cairo.
„ Nov. 12 . Left Cairo on active service in the Nile expedition. (See Chapter XII.)

Second Battalion.

„ Feb. 28 . Embarked for Malta.

First Battalion.

1885. Aug. 24 . Embarked at Alexandria.
„ Sept. 9 . Arrived at Plymouth.
„ Dec. 16 . Plymouth to Devonport.

Second Battalion.

„ Jan. 7 . Embarked at Malta for Bombay.
„ „ 26 . Arrived at Bombay.
„ Feb. 4 . Arrived at Umballa.
„ April 24 . Umballa to Subathu, with detachment at Jutogh.

First Battalion.

1886 . . . At Devonport.

Second Battalion.

No change of station, except during camp of exercise.

First Battalion.

1887. Oct. 3 . Devonport to Plymouth.

Second Battalion.

„ Nov. 4 . Subathu to Nowshera, arriving there on December 25th, detachments at Fort Attock and Cherat.

First Battalion.

1888. Oct. 11 . Plymouth to Devonport.

Second Battalion.

„ Sept. 21 . Nowshera to Derband. On active service in the Black Mountain or Hazara expedition. (See Chapter XIII.)
„ Nov. 15 . At the end of the operations, Derband to Nowshera, where the battalion arrived on 29th November.

First Battalion.

1889. May 6 . Devonport to Harwich by sea and thence to Colchester.

Second Battalion.

„ Oct. 24 . To Peshawar for a review by the Viceroy.
„ Nov. 3 . Peshawar to Nowshera.
„ Dec. 18 . Nowshera to Peshawar.

First Battalion.

1890 . . . At Colchester.

Second Battalion.

„ April 21 . Peshawar to Cherat ; detachment at Peshawar.
„ Oct. 1 . Cherat to Peshawar.
„ November At camp of exercise.
„ Dec. 5 . Began march to Lucknow.

FIRST BATTALION.

1891. Nov. 4 . Colchester to the Curragh.

SECOND BATTALION.

„   Mar. 3 . Arrived at Lucknow ; detachment at Fategarh.

1892-93 .   . Neither battalion changed station, except during manœuvres and camps of exercise.

FIRST BATTALION.

1894. Oct. 31 . After the summer manœuvres, the battalion made a short halt at Birr, and then proceeded to Limerick.

SECOND BATTALION.

„   Nov. 29 . Began march from Lucknow to Jubbulpore.

FIRST BATTALION.

1895 .   .   . At Limerick.

SECOND BATTALION.

„   Jan. 2 . Arrived at Jubbulpore from Lucknow ; detachment at Sangor.

FIRST BATTALION.

1896 .   .   . While the drainage of the barracks at Limerick was being modernised, part of the battalion was temporarily quartered at Templemore, and then returned to Limerick.
(A section of mounted infantry were sent to South Africa, and were employed in the Mashonaland expedition.   (See Chapter XIV.)

SECOND BATTALION.
At Jubbulpore.

FIRST BATTALION.

1897 .   .   . At Limerick.

SECOND BATTALION.

„   Sept. 15 . Jubbulpore for Rawal Pindi, on active service on the Tirah campaign. (See Chapter XIII.)

FIRST BATTALION.

1898. Aug. 30 . Limerick to Buttevant, with detachment at Clonmel.

SECOND BATTALION.

„   April . Arrived at Mhow from Rawal Pindi ; detachment at Indore.

FIRST BATTALION.

1899. Nov. 23 . Buttevant to Aldershot.
„   Dec. 16 . Embarked at Southampton for South Africa on active service. (See Chapters XIV. and XV.)

SECOND BATTALION.
At Mhow.

FIRST BATTALION.

1900 .   .   . On active service in South Africa.

SECOND BATTALION.
At Mhow.

FIRST BATTALION.

1901 . . . On active service in South Africa.

SECOND BATTALION.
At Mhow ; detachments at Indore, Kamptee, and Sitabaldee.

FIRST BATTALION.

1902. (to June 1) On active service in South Africa.

SECOND BATTALION.

„ April 28 . Mhow to Kamptee.

APPENDIX 2.

CASUALTY ROLL.

(In this Appendix an attempt has been made to collect the names of the officers, non-commissioned officers, and private soldiers of the regiment who in its many campaigns have been killed or wounded, or who died from accident or disease. The information about the losses in the wars of William III. and of Marlborough is very incomplete, for it is obvious that far greater numbers of officers and men must have perished than are recorded by Parker, Kane, and Stearne, who only mention the casualties in battles and sieges of great importance. The names of non-commissioned officers and men who, though wounded, recovered from their injuries cannot be traced further back than the Crimean war.)

(A).

WILLIAM III.'s CAMPAIGNS.

1690. 1st Siege of Limerick.
(Though seven officers are said to have been killed and eight wounded, the following are the only names that can be traced.)

Officers . Killed . . . Captains R. Needham and C. Brabazon ; Lieutenant P. Latham and Ensign —— Smith.

Died of wounds . Lieutenant-Colonel G. Newcomb (or Newcomen).

Wounded . . Colonel the Earl of Meath ; Lieutenants R. Blakeney and C. Hubblethorne.

Other ranks . . . . More than 100 killed or wounded.

1691. Battle of Aughrim.
Officers . Killed . . . Captain —— Butler.

Wounded . . A major, a captain, and two subalterns (names unknown).

Other ranks . . . . 7 killed, 8 wounded.

1695. Siege of Namur.
Officers . Killed . . . Lieutenant-Colonel A. Ormsby ; Captains B. Purefoy, H. Pinsent, N. Carteret ; Lieutenants C. Fitzmorris and S. Ramme ; Ensigns A. Fettyplace, —— Blunt, H. Baker, and S. Hayter.

Died of wounds . Captain John Southwell ; Ensign B. Lister (or Leycester) and an officer whose name cannot be traced.

Wounded . . Colonel Frederick Hamilton ; Captains R. Kane, F. Duroure, H. Seymour, and W. Southwell ; Lieutenants L. La Planche, T. Brereton, C. Hybert (or Hibbert), and A. Rolleston ; Ensigns T. Gifford, J. Ormsby, and W. Blakeney.

Other ranks . . . . The losses in killed or wounded were 380 or 271. (See Chapter I. p. 21.)

(B).

MARLBOROUGH'S CAMPAIGNS

IN THE WAR OF THE SPANISH SUCCESSION.

1704. Capture of the Schellenberg.

Officers . Wounded .	.	Captain M. Leathes ; Ensigns J. Pinsent (or Pensant), S. Gilman, and E. Walsh.
Non-commissioned officers	.	1 killed, 3 wounded.
Privates	.	11 killed, 32 wounded.

Battle of Blenheim.

Officers . Killed . .	.	Captains H. Browne and A. Rolleston ; Ensign W. Moyle.
Died of wounds	.	Captain W. Vaughan (or Vauclin).
Wounded	.	Major R. Kane ; Captains F. de la Penotière and N. Hussey ; Lieutenants W. Weddall (or Weddell), S. Roberts, J. Harvey, B. Smith, W. Blakeney, and Ensign R. Tripp.
Non-commissioned officers	.	5 killed, 9 wounded.
Privates	.	52 killed, 87 wounded.

1706. Battle of Ramillies . The regiment is said to have been "greatly mauled" in the battle. (See Chapter II. p. 44.)

1706. Siege of Menin.

Officers . Killed . .	.	2 captains and 5 subalterns.
Wounded	.	Captain-Lieutenant Parker and seven others. (Other names unknown.)
Other ranks . . .	.	About 100 killed or wounded.

1708. Battle of Oudenarde.

Officers . . Killed . .	.	1 lieutenant (name not known).
Other ranks . . .	.	8 killed, 12 wounded.

Siege of Lille.

Officers . Killed . .	.	2 captains, 3 subalterns. (Names not known.)
Wounded	.	Major and several others. (Names not known.)
Other ranks . . .	.	200 killed or wounded.

1709. Siege of Tournai. See Chapter II. p. 55. It is obvious that the regiment suffered considerably ; but the numbers are not clear.

Battle of Malplaquet.

Officers . Wounded .	.	2 (names not known).
Other ranks . . .	.	10 killed or wounded.

1710. Siege of Aire.

Officers . Killed . .	.	3 (names not known).
Wounded	.	5 (names not known).
Other ranks . . .	.	80 killed or wounded.

1711. Siege of Bouchain.

Officers . Wounded .	.	4 (names not known).
Other ranks . . .	.	About 40 killed or wounded.

(C).

THE WAR WITH THE AMERICAN COLONISTS.

1775. Retreat from Concord and Lexington.

Killed	.	.	Privates S. Lee and J. Russell.
Wounded	.	.	4 private soldiers.

Battle of Bunker's Hill.

Officers	.	Wounded	.	. Lieutenant W. Richardson.
Other ranks	Killed	.	.	. Privates D. Flynn, T. Smith, and W. Sorrel.
	Wounded	.	.	7 private soldiers.

.   .   .   .

(D).

1793.   THE DEFENCE OF TOULON.

Officers   .   Missing (prisoner
of war)   .   .   Lieutenant George Minchin.

Other ranks—
    Killed or died from wounds or of disease—
        Sergeants .   R. House, J. Russell, M. Nowlan.
        Corporal .   P. Hanson.
        Privates .   E. Murdoch, T. Griffiths, W. Briggs, W. Wilkinson, P. M'Gurke,
                J. Harper, J. Molloy, W. Allen, D. Madden, J. Shelly, C. Reed, H.
                Allen, T. Border, W. Warren, J. Church, M. M'Ilvany, J. Winch,
                A. Price, W. Sheen, T. Field, J. Mayo, P. White, J. Riddell,
                G. Lacey, J. Cruickshanks, E. Strange, P. Roberts, H. Foy, H.
                Costello, B. Blazor, J. Smith, W. Bowyer, W. Cable, B. Johnson.

.   .   .   .

(E).

1794.   CORSICA.

(Killed in action or died from wounds, accident, or disease between April 1794 and
December 1794.)

        Officers   .   Lieutenant W. Byron (killed) ; Ensign F. Pennyman, Surgeons C.
                Kennelly, and T. Jackson (died of disease).
        Sergeants .   A. White, A. Turnbull, J. Abraham, E. Turnbull, W. Taylor, J.
                Antwhiste, D. M'Donald, T. Astley, W. Slade.
        Corporals .   T. Porter, S. Kerns, W. Moran, W. Irwin, J. Bishop, W. Cooper.
        Privates .   T. Philips, C. Chaplain, J. Browning, C. Sheridan, D. Fielding. J. Eadon,
                G. M'Lean, J. Derry, J. Willington, J. Blacker, C. Turner, T.
                Hopkins, W. Bennett, J. Blake, J. Quinn, C. Riche, M. Striffen,
                M. Reilly, H. M'Mullen, J. Crowley, W. Huskins, J. Carey,

M. Lloyd, T. Walsh, H. Marshall, J. Cooke, T. Connor, J. Joyce, J. Rubb, M. Finlan, G. Diamond, E. Warr, P. Gallougher senr., P. Rian, W. O'Neill, E. Doyle, W. Keane, T. Coyle, O. Kelly, R. German, J. Henly, M. Healy, C. Stagman, P. Dunn, M. Rian, J. M'Surley, H. Collins, J. Butcher, V. Smith, T. David, D. Mott, J. Donolly, M. Martin, J. Monaghan, M. Flanaghan, B. Harrison, T. Cooper, W. Jael, J. Birch, T. Ledgerwood, W. Cooke, T. Campbell, T. Martin, W. Callaghan, S. Bland, W. Scott, J. Red, J. Eagon, T. Crumlish, W. Garilt, G. Benson, J. Thompson, J. Millar, B. Cooke, T. Abraham, F. Walsh, J. Reynolds, J. Douch, J. Carleton, G. Plumer, M. Burke, J. O'Brien, J. Edwards, J. Paterson, J. Weir, C. Harrison, F. Rearden, G. Westwood, W. Watson, F. Evans, P. Gallougher junr., T. Hughes, J. Smith, J. Shonplatter, W. Hervey, W. Honoretta, F. Lynder, T. Handley, P. Carr, D. Houlahan, A. Jordan, T. Murphy, J. Conlin, W. Bowland, J. Fisher, A. Hart, G. Texter, W. Anderson, J. Hengly, T. Tuesby, G. Nockton, J. Spense, P. Kennedy, J. Carden, W. Scullard, J. Roarke, W. Tatton, J. Nolan, T. Drinnett, C. Dyson, T. Kinch, E. Eamer, J. Campbell, D. Ford, J. Morgan, J. Branan, W. Newton, J. Duffy, J. M'Donagh, J. Gallougher, M. M'Loughlin, M. Murphy, T. Perkins, H. Loughrie, P. Cummins, J. Irwin, T. Moorhouse, W. Taggart, G. Mosey, W. Browse, W. Ellis, J. Farnsworth, J. Shields, T. Harris, G. Robinson, T. Lee, A. Pithie, R. Divers, C. Reardon, J. Mulconray, C. Reeny, T. Bergin, T. Wilson, J. Lee, J. Kelly.

.   .   .   .

(F).

1801.   EGYPT.

Killed—
    Officers   .   Captain-Lieutenant G. Jones.
    Other ranks   None.
Died of wounds, accident, or disease—
    Officers   .   Captain W. Morgue; Ensigns H. Bruley and W. Brand; Quartermaster M. M'Dermott.
    Sergeants .   T. Houlahen, P. Marten, P. Bennett, J. Maxwell, H. Francis.
    Corporals .   J. Burrows, J. Sanders, E. Cassidy.
    Drummers   T. Acton, S. Acton, G. Rutledge, J. Kyatt.
    Privates   .   J. Gallougher, L. Doyle, J. Farrell, O. Brislow, P. Robinson, M. Milkerrine, J. Clark, J. Dufree, S. Bacon, L. Delancy, P. Ennisy, J. Grimshaw, J. Hammond, P. Kiguire, T. Connolly, J. Oliver, J. Tonar, W. Hillier, G. Needhem, W. Thompson, J. Cummins, R. Graham, W. Harris, G. Newbold, W. Willington, J. Boyle, W. Dempsey, J. M'Cawley, T. Kelly, J. Mayor, W. Burgess, S. Bryan, T. Marsden, H. Athe, T. Marten, J. Hunt, D. Mahoney, P. Marsh, J. Skiene, J. Neil, D. Clarke, J. Dempsey, T. Finlin, H. Poole.

.   .   .   .

(G).

1840-2.   CHINA.

Officers . .	Killed in action .	Lieutenant - Colonel N. R. Tomlinson ; Captain C. J. R. Collinson.
	Died of disease .	Major R. Hammill (1841) ; Lieutenants H. F. Vavasour (1840), S. Haly (1841), G. W. Davis (1841), A. Wilson (adjutant) (1841), F. Swinburne (1841), J. Cockrane (1842), D. Edwardes (1842), Hon. C. H. Stratford (1842) ; Ensign L. M. T. Humphreys (1842) ; Assistant-Surgeon J. Baker.
	Wounded . .	Captain J. J. Sargent ; Lieutenants D. Edwards, G. Hilliard, A. Murray, E. Jodrell, S. Bernard.
Sergeants .	Killed . . .	Paymaster-Sergeant E. Fitzgerald.
	Died of wounds .	Colour-Sergeant W. Kiscadden.
	Died of disease .	Orderly - Room Clerk R. Bullock ; Colour - Sergeant M. Switzer, B. M'Clennon, H. Smith, J. Brady, J. Cummin, P. Molan.
Corporals .	Died of wounds .	J. Bushell.
	Died of disease .	J. M'Carthy, J. Farlow, J. Spratt, J. Wilson, J. Henry, J. M'Carthy, M. M'Entaggart, W. Peake, A. Dixon, J. Connors.
Drummers.	Died of disease .	D. Moore, E. Poulteney, P. Callopy.
Privates .	Killed . . .	J. Henry, P. Sheppard.
	Died of Wounds .	J. Mulhaven, G. Bond, P. Gorman, J. Power.
	Died from accident or drowning .	P. Mineham, A. Scott.
	Died of disease .	H. Crozier, J. Turner, G. M'Cormick, E. M'Cabe, J. Dailey, J. Short, J. Hensey, J. Warrell, M. Mackay, G. Cullwell, E. Haslam, J. Maginniss, T. Short, R. Pawell, W. Abraham, R. M'Henry, E. Gallagnet, M. Connors, H. Kelly, W. Holey, J. Spears, R. M'Carthy, J. Connell, M. M'Wheney, P. Burke, M. M'Grath, H. Crangle, M. Nowland, W. M'Keown, G. Moirow, J. Murphy, M. Fullerton, P. Haran, T. Grace, M. Harsham, H. Frederick, M. White, D. Hogan, A. Woods, M. Kenna, D. Carroll, J. Short, J. M'Combe, H. Quierland, J. Houston, J. Parry, A. Macauley, J. M'Murray, T. Denahey, J. Shaw, W. Devine, A. M'Donald, A. Meehan, J. Connell, G. Banks, A. Muldoon, R. Hayes, J. Ward, B. Thompson, D. M'Auliffe, J. Maley, D. Chambers, J. Slattery, C. Flanagan, D. Evans, G. Douglass, R. Johnston, P. Downs, M. Murray, J. Mackay, J. Coady, S. Gaffney, E. Hewitt, D. Hoolohan, T. M'Elvasey, R. M'Ginday, M. Carroll, M. M'Grath, G. Crummey, C. Burke, J. Taylor, D. Hogan, T. Paine, M. Shanahan, P. Bratman, M. Bollard, A. Carroll, L. Downey, M. Hayes, T. M'Donald, P. Meighan, J. Mulharen, M. Punlan, J. Raftery, J. Tackney, J. Higgins, I. Pratt, C. Frere, W. Harvey, W. Greay, M. Rodgers, M. Allen, F. Briscoe, P. Finn, P. Dolan, M. Casey, M. Grogan,

J. Costello, J. Connors, M. Mahony, E. Purlan, D. Delany, M. Gallagher, J. Crosby, P. Rodgers, J. Kelly (ii.), J. Tresham, C. Rourke, J. Kelly (i.), J. Murtha, H. M'Grath, T. Connor, M. Ryder, J. Morris, M. Mullaly, J. M'Dermott, W. Sheppard, W. Hamilton, H. Henry, A. Quinn, C. Ryan, W. Redmond, F. O'Connell, J. Johnston, J. Scott, J. Coon, H. M'Nabb, M. Hayes, D. Bloomfield, G. Gunning, G. Jamison, D. Conrahey, B. O'Kara, J. Moroney, M. Morgan, A. Woods, D. Carr, G. Bond, H. Forster, P. Gorman, J. M'Guire, P. Scalley, M. Callins, W. Abraham, E. Gallagher, H. Kelly, P. Horan, G. Morron, E. Poulteny, J. Shaw, J. Ward, D. M'Auliffe, P. Downes, M. Murray, G. Crummey, C. Burke, S. Buffney, J. Davies, R. Bradley, P. Hogan, J. Mulvehill, J. M'Clemnay, J. Devlin, S. Cannan, E. Bourke, J. Henry, J. Laverty, J. Meade, P. Minehan, B. Pearson, J. Power, P. Skey, A. Scott, P. Sheppard, P. Wang, E. Bourke, W. Cormack, T. Fizzell, J. Kennedy, P. Kernan, G. Lilly, P. Moran, T. Motley, J. M'Kenna, H. O'Brien, M. Parsons, W. Birby, P. Skey, P. Tunney, J. Wade, J. White, P. Daly.

.   .   .   .

(H).

1852-3.   THE SECOND WAR WITH BURMA.

Officers—
    Killed in action or died of wounds—
        Lieutenants R. Doran, W. P. Cockburn.
    Died of disease—
        Lieutenant-Colonel C. J. Coote ; Captain A. Gillespie ; Lieutenant F. Lillie.
Other ranks—
    Killed in action or died of wounds—
        Sergeant . W. M'T. Shanks.
        Corporal . M. Ganley.
        Drummer . W. Brown.
        Privates . M. M'Dermott, J. Noland, G. Roarke, J. Sweeny, J. Tuppy, T. Cooney, J. Crossin, T. Dowd, T. Egan, J. M'Goughlin, J. Ryan (2), J. Ryder, W. Wall (2).
    Died of disease or from accident—
        Sergeants . Quartermaster-Sergeant C. Harman ; Orderly - Room Clerk J. Ford ; Drum - Major R. Harringan ; Colour - Sergeants S. Fullerton, M. Dutton, P. Hackett, J. Hogan ; Sergeants C. D. Carry, A. Owens, T. Gaffney, A. M'Clean, O. Manus, J. Murray, C. Quinn, S. M. Thackery, G. Cary.
        Corporals . W. Bowles, J. H. Briscoe, T. Donaher, R. Moore, J. Kelly, C. M'Cracken, P. Luthervill, M. Rodgers, J. Brady, W. Wheeldon, P. Fladdeny.
        Drummers W. Nelligan, J. Lyons, E. Lyon, J. Storan.

Privates . P. Burke, T. Bourke, W. Canty, P. Carroll, G. Cooper, M. Crannich, E. Crow, P. Dalton, B. Daly, T. Daly, M. Donnell, M. Doyle, J. Dwyer, T. Fox, T. Foy, W. Kelly (iii.), P. Kennedy, P. Kiley, W. Lesinane, J. Lynch, W. Lynch, R. M'Knight, J. Maher, J. Mathews, P. Meighan, J. Moran, J. P. Murphy, M. Nicholas, M. O'Brien, P. O'Loughlin, M. Phelan, T. Pilkington, M. Power, N. Power, T. Rubie, J. Shaw, J. Shea, M. Shean, J. Simmons, J. Toole, M. Tynan, R. Williams, W. Ball, G. Browne, T. Calligan, M. Carragher, M. Casgrove, E. M. Devine, D. Dowd, J. Doyle, W. Duggan, T. Dunne, J. Ferguson, D. Flannedy, M. Gleeson, S. Griffin, L. Hardiman, J. Harris, T. Harrington, P. Healy, J. Heffirnan, M. Hogan, J. Kelly, J. M'Donald, Patrick M'Kenna, Phelix M'Kenna, L. M'Loughlin (drowned), D. Murphy, L. Nolan, T. Noland, T. Parsons, W. M. Roden, T. Ryan (ii.), R. Ryder, T. Shea, D. Sullivan, M. Tierney, M. Walsh (ii.), G. Alcock, W. Allen, S. Archbold, P. Barry (i.), P. Bennett, P. Boylan, M. Brien, J. Bralley, M. Butler, J. Cain, S. Campbell, J. Cushman (drowned), T. Collins, W. Connelly, R. Cotter, P. Coughlan, J. Cummins, T. Cummins, E. Deakins, M. Dee, P. Donnelly, M. Duggan, T. Fenton, M. Fitman, E. Fitzgerald, C. Flanagan, J. Fleming, W. Fullerham, P. Gallagher, J. Gallagher, J. Glavin, J. Hamilton, J. Hopkins, E. Hunter, M. Kelly, T. Kelly, J. Lawler, T. Leahy, T. Leary, J. M'Cabe, E. Macken, D. Meade, J. Mulholland, J. Murphy (iii.), M. Murphy, T. Mead, T. Parken, P. Power, P. Ryan (ii.), P. Ryan, W. Smart, H. Stewart, J. Storen, M. Sullivan, M. Tooney, J. Warren, R. Welch, J. Williams, W. Wingrove, M. Barrett, M. Baulden, F. Browne, J. Byrne, D. Cahal, J. Callaghan (ii.), J. Carty, M. Coan, M. Cooney, H. Copley, J. Cramteh, R. Creery, J. Currey, P. Derkin, M. Devine, J. Donnelly, J. Duggan (ii.), P. Dugan, W. H. Edwards, P. English, J. Farrell, D. Fennell, P. Fenton, P. Finigan, M. Fitzgerald, J. Flynn, L. Foley, M. Gannon, J. Gibney, P. Glynn, W. Hamilton, S. Harrington, M. Hayes, J. Hill, E. Hogan, J. Hunt, J. Ingles, M. Kain, J. Kavanagh, J. Kearley, P. Kelly, C. Kennally, J. Kettewell, G. King, J. M'Cabe, J. M'Cormick, R. M'Farland, A. M'Gill, J. M'Glynn, J. Mahony, J. May, N. Moore, J. Mulhern, M. Murphy, M. Murphy (ii.), W. Murray, J. Neil, C. Pendergrast, P. Plant, R. Power, J. Reidy, D. Roche, D. Ronan, J. Scally, P. Sheehan, T. Sheehan, P. Sheridan, M. Sullivan, G. Taylor, W. Taylor, J. Vanee, H. Vaughan, N. Walsh, J. Walsh, J. Wilkinson, D. Baxan, R. Barratt, J. Bourke, M. Boyle, P. Byrne, T. Caffrey, R. Calvert, J. Carrall (ii.), M. Cavanagh, J. Collins, J. Cormick, P. Daly (ii.), R. Donovan, M. Flaherty, M. Foley, W. Gore, J. Gough, J. Green (i.), J. Griffen, W. Hallinan, E. Hauranan, J. Harnan, P. Hassett, O. Hederman, R. Kavanagh, H. Kelly, W. Keris, J. Lonsdale, J. M'Corvill, J. M'Cormick, F. M'Guire, W. M'Kernon, R. M'Kirn, E. M'Manus, M. M'Mamara, S. Maggs, C. Mahoney, J. Mooney, J. Moore, J. Morgan, T. O'Dea, R. Olliver, W. Pedlow, E. Penrose, J. Rahally, J. Ready, J. Reardon (i.), W. Roberts, D. Ryan, T. Sullivan, P. Tancred, W. Wall, W. Whipple, J. Worrell, A. Edmonds, D. Bourke, J. Broderick, J. Brown, J. Costigan, J. Daly, T. Delahunty, J. Dunn, J. Durnin, E. Flinter, A. Harrington, C. Heffernan, S. Honrihan,

A. Horragan, J. Kelly (ii.), W. Kelly (ii.), D. Kelly, D. Kennedy, J. King, J. Kyley, J. Langston, J. Lanregan, S. Lightbody, J. M'Cracken, J. Moran, P. Murphy, M. Murphy, F. Murray, D. Murray, J. Nolan, J. O'Trien, J. Quigley, M. Quinn, E. Ready, W. Sherridan, F. Stewart, H. Tate, J. Taylor, P. Ternon, J. Tierney, J. Todd, L. Walsh, J. Weir, J. Barnwill, J. Buckley, R. Delahunty, P. Garrity, P. Hardiman, M. Hayes, C. Henry, J. Lamb, O. Reagan, J. Toohey.

.   .   .   .

(I).

1854-6.   THE WAR IN THE CRIMEA.

Officers—
Killed   .   . Lieutenant J. W. Meurant.
Died of disease . Lieutenant E. D. Ricard.
Wounded .   . Major J. Clarke Kennedy ; Captains A. Armstrong, J. Cormick, M. J. Hayman, H. F. Stephenson, J. G. Wilkinson ; Lieutenants W. O'B. Taylor, F. Fearnley, C. Hotham, W. Kemp.

Other ranks—
Killed—
Sergeant   . Colour-Sergeant T. Mallow.
Corporals . M. Hartigan, G. Morgan, J. Watson.
Privates   . O. Whelan, W. Birmingham, J. Cashman, M. Cantlin, T. Cotter, F. Degnan, P. Dowd, K. Flynn, K. Gordon, M. Gorman, C. Hannagan, A. Keane, P. Kearns, L. Keelan, J. Lynch, T. M'Cormick, W. M'Cormick, S. M'Evoy, J. Malony, M. Murphy (ii.), P. Malony, J. Murray, D. O'Brien, G. Pugh, B. Quinn, J. Rodgers, D. Walpole, T. Cavanagh, J. Clarke, T. Donovan, P. Kelcher, J. Nolan, R. Nugent, J. Reeves, J. Reilly, D. Rourke, P. Smith.

Died of wounds—
Sergeant   . Colour-Sergeant G. Wildenham, T. Studdart.
Corporal   . J. Leahy.
Drummer . W. Cardwell.
Privates   . M. Keane, J. Ahern, P. Bryan, J. Carroll, A. Church, J. Dolan, T. Edmonds, R. Entwistle, T. Fragan, R. Fenton, M. Hallinan, M. Hanrahan, M. Kennally, H. M'Cabe, M. M'Gawley, J. M'Gowan, P. Masterson, M. Moriarty, W. Quinn, W. Rainey, J. Ryan, G. P. Storey, J. Tigue, P. Tobin, J. Wiggins, J. Woods, P. Leary, J. Doyle, W. Hamilton, W. Howes, D. M'Carthy, H. M'Guinness, D. Murray, T. O'Leary, P. Ryan, J. Sessnan, M. Sheehan, T. Smyth, R. Walsh, J. Sullivan.

Died of disease—
Sergeants . Hospital-Sergeant J. M'Gill ; Sergeants J. Bogle, A. M'Cormick.
Corporals . J. Brimage, J. Lacey, P. Kilkelly.
Privates   . G. Beckett, T. Carmode, M. Carmody, P. Carroll, R. Clark, P. Collins, I. Cooke, W. Davis, W. Deane, J. Develin, J. Exham, W. Fry, J. Garvey, J. Grogan, A. Haigh, H. Hobson, T. Halt, M. Keeffe, A. Killeen, R. Lowe, T. M'Namara, P. Mangan, J. Mangner, J. Mathews, J. Manning, M. Mulcaby, M. Murphy, J. O'Brien, J. O'Neill, W. Pelitt, M. Purcell, P. Quealy, D. A. Shehin, J. Smith

(ii.), W. Smyth, R. T. Young, M. Walsh, W. Deegan, E. Ridgeway, J. Blair, J. Byrnes, J. Fragan, W. Foord, J. Harte, A. Hickey, S. M'Namara, P. Murtha, B. Ready, J. Russell, A. Scott, C. Slattery, G. Ablett, G. Coxall, E. Green, M. M'Donald, G. M'Kone, J. Morris, J. Shea, J. Secrett, J. Hilton, J. Brien, T. Farrelly, J. Fleming, H. Neill, D. Leary, W. Barlow, M. Cash, T. Caffey, G. Scales, T. Sullivan, J. Whelan, P. Rooney, H. Palmer.

Wounded—

Sergeants . Colour-Sergeants J. Orchard, J. Proctor ; Sergeants N. Hunter, J. Hobbs, M. M'Key, F. Bartlett, P. Carroll, G. Clarke, E. Dunne, J. Gleeson, J. Grant, J. Hallissey, C. Keenan, T. M'Carthy, H. Morton, T. O'Donnell, E. Owen, W. Reside, R. Sheehan, W. Stewart, W. Stuart, P. Collins, J. Harvey, J. Jackson, C. Keenan.

Corporals . J. Ryan, D. Murphy, J. Maddigan, J. Dillon, P. Kuniare, C. Newman, M. O'Connor, H. Sherdy, R. Waters, J. Marks, M. Rourke, C. Newman.

Drummers T. M'Grath, J. Molloy.

Privates . J. Connors, H. Griffiths, T. M'Hale, M. Rowley, J. Hopkins, P. M'Guire, J. Malmey, P. Hughes, O. Sweeney, P. Brody, M. Flannery, J. Ford, T. Green, J. Hamilton, T. Ryan, D. Buckley, T. Farrelly, W. Fulham, J. M'Dermott, P. Mullhalley, P. Sullivan, F. Toole, T. Vyse, P. Abbott, R. Baglin, T. Bailey, M. Brogan, W. Browne, J. Callaghan, J. Casey, M. Cawley, C. Clancey, J. Clancey, E. Clayton, John Coleman, Jerh. Coleman, J. Collins, M. Collins, P. Collins, F. Comisky, M. Condon, M. Connell, O. Connell, J. Cotton, T. Coulter, J. Cox, P. Coyle, M. Cremine, P. Cullinan, T. Cumiskey, P. Cummins, J. Curtin, J. Dacy, J. Dennis, A. Desmond, J. Desmond, R. Doherty, P. Donohoe, P. Donovan, J. Dougherty, P. Dowd, J. Downs, Jos. Doyle, D. Driscoll, T. Dimphy, J. Duggan, J. Dunn, J. Edgill, M. Edwards, W. Fallon, J. Farrell, N. Farrell, C. Fielding, P. Finnegan, J. FitzGerald, T. Flaherty, T. Flannagan, J. Fleming, G. Foote, J. Forster, C. Fry, M. Glamson, W. Good, F. Goody, A. Gorman, P. Greeman, J. Gultry, T. Haggarty, M. Hair, A. Hardy, J. Harrington (i.), J. Harrington (ii.), R. Harris, T. Hasleton, D. Hayes, J. Hayes, J. Henry, D. Hogan, J. Houston, J. Hughes, P. Hugnes, L. Jerman, D. Keane, M. Kennedy, C. Keilly, P. Kilty, G. Killeen, J. Lancaster, E. Langton, P. Leary (ii.), T. Leary, J. Lebart, G. Lucas, J. Lynch, C. M'Carthy, J. M'Carthy, J. M'Cawley, J. M'Garagle, H. M'Gavin, M. M'Gawley, J. M'Gowen, M. M'Guire, J. M'Guinness, T. M'Hales, O. M'Kevill, J. M'Longlin, J. M'Nally, O. M'Nally, M. Mackay, J. Maher, W. Maher, W. Malley, T. Mangan, H. Mansfield, J. Marks, R. Marsh, T. Medhurst, W. Milliard, C. Moreland, J. Morrow, T. Mulready, P. C. Murphy, J. Murphy, P. Murphy, T. Murphy (i.), T. Murphy (ii.), H. Nanton, H. Neill, J. Nunn, J. O'Brien, P. O'Brien, J. O'Reegan, J. O'Sullivan, H. Powell, M. Prior, A. Quillan, T. Quillan, W. Rainey, J. Reagan, J. Reeves, J. Roach, T. Roberts, D. Robinson, T. Rohan, D. Rourke, J. Ryan (ii.), M. Ryan, E. Scanlon, M. Shaw, C. Sheehan, J. Sherrook, J. Shihy, T. Singleton, J. Slowey, A. Small, Pat. Smith, Phillip Smith, J. Spright, T. Sullivan, H. Spaulding, J. Swift, P. Taffe, T. Talbot, H. Thompson, E. Walsh, R. Walsh, W. Warwick,

J. Whelan, P. Winne, T. Wyse, P. Bannan, M. Byrnes, J. Crowley,
J. Jordon, T. O'Brien, D. Quill, H. Spaulding, H. Tue, D. Quilley,
E. Ashton, J. Buckley, B. Keffe, J. Lyons, P. Burley, M. Dignam,
T. M'Mahon, J. Morrow, B. Flanahan, J. O'Brien, W. Fallan, C.
Fry, J. Cantlin, T. Medhurst, D. O'Connell, J. Stanley, T. M'Mahon,
J. Halinan, M. Collins, G. Baker, W. Hamilton, J. Lawlor, T.
Singleton, J. Kerry, W. M'Crackin, M. Glamson, R. Keefe, J. Curry,
D. Kane, H. M'Cann, M. Quigley, J. Quilligan, J. Butler, T. Linihan,
J. Sullivan, J. Murphy, J. O'Rogan, P. O'Donnell.

(J).

1858-9.   OPERATIONS DURING THE MUTINY IN INDIA.

Deaths from disease—
   Officers   . Captain W. F. G. Forster; Lieutenant T. Watt; Assistant-Surgeon
                   C. E. Porteous.
Other ranks—
   Privates   . J. Jones, P. M'Caskir, G. Sutton, P. Travers, T. Gayner, T. Hogan, W.
                   M'Kenna, J. Shihey, J. Cronin, G. Drakin, J. D. Finne, C. Walker,
                   T. Williams, R. Allen, H. Bloomer, F. Carter, E. Clayton, T.
                   Gallagher, J. Hinley, J. Jennings, J. Lee, P. Loughrey, T. Murphy,
                   A. Scott, T. Slater, J. Sweeney, J. Wilkinson.

(K).

1863-1867.   NEW ZEALAND.

Officers—
   March 30-April 2, 1864. Capture of the *pah* at Orakau.
       Mortally wounded—Brevet-Major J. T. Ring.
       Died of accident or disease during the war—
           Lieutenants F. P. Leonard (1864) and O. R. Lawson (drowned 1865); Ensign
               G. B. Jenkins (drowned 1865).
Other ranks—
   July 17th 1863. Attack on a convoy in the Hunua forest.
       Killed   . Privates A. Jamieson, F. Macgrath, J. Scott, J. Limerick.
       Wounded . Sergeant W. Lawson; Corporals Flinn and Kee; Lance-Corporal
                   Kavanagh; Privates Keene, Gibbons, H. Hurst, H. Ryan, A. M.
                   Cague, T. Connors.
   July 22nd 1863. Affair at Keri-Keri.
       Killed   . Private John Ewins.
       Wounded . Privates J. Hamilton, T. Dunbar, —— Conroy, J. FitzGerald.
   August 25th 1863. Affair in the Hunua forest.
       Wounded . Private L. Glover.
   March 30th-April 2nd 1864. Capture of the *pah* at Orakau.
       Killed   . Sergeant W. Lawson; Privates T. Carroll, M. Bellaine, T. Traynor,
                   H. Cassedy.
       Died of wounds—Privates J. O'Donnell, T. Hannon, G. Gallagher.
       Wounded . Corporal Johnson; Drummer Lyon; Lance-Corporal G. Carroll;
                   Privates J. Close, G. Thomas, P. Fax, J. Carlisle, J. Stainton,
                   E. Jenkins.

January 24th-25th 1865. The affair at Nukumaro.

Officers—No losses.

Other ranks—

Killed   . Privates P. Conlin, J. Brien, S. Heathwood.

Died of wounds—Private T. Graham.

Wounded . Lance-Corporal J. Scott ; Privates J. Boyle, C. Rivers, J. Dorez, C. Gallagher, P. Cranny, T. Lock, F. Trevor, D. Watkins, R. High, P. Wheelon.

Died of accident or disease during the war—

Sergeants . Colour-Sergeant J. J. Hawkesby.

Corporal . T. Armstrong.

Drummer . A. Cassedy.

Privates . D. Carrall, T. Connell, D. Aldecroft (drowned), P. Kennedy, J. Moran, J. Murray, J. O'Meally (drowned), J. O'Neil (drowned), W. Carroll, W. M'Dowell, W. O'Rourke (drowned), M. Cussen, B. Bolton, A. Conner, J. Hallman, W. M'Carton, M. Quinn, M. Staunton, J. Hennesery, P. Leslie, J. Plunket, G. Ridgway (drowned), M. Slattery (drowned), J. Lockling, C. Roarke (drowned), E. Smith (drowned), G. Clarke, H. Kilroy, J. Sadler, P. Shea, E. Lawlor, T. Crosson, J. Harrity, J. M'Enerney, S. Welbey, C. Devling.

(L).

1878-80.   AFGHAN WAR.

Losses of the first Battalion from accident or disease while on the line of communication in the Khyber Pass.

Officer—

Quartermaster . . . R. Barrett.

Non-commissioned officers, &c.—

Quartermaster-Sergeant . A. Keating ; Colour-Sergeant A. Bagnall ; Sergeants J. Mann and J. M'Connell.

Corporals . . . . J. Connelly and J. Cox.

Drummer . . . . J. Manley.

Privates . . . . P. Darmody, M. Delaney, R. Dillon, W. Fitzgerald, M. Kehoe, H. King, G. M'Donnell, D. M'Guill, W. Milne, J. Monaghan, P. Shea, R. Bolger, J. Burke, T. Carthy, J. Cleary, P. Dumphy, J. Freeman, M. Haldon, J. Lee, J. Madden, J. O'Brien, R. Keeffe, J. Poe, A. Thompson, P. Carroll, J. M'Guire, J. Galavin, T. O'Connell, M. Downey, T. Graham, J. Kenny, T. Reiddy, P. Traynor, M. O'Donnell, P. Hudson, T. Preston, J. Kennedy, A. Newman, J. Perkins, J. Moore, W. Johnson, G. Kelly, T. Kelly, A. Keefe, J. Barry, J. Gorman, T. Murphy, T. Dunne, B. Farrell, P. Hackett, M. Keane, A. Pinner, M. Whelan.

(M).

1882.   EGYPT.

Kassasin.   9th September 1882.

Wounded   .   .   Captain H. H. Edwards (attached from Royal Welsh Fusiliers);
Privates Richard Keough and Richard Burke.

Tel-el-Kebir.   13th September 1882.

Officers and other ranks—

Killed   .   .   .   Captain C. M. Jones (attached from the Connaught Rangers);
Lance-Corporal F. B. Devine; Privates P. Milligan and
P. Stars.

Mortally wounded . Privates C. Looby, J. Woodall, P. Maher, H. Lines.

Wounded   .   .   Lieutenants A. G. Chichester and H. H. Drummond-Wolff
(attached from the Royal Fusiliers); Colour-Sergeant W.
Savage; Sergeant M. Darmedy; Privates P. Ryan, J. Shea,
P. Connelly, J. Sexton, P. Neill, M. Fleming, J. Mannering,
P. Malone, P. Gough, J. Goulding, T. Dalton, and J. Cannon.

The following died from accident or disease during the campaign—

Armourer-Sergeant T. Gillson; Sergeants M. Harper, T. Holmes,
C. Whiteside; Drummer J. O'Connor; Boy A. Paradine;
Privates J. Brophy, M. Callaghan, N. Fardy, H. Gardner,
J. Gulliver, P. Jordan, P. Joyce, J. Maher (drowned), J.
Ryan (1), J. Ryan (2), E. Street, J. Willis, E. Whelan.

(N).

1884-5.   THE CAMPAIGN ON THE NILE.

Casualties at Abu Klea on 16th and 17th February 1885.

16th.

Officer—

Severely wounded . Quartermaster and Honorary Lieutenant Jamieson.

Other ranks—

Severely wounded . Sergeant Hanraham.

Slightly wounded . Corporal Farrell; Privates Kerwick, Daveney, Daley, M'Loughlin,
Murphy, Porter.

17th.

Privates Norris, Healey, M'Keevor, Glashier, M'Guire.

Deaths from accident or disease during the campaign—

Sergeant R. Squire.

Corporal J. Kennedy; Lance-Corporal T. Kennedy.

Privates P. Breen, P. Burden, P. Carr, J. Coughlin, J. Coulter, D.
Dandridge, E. Dooey, E. Dyer, P. Farrell (drowned), T. Finn,
P. Fortune, L. Jones, W. Knapp, E. Lewis, W. Lynch, J.
Mackay (drowned), H. Morgan, G. Noyce, W. Roach.

(O).

1888. ### BLACK MOUNTAIN OR HAZARA CAMPAIGN.

Killed in action . . . . Privates P. M. C. Loughlin and J. Johnson.
Killed by falling over a precipice . Privates —— Gibson and —— M'Grath.
Wounded . . . . . Privates P. Martin, P. Ryan, and T. Gavin.

(P).

1896. ### MASHONALAND.

Killed . . . Private W. Wickham.
Died of disease . Private E. Lyons.
Wounded . . Lieutenant S. G. French ; Privates T. Mahony and James M'Kay.

(Q).

1900-1902. ### SOUTH AFRICA.

CASUALTIES OF THE ROYAL IRISH REGIMENT.

Officers.

Killed—
1900.
Feb. 12. Captain S. G. French . . . Operations for the relief of Mafeking.
July 23. Captain W. Gloster . . . . Slabbert's Nek.
1901.
Jan. 7-8. Captain F. L. Fosbery . . . Monument Hill, Belfast.

Died of wounds—
1900.
June 1. Captain Sir John E. C. Power, Bart. Wounded between Kroonstad and
(5th Battalion, attached to Irish   Lindley.
Yeomanry).
July 8. Captain J. B. S. Alderson . . . Wounded at Bethlehem.
Sept. 3. Captain R. R. Arbuthnot . . . Wounded at Ottoshop, Western
Transvaal.

Died of disease—
1900.
May 24. 2nd Lieutenant A. C. S. Fletcher . Bloemfontein.
1902.
March 21. Captain G. A. Ashfordby-Trenchard Elandsfontein
(5th Battalion, attached to 23rd
Mounted Infantry).

Wounded—
1900.
Feb. 14. Major H. M. Hatchell . . . Jacobsdal.
April 29. Captain R. A. Smyth . . . Thabanchu.

May 20.	Lieutenant M. H. E. Welch .	. Near Lindley.
July 7.	Captain T. Warwick Williams .	. Bethlehem.
	(Volunteer company).	
July 23.	Captain E. F. Milner (severely) .	. Slabbert's Nek.
1901.		
Jan. 7-8.	Captain E. F. Milner (severely .	. Monument Hill, Belfast.
Oct. 24.	Lieutenant J. A. M. J. P. Kelly	. Near Koffyfontein.
Nov. 6.	Major B. J. C. Doran . .	. Strydomsvlei, near Willowmore.
	(In command of a column).	

Injured—

Captain G. Hearn (4th Battalion).

Non-Commissioned Officers and Men.

Killed—

1900.

May 4.	6435 Private P. Murphy . .	. Near Brandfort.
May 10.	4055 ,, J. M'Lean.	
	6035 ,, A. Eaton . .	. Near Winburg.
June 28.	5291 ,, P. Ryan . . .	. Klipplaat Drift.
July 7.	6512 ,, M. Donovan . .	. Bethlehem.
	3853 ,, M. Carroll . .	. ,,
July 23-24.	2343 Sergeant J. Keyton . .	. Slabbert's Nek.
	6217 Corporal T. Ryan . .	. ,,
	1049 Private J. Gardiner (3rd batt.) .	,,
	6559 ,, M. Nagle . .	. ,,
	6529 ,, M. Power . .	. ,,
	3425 ,, M. Keating . .	. ,,
July 26.	5583 Corporal C. Hogan . .	. Naauwpoort Nek.
July 28.	3493 Lance-Corporal W. O'Farrell	. Slaapkranz.
Sept. 7.	3798 Private M. Dawson . .	. Near Lydenburg.
	944 ,, J. Connolly (5th Batt.) .	,,
1901.		
Jan. 7-8.	3614 Lance-Corporal J. Denison .	. Monument Hill, Belfast.
	4348 ,, G. Dowie .	. ,, ,,
	3733 Private J. Barry . . .	. ,, ,,
	1198 ,, J. Colwell (4th batt.) .	,, ,,
	5295 ,, M. Dundon . .	. ,, ,,
	858 ,, W. Grindon (3rd batt.) .	,, ,,
	6447 ,, M. M'Grath . .	. ,, ,,
	3439 ,, J. Shea . . .	. ,, ,,
March 14.	140 ,, M. Keogh . .	. Krugerspost.
Nov. 20.	6154 Sergeant W. Brady . .	. Rietfontein.
1902.		
Jan. 27.	5062 Private T. Corbett . .	. Mexico, near Winburg.

Died of wounds—

1900.

2958 Private W. Costan . .	. Wounded at Bethlehem, July 7.
289 ,, E. Brophy (3rd batt.) .	,, ,, ,,
63 ,, H. Azelby . .	. ,, ,, ,,
6114 ,, M. Wheelan . .	. ,, ,, ,,
2066 ,, P. Stewart . .	. Wounded at Slabbert's Nek, July 23-24.

1900.	6413	Private M. Holden . . .	Wounded at Slabbert's Nek, July 23-24.
	489	„ D. Devereux (3rd batt.) .	„ „ „
1901.	4882	Sergeant J. Jones . . .	Wounded at Monument Hill, Belfast, January 7-8.
	724	Private J. Clancy (4th batt.) .	„ „ „
	3923	„ J. Donovan . . .	„ „ „
	1989	„ J. Fitzgerald . . .	„ „ „
	6331	„ T. Murphy . . .	„ „ „
	2494	„ J. Ryan (5th batt.) .	Wounded at Krugerspost, March 14.
	2744	„ L. Taylor . . .	Defence of train at Wildfontein, March 22.
1902.	1040	„ J. Brett . . .	Defence of blockhouse near Lydenburg, March 22.

Accidentally killed or drowned—

1900.			
Dec. 30.	5871	Private B. Walsh . . .	Near Zand river farm.
1901.			
Feb. 23.	6375	„ P. Murphy . . .	Modder river.
Sept. 9.	4247	„ W. Sweeney . . .	Near Jagersfontein.
Nov. 20.	5845	„ D. Kehoe . . .	„ Lydenburg.
1902.			
Feb. 22.	——	Conductor F. Stanners (attached)	„ „
March 31.	3185	Private M. Cullen (4th Batt.) .	„ „

Died of disease—

Non-commissioned officers—

3750, Orderly-Room Sergeant P. Broderic ; 2762, Sergeant-Drummer T. Morey ; 4313, Sergeant J. Cheasty ; 3157, Sergeant H. Healey ; 5804, Corporal W. Fagan ; 5130, Corporal P. Murphy.

Drummer—5672, M. Wall.

Private soldiers—

5411, J. Brennan ; 138, J. Brien (4th Batt.) ; 6260, L. Clancy ; 32, P. Carthy (3rd Batt.) ; 1858, J. Clince (3rd Batt.) ; 4106, E. Clouter ; 5400, M. Coveney ; 4256, J. Craven ; 4227, C. Daly ; 1823, P. Dempsey (3rd Batt.) ; 6606, W. Donoghue ; 3767, P. Dunne ; 6305, J. Evett ; 3146, P. Eustace ; 3951, J. Fagan ; 6346, R. Field ; 6248, J. Fenelon ; 6219, J. Fleming ; 6335, W. Foran ; 1444, J. Giltrap (3rd Batt.) ; 1918, J. Gorman (5th Batt.) ; 580, J. Hanton (3rd Batt.) ; 6797, J. Houghton ; 1578, J. Hill (5th Batt.) ; 2909, B. Holohan (4th Batt.) ; 274, P. Kane (3rd Batt.) ; 6363, A. Kavanagh ; 939, T. Kavanagh (3rd Batt.) ; 6542, P. Keating ; 586, W. Kelly (3rd Batt.) ; 6031, J. Lee ; 4719, J. M'Namara ; 83, W. M'Namara (5th Batt.) ; 6228, J. Martin ; 3846, M. Malone ; 4414, J. Moran ; 6264, J. Mulcahy ; 6153, P. Mulcahy ; 5273, G. Murphy ; 1670, J. Murphy (3rd Batt.) ; 131, P. Murphy (3rd Batt.) ; 2111, M. Murray (4th Batt.) ; 4084, M. M'Guinness ; 6513, J. O'Neill ; 6397, T. Power ; 2326, J. Pyte (4th Batt.) ; 6453, J. Quirke ; 4708, A. Stafford ; 3419, W. Scannell ; 1471, J. Sinnott (3rd Batt.) ; 4871, J. Slattery ; 3620, R. J. Walsh ; 1458, G. Webster (4th Batt.) ; 6350, W. Whitmore.

Wounded—

1900.			
Feb. 10.	4723	Sergeant W. Leggett . . .	Klip Drift.
Feb. 27.	4893	„ J. Peebles . . .	Paardeberg.
	3623	Lance-Corporal R. Foster . .	„
	5386	Private M. Connell . . .	„
	6317	„ F. Ennis . . .	„

1900.

Feb. 27.	6186	Private A. Freeman	.	.	.	Paardeberg.

1900.

Feb. 27.   6186   Private A. Freeman . . . Paardeberg.

3442   „   M. Shaughnessy . .   „

6255   „   D. Fitzgerald . . . Ramah.

6249   „   M. Delohery . . .   „

March 31.   2808   „   P. Brown . . . Sannah's Post.

5490   „   M. Cain . . .   „

5218   „   J. Everett . . .   „

April.   5878   Lance-Corporal T. Holland . March from Thabanchu to Pretoria.

May.   5108   Sergeant F. M'Tighe, severely .   „   „   „

June.   5186   Lance-Corporal H. Cross, severely   „   „   „

3167   Private R. Dwyer . . .   „   „   „

3076   „   W. Nolan, severely .   „   „   „

3094   „   J. Murray, severely .   „   „   „

3594   „   P. Maher, severely .   „   „   „

June 28.   3747   Lance-Corporal J. Maher . . Klipplaat Drift.

June 29.   3702   Private J. Doyle . . . . Drift over the Zand river.

July 6.   1426   „   T. Allen . . . Bethlehem.

4983   „   J. Keadid . . .   „

July 7.   4243   Col.-Sergt. T. Mahony, severely   „

3911   Corporal P. Smith, severely .   „

6162   „   R. Cant, severely .   „

4710   Lance-Corpl. M. Reid, severely .   „

5267   „   M. Sullivan .   „

795   Private J. Parsons, severely .   „

257   „   T. Hughes (3rd Batt.) .   „

6613   „   D. Kenny, severely .   „

1659   „   J. Giltrap (3rd Batt.), severely   „

6331   „   J. Murphy, severely .   „

3267   „   K. Sealey . .   „

6393   „   C. Meehan, severely .   „

6254   „   J. Murphy, severely .   „

6203   „   J. Noctor, severely .   „

3387   „   M. Meara, severely .   „

1845   „   J. Hartigan (3rd Batt.) .   „

5974   „   J. Mooney . .   „

866   „   W. Carley (3rd Batt.), severely   „

1724   „   P. Fitzgerald, severely .   „

99   „   J. Dahy, severely .   „

2354   „   P. Mackay, severely .   „

206   „   J. Purcell, severely .   „

3450   „   W. Ryan, severely .   „

6492   „   J. Ryan, severely .   „

3862   „   P. Whelan, severely .   „

2756   „   P. Cherry, severely .   „

3334   „   M. Kelly, severely .   „

2595   „   W. Hally, severely .   „

1330   „   P. Doyle, severely .   „

3377   „   M. Butler . .   „

5604   „   J. Crotty, severely .   „

4385   „   J. Deane, severely .   „

5974   „   J. Mooney . .   „

1900.
July 7.   410 Private J. Gardner (3rd Batt.), severely . Bethlehem.
     1456   „   J. Devereux, severely . . .   „
     2353   „   J. Lander . . . .   „
     6609   „   J. Power . . . .   „

1900.
July.   7827 Lance-Sergt. W. M'Donnell, severely . Volunteer company . Bethlehem.
     7952 Corporal W. Wilson, severely . .   „   .   „
     7895 Private P. Beaumont . . .   „   .   „
     7834   „   T. Brophy . . .   „   .   „
     7854   „   T. Carroll . . .   „   .   „
     7844   „   A. Collins, severely . .   „   .   „
     7883   „   T. M'Cormick, severely . .   „   .   „
     7879   „   R. Malone, severely . .   „   .   „
July 23-24. 1967 Sergeant T. M'Guinness, severely   Slabbert's Nek.
     3562 Lance-Corp. J. Williams, severely   „
     4506 Private J. Kavanagh, severely .   „
     4817   „   J. Coghlan . . .   „
      630   „   R. Foley (3rd Batt.), severely   „
     2456   „   H. Keogh . . .   „
     2625   „   D. Hearney . . .   „
July 26.   6230   „   F. Belford, severely .   Naauwpoort Nek.
July 28.   6489   „   W. Sinnott, severely .   Slaapkranz.
     2143   „   J. Moore, severely . .   „
     1217   „   M. Quirke (3rd Batt.),
               severely . .   „
     3848   „   P. M'Namara . .   „
     4188   „   J. Kelly, severely . .   „
Sept. 7.   1989   „   P. Connors . .   Near Lydenburg.
     3831   „   J. Fitzpatrick . .   „
Nov. 6.   4892   „   C. Wilks . .   Bothaville.
     6189   „   W. Foulkes . .   „
     6249   „   M. Delohery . .   „
Dec. 26.   6565   „   B. Boyle, dangerously .   On railway near Pan.
     1604   „   J. Dalton, slightly . .   „   „

1901.
Jan. 7-8.   5217 Sergeant W. Bullock . .   Monument Hill, Belfast.
     2608 Lance-Corporal M. Spillane, severely   „   „
     5808 Drummer C. Abbott, severely .   „   „
     6196 Private W. Burke, severely .   „   „
     1558   „   P. Cavanagh, severely .   „   „
     6129   „   W. Butler, severely .   „   „
     6200   „   T. Doyle, severely .   „   „
     2611   „   J. Flynn, severely .   „   „
     1561   „   J. Jones . . .   „   „
     2133   „   P. Lacey (3rd Batt.), severely   „   „
     1680   „   J. Lawlor . .   „   „
     6407   „   J. O'Brien, severely .   „   „
     3308   „   J. O'Brien . .   „   „
     2228   „   R. O'Brien, severely .   „   „
     4077   „   J. O'Keeffe, severely .   „   „
      878   „   W. Connors (3rd Batt.), severely   „   „

1901.

Jan.	4609	Private	W. Power, dangerously .	Monument Hill, Belfast.
	6485	,,	T. Reilly, severely . .	,, ,,
	1222	,,	J. Ryan, severely . .	,, ,,
	3053	,,	W. Ryan, severely . .	,, ,,
	3348	,,	J. Sheehan, severely .	,, ,,
	4735	,,	J. Smith, severely . .	,, ,,
Jan. 29.	3595	,,	J. Radigan . . .	Tabaksberg.
Mar. 14.	2512	,,	D. Doyle, severely . .	Kruger's Post.
	1011	,,	J. Dalton, severely . .	,,
	1914	,,	J. Kane, severely . .	,,
May 5.	5314	Drummer	G. Radford . .	Haartebeestfontein.
	4071	Private J. Cooney . . .		,,
Aug. 21.	7876	,,	T. Lea	Wonderfontein.
Oct. 7.	6753	,,	P. Walsh . . .	Witklip.
	5590	Lance-Corp. A. Clinton .		Snyman's Post.
Oct. 19.	6564	Private T. Murphy . . .		,,

1902.

Mar. 19.	3263	Sergeant	T. M'Hale, severely .	Defence of blockhouse near Lydenburg.
	3725	Private	J. Flynn (4th Batt.), severely	,, ,,
	6664	Private C. O'Neill, dangerously .		,, ,,
	3769	,,	J. Kelly, severely . .	,, ,,
	1542	,,	J. Barnes, severely . .	,, ,,
	5594	,,	S. O'Donoghue, severely .	,, ,,
	5526	,,	J. Matley, severely . .	,, ,,
	6469	,,	T. Connors, severely .	,, ,,

1900.   The following men were severely injured :—

5731 Private J. Crooke and 3413 Private C. O'Brien.

APPENDIX 3.

OFFICERS OF THE 1st AND 2nd BATTALIONS WHO DIED IN THE WEST INDIES BETWEEN 1805 AND 1816.

1805. Captains H. Snooke and J. Graham ; Lieutenants R. Hutton, G. Andrews, R. N. King, A. Baker, P. Scott ; Paymaster W. Hay ; Quartermaster J. Atkins ; Ensign J. Strang.

1806. Lieutenant J. Maguire ; Quartermaster A. Haythorn.

1807. Lieutenants F. Munro, C. Carleton, R. Hopley ; Ensign H. Kennedy ; Paymaster H. Salvin ; Quartermaster —— Cullen.

1808. Lieutenant-Colonel R. Honeyman ; Captains A. Berkeley, T. Baylis, D. Lindsay, and H. Noel ; Lieutenant J. Whitley ; Ensign L. W. Redwood.

1809. Quartermaster —— Nowlan.

1810. Captains C. O'Gorman and J. N. Maillard ; Lieutenants W. Coulson, J. Ord, R. Barry, and J. S. Owen ; Ensigns S. Bishop, W. Bell, and A. O'Loughlin ; Paymaster Drake ; Assistant-Surgeon W. Crofton.

1811. Major W. Thomlinson ; Captain J. Hoy.

1812. Lieutenants W. Hely and S. Wilders ; Ensign —— Bastall ; Quartermaster W. Simmons.

1813. Major J. E. Inston ; Captain W. Burnett ; Lieutenant J. Dwyer ; Paymaster L. T. Sumpter.

1814. Major J. B. Haffey ; Captain J. Aitken ; Lieutenant E. Campbell.

1815. Captain W. H. Whitfield.

1816. Lieutenant W. Farmerie.

APPENDIX 4.

ROLL OF OFFICERS, WARRANT OFFICERS, NON-COMMISSIONED OFFICERS, AND MEN OF THE ROYAL IRISH REGIMENT TO WHOM HAVE BEEN AWARDED THE VICTORIA CROSS, MEDALS FOR DISTINGUISHED CONDUCT IN THE FIELD, FOR MERITORIOUS SERVICE, AND FOR LONG SERVICE AND GOOD CONDUCT.

THE VICTORIA CROSS.

Rank.	Name.	Campaign.
Captain	**Thomas Esmonde**	Crimea.
Captain . . .	**Hugh Shaw** . .	New Zealand.
Private, No. 3733	**John Barry** . .	South Africa.

(Lieutenant-General Sir Henry Marshman Havelock-Allan is not included in this list, as he won his V.C. while in another regiment.)

DISTINGUISHED CONDUCT IN THE FIELD.

Rank.	Name.	Campaign.
Sergeant . . .	Henry Morton .	Crimea.
Corporal . . .	M. Egan . . .	,,
,, . . .	Thomas Murphy .	,,
Private . . .	Richard Baglin .	,,
,, . . .	Edwin Erwin .	,,
,, . . .	Thadeus Flannery .	,,
,, . . .	Henry Forrestall .	,,
,, . . .	Robert Marshall .	,,
,, . . .	William Major .	,,
,, . . .	James M. Guinness .	,,
,, . . .	Nicholas O'Neill .	,,
,, . . .	John Sessman .	,,
,, . . .	Patrick Whelan (2830) .	,,
,, . . .	Patrick Whelan (3521) .	,,

(It will be noticed that these names are also shown on the list of recipients of the good conduct medal.)

Rank.	Name.	Campaign.	
Private . . .	James Acton . .	New Zealand,	1866.
,, . . .	John Brandon .	,,	1865.
,, . . .	George Clampitt .	,,	,,
,, . . .	John Graham .	,,	,,
,, . . .	John Hennigan .	,,	1866.
,, . . .	James Kearnes .	,,	1865.
Sergeant . .	Edward O'Donnell .	Egypt, 1882.	
Sergeant-Major .	J. Bergin . .	South Africa, 1900-2.	

Rank.				Name.			Campaign.
Sergeant	.	.	.	J. O'Connor	.	.	South Africa, 1900-2.
,,	.	.	.	H. Loney	.	.	,,
,,	.	.	.	T. Connolly	.	.	,,
Corporal	.	.	.	P. Doyle	.	.	,,
,,	.	.	.	E. Lovely	.	.	,,
Lance-Corporal	.	.	.	P. Dumphy	.	.	,,
,,	.	.	.	W. Tytherleigh	.	.	,,
Private	.	.	.	W. Sweeney	.	.	,,
,,	.	.	.	T. Baker	.	.	,,
,,	.	.	.	M. Maher	.	.	,,
,,	.	.	.	J. Murphy	.	.	,,
,,	.	.	.	J. Radigan	.	.	,,

WARRANT OFFICERS AND NON-COMMISSIONED OFFICERS TO WHOM HAS BEEN AWARDED THE MERITORIOUS SERVICE MEDAL AND ANNUITY.

Rank.			Name.			Campaign.
Sergeant	.	.	John Grant	.	.	Crimea.
Colour-Sergeant		.	Martin Cummins	.	.	China, Burma, and Crimea.
Sergeant-Major		.	William Toohey	.	.	Indian Mutiny.
Sergeant	.	.	Edward Foy	.	.	
Sergeant-Major		.	J. Bergin	.	.	Afghanistan, Nile, and South Africa.
Quartermaster-Sergeant		.	A. Molloy	.	.	New Zealand.
Sergeant	.	.	Richard Ford	.	.	Burma and Crimea.

NON-COMMISSIONED OFFICERS AND MEN WHO HAVE RECEIVED THE GRATUITY AND GOOD CONDUCT MEDAL FROM 1849 TO JUNE 30, 1902.

1ST BATTALION.

Year.		No.		Rank.					Name.
1850-1	.	338	.	Sergeant	.	.	.	.	Will Bett.
,,	.	788	.	Private	.	.	.	.	John Redding.
,,	.	609	.	,,	.	.	.	.	Mat. Connors.
1851-2	.	790	.	Sergeant	.	.	.	.	William Shanahan.
,,	.	810	.	Armourer-Sergeant	.	.	.	.	Richard Ford.
1852-3	.	681	.	Private	.	.	.	.	John Priestley.
,,	.	776	.	,,	.	.	.	.	Owen Cork.
,,	.	751	.	,,	.	.	.	.	James Ward.
,,	.	697	.	,,	.	.	.	.	Thomas Morrow.
1853-4	.	806	.	Colour-Sergeant	.	.	.	.	James M'Illwain.
,,	.	832	.	Corporal	.	.	.	.	Thomas M'Gowan.
,,	.	853	.	Private	.	.	.	.	Saul Gilloe.
1854-5	.	421	.	,,	.	.	.	.	Edward Lyons.
,,	.	653	.	,,	.	.	.	.	Robert Black.
,,	.	890	.	,,	.	.	.	.	Charles Armstrong.
,,	.	929	.	,,	.	.	.	.	Thomas Creagh.
,,	.	870	.	,,	.	.	.	.	Patrick Martin.
,,	.	927	.	,,	.	.	.	.	Thomas Carroll.
1855-6	.	2315	.	Sergeant	.	.	.	.	Henry Morton.
,,	.	2451	.	Corporal	.	.	.	.	M. Egan.

Year.	No.	Rank.	Name.
1855-6	2785	Corporal	Thomas Murphy
,,	3559	Private	Nicholas O'Neill.
,,	2025	,,	Robert Marshall.
,,	3023	,,	Edwin Erwin.
,,	3707	,,	Richard Baglin.
,,	2294	,,	Thadeus Flannery.
,,	2846	,,	William Major.
,,	3053	,,	Henry Forrestall.
,,	2080	,,	James M. Guinness.
,,	2830	,,	Patrick Whelan.
,,	3346	,,	John Sessman.
,,	3521	,,	Patrick Whelan.
,,	1054	,,	Bartholomew Barnacle.
,,	1055	,,	Patrick Daly.
1856-7			
1857-8	1100	,,	Walter Lawless.
,,	1196	Sergeant	Isaac Orchard.
,,	1233	Private	John O'Brien.
,,	1260	,,	Richard Dobin.
1858-9	3259	Sergeant	William Fannon.
,,	1504	,,	Thomas Connors.
1859-60	1676	,,	John Lavin.
,,	1780	Quartermaster-Sergeant	Charles Cadman.
,,	1464	Private	Daniel Flanagan.
1860-1	1828	,,	Patrick Connolly.
,,	2955	Sergeant-Major	Alexander Stowell.
,,	3967	Private	Benjamin Dyson.
,,	1870	,,	Patrick Clancy.
,,	1877	Sergeant	William Burkett.
,,	1874	Private	John Gilhooly.
1861-2	1878	,,	Thomas Melley.
,,	1551	,,	James Morgan.
,,	1190	Colour-Sergeant	Martin Cummins.
,,	1928	Private	James O'Daniel.
,,	1568	Hospital-Sergeant	Charles S. Edwards.
1862-3	3327	Sergeant	William Iron.
,,	2039	Private	Michael Farrell.
,,	1920	,,	Nichs. Wall.
1863-4	1866	,,	Michael Walsh.
,,	2124	,,	William Cunnah.
,,	1216	Sergeant	John O'Neill.
1864-5	968	Private	William Butler.
,,	3658	,,	Andrew Nelson.
,,	2257	,,	Michael Melvin.
,,	2396	,,	Michael Coulihan.
,,	2380	Quartermaster-Sergeant	Thomas Conway.
,,	2303	Private	Michael Sweeney.
1865-6	2294	,,	Thady. Flanery.
,,	3445	,,	Michael Fraley.
,,	946	,,	John Grady.
,,	2535	,,	John Lawler.

Year.	No.	Rank.	Name.
1865-6	2155	Colour-Sergeant	James Proctor.
,,	2327	Private	Jasper Twissell.
1866-7	2388	,,	John Hutch.
,,	2565	,,	John Dumphey.
,,	2618	,,	John Harrington.
,,	846	,,	Thomas Dowd.
1867-8	2682	,,	Patrick Barry.
,,	826	Sergeant	James Cumberford.
,,	2432	Private	Thomas Rabbit.
1868-9	3566	Quartermaster-Sergeant	James Proctor.
,,	1148	Private	Patrick Wall.
1869-70	2791	Colour-Sergeant	Charles Glynn.
,,	2786	Corporal	James O'Gready.
,,	2884	Sergeant	Patrick Collins.
,,	1131	Private	John Sexton.
,,	3361	Sergeant	Thomas Pearmain.
,,	973	,,	Charles Fitch.
1870-1	2989	Private	Daniel Leahy.
,,	2922	,,	Bartholomew Millerick.
,,	1026	,,	John Sheehan.
,,	2778	Armourer-Sergeant	George Ford.
,,	2948	Hospital-Sergeant	James O'Regan.
1871-2	3147	Private	Patrick Brady.
,,	3082	,,	Thomas Hickey.
,,	3502	,,	Jonathan Taylor.
,,	3038	,,	John Sweeney.
,,	4772	,,	John Toole.
,,	3138	Sergeant	Daniel Corbet.
1872-3	3300	,,	James Roddy.
,,	4089	Private	Samuel Card.
,,	1056	,,	Michael Doyle.
,,	3219	,,	Francis Boyle.
,,	3296	Corporal	John Pratt.
,,	3829	Sergeant	William Hudson.
,,	4019	Colour-Sergeant	Stephen Bowen.
,,	4158	,, ,,	Michael Murphy.
,,	4159	Private	James Fox.
1873-4	121	,,	Patrick Broderick.
,,	4300	,,	Moses Green.
,,	4653	,,	Anthony Hynes.
,,	4404	,,	John Stephens.
,,	146	,,	Michael Mahon.
,,	4709	,,	James Cuddy.
,,	2780	Sergeant	Richard Ford.
,,	2972	Corporal	Michael Duggan.
,,	4050	Private	John Cross.
1874-5	69-B. / 729	Corporal	Jerh. Donovan.
,,	1003	,,	David Roche.
,,	3852	Sergeant	Thomas Mathews.
,,	128	,,	Pat. M'Guinness.

Year.	No.	Rank.	Name.
1874-5	3149	Sergeant	John Hynes.
1875-6	75	Quartermaster's Clerk	Edward Foy.
,,	669	Sergeant	Thomas Spring.
,,	375	,,	John Fennely.
,,	173	Private	Patrick Keelehan.
,,	229	,,	Robert Cumberford.
,,	1062	,,	Michael Ryan.
,,	50	,,	Patrick M'Shean.
,,	234	,,	Michael O'Hanlon.
,,	1548	Sergeant	William Dickson.
1876-7	816	Quartermaster-Sergeant	William Sparrow.
,,	69-B. / 941	Private	Martin Burke.
,,	4559	Sergeant	Thomas Wright.
,,	951	Private	Alexander Sutton.
,,	4786	,,	Rody Walsh.
1877-8	69-Bde. / 508	,,	Joseph Davy.
,,	69-Bde. / 615	,,	Thomas O'Connor.
,,	355	,,	Dennis O'Brien.
,,	69-Bde. / 616	,,	Michael Quiligan.
,,	286	,,	Patrick Burke.
,,	69-B. / 931	,,	John Commons.
,,	1527	Bandmaster	Charles Fitzpatrick.
,,	4388	Sergeant	James Pearson.
,,	671	Private	William M'Conville.
,,	45	,,	Michael M'Loughlin.
,,	69-B. / 556	,,	John Byrne.
,,	1702	,,	Robert Shields.
,,	4788	Sergeant-Major	William Toohey.
1878	69-B. / 506	Private	Patrick Smith.
,,	69-B. / 503	,,	Patrick Croke.
,,	69-B. / 511	,,	Michael M'Cabe.
,,	69.B. / 663	,,	James Rodham.
1879	69-B. / 109	,,	Joseph Gleeson.
,,	69-B. / 653	,,	John M'Dermott.
1880	69-B. / 1460	,,	James Smith.
1881-2	1018	Sergeant-Instructor of Gymnastics	Edward Kenruly.
,,	1009	Sergeant	John M'Whurter.
,,	1242	Private	Michael Morrissey.

Year.	No.	Rank.	Name.
1882-3	1052	Sergeant	William Hayden.
,,	564	Private	Michael Mulhare.
1883-4	544	Corporal	Patrick Guinan.
,,	560	Private	Charles M'Carthy.
,,	1288	,,	John Beehan.
,,	1217	,,	Philip Walsh.
,,	1220	Sergeant	William Williams.
1884-5	1211	Private	Andrew Cahill.
,,	203	Sergeant	Charles O'Brien.
,,	281	Private	Patrick O'Brien.
,,	994	Corporal	Thomas Toomey.
,,	1412	Sergeant	Henry A. Hills.
1885-6	370	Corporal	Peter Byrnes.
,,	1196	Private	John Brennan.
,,	2158	Sergeant	Thomas L. Folley.
1886-7	1511	Musician	Robert Hughes.
,,	1545	Colour-Sergeant	Paul Stokes.
,,	974	,, ,,	John Kenely.
,,	1574	Sergeant-Cook	Robert Dillon.
1887-8	1549	Band-Sergeant	Charles Tribe.
,,	1719	Private	Thomas MacNamara.
,,	1202	,,	Edward Neville.
,,	2064	Orderly-Room Sergeant	Owen R. Williams.
1888-9	1140	Private	F. Dougherty.
,,	1575	Colour-Sergeant	A. Stevens.
,,	1896	Drummer	Patrick Nicholson.
,,	1152	Private	Thomas Raper.
,,	1873	,,	Hugh Cunningham.
,,	662	Quartermaster-Sergeant	Albert Hendy.
,,	1728	Private	S. Breadon.
,,	1760	,,	J. Byrne.
,,	501	,,	A. Ingram.
,,	2178	,,	A. Kirkpatrick.
,,	1146	Lance-Sergeant	J. O'Keefe.
,,	1209	Private	M. Tobin.
,,	1139	Colour-Sergeant	J. Bergen.
,,	645	,, ,,	S. Wills.
1890-1	1874	Private	Henry Walker.
1891-2	1879	,,	M. O'Neill.
1892-3	2205	Bandsman	J. Plunkett.
,,	2256	Private	T. Condon.
,,	2463	,,	J. Fitzsimons.
,,	1872	Bandsman	P. Bagge.
,,	2579	,,	G. Chaney.
,,	2578	,,	A. Hyam.
1893-4	2076	Colour-Sergeant	J. Cooper.
,,	1918	Quartermaster-Sergeant	W. E. Harradine.
1894-5	2882	Colour-Sergeant	W. Byrne.
,,	1012	Sergeant	P. Ward.
,,	2826	Private	M. Day.
,,	2099	,,	J. Sullivan.

Year.	No.	Rank.	Name.
1894-5	2100	Private	W. Bryan.
,,	2829	Colour-Sergeant	E. Tobin.
,,	2791	Bandsman	John Mould.
1895-6	3046	Sergeant-Instructor of Musketry	J. P. O'Brien.
,,	2790	Private	G. S. Simonite.
,,	1063	Lance-Corporal	Daniel Lowther.
,,	1498	Quartermaster-Sergeant	James Smith.
,,	2686	Private	Edward Naper.

2ND BATTALION.

Year.	No.	Rank.	Name.
1858-9	434	Colour-Sergeant	Dexter Johnson.
,,	403	,, ,,	Robert Meredith.
1859-60	369	,, ,,	Henry Backley.
,,	194	Sergeant	Francis O'Hare.
,,	1160	,,	Walter Thomson.
,,	1	Private	Patrick Shehan.
,,	3	,,	James Russell.
1860-1	4	Corporal	Michael Horrigan.
,,	49	Private	Michael Cawley.
1861-2	11	,,	John Power.
1862-3	310	Sergeant	Timothy M'Carthy.
,,	18	Corporal	Robert Philips.
1864-5	1401	Colour-Sergeant	John Gleeson.
1865-6	1412	Private	Philip Ryan.
,,	1391	Corporal	Peter Moloy.
1866-7	1594	Private	Jeremiah Bishhagra.
,,	1589	,,	Michael Ward.
,,	409	Colour-Sergeant	William Heald.
,,	386	Private	Andrew Murray.
1867-8	1795	Sergeant-Major	John Prendergast.
,,	1887	Private	Jeremiah Murphy.
,,	1400	,,	Thomas Gilloyley.
,,	1902	,,	Thomas Foley.
1868-9	1404	Sergeant-Instructor of Musketry	Samuel Chandler.
,,	144	Colour-Sergeant	William Darby.
1869-70	1896	Private	Edward Crowley.
,,	1893	,,	Patrick Connors.
,,	311	,,	Jeremiah Connors.
,,	1674	,,	Robert M'Dermott.
1870-1	1681	,,	Richard Fitzwilliam.
,,	1472	Colour-Sergeant	Alexander Nicholas.
1871-2	1851	Drum-Major	William Henry Hale.
,,	1606	Private	William Connell.
,,	1729	,,	William Arnett.
,,	16	,,	Michael M'Carthy.
1872-3	1653	Sergeant	Thomas Rooney.
,,	422	Colour-Sergeant	John Hart.
1873-4	1830	Private	George Lucas.
,,	2299	,,	Henry Carragher.
,,	1619	,,	Anthony Cushen.

Year.	No.	Rank.	Name.
1873-4	2518	Sergeant	Joseph Day.
,,	1516	,,	George Copley.
1874-5	1817	Private	Stephen Maloney.
1875-6	1809	Sergeant-Major	Charles Brain.
,,	65	Sergeant	James Mylan.
,,	2315	Private	John Fahey.
,,	1040	,,	John Reilly.
,,	70	Corporal	John Power.
,,	69-B./789	Private	Patrick Keefe.
,,	83	,,	Patrick Walsh.
,,	741	Colour-Sergeant	Patrick Dowling.
,,	43	,, ,,	Edward Molloy.
,,	78	Private	James Butler.
,,	2566	Corporal	John Syberry.
1876-7	1925	Armourer-Sergeant	John Smith.
,,	1247	Sergeant	Robert Waters.
,,	2344	Private	Patrick M'Cormack.
,,	2235	,,	Patrick Bryan.
,,	2385	,,	Michael Walsh.
,,	1924	,,	William Ferguson.
,,	145	Canteen-Sergeant	Patrick Maloney.
,,	176	Colour-Sergeant	William Forsythe.
,,	228	Sergeant	John Nixon.
,,	229	,,	John Dillon.
,,	372	,,	Michael Dowling.
,,	288	Corporal	Bernard M'Keown.
,,	1344	Drummer	Laurence Kavanagh.
,,	184	,,	John Smith.
,,	1797	Private	James Armitage.
,,	2325	,,	John Graham.
,,	2375	,,	Michael Whelan.
,,	2275	,,	Henry Ward.
,,	277	,,	John Keane.
,,	404	,,	Anthony Canavan.
,,	968	Sergeant	Joshua Forsythe.
,,	427	Private	William Gibbons.
,,	473	,,	James Kyle.
,,	592	,,	John M'Enerney.
,,	2381	Sergeant	John Ryan.
,,	426	Colour-Sergeant	Thomas F. Walshe.
,,	69-Bde./775	Private	Edward Graham.
1877-8	2308	Colour-Sergeant	Timothy Dempsey.
,,	743	Corporal	Timothy Troy Guder.
,,	959	Sergeant	William Mosgrove.
,,	381	,,	William Wilson.
,,	750	Private	John Barry.
,,	562	,,	Patrick Daly.
,,	830	Sergeant	Joseph Dundas.
,,	1073	Private	David Thompson.

Year.	No.	Rank.	Name.
1877-8	1090	Sergeant-Instructor of Musketry	James Stapleton.
,,	1025	Colour-Sergeant	Francis Birch.
,,	1000	Sergeant-Major	George Hawkesby.
,,	1019	Colour-Sergeant	Thomas MacMillan.
,,	993	,, ,,	Arthur Molloy.
1878	956	Private	Harry Carroll.
,,	1305	,,	Patrick Clifford.
,,	1407	Sergeant	Owen Connell.
,,	1334	Colour-Sergeant	Richard Brien.
,,	1356	Private	James Butler.
,,	1335	,,	John Kennedy.
,,	801	,,	Felix Logan.
,,	1474	Sergeant	Robert Markham.
,,	1480	Private	William Rowe.
,,	270	,,	John Corcoran.
,,	1369	,,	Thomas Quinlan.
,,	2374	,,	Joseph Walker.
,,	2304	,,	John Culligan.
,,	1631	Colour-Sergeant	Charles Tadd.
1879	1337	,, ,,	Clement Eaton.
,,	2341	Private	William Kennedy.
,,	69-B. / 1125	Sergeant	William Savage.
,,	1508	Private	John Murphy.
1880	1304	Sergeant	Thomas Kelly.
1880-1	1095	,,	William M'Intosh.
1881-2	2295	,,	Maurice Breen.
1882-3	529	Private	Daniel Allen.
1887-8	972	Sergeant	Charles Stokes.
,,	1944	Quartermaster-Sergeant	William Dundas.
,,	2042	Private	Samuel Pettit.
1888-9	2466	Lance-Sergeant	H. Clements.
,,	2397	Sergeant Drummer	J. Frost.
,,	416	Private	T. Pettit.
,,	2468	Colour-Sergeant	J. Chambers.
,,	2703	Band-Sergeant	W. Nash.
,,	2722	Corporal	E. Avery.
1890-1	2736	Sergeant	Martin Lepper.
,,	1927	Colour-Sergeant	John Perrin.
,,	2704	Sergeant Drummer	Francis Weeks.
,,	646	Private	Matt. Akins.
1892-3	2079	Colour-Sergeant	J. M'Namara.
1894-5	3199	Corporal Lance-Sergeant	Robert Smith.
,,	1576	Lance-Corporal	Matthew Doyle.
1895-6	3195	Quartermaster-Sergeant	J. Cremen.
,,	3246	,, ,,	J. Richings.
1896-7	2576	,, ,,	H. W. Walshe.

(From this date the official returns do not specify to which battalion the recipient of the medal belonged.)

1897-8	2072	Sergeant-Major	William Moffatt.
,,	3761	Private	Joseph Kennedy.

Year.	No.	Rank.	Name.
1897-8	3781	Colour-Sergeant	Henry Fitzgerald.
,,	3149	,, ,,	Patrick O'Brien.
,,	3430	Sergeant-Instructor of Musketry	David Morrissey.
,,	3231	Private	Robert Harwood.
,,	4288	Colour-Sergeant	Randal O'Driscoll.
,,	3576	Lance-Corporal	Frank Sherwin.
1898-9	3849	Private	Michael Callaghan.
,,	2806	Sergeant Drummer	Henry Tidy.
,,	3228	Sergeant	Edward Donovan.
,,	657	Private	Barthol. Castles.
,,	3247	Colour-Sergeant	John O'Brien.
,,	3982	Sergeant Drummer	Henry Williams.
1899-1900.	4285	Private	Patrick Broderick.
,,	4286	Sergeant of the Band	Otto Dusseldorf.
,,	4097	Private	Timothy Mockler.
,,	3572	,,	John Redmond.
,,	178	Quartermaster-Sergeant	Robert Lewry.
1900-1	548	Private	Edward Mulderig.
,,	568	Sergeant	J. Macpherson.
1901-2	1321	Private	William Ryan.
,,	547	Colour-Sergeant	E. Dougherty.
,,	1375	Lance-Corporal	C. J. Beresford.

APPENDIX 5.

TIRAH, 1897-8.

COLONEL LAWRENCE'S ORDER OF JUNE 8, 1898, WITH EXTRACT FROM THE ADJUTANT-GENERAL'S LETTER EXCULPATING THE SECOND BATTALION, ROYAL IRISH REGIMENT.

(Extract.)

"I am directed by the Secretary of State to inform you that a perusal of the papers connected with the withdrawal of the 2nd Battalion Royal Irish Regiment from the field force on the North-Western Frontier has satisfied the Commander-in-Chief that a grave injustice was done to the 2nd Battalion Royal Irish Regiment when it was recalled from field service.

"(Signed)   EVELYN WOOD, A.-G."

"Knowing that many present here with these battalions have sons, brothers and other relations and friends serving in the second battalion, and that also there are many here who have served in it, he thinks that this will be interesting and satisfying to all.

"The 2nd battalion left Jubbulpore for the front in August last, and when assembled at Rawal Pindi, all detachments having joined headquarters, was over 800 strong.

"The regiment moved thence by rail to Khasalgurh, from thence by march route to Hangu, the two last marches (twenty-six miles) being done in one day, guarding a convoy some five miles long, with the enemy reported as lying in wait to attack, which, however, they did not do.

"The battalion was detained at Hangu, in the Miranzai Valley for two or three weeks, and it was in this place, owing to the heat and unhealthiness of the valley, it being the most unhealthy time of the year, that malarial fever became prevalent, and few escaped sickness.

"From there the regiment was broken up into detachments, 100 men garrisoning the friendly village of Shahu Khel, in the Khanki Valley, and 150 being detached to the Kurrum. These latter, supposed to be sickly or weakly men, averaged twenty-two miles a day for six days. 'B' Company under Captain King, on one occasion marched seventeen miles to meet and escort back artillery; thirty men, under Lieutenant Potter, volunteered, after three hours' rest to march back as escort, which they did, the remainder following a few hours later, thirty-four miles in one day.

"On September 9th 'A' and 'C' companies from Hangu, with three native battalions, marched to Fort Lockhart, escorting a convoy, and in the return march were successfully engaged with the enemy on Gogra Hill.

"On September 12th the headquarters, 295 strong, took part in the relief of Gulistan, on which occasion three actions were fought between Hangu and that fort, at Gogra, Saragari, and Gulistan, the enemy being cleared off the Samana Ridge.

"The headquarters remained at Fort Lockhart awaiting the further advance. No hint that the regiment was to be sent back reached the ears of any one belonging to it until the day on which it was published in orders.

"As soon as he heard of it, the Commanding Officer and Second-in-command at once interviewed the General, who informed them that the reason of the recall was 'that the regiment was saturated with malarial fever.'

"The Commanding Officer, well knowing that at the time sickness had almost entirely disappeared, asked for a medical board, the result being that the board passed 523 men as absolutely fit, and above the average in physique. Thirty only were rejected at Fort Lockhart ; most of the remainder were at Kohat and Hangu and were not examined.

"Every effort was made to get the order cancelled, but without avail. The battalion marched into Rawal Pindi over 700 strong.

"A court of enquiry was applied for, and refused.

"In the end the battalion was ordered back to the front, but too late to take part in any further important operations. It thus lost the chance of adding fresh laurels to its name, through no fault of its own.

"It was not long before certain libellous newspaper writers, eager for scandal, commenced their attacks on the fair fame of the regiment, but no one who knows the material of which it consisted, men from the counties of Wexford, Tipperary, Kilkenny, and Waterford, ever for a moment gave credence to their tales.

"No steps have been left untaken to have this great wrong righted. His lordship, the Commander-in-Chief has given the above decision, and every man who wears or who has ever worn the uniform of the Royal Irish owes a debt of gratitude to his lordship which can never be sufficiently repaid for the trouble he has taken in our cause.

"Colonel Lawrence would like to make it known to the battalions here at Kilworth that he never heard or heard of, a complaint from any one during these operations, though the heat, hard work, and long marches were particularly trying. On the contrary, the men were conspicuous for cheery willingness and good temper, and their eager keenness to meet the enemy.

"CAMP, KILWORTH, *June 8th* 1898."

APPENDIX 6.

THE SOLDIER'S KIT IN SOUTH AFRICA.

Extract from Regimental Orders of 4th of January 1900—

s.s. *Gascon*.

"The valise equipment will be drawn to-morrow. The valises will be packed with the following articles: Clothes' brush; field cap (to be carried in haversack on moving); hold-all, with knife, fork, spoon, shaving brush, razor and case, and comb; Housewife; flannel shirt; socks (2 pair); one suit drab serge; towel and soap; worsted cap; canvas shoes; boot-laces (spare); small-book; tin of grease; flannel belt.

"ARTICLES WORN OR CARRIED BY THE SOLDIER.

"Full dress: head dress and cover; frock; flannel shirt; trousers; braces; socks; flannel belt; ankle boots; putties; haversack, with balance of day's ration; valise packed, straps and braces; waistbelt and frog; pouches; pocket-knife and lanyard; water-bottle (full), with strap; mess tin and strap; Field dressing and description[1] card; rifle, with sling, pull-through, full oil-bottle, and sight protector; bayonet and scabbard; greatcoat and straps; entrenching tools (if in possession, 16 picks and 33 shovels in each company).

"Articles to be packed in the sea kit-bags: 1 frock (H.P.); 1 pair ankle boots; 1 pair trousers (H.P.); 1 black kit-bag."

By Regimental Order dated April 19, 1900, the weight was reduced—
"The following articles only will be carried on the person of the soldier when the battalion moves (viz.): Khaki serge (trousers and jacket); flannel shirt; flannel belt; putties; socks and boots; helmet; drawers (if in possession); waistbelt; braces; two pouches with 50 rounds of ammunition in each; bayonet and frog; rifle and sling; haversack on back; mess tin; water-bottle; one blanket rolled on belt; jersey, either worn on person or rolled on the blanket; woollen cap (if in possession) in the haversack.

"If rations are carried, meat in mess tins, biscuit in haversack.

"All small kit must be carried in the haversack.

"In company waggon the following will be carried, viz.: greatcoat with one shirt and one pair of socks in the pockets; one blanket; one waterproof sheet."

[1] *I.e.*, identity card.

APPENDIX 7.

INSTRUCTIONS FOR THE DEFENCE OF TRAINS, IN ORDERS FOR DECEMBER 6, 1900.

"The following C. of S. circular memo., No. 25 of Pretoria 27-11-00 is published for information.

1. All officers and men travelling by train on all occasions must be armed.
2. The senior officer travelling on a train is responsible for its defence, if attacked.
3. For this purpose every officer travelling should satisfy himself whether he is the senior officer on the train or not.
4. The senior officer on the train should see that the men travelling by the train have their rifles handy, and that one or two men are detailed to keep a look-out.
5. It has lately been noticed that the enemy, when they attempt the capture of a train, ride up behind the train when it is going slowly up a grade, and detach the vacuum hose from the rear of the brake-van. They then open fire along both sides of the train, to prevent any one getting out.
6. To avoid this, a truck is attached to the rear of each train, with the vacuum hose disconnected. If any troops are travelling on the train, the senior officer should see that some of them are posted, if possible, on the rear truck.
7. Engine drivers have instructions to blow a long blast on the base whistle, if they have any reason to think that anything is wrong. Troops should be instructed to stand to arms on hearing this warning."

In orders of February 22, 1901, appeared the following instructions for officers and men travelling by train.

"1. A commander is to be detailed in each truck in which there are troops.
2. Officers travelling with troops are to be distributed throughout the train : they are not all to travel together in one truck.
3. The men are to keep their ammunition on, and their rifles beside them. The rifles are not to be stacked in a corner of the truck.
4. The men in the rear truck are to be mounted as a guard with a sentry, and magazines charged.
5. The officer in command of the train should enquire of the Commandant or R.S.O. which are the most dangerous parts of the line and warn all under his command.
6. Goods and bales on the trucks are to be arranged as breastworks as far as possible, in the rear truck especially.
7. R.S.O.'s are to arrange that these orders are shown to the Commander of every train. When small parties without an officer or N.C.O. are on the train, he should appoint one man in charge."

APPENDIX 8.

OPERATIONS IN THE NORTH OF THE TRANSVAAL.

EXTRACT FROM THE "RECORD OF SERVICE," FROM APRIL 12, 1901, TO SEPTEMBER 30, 1901, SHOWING THE MOVEMENTS OF THE FIRST BATTALION DAY BY DAY DURING THIS PERIOD.

1901.

12th April . Came under command of Colonel Park forming part of Park's column

13th „ . together with 1/ Gordon Highlanders, 53rd Battery, Royal Field Artillery, 4th M.I., one Company 4th Divisional M.I. The battalion fell in at 6.15 P.M. The infantry got into ox waggons after crossing Mission Drift and rode 5 miles to Gun Hill : marched from there to Vlakfontein and halted till dawn, then marched across Klipplaats drift, total distance 27 miles.

14th „ . Marched at 5 A.M. to De Groot boom, crossing Speckboom River. No opposition ; some casualties in the Mounted Infantry who acted as rear-guard ; road very bad in places.

15th „ . Battalion fell in at 5.15 with orders to take and hold the ground commanding Oliphant's Poort road. No opposition. Camped at Doornhoek.

16th „ . Marched at 5.30 A.M. expecting to attack laager at Bergfontein, no opposition ; laager vacated except by women and children. Road extremely bad.

17th „ . Marched at 2 P.M. for Reitfontein.

18th „ . F, G, and H Companies, 1 gun R.F.A., one Company Mounted Infantry, under Lt.-Col. Guinness ; A, B, C, and D companies (under Capt. Grogan), 1 pom-pom, 1 company Mounted Infantry, under Major Eustace, King's Royal Rifles, formed two separate columns ; the former to work to the N.W., the latter to the S.W. to round up D. Shuman reported in kloof to the west. Col. Guinness' column marched to Dwars River East, Major Eustace's to Boschfontein. Colonel Guinness' column met no opposition. Major Eustace's was sniped. No casualties amongst the Royal Irish.

19th „ . Having received information that D. Shuman was in kloof about 8 miles away, Col. Guinness' column marched at 6.15 A.M. up the Dwars River West. Met no opposition and halted about 7 miles from former camp up Dwars River West. Major Eustace's column proceeded at 5 A.M. through nek west of Boschfontein ; C Company under 2nd Lieut. Hon. H. Deane-Morgan captured 24 Boers and 900 cattle.

20th „ . Lieut.-Colonel Guinness' column marched at 7 A.M. to camping ground of 18th inst. Major Eustace's column after farm clearing returned to Boschfontein.

21st April . Lieut.-Colonel Guinness' column marched to Reitfontein ; Major Eustace's column to Boschoek ; total bag of combined columns 92 Boers, and 1200 cattle.

22nd ,, . Major Eustace's column halted at Boschoek.

23rd ,, . Major Eustace's column marched to Modder Spruit, parts of a blown-up " Long Tom " brought into camp.

24th ,, . Major Eustace's column marched to Reitfontein, A, B, C, and D companies rejoining Headquarters.

25th ,, . F and H companies under Captain White proceeded on convoy duty to Steelpoort drift. A, B, C, and G Companies with Headquarters fell in at 6.15 P.M. and, with Colonel Park and one 15-pounder gun and one company mounted infantry, marched to Nek about 5 miles due east of Reitfontein, there to bivouac and co-operate next day with Major Gough from Lydenburg and Colonel M'Bean, Gordon Highlanders, to S. and S.E.

26th ,, . Fell in at 5.30 A.M. and captured by combined movement about 60 prisoners, 1 pom-pom, and 600 cattle. Returned to camp *via* Drepgezat and Modder Spruit, a very exhausting day. F and H companies returned from convoy duty. No casualties.

28th ,, . B and D companies under Lieut. Farmer proceeded on convoy duty to Magnet Heights.

4th May . . Marched at 7 A.M. for Boschfontein. No opposition.

5th ,, . . Marched at 4.30 A.M., A and G Companies under Major Orr proceeding by Kopjes Kraal and Kraaibosch occupying Nek between latter Kaffir Kraal, for Kaffir Kraal Valley. There was some firing at mounted infantry in valley, but no casualties. Camped on Oshoek.

6th ,, . . Marched to Boschoek (1341).

10th ,, . . March at 7 A.M. for Lydenburg.

15th ,, . . ,, 3 A.M. for Manchberg.

16th ,, . . ,, 5 A.M. for Klipgat (209).

17th ,, . . ,, 9 A.M. for Tweefontein (520).

18th ,, . . ,, 7 A.M. for Bosjes Kop (199).

19th ,, . . ,, 9 A.M. for Nelspruit.
A, B, C, and D Companies proceeded to Godwan, Nooitgedacht, Alkmaar, and Elandshoek respectively on detachment to guard the line.

23rd ,, . . A, B, C, and D companies rejoined Headquarters.

25th ,, . . Marched at 8 A.M. to camp near Bosjes Kop, crossing Crocodile Drift.

26th ,, . . Marched at 6 AM. for Doorn Kraal.

27th ,, . . Marched at 8 A.M. for Tweefontein, camped S.E. of Nelspruit Drift.

28th ,, . . A, B, C, D, and F companies paraded at 6 A.M. and proceeded with Colonel Park to burn farms, &c., D company proceeding across Nelspruit to piquet hills to N.W., B and C companies to hills to W., and A and F companies to Krugers farm.

29th ,, . . Marched at 4.40 A.M. for Bosjes Kop.

30th ,, . . Marched at 8.30 A.M. for Alkmaar. Half the force got across the drift (which was rapid and difficult) and camped on south side, remainder camped on north side.

31st ,, . . Marched into Alkmaar.

10th June . Marched at 8.30 A.M. and crossed the Crocodile by drift, infantry by sheep bridge.

11th ,, . Marched at 8 A.M. for Heidelburg, and camped with Burney's column, with which was General Spens.

12th June	. Marched at 8.15 A.M. to Tweefontein.
13th ,,	. Marched at 8.30 A.M. for Reitvallei.
15th ,,	. Marched at 6 A.M. for Houtboschtoop.
16th ,,	. Marched at 9 A.M. for Elandsdrift over very bad road.
17th ,,	. A Company proceeded on convoy duty to Lydenburg. B, D, F, G, and H Companies searched kloofs to the west running up Drakensberg range. Bag 5 prisoners : no opposition.
18th ,,	. Marched at 6.30 A.M. to Kalmoesfontein : very bad road.
19th ,,	. Erected blockhouses in the Nek south of camp and also S.W. of camp.
20th ,,	. Moved camp about 3 miles to the east. D company under Captain Milner with one gun R.F.A. proceeded on convoy duty to Kaffirfootpad to meet convoy with A company.
21st ,,	. A and D companies rejoined with convoy from Lydenburg.
22nd ,,	. A, C, D, F, and G companies under Lieutenant-Colonel Guinness with 1 Company Mounted Infantry and 1 gun R.F.A. paraded at 6.30 A.M., and marched to ground overlooking Crocodile valley with the intention of stopping the enemy retiring from Colonel Benson's column, operating on Somerset and Kodoeshoek. No Boers.
24th ,,	. A, B, C, and H Companies with mounted infantry and one section R.F.A. carried out the same duty as on 22nd inst. No Boers.
25th ,,	. A, B, C, and F Companies performed manœuvres much similar to those of yesterday. No Boers. Some farms cleared of women and children.
26th ,,	. Battalion (except G Company) fell in at 6.30 A.M. D Company proceeded with 1 gun R.F.A. under Major Gavin to occupy spur overlooking Buffels Kloof, Kleinfontein. The remainder moved west across Buffels Kloof and to Crocodile valley. Heavy climbing. No Boers. Some cattle captured.
27th ,,	. Marched at 8 A.M. for Kaffirfootpad.
28th ,,	. Marched at 6.30 A.M. for Lydenburg.
2nd July	. A, B, C, and D Companies fell in under Major Gavin at 10 P.M. for a turning movement on Vosloo's Farm near Kruger's Post. F, G, and H Companies under Lieutenant-Colonel Guiness, C.B., fell in at 11.15 P.M. The former party proceeded on foot across the country, the latter along the Lydenburg-Kruger's Post road together with guns and mounted infantry. Surrounded Vosloo's Farm by dawn 3rd inst., but piquet had gone.
3rd ,,	. Moved on to Kruger's Post and bivouacked there, some casualties in M.I., but enemy not in force.
4th ,,	. Marched at 7 A.M. for Lydenburg. The enemy followed up the rear-guard. There were no casualties.
5th ,,	. Rendezvoused at 12 noon, and marched to Witklip, 2 companies M.I., 2 guns, 42nd Batty. R.F.A., and 1 pom-pom.
6th ,,	. Marched at 4 A.M. for Wemers Hoek.
7th ,,	. Marched at 8.30 A.M. for Balmietfontein.
8th ,,	. A, D, F, G, and H companies under Lieutenant-Colonel Guinness, C.B., "fell-in" at 6.55 A.M. and with M.I. and 2 guns R.F.A. proceeded south to burn farms and collect families. No opposition.
9th ,,	. Marched at 8.30 A.M. for Klipbank Spruit.
10th ,,	. ,, to Oshoek.
12th ,,	. ,, to Weemershoek.
13th ,,	. ,, to Lydenburg.
26th ,,	. ,, at 6.30 A.M. for Zwaggershoek.
27th ,,	. ,, to Elandspruit.

28th July   .   Marched to Dulstroom, and were joined by 4th Battalion M.I. and 2 guns R.F.A.

29th ,,   .   ,,   to Witpoort.

30th ,,   .   ,,   to Blinkwater.

3rd August   .   Blinkwater. D and F companies with two guns R.F.A. marched at 4.30 A.M. for Konterdanskloof, the M.I. having gone on at 1.30 A.M. 2 Boers killed, 3 wounded, 200 cattle, 400 sheep captured.

4th ,,   .   Marched at 10 A.M. for Roos Senekal.

7th ,,   .   Marched at 9 A.M. for Paardekloof.

8th ,,   .   At 12 midnight A, B, C, and H companies with machine gun under Lieutenant-Colonel Guinness, C.B., marched by Kaffir path over the eastern spur of the Tantesberg at midnight to the N.N.E. to surprise and capture Boers and cattle. Two Companies M.I., one section R.F.A., and pom-pom under Colonel Park moved by road more to the east. Captured 136 cattle and about 20 horses.

11th ,,   .   Got waggons up Tantesberg and marched on about 6 miles.

12th ,,   .   Marched to Goedgedacht to remain there with a view of stopping the roads to the east and south-east.

17th ,,   .   Five companies and two guns marched at 8.30 A.M., news being brought in that Boers and cattle were at Paarde Plaatz. Force got there too late.

22nd ,,   .   Marched to Paardekloof.

25th ,,   .   Marched to Roos Senekal.

26th ,,   .   H company and the 4th Battalion M.I. went along Lydenburg Road to co-operate with us the next day.

27th ,,   .   A, B, D, F, and G companies, 1 section R.F.A., pom-pom, and 2 companies M.I., under Lieutenant-Colonel Guinness, C.B., marched at 3 A.M. along road leading to the sources of the Tonteldos. Met Major Walker's party at about 10 A.M. They had been sniped. Camped at Schoongezicht.

28th ,,   .   Marched at 2 P.M. for Roos Senekal.

30th ,,   .   ,,   to Paarde Kop.

2nd Sept.   .   ,,   ,, Blinkwater.

6th ,,   .   ,,   ,, Groot Reit Vlei.

7th ,,   .   ,,   ,, Hoed Spruit.

9th ,,   .   ,,   ,, Bankfontein.

10th ,,   .   ,,   ,, Gun Hill, about 2 miles N.E. of Middelburg.

13th ,,   .   ,,   ,, Moved to camp where Colonel Benson had been, about 1 mile N. of Middelburg.

16th ,,   .   ,,   ,, Pan.

17th ,,   .   ,,   ,, Wonderfontein.

18th ,,   .   ,,   ,, Bergendal.

19th ,,   .   ,,   ,, Machadodorp.

23rd ,,   .   ,,   ,, Helvetia.

24th ,,   .   ,,   ,, Shumans Kloof.

27th ,,   .   ,,   ,, Badfontein.

28th ,,   .   ,,   ,, Witklip.

29th ,,   .   ,,   ,, Lydenburg.

APPENDIX 9.

SUCCESSION OF COLONELS OF THE REGIMENT.

COLONEL-IN-CHIEF.

Field-Marshal The Right Hon. G. J., Viscount Wolseley, K.P., G.C.B.,
O.M., G.C.M.G. 1898

COLONELS.

1. Arthur Forbes, Earl of Granard 1684
2. Arthur, Lord Forbes 1686
3. Colonel Sir John Edgworth 1688
4. Edward Brabazon, Earl of Meath 1689
5. Major-General Frederick Hamilton 1692
6. Lieutenant-General Richard Ingoldsby 1705
7. Brigadier-General Robert Stearne 1712
8. Brigadier-General William Cosby 1717
9. Colonel Sir Charles Hotham, Bart. 1732
10. Major-General John Armstrong 1735
11. General Sir John Mordaunt, K.B. 1742
12. Lieutenant-General John Folliott 1747
13. General Sir John Sebright, Bart. 1762
14. General Sir James Murray, Bart. (later Pulteney) . . . 1794
15. General John Hely Hutchinson, Earl of Donoughmore, K.B. . . 1811
16. General Matthew Aylmer, Lord Aylmer, G.C.B. . . . 1832
17. Field-Marshal Sir John Forster Fitzgerald, G.C.B. . . . 1850
18. Lieutenant-General Clement Alexander Edwards, C.B. . . 1877
19. General Sir Alexander Macdonell, K.C.B. 1882
20. General Sir Richard Denis Kelly, K.C.B. 1886
21. General George Frederick Stevenson Call, C.B. . . . 1889
22. General Robert Walter M'Leod Fraser 1895
23. Lt.-General Sir Henry Marshman Havelock-Allan, Bart., V.C., G.C.B. 1895
24. Major-General Charles Frederick Gregorie, C.B. . . . 1897

BIOGRAPHIES OF THE COLONELS.

COLONEL-IN-CHIEF.

Field-Marshal The Right Hon. G. J., Viscount Wolseley, K.P., G.C.B., O.M., G.C.M.G.

Garnet Joseph Wolseley, the eldest son of Major Wolseley, 25th The King's Own Scottish Borderers, was born on the 4th of June, 1833, and was appointed Ensign in the 80th Regiment on the 12th of March, 1852. He served with that regiment in the Burmese War of 1852-53 (Medal); he was with the expedition under Sir John Cheape against the robber chief Myat Toon, and was severely wounded when leading a storming party (Mentioned in despatches). In this campaign Ensign Wolseley fought shoulder to shoulder with the men of the 18th Royal Irish, and thus, early in his military career, formed acquaintance with the regiment of which he was destined to become Colonel-in-Chief, and which has since served through campaigns in armies under his command.

Lieutenant Wolseley's next active service was in the Crimea with the 90th Light Infantry. Landing in December, 1854, he was employed in the trenches as Acting Engineer until the fall of Sebastopol, and was engaged in the assault and defence of the Quarries on June 7th, the attack of June 18th, and the sortie of August 30th, when he was severely wounded (Several times mentioned in despatches, Medal with clasp, Knight of the Legion of Honour, 5th Class of the Medjidie, and Turkish Medal).

Captain Wolseley served through the Indian Mutiny, and was present at the relief of Lucknow, the defence of the Alumbagh, the siege and capture of Lucknow, the affair of Baree, and the action at Nawabgungee (Repeatedly mentioned in despatches, promoted to be Major with Brevet of Lieutenant-Colonel, Medal with clasp).

Lieutenant-Colonel Wolseley served on the staff of Sir Hope Grant in the war of 1860 in China, and was present at the assault of the Taku Forts, and in all the other engagements throughout the campaign (Medal with two clasps).

During service on the staff in Canada, Colonel Wolseley was employed from 1868 to 1870 in dealing with the Fenian raids (Medal with two clasps), and he commanded the expedition sent in 1870 from Canada to the Red River Territory for the suppression of the Rebel Government at Fort Garry (K.C.M.G., C.B., Clasp).

Sir Garnet Wolseley was Governor of the Gold Coast and Commander of the Forces during the Ashanti War of 1873-74. For this service he received the thanks of both Houses of Parliament, was promoted to be Major-General for Distinguished Service in the Field, and was awarded the G.C.M.G., K.C.B., and Medal and clasp.

In June, 1879, Sir Garnet Wolseley went to South Africa as Governor and High Commissioner of Natal; he completed the subjugation of the Zulus, brought the war to an end, and afterwards overpowered Sekukuni's forces, and destroyed their stronghold (G.C.B., Medal and clasp).

Lieutenant-General Sir Garnet Wolseley was Commander-in-Chief of the British Expeditionary Army throughout the Egyptian War of 1882, in which campaign that army in the space of twenty-five days effected its disembarkation at Ismailia, traversed the desert, fought the decisive battle of Tel-el-Kebir, and seized Cairo, the capital. He received the thanks of both Houses of Parliament, was raised to the Peerage, and promoted to be General for Distinguished Service in the Field (Medal with clasp, 1st Class of the Osmanieh, and Khedive's Star).

Lord Wolseley commanded the Forces in the Nile Expedition of 1884-85. He received the thanks of both Houses of Parliament, was raised to be Viscount in the Peerage, and was awarded two clasps. The prize which Lord Wolseley offered to the Battalion which made the fastest passage up the Nile was won by the 1st Battalion of the 18th Royal Irish.

On his return from the Soudan, Viscount Wolseley resumed his post of Adjutant-General to the Forces, which he held until 1890, when he was appointed Commander-in-Chief of the Forces in Ireland. He was promoted to be Field-Marshal on the 26th of May, 1894. In 1895, Lord Wolseley was appointed to succeed H.R.H. the Duke of Cambridge as Commander-in-Chief, and held this post for five years. On the 20th of July, 1898, Lord Wolseley was appointed by Her Majesty Queen Victoria to be Colonel-in-Chief of The Royal Irish Regiment.

COLONELS.

1. Arthur Forbes, Earl of Granard.

Arthur Forbes, the eldest son of Sir Arthur Forbes, Bart., of Castle Forbes, Co. Longford, was born in 1623, and was a cavalry officer in the Royal Army during the rebellion in the reign of King Charles I. He attained the rank of Colonel in 1646, and held a command in

Scotland under Montrose. Having zealously espoused the royal cause, he was, after the Restoration sworn a member of the Privy Council and appointed Marshal of the Army in Ireland. He was raised to the peerage of Ireland by patent, dated 22nd of November, 1675, as Baron Clanehugh and Viscount Granard. In 1684, the independent companies of foot in Ireland were formed into seven infantry regiments, and the Colonelcy of one of these corps was conferred upon Viscount Granard, who was promoted to the rank of Lieutenant-General. Lord Granard's regiment, afterwards the 18th Royal Irish, and now The Royal Irish Regiment, is the only one of the regiments then formed which has continued in the service of the British crown. In December, 1684, Viscount Granard was created Earl of Granard. In 1686, he resigned the Colonelcy of his regiment in favour of his son, Arthur, Lord Forbes.

2. Arthur, Lord Forbes.

Lord Forbes served under Marshal Turenne, and took part in the battle of Saspach. He was present at the siege of Buda. He obtained the command of Lord Granard's regiment on the 1st of March, 1686, and commanded it when it came to England at the time of the Revolution in 1688. The regiment marched from Chester to London, where it was quartered in the borough of Southwark. Soon after the abdication of King James II., Lord Forbes retired from the service.

3. Colonel Sir John Edgworth.

This officer was Captain of one of the independent companies of pikemen and musketeers in Ireland, and was promoted to be Major of the Earl of Granard's regiment. On the retirement of Lord Forbes, the Colonelcy of the regiment was conferred on Sir John Edgworth by the Prince of Orange. In consequence of irregularities concerning the supply of clothing to recruits, Sir John was deprived of his commission in 1689.

4. Edward Brabazon, Earl of Meath.

The Hon. Edward Brabazon was originally Captain of one of the Irish independent companies. In 1684, he succeeded, on the death of his brother, to the dignity of Earl of Meath. He joined the Prince of Orange at the Revolution of 1688, and, in the following year, was appointed to the Colonelcy vacated by Sir John Edgworth. The regiment being selected for service in Ireland with Duke Schomberg's army, he commanded it at the siege of Carrickfergus and at the battle of the Boyne. He showed great gallantry at the siege of Limerick, where he was wounded. At the close of the campaign in Ireland the Earl of Meath retired from the service.

5. Major-General Frederick Hamilton.

Frederick Hamilton commenced his military career in one of the companies of pikemen and musketeers which were incorporated in Lord Mountjoy's regiment. In 1688, he was given a company in Lord Forbes' regiment by King William III., and promoted to be Major. He served with the regiment through the campaign in Ireland, and, when Lieut.-Colonel Newcomb was mortally wounded at the storming of Limerick, he succeeded to the Lieut.-Colonelcy of the regiment, and commanded it at Athlone, Aughrim, and second siege of Limerick. In 1692, he succeeded the Earl of Meath in the Colonelcy. He commanded the regiment throughout the campaign of King William III. in Flanders, and was wounded at the memorable assault upon the castle of Namur. In 1702, Colonel Hamilton was promoted to be Brigadier-General in the Duke of Marlborough's army, and his brigade, which included his own regiment, was engaged at the sieges of Venloo, Ruremonde, and Liege. Brigadier-General Hamilton again commanded a brigade during the campaigns of 1703 and 1704, and, as a Major-General, he took part in the battles of Schellenberg and Blenheim. In 1705, he received Queen Anne's permission to sell the Colonelcy of his regiment.

6. Lieutenant-General Richard Ingoldsby.

Richard Ingoldsby entered the army in the reign of King Charles II., his first commission being dated 13th of June, 1667. He joined the Prince of Orange at the Revolution, and after serving in the campaigns of King William III., he was appointed to the Colonelcy of the 23rd Regiment. He commanded that regiment at Namur, and was promoted to the rank of Brigadier-General in 1696. On the outbreak of war in 1701, he was sent to Holland with a command in the Duke of Marlborough's army, and highly distinguished himself during several campaigns. As a Lieutenant-General he was present at the battles of Schellenberg and Blenheim. On the 1st of April, 1705, General Ingoldsby was appointed Colonel of the 18th Royal Irish, and was afterwards nominated one of Her Majesty's Lords Justices, and Master of the Horse for Ireland. He died on the 29th of January, 1712.

7. Brigadier-General Robert Stearne.

Robert Stearne belonged to one of the independent companies in Ireland that were incorporated into Lord Granard's Regiment in 1684. His journal, which relates the stirring events in which he participated with the regiment from 1684 to 1717, is now one of the most valued possessions of The Royal Irish. He accompanied the regiment to England at the Revolution in 1688, and became Captain of his company in the following year. At the close of King William's campaign in Ireland he was promoted to be Major. He served in the Flanders campaigns of 1695 and 1696. At the storming of Namur, where the regiment so greatly distinguished itself and acquired the title of The Royal Regiment of Ireland, Lieut.-Colonel Ormsby was killed, and Major Stearne was promoted by King William to the lieut.-colonelcy. He served in the Netherlands and Germany throughout the whole of the wars of Queen Anne's reign, and commanded the regiment at the battles of Schellenberg, Blenheim, Ramillies, Oudenarde, and Malplaquet ; also in numerous sieges and engagements. Colonel Stearne became Brigadier-General in 1711, and in 1712 he was rewarded with the Colonelcy of his regiment, and was also appointed Governor of the Royal Hospital at Dublin. He concludes his journal in the following words : " In the month of May, 1717, the regiment received orders to march to Portsmouth, and there I take my leave of them, for, in the month of January following, His Majesty gave me leave te resign my regiment to Colonel William Cosby, after having served six crowned heads of England, and been forty years attached to one company without ever being removed from it ; having made twenty-one campaigns ; having been in seven field-battles—fifteen sieges—seven grand attacks on counterscarps and breaches—two remarkable retreats—at the passing of four of the enemy's lines—besides several other petty actions ; and, through God's assistance, never had one drop of blood drawn from me in all those actions." Brigadier-General Stearne died on the 1st of November, 1732.

8. Brigadier-General William Cosby.

William Cosby served for many years as an officer of the Life Guards, and rose to the rank of Lieut.-Colonel. He was promoted to the Colonelcy of the 18th Royal Irish in December, 1717, and accompanied the regiment to Minorca. He commanded a detachment of the troops sent from that island to Gibraltar, when the Spaniards besieged the fortress in 1727. Colonel Cosby was afterwards appointed Governor of the Leeward Islands, and, in 1732, he became Captain-General and Governor-in-Chief of New York and New Jersey, when he relinquished the Colonelcy of his regiment.

9. Colonel Sir Charles Hotham, Bart.

Charles Hotham entered the army in the reign of Queen Anne, and served on the Continent in the campaigns of the Duke of Marlborough. He was a great friend of the

Prince of Wales, afterwards George II., who, on his accession to the throne, appointed Sir Charles to be a Groom of the Bedchamber. He was subsequently Envoy Extraordinary and Plenipotentiary to King Frederick the Great, of Prussia. Sir Charles Hotham was appointed Colonel of the 18th Royal Irish in January, 1732, and, in 1735, he was removed to the Colonelcy of the Horse Grenadier Guards.

10. Major-General John Armstrong.

This officer entered the army in 1704, and served with reputation throughout the Duke of Marlborough's campaigns. He was promoted to the rank of Colonel in December, 1712. At various periods he held the appointments of Surveyor-General of H.M.'s Ordnance, Chief Engineer of England, and Quartermaster-General. In 1735, he was rewarded with the Colonelcy of the 18th Royal Irish, and was advanced to the rank of Major-General in 1739. He died on the 15th of April, 1742.

11. General Sir John Mordaunt, K.B.

John Mordaunt entered the army on the 25th of August, 1721, and rose to the rank of Captain and Lieut.-Colonel in the Third Foot Guards, from which he was removed to the Colonelcy of the 18th Royal Irish in 1742. He was promoted to be Brigadier-General in 1745, and commanded a brigade at the battle of Falkirk. He afterwards served under H.R.H. the Duke of Cumberland, and commanded a brigade at the decisive battle of Culloden. His next service was in the Netherlands, where he distinguished himself at the battle of Val in 1747. In the same year he was promoted to be Major-General, and soon afterwards was removed to the 12th Dragoons.

12. Lieutenant-General John Folliott.

After service in the junior ranks, John Folliott became Lieut.-Colonel of the 7th Horse in June, 1737, and, for his efficient command of that corps was rewarded in June, 1743, with the Colonelcy of the 62nd Regiment, from which he was transferred, in December, 1747, to the 18th Royal Irish. He became Major-General in 1754, and Lieut.-General in 1758. He was appointed Governor of Ross Castle, and at the time of his death, in 1762, was M.P. for Sligo.

13. General Sir John Sebright, Bart.

John Sebright was an officer in the First Foot Guards, in which corps he became Captain and Lieut.-Colonel in 1749. Having been promoted to the rank of Major-General in 1761, he was given the Colonelcy of the 18th Royal Irish in the following year. In 1765 he succeeded to the family baronetcy. He was promoted to be Lieut.-General in 1770, and General in 1782. Sir John Sebright died in 1794.

14. General Sir James Murray, Bart.

James Murray served in the Seven Years' War, and became Major in the 97th Regiment in 1762. In 1771 he succeeded, on the decease of his father, to the dignity of Baronet. He served through the American war, and distinguished himself at the defence of St Christopher. In 1789, he was appointed A.D.C. to the King, with the rank of Colonel. In 1793, he became Adjutant-General of the army in Flanders under the command of H.R.H. the Duke of York, and was promoted to be Major-General. Whilst in Flanders he was nominated to be Colonel of the 18th Royal Irish. On his marriage to the Countess of Bath, Sir James assumed the surname and arms of Pulteney. In 1800 he commanded an expedition against Ferrol, and subsequently joined the army under Sir Ralph Abercromby. In 1807, Sir James Pulteney became Secretary at War, and was promoted to be General in 1808. He died in April 1811.

15. General Lord Hutchinson, K.B.

The Honourable John Hely Hutchinson entered the army in January, 1774, as Cornet in the 18th Light Dragoons. In 1781, he became Major in the 77th Atholl Highlanders, in which corps he rose to the rank of Lieut.-Colonel in 1783. He served through two campaigns in Flanders as A.D.C. to Sir Ralph Abercromby, and was promoted to be Major-General in 1796. During the rebellion of 1798 in Ireland, he was second in command at the action at Castlebar. Major-General Hutchinson's next active service was in the expedition of 1799 to Holland when he was mentioned in despatches. In 1800, he was appointed second in command of the expedition to Egypt under Sir Ralph Abercromby. After the death of that officer, from wounds received in the action of the 21st of March, the command of the troops devolved upon Major-General Hutchinson. In the subsequent operations he evinced great talent and energy, and ultimately forced the French " Army of the East " to evacuate Egypt. For his services he received the thanks of both Houses of Parliament, and was raised to the peerage as Baron Hutchinson of Alexandria and of Knocklofty in the county of Tipperary. In 1803, Lord Hutchinson was promoted to be Lieut.-General, and, on the 27th of April, 1811, he was appointed Colonel of the 18th Royal Irish, which regiment had served under his command in Egypt. In 1813 he became General, and, in 1825, he succeeded to the title of Earl of Donoughmore. He died on the 6th of July, 1832.

16. General Lord Aylmer, G.C.B.

The Honourable Matthew Aylmer was born on the 25th of May, 1775, and succeeded his father as fifth Baron Aylmer on the 22nd of October, 1785. He entered the army in 1787, and served in the expedition to St Domingo in 1793 and 1794 ; he was present at the attacks upon Tiburon, at the storming of the Fort de l'Aeul (wounded), at the affair of Bombard, and at the reduction of Port au Prince. Lord Aylmer was present at the descent near Ostend in May, 1798, and remained a prisoner in France for six months. In 1700, he served in Holland, and was present at the battle of the Helder, the attack on the British lines of the 10th of September, and the battles of the 19th of September and the 2nd of October. He was with the Coldstream Guards in the North of Germany under Lord Cathcart in 1805, and at the taking of Copenhagen in 1807. He served on the staff of the army during the Peninsular War, and also in command of a brigade. He received a cross and clasp for Talavera, Busaco, Fuentes d'Onor, Vittoria, and the Nive. Lord Aylmer was appointed to be Colonel of the 18th Royal Irish on the 23rd of July, 1832. He died on the 3rd of February, 1850.

17. Field-Marshal Sir John Forster Fitzgerald, G.C.B.

Sir John Fitzgerald held a commission in the army for the almost unprecedented period of 84 years. He was the son of Edward Fitzgerald, Esq., of Carrigoran, M.P. for Clare in the Irish Parliament, and was born in 1786. He was gazetted to an ensigncy in October, 1793, and joined the 46th Regiment in 1801. He served throughout the Peninsular War and became Lieutenant-Colonel in 1810. He commanded his regiment at the battle of Salamanca, and subsequently a brigade in the Peninsula. He received the gold cross for Badajoz, Salamanca, Vittoria, and the Pyrenees. As a Major-General he did good service on the staff at Bombay, and became Lieutenant-General on the 23rd November, 1841. On March 9th, 1850, he was appointed Colonel of the 18th Royal Irish, and was promoted to be General in 1854. Sir John Fitzgerald was M.P. for Clare from 1852 to 1857. He was promoted to be Field-Marshal on the 29th of May, 1875, in the same gazette with General H.R.H. Albert Edward, Prince of Wales. Sir John died at Tours on March 24th, 1877.

18. Lieutenant-General Clement Alexander Edwards, C.B.

Clement Alexander Edwards, the son of Colonel C. M. Edwards, Military Secretary to the Duke of York, was born in London on the 13th of November, 1812. He joined the Royal Military College at Sandhurst when only fourteen, and, passing out first on the list, was gazetted to the 18th Royal Irish on June 11th, 1829. He served with the regiment through the war in China of 1840-42 (Medal), and was present at the attack upon Canton, the taking of Amoy, Chapoo, Woosung, Shanghai, and Chinkiangfu ; and was afterwards appointed by Lord Gough to be A.Q.M.G. to the force in China. He next served with the 18th Royal Irish in the Burmese War from July, 1852, to the conclusion ; he was at the taking of Prome, and was given a detached command for several months, during which after much fighting and severe marches the provinces of Padoung and Kangheim were cleared of the enemy. In January, 1853, he led a party on special service from Prome to Arracan, for which the Government of India recorded its approbation (Medal with clasp for Pegu, and brevet of Lieutenant-Colonel). Lieutenant-Colonel Edwards served in the Crimea with the 18th Royal Irish from the 30th of December, 1854, including the siege and fall of Sebastopol (Medal with clasp, C.B., Brevet of Colonel, Knight of the Legion of Honour, 3rd class of the Medjidie, and Turkish Medal). He succeeded to the command of the regiment on the 9th of March, 1855. Colonel Edwards afterwards proceeded to India with his regiment, and commanded a brigade at Mhow. At the termination of the Mutiny, he received the thanks of the Governor-General in Council for the promptness of the measures whereby the rebels under Tantia Topee were prevented from entering Khandeish. Colonel Edwards was awarded the Distinguished and Meritorious Service Reward in January, 1860. After the Mutiny he exchanged to the 49th Regiment, and commanded it until August, 1863. He was Inspector-General of Recruiting from July, 1867, to August 1873. On the 25th of March, 1877, Lieutenant-General Edwards was appointed to the Colonelcy of the 18th Royal Irish, with which he had served so long and with such distinction. He died on the 29th of July, 1882.

19. General Sir Alexander Macdonell, K.C.B.

Alexander Macdonell joined the army in 1837, and served with the Rifle Brigade in the Kaffir War of 1846-47 (Medal). Also throughout the Crimean campaign as A.D.C. to Sir George Brown, and was present at the affair of Bulganac, capture of Balaklava, and the battles of Alma and Inkerman. He commanded the 2nd Battalion of the Rifle Brigade from May, 1853, to the fall of Sebastopol (Medal with three clasps, Brevets of Major and Lieutenant-Colonel, Knight of the Legion of Honour, Sardinian and Turkish Medals, and 5th class of the Medjidie). Colonel Macdonell commanded the 3rd Battalion of the Rifle Brigade during the Indian Mutiny, including the siege and capture of Lucknow (Brevet of Colonel, Medal and clasp). He rose to the rank of General in April, 1882, and, in recognition of his distinguished services, was awarded the K.C.B., and was appointed to the Colonelcy of the 18th Royal Irish on the 30th of July, 1882.

20. General Sir Richard Denis Kelly, K.C.B.

Richard Denis Kelly was born on the 9th of March, 1815, and obtained his first commission in 1834. He served with the 34th Regiment in the Crimea, and was wounded at the siege of Sebastopol (Twice mentioned in despatches, Medal and clasp, Knight of the Legion of Honour, 5th class of the Medjidie, and Turkish Medal). He served in the Indian Mutiny, 1857-59, and commanded the 34th Regiment in the actions at Cawnpore (wounded), capture of Meeangunge, siege and capture of Lucknow, and relief of Azimghur. Commanded a column during the operations in Oude. Commanded a field force on the Nepaul Frontier, and defeated the rebels near Bootwull (horse shot). Colonel Kelly was frequently mentioned in despatches, and received the thanks of the Governor-General and Commander-in-Chief (Medal and clasp, C.B., K.C.B.) Sir Richard Kelly attained the rank of General in November, 1880, and was appointed to the Colonelcy of the 18th Royal Irish on the 24th of January, 1886.

21. General George Frederick Stevenson Call, C.B.

George Call received his first commission as Ensign in the 18th Royal Irish on April 7th, 1837, and served with it during the war in China of 1840-42. He was present at the first capture of Chusan, the attack of the forts on the Canton River, the storming of the heights and fort of Canton, and the capture of Amoy (Medal). He proceeded to Burmah with the 18th Royal Irish, and served on the staff throughout the war of 1852-53 as Brigade Major of the 1st Bengal Brigade, and afterwards as A.A.G. of the Pegu Division. He was present at the destruction of the stockades on the Rangoon River, at the storming of the citadel of Rangoon, and at the capture of Prome (Medal with clasp for Pegu). Major Call served in the Crimea with the 18th Royal Irish from December, 1854, to the end of the war, including the siege and fall of Sebastopol (Medal with clasp, Brevet of Lieutenant-Colonel, Sardinian and Turkish Medals, and 5th class of the Medjidie). Colonel Call was awarded the C.B., and attained the rank of General on July 1st, 1881. He was appointed to the Colonelcy of the 18th Royal Irish on March 9th, 1889.

22. General Robert Walter M'Leod Fraser.

General Fraser acted as Staff Officer to a Detachment sent in 1837 against the rebels in Canada. He also served with the 6th Regiment in the Kaffir War of 1846-47 (Medal). In October 1857, he was commissioned to raise the 2nd Battalion of the 6th Regiment, and, having within one month obtained upwards of a thousand recruits, he was gazetted on the 25th of November, 1857, to be Lieutenant-Colonel of the Battalion. He became Major-General in 1868, Lieutenant-General in 1880, and General in 1881. General Fraser was appointed to the Colonelcy of the 18th Royal Irish on the 8th of January, 1895.

23. Lieutenant-General Sir Henry Marshman Havelock-Allan, Bart., V.C., G.C.B.

Henry Marshman Havelock, the eldest son of Sir Henry Havelock, K.C.B., the hero of the Indian Mutiny, was born on the 6th of August, 1830, and obtained his first commission as Ensign in the 10th Lincoln Regiment on the 31st of March, 1846. His first active service was in the Persian Expedition as D.A.Q.M.G. from the 15th of February, 1857, including the bombardment and capture of Mohumrah (Medal).

Captain Havelock next served throughout the Indian Campaigns of 1857-59; as A.D.C. to General Havelock in the actions of Futtehpore, Aoung, Pandoo Nuddee, and Cawnpore; and afterwards as D.A.A.G. in numerous engagements including Oonao, Nawabgunge, Bithoor, Alumbagh, and relief of Lucknow on the 25th of September—dangerously wounded and horse shot—defence of the Residency until relieved by Sir Colin Campbell on the 17th of November, on which day he was again severely wounded. With the Jounpore Field Force, as D.A.A.G., he was present at the actions of Misrutpore, Chanda, Umeerpore, and Sultanpore. He then served with the 4th Division before Lucknow from the 4th of March until its fall. As D.A.A.G. with Lugard's Column, he was present at the relief of Azimghur. Later in the campaign he commanded the 1st Regiment of Hodson's Horse. He was repeatedly mentioned in despatches, and received the brevets of Major and Lieutenant-Colonel, a year's service for Lucknow, and the Medal with two clasps. For his gallant conduct at the battle of Cawnpore in leading a direct attack upon artillery in action at close range, he was awarded the Victoria Cross.

Lieutenant-Colonel Havelock was created a Baronet on the 22nd of January, 1858.

Sir Henry Havelock served with the 18th Royal Irish in the New Zealand War of 1863-64; he was employed on the Staff and was present at Rangariri, Paterangi, and Orakau (Medal).

He attained the rank of Colonel on the 17th of June, 1868, and was employed on the Staff in Canada and at Dublin. He became Major-General on the 18th of March, 1878, and commanded the 3rd Infantry Brigade at Aldershot in 1880-81.

Sir Henry Havelock assumed by royal license, dated the 17th of March, 1880, the additional surname and arms of Allan.

His love of adventure led him as a spectator to the battles of Sedan, Plevna, and Tel-el-Kebir.

Sir Henry Havelock-Allan was promoted to be Lieutenant-General on the 9th of December, 1881 ; and was appointed to be Colonel of the 18th Royal Irish Regiment on the 27th of November, 1895, and was awarded the G.C.B. in 1897. He was killed by the Afridis when riding through the Khyber Pass on the 30th of December, 1897.

24. Major-General Charles Frederick Gregorie, C.B.

Charles Frederick Gregorie was born on the 25th of November, 1834, and was educated at Westminster School. He joined the 23rd Royal Welsh Fusiliers in the Crimea on the 16th of September, 1855, and served there to the end of the war. He was appointed Adjutant of the Regiment in May, 1857, and embarked with it in the following month at Portsmouth for China. On arrival at Cape Town, the destination of the Regiment was changed to Calcutta in consequence of the outbreak of the Indian Mutiny. He was present at the Relief of Lucknow, by Sir Colin Campbell, in November, 1857 ; at the defeat of the Gwalior Contingent at Cawnpore in December, 1857 ; and at the Capture of Lucknow in March, 1858 (Medal and two clasps). He was appointed Adjutant of the 7th Rifle Depôt Battalion at Winchester on the 8th of October, 1861. Major Gregorie exchanged to the 18th Royal Irish Regiment on the 31st of October, 1871, and succeeded to the command of the Second Battalion on the 14th of September, 1878. He commanded this Battalion throughout the campaign of 1882 in Egypt, and was present at the action of Kassasin and the battle of Tel-el-Kebir (Mentioned in despatches, C.B., Medal and clasp, and 3rd class of Medjidie). Colonel Gregorie was appointed in 1883 to the command of the 35th Regimental District at Chichester, and served there until, on the 17th of November, 1885, he became A.A. and Q.M.G. of the South-Eastern District, and held this appointment until promoted to be Major-General on the 18th of June, 1890. He commanded the 1st Infantry Brigade at Aldershot from April, 1891, until his retirement in December, 1894. He was selected for the Reward for Distinguished and Meritorious Service in June, 1894. Major-General Gregorie was appointed Colonel of The Royal Irish Regiment on the 31st December, 1897.

APPENDIX 10.

MEMORIALS OF THE ROYAL IRISH REGIMENT.

IN THE NORTH TRANSEPT OF ST PATRICK'S CATHEDRAL, DUBLIN.

I. MONUMENT COMMEMORATIVE OF CHINA WAR, 1840-42.[1]

II. VOTIVE CROSS COMMEMORATIVE OF SOUTH AFRICAN WAR, 1899-1902.

III. SARCOPHAGUS COMMEMORATIVE OF THE CAMPAIGN IN EGYPT, 1801.

IV. MONUMENT COMMEMORATIVE OF BURMAH WAR, 1852-53.

V. STAINED-GLASS WINDOW COMMEMORATIVE OF SOUTH AFRICAN WAR, 1899-1902.

VI. STAINED-GLASS WINDOW COMMEMORATIVE OF CRIMEAN WAR, 1855-56.

VII. FOUR PAIRS OF REGIMENTAL COLOURS.

MEMORIAL TABLETS AND BRASSES.[2]

GENERAL CLEMENT ALEXANDER EDWARDS, C.B.

LIEUT.-GENERAL SIR HENRY MARSHMAN HAVELOCK-ALLAN, BART., V.C., G.C.B.

MAJOR A. W. S. F. ARMSTRONG.

BREVET-MAJOR JAMES TARRANT RING.

CAPTAIN ARTHUR J. MILNER.

[1] The Memorials are enumerated, and described in the order that they appear in the frontispiece, commencing on the left.

[2] These are grouped round the South African Window.

I. THE CHINA MONUMENT.

The upper portion of the Monument consists of a sculptured representation of the Crest of the Regiment with crossed Colours and the Regimental Badges.

Beneath is the following inscription :—

DEATH OF LIEUTENANT-COLONEL TOMLINSON,
COMMANDING 18TH (ROYAL IRISH) REGIMENT,
AT CHAPPOO, 18TH MAY, 1842.

A sculptured representation of the death scene.

On the tablet below is the inscription :—

To the Memory of

THE OFFICERS, NON-COMMISSIONED OFFICERS,
DRUMMERS, AND PRIVATES,
18TH (ROYAL IRISH) REGIMENT,
WHO FELL DURING 1840-41-42 IN THE
CHINA WAR.
ERECTED BY THEIR COMRADES.

"THE TRUMPET SHALL SOUND, AND THE DEAD SHALL BE RAISED INCORRUPTIBLE.
THANKS BE TO GOD WHICH GIVETH US THE VICTORY THROUGH OUR LORD JESUS CHRIST."

—1 COR. XV.

On the scroll at the base of the Monument is the following inscription :—

THE REGIMENT LOST DURING THIS WAR BY DEATH IN THE FIELD,
FROM CASUALTIES OR FROM SICKNESS ATTENDING, AS UNDERNEATH.

LIEUT. F. VAVASOUR—12TH OCTOBER 1840.
MAJOR R. HAMMILL—7TH FEBRUARY 1841.
LIEUT. A. WILSON, ADJUTANT—19TH JUNE 1841.
LIEUT. F. SWINBURN—11TH SEPTEMBER 1841.
LT.-COL. R. TOMLINSON—18TH MAY 1842. KILLED IN ACTION.
CAPTAIN C. J. COLLINSON—21ST JULY 1842.
LIEUT. D. EDWARDES—21ST JULY 1842.
LIEUT. J. COCHRANE—29TH AUGUST 1842.
ENSIGN J. HUMPHREYS—16TH AUGUST 1842.
19 NON-COMMISSIONED OFFICERS.
158 DRUMMERS AND PRIVATES.

II. THE SOUTH AFRICAN VOTIVE CROSS.

This Memorial, which stands on the north wall of the north transept of St Patrick's Cathedral between the China and Burma Monuments, was unveiled on May 24th, 1907, by Colonel Beauchamp J. C. Doran, C.B., in the unavoidable absence of Lord Wolseley, the Colonel-in-Chief, and Major-General Gregorie, C.B., the Colonel of the Regiment. The Very Rev. the Dean of St Patrick's responded to Colonel Doran's speech.

The Celtic mural Cross, which is nine feet high, is of white marble, laid on a mosaic background, with a frame of Carlow limestone. It was designed by Sir Thomas Drew, and made by Messrs Sharp and Emery, of Great Brunswick Street, Dublin.

A brass tablet, mounted on mahogany, is placed below the Cross. It bears the Crest of the Regiment and the following inscription :—

In Memory of

OUR COMRADES WHO FELL IN THE
SOUTH AFRICAN WAR.
MDCCCXCIX-MDCCCCII.

III. SARCOPHAGUS. EGYPT, 1801.

On a black marble slab mid-way between the China and Burmah Monuments, and immediately below the South African Mural Cross, is placed a grey stone Sarcophagus, having a Sphinx embossed on the front, with the date, 1801.

IV. THE BURMA MONUMENT.

The upper portion of this is identical with the China Monument.

Beneath the crossed sculptured Colours is the following inscription :—

STORMING THE SHOE DAGON PAGODA, RANGOON.
14TH APRIL 1852.

A sculptured representation of the storming.

On the tablet below is the inscription :—

To the Memory of

THE OFFICERS, NON-COMMISSIONED OFFICERS,
DRUMMERS, AND PRIVATES,
18TH (ROYAL IRISH) REGIMENT,
WHO FELL DURING 1852-53 IN THE
BURMA WAR.
ERECTED BY THEIR COMRADES.

"THY DEAD MEN SHALL LIVE, TOGETHER WITH MY DEAD BODY SHALL THEY RISE."

On the scroll at the base of the Monument is the following inscription :—

THE REGIMENT LOST DURING THIS WAR BY DEATH IN THE FIELD,
FROM CASUALTIES OR FROM SICKNESS ATTENDING, AS UNDERNEATH.
LIEUT. R. DORAN (ADJUTANT)—14TH APRIL 1852. KILLED IN ACTION.
CAPTAIN A. GILLESPIE—11TH DECEMBER 1852.
CAPTAIN W. P. COCKBURN—20TH MARCH 1853. DIED OF HIS WOUNDS.
LT.-COLONEL C. J. COOTE—24TH MAY 1853.
LIEUT. F. LILLIE—6TH JUNE 1853.
27 NON-COMMISSIONED OFFICERS.
333 DRUMMERS AND PRIVATES.

On the floor, extending along the whole front of the Memorials of China, South Africa, Egypt, and Burma, is a black marble slab four feet wide, having four Irish Wolf Hounds in cut stone crouching thereon. Above this is a band of grey dressed stone two feet wide, with

2 E

a black marble border along the top. A wide space of the wall above is faced with polished alabaster, and this is surmounted by a white marble border.

The words CHINA—S. AFRICA—BURMA are inset in gold on the black marble slab opposite the respective Monuments.

V. THE SOUTH AFRICAN WINDOW.

The picture at p. 305 shows this Memorial directly in front. The window is a lancet, thirteen feet high and three feet six inches wide. It was designed by Miss Sara Purser, and made at her stained-glass works in Pembroke Street, Dublin. The figure in the centre represents King Cormac of Cashel—bishop, warrior, and scribe. Miss Purser writes : " He is standing leaning on his sword, with his warriors behind him ; one holds his shield, and another a banner with a dragon of an interlacing Celtic design. At the top of the window two angels support his mitre. In a panel at the base, a mourning angel leans over a shield bearing a badge of the Regiment—the Lion of Nassau. On a scroll is the Regimental motto —'Virtutis Namurcensis Præmium'—and the Harp and Crown ; the Sphinx and the Dragon are also worked into the ornament."

At the bottom of the window is inscribed on the glass :—

IN MEMORY OF THE OFFICERS, NON-COMMISSIONED OFFICERS, AND MEN

OF THE ROYAL IRISH REGIMENT WHO FELL IN THE

SOUTH AFRICAN WAR, 1899-1902.

As the Dêpot of the Regiment is at Clonmel, in the diocese of Cashel, the choice of the subject of the window is very appropriate, and Miss Purser has been most successful in introducing the various regimental devices into the design ; the jewel-like colours of the glass are also admirable.

VI. THE CRIMEAN WINDOW.

This is just visible in the picture to the right of the South African Window. It is a lancet ; at the top is the Harp and Crown, with wreath of shamrocks, and a scroll bearing the regimental motto. In the centre is a view of Sebastopol Harbour, and at the base an ornamental design.

On a scroll below the window is the following inscription :—

THIS MEMORIAL WINDOW

WAS ERECTED

TO THE MEMORY OF THOSE OF THE

18TH (ROYAL IRISH) REGIMENT

WHO FELL IN THE CRIMEA

1855-56.

KILLED OR DIED OF THEIR WOUNDS—

LIEUT. J. W. MEURANT,

IN ACTION, 18TH JUNE 1855.

THREE SERGEANTS, ONE DRUMMER,

AND 85 RANK AND FILE.

DIED OF DISEASE—

ENSIGN E. D. RICARD, 5TH MAY 1856.

3 SERGEANTS AND 77 RANK AND FILE.

" HE THAT BELIEVETH IN ME THOUGH HE WERE DEAD YET SHALL HE LIVE."

—GOSPEL OF ST JOHN, XI. C., 25TH V.

VII. REGIMENTAL COLOURS.

1. Above the China Memorial. A Pair of Colours.
   With Shield bearing the inscription—

1ST BATTALION, THE ROYAL IRISH REGIMENT, 1886.

2. Above the Burma Memorial. A Pair of Colours.
   With Shield bearing the inscription—

THE COLOURS OF THE 1ST BATTALION, ROYAL IRISH REGIMENT
CARRIED FROM 1837 TO 1856, IN THE WARS OF
CHINA, BURMA, AND THE CRIMEA.

3. On the East Side. A Pair of Colours.
   With Shield bearing the inscription—

2ND BATTALION, THE ROYAL IRISH REGIMENT, 1904.

4. On the West Side. A Pair of Colours.
   With Shield bearing the inscription—

3RD BATTALION, THE ROYAL IRISH REGIMENT, 1908.

MEMORIAL TABLETS AND BRASSES.

1. Brass Tablet placed below the South African Memorial Window bearing the following inscription :—

In Memory of

GENERAL CLEMENT ALEXANDER EDWARDS, C.B.,
KNIGHT OF THE LEGION OF HONOUR.
BORN NOVEMBER 13TH, 1812 ; DIED JULY 29TH, 1882.
COLONEL OF THE ROYAL IRISH REGIMENT,
IN WHICH HE SERVED UPWARDS OF 53 YEARS,
WAS PRESENT WITH ITS 1ST BATTALION IN
THE WARS OF CHINA, 1842 ; BURMA, 1852 ;
THE CRIMEA, 1854 ; THE INDIAN MUTINY, 1857.

THIS TABLET IS ERECTED BY HIS BROTHER OFFICERS.

(The Tablet bears the private Crest of General Edwards and the Regimental Crest.)

2. Brass tablet placed to the left of the South African Memorial Window bearing the following inscription :—

In Memory of

LIEUT.-GENERAL SIR HENRY MARSHMAN HAVELOCK-ALLAN,

BARONET, V.C., G.C.B., M.P., D.L.,

COLONEL OF THE ROYAL IRISH REGIMENT.

SON OF

MAJOR-GENERAL SIR HENRY HAVELOCK, K.C.B.,

OF LUCKNOW.

A GALLANT AND HEROIC SOLDIER, HE SERVED

WITH GREAT DISTINCTION IN THE PERSIAN AND

INDIAN MUTINY CAMPAIGNS, AND THE

NEW ZEALAND WAR OF 1863-65.

HE WAS KILLED BY THE AFRIDIS IN THE KYBER PASS ON

30TH DECEMBER, 1897.

THIS TABLET IS ERECTED IN GRATEFUL RECOGNITION OF HIS

DEVOTION TO THE REGIMENT OF WHICH HE WAS CHIEF

BY THE OFFICERS PAST AND PRESENT, WARRANT OFFICERS,

NON-COMMISSIONED OFFICERS. AND MEN OF

THE ROYAL IRISH REGIMENT.

(The tablet bears the private Crest of Sir H. Havelock-Allan and the Regimental Crest.)

3. Brass tablet also placed on the left of the South African Memorial Window bearing the following inscription :—

In Memory of

CAPTAIN ARTHUR J. MILNER,

18TH THE ROYAL IRISH,

DIED AT PALAMPORE,

PUNJAB, INDIA,

17TH SEPTEMBER 1879,

AGED 31 YEARS.

THIS TABLET IS ERECTED

BY THE OFFICERS, N.-C. OFFICERS, AND MEN OF

THE REGIMENT BY WHOM

HE IS DEEPLY REGRETTED.

(The tablet bears the private Crest of Captain Milner and the Regimental Crest and Motto.)

4. Stone inset placed on the right of the South African Memorial Window bearing the following inscription :—

Sacred to the Memory of

BREVET-MAJOR JAMES TARRANT RING,

18TH ROYAL IRISH,

WHO WAS MORTALLY WOUNDED WHEN GALLANTLY
LEADING THE ASSAULT ON THE ENEMY'S POSITION
AT ORAKAU PAH ON THE 2ND APRIL, 1864.
HE ON SEVERAL OCCASIONS DISTINGUISHED HIMSELF
DURING HIS SERVICE IN THE NEW ZEALAND WAR,
AND ENJOYED THE CONFIDENCE AND RESPECT
OF BOTH THE OFFICERS AND MEN OF THE REGIMENT,
BY WHOM THIS MEMORIAL IS ERECTED.

5. Brass tablet also placed on the right of the South African Memorial Window bearing the following inscription :—

In Memory of

MAJOR A. W. S. F. ARMSTRONG,

18TH ROYAL IRISH,

KNIGHT OF THE LEGION OF HONOUR,

WHO, AFTER SERVING WITH DISTINCTION
IN CHINA, INDIA, BURMA,
AND THE CRIMEA,
DIED AT SHORNCLIFFE CAMP,
ON THE 13TH DECEMBER, 1860.

THIS TABLET IS ERECTED
BY HIS BROTHER OFFICERS
IN TOKEN OF THEIR REGARD AND ESTEEM.

"CHRIST IS ALL, AND IN ALL."—COLS. III. XI.

(The tablet bears the private Crest of Major Armstrong and the Regimental Crest and Motto.)

All connected with the Regiment, both in the past and the present, who may not have visited St Patrick's Cathedral in recent years, will be struck by the vast improvement lately effected through the rearrangement and artistic grouping of the numerous Regimental Memorials.

Upon this subject, Sir Thomas Drew wrote on August 20th, 1907 : "The real Memorial work was the collection of the previous Memorials of the Regiment, which were casual and scattered, and rearranging them with some general regard into a trophy in which the older Burmah and China monuments of the Pagan and Early Victorian Era were grouped with the dominant South African Votive Cross. They lent themselves, I thought, very happily to component parts of one Regimental Memorial of historic interest, to which the North Transept of the Cathedral is dedicated now. As a whole, and properly photographed, I could conceive no more effective frontispiece to a book on the Royal Irish Regiment."

The Very Reverend The Dean of St Patrick's, in the course of his speech at the ceremony of the unveiling of the South African Memorial, said : " It is the privilege of the Chapter of the National Cathedral to be the guardians of many memorials of distinguished Irish regiments. But with no regiment are our ties so manifold and so intimate as with the famous regiment which offers us to-day the custody of its Memorial of the comrades who fell in South Africa. We are surrounded at this end of the North Transept by your insignia and the memorials of your past. In this place, hallowed by so many memories of gallant men, it is fitting that you should offer, and that we should welcome, a monument which will recall to future generations the services which the 1st Battalion of the 18th Royal Irish—the Royal Regiment of Ireland — rendered with faithfulness and devotion for two years and a half during the last great trial of our arms, the long death-roll—too long to inscribe on our walls here—shows at how great a cost your duty was fulfilled."

MEMORIALS OF THE ROYAL IRISH REGIMENT AT CLONMEL.

These consist of—
    I. A Memorial Cross commemorative of the Campaigns in Afghanistan, 1879-80 ; Egypt, 1882 ; and the Nile Expedition, 1884-85.
    II. A Monument commemorative of the South African War, 1899-1902.

THE AFGHANISTAN AND EGYPT CROSS.

This Memorial is placed in the Barrack Square at Clonmel, where the Depôt of the Regiment is stationed. The design is that of an old Celtic Cross adapted from one in Co. Sligo. It is executed in red Aberdeen granite, the height is 7 feet 6 inches, width 2 feet 9 inches, and mounted on a base 2 feet 6 inches high. The designers and executants of the work are Messrs H. Sibthorpe & Son, of 33 Molesworth Street, Dublin.

The inscription on the North face of the Cross is—

IN MEMORY OF THE OFFICERS, NON-COMMISSIONED OFFICERS, AND PRIVATE SOLDIERS OF THE 1ST AND 2ND BATTALIONS OF THE ROYAL IRISH REGIMENT, WHO DIED OF DISEASE OR WERE KILLED IN ACTION DURING THE CAMPAIGNS OF AFGHANISTAN, 1879-80, AND EGYPT, 1882.

THIS MEMORIAL IS ERECTED BY THEIR COMRADES.
ALSO IN MEMORY OF NILE EXPEDITION, 1884-85.

The names inscribed on the East, West, and South faces are given in Appendix 2.
There was no public ceremony at the unveiling of this Memorial.
A picture of the Cross is at page 252.

THE SOUTH AFRICAN WAR MEMORIAL, CLONMEL.

The ceremony of unveiling this Memorial was performed at the Barracks, Clonmel, on October 5th, 1908, by the Marquis of Ormonde, Honorary Colonel of the original 5th Battalion, now the 4th Special Reserve Battalion, of the Royal Irish Regiment. About 350 men of the 2nd Battalion, under command of Colonel A. S. Orr, D.S.O., travelled from Buttevant with the band and colours, and formed up on the Barrack Square with the 3rd Special Reserve Battalion, under command of Major R. O. Kellett.

After carrying out the ceremony of unveiling, the Marquis of Ormonde addressed the troops, and recounted the services of the Regiment during the War in South Africa. He made special mention of the gallant deed of No. 3733, Private J. Barry, a Kilkenny man, who was killed at Monument Hill on the night of January 6th, 1901. Private Barry was awarded the Victoria Cross, and it was given to his widow. Lord Ormonde further alluded to the fine fighting record of the Royal Irish in all parts of the British Empire during two and a quarter centuries.

Colonel A. S. Orr, D.S.O., responded on behalf of the Regiment.

DESCRIPTION OF THE MEMORIAL.

Designer—R. CAULFEILD ORPEN, Esq., B.A., F.R.I.A.I., 13 South Frederick Street, Dublin.

Executants—Messrs C. W. HARRISON & SONS, 178 Great Brunswick Street, Dublin.

The Memorial consists of three stone seats, forming a triangle, set on a circular platform, reached by three broad circular steps. Above the backs of the seats, and filling the space which they enclose, rises a triangular block of masonry having sunk panels on each of its faces, the whole being surmounted by a carved stone cornice.

The work is executed throughout in fine selected Irish limestone from the Stradbally quarries.

The height of the entire structure is fifteen feet, and the sides of the triangle are eight feet.

The front panel on the triangle bears a female figure executed in bronze in relief. The figure was designed and modelled by Miss Beatrice Elvery, of Dublin, who also made the models for the bronze wreaths and escutcheons which surround the Memorial immediately below the carved stone cornice; the escutcheons show the regimental badges. The two side panels on the triangle, which correspond in size with the front panel, are filled with the roll of Officers, Non-Commissioned Officers, and Men who fell in the Campaign.

On the panels behind the three seats the following inscriptions are placed :—

Front—

> SOUTH AFRICA, 1899-1902.   TO THE MEMORY OF THE OFFICERS,
> NON - COMMISSIONED OFFICERS, AND MEN OF THE ROYAL IRISH
> REGIMENT WHO WERE KILLED IN ACTION AND DIED OF WOUNDS
> OR DISEASE DURING THE CAMPAIGN.

On the Right Side—

> 1899-1900.   RELIEF OF KIMBERLEY, PAARDEBURG, JOHANNESBURG,
> DIAMOND HILL, WITTEBERGEN.

On the Left Side—

> 1901-1902.   CAPE COLONY, BELFAST, WITTEBERGEN, SOUTH AFRICA, 1901,
> SOUTH AFRICA, 1902.

The names inscribed on the two side panels of the triangle are given in Appendix 2.

A picture of the Memorial is at page 374.

APPENDIX 11.

TABLE SHOWING THE FORMER NUMBERS AND PRESENT NAMES OF THE INFANTRY REGIMENTS OF THE REGULAR ARMY.

Old Numbers.		Present Names.
1st .	.	The Royal Scots (Lothian regiment).
2nd	.	The Queen's (Royal West Surrey regiment).
3rd	.	The Buffs (East Kent regiment).
4th	.	The King's Own (Royal Lancaster regiment).
5th	.	The Northumberland Fusiliers.
6th	.	The Royal Warwickshire regiment.
7th	.	The Royal Fusiliers (City of London regiment).
8th	.	The King's (Liverpool regiment).
9th	.	The Norfolk regiment.
10th	.	The Lincolnshire regiment.
11th	.	The Devonshire regiment.
12th	.	The Suffolk regiment.
13th	.	The Prince Albert's (Somersetshire Light Infantry).
14th	.	The Prince of Wales' Own (West Yorkshire regiment).
15th	.	The East Yorkshire regiment.
16th	.	The Bedfordshire regiment.
17th	.	The Leicestershire regiment.
18th	.	The Royal Irish regiment.
19th	.	Alexandra, Princess of Wales' Own (Yorkshire regiment).
20th	.	The Lancashire Fusiliers.
21st	.	The Royal Scots Fusiliers.
22nd	.	The Cheshire regiment.
23rd	.	The Royal Welsh Fusiliers.
24th	.	The South Wales Borderers.
25th	.	The King's Own Scottish Borderers.
26th	.	1st batt. The Cameronians (Scottish Rifles).
27th	.	1st „ The Royal Inniskilling Fusiliers.
28th	.	1st „ The Gloucestershire regiment.
29th	.	1st „ The Worcestershire regiment.
30th	.	1st „ The East Lancashire regiment.
31st	.	1st „ The East Surrey regiment.
32nd	.	1st „ The Duke of Cornwall's Light Infantry.
33rd	.	1st „ The Duke of Wellington's (West Riding regiment).
34th	.	1st „ The Border regiment.
35th	.	1st „ The Royal Sussex regiment.
36th	.	2nd „ The Worcestershire regiment.
37th	.	1st „ The Hampshire regiment.

Old Numbers.			Present Names.
38th	.	1st batt.	The South Staffordshire regiment.
39th	.	1st „	The Dorsetshire regiment.
40th	.	1st „	The Prince of Wales' Volunteers (South Lancashire regiment).
41st	.	1st „	The Welsh regiment.
42nd	.	1st „	The Black Watch (Royal Highlanders).
43rd	.	1st „	The Oxfordshire and Buckinghamshire Light Infantry.
44th	.	1st „	The Essex regiment.
45th	.	1st „	The Sherwood Foresters (Nottingham and Derbyshire regiment).
46th	.	2nd „	The Duke of Cornwall's Light Infantry.
47th	.	1st „	The Loyal North Lancashire regiment.
48th	.	1st „	The Northamptonshire regiment.
49th	.	1st „	Princess Charlotte of Wales' (Royal Berkshire regiment).
50th	.	1st „	The Queen's Own (Royal West Kent regiment).
51st	.	1st „	The King's Own (Yorkshire Light Infantry).
52nd	.	2nd „	The Oxfordshire and Buckinghamshire Light Infantry.
53rd	.	1st „	The King's (Shropshire Light Infantry).
54th	.	2nd „	The Dorsetshire regiment.
55th	.	2nd „	The Border regiment.
56th	.	2nd „	The Essex regiment.
57th	.	1st „	The Duke of Cambridge's Own (Middlesex regiment).
58th	.	2nd „	The Northamptonshire regiment.
59th	.	2nd „	The East Lancashire regiment.
60th	. . .		The King's Royal Rifle Corps.
61st	.	2nd batt.	The Gloucestershire regiment.
62nd	.	1st „	The Duke of Edinburgh's (Wiltshire regiment).
63rd	.	1st „	The Manchester regiment.
64th	.	1st „	The Prince of Wales' (North Staffordshire regiment).
65th	.	1st „	The York and Lancaster regiment.
66th	.	2nd „	Princess Charlotte of Wales' (Royal Berkshire regiment).
67th	.	2nd „	The Hampshire regiment.
68th	.	1st „	The Durham Light Infantry.
69th	.	2nd „	The Welsh regiment.
70th	.	2nd „	The East Surrey regiment.
71st	.	1st „	The Highland Light Infantry.
72nd	.	1st „	Seaforth Highlanders (Ross-shire Buffs, the Duke of Albany's).
73rd	.	2nd „	The Black Watch (Royal Highlanders).
74th	.	2nd „	The Highland Light Infantry.
75th	.	1st „	The Gordon Highlanders.
76th	.	2nd „	The Duke of Wellington's (West Riding regiment).
77th	.	2nd „	The Duke of Cambridge's Own (Middlesex regiment).
78th	.	2nd „	Seaforth Highlanders (Ross-shire Buffs, the Duke of Albany's).
79th	.	1st „	The Queen's Own Cameron Highlanders.
80th	.	2nd „	South Staffordshire regiment.
81st	.	2nd „	Loyal North Lancashire regiment.
82nd	.	2nd „	The Prince of Wales' Volunteers (South Lancashire regiment).
83rd	.	1st „	The Royal Irish Rifles.
84th	.	2nd „	The York and Lancaster regiment.
85th	.	1st „	The King's (Shropshire Light Infantry).
86th	.	2nd „	The Royal Irish Rifles.
87th	.	1st „	Princess Victoria's (Royal Irish Fusiliers).
88th	.	1st „	The Connaught Rangers.

Old Numbers.   Present Names.

89th	.	2nd batt.	Princess Victoria's (Royal Irish Fusiliers).
90th	.	2nd ,,	The Cameronians (Scottish Rifles).
91st	.	1st ,,	Princess Louise's (Argyll and Sutherland Highlanders).
92nd	.	2nd ,,	The Gordon Highlanders.
93rd	.	2nd ,,	Princess Louise's (Argyll and Sutherland Highlanders).
94th	.	2nd ,,	The Connaught Rangers.
95th	.	2nd ,,	The Sherwood Foresters (Nottingham and Derbyshire regiment).
96th	.	2nd ,,	The Manchester regiment.
97th	.	2nd ,,	The Queen's Own (Royal West Kent regiment).
98th	.	2nd ,,	The Prince of Wales' (North Staffordshire regiment).
99th	.	2nd ,,	The Duke of Edinburgh's (Wiltshire regiment).
100th	.	1st ,,	The Prince of Wales' Leinster regiment (Royal Canadians).
101st	.	1st ,,	The Royal Munster Fusiliers.
102nd	.	1st ,, }	The Royal Dublin Fusiliers.
103rd	.	2nd ,, }	
104th	.	2nd ,,	The Royal Munster Fusiliers.
105th	.	2nd ,,	The King's Own (Yorkshire Light Infantry).
106th	.	2nd ,,	The Durham Light Infantry.
107th	.	2nd ,,	The Royal Sussex regiment.
108th	.	2nd ,,	The Royal Inniskilling Fusiliers.
109th	.	2nd ,,	The Prince of Wales' Leinster regiment (Royal Canadians).
			The Rifle Brigade.

MAP Nº 10.

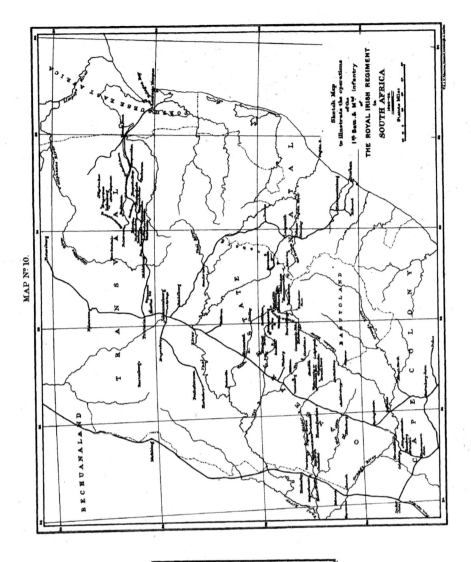

Sketch Map
to illustrate the operations
of the
1st Batn. & 2nd Infantry
of
THE ROYAL IRISH REGIMENT
in
SOUTH AFRICA

Scale of Miles

TRANSVAAL

ORANGE RIVER COLONY

BECHUANALAND

CAPE COLONY

BASUTOLAND

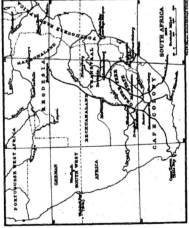

SOUTH AFRICA

PORTUGUESE WEST AFRICA

GERMAN
SOUTH WEST
AFRICA

RHODESIA

BECHUANALAND

CAPE COLONY

INDEX.

2 F

Printed in the United Kingdom
by Lightning Source UK Ltd.
123064UK00001B/59/A